Dominican Republic and Haiti
country studies

Federal Research Division
Library of Congress
Edited by
Helen Chapin Metz
Research Completed
December 1999

North Atlantic Ocean

HAITI

DOMINICAN REPUBLIC

Santo Domingo ✪

✪
Port-au-Prince

Caribbean Sea

On the cover: Hispaniola (La Isla Española)

Third Edition, First Printing, 2001.

Library of Congress Cataloging-in-Publication Data

Dominican Republic and Haiti : country studies / Federal Research Division, Library of Congress ; edited by Helen Chapin Metz.
    p. cm. — (Area handbook series, ISSN 1057–5294) (DA pam ; 550–36)
    "Research completed December 1999."
    Includes bibliographical references and index.
    ISBN 0–8444–1044–6 (alk. paper)
    1. Dominican Republic. 2. Haiti. I. Metz, Helen Chapin, 1928– .
II. Library of Congress. Federal Research Division. III. Series. IV.
Series: DA pam ; 550–36

    F1934.D64 2001
    972.93—dc21

                 2001023524

Headquarters, Department of the Army
DA Pam 550–36

Foreword

This volume is one in a continuing series of books prepared by the Federal Research Division of the Library of Congress under the Country Studies/Area Handbook Program sponsored by the Department of the Army. The last two pages of this book list the other published studies.

Most books in the series deal with a particular foreign country, describing and analyzing its political, economic, social, and national security systems and institutions, and examining the interrelationships of those systems and the ways they are shaped by historical and cultural factors. Each study is written by a multidisciplinary team of social scientists. The authors seek to provide a basic understanding of the observed society, striving for a dynamic rather than a static portrayal. Particular attention is devoted to the people who make up the society, their origins, dominant beliefs and values, their common interests and the issues on which they are divided, the nature and extent of their involvement with national institutions, and their attitudes toward each other and toward their social system and political order.

The books represent the analysis of the authors and should not be construed as an expression of an official United States government position, policy, or decision. The authors have sought to adhere to accepted standards of scholarly objectivity. Corrections, additions, and suggestions for changes from readers will be welcomed for use in future editions.

Robert L. Worden
Chief
Federal Research Division
Library of Congress
Washington, DC 20540–4840
E-mail: frds@loc.gov

Acknowledgments

The authors wish to acknowledge the work of Frederick J. Conway, Melinda Wheeler Cooke, Georges A. Fauriol, Richard A. Haggerty, Patricia Kluck, Daniel J. Seyler, Glenn R. Smucker, and Howard J. Wiarda, who contributed to the 1991 edition of *Dominican Republic and Haiti: Country Studies.* Their work served as a framework for various chapters of the present volume. The authors also are grateful to individuals in various agencies of the United States government and international and private institutions who gave their time, research materials, and special knowledge to provide information and perspective.

The authors also wish to thank those who contributed directly to the preparation of the manuscript. These include Sandra W. Meditz, who reviewed all drafts and served as liaison with the sponsoring agency and printer; Marilyn Majeska, who edited all chapters and managed production of the manuscript; and Janie L. Gilchrist, who did the word processing and prepared the camera-ready copy.

Maryland Mapping and Graphics provided invaluable graphics support, including the preparation of maps, charts, photographs, and cover and chapter illustrations. Kimberly A. Lord prepared the illustrations for the title pages of the chapters on Haiti. Various individuals, libraries, and public agencies, especially the Inter-American Development Bank, provided photographs.

Finally, the authors would like to thank Tim Merrill, who checked the rendering of foreign names and terms.

Contents

Chapter 4. Dominican Republic: Government and
Politics 159
Jonathan Hartlyn

List of Figures

Preface

Like its predecessors, these studies represent an attempt to treat in a compact and objective manner the dominant contemporary social, political, economic, and military aspects of the Dominican Republic and Haiti. Sources of information included scholarly books, journals, and monographs; official reports of governments and international organizations; numerous periodicals; the authors' previous research and observations; and interviews with individuals who have special competence in Dominican, Haitian, and Latin American affairs. Chapter bibliographies appear at the end of the book; brief comments on sources recommended for further reading appear at the end of each chapter. To the extent possible, place-names conform with the system used by the United States Board on Geographic Names (BGN). Measurements are given in the metric system; a conversion table is provided to assist readers unfamiliar with metric measurements (see table 1, Appendix). A glossary is also included.

Although there are numerous variations, Spanish surnames generally consist of two parts: the patrilineal name followed by the matrilineal one. In the instance of Joaquín Balaguer Ricardo, for example, Balaguer is his father's surname and Ricardo, his mother's maiden name. In nonformal use, the matrilineal name is often dropped. Thus, after the first mention, just Balaguer is used. A minority of individuals use only the patrilineal name.

Creole words used in the text may be presented in forms that are unfamiliar to readers who have done previous research on Haiti. The Creole orthography employed in this volume is that developed by the National Pedagogic Institute (Institut Pédagogique National–IPN), which has been the standard in Haiti since 1978.

The body of the text reflects information available as of December 1999. Certain other portions of the text, however, have been updated: the Introduction discusses significant events that have occurred since the completion of research, the Country Profiles and the tables include updated information as available, and the Bibliography lists recently published sources thought to be particularly helpful to the reader.

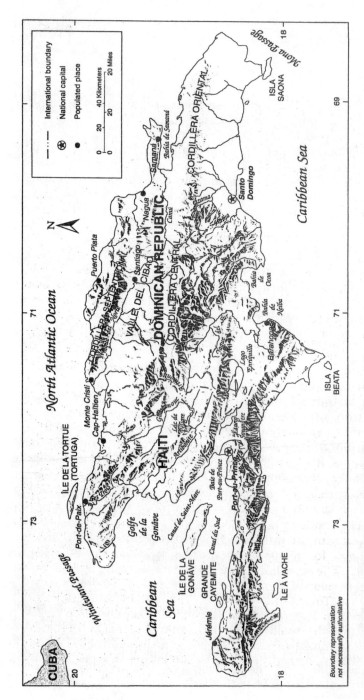

Figure 1. Dominican Republic and Haiti: Topography and Drainage

Introduction

THE HISTORIES OF THE TWO countries on the island of Hispaniola, the Dominican Republic and Haiti, have been inextricably intertwined. However, despite their similarities in some areas, they have important differences. The whole island, the first Spanish settlement in the New World and named Santo Domingo by Christopher Columbus in 1492, experienced decimation of its indigenous Indian, primarily Taino, population as a result of the Indians' treatment by colonial settlers. African slaves were brought to both sides of the island as early as the first part of the sixteenth century to supply the needed labor force for sugar plantations. Spain ruled the entire island until 1697, when, under the Treaty of Ryswick, it ceded the western third of the island, which then became known as Saint-Domingue, to France.

During the eighteenth century, important demographic differences emerged. The population of Santo Domingo grew rapidly as trade reforms occurred, and by 1790 the country had some 100,000 people, roughly equal numbers of whites, free coloreds, and slaves. In contrast, Saint-Domingue, the most prosperous agricultural colony in the Western Hemisphere, had some 30,000 whites, 27,000 freedmen, and 400,000 black slaves. Differences in the economies of the two countries affected the makeup of the population. Santo Domingo engaged primarily in subsistence agriculture, requiring fewer slaves, and Spanish legislation enabled slaves to buy their freedom for relatively small sums. The result was a more egalitarian society than that of Saint-Domingue, which featured a more racially stratified population.

The resultant race-based tensions in Saint-Domingue, combined with the influences of the French Revolution, led to a struggle for independence from France that started in August 1791. The rebellion began as a slave uprising against whites and developed into the Haitian Revolution, headed by such figures as Toussaint Louverture. The uprising ultimately culminated in Haiti's proclamation of independence in 1804. Meanwhile, Spain, which had suffered setbacks on the European continent and was unable to maintain its hold on Santo Domingo, turned the area over to France in a peace treaty in 1795. Toussaint entered Santo Domingo in January 1801 and abolished slavery; later, however, the French reinstituted slavery in the area under their control in the east. The return of Spanish landowners to Santo Domingo in the early 1800s and the blockade by the British of the port of Santo Domingo led to the final departure of the French in 1809 and the return of Spanish rule. This rule was short-lived, however, because Jean-Pierre Boyer, as president of now independent Haiti, invaded Santo Domingo in 1822, and Haiti occupied the country for twenty-two years.

Subsequent Dominican leaders have revived memories of Haiti's harsh treatment of the inhabitants during its occupation of Santo Domingo, fueling Dominican dislike of Haitians. Moreover, during the occupation, Haitians, who associated the Roman Catholic Church with their colonial oppressors, confiscated Dominican Roman Catholic churches and property and severed the church's connection to the Vatican. Such historical experience caused Dominicans to see themselves as culturally and religiously different from Haitians and promoted a desire for independence. Building on this sentiment, Juan Pablo Duarte founded in 1838 a secret movement whose motto was "God, Country, and Liberty," defining Dominican nationality in religious and Hispanic terms. The overthrow of Boyer in the Haitian Revolution of 1843 further helped activate the Dominican struggle for independence, which occurred in February 1844.

Independence, however, did not bring either the Dominican Republic or Haiti a democratic central government organization but rather the rule of a series of strong men, or caudillos. Independence was also accompanied by political instability and interspersed with interference and sometimes occupation by one or another of the major powers, including the United States. In addition to taking charge of the finances of both countries on different occasions to ensure that the United States sphere of influence was not invaded by European powers seeking to recover debts that had not been paid, the United States occupied Haiti from 1915 to 1934 and the Dominican Republic from 1916 to 1924. Although strongman rule was accompanied frequently by liberal-sounding constitutions (since 1844 the Dominican Republic has had thirty-two constitutions, while Haiti has had twenty-four constitutions since 1804), such documents were ignored when it was convenient to do so, altered unilaterally, or negated by sham plebiscites. Major instances of such strongman regimes were those of

Rafael Trujillo in the Dominican Republic from 1930 to 1961, and François Duvalier, followed by his son Jean-Claude Duvalier, in Haiti from 1957 to 1986.

Accompanying these political developments was the grinding poverty of the vast majority of the population in both countries, apart from a small wealthy landowning class. Although the Dominican Republic has succeeded in improving its lot, Haiti today is considered by the World Bank (see Glossary) to be the poorest nation in the Western Hemisphere, and extensive malnutrition continues to be a serious concern. Moreover, a 1998 study done under the auspices of the United Nations Population Fund concluded that at an average of 4.8 births per woman, Haiti had the highest birthrate in the Western Hemisphere, double that of Latin America as a whole. Haiti's infant mortality rate of seventy per 1,000 is twice as high as that of the Dominican Republic, and Haiti's gross domestic product (GDP—see Glossary), variously given as between $200 and $400 per person, is less than one-fourth that of the Dominican Republic.

Haiti's high birth rate has put enormous pressure on the land, given the country's small amount of arable land in relation to the size of the population. National data gathered in 1995 revealed that 48 percent of the total land area in Haiti was being cultivated, although only 28 percent of the country's land is suitable for farming. The situation has resulted in serious soil erosion, loss of forest cover, and meager incomes for rural dwellers, who are estimated to represent some 59 percent of the population. Agriculture produces only about 25 percent of gross national product (GNP—see Glossary), yet agricultural work engages about two-thirds of the national labor force.

Haiti's economy has suffered not only from inefficiency and corruption but also from the three-year United Nations (UN) embargo placed on the country following the ouster of the democratically elected government of Jean-Bertrand Aristide (1991–94). To obtain needed funds from the United States and the International Monetary Fund (IMF—see Glossary), Haiti promised in 1994 to make such reforms as privatization and reductions in the size of its civil service. In practice, however, the Haitian administration found it politically unwise to maintain these commitments. Nevertheless, Haiti continues to receive international aid, including World Bank funding for two projects seeking to assist the poorest elements of the population—a1 Employment Generation Project and a Basic Infrastructure Project designed to improve social services. In addition, the United States Agency for International Development spent more than US$300 million in Haiti over the period from 1994 to 1999, vaccinating people, providing food for school children, improving hillside agriculture to increase farmer income, grafting fruit trees, and repairing roads. In general, however, since the restoration of democratically elected government in 1994, Haiti has experienced political instability and as a consequence, difficulty in attracting foreign investment or tourists.

Progress in the Dominican Republic's economic sphere, albeit more positive than Haiti's, has been uneven. Such sectors as the free-trade zones in which assembly plants are located and tourism are doing relatively well. Growth in tourism has been significant and steady, featuring an increase of 10 percent in 1999 over 1998 and an announcement by the Secretariat of State for Tourism that the number of tourists for the first three months of 2000 represented a 25 percent gain over 1999. Despite this progress, according to the Third National Survey of Household Expenditures and Incomes announced in November 1999, some 21 percent of the Dominican population is estimated to live in extreme poverty, including 33 percent of citizens in rural areas. Most residents of such areas lack access to potable water and some 25 percent lack electricity. Furthermore, a significant part of the population is affected by deficiencies in health care, housing, sanitation, and education. General dissatisfaction over lack of water supply, power outages, insufficient housing construction, and failure to repair roads led to strikes and popular demonstrations in 1999 and early 2000. The aftermath of Hurricane Georges that hit in September 1998 has aggravated the situation. Recovery is as yet incomplete despite international assistance, including the deployment of 3,000 United States Army personnel in 1999 to participate in Operation Caribbean Castle to rebuild destroyed bridges and rural schools.

The economy of the Dominican Republic is strongly affected by the legacy of the country's troubled relationship with Haiti and its people. On the one hand, Haitian workers are needed for Dominican coffee and sugar harvests and for unskilled construction work. On the other hand, the Dominican government institutes regular deportations of Haitians and Dominico-Haitians born in the Dominican Republic. At present, some 2,000 to 3,000 Haitians are deported monthly. In late 1999,

30,000 Haitians were reportedly deported, causing problems for the subsequent coffee harvest, which usually employs some 35,000 Haitian coffeepickers.

Recognizing that Haiti not only constitutes a significant source of the Dominican unskilled work force but also represents a market for Dominican goods, some Dominican leaders have begun to urge that the Dominican Republic join other countries in providing aid to Haiti. In an address to a graduating class of Dominican diplomats in 1999, President Leonel Fernández Reyna stated that the international community needed to promote Haiti's social and economic development. Earlier, in August 1999, the Dominican deputy minister of state for foreign affairs predicted that Haitians would continue their illegal migration to the Dominican Republic until political stability, economic progress, and a more equitable distribution of wealth were achieved in Haiti. However, in January 2000 the Dominican secretary of state for labor announced that no new work permits would be given to Haitians to enter the Dominican Republic to cut sugarcane. Instead, he advised Dominican employers to improve working conditions in the cane fields in order either to induce Haitians already in the Dominican Republic—500,000 Haitians are reportedly in the Dominican Republic—to work there or to attract indigenous Dominican workers. That a sizeable pool of potential Haitian workers exists in the Dominican Republic is suggested by the fact that in late 1999, the Haitian embassy in Santo Domingo issued 44,000 birth certificates to Haitians living in the Dominican Republic. Although the possession of a birth certificate does not give a Haitian legal status in the Dominican Republic, it enables the person to acquire a Haitian passport, which is a prerequisite for obtaining temporary work. Concern over the living conditions of Haitian workers in the Dominican Republic caused a number of Dominicans in the spring of 2000 to organize a peace march through Haiti to promote better conditions for such workers.

Drug trafficking continues to plague both the Dominican Republic and Haiti. Concern over increased smuggling of cocaine and heroin from Colombia through the Dominican Republic and Haiti, to the greater New York area via Puerto Rico and South Florida for East Coast distribution, has resulted in a series of efforts to disrupt the traffic. One is a coordinated plan by the United States and the Dominican Republic to deploy soldiers in cities and military outposts along the 223-

mile Dominican-Haitian border. The new Dominican inter-agency border patrol unit, which was formed in January 2000, will also act against illegal Haitian immigration and shipments of contraband weapons. In December 1999, the Dominican and Haitian police agreed to cooperate to fight drug trafficking, car theft, money laundering, and illegal immigration along their common border. To these ends, the Dominican Republic is setting up computerized police posts along the frontier. The chief of the United States Coast Guard visited the Dominican Republic in late March 2000 to coordinate implementation of the anti-drug efforts with the Dominican navy and the Secretariat of State for the Armed Forces. To date the various efforts are reportedly proving ineffective against corruption and the increased assault by traffickers on the vulnerable borders and institutions of Hispaniola. With regard to immigration control, in March 1999, the Dominican president and the governor of Puerto Rico met to strengthen measures against illegal Dominican immigration to Puerto Rico and thence to the United States mainland (Dominicans are the largest immigrant group in New York City).

Political instability and corruption have plagued both Haiti and the Dominican Republic. The problem has been particularly severe in Haiti since the end of the Duvalier regime. Following Jean-Claude Duvalier's ouster in 1986, a group of generals, for years Duvalier loyalists, played a major role in the interim government. During elections in November 1987, Duvalierist supporters killed numerous Haitians waiting to vote, causing all the candidates to condemn the interim government. Several fraudulent elections or seizures of power by military figures followed, prior to the election of a Roman Catholic priest, Jean-Bertrand Aristide, in December 1990. Identified with the poor, Aristide represented a threat to the country's establishment and was overthrown by a military coup after being in office less than a year. Following a United Nations-sanctioned, multilateral military intervention, Aristide was restored to office in October 1994. When Aristide's term expired in 1996, he was succeeded by René Préval. A bitter power struggle between Préval and the parliament, however, paralyzed Haiti's government and resulted in total governmental gridlock in 1997 and 1998. In consequence, Haiti again began to experience popular unrest, opposition-incited incidents, and a stagnating economy. In December 1998, Préval's candidate for prime minister, Jacques Édouard Alexis, was confirmed by a sharply divided legislature. In January 1999, Préval dissolved parliament because the electoral terms for most officials had expired, appointed municipal officials as "interim executive agents" of the Ministry of Interior, and began to rule by decree until elections could be held.

Complexities involved in setting up national elections resulted in three postponements from the original November 1998 election date. To facilitate elections, the United States provided $3.5 million in aid for voter registration and allocated an additional $10–15 million toward the estimated election cost of $18.5 million. Haiti contributed a further $9 million.

Haiti's sporadic violence, including shootings and other political disturbances—and the resulting danger to United States personnel—led Marine General Charles E. Wilhelm of the United States Southern Command, in February 1999 closed-door testimony before a subcommittee of the House of Representatives Appropriations Committee, to advocate the withdrawal from Haiti of remaining United States troops. These 500 military personnel, remnants of the 20,000-strong force that went to Haiti during the international intervention of September 1994, had assisted Haiti by providing medical care to the populace, constructing schools, repairing wells, and training police. The last United States forces permanently stationed in Haiti left in February 2000, but periodic training visits of United States military personnel, including the use of armed forces reservists, continue.

A UN mission continues training the Haitian police force. Haitian faith in the rule of law has been severely tested, however, because of police abuses that are exacerbated by a dysfunctional judiciary. Violence can reach alarming levels in Haiti, as it did in the period preceding the May 2000 elections. Human rights activists have pressured former president Aristide to use his stature to denounce the use of violence. To date, Aristide has been unwilling to follow such a course, preferring to take steps behind the scenes as opposed to making public statements.

In May 2000, Haiti held elections for 7,500 posts, including the entire Chamber of Deputies and two-thirds of the Senate as well as numerous municipal offices. Twenty-nine thousand candidates from a wide spectrum of political parties and organizations participated. Several hundred international observers joined a well organized national network of several thousand domestic observers. Voter turnout was at least 60 percent of the

4 million persons eligible. Despite delays, loud complaints from among the losing parties, some incidents, and various apparent irregularities in voting, the elections held on May 21 were termed "credible" by international and domestic observers and by the Organization of American States (OAS) Election Observation Mission.

Although the Lavalas Family, the party of Aristide, apparently gained a substantial election victory at the ballot box, the OAS subsequently discovered a serious error in the method of determining the winners of Senate races as announced by the Provisional Electoral Council. The OAS asked the Council to recalculate the percentage of votes won by all candidates, an action that could force several declared Senate winners to take part in runoff voting. The runoff election was rescheduled for July 9. The Council, with strong support from the presidential palace, refused to accept the OAS recommendations, however, creating an emerging international confrontation. This conflict is only the latest chapter in Haiti's troubled quest for post-dictatorial democracy.

Conditions are somewhat better in the Dominican Republic, although there, too, political instability has existed. Leonel Fernández won the 1996 runoff elections, but he has been unsuccessful in implementing many of his programs because of his party's small representation in Congress. In the 1998 elections, following the death of José Peña Gómez, his opposition party, the Democratic Revolutionary Party (Partido Revolucionario Dominicano—PRD), made sweeping gains. As a result, Congress in 1998 passed a new law abolishing the security of tenure of judges that Fernández had achieved and making judges subject to reappointment every four years. A poll taken in April 2000 showed that no candidate for the May 2000 presidential elections had the just over 50 percent needed for election (Fernández was ineligible to run again). As it developed, with 99 percent of the ballots counted, the Electoral Council announced the evening of May 17 that the opposition PRD candidate, Hipolito Mejía, had received 49.87 percent of the vote. His nearest opponent, Danilo Medina of the governing Dominican Liberation Party, had 24.94 percent of the vote, and seven-time former president Joaquín Balaguer had 24.6 percent. At a press conference on May 18, Medina stated that a June 30 runoff election would cost too much in time, money, and tension and that a continued campaign would hurt the economy. Therefore he "acknowledged the victory of the

PRD," laying the groundwork for Mejía's inauguration on August 16.

The latest round of Hispaniola's elections indicates that while each side of the island has moved away markedly from the strong-man role of the past, the transition to the peaceful, transparent, and capable democratic governance required for much-needed sustained social and economic development will continue to be fraught with problems.

June 30, 2000   Helen Chapin Metz

Dominican Republic: Counry Profile

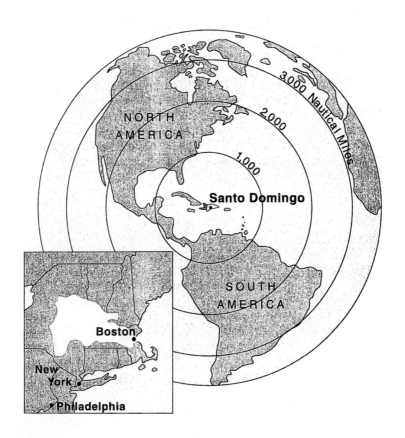

Country

Formal Name: Dominican Republic.

Short Form: Dominican Republic.

Term for Citizens: Dominicans.

Capital: Santo Domingo.

Geography

Size: Approximately 48,442 square kilometers.

Topography: Mountain ranges divide country into three regions: northern, central, and southwestern. Seven major drainage basins, most important that of Yaque del Norte River. Largest body of water, Lago Enriquillo (Lake Enriquillo), in southwest. Highest mountain peak, Pico Duarte, rises in Cordillera Central (Central Range) to height of 3,087 meters.

Climate: Primarily tropical, with temperatures varying according to altitude. Seasons defined more by rainfall than by temperature. For most of country, rainy season runs roughly from May through October; dry season, from November through April. Rainfall not uniform throughout country because of mountain ranges. Tropical cyclones strike country on average of once every two years and usually have greatest impact along southern coast.

Society

Population: Annual rate of increase has been declining; was 1.6 percent in mid-1990s. Total population estimated at just over 8 million in 1997.

Language: Spanish.

Ethnic Groups: Approximately 75 percent of mid-1990s population mulatto, a legacy of black slavery during colonial period. Approximately 10 percent white; 15 percent black.

Education and Literacy: An estimated 82 percent of population literate in 1997. Education system includes six years of compulsory primary education, an additional six years of secondary education, and higher education at one of more than twenty-seven postsecondary institutions. Major university and sole public institution is Autonomous University of Santo Domingo (Universidad Autónoma de Santo Domingo— UASD), with four regional centers in 1990s.

Health: State-funded health programs reach 80 percent of population in theory (but 40 percent in reality). Facilities concentrated in Santo Domingo and Santiago de los Caballeros (Santiago); service in rural areas suffers accordingly. Main causes of death: pulmonary, circulatory, and cardiovascular diseases. Average life expectancy seventy years for 1990–95 period.

Religion: More than 80 percent Roman Catholic. Protestant groups also active; evangelicals have been most successful in attracting converts.

Economy

Gross Domestic Product (GDP): About US$5.8 billion in 1996, or approximately US$716 per capita.

Agriculture: Declining in significance since 1960s when agriculture employed almost 60 percent of workforce, accounted for 25 percent of GDP, and generated 80 to 90 percent of total exports. By 1992 sector's share of exports had dropped to 43 percent and it employed 28 percent of labor force. By end 1995, agriculture's share of GDP at 12.7 percent and it employed 12.9 percent of workforce. Importance of sugar, traditionally major crop, has declined steadily; other significant crops: coffee, cocoa, and tobacco. Implementation of Caribbean Basin Initiative (CBI) (see Glossary) provided reduced tariff access to United States market for such items as ornamental plants, winter vegetables, spices, nuts, citrus, and tropical fruits.

Industry: Domestic manufacturing and assembly operations in free zones accounted for 18.3 percent of GDP in 1998. Domestic manufacturing, including consumer goods, food, and cigar production, grew by 10.1 percent in first half 1998. Growth resulted partly from dramatic increase in United States demand for cigars, for which Dominican Republic is leading supplier. Industrial free zones numbered thirty-three by 1995 and employed some 165,000 workers in 469 companies; number of employees increased to 182,000 in 1997, but number of firms operating in free zones dropped to 434. Free-zone exports generated needed foreign exchange: US$2 billion in 1996 and US$3.8 billion in 1997—almost 75 percent of total Dominican export earnings.

Services: Tourism leading service industry; generated more than US$1.55 billion in foreign exchange in 1995 and US$2.1 billion in 1997. Sector employed 44,000 hotel workers directly and additional 110,000 indirectly. Number of tourists almost tripled in ten years, from 278,000 in 1975 to 792,000 in 1985, surpassed 1 million in 1987, and jumped to 1,766,800 in 1994 to 1,930,000 in 1996 to 2,211,000 in 1997. In 1997 country became second largest earner of tourism dollars in Caribbean, after Mexico.

Currency: Issued by Central Bank of the Dominican Republic

3

since 1948, Dominican Republic peso (RD$) was officially maintained on par with US$ until 1985, when it was floated (and devalued) against the dollar until it stabilized at US$1 = RD$6.35 in 1989. After experiments with multiple exchange rates, all rates were unified in 1997 on free-market basis and at initial rate of US$1 = RD$14. After Hurricane Georges, official rate dropped to US$1 = RD$15.46. Commercial rate was US$1 = RD$16.25 in January 2000.

Imports: Total imports in 1998: US$3,403.1 million. Deep plunge in oil prices reduced Dominican fuel bill by about 20 percent to US$336 million in first half 1998, but total value of imports increased by 15 percent over 1997 as aftermath of Hurricane Georges, which left 300 people dead and hundreds of thousands homeless. Government officials estimated surge in imports related to reconstruction effort at US$700 million through 1999.

Exports: Total exports in 1998: US$2,457.6 million. Sharp decline in world commodity prices caused by 1997 Asian currency crisis created negative impact on trade deficit. Exports of nickel, major Dominican earner of foreign exchange, suffered 27 percent price drop and fell 38.4 percent in 1998. Coffee exports adversely affected by 10 percent decline in international prices. Export of sugar and sugar products in 1998 decreased 29.6 percent, mainly as result of 24 percent cut in Dominican international sugar quota.

Balance of Payments: Trade deficits continued into 1990s, hitting record US$1.639 billion in 1993, 1.4 percent increase over 1992, and exceeding US$1.5 billion in 1994. Deficits registered continued deterioration: from US$832 million in first half 1997 to US$945 million in first half 1998.

Fiscal Year: Calendar year.

Fiscal Policy: President Leonel Fernández Reyna's campaign against tax evasion (upon taking office in 1996) proved successful: budgetary income in 1997 was 31 percent higher than in 1996. Reforms in late 1990s included strengthening Central Bank's autonomy and tightening credit and wage systems. Inflation plunged from 80 percent in 1990 to 9 percent in 1995. External public debt as share of GDP more than halved (to 33 percent) in same period. Unemployment rate declined from about 20 percent in 1991–93 to about 16 percent in 1995.

Transportation and Communications

Roads: Most roadways of 17,200-kilometer network narrow and flood easily. Worsening conditions prompted World Bank (see Glossary) and Inter-American Development Bank to finance better maintenance systems. Major road construction program initiated in late 1990s to develop intercity routes and urban projects in Santo Domingo.

Railroads: 1,600-kilometer railroad system, one of longest in Caribbean, most of which owned by state sugar enterprise. Several private rail companies also serve sugar industry.

Ports: Of fourteen ports, only five are major. Largest, Santo Domingo, handles 80 percent of imports; has cruiseliner berth enlarged in 1997. Other major ports include Haina, Boca Chica, and San Pedro de Macorís on south coast, and Puerta Plata on north coast.

Airports: Five international airports: Santo Domingo, Puerta Plata, Punta Cana, La Romana, and Barahona. Sixth airport under construction at Samaná in late 1990s. Puerto Plata and Punta Cana main airports for charter flights; Las Américas near Santo Domingo for scheduled flights. American Airlines dominant carrier, with routes to many United States cities, chiefly Miami and New York.

Telecommunications: Industry fastest growing element of economy, doubling share of GDP to 4.6 percent since government opened sector to competition in 1990. In first half 1998, grew by 20.8 percent. Telephone system includes direct domestic and international dialing, toll-free access to United States through 800 numbers, high-speed data transmission capabilities, fiber-optic cables, and digital switching.

Government and Politics

Government: Republic with elected representative governmental system. Executive is dominant branch. Presidents serve four-year terms and, following a 1994 constitutional reform, cannot be reelected immediately. Legislature, known formally as Congress of the Republic, consists of Senate and Chamber of Deputies. Judicial power exercised by Supreme Court of Justice and by other courts created by 1966 constitution and by law. Following a 1994 constitutional reform, Supreme Court judges are chosen by a Council of the Magistrature, with membership from all three branches of government; other judges are chosen by the Supreme Court. Provincial (state) governors appointed by president; municipalities (counties) governed by elected mayors and municipal councils.

Politics: Following independence from Haiti in 1844, country characterized by instability for almost a century. Dictator Rafael Leónidas Trujillo Molina took power in 1930 and ruled in repressive authoritarian fashion until his assassination in 1961. Brief civil war in 1965 between liberal Constitutionalists—supporters of 1963 constitution promulgated during short-lived presidency of Juan Bosch Gaviño—and conservative Loyalist military factions. Subsequent elections brought Trujillo protégé Joaquín Balaguer Ricardo to presidency, an office he held for twelve years. Balaguer's attempt to nullify 1978 elections thwarted by pressure from Washington, allowing Silvestre Antonio Guzmán Fernández of social democratic Dominican Revolutionary Party (Partido Revolucionario Dominicano—PRD) to assume nation's leadership. PRD also won 1982 elections with lawyer Salvador Jorge Blanco as its standard bearer. Both PRD governments plagued by economic difficulties that forced them to institute austerity measures instead of social reforms they initially advocated. Declining popularity of Jorge Blanco government contributed to Balaguer's election for a fourth term beginning in 1986. Balaguer retained power through increasingly conflictual and questioned elections in 1990 and 1994; he agreed to shorten his term in 1994 to two years and accept constitutional reforms including no immediate reelection. Leonel Fernández Reyna of the Party of Dominican Liberation (Partido de la Liberación Dominicana—PLD) won 1996 presidential elections.

International Relations: Diplomatic activities concentrated on Caribbean, Latin America, United States, and Western Europe. Relations with neighboring Haiti traditionally strained as a result of historical conflicts, cultural divergences, and most recently, increased migration into the Dominican Republic from Haiti. Most important international relationship with United States, on which Dominican Republic has political, economic, and strategic dependence.

International Agreements and Memberships: Signatory of Inter-American Treaty of Reciprocal Assistance (Rio Treaty)

6

and all major inter-American conventions. Member of United Nations and its specialized agencies, Organization of American States, International Monetary Fund (see Glossary), Inter-American Development Bank, and other multilateral financial institutions. Also member of World Trade Organization, African, Caribbean, and Pacific Group of Nations, and other regional trade groupings.

National Security

Armed Forces: Dominican armed forces consist of army, navy, and air force. Total personnel in 1999 reported to be 24,300.

Organization: President is constitutional commander in chief. Chain of command extends downward to secretary of state for the armed forces, then to deputy secretaries of state for individual branches of service, each of which administered through a chief of staff and a general staff. Chiefs of staff exercise operational control except in emergencies. Country divided into three defense zones: Southern Defense Zone, Western Defense Zone, and Northern Defense Zone.

Equipment: Army equipment includes twenty-four French and United States light tanks, armored vehicles, half-tracks, and towed howitzers, largely outmoded and poorly maintained. Dominican navy in 1999 consisted primarily of twelve armed patrol vessels, mostly United States-made craft of World War II vintage. Dominican air force organized into three flying squadrons: one of Cessna A–37B Dragonfly jets, one of C–47 transports, and one of helicopters.

Police: Internal security responsibility shared by armed forces and National Police. Total police manpower in 1998 about 15,000. Commanded by director general subordinate to secretary of state for interior and police. National Department of Investigations, a domestic intelligence unit, and National Drug Control Directorate are independent bodies reporting directly to president.

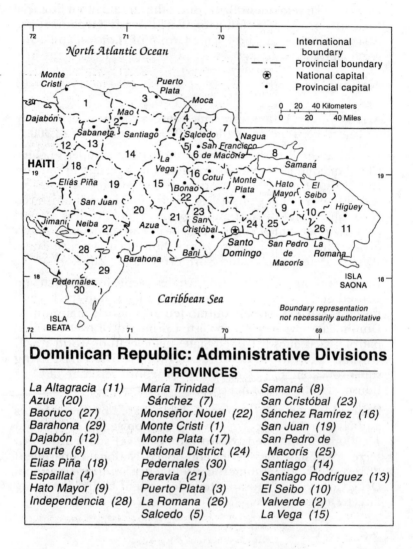

Dominican Republic: Administrative Divisions
——————————— PROVINCES ———————————

La Altagracia (11)   María Trinidad   Samaná (8)
Azua (20)   Sánchez (7)   San Cristóbal (23)
Baoruco (27)   Monseñor Nouel (22) San Juan (19)
Barahona (29)   Monte Cristi (1)   San Juan (19)
Dajabón (12)   Monte Plata (17)   San Pedro de
Duarte (6)   National District (24) Macorís (25)
Elías Piña (18)   Pedernales (30)   Santiago (14)
Espaillat (4)   Peravia (21)   Santiago Rodríguez (13)
Hato Mayor (9)   Puerto Plata (3)   El Seibo (10)
Independencia (28) La Romana (26)   Valverde (2)
               Salcedo (5)   La Vega (15)

Figure 2. Dominican Republic: Administrative Divisions, 1999

8

Table A. Dominican Republic: Chronology of Important Events

Period		Description
1492		Columbus lands at present-day Môle Saint-Nicolas, Haiti; establishes first permanent Spanish New World settlement at site of Santo Domingo.
1492–1697		Spain colonizes Hispaniola.
1503		Nicolás de Ovando named governor and supreme justice; institutes *encomienda* system. Importation of African slaves begins.
1586		Sir Francis Drake captures city of Santo Domingo, collects ransom for returning it to Spain.
1697		Spain, under Treaty of Ryswick, cedes western third of Hispaniola (Saint-Domingue—modern Haiti) to France.
1801		Toussaint Louverture invades Santo Domingo, abolishes slavery.
1802		France occupies the Spanish-speaking colony, reinstituting slavery in that part of the island.
1809		Spanish rule is restored.
1818–43		Under presidency of Jean-Pierre Boyer, Haiti invades and occupies Santo Domingo; abolishes slavery.
1821		Spanish lieutenant governor José Núñez de Cáceres declares colony's independence as Spanish Haiti.
1838		Juan Pablo Duarte creates secret independence movement, La Trinitaria.
1844	February 27	La Trinitaria members and others rebel; Santo Domingo gains independence.
	July 12	Pedro Santana's forces take Santo Domingo and proclaim Santana ruler.
1849		Buenaventura Báez Méndez becomes president; Santana expels him in 1853. (Báez resumes presidency 1865–66, 1868–74, 1878–79).
1861	March 18	Santana announces annexation of Dominican Republic by Spain.
1865	March 3	Queen of Spain approves repeal of Santo Domingo annexation.
1882–99		Ulises Heureaux rules as president/dictator.
1905		General Customs Receivership established; United States administers Dominican finances.
1916–24		United States marines occupy Dominican Republic
1930–61		Rafael Leónidas Trujillo Molina, head of National Guard, becomes president/dictator; rules directly or indirectly until assassinated.
1937		Dominican military massacre some 15,000–20,000 Haitians near Dominican-Haitian border.
1942		Dominican women given suffrage.
1965	April 28	United States intervenes, fearing a potential communist takeover because Dominican troops are unable to control a civil war.
1966–78		Joaquín Balaguer Ricardo becomes president in 1966, and United States troops leave.
1978–82		Antonio Guzmán Fernández becomes president; creates a more democratic regime.
1982–86		Salvador Jorge Blanco elected president.
1986–96		Balaguer returns to presidency.
1996		In free elections, Leonel Fernández Reyna is elected in second round.

Table A. (Cont.) Dominican Republic: Chronology of Important Events

Period		Description
1997		Newly created Council of the Magistrature appoints a distinguished new Supreme Court.
1998	May	Fair congressional and municipal elections held one week after death of noted politician José Francisco Peña Gómez.

Chapter 1. Dominican Republic: Historical Setting

Tomb of the three fathers of the Dominican Republic in Santo Domingo

IN THE DOMINICAN REPUBLIC, the past has weighed heavily on current political practices. The country's historical evolution, for example, has proved particularly inimical to democratic development, deviating significantly from patterns viewed as optimum for the development of democracy. Political scientist Robert Dahl has argued that sequences in which successful experiences with limited liberalization are followed by gradually greater inclusiveness appear to favor democracy. The analyst Eric Nordlinger has asserted that the pattern most promising for the development of democracy is one in which national identity emerges first, then legitimate and authoritative state structures are institutionalized, and ultimately mass parties and a mass electorate emerge with the extension of citizenship rights to non-elite elements.

The pattern followed by the Dominican Republic was very different. The country's colonial period was marked by the decimation of the indigenous population, and then by poverty and warfare. National integration was truncated, first by a Haitian invasion and then by the attempts of some Dominican elites to trade nascent Dominican sovereignty for security by having foreign powers annex the country, while enriching themselves in the process. State building also suffered under the dual impact of international vulnerability and unstable, neopatrimonial, authoritarian politics. Both integration and state building were also impaired by bitter regional struggles based on different economic interests and desires for power that accentuated the politics of the country. In this context, the failure of early efforts to extend liberal guarantees and citizenship rights to vast sectors of the population served to reinforce past patterns of behavior. Nonetheless, reform efforts continually reemerged.

Indeed, a Dominican state arguably did not emerge until the late nineteenth century or even the era of Rafael Leónidas Trujillo Molina (1930–61). Trujillo's emergence, in turn, was unquestionably facilitated by changes wrought by the eight-year United States occupation of the Dominican Republic at the beginning of the twentieth century. Trujillo's pattern of rule could not have been more hostile to democratic governance. His centralization of power, monopolization of the economy, destruction or co-optation of enemies, and astonishing constitutional hypocrisy were, however, combined with the forging of national integration, the establishment of state institutions, and the beginnings of industrialization, although in a distorted manner.

Thus, the country essentially had no history of democratic rule prior to 1961, despite the presence of a liberal constitutional tradition. In the context of contradictory and extensive United States actions both to foster democracy and to block perceived communist threats, efforts toward democratic transition following the death of Trujillo ultimately failed. The short-lived democratic regime of Juan Bosch Gaviño (1962) was followed by unstable governments and ultimately by United States intervention in 1965 out of fear of a "second Cuba." A key figure from the Trujillo era, Joaquín Balaguer Ricardo, was to govern the country for twenty-two of the next thirty years, from 1966 to 1978 and again from 1986 to 1996. His rule combined political stagnation with dramatic socioeconomic transformation. The 1978 democratic transition following Balaguer's authoritarian twelve-year period in office ended in return to the pre-democratic status quo. Although Balaguer was ushered back into office through democratic elections in 1986, his increasingly authoritarian rule finally ended when he stepped down from the presidency in 1996.

The Dominican Republic is entering the new millennium bolstered by potential changes in political leadership, significant evolution in the country's social structure, and an international environment more favorable to political democracy. However, the country also faces formidable challenges in terms of continued political fragmentation, difficult economic adjustments, and corruption and criminal violence associated in part with drug trafficking.

The First Colony

The island of Hispaniola (La Isla Española) was the first New World colony settled by Spain. Christopher Columbus first sighted the island in 1492 toward the end of his first voyage to "the Indies." Columbus and his crew found the island inhabited by a large population of friendly Taino (Arawak) Indians, who made the explorers welcome. The land was fertile, but of greater importance to the Spaniards was the discovery that gold could be obtained either by barter with the natives or by extraction from alluvial deposits on the island.

Spain's first permanent settlement in the New World was established on the southern coast at the present site of Santo Domingo. Under Spanish sovereignty, the entire island bore the name Santo Domingo. Indications of the presence of gold—the lifeblood of the nascent mercantilist system—and a population of tractable natives who could be used as laborers combined to attract Spanish newcomers interested in acquiring wealth quickly during the early years. Their relations with the Taino Indians, whom they ruthlessly maltreated, deteriorated from the beginning. Aroused by continued seizures of their food supplies, other exactions, and abuse of their women, the formerly peaceful Indians rebelled—only to be crushed decisively in 1495.

Columbus, who ruled the colony as royal governor until 1499, devised the *repartimiento* system of land settlement and native labor under which a settler, without assuming any obligation to the authorities, could be granted in perpetuity a large tract of land together with the services of the Indians living on it.

In 1503 the Spanish crown instituted the *encomienda* system. Under this system, all land became in theory the property of the crown, and the Indians were considered tenants on royal land. The crown's right to service from the tenants could be transferred in trust to individual Spanish settlers (*encomenderos*) by formal grant and the regular payment of tribute. The *encomenderos* were entitled to certain days of labor from the Indians, and they assumed the responsibility of providing for the physical well-being of the Indians and for their instruction in Christianity. Although an *encomienda* theoretically did not involve ownership of land, in practice it did—ownership was just gained through other means.

The privations that the Indians suffered demonstrated the unrealistic nature of the *encomienda* system, which the Spanish authorities never effectively enforced. The Indian population died off rapidly from exhaustion, starvation, disease, and other causes. When the Spanish landed, they forced an estimated 400,000 Tainos (out of a total Taino population of some 1 million) to work for them; by 1508 the Tainos numbered only around 60,000. By 1535 only a few dozen were still alive. The need for a new labor force to meet the growing demands of sugarcane cultivation in the 1520s prompted an increase in the importation of African slaves, which had begun in 1503. By

1546 the colony had some 12,000 slaves and a white population of under 5,000.

The granting of land without any obligation to central authorities, as was done under the *repartimiento* system, led to a rapid decentralization of power. Power was also diffused because of the tendency of the capital city, Santo Domingo (which also served as the seat of government for the entire Spanish Indies), to orient itself toward continental America, which provided gold for the crown, and toward Spain, which provided administrators, supplies, and immigrants to the colonies. With little contact existing between the capital and the hinterland, local government was doomed to be ineffective, and for practical purposes the countryside fell under the sway of the large local landowners.

As early as the 1490s, the landowners among the Spanish colonists successfully conspired against Columbus. His successor, Francisco de Bobadilla, was appointed chief justice and royal commissioner by the Spanish crown in 1499. Bobadilla sent Columbus back to Spain in irons; Queen Isabella soon ordered him released. Bobadilla, who had proved an inept administrator, was replaced in 1503 by the more efficient Nicolás de Ovando, who assumed the titles of governor and supreme justice. Because of his success in initiating reforms desired by the crown—the *encomienda* system among them—Ovando received the title of Founder of Spain's Empire in the Indies.

In 1509 Columbus's son, Diego, was appointed governor of the colony of Santo Domingo. Diego's ambition aroused the suspicions of the crown, which in 1511 established the *audiencia*, a new political institution intended to check the power of the governor. The first *audiencia* was simply a tribunal composed of three judges whose jurisdiction extended over all the West Indies. The tribunal's influence grew, and in 1524 it was designated the Royal Audiencia of Santo Domingo (Audiencia Real de Santo Domingo), with jurisdiction in the Caribbean, the Atlantic coast of Central America and Mexico, and the northern coast of South America. As a court representing the crown, the *audiencia* was given expanded powers that encompassed administrative, legislative, and consultative functions; the number of judges increased correspondingly. In criminal cases, the *audiencia*'s decisions were final, but important civil suits could be appealed to the Royal and Supreme Council of the Indies (Real y Supremo Consejo de Indias) in Spain.

The Council of the Indies, created by Charles V in 1524, was the Spanish crown's main agency for directing colonial affairs. During most of its existence, the council exercised almost absolute power in making laws, administering justice, controlling finance and trade, supervising the church, and directing armies.

The arm of the Council of the Indies that dealt with all matters concerned with commerce between Spain and the colonies in the Americas was the House of Trade (Casa de Contratación), organized in 1503. Control of commerce in general, and of tax collection in particular, was facilitated by the designation of monopoly seaports on either side of the Atlantic Ocean. Trade between the colonies and countries other than Spain was prohibited. The crown also restricted trade among the colonies. These restrictions hampered economic activity in the New World and encouraged contraband traffic.

The Roman Catholic Church became the primary agent in spreading Spanish culture in the Americas. The ecclesiastical organization developed for Santo Domingo and later established throughout Spanish America reflected a union of church and state closer than that which actually prevailed in Spain itself. The Royal Patronage of the Indies (Real Patronato de Indias, or, as it was called later, the Patronato Real) served as the organizational agent of this affiliation of the church and the Spanish crown.

Santo Domingo's importance to Spain declined in the first part of the sixteenth century as the gold mines became exhausted and the local Indian population was decimated. With the conquest of Mexico by Hernán Cortés in 1521 and the discovery there, and later in Peru, of great wealth in gold and silver, large numbers of colonists left for Mexico and Peru, and new immigrants from Spain also largely bypassed Santo Do-mingo.

The stagnation that prevailed in Santo Domingo for the next 250 years was interrupted on several occasions by armed engagements, as the French and British attempted to weaken Spain's economic and political dominance in the New World. In 1586 the British admiral, Sir Francis Drake, captured the city of Santo Domingo and collected a ransom for its return to Spanish control. In 1655 Oliver Cromwell dispatched a British fleet commanded by Sir William Penn to take Santo Domingo. After meeting heavy resistance, the British sailed farther west and took Jamaica instead.

The withdrawal of the colonial government from the northern coastal region opened the way for French buccaneers, who had a base on Tortuga Island (Île de la Tortue), off the northwest coast of present-day Haiti, to settle on Hispaniola in the mid-seventeenth century. The creation of the French West India Company in 1664 signaled France's intention to colonize western Hispaniola. Intermittent warfare went on between French and Spanish settlers over the next three decades; Spain, however, was hard-pressed by warfare in Europe and could not maintain a garrison in Santo Domingo sufficient to protect the entire island against encroachment. In 1697, under the Treaty of Ryswick, Spain ceded the western third of the island to France. The exact boundary of this territory (Saint-Domingue—modern Haiti) was not established at the time of cession and remained in question until 1929.

During the first years of the eighteenth century, landowners in the Spanish colony did little with their huge holdings, and the sugar plantations along the southern coast were abandoned because of harassment by pirates. Foreign trade all but ceased, and almost all domestic commerce took place in the capital city.

The Bourbon dynasty replaced the Habsburgs in Spain in 1700. The new regime introduced innovations—especially economic reforms—that gradually began to revive trade in Santo Domingo. The crown progressively relaxed the rigid controls and restrictions on commerce between the mother country and the colonies and among the colonies. By the middle of the century, both immigration and the importation of slaves had increased.

In 1765 the Caribbean islands received authorization for almost unlimited trade with Spanish ports; permission for the Spanish colonies in America to trade among themselves followed in 1774. Soon duties on many commodities were greatly reduced or removed altogether. By 1790 traders from any port in Spain could buy and sell anywhere in Spanish America, and by 1800 Spain had opened colonial trade to all neutral vessels.

As a result of the stimulus provided by the trade reforms, the population of the colony of Santo Domingo increased from about 6,000 in 1737 to approximately 100,000 in 1790, with roughly equal numbers of whites, free coloreds, and slaves. The size and composition of Santo Domingo's population contrasted sharply, however, with that of the neighboring and far more prosperous French colony of Saint-Domingue, where some 30,000 whites and 27,000 freedmen extracted labor from some 400,000 black slaves.

The Struggle for Formal Sovereignty

The nineteenth-century struggle for independence of what was to become the Dominican Republic was an incredibly difficult process, conditioned by the evolution of its neighbor. Although they shared the island of Hispaniola, the colonies of Saint-Domingue and Santo Domingo followed disparate paths, primarily as a result of economic factors. Saint-Domingue was the most productive agricultural colony in the Western Hemisphere, and its output contributed heavily to the economy of France (see French Colony of Saint-Domingue, 1697–1803, ch.6.) Prosperous French plantation owners imported great numbers of slaves from Africa and drove this captive work force ruthlessly. By contrast, Santo Domingo was a small, unimportant, and largely ignored colony with little impact on the economy of Spain.

Although by the end of the eighteenth century economic conditions were improving somewhat, landowners in Santo Domingo did not enjoy the same level of wealth attained by their French counterparts in Saint-Domingue. The absence of market-driven pressure to increase production enabled the domestic labor force to meet the needs of subsistence agriculture and to export at low levels. Thus, Santo Domingo imported far fewer slaves than did Saint-Domingue. Spanish law also allowed a slave to purchase his freedom and that of his family for a relatively small sum. This fact contributed to the higher proportion of freedmen in the Spanish colony than in Haiti; by the turn of the century, freedmen actually constituted the majority of the population. Again, in contrast to conditions in the French colony, this population profile contributed to a somewhat more egalitarian society, plagued much less by racial schisms.

With a revolution against the monarchy well underway in France, the inevitable explosion took place in Saint-Domingue in August 1791 (see Fight for Independence, 1791–1803, ch. 6). The initial reaction of many Spanish colonists to news of the slaughter of Frenchmen by armies of rebellious black slaves was to flee Hispaniola entirely. Spain, however, saw in the unrest an opportunity to seize all or part of the western third of the island through an alliance of convenience with the British. These intentions, however, did not survive encounters in the field with forces led by the former slave François Dominique Toussaint Louverture. By mid-1795, Spain had signed a peace treaty with France in which it surrendered the eastern part of the island; the terms of the treaty reflected Spain's setbacks in Europe and its relative decline as a world power. In recognition of his leadership against the Spanish (under whose banner he had begun his military career), British, and rebellious royalists and mulattoes, Toussaint was named governor general of Saint-Domingue by the French Republic in 1796. After losing more than 25,000 troops, Britain withdrew from the island in April 1798. Toussaint marched into Santo Domingo in January 1801; one of his first measures was to abolish slavery.

France occupied the devastated Spanish-speaking colony in February 1802. The Spanish and Dominican elites on the Spanish part of the island allied themselves with the French, who reinstituted slavery in that part of the island. However, the expeditionary force dispatched by Napoleon Bonaparte was defeated by the forces of the former French slaves, led by Toussaint —and later by Jean-Jacques Dessalines. Yellow fever, malaria, and war led to the loss of 52,000 French soldiers. Upon defeating the French, Dessalines and his followers established the independent Republic of Haiti in January 1804 (see Fight for Independence, 1791–1803, ch.6). A small French presence, however, remained in the former Spanish colony, in spite of Haitian pressures.

By 1808 a number of émigré Spanish landowners had returned to Santo Domingo. These royalists had no intention of living under French rule, however, and sought foreign aid and assistance to restore Spanish sovereignty. Help came from the Haitians, who provided arms, and the British, who occupied Samaná and blockaded the port of Santo Domingo in 1809. The remaining French representatives fled the island in July 1809.

The 1809 restoration of Spanish rule ushered in an era referred to by some historians as España Boba (Foolish Spain). Under the despotic rule of Ferdinand VII, the colony's economy deteriorated severely. Some Dominicans began to wonder if their interests would not best be served by the sort of independence movement that was sweeping the South American colonies. In keeping with this sentiment, Spanish lieutenant governor José Núñez de Cáceres announced the colony's independence as the state of Spanish Haiti on November 30, 1821. Cáceres requested admission to the Republic of Gran Colombia (consisting of what later became Colombia, Ecuador, Venezuela, and Panama), recently proclaimed established by Simón Bolívar and his followers. While the request was in transit, however, the president of Haiti, Jean-Pierre Boyer, decided to invade Santo Domingo and to reunite the island under the Haitian flag.

The twenty-two-year Haitian occupation that followed (1822–44) is recalled by Dominicans as a period of brutal military rule, although the reality is more complex. Haiti's policies toward Santo Domingo were induced in part by international financial pressures because Haiti had promised in an 1825 treaty to indemnify former French settlers in return for French recognition of Haitian independence. Ultimately, it was a period of economic decline and of growing resentment of Haiti among Dominicans. The main activity was subsistence agriculture, and exports consisted of small amounts of tobacco, cattle hides, caoba wood (Dominican mahogany), molasses, and rum; the population, in turn, had declined precipitously by 1909 to some 75,000 people. Boyer attempted to enforce in the new territory the Rural Code (Code Rural) he had decreed in an effort to improve productivity among the Haitian yeomanry; however, the Dominicans proved no more willing to adhere to its provisions than were the Haitians (see Early Years of Independence, 1804–43, ch. 6). Increasing numbers of Dominican landowners chose to flee the island rather than live under Haitian rule; in many cases, Haitian administrators encouraged such emigration.

Dominicans also resented the fact that Boyer, the ruler of an impoverished country, did not (or could not) provision his army. The occupying Haitian forces lived off the land in Santo Domingo, commandeering or confiscating what they needed. Racial animosities also affected attitudes on both sides; black Haitian troops reacted with resentment toward lighter-skinned Dominicans, while Dominicans came to associate the Haitians' dark skin with the oppression and abuses of occupation. Furthermore, Haitians, who associated the Roman Catholic Church with the French colonists who had so cruelly exploited and abused them before independence, confiscated all church property in the east, deported all foreign clergy, and severed the ties of the remaining clergy to the Vatican. The occupation reinforced Dominicans' perception of themselves as different from Haitians with regard to culture, religion, race, and daily practices.

Scattered unrest and isolated confrontations between Haitians and Dominicans soon began; by 1838 significant organized movements against Haitian domination formed. The most important was led by Juan Pablo Duarte of a prominent Santo Domingo family who returned from seven years of study in Europe to find his father's business had been ruined under Haitian occupation. Unlike many of the country's subsequent caudillo rulers, Duarte was an idealist, an ascetic, and a genuine nationalist. Although he played no significant part in its rule, he is considered the father of his country. He certainly provided the inspiration and impetus for achieving independence from Haiti.

In July 1838, Duarte led the effort to create a secret movement, dubbed La Trinitaria (The Trinity). Its original nine members had organized themselves into cells of three; the cells went on to recruit as separate organizations, maintaining strict secrecy. At the same time, the name clearly evoked the Holy Trinity. Its motto was "Dios, Patria, y Libertad" (God, Country, and Liberty), and the movement's flag and shield had a cross and an open Bible—all of which became national symbols. Dominican nationality became defined in religious and Hispanic terms, which permitted contrast to Haiti. As the country's principal enemy was the anti-Catholic and non-Spanish-speaking Haiti, and perhaps because the Catholic Church was very weak in the country, Dominican liberals were largely pro-church, in contrast to their counterparts in the rest of Central and South America.

The catalyst that helped set off the Dominican struggle for independence was the overthrow of Boyer in the Haitian Revolution of 1843. Initially good relations between liberal Haitians and liberal Dominicans in Dominican territory, however, soon grew tense. General Charles Rivière-Hérard successfully cracked down on the Trinitarios, forcing Duarte to flee in August 1843. However, Francisco del Rosario Sánchez, Duarte's brother Vicente, and Ramón Mella helped to reestablish the Trinitaria movement. They planned an independence effort built around arms that a returning Duarte was to bring in late December; however, Duarte failed in his efforts to gain the necessary weapons and was forced to postpone his return home because of a serious illness. Concurrently, other conspiracies flourished, particularly one seeking to gain the support of France. When Duarte had not returned by February 1844, the rebels agreed to launch their uprising without him.

On February 27, 1844—thereafter celebrated as Dominican Independence Day—the rebels seized the Ozama fortress in the capital. The Haitian garrison, taken by surprise and apparently betrayed by at least one of its sentries, retired in disarray. Within two days, all Haitian officials had departed Santo Domingo. Mella headed the provisional governing junta of the new Dominican Republic. Duarte returned to his country on March 14, and on the following day entered the capital amidst great adulation and celebration. However, the optimism generated by revolutionary triumph would eventually give way to the more prosaic realities of the struggle for power.

Ambivalent Sovereignty, Caudillo Rule, and Political Instability

The decades following independence from Haiti were marked by complex interactions among Dominican governing groups, opposition movements, Haitian authorities, and representatives of France, Britain, Spain, and the United States. Duarte and the liberal merchants who had led the initial independence effort were soon swept out of office and into exile, and the independent tobacco growers and merchants of the northern Cibao valley, who tended to favor national independence, were unable to consolidate control of the center. Government revolved largely around a small number of caudillo strongmen, particularly Pedro Santana Familias and Buenaventura Báez Méndez (allies who became rivals), and their intrigues involving foreign powers in defense against Haiti and for personal gain. All these factors meant that neither a coherent central state nor a strong sense of nationhood could develop during this period.

The Infant Republic, 1844–61

Santana's power base lay in the military forces mustered to defend the infant republic against Haitian retaliation. Duarte, briefly a member of the governing junta, for a time commanded an armed force as well. However, the governing junta trusted the military judgment of Santana over that of Duarte, and he was replaced with General José María Imbert. Duarte assumed the post of governor of the Cibao, the northern farming region administered from the city of Santiago de los Caballeros, commonly known as Santiago. In July 1844, Mella and a throng of other Duarte supporters in Santiago urged him to take the title of president of the republic. Duarte agreed to do so, but only if free elections could be arranged. Santana, who felt that only the protection of a great power could assure Dominican safety against the Haitian threat, did not share Duarte's enthusiasm for the electoral process. His forces took Santo Domingo on July 12, 1844, and proclaimed Santana ruler of the Dominican Republic. Mella, who attempted to mediate a compromise government including both Duarte and Santana, found himself imprisoned by the new dictator. Duarte and Sánchez followed Mella into prison and subsequently into exile.

The country's first constitution in 1844 was a remarkably liberal document. It was influenced directly by the Haitian constitution of 1843 and indirectly by the United States constitution of 1789, by the liberal 1812 Cadiz constitution of Spain, and by the French constitutions of 1799 and 1804. Because of this inspiration, it called for presidentialism, a separation of powers, and extensive "checks and balances." However, Santana proceeded to emasculate the document by demanding the inclusion of Article 210, which granted him extraordinary powers "during the current war" against Haiti.

Santana's dictatorial powers continued throughout his first term (1844–48), even though the Haitian forces had been repelled by December 1845. He consolidated his power by executing anti-Santana conspirators, by rewarding his close associates with lucrative positions in government, and by printing paper money to cover the expenses of a large standing army, a policy that severely devalued the new nation's currency. Throughout his term, Santana also continued to explore the possibility of an association with a foreign power. The governments of the United States, France, and Spain all declined the offer.

Santana responded to a general discontent prompted mainly by the deteriorating currency and economy by resigning the presidency in February 1848 and retiring to his *finca* (ranch) in El Seibo. He was replaced in August 1848 by minister of war Manuel Jiménez, whose tenure ended in May 1849. The violent sequence of events that culminated in Jiménez's departure began with a new invasion from Haiti, this time led by self-styled emperor Faustin Soulouque (see Increasing Instability, 1843–1915, ch. 6). Santana returned to prominence at the head of the army that checked the Haitian advance at Las Carreras in April 1849. As the Haitians retired, Santana pressed his advantage against Jiménez, taking control of Santo Domingo and the government on May 30, 1849.

Although Santana once again held the reins of power, he declined to formalize the situation by running for office. Instead, he renounced the temporary mandate granted him by the Congress and called for an election—carried out under an electoral college system with limited suffrage—to select a new president. Santana favored Santiago Espaillat, who won a ballot in the Congress on July 5, 1849; Espaillat declined to accept the presidency, however, knowing that he would have to serve as a puppet so long as Santana controlled the army. This refusal cleared the way for Báez, president of the Congress, to win a second ballot, which was held on August 18, 1849.

Báez made even more vigorous overtures to foreign powers to establish a Dominican protectorate. Both France (Báez's personal preference) and the United States, although still unwilling to annex the entire country, expressed interest in acquiring the bay and peninsula of Samaná as a naval or commercial port. Consequently, in order to preserve its lucrative trade with the island nation and to deny a strategic asset to its rivals, Britain became more actively involved in Dominican affairs. In 1850 the British signed a commercial and maritime treaty with the Dominicans. The following year, Britain mediated a peace treaty between the Dominican Republic and Haiti.

Báez's first term established the personal rivalry with Santana that dominated Dominican politics until the latter's death in 1864. President Báez purged Santana's followers (*santanistas*) from the government and installed his own followers (*baecistas*) in their place, pardoned a number of Santana's political opponents, reorganized the military in an effort to dilute Santana's power base, and apparently conceived a plan to create a militia that would serve as a counterforce to the army.

Seeing his influence clearly threatened, Santana returned to the political arena in February 1853, when he was elected to succeed Báez. The general moved quickly to deal with Báez, who had once been a colonel under his command, denouncing him for ties to the Haitians and as a threat to the nation's security. Exercising his authority under Article 210 of the constitution, Santana expelled the former president from the Dominican Republic.

Although he enjoyed considerable popularity, Santana confronted several crises during his second term. In February 1854, a constituent assembly promulgated a new, even more liberal constitution than that of 1844, which also eliminated the dictatorial powers granted by Article 210. However, it was almost immediately modified to place all control over the armed forces directly in the hands of the president. With his control over the army restored, Santana readily forced the adoption by the Congress of a much more authoritarian constitutional text later that year.

On the international front, renewed annexation talks between the Dominican and United States governments aroused the concern of Haitian emperor Soulouque. Motivated at least in part by a desire to prevent the acquisition of any portion of Hispaniola by the slaveholding United States, Soulouque launched a new invasion in November 1855. However, Dominican forces decisively defeated the Haitians in a number of engagements and forced them back across the border by January 1856.

The final crisis of Santana's second term also originated in the foreign policy sphere. Shortly after the Haitian campaign, the Dominican and United States governments signed a commercial treaty that provided for the lease of a small tract in Samaná for use as a coaling station. Although Santana delayed implementation of the lease, its negotiation provided his opponents—including *baecistas* and the government of Spain—the opportunity to decry Yankee imperialism and demand the president's ouster. Pressure built to such an extent that Santana felt compelled to resign on May 26, 1856, in favor of his vice president, Manuel de la Regla Mota.

Regla Mota's rule lasted almost five months. An empty treasury forced the new president to discharge most of the army. Thus deprived of the Dominican rulers' traditional source of power, his government all but invited the return of Báez. With the support of the Spanish, Báez was named vice president by Regla Mota, who then resigned in Báez's favor. Not a forgiving man by nature, Báez lost little time in denouncing ex-president Santana and expelling him from the country. Once again, Báez purged *santanistas* from the government and replaced them with his own men.

Báez had little time in which to savor his triumph over his rival, however. Reverting to the policies of Báez's first term, the government flooded the country with what rapidly became all but worthless paper money. Farmers in the Cibao, who objected strongly to the purchase of their crops with this devalued currency, rose against Báez in what came to be known as the Revolution of 1857. Their standard-bearer, not surprisingly, was Santana.

Pardoned by a provisional government established at Santiago, Santana returned in August 1857 to join the revolution. He raised his own personal army and soon dominated the movement. A year of bloody conflict between the governments of Santiago and Santo Domingo took a heavy toll in lives and money. Under the terms of a June 1857 armistice, Báez once again fled to Curaçao with all the government funds he could carry. Santana proceeded to betray the aspirations of some of his liberal revolutionary followers by restoring the dictatorial constitution of 1854. *Santanismo* again replaced *baecismo*; only a small group of loyalists realized any benefit from the exchange, however. Politically, the country continued to walk a treadmill. Economically, conditions had become almost unbearable for many Dominicans. The general climate of despair set the stage for the success of Santana's renewed efforts to obtain a protector for his country.

Annexation by Spain, 1861–65

On March 18, 1861, Santana announced the annexation of the Dominican Republic by Spain. A number of conditions had combined to bring about this reversion to colonialism. The Civil War in the United States had lessened the Spanish fear of retaliation from the north. In Spain itself, the ruling Liberal Union of General Leopoldo O'Donnell had been advocating renewed imperial expansion. And in the Dominican Republic, both the ruler and a portion of the ruled were sufficiently concerned about the possibility of a renewed attack from Haiti or domestic economic collapse to find the prospect of annexation attractive.

Support for annexation did not run as deep as Santana had represented to the Spanish, however. The first rebellion against Spanish rule broke out in May 1861, but was quashed in short order. A better organized revolt, under the leadership of *baecista* General Francisco del Rosario Sánchez, sprang up only a month later. Santana, now bearing the title of captain general of the Province of Santo Domingo, was forced to take to the field against his own countrymen as the representative of a foreign power. The wily Santana lured Sánchez into an ambush, where he was captured and executed. Despite this service, Santana found his personal power and his ability to dole out patronage to his followers greatly restricted under Spanish rule. As a result, he resigned the captaincy general in January 1862.

Resentment and rebellion continued, fed by racial tension, excessive taxation, the failure to stabilize the currency, the uncompensated requisition of supplies by the Spanish army, heavy-handed reform of local religious customs by an inflexible Spanish archbishop, and the restriction of trade to the benefit of the Spanish metropolis. The Spaniards quelled more uprisings in 1863, but guerrilla actions continued. In response to the continuing unrest, a state of siege was declared in February 1863.

Rebellious Dominicans set up a provisional government in Santiago, headed by General José Antonio Salcedo, on September 14, 1863. Their proclamation of an Act of Independence launched what is known as the War of Restoration. For their part, the Spanish once again turned to Santana, who received command of a force made up largely of mercenaries. However, by this time, his popularity had all but disappeared. Indeed, the provisional government had denounced Santana and condemned him to death for his actions against his countrymen. On June 14, 1864, a broken and despondent Santana saved the rebels the trouble of carrying out their sentence by dying (or, unproven speculation asserts, by committing suicide).

Meanwhile, the guerrilla war against the Spanish continued. The rebels further formalized their provisional rule by replacing Salcedo (who had advocated the return of Báez to rule a restored republic), and then holding a national convention on February 27, 1865, which enacted a new constitution and elected Pedro Antonio Pimentel Chamorro president.

Several circumstances began to favor a Spanish withdrawal. One was the conclusion of the Civil War in the United States, which promised new efforts by Washington to enforce the Monroe Doctrine. Another was that the Spanish military forces, unable to contain the spread of the insurrection, were losing even greater numbers of troops to disease. The O'Donnell government had fallen, taking with it any dreams of a renewed Spanish empire. On March 3, 1865, the queen of Spain approved a decree repealing the annexation of Santo Do-mingo, and by July all Spanish soldiers had left the island.

The Contest for Power, 1865–82

The Spanish left both economic devastation and political chaos in their wake. In the period from 1865 to 1879, there were twenty-one different governments and at least fifty military uprisings. A power struggle began between the conservative, cacique-dominated south and the more liberal Cibao, where the prevalence of medium-sized landholdings contributed to a more egalitarian social structure. The two camps eventually coalesced under the banners of separate political parties. The *cibaeños* adhered to the National Liberal Party (Partido Nacional Liberal), which became known as the Blue Party (Partido Azul). The southerners rallied to Báez and the Red Party (Partido Rojo).

The conservative Reds effectively employed their numerical superiority in the capital to force the restoration of Báez, who returned triumphantly from exile and assumed the presidency on December 8, 1865. However, he was unable to assert the kind of dictatorial control over the whole nation that he and Santana had once alternately enjoyed because power had been diffused, particularly between the opposing poles of the Cibao and the south.

After a successful uprising that forced Báez to flee the country in May 1866, a triumvirate of *cibaeño* military leaders, the most prominent of whom was Gregorio Luperón, assumed provisional power. General José María Cabral Luna, who had served briefly as president in 1865, was reelected to the post on September 29, 1866. The *baecistas*, however, were still a potent force in the republic; they forced Cabral out and reinstalled Báez on May 2, 1868. Once again, his rule was marked by peculation and efforts to sell or lease portions of the country to foreign interests. These included an intermittent campaign to have the entire country annexed by the United States, which President Ulysses S. Grant also strongly supported. However, the United States Senate rejected the 1869 treaty calling for annexation, giving President Grant his first major legislative defeat. Grant continued efforts to annex Dominican territory until 1873. Báez, in turn, was again overthrown by rebellious Blues in January 1874.

After a period of infighting among the Blues, backing from Luperón helped Ulises Francisco Espaillat Quiñones win election as president on March 24, 1876. Espaillat, a political and economic liberal and the first individual who was not a general to reach the presidency, apparently intended to broaden personal freedoms and to set the nation's economy on a firmer footing. He never had the opportunity to do either, however. Rebellions in the south and east forced Espaillat to resign on

December 20, 1876. Ever the opportunist, Báez returned once more to power. The most effective opposition to his rule came from guerrilla forces led by a politically active priest, Fernando Arturo de Meriño. In February 1878, the unpopular Báez departed his country for the last time; he died in exile in 1882.

Both Santana and Báez had now passed from the scene. They had helped create a nation where violence prevailed in the quest for power, where economic growth and financial stability fell victim to the seemingly endless political contest, and where foreign interests still perceived parts of the national territory as available to the highest bidder. This divisive, chaotic situation invited the emergence of an able military leader and a shrewd, despotic political leader who would dominate the country over a seventeen-year period.

Ulises Heureaux, Growing Financial Dependence, and Continued Instability

Ulises Heureaux, 1882–99

Ulises Heureaux, Luperón's lieutenant, stood out among his fellow Dominicans both physically and temperamentally. The illegitimate son of a Haitian father and a mother originally from St. Thomas, he, like Luperón, was one of the few black contenders for power. As events would demonstrate, he also possessed a singular thirst for power and a willingness to take any measures necessary to attain and to hold it.

During the four years between Báez's final withdrawal and Heureaux's ascension to the presidency, seven individuals held or claimed national, regional, or interim leadership. Among them were Ignacio María González Santín, who held the presidency from June to September 1878; Luperón, who governed from Puerto Plata as provisional president from October 1879 to August 1880; and Meriño, who assumed office in September 1880 after apparently fraudulent general elections. Heureaux served as minister of interior under Meriño; his behind-the-scenes influence on the rest of the cabinet apparently exceeded that of the president. Although Meriño briefly suspended constitutional procedures in response to unrest fomented by some remaining *baecistas*, he abided by the two-year term established under Luperón and turned the reins of government over to Heureaux on September 1, 1882.

Heureaux's first term as president was not particularly noteworthy. The administrations of Luperón and Meriño had achieved some financial stability for the country; political conditions had settled down to the point where Heureaux needed to suppress only one major uprising during his two-year tenure. By 1884, however, no single successor enjoyed widespread support among the various caciques who constituted the republic's ruling group. Luperón, still the leader of the ruling Blue Party, supported General Segundo Imbert for the post, while Heureaux backed the candidacy of General Francisco Gregorio Billini. A consummate dissembler, Heureaux assured Luperón that he would support Imbert should he win the election, but Heureaux also had ballot boxes in critical precincts stuffed in order to assure Billini's election.

Inaugurated president on September 1, 1884, Billini resisted Heureaux's efforts to manipulate him. Thus denied de facto rule, Heureaux undermined Billini by spreading rumors to the effect that the president had decreed a political amnesty so that he could conspire with ex-president Cesáreo Guillermo Bastardo (February 27–December 6, 1879) against Luperón's leadership of the Blues. These rumors precipitated a governmental crisis that resulted in Billini's resignation on May 16, 1885. Vice President Alejandro Woss y Gil succeeded Billini. Heureaux assumed a more prominent role under the new government. A number of his adherents were included in the cabinet, and the general himself assumed command of the national army in order to stem a rebellion led by Guillermo. The latter's death removed another potential rival for power and further endeared Heureaux to Luperón, a longtime enemy of Guillermo.

Luperón accordingly supported Heureaux in the 1886 presidential elections. Opposed by Casimiro de Moya, Heureaux relied on his considerable popularity and his demonstrated skill at electoral manipulation to carry the balloting. The blatancy of the fraud in some areas, particularly the capital, inspired Moya's followers to launch an armed rebellion. Heureaux again benefited from Luperón's support in this struggle, which delayed his inauguration by four months but further narrowed the field of political contenders. Having again achieved power, Heureaux maintained his grip on it for the rest of his life.

Several moves served to lay the groundwork for Heureaux's dictatorship. Constitutional amendments requested by the president and effected by the Congress extended the presidential term from two to four years and eliminated direct elections in favor of the formerly employed electoral college system. To expand his informal power base, Heureaux (who became popularly known as General Lilís, thanks to a common mispronunciation of his first name) incorporated both Reds and Blues into his government. The president also established an extensive network of secret police and informants in order to avert incipient rebellions. The press, previously unhampered, came under new restrictions.

In the face of impending dictatorship, concerned Dominican liberals turned to the only remaining figure of stature, Luperón. The elections of 1888 therefore pitted Heureaux against his political mentor. If the dictator felt any respect for his former commander, he did not demonstrate it during the campaign. Heureaux's agents attacked Luperón's campaigners and supporters, arresting and incarcerating considerable numbers of them. Recognizing the impossibility of a free election under such circumstances, Luperón withdrew his candidacy, declined the entreaties of those of his followers who urged armed rebellion, and fled into exile in Puerto Rico.

Although plots, intrigue, and abortive insurrections continued under his rule, Heureaux faced no serious challenges until his assassination in 1899. He continued to govern in mock-constitutional fashion, achieving reelections through institutionalized fraud, even as repression worsened. Like Santana and Báez before him, Heureaux sought the protection of a foreign power, principally the United States. Although annexation was no longer an option, the dictator offered to lease the Samaná Peninsula to the United States. The arrangement was never consummated, however, because of opposition from the liberal wing of the Blue Party and a number of concerned European powers. In spite of protests from Germany, Britain, and France, in 1891 Washington and Santo Domingo concluded a reciprocity treaty that allowed twenty-six United States products free entry into the Dominican market in exchange for similar duty-free access for certain Dominican goods.

Under Heureaux, the Dominican government considerably expanded its external debt, even as there was considerable blurring between his private holdings and the state's financial affairs. Some improvements in infrastructure resulted, such as the completion of the first railroads. Initial attempts at professionalizing the army and bureaucratizing the state were made, and educational reforms were introduced. As a result of favorable state policies, modern sugar estates began to replace cattle-ranching estates, even as exports of coffee and cocoa expanded. Yet, onerous terms on the major external loan, corruption and mismanagement, and a decline in world sugar markets, all exacerbated both domestic budget deficits and external balance of payments shortfalls.

Despite the dictator's comprehensive efforts to repress opposition—his network of spies and agents extended even to foreign countries—opposition eventually emerged centered in the Cibao region, which had suffered under Heureaux's policies favoring sugar interests in Santo Domingo and San Pedro de Macorís. An opposition group calling itself the Young Revolutionary Junta (Junta Revolucionaria de Jóvenes) was established in Puerto Rico by Horacio Vásquez Lajara, a young adherent of Luperón. Other prominent members of the group included Federico Velásquez and Ramón Cáceres Vásquez. The three returned to their plantations in the Cibao and began to lay the groundwork for a coordinated rebellion against the widely detested Heureaux. The impetuous Cáceres, however, shot and fatally wounded the dictator when he passed through the town of Moca on July 26, 1899. Cáceres escaped unharmed.

Growing Financial Dependence and Political Instability

Heureaux left two major legacies: debt and political instability. It was these legacies that finally helped usher in the United States military occupation of 1916. In the six years after Heureaux's assassination in 1899, the country experienced four revolts and five presidents. National politics came to revolve primarily around the conflict between the followers of Juan Isidro Jimenes Pereyra, called *jimenistas,* and the followers of Horacio Vásquez Lahara, called *horacistas;* both men and both groups had been involved in plots against Heureaux.

After a brief period of armed conflict, Vásquez headed a provisional government established in September 1899. Elections brought Jimenes to the presidency on November 15. The Jimenes administration faced a fiscal crisis when European creditors began to call in loans that had been contracted by Heureaux. Customs fees represented the only significant source of government revenue at that time. When the Jimenes government pledged 40 percent of its customs revenue to repay its foreign debt, it provoked the ire of the San Domingo Improvement Company. A United States-based firm, the Improvement Company, had lent large sums to the Heureaux regime. As a result, it not only received a considerable percentage of customs revenue, but also had been granted the right to administer Dominican customs in order to ensure regular repayment. Stung by the Jimenes government's resumption of control over its customs receipts, the directors of the Improvement Company protested to the United States Department of State. The review of the case prompted a renewed interest in Washington in Dominican affairs.

Cibao nationalists suspected the president of bargaining away Dominican sovereignty in return for financial settlements. Government forces led by Vásquez put down some early uprisings. Eventually, however, personal competition between Jimenes and Vásquez brought them into conflict. Vásquez's forces proclaimed a revolution on April 26, 1902; with no real base of support, Jimenes fled his office and his country a few days later. However, conflicts among the followers of Vásquez and opposition to his government from local caciques grew into general unrest that culminated in the seizure of power by ex-president Alejandro Woss y Gil in April 1903.

Dominican politics had once again polarized into two largely nonideological groups. Where once the Blues and Reds had contended for power, now two other personalist factions, the *jimenistas* (supporters of Jimenes) and the *horacistas* (supporters of Vásquez and Cáceres), vied for control. Woss y Gil, a *jimenista*, made the mistake of seeking supporters among the *horacista* camp and was overthrown by *jimenista* General Carlos Felipe Morales Languasco in December 1903. Rather than restore the country's leadership to Jimenes, however, Morales set up a provisional government and announced his own candidacy for the presidency—with Cáceres as his running mate. The renewed fraternization with the *horacistas* incited another *jimenista* rebellion. This uprising proved unsuccessful, and Morales and Cáceres were inaugurated on June 19, 1904. Yet, conflict within the Morales administration between supporters of the president and those of the vice president eventually led to the ouster of Morales, and Cáceres assumed the presidency on December 29, 1905.

As a backdrop to the continuing political turmoil in the Dominican Republic, United States influence increased considerably during the first few years of the twentieth century. Pressures by European creditors on the Dominican Republic and the Anglo-German blockade of Venezuela in 1902–03 led to President Theodore Roosevelt's "corollary" to the Monroe Doctrine, which declared that the United States would assume the

Offices of the General Customs Receivership,
Santo Domingo, 1907
Courtesy National Archives

police powers necessary in the region to ensure that creditors would be adequately repaid. United States military forces had intervened several times between 1900 and 1903, primarily to prevent the employment of warships by European governments seeking immediate repayment of debt. In June 1904, the Roosevelt administration negotiated an agreement whereby the Dominican government bought out the holdings of the San Domingo Improvement Company. Then, following an intermediate agreement, the Morales government ultimately signed a financial accord with the United States in February 1905. Under this accord, the United States government assumed responsibility for all Dominican debt as well as for the collection of customs duties and the allocation of those revenues to the Dominican government and to the repayment of its domestic and foreign debt. Although parts of this agreement were rejected by the United States Senate, it formed the basis for the establishment in April 1905 of the General Customs Receivership, the office through which the United States government administered the finances of the Dominican Republic.

The Cáceres government became the financial beneficiary of this arrangement. Freed from the burden of dealing with creditors, Cáceres attempted to reform the political system. Constitutional reforms placed local *ayuntamientos* (town councils) under the power of the central government, extended the presidential term to six years, and eliminated the office of vice president. Cáceres also nationalized public utilities and established a bureau of public works to administer them. The curtailment of local authority particularly irked those caciques who had preferred to rule through compliant *ayuntamientos*. The continued financial sovereignty of the "Yankees" also outweighed the economic benefits of the receivership in the minds of many Dominican nationalists. Intrigues fomented in exile by Morales, Jimenes, and others beset Cáceres, who was assassinated on November 19, 1911.

The assassination of Cáceres led to another period of political turmoil and economic disorganization that was to culminate in the republic's occupation by the United States. The fiscal stability that had resulted from the 1905 receivership eroded under Cáceres's successor, Eladio Victoria y Victoria, with most of the increased outlays going to support military campaigns against rebellious partisans, mainly in the Cibao. The continued violence and instability prompted the administration of President William H. Taft to dispatch a commission to Santo Domingo on September 24, 1912, to mediate between the warring factions. The presence of a 750-member force of United States Marines apparently convinced the Dominicans of the seriousness of Washington's threats to intervene directly in the conflict; Victoria agreed to step down in favor of a neutral figure, Roman Catholic archbishop Adolfo Alejandro Nouel Bobadilla. The archbishop assumed office as provisional president on November 30.

Nouel proved unequal to the burden of national leadership. Unable to mediate successfully between the ambitions of rival *horacistas* and *jimenistas*, he resigned on March 31, 1913. His successor, José Bordas Valdés, was equally unable to restrain the renewed outbreak of hostilities. Once again, Washington took a direct hand and mediated a resolution. The rebellious *horacistas* agreed to a cease-fire based on a pledge of United States oversight of elections for members of local *ayuntamientos* and a constituent assembly that would draft the procedures for presidential balloting. The process, however, was flagrantly manipulated and resulted in Bordas's reelection on June 15, 1914.

Bordas reached out to the *jimenistas,* naming one of their leaders, Desiderio Arias, as government delegate to the Cibao. However, *horacistas* soon revolted, declaring a new provisional government under Vásquez. Subsequent mediation by the United States government led to municipal and congressional elections in December 1913. However, these elections were blatantly manipulated by Bordas, leading to renewed tensions with not only *horacistas* but also *jimenistas.*

The United States government, this time under President Woodrow Wilson, again intervened. The "Wilson Plan"—delivered as an ultimatum—essentially stated: elect a president or the United States will impose one. Bordas resigned, and the Dominicans accordingly selected Ramón Báez Machado (the son of Buenaventura Báez) as provisional president on August 27, 1914, to oversee elections. Comparatively fair presidential elections held on October 25 returned Jimenes to the presidency.

However, a combination of continued internecine political infighting and United States pressure made Jimenes's position untenable soon after his inauguration on December 6, 1914. The United States government wished him to regularize the appointment of a United States comptroller, who was overseeing the country's public expenditures, and to create a new national guard, which would be under the control of the United States military, thus eliminating the existing army controlled by Arias. At the same time, Jimenes found himself with less and less political support, as he confronted opposition first from *horacistas* and then from his own secretary of war, Desiderio Arias. Arias spearheaded an effort to have Jimenes removed by impeachment so that he could assume the presidency. Although the United States ambassador offered military support to his government, Jimenes opted to step down on May 7, 1916. At this point, the United States decided to take more direct action. United States forces had already occupied Haiti (see United States Involvement in Haiti, 1915–34, ch. 6), and this time Arias retreated from Santo Domingo on May 13, under threat of naval bombardment; the first Marines landed three days later. Although they established effective control of the country within two months, the United States forces did not proclaim a military government until November.

The country occupied by the United States Marines was one marked not only by weak sovereignty, but also by unstable political rule, fragmented and fearful economic elites, a weak church, and the absence of a central state and of a national military institution independent of individual leaders or loyalties.

From the United States Occupation (1916–24) to the Emergence of Trujillo (1930)

The United States occupation of the Dominican Republic was to be a critical turning point in Dominican history, although not for the reasons intended by the occupying forces. Led by military governor Rear Admiral Harry S. Knapp, programs were enacted in education, health, sanitation, agriculture, and communications; highways were built; and other public works were created. In addition, other programs crucial to strengthening state structures and a market economy were implemented, including both a census and a cadastral survey. The latter allowed land titles to be regularized and United States sugar companies to expand their holdings dramatically, even as infrastructure to facilitate exports was developed. The most significant measure was the establishment of a new Dominican constabulary force.

Most Dominicans, however, greatly resented the loss of their sovereignty to foreigners, few of whom spoke Spanish or displayed much real concern for the welfare of the republic. The most intense opposition to the occupation arose in the eastern provinces of El Seibo and San Pedro de Macorís. From 1917 to 1921, the United States forces battled a guerrilla movement known as *gavilleros* in that area. Although the guerrillas enjoyed considerable support among the population and benefited from a superior knowledge of the terrain, they eventually yielded to the occupying forces' superior power.

After World War I, however, public opinion in the United States began to run against the occupation, and in June 1921 United States representatives presented a withdrawal proposal, known as the Harding Plan. The plan called for Dominican ratification of all acts of the military government, approval of a US$2.5-million loan for public works and other expenses, the acceptance of United States officers for the constabulary—now known as the National Guard (Guardia Nacional)—and the holding of elections under United States supervision. Popular reaction to the plan was overwhelmingly negative. Moderate Dominican leaders, however, used the plan as the basis for further negotiations that resulted in an agreement allowing for the selection of a provisional president to rule until elections could be organized. Under the supervision of High Commissioner Sumner Welles, Juan Bautista Vicini Burgos assumed the provisional presidency on October 21, 1922. In the presidential election of March 15, 1924, Horacio Vásquez handily defeated Francisco J. Peynado; shortly after his inauguration in July, all United States marines withdrew.

The aging Vásquez governed ineffectively and corruptly, dramatically expanding public employment and extending his term in office by two years. As doubts emerged about the fairness of the 1930 elections, an uprising against the president led to the naming of Rafael Estrella Ureña as provisional president pending the elections. Rafael Leónidas Trujillo Molina, the head of the country's newly established military force, had played a critical, secretive role in ensuring the success of the rebellion against Vásquez. Trujillo soon emerged as the only presidential candidate in the elections, winning with 99 percent of the vote.

Trujillo was able to gain power and quickly consolidate a much more solid grip on power than previous Dominican rulers because of domestic and international factors. He now led a far more powerful national military institution than had previously existed while traditional powerholders remained weak and the population was largely disarmed. Moreover, he benefited from the improved transportation and communication infrastructure built during the occupation. In addition, in the 1920s, the United States moved toward a policy of nonintervention, a policy facilitated by the absence of any perceived threat to continued United States influence in the area from an outside power.

The Trujillo Era, 1930–61

Rafael Trujillo was born in 1891 and raised in San Cristóbal, a small town near the capital, in a family of modest means of mixed Spanish, Creole, and Haitian background. In less than ten years, from 1919 to 1928, he emerged from being an obscure minor officer in a newly formed constabulary force to become head of the country's army. Over the period of his rule from 1930 to 1961, he formally held the presidency from 1930 to 1938 and from 1942 to 1952; however, he always retained direct control over the military, allowing pliant individuals such as his brother Héctor to serve as president. His thirst for power was combined with megalomania (for example, Santo Domingo was renamed Ciudad Trujillo and Pico Duarte, the highest mountain in the Antilles, became Pico Trujillo) and a drive to accumulate massive wealth.

Trujillo's regime quickly moved beyond the traditional Dominican caudillo regimes of the nineteenth century. By the end of his second term, it was evident that his regime's totalitarian features went beyond those of Heureaux, its historical predecessor. Occasionally partial liberalizations occurred in response to international pressures. Such liberal episodes were particularly evident in late 1937 and early 1938, following the outcry that came after the October 1937 massacre of some 5,000 to 12,000 Haitians along the Dominican-Haitian border, and in the immediate post-World War II era. But Trujillo's accumulation of wealth and power would continue, reaching a peak in 1955. The regime's deterioration began shortly thereafter, accelerating in 1958.

Central to Trujillo's domination of the country was control over an expanding armed forces and police, which were his personal instrument rather than a national institution; the armed forces and the police grew from around 2,200 in 1932 to 9,100 in 1948 to 18,000 in 1958. In the mid-1950s, Trujillo transferred the best troops and weapons to a military service known as Dominican Military Aviation, controlled by his son Ramfis.

Yet, Trujillo's regime was not based purely on repression, although over time it increasingly became so. Ideologically, Trujillo portrayed himself with some success as a forger of the Dominican nation, builder of the state, and defender of its economic interests. His was the first prolonged period in the country's history when the country was not directly attacked or occupied by Spain, the United States, or Haiti. Trujillo built upon the country's antipathy to Haiti to help articulate a nationalist ideology appealing to traditional Hispanic and Roman Catholic values, aided by intellectuals such as Joaquín Balaguer Ricardo. In the 1930s, especially, he also articulated a vision of discipline, work, peace, order, and progress. As these values became embodied in a number of large-scale public works and construction projects, and particularly as the economy began moving out of the Great Depression of the late 1930s, Trujillo almost certainly gained respect among some elements of the population. In some cases, he also gained support because he presented himself in a messianic form. By the 1950s, and particularly after signing a concordat with the Vatican in 1954, Trujillo often attacked "international commu-

Rafael Leónidas Trujillo Molina
Courtesy Library of Congress

nism" as a threat to the country's traditional values that he
claimed he was seeking to uphold.

Trujillo also waved the ideological banner of economic
nationalism, although it sometimes cloaked his own personal
accumulation of wealth. Trujillo ended United States administration of Dominican customs (in 1941), retired the Dominican debt (in 1947), and introduced a national currency to
replace the dollar (also in 1947), even as he amassed a sizeable
personal fortune.

Economically, Trujillo eventually became the single dominant force in the country by combining abuse of state power,
threats, and co-optation. Trujillo's initial schemes to enrich
himself revolved around the creation of state or commercial
monopolies. He then gradually moved into industry, forcing
owners to allow him to buy up shares, while also enjoying
healthy commissions on all public works contracts. After World
War II, Trujillo expanded into industrial production. His most
massive investments were made in sugar, which was largely foreign-owned. The planning and implementation of Trujillo's
sugar operations, however, were so poor that had it not been
for the numerous state subsidies they received, they would have
lost money.

41

Although some of the country's economic elite maintained a degree of individual autonomy, no possibility existed for independent organization. Trujillo enjoyed humiliating those who previously had enjoyed both social prestige and economic wealth; they intensely disliked him but were forced to conform. Only in Trujillo's last two years did any concerted opposition emerge from within the economic elite. Indeed, Trujillo's economic holdings at the time of his death were staggering. Almost 80 percent of the country's industrial production was controlled by him; and nearly 60 percent of the country's labor force depended directly or indirectly on him, 45 percent employed in his firms and another 15 percent working for the state. The only organization that retained any degree of autonomy was the Roman Catholic Church; until the very end of his rule, it remained abjectly loyal to him.

Politically, Trujillo combined guile, cynicism, ruthlessness, and co-optation. He cynically deployed constitutional norms and legal requirements, which ostensibly were followed faithfully, and totally dominated a single-party apparatus. In addition, Trujillo engaged in byzantine manipulation of individuals, who were shifted around public offices in a disconcerting fashion as personal rivalries were promoted and tested. At its apogee, the Dominican Party (Partido Dominicano) had branches throughout the country, helping to keep Trujillo apprised of local realities, needs, and potential threats to his rule. The party's charitable activities, homages to Trujillo, and campaign efforts were financed largely by a percentage taken from the salaries of public employees. Trujillo made voting mandatory (not voting could be risky), and in 1942 he expanded the suffrage to women.

International factors were also important in helping Trujillo sustain his grip on power. Trujillo employed public relations firms and assiduously cultivated his military contacts and individual politicians in the United States to enhance his reputation and sustain United States support. He went to elaborate lengths to demonstrate domestically that he retained support from the United States. In some periods, United States diplomats expressed their frustration at being manipulated by Trujillo even as United States military personnel openly praised his rule. At the same time, his complex web of conspiracy, intrigue, and violence extended beyond Dominican borders; he provided support for various regional dictators and plotted against perceived foreign enemies, such as Rómulo Betancourt of Venezuela, who, in turn, provided support for exile groups plotting against Trujillo.

By the late 1950s, Trujillo faced multiple challenges, even as the country's economy was suffering and his own mental acuity was declining. Domestic opposition, agitation by exiles, and international pressures began to reinforce each other. A failed invasion attempt in June 1959 from Cuba helped spawn a major underground movement, itself brutally crushed in January 1960. As a gesture of liberalization, in August 1960 Trujillo removed his brother from the presidency, replacing him with then vice president Joaquín Balaguer.

However, domestic opposition continued to grow, the Roman Catholic Church began to distance itself from the regime, and with concerns mounting about the Cuban Revolution, the United States distanced itself as well. A summary of United States policy intentions during this period is provided in President John F. Kennedy's often-cited dictum that in descending order of preferences the United States would prefer a democratic regime, continuation of a Trujillo regime, or a Castro regime, and that the United States should aim for the first, but not renounce the second until it was sure the third could be avoided. Covert and overt pressure, including cutting off the United States sugar quota and Organization of American States (OAS—see Glossary) sanctions, were applied to the Trujillo regime. Finally, conspirators, who for the most part had largely been supporters of the regime in the past, successfully assassinated Trujillo on May 30, 1961. Following Trujillo's death, attention immediately focused on what kind of regime would replace him. It took additional threats of United States military intervention to force Trujillo's relatives from the island in November 1961 in order to allow opposition elements to emerge.

Democratic Struggles and Failures

As were the years following the assassination of Heureaux decades earlier, the immediate post-Trujillo period was a convulsive one for the country. The preexisting political institutions and practices from the Trujillo regime were clearly inimical to a successful democratic transition. Yet, a clear break with the Trujillos was achieved. In January 1962, Joaquín Balaguer, who as vice president had taken over upon Trujillo's death, was forced into exile by opposition elements. A provisional government was formed to prepare for democratic elections. The upper-class opposition to Trujillo was organized in the National Civic Union (Unión Cívica Nacional—UCN). The UCN dominated the provisional government and expected its candidate, Viriato Fiallo, to win the elections. To the UCN's surprise, it was defeated by Juan Bosch Gaviño, one of the founders of the Dominican Revolutionary Party (Partido Revolucionario Dominicano—PRD) in exile in the late 1930s, and the UCN soon disappeared. The PRD was successfully converted into a mass party with both urban and rural appeal: Bosch campaigned as the candidate of the poor and promised to implement a variety of socioeconomic and political reforms.

The Bosch administration represented a freely elected, liberal, democratic government concerned for the welfare of all Dominicans. The 1963 constitution separated church and state, guaranteed civil and individual rights, and endorsed civilian control of the military. These and other changes, such as land reform, struck conservative landholders and military officers as radical and threatening. The hierarchy of the Roman Catholic Church also resented the secular nature of the new constitution, in particular its provision for legalized divorce. The hierarchy, along with the military leadership and the economic elite, also feared communist influence in the republic, and they warned of the potential for "another Cuba."

As a result, the conservative socioeconomic forces coalesced with political, military, and church figures to overthrow President Bosch on September 25, 1963, only seven months after he assumed office; United States support for his government had also weakened. The institutional changes that Bosch, his new constitution, and his proposed reforms represented, in a situation in which his party possessed an absolute majority, were perceived as too threatening; however, middle-sector and popular-sector groups remained relatively weak and unorganized. If Bosch's regime was overthrown in 1963 ostensibly because of its alleged communist nature, weak radical leftist elements were in fact strengthened by the coup, and the country experienced further polarization over the next several years.

Following the coup, a civilian junta known as the Triumvirate, dominated by the UCN and headed by Emilio de los Santos, was formed. However, Santos resigned on December 23 and was replaced by Donald Reid Cabral, who increasingly became the dominant figure. His regime lacked legitimacy or strong support, however, and on April 25, 1965, a civil-military conspiracy sought to return Bosch to power. The Dominican government's action provoked a series of events leading to the "constitutionalist" uprising in support of Bosch. Three days later, on April 28, the United States intervened because the "loyalist" Dominican military troops led by General Elías Wessin y Wessin were unable to control the growing civil-military rebellion, often referred to as a civil war. The intervention was the result of an exaggerated fear on the part of the United States regarding a potential "second Cuba." Its unilateral nature was subsequently modified by the creation of an OAS-sponsored peace force, which supplemented the United States military presence in the republic.

Ultimately, negotiations during 1965–66 arranged a peaceful surrender of the constitutionalist forces, which were surrounded by foreign troops in downtown Santo Domingo. The negotiations also prevented a new outbreak of hostilities and provided for elections, which were overseen by a provisional government led by Hector García Godoy. However, many Dominicans viewed these elections, which permitted the United States to extricate its troops from the country, as tainted. Bosch and Balaguer (who had returned from exile in June 1965) were the two main candidates. Bosch felt betrayed by the United States, which had blocked his possible return to power and turned on his military supporters, and he ran a lackluster campaign. Balaguer, at the head of his own conservative Reformist Party (Partido Reformista—PR), campaigned skillfully and energetically, promising peace and stability. Balaguer was clearly the candidate favored by most conservative business interests and by the officer corps that retained control of the armed forces; most Dominicans also were convinced he was the candidate strongly favored by the United States. Although the civil war had been confined to urban areas, it left some 3,000 dead and the country polarized. Thus, for many Dominicans, Balaguer's administration lacked legitimacy.

Authoritarian Balaguer, 1966–78

In his authoritarian and patrimonial style, predilection for grandiose public construction projects, and emphasis on the country's Hispanic essence, Balaguer resembled Trujillo. However, Balaguer's treatment of economic, military, and political power differed from that of the strongman under whom he had served, in part because of changes in Dominican society and international circumstances.

The Balaguer period from 1966 to 1978 was one of high economic growth; the country averaged a 7.6 percent increase in
real GDP over the period. Growth was based on increased
export earnings, import-substitution in consumer goods promoted by generous tax incentives, and public investment
projects. It was facilitated by the United States sugar quota and
generous economic assistance, particularly in the early Balaguer years. Balaguer ruled in a patrimonial fashion, ensuring
that he was the central axis around which all other major political and economic forces revolved. At the same time, he eventually undermined his position by piomoting the development of
business groups separate from, even if dependent upon, the
state. Such an approach sharply contrasted with the approach
taken in the Trujillo period. However, organized labor
remained extremely weak as a result of repression, co-optation,
and very restrictive labor legislation.

Relations between business and Balaguer were complicated
by the growing incursions of the armed forces into business
and into politics. Balaguer had a commanding presence within
the military as a result of his ties to the Trujillo period, his anticommunism, his statesmanlike caudillo figure, and his acceptance of military repression as well as large-scale corruption.
However, he clearly was not the military figure Trujillo had
been. He sought to manage the military by playing off the
ambitions of the leading generals and shifting their assigned
posts. Yet, he occasionally confronted serious challenges, such
as a coup effort by Elías Wessin y Wessin in 1971, which he successfully dismantled. The two leaders were later to reconcile
politically.

The initial Balaguer years were a period of relative polarization that saw government repression and sporadic terrorist
activities by opposition groups. In a six-year period after the
1965 occupation, some 2,000 additional Dominicans were
killed. Following his electoral victory in 1966, Balaguer ran
again and won in elections in 1970 and 1974. However, in these
elections, the military placed strong pressure on opposition
candidates, most of whom ultimately withdrew prior to election
day. Balaguer also practiced a policy of co-optation, bringing
opposition figures into government. The extent and the severity of repression, particularly after 1976, were considerably less
than in the Trujillo years.

By the 1978 elections, Balaguer's drive for power, reelection-
ist aspirations, and policy decisions had alienated a number of

his former supporters. His popularity was also affected by worsening economic conditions. An economic downturn finally affected the country around 1976, when the sugar boom that had offset oil price increases faded. In addition, the country's substantial growth, industrialization, and urbanization had expanded middle-sector and professional groups, which were disgruntled by Balaguer's method of rule and apparent discrimination against newer and regional groups. The PRD, feeling the mood of the population and sensing support from the administration of United States president Jimmy Carter, nominated a moderate, Silvestre Antonio Guzmán Fernández, as its candidate to oppose Balaguer in the 1978 elections.

For these elections, the PRD also projected a more moderate image and strengthened its international contacts, particularly with the United States government and the Socialist International. The PRD's ability to project itself as a less threatening alternative to Balaguer in 1978 was facilitated by the decision of Bosch in 1973 to abandon his party and establish another, more radical and cadre-oriented party, the Party of Dominican Liberation (Partido de la Liberación Dominicana—PLD). Bosch's exit followed upon his disillusionment with liberal democracy following the 1965 United States intervention. In the 1980s, however, he was to lead his party back into the electoral arena.

Electoral victory did not come easily for the PRD. As it became evident early in the morning after election day that the party was winning by a wide margin, a military contingent stopped the vote count. In the end, the effort to thwart the elections was dismantled because of firm opposition by the Carter administration, other Latin American and European governments, and domestic groups. Yet, in the tense period between the election and the inauguration, congressional electoral results were "adjusted" to provide the exiting Balaguer with a guarantee that he would not be prosecuted. Principally this adjustment involved giving Balaguer's party, the PR, a majority in the Senate, which appointed judges, and thus was key to the successful prosecution of corruption charges.

The PRD in Power and Balaguer, Again

Unlike Balaguer, the leaders of the Dominican Revolutionary Party (PRD) promoted a democratic agenda. During the electoral campaign of 1978, the PRD conveyed the image of being the party of change (*el partido del cambio*); the party pledged to improve the living standards of the less privileged, to include those who felt politically underrepresented, and to modernize state institutions and the rule of law. As a result, the PRD's rise to power generated expectations among the Dominican people for socioeconomic and political reforms that were largely not achieved.

One threat to democracy that began to recede in 1978 was that of military incursion into politics, given that President Guzmán dismissed many of the key generals associated with repression. The armed forces have remained under civilian control. However, this control resulted primarily from the personal relations top military officers had with the president and the divided political loyalties within the officer corps. Even when Balaguer returned to power in 1986, however, the military did not regain the level of importance and influence it had had during his first twelve years in office.

The Guzmán administration (1978–82) was viewed as transitional because it faced a Senate controlled by Balaguer's party and growing intraparty rivalry in the PRD, which was led by Salvador Jorge Blanco. Yet, the PRD was able to unify around Jorge Blanco's presidential candidacy (Guzmán had pledged not to seek reelection) and defeat Balaguer and Bosch in the May 1982 elections. Tragically, Guzmán committed suicide in July 1982, apparently because of depression, isolation, and concerns that Jorge Blanco might pursue corruption charges against family members; vice president Jacobo Majluta Azar completed Guzmán's term until the turnover of power in August.

Initial hopes that the Jorge Blanco administration (1982–86) would be a less personalist, more institutional, reformist presidency were not realized. A major problem was the economic crisis that not only limited the resources the government had available and demanded inordinate attention, but also forced the government to institute unpopular policies, sometimes by executive decree. Problems had begun under Guzmán: prices sharply increased following the second Organization of the Petroleum Exporting Countries (OPEC) oil shock, interest rates skyrocketed, and exports declined. In addition, sugar prices fell in 1977–79, rebounded in 1980, and then fell sharply again even as the United States sugar quota was being reduced and as prices of other Dominican exports also declined.

Significant steps toward economic stabilization were taken under the Jorge Blanco administration, although not without difficulty. In April 1984, the government imposed price increases on fuel, food, and other items as part of a package of measures negotiated with the International Monetary Fund (IMF—see Glossary) to renew international credit flows. Protests against these measures escalated into full-scale riots that were tragically mismanaged by the armed forces, leading to scores of deaths and the suspension of the measures. In the face of growing international constraints, the administration successfully complied with an IMF stand-by program over 1985 and 1986. However, the economic measures induced a sharp recession in the country. Another problem was executive-congressional deadlock, now driven by intraparty factionalism. The PRD was increasingly divided between followers of Salvador Jorge Blanco and José Francisco Peña Gómez on the one hand, and Jacobo Majluta Azar, on the other. Other difficulties resulted from the reassertion of patronage and executive largesse.

The situation in the country was perhaps responsible for the outcome of the May 1986 elections: Balaguer emerged victorious with a slim plurality, defeating Majluta of the PRD and Bosch of the PLD; Bosch had nevertheless received 18 percent of the vote, double the percentage from four years earlier. Balaguer had merged his party with several smaller Christian Democratic parties to form the Reformist Social Christian Party (Partido Reformista Social Cristiano—PRSC). However, the promise of a more coherent ideological base for his party was never realized.

Balaguer began his 1986 term by denouncing the mistakes and irregularities carried out by his predecessors. His denunciation led ultimately to the arrest of former president Jorge Blanco on corruption charges. The administration did nothing to remove the factors that fostered corruption, however, seemingly satisfied with discrediting the PRD and particularly Jorge Blanco.

Balaguer also sought to revive the economy quickly, principally by carrying out a number of large-scale public investment projects. He pursued a policy of vigorous monetary expansion, fueling inflationary pressures and eventually forcing the government to move toward a system of exchange controls. Inflation, which had been brought down to around 10 percent in 1986, steadily climbed through Balaguer's first term. Balaguer also faced increasing social unrest in the late 1980s. Numerous strikes, such as a one-day national strike in July 1987, another in March 1988, and another in June 1989, took place between 1987–89; in 1990 Balaguer faced two general strikes in the summer and two others in the fall. Through a patchwork quilt of policies, the administration was able to limp through the May 1990 elections without a formal stabilization plan.

In spite of the country's problems, Balaguer achieved a narrow plurality victory in 1990. In elections marred by irregularities and charges of fraud, the eighty-three-year-old incumbent edged out his eighty-year-old opponent, Bosch, by a mere 24,470 votes. Peña Gómez, the PRD candidate, emerged as a surprisingly strong third candidate. By 1990 the PRD was irreparably split along lines that had formed during the bitter struggle for the 1986 presidential nomination. Peña Gómez had stepped aside for Jacobo Majluta in 1986 but had vowed not to do so again. The failure of numerous efforts since 1986 to settle internal disputes, as well as extensive legal and political wrangling, eventually left Peña Gómez in control of the PRD apparatus. Majluta ran at the head of a new party and came in a distant fourth.

Once Balaguer was reelected, he focused on resolving growing tensions between his government and business and the international financial community. In August 1990, Balaguer commenced a dialogue with business leaders and signed a Solidarity Pact. In this pact, Balaguer agreed to curtail (but not abandon) his state-led developmentalism in favor of more austerity and market liberalization. He reduced public spending, renegotiated foreign debt, and liberalized the exchange rate, but he did not privatize state enterprises. An agreement with the IMF was reached in 1991, and ultimately what had been historically high rates of inflation in the country (59 percent in 1990 and 54 percent in 1991) receded. Levels of social protest also decreased, as the country looked toward the 1994 elections.

In the 1994 campaign, the main election contenders were Balaguer of the PRSC and Peña Gómez of the PRD, with Bosch of the PLD running a distant third. In spite of suspicion and controversies, hopes ran high that with international help to the Electoral Board, a consensus document signed by the leading parties in place, and international monitoring, the 1994 elections would be fair, ending a long sequence of disputed elections in the Dominican Republic. Much to the surprise of many Dominicans and international observers, irregularities in voter registry lists were detected early on election day, which prevented large numbers of individuals from voting. In what turned out to be extremely close elections, the disenfranchised appeared disproportionately to be PRD voters, a situation that potentially affected the outcome. The prolonged post-election crisis resulted from the apparent fraud in the 1994 elections. Balaguer had ostensibly defeated Peña Gómez by an even narrower margin than that over Bosch in the 1990 elections. This situation caused strong reactions by numerous groups inside and outside the country: the United States government, the OAS, international observer missions, business groups, some elements of the Roman Catholic Church, and the PRD, among others. The severe criticism led to the signing of an agreement, known as the Pact for Democracy, reached among the three major parties on August 10, 1994. The agreement reduced Balaguer's presidential term to two years, after which new presidential elections would be held. The agreement also called for the appointment of a new Electoral Board as well as numerous constitutional reforms. The reforms included banning consecutive presidential reelection, separating presidential and congressional-municipal elections by two years, holding a run-off election if no presidential candidate won a majority of the votes, reforming the judicial system, and allowing dual citizenship.

A New Beginning?

The 1994 agreement and constitutional reforms, reinforced by increased vigilance by elements of Dominican civil society and by international actors, led to successful, free elections in 1996. None of the three main contenders in 1996 received the absolute majority necessary to win in the first round. Peña Gómez of the PRD reached the highest percentage with 45.9 percent, followed by Leonel Fernández of the PLD with 38.9 percent (Bosch had finally stepped down as party leader because of age and health), and Jacinto Peynado of the PRSC with 15 percent. Balaguer, who had not endorsed his party's first-round candidate, in the second round joined with the PRSC to officially endorse the candidacy of Leonel Fernández of the PLD in a "Patriotic Pact." The pact's spokesmen, who called for the preservation of national sovereignty and Dominicanness, were, in effect, articulating racial and anti-Haitian themes in their campaign against Peña Gómez, who was of Haitian ancestry. Aided by the PRSC endorsement, Leonel Fernández Reyna was able to defeat Peña Gómez in the second round.

Fernández's arrival to the presidency illustrated many of the dramatic changes that had taken place in the country. At the time of the death of Trujillo in 1961, the Dominican Republic was a predominantly rural country with a population isolated from international contact and an economy largely dependent on the export of sugar and other agricultural crops. By 1996 the country was mostly urban, and its economy and culture were far more linked to the outside world. Sugar was fading in importance; the country's major sources of foreign exchange were now tourism, exports from free trade zones, and remittances from overseas migrants. Indeed, the new president had spent part of his youth as a migrant in New York, where as many as one in fourteen Dominicans currently live; he could converse comfortably in English or Spanish about the implications of economic globalization, the threat of drug trafficking routes through the island republic, or the records of the dozens of Dominican baseball players in the major leagues of the United States.

The 1996 elections were the first in the country since 1962 when neither Balaguer nor Bosch was a candidate. Political change was evident, as were elements of continuity and conflict. Fernández obtained the presidency, but the new electoral calendar established by the 1994 reform meant that congressional elections would now be held at the midpoint of the presidential term. Indeed, his party had a very small representation in Congress because of its poor performance in the 1994 elections. Soon after Fernández's electoral victory, Balaguer's PRSC negotiated a pact with the PRD to obtain leadership positions in Congress. Without congressional support, however, as of mid-1998 the Fernández administration was stymied in its efforts to pass legislation.

Midway through his presidential term in office, Fernández had been governing in a more democratic fashion than Balaguer. As of mid-1998, the Fernández administration had had two major political successes. One was the appointment in August 1997 of a new Supreme Court—widely viewed as comprising many distinguished jurists—in a much more open process through a Council of the Magistrature established by the constitutional reform of 1994. The other was the holding of fair congressional and municipal elections on May 16, 1998. At the same time, the death of Peña Gómez, one of the country's political leaders, on May 10, 1998, was an indicator of the transition in Dominican politics at the close of the twentieth century. Because of Peña Gómez's death one week before the elections, the PRD won by an even wider margin than polls had suggested, gaining 80 percent of Senate seats, 56 percent of seats in the Chamber of Deputies, and 83 percent of mayoral races. Although Fernández's own PLD improved its congressional representation compared to 1994, it was not nearly to the level expected by the party; the PRSC also did very poorly.

Thus, the Dominican Republic is entering the new century seeking to strengthen still fragile democratic institutions, building on the successful democratic transition represented by the 1996 elections. The country is also having to learn how to manage the bitter interparty wrangling reflected in tense executive-congressional relations while also managing leadership changes in the major parties and confronting continuing serious socioeconomic challenges.

* * *

An excellent one-volume historical overview in English is Frank Moya Pons's *The Dominican Republic: A National History.* Also useful are the chapters by Frank Moya Pons and H. Hoetink found in *The Cambridge History of Latin America* (in volumes 2, 5, and 7, including their bibliographical essays). On the nineteenth century, see also H. Hoetink, *The Dominican People 1859–1900: Notes for a Historical Sociology*; Sumner Welles, *Naboth's Vineyard: The Dominican Republic, 1844–1924*; and Emelio Betances, *State and Society in the Dominican Republic*. Bruce J. Calder's *The Impact of Intervention* is an excellent study of the United States occupation and its effects. On Trujillo, Robert Crassweller's *Trujillo: The Life and Times of a Caribbean Dictator* is highly recommended. Howard Wiarda has written extensively on the Dominican Republic; his most detailed work is a three-volume study, *Dictatorship, Development and Disintegration: Politics and Social Changes in the Dominican Republic*. Rosario Espinal has published many valuable articles, including "An Interpretation of the Democratic Transition in the Dominican Republic." Recent analyses of Dominican politics include those by Jan Knippers Black, *The Dominican Republic*; James Ferguson, *The Dominican Republic: Beyond the Lighthouse*; and Jonathan Hartlyn, *The Struggle for Democratic Politics in the Dominican Republic*. (For further information and complete citations, see Bibliography.)

Chapter 2. Dominican Republic: The Society and Its Environment

A bohío, *or rural hut*

DOMINICAN SOCIETY OF THE late 1990s reflects the country's Spanish-African-Caribbean heritage. It manifests significant divisions along the lines of race and class. A small fraction of the populace controls great wealth, while the vast majority struggles to get by. The small emerging middle class works both to maintain and to extend its political and economic gains. Generally speaking, Dominican society offers relatively few avenues of advancement; most of those available allow families of modest means only to enhance slightly or consolidate their standing.

The majority of the population is mulatto, the offspring of Africans and Europeans. The indigenous Amerindian population had been virtually eliminated within half a century of initial contact. Immigrants—European, Middle Eastern, Asian, and Caribbean—arrived with each cycle of economic growth. In general, skin color determines placement in the social hierarchy: lighter skin is associated with higher social and economic status. European immigrants and their offspring find more ready acceptance at the upper reaches of society than do darker-skinned Dominicans.

The decades following the end of the regime of Rafael Leónidas Trujillo Molina (1930–61) have been a time of extensive changes as large-scale rural-urban and international migration have blurred the gulf between city and countryside. Traditional attitudes persist: peasants continue to regard urban dwellers with suspicion, and people in cities continue to think of rural Dominicans as unsophisticated and naive. Nonetheless, most families include several members who have migrated to the republic's larger cities or to the United States. Migration serves to relieve some of the pressures of population growth. Moreover, cash remittances from abroad permit families of moderate means to acquire assets and maintain a standard of living far beyond what they might otherwise enjoy.

The alternatives available to poorer Dominicans are far more limited. Legal emigration requires assets beyond the reach of most, although some risk the water passage to Puerto Rico. Many rural dwellers migrate instead to one of the republic's cities. These newcomers, however, enjoy financial resources and training far inferior to those prevailing among families of moderate means. For the vast majority of the republic's population, the twin constraints of limited land and limited employment opportunities define the daily struggle for existence.

In the midst of far-reaching changes, the republic continues to be a profoundly family oriented society. Dominicans of every social stratum rely on family, kin, and neighbors for social identity and interpersonal relations of trust and confidence, particularly in the processes of migration and urbanization. At the same time, these processes often cause the family to disintegrate.

Geography

The Dominican Republic is located on the island of Hispaniola (La Isla Española), which it shares with Haiti to the west. The 388-kilometer border between the two was established in a series of treaties, the most recent of which was the 1936 Protocol of Revision of the Frontier Treaty (Tratado Fronterizo) of 1929. The country is shaped in the form of an irregular triangle. The short side of the triangle is 388 kilometers long, while the two long sides form 1,575 kilometers of coastline along the Atlantic Ocean, Caribbean Sea, and Mona Passage. The total area of the country is 48,442 square kilometers. Although the Dominican Republic boasts the highest elevations in the Antilles, it also has a saltwater lake below sea level (see fig. 1).

Natural Regions

The mountains and valleys of the Dominican Republic divide the country into three regions: the northern region, central region, and southwestern region. The northern region borders the Atlantic Ocean and consists of the Atlantic coastal plain, Cordillera Septentrional (Northern Range), Valle del Cibao (Cibao Valley), and Samaná Peninsula. The Atlantic coastal plain is a narrow strip that extends from the northwestern coast at Monte Cristi to Nagua, north of the Samaná Peninsula. The Cordillera Septentrional is south of and runs parallel to the coastal plain. Its highest peaks rise to an elevation of more than 1,000 meters. The Valle del Cibao lies south of the Cordillera Septentrional. It extends 240 kilometers from the northwest coast to the Bahía de Samaná (Samaná Bay) in the east and ranges in width from fifteen to forty-five kilometers. To the west of the ridge lies the Valle de Santiago, and to the east is the Valle de la Vega Real. The Samaná Peninsula is an eastward extension of the northern region, separated from the Cordillera Septentrional by an area of swampy lowlands. The peninsula is mountainous, with its highest elevations reaching 600 meters.

The central region is dominated by the Cordillera Central (Central Range); it runs eastward from the Haitian border and turns southward at the Valle de Constanza to end in the Caribbean Sea. This southward branch is known as the Sierra de Ocoa. The Cordillera Central is 2,000 meters high near the Haitian border and reaches an elevation of 3,087 meters at Pico Duarte, the highest point in the country. An eastern branch of the Cordillera Central extends through the Sierra de Yamasá to the Cordillera Oriental (Eastern Range). The main peaks of these two mountain groups are not higher than 880 meters. The Cordillera Oriental also is known as the Sierra de Seibo.

Another significant feature of the central region is the Caribbean coastal plain, which lies south of the foothills of the Sierra de Yamasá and the Cordillera Oriental. It extends 240 kilometers from the mouth of the Ocoa River to the extreme eastern end of the island. The Caribbean coastal plain is ten to forty kilometers wide and consists of a series of limestone terraces that gradually rise to an elevation of 100 to 120 meters at the northern edge of the coastal plains at the foothills of the Cordillera Oriental. Finally, the central region includes the Valle de San Juan in the western part of the country; the valley extends 100 kilometers from the Haitian border to Bahía de Ocoa.

The southwestern region lies south of the Valle de San Juan. It encompasses the Sierra de Neiba, which extends 100 kilometers from the Haitian border to the Yaque del Sur River. The main peaks are roughly 2,000 meters high, while other peaks range from 1,000 to 1,500 meters. On the eastern side of the Yaque del Sur lies the Sierra de Martín García, which extends twenty-five kilometers from the river to the Llanura de Azua (Plain of Azua).

The Hoya de Enriquillo, a structural basin that lies south of the Sierra de Neiba, is also within the southwestern region. The basin extends ninety-five kilometers from the Haitian border to the Bahía de Neiba and twenty kilometers from the Sierra de Neiba to the Sierra de Baoruco. The Sierra de Baoruco extends seventy kilometers from the Haitian border to the Caribbean Sea. Its three major peaks surpass 2,000 meters in height. The Procurrente de Barahona (Cape of Barahona) extends southward from the Sierra de Baoruco and consists of a series of terraces.

Drainage

The Dominican Republic has seven major drainage basins. Five of these rise in the Cordillera Central and a sixth in the Sierra de Yamasá. The seventh drainage system flows into the Lago Enriquillo (Lake Enriquillo) from the Sierra de Neiba to the north and the Sierra de Baoruco to the south. In general, other rivers are either short or intermittent.

The Yaque del Norte is the most significant river in the country. Some 296 kilometers long and with a basin area of 7,044 square kilometers, it rises near Pico Duarte at an elevation of 2,580 meters in the Cordillera Central. It empties into Bahía de Monte Cristi on the northwest coast where it forms a delta. The Yaque del Sur is the most important river on the southern coast. It rises to an elevation of 2,707 meters in the southern slopes of the Cordillera Central. Its upper course through the mountains comprises 75 percent of its total length of some 183 kilometers. The basin area is 4,972 square kilometers. The river forms a delta near its mouth in the Bahía de Neiba.

The Lago Enriquillo, the largest lake in the Antilles, lies in the western part of the Hoya de Enriquillo. Its drainage basin includes ten minor river systems and covers an area of more than 3,000 square kilometers. The northern rivers of the system are perennial and rise in the Sierra de Neiba, while the southern rivers rise in the Sierra de Baoruco and are intermittent, flowing only after heavy rainfall. The Lago Enriquillo itself varies from 200 to 265 square kilometers. Its water level oscillates because of the high evaporation rate, yet on the average it is forty meters below sea level. The water in the lake is saline.

Climate

The Dominican Republic has primarily a tropical climate, with more diurnal and local than seasonal variations in temperature, and with seasonal variability in the abundance of rainfall. The average annual temperature is 25°C, ranging from 18°C at an elevation of more than 1,200 meters to 28°C at an elevation of ten meters. Highs of 40°C are common in protected valleys, as are lows of 0°C in mountainous areas. In general, August is the hottest month and January and February, the coldest.

Seasons, however, vary more as a function of rainfall than of temperature. Along the northern coast, the rainy season lasts from November through January. In the rest of the country, it runs from May through November, with May being the wettest month. The dry season lasts from November through April, with March being the driest month. The average annual rainfall for the country as a whole is 150 centimeters. Rainfall varies, however, from region to region, from thirty-five centimeters in the Valle de Neiba to 274 centimeters in the Cordillera Oriental. In general, the western part of the country, including the interior valleys, receives the least rain.

Tropical cyclones—such as tropical depressions, tropical storms, and hurricanes—occur on the average once every two years in the Dominican Republic. More than 65 percent of the storms strike the southern part of the country, especially along the Hoya de Enriquillo. The season for cyclones lasts from the beginning of June to the end of November; some cyclones occur in May and December, but most occur in September and October. Hurricanes usually occur from August through October. They may produce winds greater than 200 kilometers per hour and rainfall greater than fifty centimeters in a twenty-four-hour period.

Population

Size and Growth

The country's total population in 1993, according to the census of that year, totaled slightly more than 7 million; its population for 1997 has been estimated to be slightly above 8 million. Growth has been high since official census-taking began in 1920. The average growth rate peaked during the 1950s at 3.6 percent per year. Since then the rate has been declining: during the 1960s, the population grew at 2.9 percent annually; during the 1970s, at 2.3 percent; during the 1980s, at 2.0 percent; and during the 1990s, at 1.6 percent (see fig. 3).

The total fertility rate, although still relatively high, declined substantially in the 1970s and then slowly in the 1980s and early 1990s: from 3.7 children per woman of child-bearing age in 1985 to 3.2 in 1990, 2.8 in 1992, and 2.7 in 1995. Official estimates indicate that half of all married women use contraceptives—the rate was reportedly 58 percent in 1984 in comparison to 32 percent in 1975. However, the Dominican Republic's existing population growth rate and field studies

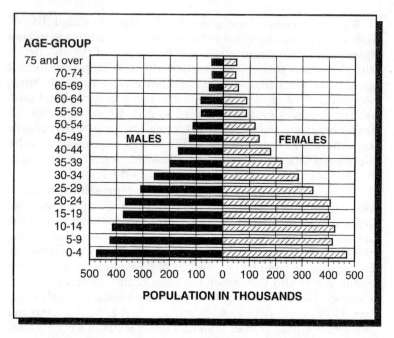

AGE-GROUP

MALES   FEMALES

500 400 300 200 100 0 100 200 300 400 500

POPULATION IN THOUSANDS

Source: Based on information from Dominican Republic, Oficina Nacional de
Estadística, *La República Dominicana en Cifras, 1997*, Santo Domingo, 1998,
52-55.

*Figure 3. Dominican Republic: Population Distribution by Age and
Sex, 1993 Census*

seem to belie this figure. A scholarly study in the 1990s indicates, for example, that whereas the use of contraceptive pills ranged from 5 to 9 percent for the 1975 to 1986 period, permanent sterilization has become the most popular birth control method among Dominican women. Their recourse to it rose from 8 to 33 percent during the above period.

Despite the opposition of the Roman Catholic Church, the government began supporting family planning in 1967 with financing from the United States Agency for International Development. The family planning program expanded rapidly, from eight clinics concentrated in the cities and larger towns to more than 500 clinics—some in small towns and rural areas—by the late 1980s. Both the Secretariat of State for Public Health and Social Welfare (Secretaría de Estado de Salud Pública y Asistencia Social—SESPAS) and the National Council on Population and Family (Consejo Nacional de Población y

Familia—Conapofa) offer family planning services. By the 1980s, both organizations were trying to make their programs more responsive to the needs of rural families. In the 1980s, the groups focused on population reduction along with maternal and child health. The focus shifted in the 1990s to achieving a balance among population level, economic development, and progress toward social well-being.

Birth control encounters strong resistance from both sexes, especially in the countryside and the smaller cities. Although women use a variety of substances believed to be contraceptives or abortifacients, there is considerable misinformation about family planning. Many men believe birth control threatens their masculinity; some women think various contraceptive methods cause sickness. Dominican migrants who travel abroad are more aware of the available options, and some women migrants use modern contraceptives.

Population Distribution

With regard to demographic distribution, the traditional (nonadministrative) subregions of the country include Valdesia and Yuma in the southeast, Enriquillo and Del Valle in the southwest, and the Central, Eastern, and Western Cibao in the north. The subregion of densest settlement is Valdesia on the southern coast, which contains the nation's capital and, according to the 1993 census, 41 percent of the population. Roughly one-third (30 percent in 1993) of all Dominicans live in the National District, the area surrounding the national capital of Santo Domingo. The other major area of settlement is the Central Cibao, which accounted for 23 percent of total population in 1993 (see table 2, Appendix).

Administrations have attempted to control population growth and distribution since the 1950s. The Trujillo regime fostered agricultural colonies scattered throughout the countryside and strung along the western frontier with Haiti. Some were coupled with irrigation projects. In the late 1970s, some new joint projects with Haiti were approved by President Silvestre Antonio Guzmán Fernández (1978–82).

Beginning in the late 1970s, the government also set up industrial free zones around the country. Although the desire to increase employment was the government's primary motivation, the establishment of free zones also had as a secondary goal the dispersal of industrialization, and thus migration, away from Santo Domingo (see Manufacturing, ch. 3). Intercensal growth rates on the subregional and provincial levels reflect these trends. Puerto Plata grew at more than twice the rate of the nation as a whole in the 1970s. This trend continued in the 1980s and early 1990s as a result of the rapidly developing and expanding tourist industry along the north coast. The southeast, especially the National District, has expanded much faster than most of the country, as has La Romana, both largely on account of the increased number of industrial free zones.

Migration

The Dominican Republic is a country of migrants. Surveys in the mid-1970s found that nearly two-thirds of city dwellers and half of those in the countryside had migrated at least once. According to the 1981 census, nearly one-quarter of the population was living in a province other than that in which they were born. A decade later, according to the 1993 census, the figure had increased to one-third of the population. Rural areas in general, especially in the Central Cibao, have experienced significant levels of out-migration. The movement of peasants and the landless into the republic's growing cities has accounted for the lion's share of migration, however. Indeed, Dominicans have even coined a word, *campuno*, to describe the rural-urban campesino migrant. In the 1970s, the industrial free zones, particularly in La Romana and San Pedro de Macorís, attracted many migrants in search of employment. According to the 1981 census, the principal destinations for migrants were the National District followed by the provinces of La Romana, Independencia, and San Pedro de Macorís (see fig. 2). In the National District, 46 percent of the inhabitants were migrants. The main destination for migrants in the 1980s, according to the 1993 Dominican census, continued to be the National District but was followed this time by the provinces of Valverde and San Cristóbal and then La Romana and San Pedro de Macorís. This census indicated the increasing urbanization of the country as well as the apparent continuing magnet effect of the industrial zones, which in 1997 numbered thirty-five and employed 182,000 Dominicans.

In the 1990s, women predominated in both rural-urban and urban-rural migration (55 to 60 percent of the workers in the industrial free zones were women, representing what two Dominican analysts call the "feminization" of labor, especially in Santo Domingo). Men, however, are more likely than women to move from city to city or from one rural area to another. According to the 1993 census, in rural areas men outnumber women until the twenty to twenty-four-year age-group, when women become more numerous; in the forty-five to fifty-year age-group, men once again become and remain in the majority. The figures reflect the fact that men in the twenty-five to forty-four-year age-group leave for the cities or for the United States. Many return two decades later. On the other hand, in the urban areas from their teens on women outnumber men.

In general, migrants earn more than non-migrants and suffer lower rates of unemployment, although underemployment is pervasive. Urban-rural migrants have the highest incomes. This category, however, consists of a select group of educated and skilled workers, mostly government officials, teachers, and the like moving from a city to assume specific jobs in rural areas. They receive higher wages as a recompense for the lack of urban amenities in villages.

Migrants speak of the migration chain (*cadena*) tying them to other migrants and their home communities. Kin serve as the links in the chain. They care for family, lands, and businesses left behind, or, if they have migrated earlier, assist the new arrivals with employment and housing. The actual degree of support families can or are willing to give a migrant varies widely, however.

The process of rural-urban migration typically involves a series of steps. The migrant gradually abandons agriculture and seeks more nonagricultural sources of income. Migrants rarely arrive in the largest, fastest-growing cities "green" from the countryside. They acquire training and experience in intermediate-sized cities and temporary nonfarm jobs en route.

International migration plays a significant role in the livelihood of many Dominicans. Anywhere from 10 to 12 percent of the total population are residing abroad. Estimates of those living and working in the United States in the 1990s range from 300,000 to as high as 800,000. Roughly 200,000 more are estimated to be in San Juan, Puerto Rico, many of them presumably waiting to get to the United States mainland. One Dominican official reported the estimated number in the late 1990s to be 700,000, which includes 75,000 illegals. In the mid-1980s, the United States admitted from 23,000 to 26,000 Dominicans annually; by 1990 the number had increased to 42,195 and by 1993 to almost 46,000. (The United States census of 1990 reported that there were 511,297 Dominicans living as permanent residents. After the Dominican constitution was amended in 1994 to allow dual citizenship, there was a Dominican rush to naturalize.) Most emigrants go to New York City (68 percent in 1990); starting in the mid-1980s their destinations also included other cities of the eastern seaboard—Boston, Providence, and Hartford—and in the South, Miami.

In the 1960s and early 1970s, many professionals emigrated because of the lack of professional opportunities, thus constituting a brain drain, one that affected some key professions. Later, the majority of those emigrating were unemployed, unskilled, and women. A sizable minority (about one-third), however, emigrated not only for economic reasons but to continue their education, especially graduate and professional, or to join other family members. Many planned to save their money and return home to start a small business. In the 1980s and 1990s, the emigrants' educational and skill levels have been changing. Whereas the majority are still unskilled, an increasing minority includes emigrants who are relatively more educated and skilled than the Dominican populace as a whole. Most come from cities, but the mid- to large-sized farms of the overpopulated Cibao also send large numbers. Working in the United States has become almost an expected part of the lives of Dominicans from families of moderate means.

This practice linking the two countries has resulted in the development of what some scholars call the "dual societies"—Dominican and United States—and the "dual identity" of Dominicans. Their moving back and forth, working and saving in the United States, being influenced by United States values, produces a north-south transnationalism. Because so many Dominicans live and work in New York City, a special word—"Domyork"—was created at home to describe those returning to visit, open a business, or retire.

Cash remittances from Dominicans living abroad have become an integral part of the national economy. Emigrants' remittances constitute a significant percentage of the country's foreign exchange earnings. Remittances are used to finance businesses, purchase land, and bolster a family's standard of living. Most emigrants see sending money as an obligation. Although some refuse to provide assistance, they come under severe criticism from both fellow emigrants and those who remain behind. The extent to which an emigrant's earnings are committed to family and kin is sometimes striking. Anthropologist Patricia Pessar has described a Dominican man in New

View of the Duarte Highway north of Santo Domingo
Courtesy Inter-American Development Bank

York who earned less than US$500 per month. He sent US$150 of this to his wife and children and another US$100 to his parents and unmarried siblings. In 1990 remittances accounted for 40 percent of Dominican family income, and 88 percent of these remittances came from New York state.

Money from abroad has had a multiplier effect; it has spawned a veritable construction boom in emigrants' hometowns and neighborhoods beginning in the mid-1970s and continuing since that time. Some of the returning "Domyorks" who survived and profited from drug trafficking have brought about a major change in traditional Dominican society with their Hollywood homes, expensive cars, noisy bars, and discos. San Francisco de Macorís is the main city that has been so transformed. The increasing emigrant investments in housing and in tourism also have challenged the traditional elite's monopoly control. Additionally, emigrants contribute significant sums to the church back home. Many parish priests make annual fund-raising trips to New York to seek donations for local parish needs.

The impact of emigration is widely felt, which is illustrated by the experience of two Dominican villages, two decades apart, whose emigrants went to New York City and Boston. In the earlier case, in one Cibao village 85 percent of the house-holds had at least one member living in New York in the mid-1970s. In the later case, a village in the southern province of Peravia, more than 65 percent of the 445 households had rela-tives in the Boston metropolitan area in the mid-1990s. Where emigration is common, it alters a community's age pyramid: eighteen to forty-five-year-olds (especially males) are essentially missing. Emigration also eliminates many of the natural choices for leadership roles in the home community. Addition-ally, anthropologist Pessar noted in a recent study the negative impact of departures upon rural society. Emigration, for exam-ple, has led to a shift from share-cropping to cattle grazing, resulting in the fragmentation of the rural economy. Although those left behind often feel isolated from their neighbors and are adrift, especially those who have left farming for cattle graz-ing, there is a constant exchange of news and information, and the maintenance of social contact between the remaining vil-lagers and their emigrant relatives. The latter's remittances economically sustain or improve the welfare of the former.

Urbanization

For most of its history, the Dominican Republic was over-whelmingly rural; in 1920 more than 80 percent of its populace lived in the countryside, and by 1950 more than 75 percent still did. Substantial urban expansion began in the 1950s and gained tremendous momentum in the 1960s, 1970s, and 1980s. Urban growth rates far outdistanced those of the country as a whole. The urban population expanded at 6.1 percent annu-ally during the 1950s, 5.7 percent during the 1960s to 1970s, 4.7 percent through the 1980s, and 3.3 percent from 1990 to 1995 (rural population has decreased 0.3 percent since 1990).

In the early decades of the twentieth century, the country was not only largely rural, but the urban scene itself was domi-nated by smaller cities and provincial capitals. In 1920 nearly 80 percent of all city dwellers lived in cities with fewer than 20,000 inhabitants. Santo Domingo, with barely more than 30,000 residents, accounted for only 20 percent of those in cit-ies. By contrast, in 1981 Santo Domingo alone accounted for nearly half of all city dwellers; it had more than double the total population of all cities of more than 20,000 inhabitants. Cities with fewer than 20,000 inhabitants—nearly 80 percent of the urban population in 1920—constituted less than 20 per-cent by 1981. According to the 1993 census, the Dominican

Republic was 56 percent urban, and Santo Domingo had 40 percent of the urban population. The *United Nations Demographic Yearbook, 1996* estimated the country to be almost 62 percent urban in 1995.

Santo Domingo approximately doubled its population every decade between 1920 and 1970. Its massive physical expansion, however, dates from the 1950s. The growth in industry and urban construction, coupled with Trujillo's expropriations of rural land, fueled rural-urban migration and the city's growth. In 1993 the city had slightly more than 2 million inhabitants. The republic's second and third largest cities, Santiago de los Caballeros and La Romana, also experienced significant expansion in the 1960s and 1970s. Santiago, the center of traditional Hispanic culture, drew migrants from the heavily populated Cibao. La Romana, in the southeast, grew as a center of employment in the sugar industry as well as a tourism center; it was also the site of the country's first industrial free zone (see Manufacturing, ch. 3). The two cities continued to grow throughout the 1980s and early 1990s while the sugar industry declined—replaced by expanding industrial free zones and tourism in La Romana. In 1993 the population of Santiago de los Caballeros stood at 488,291 and that of La Romana at 141,570.

Population growth and rural-urban migration have strained cities' capacity to provide housing and amenities. Nevertheless, in 1981 nearly 80 percent of city dwellings had access to potable water; 90 percent had limited sewage disposal; and roughly 90 percent had electricity. These percentages subsequently declined because the provision of such services did not keep up with the general increase in population as well as with the continued rural-urban migration. For example, a Pan American Health Organization (PAHO) report estimated that in 1993 the potable water supply reached 65 percent of the population: 80 percent were in urban areas and 46 percent were in rural areas (only 25 percent of rural communities had drinking water services). Sewage disposal services covered only 16 percent of the entire population, and 28 percent of the urban population had apartment or house connections. (According to the 1993 Dominican census, 214,354 of the country's 1,629,616 dwellings lacked sanitary services.) Finally, the PAHO report indicated that 81 percent of the dwellings had electricity.

By the mid-1980s, there was an estimated housing deficit of some 400,000 units; by 1990 estimates, 600,000 dwellings were uninhabitable, 800,000 needed repairs, and only 500,000 were conside¬ed adequate. The need is greatest in the National District. Squatter settlements have grown in response to the scarcity of low-cost urban housing. In Santo Domingo these settlements are concentrated along the Ozama River and on the city's periphery. When Joaquín Balaguer Ricardo returned to the presidency in 1986, 3,000 squatters were forced from the construction site of the lighthouse along the Ozama River. They were moved to the side of the construction site where a slum area developed. A high wall was built to keep the area from being seen.

Public housing initiatives date from the late 1950s, when Trujillo built some housing for government employees of moderate means. Through the 1980s, a number of different governmental agencies played a role. Often motivated to create jobs during economic crises, the Technical Secretariat of the Presidency has designed a variety of projects in Santo Domingo. The Aid and Housing Institute and the National Housing Institute bear primary responsibility for the financing and construction of housing. In general, public efforts have been hampered by extreme decentralization in planning coupled with equally extreme concentration in decision-making. The primary beneficiaries of public projects are usually lower-income groups, although not the poorest urban dwellers. Projects have targeted those making at least the minimum wage, namely the lower-middle sector or the more stable segments of the working class.

Racial and Ethnic Groups

Ethnic Heritage

The island's indigenous inhabitants were mainly the Taino Indians, an Arawak-speaking group, and a small settlement of Carib Indians around the Bahía de Samaná. These Indians, estimated to number perhaps 1 million at the time of their initial contact with Europeans, for the most part had been killed or died by the 1550s as a result of harsh Spanish treatment. The Tainos were especially ill-treated.

The importation of African slaves began in 1503. By the nineteenth century, the population was roughly 150,000: 40,000 were of Spanish descent, 40,000 were black slaves, and the remainder were either freed blacks or mulattoes. In the mid-1990s, approximately 10 percent of the population was considered white and 15 percent black; the remainder were mulattoes—75 percent (the percentages are often debated). Since then the percentage of whites has been slowly decreasing and that of mulattoes increasing; the black percentage has remained about the same, with Haitian immigration being a factor. The figures about the ethnic ratio and its changing composition are a sensitive Dominican issue because many elite and upper-class whites are anti-African (blacks and mulattoes) and seek to claim a higher, constant "white" figure. Many mulattoes, however, claim a larger percentage for themselves at the same time that many others have difficulty acknowledging their African roots.

Contemporary Dominican society and culture are primarily Spanish in origin. At the same time, much of popular culture reflects many African influences. Taino influence is limited to cultigens, such as maize or corn, and a few vocabulary words, such as *huracán* (hurricane) and *hamaca* (hammock). The African influence in society was officially suppressed and ignored by the Trujillo regime (1930–61) and then by Balaguer until the 1980s. However, certain religious brotherhoods with significant black membership have incorporated some Afro-American elements. Observers also have noted the presence of African influence in popular dance and music (see Culture, this ch.).

There has long been a preference in Dominican society for light skin, straight hair, and "white" racial features. Blackness in itself, however, does not necessarily restrict a person to a lower status position. Upward mobility is possible for the dark-skinned person who manages to acquire education or wealth. During the era of Trujillo, joining the military became a major means of upward mobility, especially for dark and light-skinned Dominicans—the white elite would not permit its sons to join). Social characteristics focusing on family background, education, and economic standing are, in fact, more prominent means of identifying and classifying individuals. Darker-skinned persons are concentrated in the east, the south, and the far west near the Haitian border. The population of the Cibao, especially in the countryside, consists mainly of whites or mulattoes.

Dominicans traditionally prefer to think of themselves as descendants of the island's Indians and the Spanish, ignoring their African heritage. Thus, phenotypical African characteristics, such as dark skin pigmentation, are disparaged. Trujillo, a

71

light-skinned mulatto who claimed that he was "white" (French and Spa⁻ish), instituted as official policy that Dominicans were racially white, culturally Spanish, and religiously Roman Catholic. Balaguer continued this policy until the 1980s when he openly recognized African cultural and social influences. He made the change because, first, he followed two opposition party governments, those of presidents Guzmán (1978–82) and Jorge Blanco (1982–86), who had officially recognized the country's African roots. Second, he was appealing for votes as he prepared for his reelection campaign in 1986. Because of Trujillo's and then Balaguer's racial conditioning, emigrants and visitors to the United States are often shocked to discover that they are viewed as "black." However, they and many back home welcomed the civil rights and black pride movements in North America in the 1960s and 1970s. Those returning brought a new level of racial consciousness to the republic because they had experienced both racial prejudice and the black pride movement. The returning emigrants who brought back Afro hairstyles and a variety of other "Afro-North Americanisms" received mixed reactions from their fellow Dominicans, however.

Modern Immigration

Although almost all immigrants assimilate to Dominican society (often with surprising speed and thoroughness), immigration has had a pervasive influence on the ethnic and racial configuration of the country. Within a generation or two, most immigrants with the exception of Haitians are considered Dominican even though the family may continue to maintain contact with relatives in the country of origin. Both the elite and the middle segments of society have recruited new members with each economic expansion. The main impetus to immigration was the rise of sugar production in the late nineteenth and early twentieth centuries. Some groups have had earlier antecedents, whereas others arrived as late as the 1970s, 1980s, and 1990s—Haitians and Chinese from Taiwan continued to enter in the late 1990s.

Nineteenth-century immigrants came from a number of sources. North American freedmen, principally Methodists, came in response to an offer of free land made during the period of Haitian domination (1822–44). Roughly 5,000 to 10,000 immigrated; most, however, were city dwellers and quickly returned to the United States. A few small settlements remained around Santiago, Puerto Plata, and Samaná. They eventually assimilated, although English is still widely used in the region of Samaná. Sephardic Jews arrived from Curaçao in the late eighteenth century and in greater numbers following Dominican independence from Haiti in 1844. They assimilated rapidly; both their economic assets and their white ancestry made them desirable additions from the point of view of both the elite and the criollos. Canary Islanders arrived during the late colonial period as well, in response to the improved Dominican economic conditions in the 1880s. Spaniards settled in the country during the period of renewed Spanish occupation (1861–65); a number of Spanish soldiers remained in the Dominican Republic after the War of Restoration. Germans also established themselves in the republic, principally in Puerto Plata. Some arrived before independence, but they mainly came after the Spanish occupation; they were involved primarily in the tobacco trade.

The expansion of the sugar industry in the late nineteenth century drew immigrants from every social stratum. Cubans and Puerto Ricans, who began arriving in the 1870s, aided in the evolution of the sugar industry as well as the country's intellectual development. In addition, the sugar industry attracted significant numbers of laborers from the British, Dutch, and Danish islands of the Caribbean. These immigrants also worked in railroad construction and on the docks. Initial reaction to their presence was negative, but their educational background (which was superior to that of most of the rural populace), their ability to speak English (which gave them an advantage in dealing with North American plantation owners), and their industriousness eventually won them a measure of acceptance. They founded Protestant churches, Masonic lodges, mutual aid societies, and a variety of other cultural organizations. Their descendants have enjoyed a considerable measure of upward mobility through education and religion. They are well represented in the technical trades (especially those associated with the sugar industry) and on professional baseball teams.

Arabs—Lebanese and lesser numbers of Palestinians and Syrians—first arrived in the late nineteenth century and prospered. Their assimilation was slower, however, and many continued for a long time to maintain contacts with relatives in the Middle East. Italians, as well as some South American immigrants, also arrived during this period and assimilated rapidly.

A few Chinese came from the other Caribbean islands and establis'-ed a reputation for diligence and industriousness. More followed with the United States occupation of the island (1916–24). They began as cooks and domestic servants; a number of their descendants are restaurateurs and hotel owners.

The most recent trickle of immigrants entered the country from the 1930s onward. Many founded agricultural colonies that suffered a high rate of attrition. Trujillo, who favored European "whites," admitted German Jews and Spanish civil war refugees (both in the 1930s), Japanese (post World War II), and Hungarians and Spaniards (both in the 1950s). More Chinese came from Taiwan and Hong Kong in the 1970s; by the 1980s, they were the second fastest growing immigrant group—Haitians being the first. Many had sufficient capital to set up manufacturing firms in the country's industrial free zones. In the 1990s, Chinese from Taiwan and Hong Kong continued to come to Haiti, along with some Japanese, Spaniards, and Venezuelans.

Haitians

Modern Haitian immigration to the Dominican Republic dates from the late nineteenth century, when increasing North American capital raised sugar production. Dominicans have never welcomed these immigrants, first, because of the legacy of the oppressive Haitian occupation and the Dominican struggle for independence and, second, because of Trujillo's and then Balaguer's views of Haitians and their anti-Haiti policies. The Haitian presence resulted from economic necessity born of the reluctance of Dominicans to perform the menial task of cane-cutting. The 1920 census listed slightly under 28,000 Haitian nationals in the Dominican Republic. Successive governments attempted to control the numbers of Haitians entering the country; the border was periodically closed in the 1910s and 1920s. But by 1935 the number had increased to more than 50,000. Trujillo ordered a general roundup of Haitians along the border in 1937, during which an estimated 5,000 to 12,000 Haitians were killed (see The Trujillo Era, ch. 1).

Since the 1960s, a series of bilateral agreements has regulated legal Haitian immigration. In 1966 Balaguer contracted with the Haitian government for 10,000 to 20,000 temporary Haitian workers annually for the sugarcane harvest. When this agreement expired in the early 1980s, there was a great labor shortage on the Dominican State Sugar Council (Consejo

Estatal del Azúcar—CEA) plantations. In response, the Dominican army rounded up Haitians in the country and forcibly took them to the CEA estates. The exploitation of the Haitian cane cutters included their being forced to live in filthy hovels, called *bateyes*. In 1983 the International Labour Organisation issued a critical report about the situation, which was followed by similar reports by human rights groups in 1989 and 1990. Balaguer's response after his 1990 reelection was the deportation of 50,000 Haitian illegals. Shortly before the May 1996 election, Balaguer ordered another roundup and deportation of Haitians, this time to play the racial and nationalist card against "black" Francisco Peña Gómez, the candidate of the Dominican Revolutionary Party (Partido Revolucionario Dominicano—PRD) (see Political Parties, ch. 4).

There is debate about the number of Haitians present in the Dominican Republic as well as the number who have entered legally or illegally because the estimates are often subject to political considerations. For example, at times the Balaguer government has claimed that as many as 75,000 to 100,000 Haitians have entered illegally. The 1960 census enumerated slightly under 30,000 Haitians living in the Dominican Republic. According to an unofficial Dominican census of 1991, the number of Haitian immigrants increased from around 97,000 in 1970 to 245,000 in 1991, with the majority still living in *bateyes*. Two well-known United States analysts have estimated that the number of Dominico-Haitians, or Dominicans of Haitian ancestry (they were not included in the 1991 figure of 245,000), increased by 100,000 between 1970 and 1991. The analysts also estimated that 500,000 Haitians and Dominico-Haitians were living in the Dominican Republic in 1995.

During the 1970s and 1980s, some Haitians rose to high positions in sugar production and in other areas of the economy. Although Haitians continue to account for the vast majority of cane cutters, roughly half of all labor recruiters and field inspectors also are Haitians. Haitians also work harvesting coffee, rice, and cocoa and in construction in Santo Domingo. By 1980 nearly 30 percent of the paid laborers in the coffee harvest were Haitian; in the border region, the proportion rose to 80 percent. A reasonably skilled coffee picker can nearly double the earnings of the average cane cutter. Overall, however, Haitians' earnings still lag; their wages average less than 60 percent of those of Dominicans.

The number of Haitian workers employed results from the shortage of Dominican workers and from the refusal of many Dominicans to do certain work or to work in certain places. For example, Dominicans look down on cutting sugarcane, work they view as fit only for Haitians, nor do they want to work near the border with Haiti. The large demand for Haitians as cane cutters declined rapidly in the 1980s, however, as the Dominican Republic shifted to tourism and the industrial free zones as major earners of foreign exchange. Haitians were mainly excluded from these areas but continued to work in construction, including the building of tourist complexes. When Balaguer returned to office in 1986, he initiated a public works program, which provided employment to a number of Haitians. The number of Haitians in the Dominican Republic was affected in 1990, 1994, 1996, 1998, and 1999 by deportation.

Urban Society

The Elite

The last 200 years have transformed the composition and configuration of the country's elite. Nonetheless, in the late 1990s the Dominican Republic remains a country where a relatively small number of families control great wealth while the majority of the population live in poverty. The middle stratum struggles, at its lower end, to maintain economic standing and expand its political participation and, at its upper reaches, to gain greater social acceptance and economic prosperity. Hispanic-Mediterranean ideals about the proper mode of life and livelihood continue to be significant. The primary social division is between two polar groups: the elite (*la gente buena* or *la gente culta*) and the masses.

The first half of the nineteenth century saw the elimination of many of the noteworthy families of the colonial era. During the period of Haitian domination, many prominent landowners liquidated their holdings and left. The War of Restoration against Spain also brought about changes, permitting lower-class persons who had enjoyed military success some social and economic upward mobility. The rise of sugarcane was another factor of change. The booming industry attracted immigrants of European extraction who assimilated rapidly. Poorer elite families saw a chance to improve their financial status through marriage to recently arrived and financially successful immigrants. Even well-to-do families recognized the advantages of wedding their lineage and lands to the monied merchant-immigrant clans. Although the Chinese were generally excluded from this process of assimilation, and the Arabs encountered resistance, almost everyone else found ready acceptance.

This pattern has repeated itself over the years. Each political or economic wave has brought new families into the elite as it imperiled the economic standing of others. By the 1990s, this privileged segment of society was no longer monolithic. The interests of the older elite families, whose wealth is based mostly on land (and whose prosperity diminished during the Trujillo years), do not always match those of families who amassed their fortunes under Trujillo, or of those whose money came from the expansion in industry during the 1960s and 1970s, or from the shift away from sugar and to the industrial free zones and tourism in the 1980s and 1990s. The 1965 civil war further polarized and fragmented many segments of the middle and upper classes (see Democratic Struggles and Failures, ch. 1). These developments have resulted in a new Dominican elite, whose wealth comes from banking, property, light industry, the professions, and tourism, one which co-exists with the earlier elites—the small traditional landed gentry, the business and commercial group that came to the fore in the late 1900s, and the wealthy group that worked with Trujillo.

Although rural elite families are relatively monolithic, in Santo Domingo and especially in Santiago there is a further distinction between families of the first and second rank (*gente de primera* and *gente de segunda*). Those of the first rank can claim to be a part of the 100 families referred to locally as the *tutumpote* (totem pole, a term implying family worship and excessive concern with ancestry). Those of the second rank have less illustrious antecedents; they include the descendants of successful immigrants and the nouveaux riches who have managed to intermarry with more established families.

Family loyalties are paramount, and the family represents the primary source of social identity. Elite families rely on an extensive network of kin to maintain their assets. In difficult times, the family offers a haven; as the situation improves, it provides the vehicle whereby one obtains political position and economic assets. Siblings, uncles, aunts, cousins, and in-laws comprise the pool from which one selects trusted business partners and loyal political allies. This process of networking pervades every level of society. The elite, however, profit to a much greater degree from kinship-based networking than do members of the lower classes.

The number of potential kin grows as an individual's net worth increases. The successful are obliged as a matter of course to bestow favors on a widely extended group of kin and colleagues. Individual success in the political arena carries along a host of hangers-on whose fortunes rise and fall with those of their patron. The well-to-do try to limit the demands of less illustrious kin and to obtain alliances with families of equal or greater status. These ties permit the extended family to diversify its social and economic capital.

The Middle Sector

The emerging influential middle sector, which includes the three components of upper-middle, middle-middle, and lower-middle class, represents roughly 25 to 35 percent of the population in the late 1990s. It is concentrated in the ranks of salaried professionals in government and the private sector. Members of the middle sector have almost no independent sources of wealth and so are responsive to changes in the buying power of wages and contractions in employment that accompany economic cycles. The middle level follows the racial stratification of the society as a whole: generally lighter-skinned as one proceeds up the social scale. As a group, the middle sector differs in lifestyle, marital stability, and occupation from the poor urban masses. Members firmly adhere to the Hispanic ideals of leisure and lifestyle espoused by the elite and consider themselves, at least in spirit, a part of *la gente buena*. As with the elite, economic expansion based on the growth of sugar production in the late nineteenth century broadened the middle reaches of the social ladder as well. Those of this new middle segment, however, are limited in their upward mobility by dark skin and/or limited finances. They are a diverse group that includes small shopowners, teachers, clerical employees, and professionals. They lack a class identity based on any sense of common social or economic interests. Moreover, any sense of mutual interest is undermined by the pervasiveness of the patron-client system. Individuals improve their status by linking up with a more privileged protector, not by joint political action for a shared goal.

The life strategy of middle-class families is similar to that of the elite. Their goals are to diversify their economic assets and to extend their network of political and social influence. As with the elite, the middle-level family solidifies its position through patronage. An influential family can offer jobs to loyal followers and supporters. People expect that those with power will use it for their own ends and to advance their own and their family's interests. Ties to government are particularly important, because the government is the source of many coveted jobs (see Interest Groups and Social Actors, ch. 4).

The Urban Poor

The limited availability of adequately paid and steady employment continues to define life for most urban Dominicans. The proportion of poor people has increased for the whole country but mainly for the urban poor, 64 percent of the population in the mid-1990s. This proportion increased from 47 percent in 1984 to 57 percent in 1989; the percentage of indigents increased from 16 to 30 percent for the same period; and by 1991, 70 percent of the population had fallen below the poverty line. In 1990, 39 percent of the population was living in the most impoverished areas of the country—in twenty-two of the thirty provinces. Unemployment in the 1980s and 1990s ranged between 25 and 30 percent of the economically active population. In addition, more than 40 percent of the workforce is considered underemployed. In Santo Domingo and Santiago, the two largest cities, roughly 48 percent of the self-employed, more than 50 percent of those paid piece rate, and 85 percent of temporary workers are underemployed. Under such conditions, those workers having regular employment constitute a relatively privileged segment of the urban populace.

Rural-urban migration has made the situation of the urban poor even more desperate because of competition for shelter and jobs. For the new arrivals, however, the chances of earning a living are slightly better in cities than in rural areas, although the advantages of an urban job must be weighed against the higher cost of food. Although landless or nearly landless agricultural laborers might find it difficult to work even a garden plot, the rural family can generally get by on its own food production. For the urban poor, however, the struggle to eat is relentless.

Under conditions of chronically high unemployment, low wages, and, until recently, a restrictive labor code, workers enjoy little power or leverage. Protective labor laws are limited in their coverage to workers in private companies with more than ten employees. Organized labor made significant gains in the early 1960s during the short-lived Juan Bosch Gaviño government (1962) and until the 1965 civil war. However, these gains were erased and severe restrictions were imposed upon workers when Balaguer took office in 1966. These restrictions and a frozen minimum wage—it was raised only once—were maintained by Balaguer until his electoral defeat in 1978. Once the PRD returned to office in 1978 under Silvestre Antonio Guzmán Fernández, labor conditions improved. For example, one of his first acts was to double the long-frozen minimum wage. However, despite the pro-labor position of both PRD presidents, Guzmán and Salvador Jorge Blanco (1982–86), the serious economic situation and the restrictive labor code kept organized labor ineffective and weak. For example, by the mid-1980s a scant 12 percent of the labor force was unionized, and no more than 15 percent were union affiliated in the mid-1990s (see Labor, ch. 3).

When Balaguer returned to power in 1986, he kept organized labor fragmented by enforcing the restrictions of the labor code and by fostering the formation of rival unions. Until the 1990s, the legal code prohibited nearly half of all workers (public employees and utility workers) from strikes and job actions. Nonetheless, the economic crises of the 1980s resulted in mobilizations and strikes against the Balaguer government, and a Popular Movement was formed. However, the urban poor, like workers in general, could not sustain an organized opposition because of Balaguer's willingness to use force against strikers, his massive public works projects, and a lack of effective leadership. The strikes, the growing activism of workers, Balaguer's interest in running for reelection in 1990, the formation in 1991 of the United Confederation of Workers, and pressure from the United States in the form of threatened trade sanctions, all led to a revision of the 1951 Labor Code. The new code, enacted in 1992, expanded the rights of workers to organize and established new courts for resolving labor disputes. Although many labor unions had been recognized between 1991 and 1993, fifty-five were recognized in the year after the new code's enactment. Union activity had been banned in the industrial free zones, but in 1994 the first union contract was signed.

Another factor affecting the life of the urban poor related to the role of women. A survey of urban households in the mid-1970s revealed that roughly one-quarter were headed by women. This figure has changed little in two decades, but it needs to be qualified because the women heading households in 1998 tended to be older—middle-aged and up. This change resulted from large numbers of younger women finding jobs in the industrial free zones. The change has occurred mainly in cities where these zones are located, namely, La Romana, San Francisco de Macorís, Puerto Plata, and Santo Domingo. Even in woman-headed families with a male breadwinner, a woman is frequently the more consistent income earner among poorer city dwellers. Women's economic activities are diverse, even if poorly remunerated. Women take in washing and ironing and do domestic work. The more prosperous sew. Some buy cheap or used items and raffle them off. A few who can muster the necessary capital run stalls selling groceries, cigarettes, and candy, but their trade is minimal. In smaller towns, women also perform a variety of agricultural processing tasks: grinding coffee, husking garlic, winnowing beans, and washing pig intestines.

Like more well-to-do city families, the poor try wherever possible to maintain ties with their kin in the countryside. Aid and assistance flow both ways. Farmers with relatives in the city stay with them on trips to town and repay this hospitality with produce from their fields. New rural-urban migrants are assisted by kin who have already made the transition. The poor are handicapped in these exchanges because they typically have fewer kin in a position to help. Nonetheless, the obligation to help is deeply felt. Women who migrate to cities return to their families in the countryside as economic conditions and family needs dictate.

The small urban neighborhood functions as the center of social life. Most sharing, mutual aid, and cooperative activity take place within the confines of a narrow circle of neighbors and kin. Most Dominicans share a belief that neighbors should assist each other in times of need.

Rural Society

Family and Social Relationships

Most small rural neighborhoods and villages were settled originally by one or two families. Extensive ties of kinship, intermarriage, and *compadrazgo* (coparenthood) developed among the descendants of the original settlers (see Family and Kin, this ch.). Most villagers marry their near neighbors. First cousins frequently marry, despite the formal legal prohibitions against this practice. The social life of the countryside likewise focuses on near neighbors, who are frequently direct blood relations. The bonds of trust and cooperation among these relatives form at an early age. Children wander at will among the households of extended kin. Peasants distrust those from beyond their own neighborhoods, and they are therefore leery of economic relations with outsiders. The development of community-wide activities and organizations has been handicapped by this widespread distrust. People commonly assume deceit in others in the absence of strong, incontrovertible proof to the contrary.

Until the latter twentieth century, most joint activities were kin-based: a few related extended families joined together for whatever needed attention. The *junta* was the traditional cooperative work group. Friends, neighbors, and relatives gathered at a farmer's house for a day's work. There was no strict accounting of days given and received. As wage labor became more common, the *junta* gave way to smaller work groups, or it fell into disuse.

In small towns, social life focuses on the central park, or the plaza; in rural neighborhoods, most social interaction among non-kin takes place in the stores, bars, and pool rooms where men gather to gossip. Six-day workweeks leave little time for recreation or socializing. Many farm families come to town on Sundays to shop and to attend mass. The women and children generally return home earlier than the men to prepare Sunday dinner; the men stay to visit, or to enjoy an afternoon cockfight or an important baseball or volleyball game.

Land and Poverty

Landholding is both concentrated among large holders and fragmented at the lower end of the socioeconomic scale. All but the largest producers face some constraints in terms of land and money. Two surveys conducted in the 1980s indicated the related problems of land and poverty. The first survey, the agricultural census of 1981, reported that 2 percent of landowners controlled 55 percent of the cultivable land while 82 percent of farmers owned only 12 percent. The second, a national survey taken in 1985, found extensive rural poverty. More than 40 percent of the households surveyed owned no land; another 25 percent had less than half a hectare. (In 1990 there were an estimated 450,000 farms, of which approximately

Rural family in Hato-Nuevo Magueyal, southwest of Santo Domingo
Courtesy Inter-American Development Bank

55 percent were less than one hectare in size.) Roughly 70 percent of all families relied on wage labor. Their poverty worsened in the early 1990s because the demand for such labor was down about 50 percent.

Land reform legislation has had little overall impact on landholding both because the reforms contained few provisions for land redistribution and because they have been poorly enforced. The Dominican Agrarian Institute (Instituto Agrario Dominicano—IAD) was created in 1962 to oversee land redistribution, which began with land accumulated by Trujillo and acquired by the state after his death. Little land was distributed to families during Balaguer's first term (1966–70). Instead, large tracts were turned over to a number of large estates for cattle-raising. Distribution to families was speeded up in the 1970s. By the early 1980s, irrigated rice farms, which had been left intact and farmed collectively, were slated for division into small, privately owned plots. However, by 1980 the IAD had distributed state land to only some 67,000 families—less than 15 percent of the rural population.

Land distribution was not actively pursued by either Guzmán or Jorge Blanco, mainly because of the serious economic situation. Jorge Blanco announced a land resettlement program in which 8,000 families were to be resettled the first year with increasing numbers to follow each year thereafter. However, he postponed this program as a part of his austerity measures.

When Balaguer returned to the presidency in 1986, he resumed a practice that he had engaged in while president in the 1970s. Namely, he devoted several weekends a year to visiting poor, rural areas and handing out land titles and distributing government-subsidized food to poor families—all with considerable publicity. Although little land was distributed (the records are incomplete), this practice, one also used as a campaign device, contributed to Balaguer's retaining the rural vote. Balaguer continued this activity in the 1990s while he was president and while he was campaigning for reelection in 1990 and 1994.

Population growth over the past century has almost eliminated the land reserves. Parents usually give children plots of land as they reach maturity so that they can marry and begin their own families. Over the generations, the process has led to extreme land fragmentation. Contemporary practices have sought to counteract such fragmentation by educating children, setting them up in business, or bankrolling their emigration. Such steps limit the number of heirs competing for the family holdings and assure that the next generation will be able to maintain its standard of living. One or two siblings (usually the oldest and the youngest) remain with the parents and inherit the farm. In other situations, siblings and their spouses stay on the parental lands; each couple farms its own plot of land, but they pool their labor for many agricultural and domestic tasks.

Emigration serves as a safety valve (see Migration, this ch.). Emigrants' remittances represent an essential component in many household budgets. These timely infusions of cash permit medium-sized landholders to meet expenses during the months before harvest; they also allow families to purchase more land. In communities with a history of fifteen to twenty years of high levels of emigration, the infusion of cash has had an inflationary impact on the local land market. For those relying on wage labor (daily or periodic cash payment) to earn a living, the impact is more ambiguous. In some communities, the increase in emigration means more casual work is available as more family members emigrate. In other instances, emigrants' families have switched to livestock raising to limit labor requirements or have hired an overseer to handle the agricultural work. Both these practices limit the overall demand for casual labor.

The vast majority (84 percent) of farm women contribute to the family's earnings. Women devise means of earning income that mesh with their domestic tasks: they cultivate garden plots, raise small livestock, and/or help tend the family's fields. In addition, many rural women work at diverse cottage industries and vending. They sell everything from lottery tickets to home-made sweets. In the late 1990s, approximately 20 percent of rural households were headed by women.

Because rural areas provide few services, working women have to add physically demanding and time-consuming domestic tasks to their work day. Single women are further handicapped by the traditional exclusion of women from mechanized or skilled agricultural work. Women work during the labor-intensive phases of harvesting and in processing crops like cotton, coffee, tobacco, and tomatoes. They usually earn piece rate rather than a daily wage, and their earnings lag behind those of male agricultural laborers.

Sugar Plantations

Most sugar mills and cane fields are concentrated in the southeast coastal plains. Four large groups, one government and three privately owned, own 75 percent of the land. They are the State Sugar Council (Consejo Estatal del Azúcar—CEA), the Central Romana (formerly owned by Gulf and Western), Casa Vicini (a family operation), and the Florida-based Fanjul group (which bought out Gulf and Western in 1985). The government created the CEA in 1966, largely from lands and facilities formerly held by the Trujillo family.

In the mid-1980s, there were roughly 4,500 *colonos* (see Glossary), who owned some 62,500 hectares. By the late 1980s, the number had increased to 8,000 *colonos* owning 85,000 hectares, which was 12 percent of the land in sugar production. These small to mid-sized landholders are independent growers who sell their harvested cane to the sugar mills. Although the *colonos'* level of prosperity varies significantly, some are prosperous enough to hire laborers to cut their cane and to buy cane from smaller producers. Their actual number fluctuates widely in response to the market for cane. There were only 3,200 in 1970; the number more than doubled by 1980, then declined by mid-decade but increased in the late 1980s. A slow decline in the number of *colonos* has occurred in the 1990s.

Some *colonos* are descendants of former small mill owners driven out of business during the expansion of sugar production in the late nineteenth to early twentieth centuries. The parents or grandparents of others were either subsistence farmers who had switched to cane cultivation in response to rising demand for sugar or successful field workers. Like almost all Dominican farmers, *colonos* face land fragmentation that increases progressively with each generation.

Sugar mills remain a major source of work for rural Dominicans, although direct employment peaked at a high of roughly 100,000 workers in the early 1970s. By the mid-1980s, the mills employed approximately 65,000 workers; by 1990 the number was around 55,000. The number has been declining since, however, primarily because of the sharp drop in the United States sugar quota and growing inefficiency in the state sugar sector as well as the government's increasing reliance on the industrial free zones and the tourist industry. The sugar industry has generated considerable indirect employment as well; some observers have estimated that as much as 30 percent of the population is directly or indirectly affected by sugar production (see Cash Crops, ch. 3). In the 1990s this figure decreased to about 20 percent. The 40,000 to 50,000 cane cutters constitute the bulk of the work force. Most are immigrant Haitians or their descendants (see Haitians, this ch.). In the highly stratified work force in the sugar industry, clear divisions exist among cane cutters, more skilled workers (largely Dominicans), clerical staff, and managers. Workers' settlements (*bateyes*) dot the mill and the surrounding fields; they usually include stores, schools, and a number of other facilities.

Mixed Farming

Landholding is less concentrated in the north and west; mixed crop and livestock raising dominate agricultural production. Much production is geared to subsistence, but growers also produce a number of cash crops such as cocoa, tobacco, coffee, and vegetables. The twin constraints of land and money affect the various strata of rural society differently depending on the precise configuration of resources a family can command. But hardship is widespread.

Those without land are the most hard pressed. Agricultural laborers rarely enjoy opportunities for permanent employment. Most work only sporadically throughout the year. During periods of high demand for labor, contractors form semiper-

Farmer preparing jute he has grown
Courtesy Inter-American Development Bank

manent work groups and contract their services out to farmers. As with much of social life, the individual stands a better chance if he can couch his request for work in terms of a personal link of kinship with the prospective employer.

Families that depend on wage labor have very limited resources at their disposal. Their diet lacks greens and protein; eggs and meat are luxury items. Such fare as boiled plantains, noodles, and broth often substitute for the staple beans and rice. Keeping children in school is difficult because their labor is needed to supplement the family's earnings.

Those with small plots of land also face very severe constraints. Although this group has enough land to meet some of the family's subsistence needs and even sell crops occasionally, they also need to resort to wage labor to make ends meet. Like the wage laborer, the smallholder has trouble leaving children in school. Moreover, children's prospects are extremely limited. Their parents can neither give them land nor educate them. The daily need for food also limits farmers' ability to work their own land. The land- and cash-poor face a double dilemma: they cannot work their lands effectively because to do so would mean foregoing wage labor needed to feed their families. A variety of sharecropping arrangements supplement

87

wage labor for those smallholders able to muster some cash or credit. Such arrangements, however, are of no use to the landless; only those who have land or money to finance a crop enter into these schemes. Smallholders and the landless live enmeshed in a web of dependent relationships: they depend on their neighbors and kin for help and assistance, on store owners for credit, and on larger landholders for employment.

Families with mid-sized holdings face slightly different problems. They often have enough land and financial resources to meet most of their families' food needs and earn cash from the sale of crops or livestock. They usually do not need to work for hire and sometimes can hire laborers themselves. They usually eat better than smallholders, and their children stay in school longer. But although mid-sized landholders earn more, they also have greater needs for cash during the year, particularly if they hire laborers before the harvest.

Even relatively large holders face seasonal shortages of cash. Their production costs—especially for hired labor—are typically higher than the costs faced by smaller landowners. Nevertheless, their standard of living is notably higher than that of those with less land. They generally eat better and can afford meat or fish more frequently. Although their holdings support them adequately, subdivision among the family's offspring typically leaves no heir with more than a hectare or two. Faced with this prospect, these farmers often encourage their children to pursue nonagricultural careers and help support them financially during their student years.

Almost all farmers depend to varying degrees on credit from local storekeepers. The landless and land poor need credit simply to feed their families. Mid-sized landholders use it to tide them over the lean months before harvest. Prevailing interest rates vary considerably, but the poorest farmers—those who cannot offer a harvest as collateral and who usually need short-term credit—generally pay the highest rates.

Farmers often depend on storekeepers to market their crops because they are usually unable to accumulate sufficient produce to make direct marketing a viable option. Most farmers commit their crops to their merchant-creditor long before harvest. Although store owners cannot legally require that someone who owes them money sell his or her crops to them, the possibility of being denied necessary credit at a time of future need acts as a powerful incentive for the farm family to do so.

Fishing cooperative, San Pedro de Macoris
Courtesy Inter-American Development Bank

The cycle of debt, repayment, and renewed debt is constant for most Dominican farmers.

Traditionally, the local storekeeper aids farmers in ways beyond the extension of credit. The storekeeper often establishes a paternalistic relationship with customers; farmers consult the storekeeper on matters ranging from land purchases to conflicts with neighbors. Such patronage carries a heavy price tag, however; farmers find it difficult to haggle about terms with a storekeeper who is also a friend or relative. Anthropologist Patricia Pessar recently pointed out, however, that this type of personal relationship has changed because of the shift from sharecropping to cattle raising. Because cattle raising requires far fewer workers per hectare, many of the sharecroppers became unemployed and left in search of jobs. Cattle raising is also much less seasonal than farming. These factors have greatly reduced dependence upon the storekeeper. For those needing it, however, credit, is expensive. Studies of coffee growers in the mid-1970s found that the cost of credit could easily take one-third to one-half of a mid-sized landholder's profits. This economic situation continued in the 1990s.

Consumer and savings and loan cooperatives sometimes offer the farmer an alternative to dealing with the local storekeeper, thus expanding the options of some rural families. The most successful cooperatives draw their membership from groups of kin and neighbors already linked by ties of trust. Although cooperatives may provide a solution for farmers vexed by the problem of cash shortfalls, they have not ameliorated appreciably the plight of the poorest rural dwellers. Cooperative loans are predicated on a family's ability to pay, which effectively excludes the landless and land poor.

Family and Kin

The family is the fundamental social unit. It provides a bulwark in the midst of political upheavals and economic reversals. People emphasize the trust, assistance, and solidarity kin owe one another. Family loyalty is an ingrained and unquestioned virtue; from early childhood, individuals learn that relatives are to be trusted and relied on, while those outside the family are, implicitly at least, suspect. In all areas of life and at every level of society, a person looks to family and kin for both social identity and succor.

Formal organizations succeed best where they are able to mesh with pre-existing ties of kinship. Distrust of those beyond the extended kin or neighborhood group hampers efforts to run community-wide activities or to establish organizations.

The history and pattern of settlement of the countryside have facilitated strong ties among related families. Many valleys and municipalities were settled by a few related families some five to eight generations ago. This core of extensively related families remains pivotal despite large-scale migration and urbanization. If anything, the ties among kin extend more widely in contemporary society because modern transport and communication allow families to maintain ties over long distances and during lengthy absences.

In general, the extent to which families interact and with whom they interact depends on their degree of prosperity. Families with relatively equal resources share and cooperate. Where there is marked disparity in families' wealth, the more prosperous branches try to limit the demands made by the poorer ones. On the one hand, generosity is held in high esteem and failure to care for kin in need is disparaged; but on the other, families wish to help their immediate relatives and give favors to those who can reciprocate.

A needy relation may receive the loan of a piece of land, some wage labor, or occasional gifts of food. Another type of assistance is a form of adoption by which poorer families give a child to more affluent relatives to raise. The adopting family is expected to care for the child and see that he or she receives a proper upbringing. The children are frequently little better than unpaid domestic help. Implicit in the arrangement is the understanding that the child's biological family also will receive assistance from the adopting family.

Kinship serves as a metaphor for relations of trust in general. Where a kin tie is lacking or where individuals wish to reinforce one, they will often establish a relationship of *compadrazgo* (coparenthood). Those so linked are *compadres* (coparents or godparents). In common with much of Latin America, strong emotional bonds link *compadres*. *Compadres* use the formal *usted* instead of *tú* in addressing one another, even if they are kinsmen. Sexual relations between *compadres* are regarded as incestuous. *Compadres* are commonly chosen at baptism and marriage, but the relationship extends to the two sets of parents. The tie between the two sets of parents should be strong and enduring. Any breach of trust merits the strongest community censure.

There are two accepted forms of marriage: religious and civil. Both serial monogamy and polygamous free unions are socially accepted, however. Annulment is difficult to obtain through the Roman Catholic Church; this fact, in addition to the expense involved, has made couples reluctant to undertake a religious marriage. Civil marriage is relatively common. Divorce in this case is relatively easy and uncomplicated. Marriage forms also reflect the individual's life cycle. Most opt for free unions when they are younger, then settle into more formal marriages as they grow older and enjoy more economic security. Class also plays a role: religious marriage is favored by the middle and upper class and thus indicates higher socioeconomic status. The ideal marriage involves a formal engagement and religious wedding followed by an elaborate fiesta.

No shame accrues to the man who fathers many children and maintains several women as mistresses. Public disapproval follows only if the man fails to assume the role of "head of the family" and to support his children. When a free union dissolves, a woman typically receives only the house she and her mate have inhabited. The children receive support only if they have been legally recognized by their father.

Families are usually more stable in the countryside. Because the partners usually reside in the midst of their kin, a man cannot desert his wife without disrupting his work relations with her family. A woman enjoys greater leverage when she can rely on her family to assist if a union fails or when she owns her own land and thus has a measure of financial independence.

In keeping with the doctrine of machismo, males usually play a dominant role within the family and receive the deference due the head of the household. There is wide variation in practice, however. In cases where a man is absent, has limited economic assets, or is simply unassertive, a woman assumes the role of head of the family.

Sex role differentiation begins early: boys are allowed to run about naked, while girls are much more carefully groomed and dressed. Bands of boys play unwatched; girls are carefully chaperoned. Girls are expected to be quiet and helpful; boys enjoy much greater freedom and are given considerable latitude in their behavior. Boys and men are expected to have premarital and extramarital sexual adventures. Men expect, however, that their brides will be virgins. Parents go to considerable lengths to shelter their daughters in order to protect their chances of making a favorable marriage.

Parent-child relationships differ markedly depending on the sex of the parent. Mothers openly display affection for their children; the mother-child tie is almost inviolate. Informal polls of money changers and studies have indicated that remittances sent from the United States for Mothers' Day exceed those sent at Christmas. Father-child relationships cover a broader spectrum. The father is an authority figure to be obeyed and respected, and he is more removed from daily family affairs than mothers. This pattern of sex roles is usually altered if one parent emigrates to the United States. When women are left at home, they typically take over many of the affairs customarily reserved for men. When women emigrate, they often become the main breadwinner and manager of the budget because they are often more employable than their husbands. Their success undermines the traditional father-husband role.

Religion

Around 80 percent of Dominicans are professed Roman Catholics. In the late 1990s, the Church organization included two archdioceses, nine dioceses, and 320 parishes. During this same period, there were 644 priests and 1,470 nuns in the Roman Catholic Church, more than 70 percent of whom belonged to religious orders. These figures yield a ratio of nominal Roman Catholics to priests of almost 11,000 to one. Among Latin American countries, only Cuba, Honduras, and El Salvador have higher ratios.

Roman Catholicism is the official religion of the Dominican Republic, established by a concordat with the Vatican. For most of the populace, however, religious practice is limited and formalistic. Few actually attend mass regularly. Moreover, popular beliefs and practices are often at odds with orthodox dogma. Nevertheless, the saints play an important role in traditional popular religious practice; people approach God through the intermediation of priests, local *curanderos* (curers), and the saints.

Foreigners, mainly from Spain, predominate among the clergy. The clergy themselves are divided between the traditional, conservative hierarchy and more liberal parish priests. At the parish level, some priests engage in community development projects and efforts to form *comunidades de base* (grassroots Christian communities) designed to help people organize and work together more effectively.

Trujillo sought and gained the support of the Roman Catholic Church, at least of the conservative hierarchy, during most of his regime. In exchange for this support, indicated by Church officials' regular presence and involvement in all official state ceremonies, he provided generous subsidies and gave the Church a free hand in religious and educational matters. This close relationship changed, however, when a pastoral letter protested the mass arrests of government opponents in 1960. This action so incensed Trujillo that he ordered a campaign of harassment against the Church. Only the dictator's assassination prevented his planned imprisonment of the country's bishops.

The Church has gradually become more socially involved. During the 1965 civil war, for example, the papal nuncio attempted to administer humanitarian aid. The bishops also issued various statements throughout the 1970s and 1980s calling for respect for human rights and an improved standard of living for the majority. In the 1970s, Bishop Juan Antonio Flores of La Vega campaigned for indemnification for peasants displaced by the expansion of the Pueblo Viejo mine. Later, Bishops Juan F. Pepen and Hugo Polanco Brito, who had helped found and served as the first rector of the Pontifical Catholic University Mother and Teacher in the 1960s, supported the efforts of peasants and sugar *colonos* to organize. Their actions reflected the Church's becoming involved in human rights issues in the 1980s, especially issues involving the poor and the treatment of Haitians. Some of the Church hierarchy also supported attempts to end corruption in government, and the Church endorsed the move for free elections in the 1990s.

In addition to Roman Catholics, the Dominican Republic has Protestants and practitioners of voodoo. Protestants first came as immigrants from North America in the 1820s. West Indian laborers added to their numbers in the late nineteenth and early twentieth centuries. By the 1920s, the various Protestant groups had organized nationally and established links with North American evangelical groups. The main evangelical groups include the Seventh Day Adventists, the Dominican Evangelical Church, and the Assemblies of God. Protestant groups expanded, mainly in the rural areas, during the 1960s and 1970s; pentecostals made considerable inroads in some regions. The growth of the pentecostal movement during the 1980s was such that it became a major topic at the Fourth General Conference of Latin American Bishops attended by Pope John Paul II, held in October 1992, following the V Centenario (500th anniversary) celebration in Santo Domingo of Columbus's first trip to the Americas. In the late 1990s, the evangelicals constitute 15 percent of the Protestant groups. With minor exceptions, relations between Protestants and the majority Roman Catholics are cordial.

Most Haitian immigrants and their descendants adhere to voodoo but have practiced it quietly because the government and the general population regard the folk religion as pagan and African. In Haiti voodoo encompasses a well-defined system of theology and ceremonialism (see Voodoo, ch. 7).

Culture

Literature

The Dominican Republic's literary history has had an impact on the country's culture. Balaguer considered Father Bartolomé de las Casas (1474–1566), protector of the Indians and author of *The Devastation of the Indies,* to have been the first Dominican historian. As such he made the first contribution to Dominican literature. However, most accounts would place the first Dominican literary work much later with the publication in 1882, almost forty years after independence, of a famous Dominican novel. The novel, *Enriquillo: Leyenda histórica dominicana* by Manuel de Jesús Galván, concerns a Taino *cacique* (chieftain), Enriquillo, who led a successful rebellion against the Spanish. (Today one can see the monument to this "First Hero of America" located in the center of the main crossroad leading to Lago Enriquillo.) *Enriquillo* stresses the oldest and first of the three racial-social themes of Dominican literature— that of nativism or Indianism (*indigenismo*); it exaggerates the Taino contributions to Dominican culture and ignores those that are African. The second theme is *hispanidad*, the Roman Catholic and "white" cultural legacy of mother country Spain; from this perspective, non-Catholic and "black" Haitians are viewed as inferior to Dominicans. The third theme is the *cultura criolla*, or mixed common culture, between Spanish and Africans.

The first theme long remained in literature and served as a means of ignoring the African roots of Dominicans. A strain of it continues today in the reluctance of many Dominican mulattoes to admit their African heritage; instead, they claim Indian heritage. The second theme, *hispanidad*, was maintained by the intellectual elite both before and during the rule of Trujillo, who made it governmental policy, and was continued by Balaguer until the 1990s. Advocates of *hispanidad* maintained that the Dominican heritage was entirely Spanish and suppressed writing by non-white Dominicans and literature that dealt favorably with non-white characters, especially Haitians. Balaguer's book, *Historia de la literatura dominicana*, includes a selection of writers who stressed the Spanish heritage. Trujillo's regime made Haitians and Haiti the antithesis of *hispanidad*— namely, African and uncivilized. Balaguer presented these views in a 1947 book, which appeared in English in 1949 as *Dominican Reality: Biographical Sketch of a Country and a Regime.* (The 1983 Spanish edition had Haiti in the subtitle.) During the Trujillo era, Juan Bosch Gaviño, a political opponent, novelist, and later president, and Pedro Mir, who became the National Poet, went into exile. Bosch became the leading Dominican short story writer and wrote favorably about blacks.

The third theme came to the fore after Trujillo's 1961 assassination and lasted until Balaguer was elected president in 1966. Before Bosch was overthrown as president in 1963, he welcomed public recognition of Dominicans' African roots and gave governmental support to creole culture. The 1965 civil war and United States intervention produced an upsurge in nationalism and pride that spawned two literary movements made up of young writers. Not only did these writers reject *hispanidad* in favor of *la cultura criolla,* but their concern about Dominican culture and identity caused them to oppose United States cultural influences, which they called "northamericanization."

Historical Monuments and Architecture

Once Balaguer was inaugurated in 1966, he reimposed the official policy of *hispanidad.* His stress on *hispanidad* took the form of a program to restore historical monuments such as those of colonial Santo Domingo and build new monuments to glorify the Spanish legacy. This program culminated in the inauguration of the Columbus Lighthouse (Faro Colón) in time for the celebration in Santo Domingo of the 500th anniversary (V Centenario) of the discovery of America in October 1992. This restoration and building program—it was also a public works program to reduce unemployment—began in the 1970s and was continued when Balaguer returned to office in 1986. The restoration of colonial Santo Domingo and the construction of the Plaza de la Cultura were completed in the 1970s.

While Balaguer was out of office, the two opposition party governments of Silvestre Antonio Guzmán Fernández (1978–82) and Salvador Jorge Blanco (1982–86) supported the acceptance of creole culture. When Balaguer returned to office in 1986, his government accepted officially the *cultura criolla,* which would now co-exist with *hispanidad.* The government initiated a new annual Festival of Culture, which combined state-supported festivals of popular culture—creole folk dances and music, and revival of the Carnival—with "high culture" *hispanidad.* Balaguer also speeded up the completion of the Columbus Lighthouse for the October 1992 anniversary celebration.

Popular Culture: Dance, Music, and Baseball

In addition to the more formal cultural elements of literature and monuments, the Dominican people enjoy various aspects of popular culture, such as dance, music, and baseball. The merengue, the most popular Dominican national dance, dates from independence and is based on African-Haitian sources; its roots had made it unacceptable to the Spanish elite. It was popularized in the post-Trujillo period by Johnny Ventura. The leading musical group in the Dominican Republic in the late 1990s, the 4.40 of Juan Luis Guerra, draws upon the African roots of Dominican culture and music.

In his 1997 book, *Quisqueya la Bella: The Dominican Republic in Historical and Cultural Perspective*, Alan Cambeira includes baseball, in addition to dance and music, as an integral part of the popular culture. The Dominicans, who are extremely proud of their skilled baseball players, learned the game from the marines during the United States occupation (1916–24). The United States major leagues began recruiting Dominican players in the 1950s. In the 1990s, more players are recruited from the Dominican Republic than from any other Latin American country. One of them, Sammy Sosa of the Chicago Cubs, became a national hero during his fall 1998 homerun battle with Mark McGwire of the St. Louis Cardinals. For a poor Dominican young man, baseball serves the same function that basketball serves for poor African-American youth—it is a possible path to fame and fortune.

It could be argued that a special creole culture has emerged from the "dual societies," operating in the Dominican Republic in the 1990s (see Modern Migration, this ch.). The common practice of Dominicans living and working in the United States, moving back and forth, and then often returning to the Dominican Republic to live has resulted in the development of a transnational creole culture that is an amalgam of Anglo-Saxon, Spanish, and African practices and values. The current Dominican president, Leonel Fernández Reyna (1996–2000), represents and personifies this creole culture. He lived for ten years as a member of the Dominican immigrant community in New York City, attended elementary and secondary school there, is fluent in English, and, as a mulatto, is proud of his African heritage.

Education

Primary and Secondary

Formal education includes primary, secondary, and higher education levels. The six-year primary cycle is compulsory. Three years of preschool are offered in a few areas, but not on a compulsory basis. There are several types of secondary school; most students (90 percent) attend the six-year *liceo*, which awards the *bachillerato* certificate upon completion and is geared toward university admission. Other secondary programs include teacher training schools, polytechnics, and vocational schools. All primary and secondary schools are under the formal jurisdiction of the Secretariat of State for Education and Culture (Secretaría de Estado de Educación y Cultura—SEEC). In 1984 there were an estimated 5,684 primary schools and 1,664 secondary schools; by 1993 the former had increased to 6,207 and the latter had risen to 4,606.

Despite the compulsory nature of primary education, only 17 percent of rural schools offer all six grades. This fact explains to some degree the low levels of secondary enrollment. For those who do go on to the secondary level, academic standards are low, the drop-out rate reportedly high; all but the poorest students must buy their textbooks—another disincentive to enrollment for many.

The government decreed major curriculum reforms at the primary and secondary levels in the 1970s in an effort to render schooling more relevant to students' lives and needs. Expanded vocational training in rural schools was called for as part of the reforms. Few changes had been fully implemented even by the mid-1990s, however. The realization that these reforms had been limited led in 1997 to the announcement of a ten-year Plan for Educational Reform, which was approved by and under the auspices of the Presidential Commission for State Reform and Modernization.

Primary-school teachers are trained in six specialized secondary schools and secondary-school teachers at the universities. In 1973 an agreement for improving teacher training was signed by three universities—the Autonomous University of Santo Domingo (Universidad Autónoma de Santo Domingo—UASD), the Pedro Henríquez Ureña National University (Universidad Nacional Pedro Henríquez Ureña—UNPHU), and the Pontifical Catholic University Mother and Teacher (Pontificia Universidad Católica Madre y Maestra—UCMM)—and the SEEC. However, although in 1982 roughly half of all teachers lacked the required academic background, there has been only modest improvement since then. A chronic shortage of teachers is attributable to low pay (especially in rural areas), the relatively low status of teaching as a career, and an apparent reluctance among men to enter the profession.

Education expanded at every level in the post-Trujillo era. Enrollment as a proportion of the primary school-aged population grew by more than 20 percent between the mid-1960s and the mid-1980s and that of the secondary school-aged population nearly quadrupled. By the mid-1980s, the eligible urban primary school population was almost fully enrolled; 78 percent attended public schools. Only 45 percent of those of secondary school age were enrolled, however. According to the Dominican census of 1993, 1,602,219 students were attending primary school and 379,096 attending secondary school; 87,636 were attending preschool (see table 3, Appendix). These attendance figures for primary and secondary school amounted to 78 percent of those eligible—81 percent in the former, a lower percentage than in the 1980s, and 24 percent in the latter.

Problems have accompanied educational expansion. Teaching materials and well-maintained facilities are lacking at every level. Salaries and operational expenses take up most of the education budget, leaving little surplus for additional investment and growth. Various recent estimates about the extent of literacy appear to be unduly high. For example, the 1993 Dominican census reported a national rate of 79 percent (85 percent urban and 72 percent rural). However, expanded educational programs and facilities continue to have a backlog of illiterates. Although there are programs in adult literacy, in 1981 fully one-third of the population more than twenty-five years of age had never attended school; in some rural areas the proportion rose to half of the population.

University

Dominican higher education has enjoyed spectacular growth. At Trujillo's death in 1961, the Dominican Republic had only one university, the Autonomous University of Santo Domingo (UASD), with roughly 3,500 students. This fact explains why for decades thousands of Dominicans went abroad to earn their graduate and professional degrees in Europe and the United States. The practice of going abroad for graduate work continued through the 1980s, but decreased in the 1990s. Since the end of the 1965 civil war, the number of universities in the Dominican Republic has increased dramatically, going from three universities in the 1960s, to seven in the 1970s, to eighteen in the 1980s, and to twenty-seven by 1997. By the late 1990s, a network of reputable universities had been established, with the private Pontifical Catholic University Mother and Teacher (UCMM) at its apex. Higher education enrollment totaled 176,000 students in 1997.

In the 1970s and 1980s, the United States Agency for International Development (USAID) and the Ford Foundation contributed to improving the quality of university education by providing funds and grants for developing programs as well as for faculty study in the United States. Legislation also created the National Council of Higher Education (Consejo Nacional de Educación Superior—Cones) in 1983 to deal with issues surrounding accreditation, the awarding of degrees, and coordination of programs on a national level.

The sole public institution of higher education in the Dominican Republic is the UASD, which traces its lineage directly to the Universitas Santi Dominici, established in 1538, and was formerly known as the Universidad de Santo Domingo. Although the university's administration is autonomous, the government provides all of its funding. This enables the UASD to offer courses free of charge to all enrolled students. The student body grew to more than 100,000 in the late 1980s. However, its Santo Domingo enrollments began to decline in the early 1990s. During this period, the UASD's four regional university centers—El Norte, El Sur, El Este, and El Oeste—and other universities, six new ones and two older ones, the Pedro Henríquez Ureña National University (UNPHU) and UCMM, expanded and offered needed courses of instruction.

The leading private institutions in the Dominican Republic are the UCMM, based on the United States model, established in Santiago in 1962 (it had three regional centers in the 1990s) and administered by the Roman Catholic Church, and the UNPHU, established in Santo Domingo in 1967. Four other private universities were established in the 1970s, eleven in the 1980s, and six in the 1990s. In the early 1980s, the UCMM had a student body of approximately 5,000, while the UNPHU enrolled approximately 10,000. By 1997 UCCM enrollment had reached 9,438 as a result of many student scholarships and its moderate tuition, whereas UNPHU enrollment had declined to 6,044 because of a combination of factors: high tuition, few scholarships, and a politically conservative reputation.

Enrollment in elementary and secondary private schools also expanded during the post-Trujillo era. Private schools, most of them operated by the Roman Catholic Church, enjoy a reputation for academic superiority over public schools. By the 1970s, they had become the preferred educational option for children of the urban middle class, the alternative being study

Student in a computer class
Courtesy Inter-American Development Bank

abroad. In the mid-1990s, the Church operated sixty-seven kindergartens (with 10,189 pupils), 203 primary schools (85,011 students), and 112 secondary schools (64,804 students). The number of students attending Church-operated higher institutes and universities totaled slightly more than 16,000.

The Dominican government's expenditures for public education in general and at different levels have tended to be low and inconsistent. Not only were expenditures low in the 1960s and 1970s, but Balaguer drastically reduced government funds to the UASD because many of its students and faculty members actively opposed his government. At the same time, he was generous with funds to the private UCMM. In the 1980s, the proportion of the government's budget devoted to education declined; it fell from 13.3 percent in 1983 to 6.7 percent in 1988. The budgetary proportion for education was increased in the 1990s—from 8.9 percent in 1992 to 13 percent in 1995.

Health and Social Security

Health

According to the Public Health Code, the Secretariat of

State for Health and Social Welfare (Secretaría de Estado de Salud Pública y Asistencia Social—SESPAS) is in charge of health services and is responsible for applying the Code. SESPAS has a regionally based, three-tiered organization for providing health care, health promotion, and preventive health services to the whole population. The three tiers are central, regional, and provincial, with the Secretariat's programs organized at and directed from the central and regional levels. There are eight regional offices that direct the services and oversee the health areas at the provincial level. The health areas have rural clinics while most provincial capitals have a hospital. Health services offered by SESPAS in theory cover about 80 percent of the population; in reality, in the late 1990s barely 40 percent were covered. The Dominican Social Security Institute (Instituto Dominicano de Seguro Social—IDSS) covers another 6.5 percent (or 15 percent of the economically active population), and the medical facilities of the Social Security Institute of the Armed Forces and National Police reach another 3 to 4 percent. The responsibility for workers' health, particularly workplace accidents and occupational diseases, is also shared with the secretariats for labor, education, agriculture, and public works. In the late 1990s, however, 22 percent of the population received no health care.

Both personnel and facilities, in the public as well as in the private sector, are concentrated in the National District and urban areas. This situation has continued since the 1970s when there were roughly 3,700 inhabitants per physician nationally. However, the figure ranged from about 1,650 inhabitants per physician in the National District to roughly 5,000 per physician in the southeast and the south-central provinces. By 1997 the number of health personnel included 17,460 physicians and 1,898 dentists; there are no details on the geographic distribution of these personnel (see table 4, Appendix). However, it was also the case that in 1997 more than half of the national total of 15,236 hospital beds were in the National District and the central Cibao.

SESPAS began a major effort to improve rural health care in the mid-1970s. By the mid-1980s, the government had set up more than 5,000 rural health clinics, health subcenters, and satellite clinics. Doctors doing their required year of social service as well as a variety of locally hired and trained auxiliary personnel staff the facilities. Critics charge that lack of coordination and inadequate management hamper the program's effectiveness, however. Preventive services offered through local health workers (who are often poorly trained in disease prevention and basic sanitation) are not coordinated with curative services. In addition, absenteeism is high, and supplies are lacking.

SESPAS responded to these criticisms and problems in 1997 when it announced as its highest priority the reversal of the long-standing shortfall in health and social spending. SESPAS declared that its primary goal would be the reduction of infant and maternal mortality, mainly by strengthening health services at the provincial level.

In 1990 SESPAS employed 3,598 physicians and 6,868 nurses; by 1994 those numbers had increased to 5,626 and 8,600, respectively. Reflecting a 47 percent increase since 1986, the Secretariat in 1992 operated 723 health care establishments—81 percent were rural clinics and dispensaries and 11 percent were health centers and local hospitals. In 1992 IDSS operated one maternity hospital, twenty polyclinics, and 161 outpatient clinics, mostly rural. The private sector operated 420 health care establishments in 1990. By 1996 the number of health care facilities in the country had risen to 1,334, with 730 of them coming under SESPAS, 184 under IDSS, and 417 under the private sector. In 1997 the government opened the Health Plaza in Santo Domingo, a modern, high-tech health complex. It has 430 beds, a diagnostic center, and hospitals for child and maternal care, geriatrics, and trauma treatment. The proper place of the health complex in the national health system is being debated.

The Roman Catholic Church plays an important role in the health and welfare field. In 1993 (the latest year for which figures are available) it operated twenty-nine hospitals, 155 dispensaries, twenty-three orphanages, twenty-five homes for the aged, twenty-one nurseries, and scores of other welfare facilities.

In terms of overall national health statistics, life expectancy at birth was seventy-one years for the 1990–95 period, sixty-nine years for males and seventy-three for females. The general mortality rate has gradually declined, falling to 5.5 percent per 1,000 population for the 1990–95 period. It is expected to decline to 5.2 percent per 1,000 population for 1995–2000. The infant mortality rate has steadily declined since 1985. The rate for the 1990–95 period was forty-two per 1,000 live births. The main causes of death in the population as a whole continue to be cardiovascular and pulmonary circulatory diseases (see tab'? 5, Appendix). The Pan American Health Organization (PAHO) reported a new leading cause of death for 1994, namely, such external causes as accidental injuries and violence, particularly among males. Enteritis, diarrheal diseases, and protein energy malnutrition are the major causes of death in those under the age of four. Maternal mortality stood at 4.8 deaths per 10,000 live births in 1986 and 4.5 in 1990. A PAHO study reported, however, that the registered rate of 4.5 in 1990 and slightly over three in 1994 was greatly "underregistered." As a result, the real maternal mortality rate might have been as high as twenty per 10,000 live births over the 1983–94 period. The main causes are toxemia (25 to 30 percent), hemorrhages, and sepsis associated with birth or abortion. Roughly 60 percent of births, mainly those in urban areas, are attended by medical personnel; midwives are still relied upon in many rural regions.

The UNAIDS/WHO Working Group on acquired immune deficiency syndrome (AIDS) estimated that in late 1999, the Dominican Republic had some 130,000 persons living with human immunodeficiency virus (HIV)/AIDS. Of these, about 67,200 were adult males (ages fifteen through forty-nine), 62,800 adult females (same ages), and 3,800 children (through age fourteen). The total estimated deaths of adults and children from AIDS in 1999 was 4,900.

Some of the above figures and health institutions are the result of a major project launched in 1993 to modernize and reform the health sector. The project came in response to the critical report of President Balaguer's 1991 National Health Commission. A number of commissions and organizations have been created to implement the project. In 1995 a new National Health Commission was created by presidential decree to draft reform and modernization proposals. The Commission on Health of the Chamber of Deputies drafted a general law on health; the Senate opposed it, and it was not passed. Also in 1995, a National Food and Nutrition Plan was approved; its implementation was delegated to the Secretariat of Agriculture. Two other high level commissions were appointed: the Presidential Commission for State Reform and Modernization in 1996 and the Executive Commission on Health Reform, which is directly under the presidency, in 1997.

Social Security

The Dominican Social Security Institute (IDSS), an autonomous organization, is responsible for social security coverage, which includes old-age pensions, disability pensions, survivors' and maternity benefits, and compensation for work injuries. General tax revenues supplement employer and employee contributions. Wage earners, government employees (under special provisions), and domestic and agricultural workers are eligible, although the benefits that most domestic and farm workers receive are quite limited. Permanent workers whose salaries exceed 122 Dominican Republic pesos (RD$—for value of the peso, see Glossary) per week and the self-employed are excluded. No unemployment benefits are provided. In 1994, 6.5 percent of the general population and 15.4 percent of the economically active population, or approximately 22 percent of wage earners, were enrolled. Most of those enrolled were in manufacturing, commerce, and construction. The social welfare of workers in the hotel and restaurant sector is provided by the Hotel Social Fund, a nonprofit public organization. Pensions and social services, including medical care, are covered by funds contributed by the government, employers, and workers. The Aid and Housing Institute also provides social services such as housing construction, medical care, and pensions to civil servants and military personnel below a certain salary level. Affiliation is compulsory for these two groups.

Although the level of government services exceeds that of the republic's impoverished neighbor, Haiti, limited resources, inefficiency, and a lagging economy until the late 1990s, have limited the overall impact of these programs. In 1985, 8.8 percent of the national budget supported health services, and an additional 6.9 percent funded social security and welfare programs. As a proportion of overall spending, the percentage rose to 9.5 in 1990, but declined to 7.8 percent for 1991–92 and remained at that level through 1995. More specifically, total spending by SESPAS declined as follows: from 86 percent to 65 percent between the periods 1979–82 to 1987–90, and to 55.5 percent in 1991. However, the Office of the President, in order partly to compensate for the decline, increased its share in health spending from 1.8 percent to 18 percent and then to 38.4 percent, respectively, during the same years. In 1991 total direct spending per doctor visit, bed, and hospital discharge was 60 to 70 percent lower than in 1980. In 1995 the combined national and local governments' public health expenditure was

28.6 percent of their combined budgets, which amounted to US$29 per capita. The public-private composition of national health expenditures in the Dominican Republic in 1995 was 38 percent and 62 percent, respectively.

Despite the various long-overdue and promising developments, there is little prospect for major improvement in the quality of life for most Dominicans for many years to come. Nonetheless, President Fernández has committed his administration to the improvement of social welfare—education, health, and social security. But whether improvements are implemented depends upon the economic situation and leadership by top government officials.

*   *   *

A wealth of information exists on rural life and the changing rural-urban context in the Dominican Republic. Jan Knippers Black's *The Dominican Republic: Politics and Development in an Unsovereign State,* James Ferguson's *Dominican Republic: Beyond the Lighthouse,* Glenn Hendricks's *The Dominican Diaspora,* Patricia R. Pessar's works, Kenneth Sharpe's *Peasant Politics,* and Howard J. Wiarda and Michael J. Kryzanek's *The Dominican Republic: A Caribbean Crucible,* all give a sense of the constraints with which most Dominicans must deal. Jan Black's book, H. Hoetink's *The Dominican People, 1859–1900,* and Frank Moya Pons's *The Dominican Republic: A National History* provide valuable background reading.

G. Pope Atkins and Larman C. Wilson's *The Dominican Republic and the United States: From Imperialism to Transnationalism,* Alan Cambeira's *Quisqueya la Bella: The Dominican Republic in Historical and Cultural Perspective,* and Hoetink's book cover the society and race and culture. Americas Watch reports, Ferguson's book, and Sherri Grasmuck's "Migration Within the Periphery: Haitian Labor in the Dominican Sugar and Coffee Industries" detail the situation of Haitians in the Republic. Emigration and immigration are discussed in José del Castillo and Martin F. Murphy's "Migration, National Identity, and Cultural Policy in the Dominican Republic," Sherri Grasmuck and Patricia R. Pessar's *Between Two Islands: Dominican International Migration,* Silvio Torres-Saillant and Ramona Hernández's *The Dominican Americans: The New Americans,* and Michael J. Kryzanek and Howard J. Wiarda's *The Politics of External Influence in the Dominican Republic.* Belkis Mones and Lydia Grant's "Agricultural Development, the Economic Crisis and Rural Women in the Dominican Republic" and Pessar's chapter, "Dominican Transnational Migration: Uneven Benefits Back Home and the Contingency of Return" in Emelio Betances and Hobart A. Spalding, Jr., editors, *The Dominican Republic Today* explain the ways in which rural women earn a living. Excellent surveys of the health and welfare situation are found in "Dominican Republic" in the Pan American Health Organization's *Health Conditions in the Americas*, 2, and *Health in the Americas*, 2. (For further information and complete citations, see Bibliography.)

Chapter 3. Dominican Republic:
The Economy

The Plaza del Mercado, Puerta Plata, ca. 1873

LONG DEPENDENT ON SUGAR, the Dominican Republic diversified its economy beginning in the late 1960s to include mining, assembly manufacturing, and tourism. In 1996 the country's gross domestic product (GDP—see Glossary) was approximately US$5.8 billion, or roughly US$716 per capita. A lower-middle-income country by World Bank (see Glossary) standards, the Dominican Republic depends on imported oil and, despite diversification, retained some vulnerability to price fluctuations in the world sugar market. Although poverty continued to be acute for many rural citizens in the 1990s, the economy had progressed significantly since the 1960s.

In the diversification process away from sugar, by 1980 the Dominican mining industry had become a major foreign exchange earner; exports of gold, silver, ferronickel, and bauxite constituted 38 percent of the country's total foreign sales. In the 1980s, the assembly manufacturing industry, centered in industrial free zones (see Glossary), began to dominate industrial activity. During this decade, the number of people employed in assembly manufacturing rose from 16,000 to nearly 100,000, and that sector's share of exports jumped from 11 percent to more than 33 percent. More recently, in the first half of 1998, free-zone exports increased 19 percent over the first half of 1997, from US$541 million to US$644 million. Tourism experienced a similarly dramatic expansion during the 1980s, when the number of hotel rooms quadrupled. Revenues from tourism surpassed sugar earnings for the first time in 1984. By 1995 tourism was the country's largest earner of foreign exchange, bringing in more than US$1.55 billion. The industry directly employed 44,000 persons and indirectly another 110,000.

In a 1997 review of the Dominican Republic's economic developments and policies, the International Monetary Fund (IMF—see Glossary) pronounced the country's economic performance in 1996 "broadly satisfactory." Over the longer period of 1990–95, the government was given credit for "strengthening the public finances, tightening credit and wage policies, and implementing structural reforms." Inflation plunged from 80 percent in 1990 to 9 percent in 1995. The external public debt as a share of GDP was more than halved (to 33 percent) during the same period. After dropping by about 6 percent in 1990, GDP rose on average by 4.25 percent a year in the period 1991–95, led by strong growth in the free trade zone manufacturing, construction, and tourism sectors. The unemployment rate declined from approximately 20 percent in 1991–93 to about 16 percent in 1995. Nevertheless, whereas the Dominican Republic had made great strides since the dictatorial rule of Rafael Leónidas Trujillo Molina (1930–61), the nation's political economy continued to be strongly influenced by patronage, graft, and a lingering lack of political will to confront the traditional institutions that continued to restrain economic performance.

A Developing Economy

Originally inhabited by Taino Indians, the island was settled by a Spanish expedition led by Christopher Columbus in 1492. Spanish mercantilists largely abandoned the island by the 1520s in favor of the gold and silver fortunes of Mexico and Peru. The remaining Spanish settlers briefly established an economic structure of Indian labor tied to land under the systems of *repartimiento* (grants of land and Indian labor) and *encomienda* (grants of Indian labor in return for tribute to the crown). The rapid decline of the Indian population ended the *encomienda* system by the mid-1500s, when the Taino Indians were nearing extinction and were being replaced by imported African slaves.

As economic activity became more sluggish in Eastern Hispaniola (the approximate site of the present-day Dominican Republic), Spanish control weakened and French buccaneers increasingly played a role not only in Western Hispaniola but also in the eastern part of the island. The French assumed control of the western third of the island in 1697 under the Treaty of Ryswick, establishing Saint-Domingue (modern-day Haiti) (see French Colony of Saint-Domingue, 1697–1803, ch. 1). Whereas Haiti developed into a productive agricultural center on the basis of black slave labor, in the eastern part of the island, cattle ranching was common. Farming, however, was limited to comparatively small crops of sugar, coffee, and cocoa.

The Spanish side of Hispaniola slowly developed a plantation economy during the nineteenth century, much later than the rest of the West Indies. For much of the century, political unrest disrupted normal economic activity and hindered development. Corrupt and inefficient government, by occupying

Haitian forces and by self-serving caudillos after the Dominican Republic achieved its independence in 1844, served mainly to increase the country's foreign debt (see Ambivalent Sovereignty, Caudillo Rule, and Political Instability, ch. 1). After failing to achieve independence from Spain in the Ten Years' War (1868–78), Cuban planters fled their homeland and settled in Hispaniola's fertile Cibao region, where they grew tobacco and later cocoa.

Plummeting tobacco prices in the late nineteenth century prompted United States companies to invest heavily in a burgeoning sugar industry, which would dominate the Dominican Republic's economy for most of the twentieth century. The influence of the United States was rising so rapidly that in 1904 it had established a receivership over Dominican customs to administer the repayment of the country's commercial debt to foreign holders of Dominican bonds.

Continuing economic difficulties and ongoing internal disorders, combined with the Dominican government's inability to maintain order and United States anxiety over Europe's (especially Germany's) spreading influence in the republic, led to United States occupation in 1916 and the establishment of a military government (see From the United States Occupation (1916–24) to the Emergence of Trujillo (1930), ch. 1). Even after the marines departed in 1924, United States economic advisers remained to manage customs revenues until 1941. Although security interests were the primary reason for the occupation, the United States did benefit commercially. Dominican tobacco, sugar, and cocoa, previously exported to French, German, and British markets, were shipped instead to the United States. The powerful United States sugar companies came to dominate the banking and transportation sectors. They also benefited from the partition of former communal lands, which allowed the companies to augment their holdings. However, although the occupation was resented politically by Dominicans, the Dominican economy also reaped some benefits: the United States presence helped stabilize the country's finances and greatly improved its infrastructure, constructing roads, sanitation systems, ports, and schools.

Another significant outcome of the United States occupation was the creation of a Dominican army, the commander of which, Rafael Trujillo, took power over the nation in 1930 and maintained absolute dictatorial control until his assassination in 1961 (see The Trujillo Era, 1930–61, ch. 1). Trujillo's agreement ending the United States customs receivership allowed him to assume the title of "Restorer of Financial Independence." High prices for Dominican produce during World War II (1941–45) enabled him to liquidate the country's outstanding debt in 1947. At the same time, he introduced a national currency, the Dominican Republic peso (RD$—for value, see Glossary).

Although Trujillo initiated substantial industrialization and public works projects, his interest in promoting economic development was largely for his own and his supporters' benefit. Corruption and blackmail helped him amass an enormous fortune and made him the country's largest landowner. His primary means of self-enrichment was the national sugar industry, which he rapidly expanded in the 1950s, despite a depressed international market. At the time of his death in 1961, Trujillo and his coterie reportedly controlled 60 percent of the total sugar, cement, tobacco, and shipping industries and owned more than 600,000 hectares of improved land. In the process of consolidating his enormous wealth, Trujillo looted the national treasury and built a personal fiefdom similar to those of the Somoza and the Duvalier families in Nicaragua and Haiti, respectively.

The Dominican economy's GDP experienced growth under Trujillo at the rate of about 6.5 percent a year from 1950 to 1958 but dropped to 0.3 percent from 1959 to 1961. However, the unequal distribution of that growth impoverished rural Dominicans. The period between Trujillo's assassination in 1961 and the 1965 civil war was both politically and economically chaotic, prompting simultaneous capital flight and increased demands for spending on social programs. Cash infusions (mostly from the United States) and loans helped to sustain the economy. During the first three presidencies of Joaquín Balaguer Ricardo (1966–78), the country experienced a period of sustained growth characterized by economic diversification and a more equitable distribution of benefits among Dominicans. During its peak growth period, from 1966 to 1976, the economy expanded at an annual rate of nearly 8 percent, one of the highest growth rates in the world at the time. But in 1979 two hurricanes killed more than 1,000 Dominicans and caused an estimated US$1 billion in damage, and by the early 1980s, rising oil prices and a forty-year low in sugar prices had stifled the local economy. The average rate of economic growth dropped to almost 1 percent a year.

The unstable economic situation compelled the administration of Salvador Jorge Blanco (1982–86) to enter into a series of negotiations with the IMF and to begin restructuring government economic policies. In 1983 the government signed a three-year Extended Fund Facility that called for lower fiscal deficits, tighter credit policies, and other austerity measures. This program paved the way for the first in a series of rescheduling agreements with foreign creditors. Although the reschedulings slowed the pace of repayments, the higher consumer prices that resulted from the agreements sparked food riots in April 1984. The government subsequently suspended the 1983 agreements.

In April 1985, however, the Jorge Blanco administration signed a new one-year IMF Standby Agreement that included more austerity measures and the floating of the Dominican Republic peso in relation to the United States dollar. The one-year loan also enabled the government to reschedule commercial bank and Paris Club (see Glossary) debts. However, repayments were abruptly suspended in 1986 because they were considered too high. The ensuing civil disorders and serious differences over the pace of reforms sealed the end of the agreement prematurely, and the electorate ousted the Jorge Blanco administration in favor of former president Balaguer, who evoked memories of the economic growth of the 1970s and was determined not to seek help from the IMF.

The Balaguer approach was to refuse to negotiate with the IMF in order to avoid the austere economic conditions its agreements usually entailed. Instead, Balaguer tried to revive the economy by initiating a large public works construction program during his 1986–90 tenure. The economy expanded rapidly in 1987, but then contracted sharply in 1988—mainly as a result of the government's spending patterns. High inflation and currency devaluation, coupled with serious problems with such basic services as transportation, electricity, and water, crippled Balaguer's reform program. His expansionary fiscal policies also fueled unprecedented inflation, causing prices to rise 60 percent in 1988 alone, which took a severe toll on the poorer segments of the population. His continued devaluation of the peso may have benefited the country's burgeoning export sector and tourist trade—but at the expense of disadvantaged Dominicans earning fixed salaries. By the late 1980s, the external debt—US$4 billion—was almost double what it had been in 1980. Finally, the government's payment problems and its inability to meet its foreign debt commitments left it no choice but to turn again to the IMF in 1990.

High levels of inflation, increasing debt, and persistent deficits masked several positive trends during the 1980s, however. The most positive development was the country's rapid diversification away from its dependence on sugar. New jobs in assembly manufacturing offset many of the local jobs in the cane fields. Employment in assembly operations grew from 16,000 in 1980 to nearly 100,000 by 1989. These figures represented the world's fastest growth in free-zone employment during the 1980s. By 1987 the value of assembly exports surpassed that of traditional agricultural exports. The Dominican Republic also enjoyed the Caribbean's fastest growth in tourism during the 1980s. Moreover, although the mining industry suffered from low prices and labor disputes, it contributed a significant percentage of foreign exchange as well. The agricultural sector also diversified to a limited degree, with a new emphasis on the export of nontraditional items such as tropical fruits (particularly pineapple), citrus, and ornamental plants to the United States under the Caribbean Basin Initiative (CBI—see Glossary).

Economic Policies

The severe imbalances in public finances and the fluctuations of deteriorating budget deficits that characterized the 1980s spilled over into the early 1990s. Problems related to servicing the debt also continued, forcing the government to follow a policy of on-again, off-again recourse to IMF interference. Although the required austerity measures usually caused public discontent and, in some cases, civil disturbances, President Balaguer, who had refused to negotiate with the IMF, changed course in 1990 and announced at the beginning of his sixth term that he was doubling basic food and fuel prices to meet the conditions for resumed IMF assistance. The following year witnessed further anti-inflationary measures, including the freezing of public-sector pay. The government also stopped its practice of printing money to pay for public spending, and the money supply contracted. The ensuing deep recession caused inflation to drop significantly and the exchange rate to stabilize. These developments in turn prompted the IMF in September 1991 to approve an eighteen-month standby arrangement, followed by an RD$31.8 million (about US$4.4 million) loan. Soon the economy registered a 3 percent increase in GDP and in 1993 an inflation rate of 5 percent; these figures contrasted with a 5 percent decrease in GDP and consumer price inflation of 100 percent in the late 1980s.

A reversal of policy seemed inevitable, however. Just prior to the 1994 election, the traditional upsurge in public-sector pay and government spending on public works programs reappeared, and Balaguer's extravagant capital projects began to deplete government revenues. The Central Bank of the Dominican Republic (Banco Central de la República Dominicana—BCRD) tried to remedy the deteriorating situation by requiring the government to pay the surcharge on fuel sales directly to the Central Bank to finance mounting foreign debt payments. With the 1996 presidential elections around the corner, however, the government totally ignored this requirement. The only way to maintain a modest fiscal surplus was to allow several state-owned public enterprises to delay their payments.

This heavy economic burden was passed on to the incoming president, Leonel Fernández Reyna. The new president pledged, upon his election in 1996, to observe tight fiscal policies and initiate a wide-ranging modernization program, including privatization of public enterprises. One of his first steps was to mount a campaign against tax evasion, which proved to be quite successful: budgetary income in 1997 was 31 percent higher than in 1996. Perhaps his immediate focus on taxes resulted from the common practice of tax evasion by wealthier Dominicans. Moreover, many businesses illegally received tax-exempt status because of political contacts while other qualified firms did not.

Fernández also reinstated payments of the fuel surcharge to the Central Bank, even though they put a strain on funds. The resumption of transfer payments to financially devastated state corporations, however, was a much larger drain on finances. The Fernández government inherited a huge domestic debt on several of these companies, especially the sugar and electricity enterprises. Restructuring these enterprises required the passage of a law permitting the capitalization (i.e., partial privatization) of public corporations, which was signed in June 1997 after a long struggle between the president and Congress.

Electricity distribution operations of the Dominican Electricity Corporation (Corporación Dominicana de Electricidad—CDE), as well as other divisions of the company, were scheduled for public auction by late 1998. That date was postponed indefinitely as a result of damage to the electricity network by

117

Hurricane Georges. However, in September 1998, the Dominican government and a consortium of three British and United States firms signed an agreement to construct three 100-megawatt combined-cycle generators. The generators, to be built by Germany's Siemens and financed by the World Bank and the Inter-American Development Bank (IDB), are to come on stream in early 2000.

The sugar parastatal corporation known as the State Sugar Council (Consejo Estatal del Azúcar—CEA) is to follow a different path from that of the electricity company. The Commission for the Reform of Public Enterprise announced in July 1998 that it had decided against partial privatization. Instead it recommended the introduction of private participation through long-term leases. An investment bank is to advise on the process, which is to be implemented in 1999. A group of milling, paints, oils, and insurance enterprises is also on the privatization list. Other economic reforms contemplated by the government include the liberalization of business legislation, aid for small enterprises, and the promotion of investment in tourism, telecommunications, mining, and the free zones. A new foreign investment law promulgated in September 1997 allows non-Dominican concerns to invest in all sectors, with the exception of those related to national security. It also provides for full repatriation of capital and profits. An older foreign investment law (August 1996) also encourages manufacturing in the tax-free zones by exempting foreign investors from import duty on inputs and by simplifying registration procedures and offering tax exemption for up to twenty years.

Fiscal Policy

Another significant reform under consideration by the Dominican Congress in the late 1990s was that of imposing restrictions on the executive's discretionary use of public finances. Meanwhile, a role would be established for the private sector in providing for social security and strengthening the Central Bank's autonomy and supervision of all banking procedures. Overseeing the country's financial system has always been the function of the Monetary Board of the BCRD. The BCRD controls the money supply, allocates credit and foreign exchange, seeks to restrain inflation, manages the national debt, and performs currency-typical central bank functions.

The Dominican Republic peso (RD$) has been issued by the BCRD since 1948 and was officially on par with the United States dollar for decades. The peso underwent a slow process of devaluation on the black market from 1963 until the government enacted a series of devaluations during the 1980s. A 1978 Dominican law had actually required that the peso equal the dollar in value, but as economic conditions worsened, authorities abandoned this policy. The most important change in Dominican exchange policy came in 1985: the Jorge Blanco government, acting in accordance with the terms of an IMF stabilization program, floated the national currency in relation to the dollar, thereby temporarily wiping out the previously extensive black market. The floating peso fell to a level of US$1 = RD$3.12, an official devaluation of more than 300 percent that proved to be a major shock to the economy. Preferential exchange rates, however, remained in force for oil imports and parastatal transactions. The devaluation caused higher domestic prices and burdened many poor citizens, while it improved the country's export sector through newly competitive prices. Rising inflation, balance-of-payments deficits, and foreign debt compelled further devaluations after 1985. The peso stabilized somewhat at US$1 = RD$6.35 by 1989, after bottoming out at nearly US$1 = RD$8 in mid-1988. As a result of these fluctuations, the Monetary Board experimented during the 1980s with a multitier fixed exchange rate, a floating exchange rate, and other systems. By 1988 it had settled on a fixed rate subject to change based on the country's export competitiveness and domestic inflation. An important provision of the exchange-rate policy of 1988 prohibited currency transactions at the country's exchange banks and channeled all foreign currency transactions into the commercial banks under BCRD supervision.

In February 1991, a new dual exchange-rate system authorized the BCRD to set the rate for official transactions and commercial banks to conduct operations at a free-market rate. Four years later, the two systems were unified, with the exception of such government transactions as debt servicing and importing fuels. The rates for these transactions were unified in 1997 on a free-market basis and at an initial rate of US$1 = RD$14. A gap between the two currencies, however, forced an adjustment in the official rate to US$1 = RD$14.2. After Hurricane Georges, the official rate dropped further to US$1 = RD$15.46; the commercial rate was US$1 = RD$16 in late November 1999.

Without changing the BCRD's basic functions as the country's central bank, a banking reform law in 1992 reduced the number of financial institutions. Instead, the law created "multi-banks," which would specialize in offering a complete range of services. The consolidation was effected by merging commercial and development banks with mortgage or savings banks. In the late 1990s, the Dominican Republic had fifteen commercial banks, of which one, the Banco de Reservas, was state-owned, and five were foreign-owned: the United States Chase Manhattan Bank and Citibank, Canada's Bank of Nova Scotia, and Spain's Banco Español de Credito and Banco Santander. The foreign investment law, which was passed in September 1997, opens up the banking sector to other potential foreign participants, although it stipulates that insurance agencies remain under majority Dominican ownership. In addition, seven development banks provide loans for housing, agriculture, and other investments.

Government Role

The role of the BCRD (an entity under the President's control) in managing the country's domestic monetary policy and dealing with pressures on the exchange rate is only one aspect of the government's traditional tight grip on the economy. Its interventionist approach is also evident in its repeated efforts to restrain inflation. But the disruptive nature and abrupt changes in governmental economic policy have contributed to sharp fluctuations in the inflation rate. To cite one example: lax fiscal and monetary policies caused inflation to rise from an average of approximately 6 percent in 1983 to 38 percent by 1985 to an average of 59.5 percent in 1990. An abrupt tightening of monetary policy resulted in a sharp inflation rate drop to 4.5 percent in 1992, but accelerated spending prior to presidential elections caused the rate to rise to 12.5 percent in 1995. That rise was brought down to 5.4 percent a year later, however, when the BCRD introduced tight monetary restraints. Rising food prices in 1997 again reversed the trend, raising the rate to almost 10 percent and leading to street demonstrations and to the imposition of government price controls. The business sector immediately accused the government of taking this restrictive measure strictly for political reasons related to elections. In imposing these controls on such basic goods as rice, milk, chicken, and cement, however, the administration has acknowledged that it lacks the means to enforce them and has suggested that they be used only as a reference point for prices.

The Dominican government's approach of imposing restrictive monetary measures dates back to the 1970s and 1980s, reflecting its concern over the rising cost of basic consumer goods. Many prices were set by the government's National Price Stabilization Institute (Instituto Nacional de Estabilización de Precios—Inespre). Despite Inespre's efforts, food prices rose faster than all other prices during the 1980s. Inespre's pricing policies responded more to political concerns than to economic realities. Prices of basic foodstuffs were maintained at unrealistically low levels, in part because urban violence often resulted from efforts to bring these prices more in line with the free market. Keeping urban consumer prices low necessitated the purchase of staple crops from Dominican farmers at less than fair value, a practice that depressed the income and the living standard of rural Dominicans.

Privatization

In the late 1990s, the government showed no evidence of relaxing its rigid hold on the country's economy. Although in March 1998 it had initiated the qualification process for firms interested in bidding for the distribution and marketing operations of the state-owned electricity enterprise, strong opposition in some government circles together with the impact of Hurricane Georges have slowed the process. Similarly, plans to privatize the generating operations of the CDE have been contradicted by the administration's decision in late 1997 to purchase new electric generators. Further proof that the government was extending the same approach to other public enterprises came in 1997, when it imported 600 buses for a new state corporation assigned to provide public transportation in the Santo Domingo area. The state sugar company, CEA, is also on the privatization list, but parcels of its land have been distributed, at questionably low prices in some cases, as part of the government's agrarian reform program. All these actions cast doubts on the administration's commitment to the concept of privatization. They may also reflect a strong difference of views within the administration, with some members—including the new director of the CDE, named in 1998—favoring the strengthening of state-owned enterprises rather than their privatization or capitalization.

Labor

The structure of the Dominican labor force began to change significantly during the post-Trujillo era as agriculture's share of output diminished. In 1950 agriculture had employed 73 percent of the country's labor, but by the end of the 1980s it accounted for as little as 35 percent. In mid-1996 the Food and Agriculture Organization (FAO) estimated that agriculture, forestry, and fishing employed only 20 percent of the labor force. Industry and services had incorporated approximately 20 percent and 45 percent, respectively, of displaced agricultural labor (see table 6, Appendix). As a consequence of gaps in the labor statistics, official estimates of the female segment of the economically active population varied widely, from 15 to 30 percent of the labor force. Whatever the total figures, the role of women, particularly in the urban economy, was growing by the late 1980s. Seventy percent of the employees in free-trade zones (FTZs) were women; as greater numbers of FTZs opened in the late 1980s, the rate of employment for females more than doubled the rate of employment for males. This shift represented a major transformation in the labor force; previously, the percentage of women in the Dominican work force had been lower than that for any other Latin American country. Men continued to dominate agricultural jobs, but these were among the lowest paid jobs in the country. The highest salaries were earned in mining, private utilities, financial services, and commerce. The distribution of income among workers was highly skewed; the top 10 percent earned 39 percent of national income, while the bottom 50 percent earned only 19 percent.

Income distribution continued to be skewed in the 1990s, with the top 20 percent of the population earning 60 percent of the country's total income in 1994, and the bottom 20 percent earning only 4.5 percent. A 1992 World Bank report classified 4.6 million Dominicans as poor, with 2.8 million living in extreme poverty. About 10 to 15 percent of the total workforce, estimated at 2.84 million in 1994, are union members. Official statistics put the average unemployment rate at 15.6 percent for the 1994–95 period, compared with 20.7 percent for the 1992–93 period. Approximately 15 percent of the economically active population are engaged in agriculture; 23 percent in industry; 27 percent in tourism, trade, and finance; and 35 percent in other services and government employ. Although the administration of President Fernández is committed in principle to reducing the level of public-sector overstaffing, it allowed government personnel recruitment to increase 6.4 percent in the first half of 1998. Moreover, the government has expressed reluctance to undertake public-sector layoffs despite a favorable economy.

In the 1980s, the most controversial labor law was the one governing the national minimum wage. Although the Congress increased minimum wages on several occasions during the decade, unusually high inflation, which reduced the real wages of workers, usually outpaced these increases. General strikes or other confrontations between labor and government frequently resulted. Government officials were reluctant to grant frequent raises in the minimum wage, in part, because they felt the need to keep Dominican wages competitive with those of other developing countries. Dominican wages did indeed remain lower than those in other Caribbean Basin countries, with the exception of impoverished Haiti.

A new labor code promulgated in May 1992, however, provided for increasing a variety of employee benefits. The minimum wage was raised twice in the next two years by a total of 20 percent, substantially more than the rate of inflation or devaluation. Public- and private-sector minimum wages were also increased by approximately 20 percent in 1997, resulting in a considerable rise in the Dominican Republic's labor costs.

Although labor unions appeared only after the Trujillo era and only in the form of poorly financed and politically divided peasant-based movements, the Dominican constitution provides for the freedom to organize labor unions and for the right of workers to strike (as well as for private-sector employers to lock out workers). All workers, except military and police personnel, are free to organize, and workers in all sectors exercise this right. Organized labor, however, represents no more than 15 percent of the work force and is divided among three major confederations, four minor confederations, and several independent unions. The government respects association rights and places no obstacles to union registration, affiliation, or the ability to engage in legal strikes.

Requirements for calling a strike include the support of an absolute majority of the workers of the company, a prior attempt to resolve the conflict through arbitration, written notification to the Secretariat of State for Labor, and a ten-day waiting period following notification before proceeding with a strike. The Labor Code specifies the steps legally required to establish a union. It calls for automatic recognition of a union if the government has not acted on its application within a specific time. In practice, the government has readily facilitated recognition of labor organizations. Unions can and do freely affiliate regionally and internationally, and they are independent of the government and political parties.

Collective bargaining is provided for by law and may be exercised in firms in which a union has gained the support of an absolute majority of the workers, but only a minority of companies have collective bargaining pacts. The Labor Code stipulates that workers cannot be dismissed because of their trade union membership or activities. In 1997 there were some seventy unions in the thirty-six established FTZs, which included 288 United States-owned or affiliated companies and employed approximately 172,000 workers, mostly women. The majority of these unions are affiliated with the National Federation of Free Trade Zone Workers, but many of them exist only on paper. And some FTZ companies, whose working conditions are generally better than others in the country, have a history of discharging workers who attempt to organize unions. The State Sugar Council (CEA), on the other hand, employs workers from more than 100 unions while it discourages additional organizing efforts. Dominican workers predominate in most of the unions, but two unions are Haitian-dominated.

The matter of Haitian migrants in the Dominican Republic has been a contentious one. Since the early twentieth century, the Dominican Republic has received both temporary and permanent Haitian migrants. Several hundred thousand Haitians were believed to reside in the Dominican Republic in the late 1990s, representing workers in the country both legally and illegally. As the result of several agreements between the Dominican and Haitian governments, numerous cane cutters were brought in legally. However, most were paid miserably low wages and experienced very poor living conditions. Many of the legal and illegal Haitian workers lived in camps on the sugarcane plantations. Because of disturbances that arose at a sugar plantation in 1985 in which several Haitians were killed, the government discontinued the official contracting of Haitian cane cutters. Reportedly, however, numerous Haitians in the Dominican Republic illegally (primarily because Dominican salaries and living conditions generally were better than those in Haiti) were picked up by the government and obliged to work in the cane fields or be forcibly repatriated. Haitians also worked as labor recruiters and field inspectors in the cane fields as well as laborers harvesting coffee, rice, and cocoa and as construction workers in Santo Domingo.

Although the law prohibits forced or compulsory labor, forced overtime in factories continues to be a problem. Employers, particularly in FTZs, sometimes lock the exit doors at the normal closing time to prevent workers from leaving. Other employers fail to inform new hires that overtime is optional. And there have been reports of some employees being fired for refusing to work overtime.

The Labor Code prohibits employment of children under fourteen years of age and places restrictions on the employment of children under the age of sixteen. These restrictions include a limitation of no more than six hours of daily work, no employment in dangerous occupations or establishments serving alcohol, as well as limitations on nighttime work. Dominican law requires six years of formal education. High levels of unemployment and lack of a social safety net, however, create pressures on families to allow children to earn supplemental income. Tens of thousands of children work selling newspapers, shining shoes, or washing cars, often during school hours.

The Labor Code authorizes a National Salary Committee to set minimum wage levels; the Congress may also enact minimum wage legislation. The minimum wage equals approximately US$75 per month. Although this amount covers only a fraction of the living costs of a family in Santo Domingo, many workers make only the minimum wage. For example, 60 percent of government employees earn only minimum wage. The Labor Code establishes a standard work period of eight hours a day and forty-four hours per week. It also stipulates that all workers are entitled to thirty-six hours of uninterrupted rest each week, and to a 35 percent differential for work above forty-four hours up to sixty-eight hours per week and double time for any hours above sixty-eight hours per week. The degree to which Labor Code provisions are enforced is uncertain.

The Dominican Social Security Institute (Instituto Dominicano del Seguro Social—IDSS) sets workplace safety and health conditions. However, the existing social security system does not apply to all workers and is underfunded. In addition, both the IDSS and the Secretariat of State for Labor have a limited number of inspectors appointed through political patronage charged with enforcing standards. In practice, for example, workers cannot remove themselves from hazardous workplace situations without jeopardizing continued employment. Conditions for agricultural workers are generally much worse, especially in the sugar industry. On many sugar plantations, cane cutters are paid by the weight of cane cut rather than by hours worked. Many cane cutters earn the equivalent of approximately US$3.70 per day. Many villages in which workers, often Haitians, gather for mutual support have high rates of disease and lack schools, medical facilities, running water, and sewerage systems.

Agriculture

The backbone of the Dominican economy for centuries, agriculture declined in significance during the 1970s and 1980s, as manufacturing, mining, and tourism began to play more important roles in the country's development. During the 1960s, the agricultural sector employed close to 60 percent of the labor force, contributed 25 percent of GDP, and provided between 80 and 90 percent of exports. By 1988, however, agriculture employed only 35 percent of the labor force, accounted for 15 percent of GDP, and generated approximately 50 percent of all exports. In 1992 the sector's share of exports dropped to 43 percent and employed only 28 percent of the total workforce. By the end of 1995, the agricultural sector's contribution to GDP stood at 12.7 percent, and it employed approximately 12.9 percent of the labor force. The declining importance of sugar, the principal source of economic activity for nearly a century, was even more dramatic. Sugar's share of total exports fell from 63 percent in 1975 to less than 20 percent by the late 1980s. Sugar exports in 1995 were 75 percent lower than in 1981, and the severe drought of 1997 also lowered production.

The transformation in agriculture paralleled the country's demographic trends. In 1960, some 70 percent of the country's population was rural; that figure was reduced to 30 percent in the 1990s. Government policies accelerated urbanization through development strategies that favored urban industries over agriculture in terms of access to capital, tariff and tax exemptions, and pricing policies. As a consequence, the production of major food crops either stagnated or declined in per capita terms from the mid-1970s to the late 1990s. However, production of some major export products, coffee and cocoa, grew by some 9 percent in the latter 1990s.

Picking cotton
Courtesy Inter-American
Development Bank

Rooftop hydroponics
Courtesy Inter-American
Development Bank

Land Policies

The uneven distribution of arable land continued to be a fundamental obstacle to the economic development of the Dominican Republic in the 1990s. Despite active attempts to reform land tenure patterns, the basic dichotomy of latifundio (see Glossary) and *minifundio* (see Glossary) continues to be the predominant feature of rural life. According to the 1981 agricultural census, 2 percent of the nation's farms occupied 55 percent of total farmland. By contrast, landholdings averaging less than twenty hectares, which represented 82 percent of all farms (314,665 units), covered only 12 percent of the land under cultivation. Land distribution on both extremes was notably worse. Some 161 farms, 0.1 percent of all farms, occupied 23 percent of all productive land, whereas tens of thousands of peasants possessed only a few *tareas* (the *tarea*, the most common measurement of land on the island, equaled one-sixteenth of a hectare).

The government is the largest landholder. The state-owned largest sugar producer, CEA, established in 1966 to manage the sugar operations acquired from the Trujillo family, and the Dominican Agrarian Institute (Instituto Agrario Dominicano—IAD), the national land reform agency, control the overwhelming share of public-sector land, most of which was derived from Trujillo's estate. The two major privately owned sugar producers, Central Romana and Casa Vicini, along with several large cattle ranches, represent the largest private landholdings.

The concentration of land ownership in the Dominican Republic, although it can trace its roots back to Christopher Columbus's parceling of land, resulted principally from the "latifundization" of land with the advent of commercial sugarcane production in the late nineteenth century. The concentration of arable land ownership increased after 1948, when Trujillo intensified his involvement in the sugar industry. In a little over a decade, Trujillo doubled the amount of land dedicated to sugarcane. The dictator and his cronies seized as much as 60 percent of the nation's arable land through colonization schemes, the physical eviction of peasants from their land, and the purchase of land through spurious means. In the aftermath of Trujillo's assassination in 1961, the government expropriated his family's landholdings by means of Decree 6988, thus setting the stage for contemporary land policy.

In 1962 the post-Trujillo Council of State created the IAD to centralize agrarian reform and land policy, charging the organization with redistributing the ruler's former holdings to peasants. Agrarian reform was hindered by the country's stormy political transitions in the 1960s, but it was strengthened in 1972 by legislation that authorized the government to expropriate unused farms in excess of 31.4 hectares under certain conditions. Despite the broad mandate for land reform, a cause strongly advocated by the Balaguer administration in the late 1980s, the IAD has made disappointing progress since 1962, according to its critics. Figures vary considerably as to the number of hectares actually distributed (reportedly, some 409,000 hectares by late 1987), with the greatest progress on redistribution occurring during the early years. Since 1988 land redistribution has been minimal.

The IAD distributed parcels of land to individuals, cooperatives, and settlements (*asentamientos*). A range of support services, including land-clearing, road construction, irrigation, agricultural extension services, and credit, were also provided in principle. However, peasants criticized the IAD's sluggish performance in transferring land titles, its distribution of mainly marginal agricultural land, and the generally inadequate level of support services caused by lack of funding and ineffectual management of the IAD. For example, only 38 percent of IAD land was actually devoted to the cultivation of crops in the late 1980s; 9 percent was devoted to livestock and 53 percent to forestry or other uses.

After decades of wrangling, the Dominican Republic completed the 1980s with the issue of land largely unresolved from the perspectives of both peasants and commercial farmers. This failure was most evident in data demonstrating an ongoing pattern of skewed land ownership. Frequent spontaneous land seizures and invasions by peasants of underused land throughout the 1980s epitomized rural frustrations. On one end of the economic spectrum, numerous rural associations, disconcerted by the pace and the quality of land reform, participated in land seizures, demanding "land for those who work it." On the other end of the spectrum, agribusiness complained of the government's inconsistent policies with regard to the expropriation of land. Some analysts viewed such inconsistencies as a deterrent to new investment in diversified agriculture and therefore as counterproductive to the republic's efforts through the encouragement of tourism and the development of mineral resources to diversify its economy away from sugar.

The agricultural sector continued to be depressed well into the 1990s, with a growth of just over 3 percent in 1997–98 (as against 9 percent the previous year). Government policies, especially those relating to agrarian reform, remained incoherent, with informal land occupations occurring more frequently toward the end of the decade. Years of high interest rates remained a serious impediment to investment, making it almost impossible to purchase replacements for antiquated equipment. The government's decision to import large quantities of major staple items at low prices in response to the 1997 drought caused setbacks to domestic agriculture, especially because no thought was given to helping domestic producers. Dairy farming was hit particularly hard by another government decision—to sell imported powdered milk at subsidized prices. The decision resulted in several bankruptcies in the dairy industry.

Hurricane Georges, which hit the Dominican Republic on September 22, 1998, had a devastating impact on the agricultural sector. The hurricane destroyed 80 percent of the banana crop and producers of sugarcane, cocoa, coffee, and citrus also experienced significant losses. In addition, the poultry industry was hard hit. Substantial imports of food were required for the remainder of 1998.

Land Use

About 57 percent of the Dominican Republic's total territory, some 27,452 square kilometers out of 48,442 square kilometers, was devoted to agriculture-related activities, including pasture land, in the late 1990s. In 1998 forest and woodland areas occupied some 6,000 square kilometers, representing about 12 percent of the total land area. Because of environmental concerns over deforestation, access to the main forest reserves is limited. The government also has created thirteen national parks and nine areas of special scientific interest. Although deforestation is steadily reducing this area, most of the soil is well-suited for cultivation, and the climate ranges from temperate to tropical. The coastal plains of the south and the east are the main sugar-producing areas. The valley of Cibao in the north and the Vega Real region northeast of Santo Domingo are the richest and most productive agricultural lands. These regions are endowed with a fair share of water from streams and rivers; however, the country's irrigation system barely covered 15 percent of the arable land, or about

139,000 hectares, in the late 1980s. By 1991 with the construction of several dams the irrigated area was estimated at 225,000 hectares.

Cash Crops

Despite ongoing diversification efforts since the late 1980s, the Dominican Republic in the late 1990s continues to be a major world producer of sugarcane. The sugar industry has an impact on all sectors of the economy and epitomizes the nation's vulnerability to outside forces. Fluctuating world prices, adjustments to United States sugar quotas, and the actions of United States sugar companies (such as Gulf and Western Corporation's sale of all its Dominican holdings in 1985) all could determine the pace of economic development for decades.

Columbus introduced sugarcane to Hispaniola, but sugar plantations did not flourish in the Dominican Republic until the 1870s, much later than on most Caribbean islands. Investment by United States sugar companies, such as the United States South Porto Rico Company and the Cuban-Dominican Sugar Company, rapidly transformed the Dominican economy. These companies had established themselves by the 1890s, and between 1896 and 1905 sugar output tripled. During the United States occupation (1916–24), the sugar industry expanded further, acquiring control of major banking and transportation enterprises.

Beginning in 1948, Trujillo constructed a string of sugar mills, many of which he owned personally. The elimination of United States sugar quotas for Cuba after the Cuban revolution of 1959 further enhanced the economic role of sugar because the Dominican Republic assumed Cuba's former status as the main supplier under the quota system.

Heavy reliance on sugar has created a number of economic difficulties. The harvest of sugarcane, the *zafra*, is arduous, labor-intensive, and seasonal, and it leaves many unemployed during the *tiempo muerto*, or dead season. Haitian laborers have harvested most of the Dominican cane crop since the late nineteenth century, by agreement between Hispaniola's two governments. Although Haitian cane cutters live under conditions of near slavery, two factors continue to draw them across the border: depressed economic conditions in Haiti and the reluctance of Dominicans to perform the backbreaking, poorly regarded work of cane cutting.

After the death of Trujillo, Dominican policy makers faced the sensitive issue of how best to manage the dictator's economic policy, which by stressing a one-crop economy represented more of a drain on national finances than a catalyst to development. These contradictions played themselves out within the CEA, an entrenched, politicized, and inefficient parastatal.

The role of sugar changed markedly in the 1980s as external conditions forced the national economy to diversify. Sugar prices had reached unprecedented highs in 1975 and again in 1979. The international recession of the early 1980s, however, pushed prices to their lowest level in forty years. Lower world prices hurt the Dominican economy, but the reduction of sales to the United States market, as a result of quota reductions that began in 1981, was even more costly because of the preferential price the United States paid under the quota system. The international market continued to be unpromising in the late 1990s. The market was glutted by overproduction, caused principally by European beet growers; major soft-drink manufacturers also began to turn to high-fructose corn sweeteners and away from cane sugar.

In the late 1980s, the CEA controlled 60 percent of the nation's sugar output through the ownership of 75 percent of the country's major sugar mills. These mills included the largest and best equipped, the Haina mill. The CEA also owned 233,000 hectares of land. However, the state-owned enterprise was operating at a loss and became so heavily indebted that it began selling off land for industrial free zones and tourism development projects. Its output fell below the production rate of the two major privately owned companies, Casa Vicini and the Central Romana Corporation.

The CEA's production has continued to decline steadily in the 1990s, dropping from 311,000 tons in 1993 to 271,533 tons in 1994 to 224,448 tons in 1995, to an all-time low of 196,826 tons in 1996. The long-term declining productivity of the CEA, which was scheduled for privatization in 1999, was compensated for by privately owned mills. For example, Central Romana reported record production of 370,000 tons in 1993 and 344,700 tons in 1996 (only figures available). The country's total sugar output in 1997, for example, was sufficient to enable it to meet its United States preferential import quota (see table 7, Appendix). This quota system, of which the Dominican Republic is the largest beneficiary, provides a preferential market for more than half of Dominican sugar exports and creates a cushion against slumps in world sugar prices.

Coffee, the second leading cash crop, continues to be subject to varying market conditions in the 1990s. Introduced as early as 1715, coffee continues to be a leading crop among small hillside farmers. In 1993 the area of coffee production was estimated at 85,000 hectares, whereas in the late 1980s it had covered 152,000 hectares over various mountain ranges. Coffee farming, like sugar growing, is seasonal and entails a labor-intensive harvest involving as many as 250,000 workers, some of whom are Haitians. The preponderance of small holdings among Dominican coffee farmers, however, has caused the coffee industry to be inefficient, and yields fall far below the island's potential. Production of coffee fluctuates with world prices. The trend in the 1990s was one of declining prices. As a result, low prices on the world market dramatically reduced production from 1.2 million sixty-kilogram bags in 1987–88 to less than half that amount—545,000 bags—in 1993–94. Export earnings for the latter period amounted only to US$28 million, whereas the earnings for the 1994 calendar year reached US$62.7 million, the highest figure since 1989. Exports reached the US$81 million mark in 1995 but fell back to US$65 million in 1996, mainly because of lower international prices.

Another factor that has influenced production is vulnerability of the coffee bushes to the hurricanes that periodically ravage the island, such as Hurricane Georges in September 1998. Furthermore, the Dominican coffee industry faces international problems that result mainly from the failure of the International Coffee Organization (ICO) to agree on quotas through its International Coffee Agreement (ICA). Although Dominicans consume much of their own coffee, they have increasingly been forced to find new foreign markets because of the ICO's difficulties. As is true of many Dominican commodities, middlemen often smuggle coffee into Haiti for re-export overseas.

Cocoa constitutes another principal cash crop, occasionally surpassing coffee as a source of export revenue. The Dominican cocoa industry emerged in the 1880s as a competing peasant crop, when tobacco underwent a steep price decline. Although overshadowed by sugar, cocoa agriculture enjoyed slow, but steady, growth until a period of rapid expansion in the 1970s. In response to higher world prices, the area covered with cacao trees rose from 65,000 hectares in 1971 to 117,000 hectares by 1980. Small farmers cultivate the most cocoa, producing some 40,000 tons of cocoa on approximately 134,000 hectares in 1987. This crop was enough to make the Dominican Republic the largest producer of cocoa in the Caribbean.

Cocoa production declined in the early 1990s, reaching 49,000 tons in 1991, but it recovered to a peak of approximately 67,000 tons in 1996. However, the crop was a casualty of the 1997 drought, which resulted in a loss of more than 17.5 percent. The 1987 level of US$66 million in exports also was reduced to a low point of US$35 million in 1991 before recovering to US$60 million in 1995. Higher cocoa prices on international markets raised export earnings to US$65 million in 1996.

Tobacco enjoyed a renaissance in the 1960s, with the introduction of new varieties and an increase in prices. Sales revenues peaked in 1978, but they declined considerably in the 1980s and 1990s because of lower prices, disease, and inadequate marketing. Black tobacco of the "dark air-cured and sun-cured" variety is manufactured into cigars for export. Numerous companies participate in the export of black tobacco. A growing number of cigar companies operate out of the country's burgeoning free zones.

Declining prices and structural changes in the international market for the Dominican Republic's traditional cash crops of sugar, coffee, cocoa, and tobacco forced the government to consider opportunities for nontraditional agricultural exports during the 1980s and 1990s. This new emphasis on nontraditional exports coincided with the implementation of the Caribbean Basin Initiative (CBI), which afforded the country reduced-tariff access to the United States market. The main categories of nontraditional exports promoted by the government included ornamental plants, winter vegetables (vegetables not grown in the United States during winter months), citrus, tropical fruits, spices, nuts, and certain types of produce popular among the growing Hispanic and Caribbean populations in the United States. However, new investments in agribusiness during the 1980s and 1990s were less successful than anticipated, particularly in comparison to the dramatic success of assembly manufacturing and tourism. Nonetheless, officials apparently succeeded in broadening the options of farmers and investors from a few crops to a diverse range of products. The government spearheaded agricultural diversification

Woman peeling papayas for jam
Courtesy Inter-American
Development Bank

Potter at work
Courtesy Inter-American
Development Bank

135

through an export promotion agency, the Dominican Center for the ⁿromotion of Exports (Centro Dominicano de Promoción de Exportaciones—Cedopex), and through cooperation with a nongovernmental organization, the Joint Agricultural Consultative Committee, which promotes agribusiness investment in the republic. By the 1990s, some success had been achieved with citrus and pineapples, but quicker growth in nontraditional agricultural exports was hindered by the slow pace of the CEA's diversification program, which had scheduled portions of the fertile sugar plains for conversion to nontraditional crop production.

As part of the national dish of rice and beans, rice was a major Dominican food crop in the late 1980s and 1990s. Rice production expanded significantly in the post-Trujillo era, and by late 1979 the country had achieved self-sufficiency for the first time. Rice production, however, waned in the 1980s and 1990s, forcing renewed imports.

The annual harvest of paddy rice reached 566,000 tons in 1992 but fell to 533,000 tons in 1994. Declines in production were related to a series of economic factors. Rice subsidies to the urban poor, who had less than two kilograms of rice a week as part of Inespre's food basket, or *canasta popular,* were generally at odds with the goal of increased output. Apart from such subsidies, the cost of rice was more than twice that on the world market. The government's land reform measures also may have had a negative impact on rice yields; IAD's rice holdings, which accounted for 40 percent of the nation's rice, were noticeably less productive than private rice holdings. In the late 1980s, the government continued to involve itself extensively in the industry by supplying irrigation systems to more than 50 percent of rice farmers as well as technical support through the Rice Research Center in Juma, near Bonao. The government also moved to increase the efficiency of local distribution in 1987; it transferred rice marketing operations from Inespre to the Agricultural Bank of the Dominican Republic (Banco Agrícola de la República Dominicana—Bagrícola) and then to the private sector.

The other principal grains and cereals consu.ned in the Dominican Republic include corn, sorghum, and imported wheat. Corn, native to the island, performed better than many food crops in the 1980s and 1990s because of the robust growth of the poultry industry, which used 95 percent of the corn crop as animal feed. The strong demand for feed notwithstanding,

Inespre's low prices for corn and other distortions in the local market caused by donated food from foreign sources decreased incentives for farmers and reduced output during the late 1970s and early 1980s. The cultivation of sorghum, a drought-resistant crop also used as a feed, expanded rapidly in the 1980s because of sorghum's suitability as a rotation crop on winter vegetable farms and as a new crop on newly idle cane fields.

Wheat is another increasingly important cereal because Dominicans are consuming ever-greater quantities of the commodity, donated primarily by the United States and France. The government is reluctant to interfere with Dominicans' preference for the heavily subsidized wheat over local cereals for fear of violent protests by poorer consumers.

Other major crops include starchy staples such as plantains and an assortment of tubers. Because of their abundance, sweet taste, and low cost, Dominicans consume large quantities of plantains, usually fried. Beans, a dietary staple and the chief source of protein for many Dominicans, are grown throughout the countryside.

Dominicans also grow cash crops that include an assortment of fruits and vegetables. In recent years, farmers, encouraged by the CEA, have diversified into such new crops as bananas, tomatoes, flowers, pineapples, and oranges. Citrus production became a growth industry in the late 1990s when it expanded its marketing to Europe and North America; its sales had been limited to the Caribbean market in the early 1990s. Similarly, banana production for export, which started only in 1990, totaled more than 104,160 tons in 1994 and shot up to 361,000 tons in 1996. Exports of fresh pineapple amounted to 65,000 tons in 1993, earning approximately US$13 million. The European Union, which had allotted the Dominican Republic a quota of 55,000 tons for 1995, almost doubled that amount in 1996.

Livestock

The raising of livestock, the basis of the economy during colonial times, continued to be a common practice in the 1990s, despite the country's warm climate and hilly interior. The predominant livestock on the island are beef and dairy cattle, chickens, and pigs. The country is essentially self-sufficient in its production of basic meat. Cattle-raising was still the primary livestock activity in the mid-1990s, and the Dominican stock contained 2.4 million head of cattle, up from 2 million head in the late 1980s. The great majority of the cattle were beef cattle, raised on medium-to-large ranches in the east.

The country also contains an undetermined, but dwindling, number of dairy cows. The decline in numbers of dairy cows because of large-scale slaughter of breeding cattle resulted from years of low government prices for milk. Implemented in an effort to keep consumer milk prices low, this policy had the unintended effect of dramatically increased milk imports.

The poultry industry, in contrast to the dairy industry, enjoyed strong growth in the 1980s. In the mid-1990s, the country had some 33 million chickens. A few large producers supplied the nation with 90,000 tons of broilers a year and with hundreds of millions of eggs. The pork industry had also rebounded by the mid-1980s, after suffering the virtual eradication of its stock from 1978 to 1982 because of an epidemic of African swine fever. Afterward, the Dominican Republic established an increasingly modern and well-organized pork industry.

By the mid-1990s, the number of pigs was estimated at 850,000. However, an attack of cholera in the late 1990s affected the national pig stock. In addition, Dominican livestock in the mid-1990s included some 574,000 goats. Livestock accounted for 5.2 percent of GDP in 1996, compared with 4.9 percent in 1991.

Forestry and Fishing

Pine, hardwood, and other tree cover, once ample, covered only 15 percent of the land by the beginning of the 1990s. To offset losses caused by the indiscriminate felling of trees and the prevalence of slash-and-burn agriculture, the government outlawed commercial tree cutting in 1967. Since then, limited development of commercial plantation forestry has occurred, but the nation continues to import more than US$30 million in wood products each year. Although not so drastic as in Haiti, deforestation and the erosion that it causes pose serious environmental concerns for the country's watersheds into the 1990s and beyond (see Land Use, this ch.). The limited amount of land occupied by forest and woodland (0.6 million hectares) continued to be steadily reduced in the late 1990s.

The fishing industry continued to be underdeveloped into the 1990s. It consists of only small coastal fishermen using small boats lacking refrigeration, who barely exploit the 1,400 kilometers of coastline. Fish production contributes little to the country's GDP (0.4 percent in 1994). In the late 1990s, the catch averaged about 22,000 tons per year.

Industry

Manufacturing

This sector consists of traditional or domestic manufacturing as well as assembly operations in free zones. One of the most important factors in accelerating the industrialization and diversification of the Dominican Republic's economy in the 1990s, manufacturing contributed 18.3 percent of GDP in 1998.

Traditional Manufacturing

During the Trujillo era, manufacturing grew more slowly than in other Latin American and Caribbean countries because of the dictatorship's disproportionate emphasis on sugar production. After the Balaguer government introduced the Industrial Incentive Law (Law 299) in 1968, domestic manufacturers for the first time received substantial tariff protection from foreign competition. Although these incentives stimulated an array of domestic industries, created jobs, and helped diversify the country's industrial base, Dominican industries tended to be heavily dependent on foreign input and proved to be inefficient and unable to compete internationally. In 1990 the government decided to drastically reduce the rates of import tariffs; all incentives provided for in Law 299 were eliminated in 1992. High interest rates caused the performance of the domestic industry subsector to contract in 1994 and 1995 so that it was growing at rates substantially below the national average of manufacturing. Consequently, the GDP share of domestic manufacturing, including sugar processing, declined from 16.6 percent in 1992 to 13.4 percent in 1997.

A reversal of the decline occurred, however, in 1998, mainly because the pressures of external competition, especially from Mexico, encouraged investment in modernizing plants. The manufacturing industry experienced a strong growth of 7.4 percent in the first half of 1998 in spite of a 13 percent drop in sugar production caused by the 1997 drought. The subsector of domestic manufacturing, which includes mostly consumer goods, food, and cigar production, grew by 10.1 percent in the first half of 1998. The growth may have resulted partially from a dramatic increase in the demand for Dominican cigars; the Domini·an Republic is the leading supplier to the United States, where cigar smoking was on the rise in the late 1990s.

Free-Zone Manufacturing

No economic process was more dynamic in the Dominican Republic during the 1980s than the rapid growth of free zones. Although the government established the legal framework for free zones in 1955, it was not until 1969 that the Gulf and Western Corporation opened the country's first such zone in La Romana. Free-zone development, which had progressed modestly in the 1970s, accelerated rapidly during the 1980s as a result of domestic incentives, such as Free-Zone Law 145 of 1983 and the United States CBI of 1984. Free-Zone Law 145, a special provision of the Industrial Incentive Law, offered liberal incentives for free-zone investment, including total exemption from import duties, income taxes, and other taxes for up to twenty years. By the close of the 1980s, the results of free-zone development were dramatically clear. From 1985 to 1989, the number of free zones had more than doubled, from six to fifteen; employment had jumped from 36,000 to nearly 100,000. The number of companies operating in free zones had increased from 146 to more than 220.

The trend was similar in the 1990s. Industrial free zones numbered thirty-three by the end of 1995 and employed approximately 165,000 workers in 469 companies. Those numbers remained at the same level at the end of 1996, but the number of firms operating in free zones stood at 434. The drop was attributed to keen competition from Mexico over United States markets. However, more than sixty applications for the establishment of new free-zone companies were approved in 1997. Although free-zone manufacturing contributes little to the country's GDP (3.4 percent in 1996 and 3.5 percent in 1997), it employs a significant portion of the industrial labor force (165,000 and 172,000 out of some 500,000 in 1996 and 1997, respectively). Moreover, free-zone manufacturing has been the major element in the growth of manufacturing since the last half of 1997 and grew by 8.3 percent in the first half of 1998. These factors may explain the creation within the Secretariat of State for Industry and Commerce of a special office for the development of free zones, the National Council for Free Zones (Consejo Nacional de Zonas Francas—CNZF). Also, free-zone exports generate badly needed foreign exchange:

Worker in textile mill
Courtesy Inter-American
Development Bank

US$2 billion in 1996 and US$3.8 billion in 1997—almost 75 percent of the island's total export earnings.

The Dominican Republic's free zones vary widely in terms of size, ownership, production methods, and location. The size of free zones ranges from only a few hectares to more than 100 hectares, with most located in the south and southeast. At least 70 percent of the free-zone companies produce garments, while others produce footwear, leather goods, electrical and electronic items, and cigars.

Mining

The mining industry enjoyed extraordinary growth in the 1970s, when the country's major ferronickel and *dore* (gold and silver nugget) operations were inaugurated. The contribution of mining to GDP rose from 1.5 percent in 1970 to 5.3 percent by 1980, where it remained until the late 1980s. Although the mining sector employed only about 1 percent of the labor force throughout this period, it became a major foreign-exchange earner in the 1980s.

Gold and silver *dore*, which occur naturally in the Dominican Republic, played a critical role in the rapid emergence of mining. Although the Spanish mined gold on the island as early as the 1520s, gold production in the Dominican Republic was insignificant until 1975, when the private firm Rosario Dominicano opened the Pueblo Viejo mine, the largest open-pit gold mine in the Western Hemisphere, on the north side of the island. In October 1979, the Dominican government, the owner of 46 percent of the shares of Rosario Dominicano, purchased the remaining equity from Rosario Resources, a New York-based company, thereby creating the largest Dominican-owned company in the country. Rosario's huge mining infrastructure, with an annual capacity of 1.7 million troy ounces of gold and silver, impelled by rapidly increasing international prices for gold, had nearly succeeded in pushing *dore* past sugar as the country's leading source of export revenue by 1980. From 1975 to 1980, gold and silver skyrocketed from 0 percent of exports to 27 percent. Declining prices for gold and silver during the 1980s, however, curtailed the extraordinary growth trend of the 1970s.

Production from the Rosario Pueblo Viejo gold and silver mine declined further as reserves in the oxide zone were being depleted. In 1992 gold production was down to 72,000 troy ounces (from a high of 412,990 troy ounces in 1981). The company suspended mining in March 1993, laying off 70 percent of its 1,300 employees. The average cost of production of gold in 1991 and 1992 was US$535 per ounce, compared with a selling price of US$352. Revenue from gold and silver exports, which had peaked at US$259.9 million in 1980, continued to decline—except for a brief recovery in 1987—until it reached a low of US$4.1 million in 1993. At that time, heavy losses caused by low export prices forced the company to suspend production for months. When Rosario suspended operations, it was in debt for more than US$90 million. However, the mine reopened in mid-1994 after renovation work financed by a foreign bank loan of US$20 million was completed. The reopening brought the year's exports up to US$19 million and increased them to US$44 million in 1995. Although gold and silver production in 1996 exceeded 117,625 troy ounces and 547,220 troy ounces, respectively, increasing export earnings to US$49 million, Rosario operations remained unprofitable (see table 8, Appendix). As of the late 1990s, the company continued to seek more foreign investment to allow mining in the lower sulfide zone.

Nickel is another Dominican export that contributed to the mining prosperity of the 1970s. From 1918 to 1956, the United States Geological Survey performed a series of mineral studies in the country. These studies encouraged the Canadian firm Falconbridge of Toronto to undertake its own nickel testing starting at the end of that period. Falconbridge successfully opened a pilot nickel plant in 1968, and by 1972 the company had begun full-scale ferronickel mining in the town of Bonao. In the late 1980s, the Bonao ferronickel mine was the second largest in the world. Buoyed by high international prices, nickel exports rose from 11 percent of total exports in 1975 to 14 percent by 1979. Although nickel exports, as a percentage of total exports, continued to climb in the 1980s, reaching 16 percent by 1987, lower world prices for nickel and a lengthy dispute between the government and Falconbridge over tax payments hampered output throughout the decade.

Nonetheless, nickel remains one of the Dominican Republic's main traditional exports, generating between US$220 million and US$240 million a year in the late 1990s. Low export prices, however, compelled Falconbridge Dominicana, which is majority-owned by the Toronto company, to suspend production for three months in 1993, reducing output to approximately 13,445 tons in that year. Production rose steadily thereafter, reaching 33,000 tons in 1997. Falconbridge Dominicana experienced difficulties that resulted in a 6.8 percent fall in nickel output in 1998 and caused the company to suspend operations during the last three months of 1998 because of low international prices. The firm indicated, however, that it would use the time to revamp and upgrade plant facilities. The combination of gold, silver, and nickel has made the Dominican Republic's mining sector the largest export earner, with the exception of the free zones, since the 1980s.

Construction

The construction industry had a major effect on the economy during the 1970s and the 1980s because government-funded public works provided thousands of jobs and improved the physical infrastructure. Construction activity boomed in the early 1970s, increasing at a rate of 16 percent annually from 1970 to 1975, faster than any other sector during that period, with the exception of mining. Public-works projects such as dams, roads, bridges, hospitals, low-income housing, and schools transformed the national infrastructure during the

1970s. The sector's rapid growth continued in the 1980s, but it was very uneven because of fluctuations in annual government spending. Private-sector construction, particularly of free-zone facilities and hotels, also boosted industry performance.

Construction firms, like many other Dominican businesses, rely heavily on personal contacts. For example, in the late 1980s the government awarded only about 15 percent of its construction contracts through a competitive bidding process. Government authorities, up to and including the president, negotiated or offered the remaining contracts as if they were personal spoils. The Balaguer administration's emphasis on construction in the late 1980s focused primarily on renovations in Santo Domingo. Projects included the construction of museums, a lighthouse, and a new suburb, all in preparation for 1992's observance of the 500th anniversary of Columbus's arrival in the New World.

The construction sector is generally self-sufficient; less than 33 percent of all construction material is imported. Domestically produced items include tiles, cables, gravel, sand, clay, piping, metals, paint, and cement. The rapid expansion of activity during the 1980s caused a serious shortage of cement that slowed the progress of some projects. The Dominican government built cement factories in Santiago and San Pedro de Macorís in 1977, in joint ventures with private investors, to complement its major plant in Santo Domingo. The new capacity quickly became insufficient, and the country was forced to begin importing cement by the mid-1980s. By the late 1980s, cement factories were operating at full capacity, a rarity among developing countries such as the Dominican Republic. The construction sector is a major employer of unskilled labor.

Although the construction sector's growth in the first half of the 1980s was uneven, it registered an impressive average annual growth of 18 percent in the last three years of the decade. The earlier growth spurt was the result of a rise in tourist-related projects, but the industry's stronger showing in 1989 was the result of an extensive public works program involving construction of public housing, a hydroelectric project, and an aqueduct for Santo Domingo. After contracting by 6.9 percent in 1990 and by 12.5 percent in 1991, the construction sector grew by 24.4 percent in 1992. The industry's growth rate fluctuations were determined by such factors as how much public spending was being devoted to infrastructure or how many rooms were being added by the tourism sector. Construction growth dropped back to 10.1 percent in 1993, 6.6 percent in 1994, and 5.7 percent in 1995 before jumping to 13 percent in 1996 and 17.1 percent in 1997, accounting for 10 percent of GDP in contrast to nearly 9 percent of GDP in 1987. The upswing resulted mainly from a sharp increase in spending on public works (about 3 percent of GDP), road construction, and large investments in the energy sector. In 1998 construction growth slowed from 10.9 percent in the first quarter to 6.2 percent for the first half as a whole. The boom in private construction during the third quarter of 1998 slowed as a result of a decrease in private investment and because of the high interest rates set in 1997 to support the peso. The drop is reflected in a 26.6 percent decrease in new construction permits.

Energy

An oil-importing country, the Dominican Republic has been impeded in its development efforts by the cost and scarcity of energy, especially when its import bill for petroleum multiplied tenfold in absolute terms during the 1970s. Although oil prices eased during the 1980s, the island faced a new energy crisis as a result of a critical shortage of electrical-generating capacity. Inadequate supplies of electricity resulted by the late 1980s in frequent power outages, frustrated consumers, and disrupted production activities.

The country's aggregate consumption of energy is low, even by Latin American standards. However, the Dominican Republic's narrow domestic energy resource base satisfies barely half the nation's energy demand, and the country continues to depend on imported crude oil and related petroleum products. The potential supply of hydropower, the most promising resource, is estimated at 1,800 megawatts (MW), but less than a quarter of that amount was being tapped in the late 1990s. Wood and charcoal use is constrained by the small size of the country's remaining forests. Biomass, mostly bagasse from sugarcane residue, is getting more use but has limited potential as a fuel.

The country's energy problems continued well into the 1990s. The electricity-generating operations of the Dominican Electricity Corporation (Corporación Dominicana de Electricidad—CDE) were severely deficient during most of the period from 1990 to 1996. Production fell to about one-half of peak demand in 1990 and 1991. By mid-1996, output was below 800 MW, compared with a peak demand of 1,200 MW. The problem was attributed to the frequent withdrawal from service for repair of antiquated generating units. Low hydroelectric production was also caused by an inefficient distribution system that resulted in one-half of the electricity produced being lost in transmission or through illegal connections. The CDE's losses were running at RD$200 million (some US$25.4 million) a month in 1996, and total debt had risen to RD$1,800 million (some US$138.5 million) by the end of the year.

Although power cuts and shortages continued into the mid-1990s, an electricity overhaul program financed by a US$148 million loan from the Inter-American Development Bank (IDB) and a US$105 million loan from the World Bank generated enough electricity to meet a demand for 1,250 MW by 1997. Privately operated power stations, including the 185-MW Smith-Enron station in Puerto Plata and the 220-MW Destec gas turbine at Los Minas, accounted for approximately half of total power generation.

Legislation was introduced in 1997 to privatize the CDE, and by mid-1998 the state-owned enterprise's generating and distribution operations were being restructured (see Economic Policies, this ch.). Transmission systems are to remain in public ownership, however. After years of neglect resulting from the lack of public investment by previous administrations, the CDE's installed capacity was estimated at 1,600 MW in late 1997. However, it was operating at a maximum capacity of 1,450 MW, 380 MW of which was hydroelectric. Private generators, which supply the CDE, have an estimated capacity of 600–700 MW.

The Dominican Republic has been developing its hydroelectric capacity, but imported oil continues to account for 85 percent of its energy sources. Oil imports amount to about 100,000 barrels a day, accounting for 20 percent of total import spending in 1997. Mexico and Venezuela have been the island country's traditional suppliers under the San José agreement, which allows 20 percent of the cost to be converted into soft loans. Both countries agreed in 1997 to more than triple their deliveries to the Dominican Republic—from 14,500 barrels a day to 45,000 barrels a day.

Services

Transportation

The Dominican Republic's relatively advanced transportation infrastructure, which had experienced sustained expan-

The Tavera Dam
Courtesy Inter-American Development Bank

sion since the 1950s, has been growing at a much faster rate since the late 1980s because of the booming tourist industry (see fig. 4). Roads are the most common medium of travel, and the national road network, which in the late 1990s totals more than 17,200 kilometers, is considered extensive by Caribbean standards. However, most roadways are narrow and flood easily. Moreover, 80 percent of all feeder roads had completely deteriorated by the mid-1980s because of lack of funding for badly needed maintenance and repair work. In the mid-1980s, steadily worsening road conditions prompted the World Bank and the Inter-American Development Bank to finance a program to develop better maintenance systems. However, Dominican road conditions remained poor well into the early 1990s. It was not until the late 1990s that a major road construction program was undertaken to develop intercity routes and urban projects in Santo Domingo. More than 470,700 vehicles were in use in 1997, including some 266,100 private cars and 133,610 trucks—compared with 405,000 in 1996 and about 242,000 in 1991.

In 1997 the Dominican Republic boasted a 1,600-kilometer railroad system, one of the longest in the Caribbean, compared with 325 kilometers in the mid-1980s. Although the CEA owns a substantial portion of the country's railroad system, several private rail companies serve the sugar industry, the largest of which is the Central Romana.

Of the fourteen seaports in the Dominican Republic, only five are considered major ports. Santo Domingo is the largest, handling about 80 percent of imports. The other three on the south coast are Haina, Boca Chica, and San Pedro de Macorís; the fifth major port is Puerto Plata on the north coast. In 1992 the country had a merchant fleet of 12,000 gross registered tons. Containerized shipping is widely used, mainly originating in Miami and New York. Port facilities were expanded and a new breakwater was opened in 1997 at Haina, which handles about 65 percent of maritime cargo traffic. An enlarged cruise-liner berth at Santo Domingo has made it one of the region's major berths for cruise ships. In 1998 the government granted a concession to a joint-venture company to build an even larger port to be used by the free-zone enterprises.

The Dominican Republic has five international airports: Santo Domingo, Puerto Plata, Punta Cana, La Romana, and Barahona. A sixth airport was under construction at Samaná in 1998. Puerto Plata and Punta Cana are the main airports for charter flights; Las Américas in Santo Domingo is the airport for scheduled flights. The government announced in September 1998 that for the first time it would grant concessions to upgrade and operate the international airports at Santo Domingo, Puerto Plata, Barahona, and Samaná. Thereby it hoped to reduce maintenance costs by RD$230 million annually and also shift much of the needed investment to private firms. The government intends to draft similar plans for the country's ports. Passenger arrivals on scheduled flights exceeded 1.45 million in 1995, compared with 632,000 on charter flights. American Airlines is the dominant carrier, with a market share of more than 50 percent on routes to many United States cities, but mostly Miami and New York.

Communications

One of the most modern and dynamic sectors of the Dominican economy is the telecommunications industry, which surpasses its counterparts in most Latin American and Caribbean nations in terms of technology. Telecommunications services, however, tend to be concentrated in urban areas. The government opened the telecommunications sector to competition in 1990. Since then it has become the fastest-growing element in the economy, doubling its share of GDP to 4.6 percent. In the first half of 1998, the industry grew by 20.8 percent.

The most impressive and technologically advanced component of the nation's telecommunications network is its telephone system. The Dominican Telephone Company (Compañía Dominicana de Teléfonos—Codetel), a wholly owned subsidiary of the United States company GTE, operates approximately 90 percent of the 250,000-unit national telephone system under the regulatory authority of the General Directorate for Telecommunications of the Secretariat of State for Public Works and Communications. Some of the advanced features of the system include direct domestic and international dialing, toll-free access to the United States through "800" numbers, incoming toll-free service or WATS, high-speed data transmission capabilities, fiber-optic cables, digital switching, and a full range of services usually available to consumers in the United States. In 1987 the Dominican Republic became the second Latin American country to boast cellular mobile telephones; it was the only developing country in the hemisphere to offer this service to the public on a national basis. Codetel and other companies also offer telex, electronic mail, telenet, and facsimile services to the public. A member of the International Telecommunications Satellite Organization (Intelsat), the Dominican Republic possesses a satellite earth station, a submarine cable to the United States Virgin Islands, and microwave stations. In 1989 a fiber-optic cable to Puerto Rico was completed to expedite sophisticated data transmission to the United States.

Codetel invested about US$500 million in the first half of the 1990s to upgrade its systems; by the late 1990s, it had more than 3,000 international and 500,000 domestic lines in use not only in Santo Domingo but across much of the country. Codetel accounted for almost 95 percent of the market. Codetel also signed an agreement in late 1997 with Northern Telecom of Canada for further modernization of its systems. Its most aggressive competition for the Dominican market by the close of the 1990s was expected to come from a United States company, Tricom, which is 40 percent owned by Motorola and which has embarked on a five-year US$200-million expansion plan.

Tourism

The Dominican tourist industry grew tremendously during the 1970s and the 1980s and continued to do so in the 1990s—

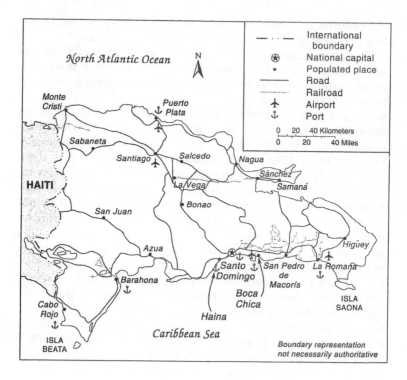

Figure 4. Dominican Republic: Transportation System, 1999

thanks to the passage in 1971 of the Tourist Incentive Law, which provided investors in tourism a ten-year tax holiday and an exemption from tariffs on imports not available locally. In 1979 the director of tourism was elevated to cabinet level, a further indication of official interest in and commitment to promoting the industry's growth. Besides its 1,400-kilometer coastline, one-third of which consists of beaches, the island also offers numerous appeals to tourists. Such attractions include the republic's inexpensive tourist accommodations and liberal divorce laws.

The number of tourists visiting the Dominican Republic almost tripled in ten years, increasing from 278,000 in 1975 to 792,000 in 1985. By 1987 the number of vacationers surpassed 1 million for the first time, and by 1997 the Dominican Republic was the second largest earner of tourism dollars in the Caribbean, behind Mexico. The country's foreign-exchange earnings from tourism also multiplied dramatically, increasing from US$430 million in 1986 to US$2.1 billion in 1997.

The tourist industry employed approximately 44,000 hotel workers in 1995; an additional 110,000 were indirectly employed by the sector. The rapid growth of tourism also had an impact on other industries, such as construction, transportation, and commerce as well as hotels, bars, and restaurants. The number of stopover tourists increased dramatically from some 850,000 in 1986 to 1,766,800 in 1994 to 1,930,000 in 1996 to 2,211,000 in 1997 (see table 9, Appendix). Most growth came from Europe, which provided about 58 percent of stopover tourists in 1997, compared with 9 percent from Canada and 23 percent from the United States. Each year during the 1980s, the United States had accounted for more than 50 percent of visitors. Stopover tourists usually stay at large hotels owned or managed by international chains from Germany, Italy, Japan, the United States, and Spain. The latter country accounts for 37 percent of Dominican hotel beds. The total number of hotel rooms available in the country was close to 40,000 in 1998, with approximately 13,000 in Puerto Plata, the island's leading resort on the north coast. Other resorts frequented by foreign tourists include Bavaro, El Cortecito, Higüey, and Punta Cana on the east coast.

Fortunately, the damage from Hurricane Georges in September 1998 affected only 5 percent of hotel rooms; the institutions affected were expected to be back in operation by December 1998. Although the number of visiting tourists continues to rise—by 15.3 percent in the first half of 1998—they are staying for shorter periods. This fact, combined with the construction of more hotel rooms, has led to lower hotel occupancy rates.

Foreign Economic Relations

Foreign Trade and Balance of Payments

Trade deficits continued to plague the Dominican Republic during the 1990s. The Dominican trade deficit exceeded US$2.7 billion in 1997 (see table 10, Appendix). The latest figures available (preliminary figures) from the Central Bank (BCRD) indicate that the trade deficit in the first half of 1998 was US$945 million. The sharp decline in world commodity prices triggered by the Asian currency crisis of 1997 undoubtedly had a strong negative impact on the Dominican Republic's

151

trade deficit. Exports of one of the country's major earners of foreign exchange, nickel, suffered a price drop of 27 percent in the first half of 1998. As a result, nickel exports fell 38.4 percent in 1998. Exports of coffee were adversely affected by a 10 percent decline in international prices. However, the price decline was offset by a 46.1 percent increase in production, which enabled coffee exports to equal their 1997 value. The 1997–98 coffee crop was one of the best in fifteen years, bringing in US$81 million from exports. Tobacco exports decreased 27.4 percent during 1998. The value of cocoa exports, however, increased by 46.1 percent as a result of world price rises and a greater volume of exports. The export of sugar and sugar products in 1998 decreased 29.6 percent as a result primarily of a 24.0 percent cut in the Dominican international sugar quota. Exports of other lesser or nontraditional products increased 7.2 percent in spite of a 20.3 percent decrease in fourth quarter production resulting from the damaging effects of Hurricane Georges. Thus, the overall decrease in value of national exports in 1998 was 12.7 percent that of 1997.

Perhaps the silver lining in the Asian crisis was the deep plunge in oil prices since 1997, which reduced the Dominican Republic's fuel bill by approximately 20 percent to US$336 million in the first half of 1998. Total domestic imports in 1998 amounted to US$7.6 billion, of which capital goods rose by 51.3 percent, and consumer goods increased by 19.3 percent. The 15 percent increase in the value of imports over 1997 is attributable in part to the effects of Hurricane Georges. Free-zone exports increased 14.0 percent, earning 18.6 percent more in 1998 than in 1997, largely the outcome of new enterprises opened in 1998. These factors kept the trade deficit from worsening.

In a measure designed to facilitate trade and improve its balance of payments, in August 1997, the Dominican Republic signed a trade agreement with the Caribbean Community and Common Market (Caricom—see Glossary). This agreement resembles the free-trade accord signed with the Central American Common Market (CACM) in April 1997 and is subject to a successful conclusion of negotiations over exemptions and liberalization of capital and labor flows between the Dominican Republic and Caricom. The two agreements aim at establishing the Dominican Republic as a bridge for promoting trade links between the Caribbean and Central America. In the late 1990s, for example, Haiti bought more than 75 percent of Dominican

Unloading lumber, port of Haina
Courtesy Inter-American Development Bank

exports to the Caribbean. The agreements would also put the Dominican Republic in a favorable position to benefit from foreign investment generated by the special agreements that the CACM and Caricom maintain with the United States and the European Union (EU).

In September 1998, Hurricane Georges cut a devastating path across the Dominican Republic, leaving about 300 persons dead, hundreds of thousands of homeless, and economic damage estimated at US$1.3 billion (8 percent of GDP). It severely damaged farming and livestock production, with total losses estimated at US$400 million during 1998–99. It also affected tourism and such key exports as sugar, coffee, cocoa, tobacco, and fruit. The government's preliminary damage assessments put the cost of repairs to basic public-sector infrastructure and low-income housing at more than US$400 million (2.5 percent of GDP).

A month later, the IMF approved the government's request for financial assistance equivalent to one-fourth of the Dominican Republic's special drawing rights (SDRs—see Glossary) quota, approximately US$56 million. The support of the Dominican government's economic adjustment program and associated rehabilitation efforts is part of the IMF policy on emergency assistance related to natural disasters.

In their request for IMF assistance, the Dominican Secretary of State for Finance and the Governor of the Central Bank said their country's adjustment policies would press ahead with a structural reform agenda including trade liberalization, reduction of inflation, pension reform, and legislation regarding tax and tariff reform. Also included was the conclusion of free-trade agreements with Central American and Caribbean countries. The officials warned that the most significant effect on the balance of payments would come from a surge in imports related to the reconstruction effort, estimated at a total of US$700 million through 1999. They promised not to introduce or intensify existing trade restrictions for balance of payments purposes. Instead, they would seek to defray construction costs by such additional measures as cutting salaries of public-sector employees by 5 to 10 percent, increasing selective consumption taxes, and requesting extensions of payment periods from bilateral creditors.

Foreign Assistance

The Inter-American Development Bank, the World Bank, and the European Union are the major multilateral aid donors to the Dominican Republic. In spite of its contentious relationship with the island nation, the IMF also has been a significant contributor. The EU has been involved only since 1990, when the Dominican Republic acceded to the Lomé Convention (see Glossary), making it eligible for EU assistance. The first protocol of 1990–95 allotted it RD$1,256 million, and the second protocol (1995–2000) increased its allocation to RD$1,565 million.

The United States and Japan are the largest bilateral donors. Other important donors include Italy, Germany, and Canada. The level of United States assistance, which dates back to the early 1960s, has tended to fluctuate widely in response to economic and political trends. It reached US$99.7 million in 1966, one of the highest levels in the region, in the aftermath of the United States occupation (see table 11, Appendix). Aid levels dropped considerably in the 1970s, however, averaging only US$18.13 million a year from 1970 through 1979. The United States Agency for International Development (USAID) augmented its program in the country during the 1980s until its assistance level averaged US$81 million a year for the decade from 1980 through 1989.

The 1990s brought a significant shift of emphasis in USAID's program priorities and strategic plans. USAID's heavy emphasis on development assistance in the 1980s gradually but consistently decreased over the years, dropping from a high of US$34.6 million in 1980 to US$18 million in 1990 to US$11 million in 1997. For a number of years, development assistance was reinforced by substantial Economic Support Funds (ESF) and Public Law–480 (PL–480—see Glossary) food aid programs. It appeared that USAID concern over the Dominican Republic's overwhelming incidence of poverty, continuing lack of economic opportunity, and social injustice led the agency to reallocate its reduced funding toward support for social-sector activities. Health and education programs, for example, accounted for 67 percent of its 1996 resources.

In outlining its five-year strategic plan for 1997–2000, USAID makes the point that "after years of keeping its distance from the government and implementing activities primarily through local NGOs (nongovernmental organizations)," one aim of its latest plan is to strengthen cooperative relations with the government in order to address long-neglected social sectors and deal with poverty issues. The country's rampant poverty (the poorest 50 percent of the population receives less than 20 percent of total income, while the richest 10 percent receives 42 percent) is caused and exacerbated by poor governance, social injustice, and extremely low social spending. Dominican public social investment is much lower than world and Latin American averages. USAID success in working directly with NGOs seems to have encouraged other donors to turn to the same organizations to help fill gaps in public services such as health, family planning, and acquired immune deficiency syndrome (AIDS) prevention. USAID's renewed cooperative relationship with such government agencies as the Secretariat of State for Public Health and Social Welfare and the Technical Secretariat of the Presidency and its Planning Office should strengthen its posture as a catalyst vis-à-vis other donors and result in better coordination.

Outlook

The disturbing aspect of the Dominican Republic's economy is that although its positive growth rate, especially in the 1990s after the sharp deterioration of the 1970s and 1980s, seems to be impressive, the economy leaves an observer with an uncomfortable feeling about how uneven it is. When various sectors are viewed separately, several appear to be doing very well. Tourism comes to mind immediately, not only because of its spectacular growth but also because of its positive impact on other industries such as construction and commerce. Free-trade zones and telecommunications are other examples of Dominican success. The aggregate of the separate components, however, seems to be unrelated to a central theme and fails to add to a cohesive whole. Perhaps other economic sectors are hobbled by a corrupt political structure, an unjust social system, outmoded institutions, flawed policies, inefficient state enterprises, or a much more basic societal malady such as poverty.

The Foundation for Economics and Development (Fondación Economía y Desarrollo—FED), a nonprofit, private economic research institute, estimates that about 21 percent of Dominicans live in poverty, surviving on less than US$1 a day. More than 20 percent of the island's families lack the income required to meet standard nutritional requirements. Approximately 65 percent of the population in rural areas lacks access to potable water and about 25 percent lacks electricity. Health, water supply, sanitation, education, and housing deficiencies affect a significant proportion of the population, with the result that the Dominican Republic trails all its neighbors in the region, with the exception of Haiti and Guyana. Historically, the level of social spending has been one of the lowest in the hemisphere, and successive administrations have cut back appropriations to the poorest elements of the population. Flawed economic policies such as protectionism and state monopolies that unfairly raise the price of basic commodities have also added disproportionately to the burden of the poor. It is estimated that the poor spend up to 45 percent of their income on protected food commodities such as rice, which costs at least twice as much as the price on world markets.

The Dominican Republic lacks a focal point that would coordinate development projects among all parties concerned—government, foreign donors, and private organizations (including businesses). The country's leadership—executive, congressional, or judiciary—needs to commit to the implementation of social programs. That the largest aid donor had to "keep its distance from the government" for years speaks volumes about the government's withdrawal and lack of serious commitment. That USAID was able to implement 85 percent of its program through private organizations is a healthy sign, especially about private initiative, but it does not compensate for full-fledged governmental participation. The lack of government participation should not be seen as an excuse for the complete dependence on the government as the engine of economic development, as occurred in the past. The government, however, must strengthen the agencies responsible for designing reform measures and delivering services to the people. Congress must be included in the process as well because after years of being largely ignored, it has become a vocal player in the country's budget and reform programs (see The Legislature, ch. 4). The judiciary also must become involved if only because it has been a key constraint to implementation of much-needed reform. Continued participation by private organizations and businesses will, of course, always be needed. Only the combination of all these ingredients will enable the Dominican Republic to effect a more equitable public resource allocation and increase funding for badly needed social programs.

*   *   *

The USAID mission in Santo Domingo is a good source of information on the general condition of the economy of the Dominican Republic. USAID reports on various aspects of the international community's development efforts in the Dominican Republic also are useful, although they tend to emphasize areas in which the mission is involved. USAID also credits many private voluntary organizations operating in the Dominican Republic and with which it cooperates closely. Another good source is the Foreign Commercial Service of the United States Department of Commerce, which prepares the Country Commercial Guide for each nation.

The Dominican Republic's Banco Central de la República Dominicana and, only since the late 1990s, the Secretariat of State for Tourism, as well as the IMF and the World Bank, are useful sources of statistical data. Those interested in following the Dominican Republic's economic development on a regular basis should consult the Economist Intelligence Unit's annual and quarterly reports. (For further information and complete citations, see Bibliography.)

Chapter 4. Dominican Republic: Government and Politics

View of the Alcázar de Colón, the home of Spanish governor Diego Columbus

THE DOMINICAN REPUBLIC IN the late 1990s could be considered a political democracy, albeit one that remained fragile and uninstitutionalized. This chapter focuses on contemporary issues and patterns in the country's government and politics. It briefly reviews the emergence of democratic politics in the country, examines the country's system of government and political institutions, analyzes the major political and socioeconomic actors, and discusses major issues in foreign relations.

Three major themes are underscored. First, the discussion notes that various historical, socioeconomic, and international factors have been unfavorable to the development of democracy in the country, although dramatic changes have taken place over the past several decades. Second, this historical experience is crucial to understanding how the country's system of government comprises both formal rules (such as the constitution and elections) and informal norms often at variance with the formal rules. The formal rules have frequently been ignored, manipulated, or changed by political actors as part of the struggle for power. Informal norms regarding both the use of the state for personal power and accumulation of wealth and the invocation of formal rules have often been more important. Following Max Weber, we may say that these norms reflect patrimonial politics, where a ruler governs a country as if it were simply an extension of his household, thus blurring public purposes and private interests. Typically, this type of ruler seeks to reduce the autonomy of his followers through complex ties of dependence and loyalty commonly involving patronage and clientelist ties. The third theme is that, as a consequence, the struggle for political democracy in the country has been a struggle not only for greater respect for civil liberties and political rights of the population as a whole, but also for the construction of a more coherent and accountable set of state and political institutions, with greater respect for a democratic rule of law.

Historical Legacies of Authoritarian Rule

The Dominican Republic has had a tragic history particularly inimical to the development of democratic politics. This fact is evident in the country's Spanish colonial experience, which was followed in the nineteenth century by foreign invasion and occupation by neighboring Haiti, a brief reoccupation by Spain, numerous civil wars, and economic ruin. These factors inhibited the possibility of national integration or the construction of a viable central state. As a result, the country experienced considerable political instability even as all early efforts to extend liberal rule in the country failed. According to Dominican historian Mu-Kien Sang, between 1840 and 1900 the Dominican Republic had fifty-six governments, of which only four comprised administrations that were able to complete their constitutional period; furthermore, seventeen individuals governed for less than a year, and 271 rebellions or armed uprisings occurred. The country ended the nineteenth century with the increasingly despotic seventeen-year rule of Ulises Heureaux (1882–99); his assassination, in turn, led to a renewed period of tremendous upheaval, aggravating the country's debt problems. Into the twentieth century, the country was marked by a weak church, insecure economic elites, and the absence of an effective national military institution, as well as by high levels of poverty and low levels of social or political organization.

The turn of the century was also marked by increasing dependence on the United States, which ultimately led to the United States occupation of 1916–24. This occupation in turn, through its establishment of a constabulary force with Rafael Trujillo Molina at its head and its improvements in the country's transportation and communications infrastructure, helped set the stage for the rise and the consolidation in power of Trujillo in 1930 (see The Trujillo Era, 1930–61, ch. 1). Trujillo governed the country from 1930 to 1961; during that time, he built a state and constructed a nation, although his methods were brutal and his discourse racist. Under Trujillo, there was seemingly complete respect for the forms of democracy. The country had a congress, a judiciary, regular elections, and the formal passage of laws, but these institutions were a meaningless charade carefully manipulated by Trujillo. His massive economic holdings, which became state patrimony upon his death, evolved into major economic liabilities for the country. In addition, Trujillo's political style of centralization of power, cynical manipulation of individuals, and constitutional hypocrisy had a profoundly negative impact on the country's political culture.

A successful transition to democracy following the death of Trujillo in 1961 faced numerous obstacles given the extent and nature of Trujillo's domination of the island republic. The military was essentially Trujillo's personal instrument, no independent societal organizations existed (with the partial exception of the Roman Catholic Church), and no political opposition was countenanced. Furthermore, the country was relatively poor, rural, and isolated. Yet, in part because of the involvement of the United States, democracy advanced further in the nation at this time than might have been expected based on the country's history and the legacies of the Trujillo era. In the period before and after Trujillo's assassination, the United States once again became deeply enmeshed in Dominican internal affairs, motivated both by anticommunist objectives (which remained central) and a desire to promote democracy. An initial result was a surprisingly successful democratic election in 1962, with the victory of Juan Bosch Gaviño and his Dominican Revolutionary Party (Partido Revolucionario Dominicano—PRD). However, Bosch was overthrown after only seven months in office by a coalition of conservative social and political forces and the military; because of Cold War fears about communism and concerns about the nature of Bosch's leadership (including the belief that Bosch himself was not sufficiently anticommunist), the United States did not forthrightly defend his government.

Following Bosch's overthrow, the country entered a deeply tumultuous period, marked in 1965 by a brief civil war and United States intervention that originated in an exaggerated fear of a "second Cuba" in the Western Hemisphere. The United States arranged the formation of a provisional government and the holding of elections in 1966. These elections were won by Joaquín Balaguer Ricardo, a prominent figure from the Trujillo era, and his Reformist Party (Partido Reformista—PR). Balaguer handily defeated a dejected Bosch, who ran a desultory campaign. Balaguer was to become the dominant figure of Dominican politics for the next three decades, serving as president from 1966 to 1978 and again from 1986 to 1996.

Under Balaguer, patrimonial politics emerged once more, although Balaguer never sought or achieved the degree of personal control that Trujillo had attained. Balaguer was an astute politician with an astounding drive for power. He was willing to be ruthless if necessary, but not over-eager to employ repression and violence. He emphasized themes of order and stability, and he continued to link Dominican nationalism to what he viewed as its Hispanic, Roman Catholic essence and to anti-Haitian themes. He was both a realist about power politics and a conservative nationalist; he recognized the overwhelming reality of the United States presence, but retained a certain disdain for that country and its leaders. Although he was willing to take United States aid, Balaguer had conservative instincts and a nationalist interpretation of Dominican history that led him generally to be, like Trujillo, a fiscal conservative.

During the period from 1966 to 1978, Balaguer governed in an authoritarian fashion. In both 1970 and 1974, in the face of open military harassment, most opposition forces opted to abstain from participation in elections. In 1973 Bosch—skeptical about liberal democracy and critical of the United States—left the PRD to found the more radical cadre-oriented Party of Dominican Liberation (Partido de la Liberación Dominicana—PLD). In 1976, however, in the face of growing United States pressure, mounting economic problems, and increasing domestic discontent, Balaguer began a process of political liberalization. Meanwhile, the PRD sought to moderate its image within the country, build support across all social sectors, and strengthen its international ties. All this set the stage for Balaguer's electoral defeat in 1978 and a transition to democracy.

The Contemporary Struggle for Democracy

The Dominican Revolutionary Party (PRD) came into office in 1978 as a party committed to strengthening democracy and fostering reform. However, the party's eight years in office were ultimately to be a disappointment. The PRD's most significant achievement was that one major threat to democracy, that of military incursion into politics, receded considerably, beginning in 1978 when President Silvestre Antonio Guzmán Fernández forcibly removed high military officers favorable to Balaguer. Even when Balaguer returned to power in 1986, the military never regained the level of importance or of influence it had had during his first twelve years in office.

In other respects, however, PRD administrations were not as successful. The Guzmán administration (1978–82) was limited in its reform agenda because it faced a Senate controlled by Balaguer's party and then experienced growing intraparty rivalry in the PRD. Initial hopes that the administration of Salvador Jorge Blanco (1982–86) could be an important example

President Joaquín Balaguer visits military installations.
Courtesy United States Department of Defense

of a less personalist, more institutional, reformist presidency
fell short as well under the impact of the country's economic
crisis. The situation was a result of the world oil crisis, executive-congressional deadlock now driven by intraparty factionalism, and the reassertion of patrimonialism from the
presidency.

By the end of Jorge Blanco's term, the PRD was a factional-
ized organization that had been forced to oversee a brutal economic adjustment and that was facing widespread accusations
of corruption and mismanagement. Although civil liberties
had generally been respected, there were no significant
advances in democratic institutionalization or participation
nor were there reforms of a social or economic nature during
the PRD years. Rather than leaving a legacy of lasting political
and economic changes implemented by a social-democratic
party, the PRD rule had continued patronage politics. Jorge
Blanco's government faced wrenching economic problems,
and its attempt to stabilize the economy involved extensive
negotiations with the International Monetary Fund (IMF—see
Glossary) and other international creditors. The situation led
to bitter party wrangling and the eventual division of the PRD.

Economic decline and divisions within the PRD paved the way for 'he unexpected presidential comeback of Joaquín Balaguer in 1986. A loyal electorate, especially older, less educated, rural, and female voters, and splits within and between the opposition parties permitted Balaguer to win the 1986 elections. Aided, it was charged, by electoral fraud, Balaguer was able to eke out narrow victories in 1990 and 1994 as well.

The 1990 elections were marred by irregularities and charges of fraud, as the eighty-three-year-old incumbent Balaguer edged out his eighty-year-old opponent, Juan Bosch, by a mere 24,470 votes. With the PRD still recovering from its factional strife, José Francisco Peña Gómez came in a surprisingly strong third place. The 1994 elections were even more crisis-ridden than those of 1990 because of an extremely tense and bitter campaign between Balaguer and Peña Gómez. When thousands of voters were prevented from voting because their names did not appear on electoral rolls, domestic protest and international pressure led to a drawn-out crisis. Between 1994 and 1996, the political efforts of opposition parties, Dominican civil society (including substantial elements of the business community), and the international community (the United States in particular) focused on how to secure the holding of fair elections in 1996 and how to block any effort by Balaguer to extend his term in office, either unconstitutionally or by modifying the constitution. The crisis was finally resolved when Balaguer agreed to reduce his term to two years and accept a number of constitutional reforms, including a prohibition on immediate presidential reelection. As a consequence, the eighty-eight-year-old Balaguer finally left the presidency in 1996, handing power over to the PLD's Leonel Fernández Reyna, whom Balaguer had tacitly supported and then openly endorsed (age and illness had led to Bosch's retirement in 1994).

The 1996 elections proceeded according to strict guidelines. In 1996, unlike the previous two elections, presidential reelection was not an issue, and the Central Electoral Board was staffed by professional nonpartisans. Furthermore, in addition to the oversight provided by several high-profile .nissions of international observers, civil society mobilized far more extensively in support of free and fair elections than it had done in the past.

The 1996 elections were held under new rules requiring a second-round election if no candidate received more than 50 percent of the votes in the first round. With a renewed PRD under his tight leadership, Peña Gómez performed well. However, he only gained 45.9 percent of the vote. He was followed by Leonel Fernández of the PLD with 38.9 percent, and Jacinto Peynado of the Reformist Social Christian Party (Partido Reformista Social Cristiano—PRSC) with 15 percent. Balaguer did not endorse his party's candidate (indeed, he did not even vote in the first round), instead providing his implicit support to Fernández during the first round. For the second round, Balaguer and the PRSC officially endorsed the candidacy of Leonel Fernández in a "Patriotic Pact" calling for the preservation of national sovereignty and Dominicanness, against the candidacy of Peña Gómez. Fernández defeated Peña Gómez in the second round.

Fernández obtained the presidency, but his party had a very small representation in Congress as a result of its poor performance in the 1994 elections. The new electoral calendar established by the 1994 reform meant that congressional elections would now be held at the midpoint of the presidential term. And, soon after Fernández's electoral victory, the PRSC negotiated a pact with the PRD to secure leadership positions in Congress.

Without congressional support, the Fernández administration has faced serious difficulties in obtaining the passage of a number of desired reforms, although some progress has been made on a number of important fronts. The legislative attempt to reform the economy in late 1996 failed when Congress refused to agree on a set of policy proposals to liberalize the economy, including lower tariffs and a higher value-added tax. Congressional deadlock prevented an agreement over the national budget for 1997, which led President Fernández to withdraw the budget bill from Congress and use the 1996 budget agreement to apply in 1997, as stipulated by the constitution when no agreement is reached between the executive and the legislative branches over revenues and expenditures.

Yet, Fernández has governed in a more democratic and institutional fashion than Balaguer, without renouncing the use of patronage or clientelist mechanisms. Some important legislative measures also have been approved to which he can point. Furthermore, the country has been able to maintain high rates of economic growth with moderate inflation, and the state has modestly expanded its investments in education, health, and housing.

With regard to greater respect for democratic institutions, several important successes occurred during Fernández's first three years in office. One has to do with improvements in the judicial branch. A crucial step was the appointment of a new Supreme Court composed of distinguished jurists in a much more open process through a Council of the Magistrature established by the constitutional reform of 1994. This Supreme Court has sought to review and improve the qualifications of judges throughout the country. In August 1998, Congress also approved a law establishing a judicial career service; the implementation of such a career service is expected to further professionalize and improve the judiciary. Another success was the fact that the congressional and municipal elections held on May 16, 1998, were viewed as free and fair, although the results were disappointing for Fernández. The death of PRD leader Peña Gómez a week before the elections probably helped the PRD win by an even wider margin than expected; with 51.4 percent of the vote, the PRD gained twenty-four of thirty Senate seats, and eighty-three of 149 Chamber of Deputies' seats. The PLD won 30.4 percent of the vote, winning only four Senate seats and forty-nine Chamber seats (sufficient to permit it to uphold a presidential veto). The PRSC, in turn, continued its decline, winning only 16.8 percent of the vote, and electing two senators and seventeen representatives.

As a result of the election, President Fernández was completing his term with continued strong opposition in Congress. In the course of 1999, both the PRD and the PLD were able to choose presidential candidates without causing party splits, even as the PRSC remained beholden to its now nonagenarian leader, Joaquín Balaguer. As of November 1999, the May 2000 presidential elections appeared to be polarized between Hipólito Mejía, the candidate of the PRD, and Danilo Medina, the candidate of the PLD. As neither appeared able to attain a majority in the first round, both were courting Balaguer and the PRSC for potential support in the second round. Thus, the state of the country's political parties (especially the PRSC) and the party system remained in flux as the country prepared for the challenges of the next century.

System of Government

Especially in the period since 1978, the Dominican Republic has had important experiences with democratic politics. At the same time, democracy has been marred by the weakness of institutions and formal rules, including flawed and sometimes fraudulent elections. Democratization also has been hindered by the lack of sustained progress in strengthening a more democratic and plural civil society, democratizing political institutions, and making state institutions more coherent and more accountable.

To understand the system of government in the Dominican Republic, as well as some of the major challenges political democracy confronts, it is crucial to understand the formal rules as defined by the constitution and electoral and other key laws. It is equally important to understand the informal norms, legacies of patrimonial politics, and strong-man rule under which politics has operated. Laws and legal procedures have often been ignored, manipulated, or changed in the pursuit of power and of policy, including in negotiations to facilitate political transitions or to control the military.

This tension between the formal rules and the informal norms of politics was especially evident during the presidential periods of Balaguer, even when he governed in a somewhat more democratic fashion during the 1986–96 period. Over time, there has been a growing demand from the institutional voices of business and from elements of civil society, particularly those representing middle-sector groups, for a change in this political style. Such elements seek a greater respect for institutionality and the rule of law, both within the state and within political parties. Dominican business people and civil society in general have increasingly recognized that effective citizenship requires reductions in severe poverty and marked inequality as well as improvements in education and health.

Yet, for various reasons, movement away from the informal norms of patrimonial, clientelist politics has been difficult, and much remains to be done. Even presidents who may not have entered office intending to foster these norms have often employed or succumbed to them. Many politicians across all the major parties have continued to pursue political office as much for personal or narrow parochial gain as for the pursuit of ideological or policy goals. Given high levels of poverty, weak societal organizations, and the country's historical patterns, many of the politicians' followers expect them to satisfy demands in a personalist, clientelist fashion, rather than in an institutional, impersonal one. Even as business organizations encourage reform and many companies largely respect the rules, other firms have grown accustomed to operating in an informal environment and deriving profit from it. And, many groups in civil society have also responded more to clientelist modes of politics than to more participatory, democratic ones.

The Evolution of Constitutional Doctrine

Liberal ideas did not penetrate deeply into the country in the nineteenth century. Constitutions and formal legal institutions were often either ignored or given ex post facto rationalizations; such documents and institutions kept liberal doctrines alive but at the cost of hypocrisy and cynicism. The Dominican Republic appears to fit the general pattern in Latin America in that the number of constitutions correlates inversely with a country's democratic experience. Having had practically no democratic history until well into the second half of the twentieth century, the country has, nevertheless, experienced a substantial number of new constitutions and other modifications. As was the case in other authoritarian countries, in the Dominican Republic the adoption of a new constitution, especially in the late nineteenth century, often reflected an authoritarian leader's effort to legitimize or extend his rule. This pattern was to continue well into the twentieth century. However, at times, as elsewhere on the continent, new constitutions in the Dominican Republic also were generated during democratic "turning points," although these tended to be short-lived. Thus, for nearly all of Dominican history, unconstitutional regimes have used constitutionalism to augment their claims to legitimacy rather than employing them to establish general "rules of the game" to which they or other major power holders in the society would commit themselves. At the same time, reformers and democratic leaders sought to generate liberal constitutional texts and to live by them.

The country's first constitution in 1844 was a remarkably liberal document. It was influenced directly by the Haitian constitution of 1843 and indirectly by the United States Constitution of 1789, the liberal 1812 Cadiz Constitution of Spain, and the French constitutions of 1799 and 1804. Because of these influences, the 1844 constitution called for presidentialism, separation of powers, and extensive "checks and balances." But its liberal nature was to be short-lived. General Pedro Santana, claiming that the legislative restrictions on the executive were excessive in a period of war, forced the Constitutional Assembly to add an article granting the president extraordinary powers. Also, although the constitution did not permit immediate presidential reelection, the Assembly elected Santana to two consecutive terms. These actions initiated a pattern in which a strong executive imposed constitutional hypocrisy; careful attention to form went hand in hand with violation of the substance of democratic process and rights.

Genuine efforts to put in place more liberal constitutions that restricted centralized, authoritarian power continued, however. Thus, an even more liberal constitution was prepared in 1854. It, too, was almost immediately modified to vitiate it of an effective legislative check on executive authority: all control over the armed forces was placed directly in the hands of the president. Later in 1854, an essentially authoritarian constitutional text was enacted because Santana, eager to ensure himself even more constitutional authority, successfully pressured the Congress for the change. The change reduced Congress from two chambers to a single, seven-member Senate that was to meet only three months a year; moreover, the president could suspend civil and political rights if deemed necessary. Meanwhile, the country soon descended into a lengthy civil war in which figures from the Cibao region emerged victorious. In 1858 in Moca, an even more liberal and democratic constitutional text was enacted, although, as in 1854, it was never implemented. For the first time in the country's history, however, the constitution called for direct elections for major elected posts; it also prohibited presidential reelection, decentralized authority, and prohibited the death penalty for political crimes.

From the enactment of a Dominican constitution in 1865, following the forced departure of the Spanish, until the United States military entered the country in 1916, sixteen additional constitutional changes took place. Most of these were associated with a change in leadership or with an effort by a leader to provide a legal cover for the extension of his term in office. Yet, they also represented a struggle between the two different constitutional traditions represented by the constitutions of 1854 and 1858. Thus, when Buenaventura Báez Méndez and the Red Party (Partido Rojo) took power in 1865, they forced the Congress to enact a more authoritarian text, in imitation of that of 1854; when Báez was overthrown a year later, a more liberal text was decreed. In turn, when Báez resumed the presidency in 1868, a constitutional shift again occurred. Constitutional changes occurred each year from 1874 to 1879 reflecting the revolts and changes in government that took place. The pattern continued in the next decade, when the leader of the Blue Party (Partido Azul), Gregorio Luperón, called for a National Convention to enact a new liberal constitution. The new constitution was enacted in 1880. This text, in turn, was reformed three more times before the end of the century (in 1881, 1887, and 1897). In 1907 and 1908, political changes were once again associated with constitutional modifications. By 1880, however, the liberal constitutional *doctrine*, although not the practice, had emerged triumphant.

Constitutional manipulation and hypocrisy continued in the twentieth century, particularly during Trujillo's period in power, when seven constitutional reforms occurred. There was formal obedience to constitutional and electoral requirements, although neither Congress nor the courts were autonomous, the population had no basic rights, and election results were carefully orchestrated. For example, in response to international pressure for democratization following the end of World War II, Trujillo permitted two regime-sponsored opposition parties to run in the 1947 elections; each officially received a similar vote of just under 4 percent of the total, which was carefully distributed so that each could win exactly one deputy seat.

In 1963, following his decisive victory in the presidential elections and his comfortable majority in Congress, Bosch decided to proceed with a significant revision of the country's constitution. The new constitution was promulgated in May 1963. In many ways, the constitution, which included prohibition of presidential reelection, was a model democratic text. However, it drew sharp attacks from conservative and business forces because it curtailed some of the traditional rights of the church and foresaw the possibility of expropriation of property and control of foreign investment. One of the first actions by the military that overthrew Bosch was to declare the new constitution "nonexistent." In turn, over the next several years Bosch sought to "return to constitutional power without elections," ultimately setting the stage for the 1965 conflict between "constitutionalist" and "loyalist" forces that led to the United States intervention.

Following his inauguration as president, Balaguer proceeded to enact a new constitution through Congress. The November 1966 constitution (with important modifications made in 1994) is the text under which the country's democracy currently operates. The new text enhanced presidential powers and permitted unlimited presidential reelection (until 1994), while removing material objectionable to church and business interests.

The Executive

Within the Dominican Republic, the 1966 constitution is widely viewed as giving the president extraordinary powers (see fig. 5). Although the formal powers of the president are fairly extensive, in fact they are more limited than in several other Latin American countries, given the absence of extensive decree powers, constitutional budgetary powers, a partial veto, and the ability to force referenda.

The president has often been perceived as having near-dictatorial powers because of the willingness of some incumbents, particularly Balaguer, to abuse the powers of their office in the absence of effective checks from the legislature or the judiciary. In doing so, such incumbents built upon historical patterns of patrimonialism and strong-man rule that had gained a degree of support in society. Thus, Balaguer and, to a much lesser extent, other presidents during this period assumed vast informal (and sometimes unconstitutional) powers to create taxes, set budgets by decree, spend money, and ignore numerous laws. In contrast, when presidents have sought to govern in a fashion that is more democratic and more respectful of the other branches of government, such as is largely the case with Leonel Fernández Reyna, who has governed with only minority support in Congress and with a more independent judiciary, their power has appeared more limited and constrained.

The constitution vests executive power in a president who is elected by direct popular vote and whose term of office is four years. Until 1994 nothing in the constitution prohibited a president from seeking reelection. Balaguer was reelected in 1970 and in 1974; following defeats in 1978 and 1982, he was elected again to the presidency in 1986. He was reelected in 1990 and again in 1994. Well-documented allegations of fraud, however, led to international pressure and an internal political crisis that was finally resolved by negotiation and constitutional reform: Balaguer's presidential term was shortened to two years, and the constitution was amended to prohibit immediate presidential reelection. The 1994 reform also introduced a mandatory second round among the top two vote getters in presidential elections if no candidate received a majority of the votes cast in the first round.

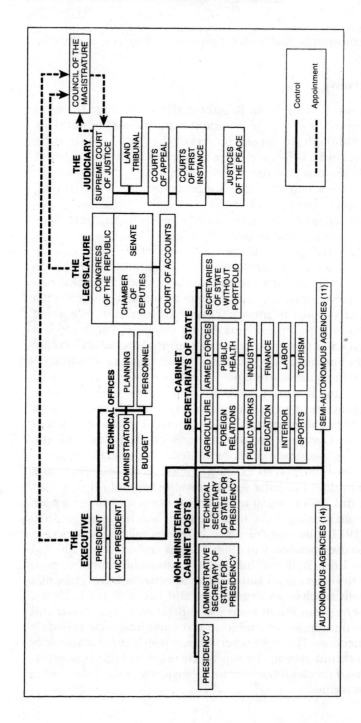

Figure 5. Dominican Republic: Structure of the Government, 1999

The constitution requires that presidential candidates be Dominican citizens by birth or origin, at least thirty years old, and in possession of all political and civil rights. A candidate cannot have been a member of the military or the police for at least one year prior to election. Vice presidential candidates must meet the same qualifications. The vice president may assume the office of president when the chief executive is ill, outside the country, or otherwise unable to perform the duties of the office. If the president dies or becomes permanently unable to carry out the functions of the office, the vice president serves until the next scheduled election. If the vice president is also unable to fill the office, the president of the Supreme Court serves temporarily. Within fifteen days, the president of the Supreme Court must convene the National Assembly (which consists of both houses of the Congress), which must then select a substitute to fill out the term.

The Dominican constitution takes twenty-seven paragraphs in Article 55 to spell out the president's extensive powers. Among the most important are those that grant the president authority over almost all appointments and removals of public officials and that empower him to promulgate the laws passed by Congress; to engage in diplomatic relations; to command, deploy, and make appointments in the armed forces; and to extend pardons. The president also has the right to declare a state of siege or a state of national emergency when Congress is not in session, and to assume special emergency powers against unions and strikes in the face of threats to public order or state security. Historically, the exercise of these emergency powers usually has been the prelude to dictatorship. The few limitations the constitution places on presidential authority focus primarily on the requirement that the president obtain congressional consent to certain appointments, treaty negotiations, and the exercise of emergency powers. In recent years, perhaps the most important constraint on the executive has been the constitutional provision that certain contracts, including foreign assistance loans from international financial institutions, require congressional approval.

The constitution of 1966 provides for cabinet secretaries of state and subcabinet secretaries of state to assist in public administration. These officials must be Dominican citizens, at least twenty-five years of age, with full civil and political rights. The powers of these officials are determined by law and are not set forth in the constitution. However, the president is constitutionally responsible for the actions of such officials. Secretaries of state serve at the president's discretion, can be removed by the president, and function both as administrators of their secretariats and as agents of presidential authority.

The extent to which presidents have sought to employ the cabinet as a functioning executive body to organize and implement policy has varied considerably. Balaguer rotated individuals in and out of such cabinet positions with great frequency and sometimes appointed people with little relevant background; he also granted the rank of secretary of state to large numbers of individuals other than cabinet ministers. Thus, alongside the formal bureaucratic structure of the state and cabinet with its constant rotation of office-holders, there were the informal cliques of Balaguer's true confidants. The governments of the PRD and of the PLD differed from this pattern, while still retaining a high degree of personalism, and, in the case of Silvestre Antonio Guzmán Fernández, nepotism.

The Legislature

The 1966 constitution confers all legislative powers on the Congress of the Republic, which consists of a Senate and a Chamber of Deputies. The election of senators and deputies is by direct vote every four years. Until 1994 congressional terms were coterminous with presidential terms. This fact greatly increased the possibility that the president's party would enjoy a majority in the legislature, particularly in the Senate. As a consequence of the 1994 constitutional reform that called for new presidential elections—but not congressional or local ones—in 1996, the electoral calendar now separates presidential elections by two years from elections for congressional and local-level positions. This nonconcurrent timing decreases the likelihood that a president will have majority support in Congress. Under Balaguer the possession of such majorities, at least in the Senate, permitted not only the use but also the abuse of presidential power. However, as a result of the 1994 reform, the country faces the opposing risk of potential deadlock and ungovernability because of executive-legislative confrontation between a minority administration and a Congress dominated by opposition parties.

One senator is elected from each of the country's provinces and from the National District (Santo Domingo); in 1998 the Dominican Senate had thirty members (see fig. 2). This electoral rule provides for significant rural overrepresentation in the Senate. Deputies also represent provinces, but their seats are appointed on the basis of population. According to the constitution, there should be one deputy for each 50,000 inhabitants in a province, with no fewer than two per province; in reality, adjustments based on census figures have often been delayed. Nevertheless, the more populous provinces and the National District do have larger delegations. In 1998 there were 149 representatives in the Chamber of Deputies, forty-four of whom came from the National District of Santo Domingo. An electoral law approved in 1997 (Law 275–97) calls for the creation of single-member electoral districts in the larger provinces of between 25,001 and 50,000 inhabitants, beginning with the elections of 2002.

Deputies and senators must be Dominican citizens, at least twenty-five years old, with full civil and political rights. They must be natives or residents for at least five years of the province they wish to represent. Naturalized citizens are eligible to run for Congress if they have been Dominican citizens for ten years. Senators and deputies are not allowed to hold another public office concurrently.

The Senate and Chamber of Deputies may meet together as the National Assembly on certain specific occasions cited by the constitution—for example, when both the president and vice president are unable to complete their terms of office and a successor must be designated, or in order to amend the constitution itself. By a three-fourths vote, the Chamber of Deputies may bring accusations against public officials before the Senate, but it has no other exclusive powers. In contrast, the Senate has several exclusive powers. These currently include: choosing the president and members of the Central Electoral Board, electing the members of the Controller's Office, approving diplomatic appointments made by the president, and hearing cases of public misconduct brought before it by the Chamber of Deputies, with removal possible with a three-fourths vote. As a result of the 1994 constitutional reform, the Senate lost an important prerogative it previously had had, the appointment of judges to the Supreme Court (see The Judiciary, this ch.).

The Congress has broad powers to levy taxes, change the country's political subdivisions, declare a state of emergency, regulate immigration, approve or reject extraordinary expenditures requested by the executive, legislate on all matters concerning the public debt, examine annually all the acts of the executive, interrogate members of the cabinet, and legislate on all matters not within the constitutional mandate of other branches of government or contrary to the constitution. By a two-thirds vote of the full membership in each chamber, the Congress can also override a presidential veto of a law previously approved by simple majority.

Historically, the Dominican Congress has been a weak, submissive branch. Its facilities, staffing, offices, and library have been woefully inadequate; in addition, the Court of Accounts, which examines the country's finances and reports to the Congress, has not provided complete or timely information. In the past several years, some modest steps toward improvement have been taken. Because the selection of candidates to the party lists has been determined by party leaders, legislators have tended to be more responsive to these leaders than to voters. Turnover has been extremely high: from 1970 to 1998, only 18 percent of incumbent senators and only 17 percent of incumbent deputies were reelected to a subsequent term. The turnover has further encouraged legislative weakness and executive predominance. Many legislators have seen their position in Congress as temporarily providing them with an opportunity to focus on issues of personal and parochial gain, rather than on broader ideological or policy issues. The high turnover has also tended to discourage emphasis on building up the institution of the Congress itself. Finally, because the judicial branch until very recently has also tended to be extremely submissive to the executive branch, there has been little the legislature could actually do to prevent abuse of power by the president. This was especially the case with Balaguer, who governed the country with considerable discretion and little effective congressional oversight.

Congress showed more independence during the PRD governments of Antonio Guzmán and Salvador Jorge Blanco between 1978 and 1986, and again under the PLD government of Leonel Fernández (1996–2000). In addition, during his 1986–96 period in office, Balaguer was more limited in his ability to ignore or sidestep Congress than he had been during the 1966–78 period when he had comfortable majorities in both chambers. Even the earlier Balaguer administrations occasionally confronted an obstructionist Congress, however. Indeed, the major power of Congress has been to obstruct and to delay—whether in the pursuit of personal or parochial gain, responding to the wishes of interest groups or other societal allies, or as a result of genuine policy or ideological differences. The PRD governments were especially frustrated by factions within their own parties, although they also faced opposition from the PRSC and PLD representatives. President Fernández, in turn, has been confronted particularly with opposition from the PRD, especially after it gained congressional seats in the 1998 election.

The Judiciary

Judicial power is exercised by the Supreme Court of Justice and by other courts created by the constitution and by law. The country has general courts, which consider civil, criminal, commercial, and labor issues (except for labor matters in the major urban areas of Santo Domingo, Santiago, San Francisco de Macorís, and San Pedro de Macorís), and certain specialized courts, namely land courts, labor courts (in the country's four major urban areas), tax courts, and new children's courts that were mandated by a 1994 law. The country also has other courts or offices with judicial functions, which do not form a part of the judicial branch. These include the Police Tribunal, the Military Tribunal, and the Central Electoral Board, which administers elections and is the unappealable arbiter of all disputes related to elections, with complaints being heard in the first instance by municipal electoral boards.

Under the Supreme Court there are nine Courts of Appeals, which hear appeals of decisions from Courts of First Instance. There are eighty-three of these Courts of First Instance, which, unlike the Supreme Court or the Appeals Courts, are presided over by only one judge. There are also 214 justices of the peace, who hear cases of small claims or minor crimes. In addition, there are also four Labor Courts of Appeal, and single Courts of Appeal for tax and for land issues; under these are the respective specialized courts of first instance.

Centralized and hierarchical, the Dominican legal system is patterned after the French system; its basic codes for criminal and civil procedure date back to 1884. The legal system has employed a code-law legal system rather than a common law system such as the one used in the United States. Detailed and comprehensive, the codes leave little room for United States-style judicial activism or citation of precedent. Legal reasoning is deductive (from the codes), rather than inductive or based on past cases.

Until a 1994 constitutional reform enacted substantial changes to the 1966 constitution, the judiciary was particularly dependent upon the other branches of government. Prior to the reform, judges were chosen by the Senate, not by the president, ostensibly to limit executive power. The Senate also selected judges for the lower courts. Because judges were not named for any specific term of office, the result was a highly politicized process of nomination and rotation in office. Furthermore, the president could name all public employees in the judicial branch, as well as temporarily name judges if vacancies occurred. Other problems cited as affecting the judiciary have included low pay, poor working conditions, staff shortages, and allegations of corruption and influence-peddling.

The 1994 constitutional reform was intended to enhance the independence and autonomy of the judiciary. It called for the establishment of a Council of the Magistrature (Consejo de la Magistratura) whose sole purpose is to name the judges of the Supreme Court. The Council consists of the president, the president of the Senate, a senator chosen by the Senate from a political party different from the president of the Senate, the president of the Chamber of Deputies, a representative chosen by the Chamber from a party different from the president of the Chamber, the president of the Supreme Court, and another judge from the Supreme Court, chosen by the Court. The reform gave the Supreme Court the power to select judges for all the courts under it, as well as to name administrative personnel for the judicial branch. Furthermore, it called for the establishment of a judicial career (judicial civil service), and for life tenure for judges in the context of this judicial civil service. And, it enabled the president, the president of the Senate or the Chamber, or any interested party to appeal to the Supreme Court to review the constitutionality of a law. After the new court was installed, it held public hearings to evaluate all sitting judges and replaced about two-thirds of them.

Requirements for appointment as a Supreme Court justice and other powers of the Court remain as established by the 1966 constitution. Supreme Court justices must be Dominican citizens by birth or origin, at least thirty-five years old, with full political and civil rights. They are required to have a law degree and to have practiced law or held judicial office for at least twelve years. These requirements become progressively less strict for lower-court justices. The Supreme Court has the exclusive power to assume jurisdiction in matters affecting the president and other high officials, act as a court of cassation, serve as a court of last instance in matters forwarded from appellate courts, exercise final disciplinary action over other members of the judiciary, and transfer justices from one jurisdiction to another.

Implementation of the 1994 constitutional reforms has been slow but significant. The Council of the Magistrature was formed in late 1996, and in August 1997 new members of the Supreme Court were named. This new Supreme Court is widely viewed as professional and nonpartisan, and for the first time in the country's history, business, professional, and middle-sector groups from civil society played an active role in the nomination and screening process. Critical judicial reforms have also made gradual progress. The Supreme Court evaluated and replaced many of the country's judges, leading to improvements in the system's efficiency and effectiveness. A law establishing a judicial career service was promulgated in August 1998, and in August 1999 a National School for the Judiciary was established to improve the training and the quality of the country's judges. With these changes, the quality of the country's judiciary and the historical subservience of the courts to the government in power appears to be changing slowly.

Public Administration

Historically, the Dominican Republic has been marked by a public administration dominated by patronage and clientelist relations, with nepotism, corruption, and inefficiency as common features. Although initial civil service legislation was passed under the United States military occupation of 1916–24, and changed several times thereafter, the legislation was never truly implemented. Indeed, the legislation was actually abolished in 1951 by President Trujillo. Under Trujillo, the state was largely an instrument for the benefit of the dictator; this meant there was little localized or decentralized corruption not countenanced by Trujillo or his closest cronies.

Following the fall of Trujillo, no ruler retained as full a personalist control over the state and its personnel as he had experienced. Balaguer (1966–78; 1986–96) came closest, especially in his first twelve years in office. Under Balaguer's administration, the executive centralized expenditures and power through contracts and patronage networks, and widely ignored administrative regulations and bureaucratic norms. Although the governments of Guzmán (1978–82) and Jorge Blanco (1982–86) did not attain as extreme a level of centralization, their administrations were marked by clientelist favoritism, nepotism, and corruption. Fernández's government has sought to initiate significant state reforms, while not totally ignoring clientelist uses of the state; one of its first measures was to increase the salary offered for high posts in government from the extremely low levels to which they had fallen under Balaguer.

In addition to receiving low salaries, Dominican public officials historically had little protection in their jobs. A civil service law was approved in 1991 and finally implemented by the executive in 1994. However, at that time only an extremely limited number of employees, primarily those working in fields related to insurance and banking services, were allowed to seek incorporation into the civil service. Under the Fernández administration, the civil service was expanded to include employees in several secretariats of state, including the Technical Secretariat of the Presidency, Labor, Foreign Affairs, and the Attorney General's office. Indeed, without further restructuring that set guidelines for determining professionalism, qualifications, and salary rates in other areas of the public sector, such a law could conceivably complicate public-sector efficiency rather than improve it.

From the cabinet level to the lowest ranks, traditionally almost all civil servants have been appointed, served, and could be removed largely at the will of the president. The result was a patronage-dominated system in which public-sector jobs were given out in return for loyalty and service. Hence merit, achievement, and competence were not always the main criteria guiding government appointments. The public bureaucracy was often characterized by incompetence even at the highest levels. Nepotism and corruption—a favor in return for a favor, the granting of special governmental privileges to favored persons, private enrichment stemming from public service, outright bribery—were also widespread. Those who tried to be honest were scorned and considered foolish by their colleagues. Indeed, for some, government service was thought of not so much as an honored career but as a brief opportunity to indulge oneself at the public trough. The frequent failure of government programs could often be attributed directly to the corruption and incompetence of the bureaucracy. And, just as the use and abuse of state funds were common at election time, a public-sector worker was often expected to do political work for his or her patron.

The abuse of the public sector and of public administration was particularly evident during Balaguer's governments. Although he insisted that corruption stopped "at the door of his office," he openly acknowledged the legitimacy of what he politely termed "commissions," allowing his family members to accept ostensible donations and gifts by favored contractors. Balaguer rarely called cabinet meetings, although he named dozens of people as secretaries of state without portfolio. Around election time, in particular, he openly countenanced corruption and the abuse of state resources. Balaguer's policy of rotating individuals in and out of government positions extended to the appointment of governors of the Central Bank; indeed, in a sample of fifty-eight countries over the past several decades, the Dominican Republic had the second lowest average tenure, around twenty-one months, for a Central Bank governor (only Argentina was lower). The PRD administrations, particularly that of Jorge Blanco, were not free of these problems, although they tended to be more rational in their naming of cabinet officials.

Under President Fernández, until August 1999 there were fifteen secretaries of state: an administrative secretary of state for the presidency, a technical secretary of state for the presidency, and twelve additional secretaries of state administering various secretariats. In August 1999, Congress approved the establishment of a new secretary of state for women. In addition, as of year-end 1999, the Central Bank governor named by Balaguer in 1994 had retained his position.

In addition to the cabinet secretaries of state, in 1999 the country had some two dozen autonomous and semiautonomous agencies. The autonomous and semiautonomous agencies were established in the early 1960s to administer new public programs as well as the vast properties and enterprises inherited by the state after the death of Trujillo. These agencies administer an array of programs and enterprises, ranging from farm loans to cooperatives to vast sugar lands. The largest of these is the State Sugar Council (Consejo Estatal del Azúcar—CEA), which at one time had 85,000 employees, making it the largest employer in the country and its most important exporter. Among the others are the Dominican State Enterprises Corporation (Corporación Dominicana de Empresas Estatales– Corde), in which twenty-three state-owned enterprises that had belonged to Trujillo were consolidated, and the Dominican Electricity Corporation (Corporación Dominicana de Electricidad—CDE) (see Industry, ch. 3).

These agencies traditionally have been dominated by patronage considerations, plagued by corruption and inefficiency, and sometimes plundered for electoral purposes. By the end of Balaguer's last term in office in 1996, even enterprises that once had been profitable were plagued with deficits. The government was being forced to subsidize the CEA, which had once provided the government with a steady stream of revenue. In addition, the CDE confronted a situation in which more than half of the electricity that it sold was either lost in transmission or distribution or not paid for, even as the country was plagued with frequent outages.

Under President Fernández, some steps toward rationalization of some public enterprises and the privatization of others were initiated during his first three years in office, following passage of the Public Enterprise Reform Law of 1997. However, in the face of protests from nationalists and workers at the firms, as well as resistance from opposition parties that feared the administration might use funds received from privatization for partisan political purposes, the government was proceeding slowly. By the end of 1999, steps had been taken to privatize the distribution of energy; to further privatize some of the production of electricity; to allow private investments in some CEA lands, with the expectation that many of the state's sugar mills would be leased to the private sector; and to permit greater private-sector involvement in areas such as the management of the country's seaports and airports.

Local Government

The Dominican system of local government, like the Dominican legal system, has been based on the French system of top-down rule and strong central authority. In late 1999, the country was divided into twenty-nine provinces plus the National District (Santo Domingo). The provinces in turn were subdivided into a total of 108 municipalities. Each province is administered by a civil governor appointed by the president. A governor must be a Dominican citizen, at least twenty-five years old, and in full possession of civil and political rights. The powers and duties of governors are set by law. The constitution establishes the structure of local government; its specific functions are enumerated in the municipal code.

*Dr. Leonel Fernández Reyna,
President of the Dominican
Republic, 1996–2000
Courtesy Embassy of the
Dominican Republic*

The municipalities and the National District are governed by mayors (called *síndicos*) and municipal councils, both popularly elected to four-year terms. The size of the council depends on the size of the municipality, but each is required to have at least five members. The qualifications of local officials as well as the powers and duties of mayors and councils are set by law. Naturalized citizens can hold municipal office provided they have lived in the community at least ten years.

Neither provinces nor municipalities have any significant independent power to levy taxes. As a result, historically few services have been initiated at the local level. There are no local police departments, only a single national force. Policy and programs relating to education, social services, roads, electricity, and public works likewise are administered at the national level, rather than at the provincial or municipal level. Local government, therefore, has been weak and ineffective, not only because it has lacked taxing authority, but also because in the Dominican system the central government sets almost all policy.

Starting in the early 1960s, the Bosch government made various efforts to strengthen Dominican local government. A new Dominican Municipal League came into existence in 1962, and efforts were made to develop community spirit, local initiative, and self-help projects. These projects were not wholly successful, in large part because of the traditional arrangement under which almost all power flowed downward from the central government. A small step was taken with the passage of a law in 1983 that mandated that a percentage of the country's taxes be distributed to municipalities. Enforcement of the law, particularly under President Balaguer, was uneven, however.

In the 1990s, as a consequence of the focus of international aid agencies on decentralization, the emergence of groups in Dominican civil society pressuring for change, and the desire of some opposition political parties to coordinate local development efforts, additional pressure for change emerged. An important potential advance took place with the passage of a January 1997 law providing that 4 percent of the central government's national budget be transferred to municipal governments. The law did not clearly specify the functions or responsibilities of a municipality, however.

Decentralization efforts under President Fernández, however, became mired in partisan politics. Following the 1998 local elections, which led to PRD plurality victories in more than half of the country's municipalities, the PRD expected to retain control of the secretary generalship of the Dominican Municipal League and thus of the enhanced resources provided for under the new law, which promised to be a key source of patronage. However, the PRD publicly accused the Fernández administration of attempting to bribe electors in order to take control of the League by supporting a candidate from the PRSC. In January 1999, following several tense incidents between riot police and PRD party members, two parallel assemblies elected two different persons as secretary general to head the League, through which would flow approximately US$400 million. The candidate of the PRSC supported by the PLD ultimately gained control of the League offices. In February 1999, President Fernández proposed a political dialogue in order to resolve several critical issues including this one, others such as the composition of the Central Electoral Board leading up to the 2000 elections, and various key administrative bills stalemated in Congress (see Electoral System, this ch.). With regard to the Dominican Municipal League, an ad-hoc committee of notables was formed to help determine how funds should be disbursed.

Electoral System

Voting is free, secret, and obligatory for both men and women. Suffrage is available to anyone eighteen years old or older, or any married person regardless of age. Members of the police or armed forces are ineligible to vote, as are those who have lost their political and civil rights, for example, incarcerated criminals. Polls are open from 6 am to 6 pm on the day of elections, which is not a working day. The method of voting has frequently been changed. In the 1996 and 1998 elections, women have voted in the morning and men in the afternoon. The process was as follows: on election day voters went to their voting station to register; once registration closed, voting began. This process (known as *colegios cerrados*) was mandated by a 1994 constitutional reform, and was intended to prevent the possibility of double voting. And, on the basis of a 1997 law, for the first time in 1998, political parties received public funding. For other provisions of the 1997 law, see below.

Elections in the Dominican Republic historically have been highly problematic and crisis-ridden. Opposition parties have usually questioned the use and abuse of state resources by the governing party, and the campaign period leading up to election day has often been marked by widespread distrust, allegations of fraud, and violence associated with campaign events. In recent years, as a consequence of fraud and protest, particularly in the 1990 and 1994 elections, important modifications in the electoral law have been made.

At the center of the problem with elections has been doubts about the objectivity, capability, and autonomy of the country's Central Electoral Board (Junta Central Electoral—JCE), which, along with its subsidiary municipal boards, is responsible for overseeing elections. These agencies combine administrative, regulatory, and judicial functions. The JCE is responsible for managing the voter registry list, regulating the campaign and administering the elections; it is also the unappealable arbiter of all disputes related to elections, with complaints being heard in the first instance by municipal electoral boards. The autonomy and credibility of the JCE have been affected by a number of factors. Its judges are named by the Senate (or by the president if the Senate is not in session and does not subsequently act) for terms that can be coterminous with each electoral period; partisan political criteria often have been uppermost. In a number of elections, an imperfect alternative to a strong

JCE was the use of ad-hoc mediating and support commissions or international observers or mediators.

As a consequence of the 1990 electoral crisis, an electoral law was passed in 1992 that instituted a number of reforms. This law provided the JCE with greater legal budgetary independence. It also provided that henceforth Dominican citizens would receive a single card that would serve both as an identity card and an electoral card; prior to this law, the JCE shared responsibility with the executive branch for the management of the offices that provided the personal identification cards that citizens had to present along with electoral cards distributed by the JCE in order to vote. Naturally, this enhanced fears by opposition parties that the emission of identity cards could be manipulated to favor the government party. Like much of the rest of the state, the JCE has also paid woefully low salaries, a situation that has improved somewhat since 1996.

As a consequence of the 1992 law, building up to the 1994 elections the JCE leadership was expanded from three to five judges—three chosen by the governing PRSC party and two by opposition parties. The JCE also issued a new national and electoral identity card and prepared a new electoral roll, which ended up being flawed and at the center of significant fraud in the elections carried out that year. Thus, the JCE remained an institutionally weak, politicized institution.

For the 1996 elections, rather than choosing JCE judges with partisan criteria paramount, independent figures were named, who remained in place for the 1998 elections. Both these elections were relatively trouble free. However, partisan criteria again played a hand when JCE judges were chosen to oversee the presidential election of the year 2000. In August 1998, the PRD-dominated Senate named all five of the JCE judges without consultation with the opposition parties. This action once again made the composition of the JCE an issue of serious contention among the country's major political parties. Finally, after extensive negotiations, in June 1999 the Senate named two additional JCE judges, one identified with the PLD and the other with the PRSC.

The electoral law of 1997 (Law 275–97) mandated a number of important changes in electoral procedures. In addition to requiring public funding of political parties, the law instituted a 25 percent quota for female candidates. The requirement helped improve female representation in the Chamber of Deputies, which went from 8.6 percent female representation in

1994 to 16.1 percent in 1998, and in the municipal councils, which went from 14.7 percent female representation in 1994 to 26.5 percent in 1998. The law also called for the creation of electoral subdistricts of three to four representatives each in large multimember provinces such as Santo Domingo and Santiago, to begin in 2002. Furthermore, the 1997 law permits Dominicans abroad to vote in presidential elections, beginning in the year 2000.

Political Parties

For a country with relatively limited experience with political democracy, the Dominican Republic has a surprisingly strong set of political parties. However, the party system is currently in a state of flux as the parties confront the risks of potential fragmentation over leadership succession issues. Since the 1960s, the country has had two important political parties: the Reformist Party (Partido Reformista—PR), now the Reformist Social Christian Party (Partido Reformista Social Cristiano—PRSC), and the Dominican Revolutionary Party (Partido Revolucionario Dominicano—PRD). A third party, the Party of Dominican Liberation (Partido de la Liberación Dominicana—PLD), was formed in 1973 and gradually became electorally important in the course of the 1980s. In addition to these three parties, numerous other minor parties have occasionally garnered support.

Prior to the Trujillo period (1930–61), parties were weakly organized, had insubstantial leadership, were neither very ideological nor programmatic, and were generally based on personalist followings rather than concrete programs. Trujillo organized the Dominican Party (Partido Dominicano) to provide himself with support, even though elections were fraudulent. Following Trujillo's assassination and the forced exile of his brothers and then of Balaguer, the party was officially banned.

When Balaguer returned from exile to campaign for the presidency in 1966, he recaptured central elements of the conservative constituency that had formed the bulwark of Trujillo's support among rural, less-educated, older, and female voters. He further sustained their loyalty and support by employing the power of the presidency and state resources on their behalf. During the 1966–78 period when he was president, several high-level military figures also played a prominent role in the party. Moreover, military pressure eased Balaguer's reelection in 1970 and 1974; nearly all of the opposition ultimately refrained from participating. Balaguer also consistently retained the support of the conservative Roman Catholic hierarchy within the country. The PR was Balaguer's personal machine, largely ignored when he was in office, except at election time. As such, it lacked a clear-cut program or coherent ideology, although Balaguer continued to reiterate themes of order, nationalism, religiosity, and anti-Haitianism.

In 1986 Balaguer supported the merging of his party with existing minor Christian Democratic parties, opening the way for the integration of his newly named PRSC (the former PR party) into the Christian Democratic Union. As with the much longer lasting and more deeply rooted link between the PRD and the Socialist International, this association brought the PRSC international visibility, financial and technical assistance, and the promise, never realized, of an ideological basis for the party. Although the merger did assist Balaguer in his electoral comeback that year, from 1978 to 1994, electoral support for the PR (or PRSC since 1986) oscillated fairly narrowly between around 35 percent and 42 percent of the vote. The party won elections for the most part because of divisions in the opposition and some use of fraud.

Throughout his political career, Balaguer has consistently retained absolute control over the PRSC, forcing out or weakening potential adversaries within the party. In 1996, when he was constitutionally barred from running for the presidency again, he refused to campaign for or ultimately vote for his own party's candidate in the first round of the presidential ballot; instead, he first quietly supported Leonel Fernández of the PLD, and then openly endorsed him for the second-round ballot. In 1996 support for the party dropped precipitously to only 15 percent in the first-round presidential election, and it has remained at that low level. Although Balaguer turned ninety-two in 1999, he retains control of the PRSC. There are serious questions about the future of the party once Balaguer dies.

Another major party is the PRD, which was founded in 1939 by exiles from the Trujillo dictatorship, including Juan Bosch. It functioned as an exile organization for twenty-two years before returning to the Dominican Republic in 1961 after Trujillo's assassination. The PRD was able to win an impressive victory in the 1962 elections, through extensive organizational work and a campaign that focused on helping the poor. This electoral victory led to the ephemeral government of Juan

Bosch, which was overthrown after only seven months in office. Yet, the PRD as a strong party was ultimately forged through this initial victory and overthrow, and the further heroics of civil war, foreign intervention, and subsequent repression under Balaguer. The struggle for democracy during the 1970s under these conditions and the hard bureaucratic work associated with it helped to build a strong organization led by José Francisco Peña Gómez, who often served as the party's secretary general. The party continued to prosper in spite of Bosch's departure in 1973 in order to create a new party. Bosch, who had become radicalized as a consequence of the 1965 United States intervention, was promoting the notion of "dictatorship with popular support."

Following Bosch's departure, the PRD pursued a three-pronged strategy to assume power in 1978. It continued its extensive organizational work, particularly in the country's major urban areas where the bulk of its supporters were found. The party also moderated its nationalist, statist, and reformist program and purposely named a very moderate figure, Guzmán, as its presidential candidate. In addition, it assiduously strengthened its international contacts, both with the Socialist International and with liberal politicians in the United States. As a consequence, when the Dominican military sought to block the vote count and prevent a PRD victory in 1978, the party was able to draw upon support from the United States and other international allies, as well as from a variety of domestic groups and to secure the presidency. In 1982, with Jorge Blanco as its presidential candidate, the PRD was once again able to win the country's national elections.

The eight-year period during which the PRD held the presidency turned out to be an acute disappointment for the country and for the party, however. The party was forced to oversee a difficult period of economic stabilization as a result of the debt crisis. At the same time, each of the presidencies became marked by bitter intraparty division as the party increasingly lost its ideological moorings and its factions fought for power and spoils. The first term was marked by the tragic suicide of Guzmán near the end of his term. Guzmán had bitterly opposed Jorge Blanco's nomination as the party's candidate for president, and as he became increasingly isolated within the party, he feared retribution and corruption charges against family members by the incoming administration. The term presided over by Jorge Blanco saw an increase in levels of corrup-

191

tion, clientelist practices, and infighting by PRD leaders. Combined with the country's economic decline, these practices helped lead to the electoral comeback of Balaguer in 1986. The prosecution and conviction of Jorge Blanco on corruption charges by Balaguer (a case still under appeal as of year-end 1999), further weakened the party. Factional divisions finally led to a formal party split in the period leading up to the 1990 elections. Peña Gómez retained the party name and symbols, while the party's 1986 candidate, Jacobo Majluta Azar, formed the Independent Revolutionary Party (Partido Revolucionario Independiente—PRI). The latter party received only 7.0 percent of the vote in the 1990 elections and subsequently declined further.

During the 1990s, Peña Gómez gradually supplanted formal notions of internal party democracy and assumed the role of uncontested leader within the PRD. He failed to attain the presidency, however. In 1994 it is likely that fraud robbed him of the margin of victory. In 1996 the introduction of a second-round presidential election—held because no party had received a majority in the first round—and an effective alliance between the PLD and the PRSC in the second round prevented him from winning. Peña Gómez's death just a week before the 1998 congressional and local elections helped the PRD to gain 51.4 percent of the vote, which translated into twenty-four of the country's thirty Senate seats and eighty-three representatives in the Chamber of Deputies. The party also won majorities in many municipalities. The PRD then successfully limited factional infighting and maintained organizational coherence while selecting its presidential nominee for the May 2000 elections, something it had not been able to do leading up to the elections of 1986 and 1990. Hipólito Mejía handily won a presidential primary the party held in June 1999, and successfully incorporated the two major losing candidates, Rafael Suberví and Hatuey DeCamps, into high-level positions within the party.

Remarkably, Juan Bosch is the founder of two of the country's three major parties. In 1973 he left the PRD to found the PLD, positioning it as a more radical, cadre-oriented, ideologically coherent, and organizationally solid party. Its major initial strength was among educated, nationalist, radicalized urban middle-sector and labor groups. Gradually, as the country's economic situation declined during the 1980s and the PRD was weakened by internecine struggles, Bosch and the PLD reentered the electoral arena. From a mere 1.1 percent of the vote in 1978, the PLD's support grew to 9.9 percent in 1982 and 18.4 percent in 1986. In 1990 a much more moderate PLD campaigned on promises of honesty, efficient government, and gradual reform. It gained 33.9 percent of the vote, losing the presidency to Balaguer by a very slim margin, which many Dominicans are convinced was the result of fraud. Although the PLD continued to retain a more complex organizational structure and a greater respect for internal party norms than did Balaguer's PRSC, Bosch remained its unquestioned leader; individuals perceived as potential threats were occasionally forced out of the party.

During the 1990s, the PLD continued to moderate its ideological position. Retaining a modest nationalism and focus on good governance, as well as a strong organizational structure, the party sought to reach out more effectively to broader sectors of Dominican society. In 1994 an aging and ailing Bosch was able to capture only 13.1 percent of the vote. As a result of the agreement following that election, Balaguer's term was shortened by two years, and he agreed not to seek reelection. Because of his age and poor health, Bosch agreed to step down as leader and presidential candidate for the PLD and endorsed the party's nominee, Leonel Fernández. With Fernández's victory in the 1996 presidential elections, the PLD reached the country's highest office; ironically, however, the once radical party did so by defeating the PRD through a coalition with the conservative Balaguer. The PLD, however, has been stymied by its lack of support in Congress. In the 1998 elections, it received 30.4 percent of the vote, slightly increasing its presence in Congress, especially in the Chamber of Deputies where it was able to elect forty-nine representatives, just enough to uphold a presidential veto. Nevertheless, President Fernández has remained a generally popular figure. And, his favored candidate within the PLD, his close adviser and Secretary of the Presidency Danilo Medina, won the party's nomination through a closed party primary in June 1999 to be the PLD candidate for the May 2000 elections. The major future challenges for the PLD are consolidating its support among the parts of the electorate it won over from the PRSC and winning over new voters, while preventing factional strife and division.

In addition to these major parties, the PRSC, the PLD, and the PRD, the Dominican Republic has had multiple minor parties. Some of these have been little more than personalist vehicles that have permitted their leaders to maintain a certain presence in the national arena, sometimes by establishing alliances with one of the major parties. Others have been created by leaders who have lost factional struggles within one of the major parties. Extreme-left and communist parties have never had much of a popular following in the country, and they have often been consumed by internecine conflicts and by bitter attacks against the PRD and then the PLD. Following the end of the Cold War, these parties declined even further as electoral vehicles, when some of their leaders joined the PRD or the PLD, and others focused more of their attention on social movements.

As the Dominican Republic enters the new century, each of its major parties confronts challenges that could lead to significant changes in the party system. And, as elsewhere on the continent and, indeed, in the world, political parties in the country confront high levels of skepticism within an electorate that often perceives them as inefficient, self-serving organizations rather than as effective means of representing their interests. The PRD remains the party with the strongest membership and following, but it knows it risks a repeat of factional division cr loss of support because of poor performance in government. The PRSC has experienced sharply declining electoral support as its aging leader was forced from the presidency, yet Balaguer retains a firm grip on the party. It is unlikely that any other leader will be able to retain the loyalty of this electorate to the degree that Balaguer did, and the fate of the party is very much in question cnce he dies. Meanwhile, as its relatively lackluster performance in the 1998 congressional elections indicates, the PLD has not yet consolidated support among the voters who gave it a presidential victory in 1996.

Interest Groups and Social Actors

In the Dominican Republic, numerous factors have militated against the establishment and maintenance of a dynamic civil society characterized by a multiplicity of interest groups and associations. Historically, the most important factors that explain this lack include poverty and low rates of education, high levels of inequality, repressive governments such as that of Trujillo (1930–61), which quashed any independent organizations, and the reliance of political actors on clientelism and patronage. Since 1961, and especially since the early 1980s, socioeconomic changes and international influences have had contradictory consequences regarding the development of civil society. Urbanization, education, economic growth, the growth of middle-sector groups, some return migration, and support from international aid and nongovernmental organizations (NGOs) have all helped the development of civil society. At the same time, economic crisis and wrenching economic changes have helped weaken labor and popular-sector organizations, and large-scale migration has also involved a significant "brain drain" of many talented Dominicans.

Overall, this sector remains quite weak, with business and middle-sector groups overrepresented. Yet, during the past several decades, more interest groups and a more self-consciously identified civil society have emerged. This civil society has played an important role in seeking to strengthen Dominican democracy, both in terms of political rights and a greater respect for institutionality and the rule of law. Its influence has been apparent in efforts to generate national agendas for reform and in more specific areas such as electoral reform (including the pursuit of gender equality through measures such as quotas for women on electoral lists), electoral observation, and judicial reform. At the same time, the role of two traditionally powerful actors, the Roman Catholic Church and the armed forces, has also evolved during the past several decades. The church has moderated its position and seen some of its influence wane in the face of the growth of Protestantism and secularization, and the role of the military in domestic affairs has declined although institutionalized, democratic, civilian control over the military yet remains to be achieved.

Economic Elites

The Dominican Republic's economy has undergone a major transformation, especially in the period since the mid-1980s. Until the 1970s, the country's economy was fundamentally based on the export of selected agricultural crops such as sugar, tobacco, coffee, and cocoa, and of minerals such as ferronickel. A set of industrialists who produced goods for a heavily protected domestic market also existed. However, during the 1980s, as sugar exports declined drastically, dramatic growth occurred in light industry for export in free-trade zones and in tourism. As a consequence, the once important Association of Landowners and Agriculturists (Asociación de Hacendados y Agricultores) was gradually overshadowed in importance by associations related to industry, finance, real estate, telecommunications, tourism, and free-trade zones; importers and commercial interests continued to retain powerful organizations, however. Behind the array of seemingly formal organizational structures lies the reality that many sectors of the economy are dominated by a few large firms that often form part of family conglomerates that sometimes have complex histories of collaboration and rivalry.

Efforts to construct a powerful, united umbrella organization of private-sector interests has had mixed results. The closest approximation is the National Council of Private Enterprise (Consejo Nacional de la Empresa Privada—Conep), which, however, has seen defections during the 1990s as a result of tensions over the nature and pace of the opening up of the economy. Such tensions have divided local industrialists from importers.

Middle Class

By the 1990s, Dominican society no longer consisted of a small landed elite at the top and a huge mass of peasants at the bottom, with almost no one in between. In large part as a result of the economic development and modernization that had occurred since the end of the Great Depression, a sizable, heterogenous middle class had emerged that comprised 30 to 35 percent of the population (see Urban Society, ch. 2).

The middle class consists of shopkeepers, government officials, clerks, military personnel, white-collar workers of all kinds, teachers, professionals, and the better-paid members of the working class. Most of the middle class resides in Santo Domingo, but secondary cities like Santiago, Barahona, Monte Cristi, La Romana, San Francisco de Macorís, and San Pedro de Macorís have also developed sizable middle-class populations.

The middle class has come to predominate within the country's major political institutions: the Roman Catholic Church, the military officer corps, government service, political parties, interest groups, and even trade union leadership. It also has provided important leadership for civil society organizations committed to good governance and clean government, and has supported women's and environmental issues and community development. Yet, many in the middle class remain quite conservative, reflecting the fact that this social group has often been divided on social and political issues. Generally, its members advocate peace, order, stability, and economic progress, although increasingly many also want democracy and respect for institutions and the rule of law.

During the late 1960s and early 1970s, many middle-class elements supported Balaguer because he was thought to stand for those things they wanted; later, chafing under Balaguer's personalism and economic decline, they supported the PRD governments of Guzmán and Jorge Blanco. As a result of the failure of these governments to reform conditions in the country, which led thousands in the middle class to migrate, they turned away from the PRD, toward either the PRSC or the PLD. Partly, their turn from the PRD came because many held anti-Haitian sentiments and thus did not wish to support the PRD's Peña Gómez. In 1996 many supported the PLD.

Trade Unions and Popular Organizations

Organized labor in the Dominican Republic has always been weak (see Labor, ch. 3). Labor was repressed under Trujillo, who passed very restrictive legislation in 1951; labor also experienced severe restrictions under Balaguer in the 1966–78 period. Although a labor code passed in May 1992 established new rights for workers and unions, organized labor remains weak and politically divided in three larger and several smaller labor confederations that represent 12 percent of the work force. Even following passage of the 1992 labor code, many employers replace workers who try to organize. They can do so because the country has high rates of unemployment and underemployment and a surplus of unskilled labor. The practice of replacing workers is especially prevalent in the country's export-oriented free-trade zones, where unionization and collective bargaining are largely absent. Some of the strongest unions are found among middle-sector professionals employed by the public sector, such as medical personnel and teachers; such professionals often obtain salary increases only after threatened or actual work stoppages.

Trade union organizations have often been closely allied with individual political parties; in recent years, however, identification of the major confederations with individual political parties has declined. Rivalry across trade union federations has often been intense, and most of the union organizations have suffered from weak funding and limited staff. In recent years, support from international labor federations and NGOs has supplemented more modest domestic revenue sources. Sometimes employers have engaged in what could be described as union-breaking activities, including the summoning of police to put down union activities. These and other conditions have both weakened and politicized the labor movement. Because collective bargaining is limited to only a few of the larger firms, political action, such as street demonstrations, marches to the National Palace, and general strikes, is a widely used tactic. These tactics are meant to put pressure on the government to side with the workers in labor disputes.

During the 1980s, a number of important urban, neighborhood-based protest organizations emerged. Their emergence was facilitated by greater democratic freedoms under PRD governments, and sometimes by the assistance of local church and other activists as well as by international aid. The activism of these groups was enhanced by the country's growing economic crisis. Typically, they focused on local-level demands such as salary increases, price reductions for basic products, and improvements in public transportation, water, and electricity services. Despite various efforts by the organizations during the 1980s and 1990s to move toward more effective, centralized, unified action, such efforts largely failed. Tensions within the organizations and between them and the already divided labor movement were also sometimes exploited by the government, particularly under Balaguer, who was a master at employing patronage and clientelism to coopt leaders and divide and weaken popular movements.

Similarly, independent peasant groups have been limited, weak, and often politically fragmented. Balaguer excelled at such political fragmentation. He retained loyal support among many in the rural sector through his appeals for a conservative, Roman Catholic nationalism and for order and stability. He also occasionally distributed land titles and other personalist benefits, even as the urban bias of many government policies led to massive rural to urban migration as well as emigration overseas. Furthermore, trade union and peasant organizations have rarely succeeded in forming a workable joint organization composed of Dominicans and Haitian migrants. Indeed, during 1999, the Dominican government took steps to try to limit the influx of Haitians and to repatriate some it considered to be in the country illegally. The increased presence of Haitians, in part because of the deteriorating situation in that country, once again became a sensitive issue domestically.

Mass Media

Starting in the early 1960s, the Dominican Republic experienced a communications revolution. The spread of radio, television, and newspapers awakened the previously isolated countryside, stimulated rapid urbanization, and led to the political mobilization of millions of persons who had never participated in politics before. In addition, since Trujillo's death in 1961, the Dominican media have been among the freest in Latin America.

In the 1990s, Dominicans have access to a multiplicity of radio and television stations domestically, including several that are state-owned and managed; many Dominicans also have access to major United States, Spanish, and Latin American networks through various satellite cable companies. All radio and television stations are government-licensed, a situation that has sometimes led to charges of undue pressure and manipulation. Furthermore, at election time, the state-owned media have usually been blatantly partisan in favor of the incumbent administration's candidates. As ownership of television units has grown, television has become the major medium through which the public receives its news. Those who cannot afford a set of their own often watch at neighbors' houses or in public places such as bars or shops.

The country's major newspaper is the *Listín Diario,* founded in 1889 and revived in 1964. Santo Domingo boasts a number of other significant dailies as well, including *Hoy, El Siglo, El Caribe, El Nacional,* and *Última Hora.* These newspapers circulate nationally, although other cities also have smaller papers. Ownership of newspapers tends to be concentrated in family-held conglomerates, which sometimes use their control of the press to advance the interests of their firms or to attack those of their rivals. Journalists are not always well paid and sometimes accept additional remuneration from government offices, political parties, or firms. Not surprisingly, objectivity in reporting sometimes suffers. At the same time, investigative reporting of alleged corruption, abuse, and negligence by government and by private-sector firms, previously almost unknown, has gained impetus over the past decade in these daily newspapers and also in the weekly newsmagazine, *Rumbo.*

Roman Catholic Church

The Dominican Republic remains about 80 percent Roman

Catholic despite major gains by Protestant groups, especially evangelical, charismatic, and spiritualist sects (see Religion, ch. 2). The Dominican Roman Catholic Church historically has been conservative and traditionalist, generally supporting the status quo and the existing power structure. But the Roman Catholic Church also has been weak institutionally, with few priests (fewer than 200 in the entire country), little land, few educational or social institutions, and little influence over the daily lives of most Dominicans.

Since the 1960s, the Roman Catholic Church has ceased to identify wholly with the status quo. Rather, it has tended to advocate moderate change. It has organized mainstream Catholic political parties, trade unions, student groups, peasant leagues, and businessmen's associations.

Liberation theology has made few inroads in the Dominican Republic. A few priests espouse liberationist ideas, but they are not considered to be in the mainstream of the clergy. Nor have there been calls by church officials for an alliance with Marxist groups, let alone calls for guerrilla struggles or other militant action against the system. During the 1980s and 1990s, the church often played a mediating role in political and social conflicts, particularly through Monsignor Agripino Núñez Collado, rector of the Pontifical Catholic University Mother and Teacher.

As the Dominican Republic has modernized and secularized, the church has lost some of its influence. The country legalized divorce in 1963 and instituted government-sponsored family planning in 1967, two measures that the church had opposed. The church seldom has succeeded in mobilizing voters in support of its favored programs. With only some 10 percent of the population engaged as active, practicing Catholics, and with Protestant groups continuing to grow rapidly, church influence has continued to decline during the 1990s. While Balaguer was in office, there was a particularly strong link between his government and the conservative cardinal and Archbishop of Santo Domingo Nicolás de Jésus López Rodríguez. However, increasingly the importance of Protestant voices within organized religion is recognized, and secular influences in culture and education continue to grow.

Armed Forces

One of the most significant changes in the Dominican Republic during the past several decades has been the lessening of the threat of military incursion into politics. Trujillo assumed power in 1930 as head of the country's military; during the thirty-one years he controlled the country, he vastly expanded the budget of the armed forces, while manipulating the military to his advantage. Following his assassination, the military retained considerable influence, and during the 1960s became deeply enmeshed in civil-military plots. Under the Balaguer presidency during the 1966–78 period, the military remained a powerful support group of the government and occasionally a potential threat to Balaguer. Numerous generals were forced to resign under PRD governments (1978–86), however.

In the 1990s, as a result of the successive changes, the Dominican military combined patrimonial elements, partisan balance, and financial constraints. The military was not the professional, partially insulated, democratically controlled armed forces that reformers had sought to develop. Different administrations also carried out their relations with the military ignoring established legal norms. The PRD administrations managed to weaken the institution of the military and to promote individuals loyal to the president to high posts. Following this pattern, Balaguer brought back to active service officers who had been loyal to him. However, during the ten years of his presidency (1986–96), the armed forces increasingly became a weak, underpaid, top-heavy, and largely unprofessional institution.

The first dramatic change to the military came on the day of Guzmán's inauguration in 1978 when he forced the resignation of several generals who could have proved a threat to his regime (see The PRD in Power and Balaguer, Again, ch. 1). During the next two years, more than thirty generals either were retired, demoted, or sent abroad. In addition to taking additional steps to remove the military from partisan politics, Guzmán also instituted a more concerted policy of rotating officers to break up regional pockets of civilian-military alliances that had become established under Balaguer. Guzmán earned the trust of the remaining military both through his conservative views and anticommunist policies and his endorsement of Balaguer's last-minute generous salary increases for the military, as well as additional modest budget increases. By the end of his administration, Guzmán could number several military among his closest and most loyal associates.

Jorge Blanco (1982–86) transformed the armed forces even more, while also establishing close relations with certain top officers. He weakened the military structure by accelerating a pattern of massive retirements, typically after first rapidly promoting officers. To outside observers, the logic was not always clear because some of those retired appeared to be professional, well-trained individuals; the United States, for example, complained that its military training funds were being wasted as careers were cut short. In addition to further limiting the ability of the military to participate in politics, Jorge Blanco's actions constrained the maneuvering room of any incoming administration regarding promotions. The result was a military force that was institutionally weak and no longer a direct political threat. And, as all the major political parties moderated their policy positions, the support for military intervention declined throughout all groups in society.

In the same way, however, that Balaguer's maneuvers in 1978 largely did not prevent Guzmán from taking steps against certain officers, so Jorge Blanco's actions ultimately did not limit Balaguer's options in 1986. Balaguer, also, had little interest in unduly strengthening the military. By the time he returned to power in 1986, he was prepared to accept his inability to retain power either by overt military pressure or through a coup, given United States pressure and the extent of organized domestic opposition. What Balaguer wanted was a military that was loyal to him. Thus, when he resumed the presidency in 1986 and in subsequent years, he simply brought a number of officers who had been close to him back into active service. Because many of these previously retired officers continued to age while ostensibly on active duty, Balaguer's strategy became known as *abuelismo* (from the word for "grandfather"). Although recalling previously retired officers was in open violation of the Organic Law of the Armed Forces, as many of Guzmán's actions had been, no effective judicial challenge could be mounted given Balaguer's sway over the judiciary and possible alternative interpretations of presidential constitutional powers.

During the 1986–96 period, the military receded further as important political, strategic, or economic players, especially in contrast to the role they had played during Balaguer's first twelve years in power. The contexts were substantially different. In 1966 Balaguer took office shortly after a civil war that had provoked serious intramilitary rifts and left a legacy of polarization and continued commitment to violence among some. In 1986 there were no active political forces committed to the use of violence. As in his first period as president, Balaguer sought to place officers he trusted in key places, occasionally rotating them to keep them off balance. However, far more than in the 1960s and 1970s, he now made a mockery of any sense of military professionalism or career path. Balaguer also permitted the budget to decline; paid the military appallingly low salaries, thus inviting corruption; allowed the armed forces to become one of the most top heavy on the continent; and made generals out of individuals such as his personal chauffeur.

The decline in military professionalism continued to deteriorate the longer Balaguer remained in office. Not surprisingly, given the low salaries and lack of official functions for many officers, corruption was alleged to be rampant. For example, because of their presence along the Haitian border, the Dominican military played an important role in acquiring Haitian labor for state sugar mills, for which bribery was often involved, and also in "facilitating" contraband trade between the two countries (especially during the period of the international embargo of Haiti in 1993 and 1994).

Balaguer's policies helped provoke unhappiness within the ranks of the military, especially among frustrated individuals in the lower ranks who perceived their chance of advancement as blocked by individuals who had been brought back from retirement and remained in place. Although some military might have been willing to support Balaguer by force of arms if called to do so, during the 1990s it appears that the Dominican armed forces were becoming increasingly divided in their political loyalties. In both the 1994 and 1996 elections, all the major presidential candidates and parties possessed the support of at least some military officers. Opposition parties did not complain of centralized military harassment against them, although evidence of local-level military bias was present.

In sum, as a result of the actions of the PRD and the more cautious and cynical steps subsequently by Balaguer, the Dominican armed forces were largely not a political threat to democracy. Yet, occasionally, firm action was still required by the president: soon after assuming the presidency in August 1996, President Fernández was forced to dismiss the head of the air force, General Juan Bautista Rojas Tabar, when the general challenged the president's political authority. President Fernández has been seeking to improve the degree of professionalism of the armed forces. Yet, the military institution (or parts of it) remains a potential instrument of the president in power because it has not yet developed into a professional, well-organized semiautonomous but democratically account-able state institution. Furthermore, in the absence of a profes-sional, apolitical ethos, it is also possible for politically ambitious individuals within the military to rise through the ranks and represent a potential threat to civilian authority.

Foreign Relations

The Dominican Republic is a relatively small and weak coun-try, heavily dependent on the outside world economically and strategically, and located in the center of what was an impor-tant area for Cold War conflict in the world—the volatile Carib-bean. Because of these factors, various outside actors have long exercised a significant degree of influence in the island nation's internal politics.

In the early nineteenth century, the principal outside actors were Spain, France, and Britain; toward the end of the century, Germany and the United States had also become involved in Dominican affairs. The United States has remained a central actor in Dominican affairs ever since. Because the Dominican Republic shares the island of Hispaniola with Haiti, and because Haiti represented a constant threat to the Dominican Republic both before and after the Haitian occupation of 1822–44, Haiti also has exerted significant influence (see The Struggle for Formal Sovereignty and Ambivalent Sovereignty, Caudillo Rule, and Political Instability, ch. 1). In recent years, the economic importance of Europe has grown for the coun-try, particularly because of increased European aid flows and the large number of Europeans who vacation in the country.

Various transnational actors have played a significant role in Dominican politics. These include private economic actors such as multinational corporations, and financial institutions such as the International Monetary Fund, the World Bank (see Glossary), and the Inter-American Development Bank. They also include other international political or state actors such as the Socialist International (the international grouping of social democratic parties, which was highly involved in Dominican affairs during the 1970s and 1980s), the international Christian Democratic Union, the Vatican, and European assistance orga-nized through the Lomé Convention (see Glossary). In recent years, they have included NGOs, principally from Europe and from the United States, including such organizations as the American Federation of Labor-Congress of Industrial Organizations (AFL-CIO) and Human Rights Watch, which played an important role in applying pressure for passage of the 1992 Labor Code in the Dominican Republic. In addition, overseas Dominicans must now be considered as important actors within the Dominican Republic because their remittances are a crucial source of foreign exchange and because Dominican political parties avidly seek their funding. The Dominican diaspora has also recently been given the right to vote in Dominican presidential elections, even as the diaspora also is beginning to have more of a presence in local politics in New York City and elsewhere where its numbers are concentrated.

With regard to relations between the United States and the Dominican Republic, in the past issues that were central focused primarily on security concerns, protection of United States private economic actors, and expectations of political solidarity. Such issues are being increasingly superseded by new issues related to market-oriented reforms, democracy and human rights, drug trafficking, and migration. From the perspective of the Dominican Republic, Dominican policy makers worry that the country is marginal to the concerns of United States policy makers; they also are concerned about unilateralism and potential pressure by the United States, no longer because of anticommunism, but as a consequence of issues such as narcotics, democracy, and human rights. Finally, the Fernández government is putting forth efforts to enhance hemispheric cooperation around such issues as trade and respect for democracy.

As a small, economically vulnerable country, the Dominican Republic has continually been forced to adapt to sudden changes in the world economy. Globalization has had contradictory effects on the country. On the one hand, it has generated sometimes wrenching economic changes, weakening previously strong popular-sector organizations and stimulating further inequality, at least in the short term. The dramatic shift away from sugar exports toward tourism and free-trade zones is one example, as is the significant increase in emigration that was spurred in the 1980s and continues to this day. On the other hand, globalization has deepened the country's links to the outside world, providing external support for organizations committed to building or strengthening democratic accountability within the country. This effect has been seen in the international support for electoral observers and for NGOs in areas such as labor, women's rights, and environmental issues.

The country's major trade relations are with the United States, its primary partner, and with Japan, Venezuela, Mexico, and the European Union. In addition to sustaining diplomatic relations with these countries, the Dominican Republic maintains embassies throughout the Western Hemisphere and in selected other countries, including the Republic of China (Taiwan) and Israel.

The Dominican Republic is a signatory to the Charter of the Organization of American States (OAS), the Inter-American Treaty of Reciprocal Assistance (the Rio Treaty), the Pact of Bogotá, and all major inter-American conventions. Historically, its ties to and involvement in the OAS were stronger than its relations with the United Nations (UN), although under President Fernández this is changing.

The Dominican Republic is a member of the UN and its Economic Commission for Latin America and the Caribbean (ECLAC), the United Nations Educational, Scientific, and Cultural Organization (UNESCO), the International Labour Organisation (ILO), the World Health Organization (WHO), and the International Court of Justice. It subscribes to the IMF, the World Bank, the International Finance Corporation (IFC—see Glossary), the Inter-American Development Bank (IDB), the International Development Association (IDA—see Glossary), and the International Telecommunications Satellite Organization (Intelsat). It is also a participant in the International Civil Aviation Organization (ICAO), the Universal Postal Union (UPU), and the International Telecommunications Union (ITU), and is a member of the International Atomic Energy Agency (IAEA).

The Dominican Republic faces significant foreign policy challenges. Under President Balaguer, the country had a low international profile and increasingly tense relations with the United States. Because of his age and his health, President Balaguer traveled abroad very little. A conservative nationalist, President Balaguer accepted the fact that the Dominican Republic was in the sphere of influence of the United States, yet he also resented its presence and its influence. Relations became especially tense around questions of democratic elections and also with regard to Haiti, particularly when the United States was seeking to force the Haitian military to leave in order for the deposed Jean-Bertrand Aristide to return to office.

The country's international profile and its relations with the United States have changed considerably since President Fernández assumed office in August 1996. In his first two years in office, President Fernández has made foreign policy and international relations an important priority. He has worked to strengthen the country's Secretariat of State for Foreign Relations and its diplomatic capabilities in terms of personnel and equipment. He has reached out to the country's Caribbean and Central American neighbors, seeking to have the Dominican Republic serve as a bridge between the two areas. He has reestablished diplomatic relations with Cuba. He has also worked with his Caribbean and Central American neighbors to find common ground on issues that affect their relations with each other and with the United States, such as drug trafficking, economic integration, improved access to United States markets, and the treatment of their emigrants in the United States, including concerns about the forced repatriation of convicted criminals to their country of origin.

The growing international profile of President Fernández and of the Dominican Republic is demonstrated by the fact that the country now presides over the African, Caribbean, and Pacific group of nations (under the Lomé Convention that obtains aid for these countries from the European Union). Furthermore, the second summit meeting of heads of state of these nations was held in Santo Domingo in November 1999. In addition, the Dominican Republic presented the requests of this group to the meeting of the World Trade Organization in Seattle, which began in late November 1999.

One of the most challenging relationships has been with Haiti. Although in general President Fernández has sought to improve relations with Haiti, he has also responded to domestic fears and pressures revolving around the growing presence of Haitian migrants in the country. As Haiti's economic situation has continued to deteriorate and Haitians have found it increasingly difficult to migrate to the United States, they increasingly attempt to enter the Dominican Republic. Large-scale deportations of Haitians during 1998 and 1999 met with protests; many deportees complained that they were not allowed to demonstrate that they were legally resident in the Dominican Republic and criticized their treatment while being transported out of the country.

Beginning with President Fernández, awareness has grown in the Dominican Republic that maintaining an informed role in world affairs is crucial to helping the country confront the challenges it faces in an increasingly globalized world. The Dominican Republic's global outlook is facilitated by the extent of contact that broader elements of the Dominican population have with that world through family members who have emigrated abroad, tourism, the media, and travel.

*   *   *

Many useful books are available on the government and politics of the Dominican Republic. On the formative Trujillo era, see Jesús Galíndez's *The Era of Trujillo*, the excellent biography by Robert Crassweller entitled *Trujillo*, and Howard J. Wiarda's *Dictatorship and Development: The Methods of Control in Trujillo's Dominican Republic*. Post-Trujillo developments are treated in detail in John Bartlow Martin's *Overtaken by Events*, and Howard J. Wiarda's three-volume *Dictatorship, Development, and Disintegration: Politics and Social Change in the Dominican* Republic. The 1965 revolution and intervention are well covered in Piero Gleijeses's *The Dominican Crisis*, Dan Kurzman's *Santo Domingo: Revolt of the Damned*, Abraham Lowenthal's *The Dominican Intervention*, and Jerome Slater's *Intervention and Negotiation: The United States and the Dominican Republic*.

For the Balaguer era of the 1960s and 1970s, see G. Pope Atkins's *Arms and Politics in the Dominican Republic*, Ian Bell's *The Dominican Republic*, Rosario Espinal's "An Interpretation of the Democratic Transition in the Dominican Republic," and Howard J. Wiarda and Michael J. Kryzanek's *The Dominican Republic: A Caribbean Crucible*. More recent developments are analyzed in Jan Knippers Black's *The Dominican Republic: Politics and Development in an Unsovereign State*, James Ferguson's *The Dominican Republic: Beyond the Lighthouse*, a special issue of the North American Congress on Latin America (NACLA) Report on the Americas entitled "The Dominican Republic After the Caudillos," Jonathan Hartlyn's *The Struggle for Democratic Politics in the Dominican Republic*, and Rosario Espinal and Jonathan Hartlyn's "The Dominican Republic: The Long and Difficult Struggle for Democracy." (For further information and complete citations, see Bibliography.)

Chapter 5. Dominican Republic: National Security

The Torre del Homenaje, Santo Domingo

BY TRADITION, THE DOMINICAN Republic's armed forces have been active in the competition for national political power and have often functioned as a praetorian guard for the government holding power. The turbulent period of the early 1960s led to three coups against the civilian government by the military leadership. Violence between reformist and conservative military elements brought the country close to civil war in 1965, and intervention by the United States was required to restore order. However, it appeared that during the 1970s and the 1980s, successive governments were able to reduce the military's former role in national political life as self-appointed final arbiter of public policy.

By the late 1980s, the stature of the armed forces had been reduced to that of an important interest group competing with other such groups for power and influence within the nation's increasingly pluralistic political system. It would be premature, however, to conclude that the goal of developing an institutionalized and apolitical military establishment had been completely realized by 1999. Individual military officers continued to exert considerable political influence, and armed forces units continued to be employed overtly during political campaigns. Nevertheless, the military's explicit support of civilian governments during the 1980s, and particularly of Joaquín Balaguer Ricardo, who served as president between 1986 and 1996, suggested that the armed forces had accepted the principle of civilian control. The military leadership benefited financially during Balaguer's rule, but could not act independently of the president. Balaguer's successor, Leonel Fernández Reyna, began his term by dismissing or retiring many generals in what was seen as part of an effort to restore higher standards to a military institution whose standards had slackened under Balaguer.

The armed forces have as their primary mission the defense of the nation's territorial integrity. However, as of 1999, the country faced no credible external threat, and the military served more as an internal security force, working with the National Police and the narcotics police to maintain domestic order, to combat the increasingly serious problem of narcotics trafficking, and to control contraband and illegal immigration from Haiti.

Although the Dominican Republic no longer faces a domestic insurgency threat, popular economic discontent has resulted in frequent protests and strikes that occasionally have become violent, resulting in injuries and some deaths. Soldiers are routinely assigned to help the police and have sometimes been accused of excessive force in clashes with demonstrators. Most of these disturbances are rooted in despair over the constant deterioration of living conditions for ordinary citizens as well as a decline in the level and quality of public services.

The country's security forces often have been called upon to prevent violence and disturbances in connection with political campaigns and elections by measures that included detentions of antigovernment figures. In 1996, however, presidential power was transferred peacefully and smoothly after elections described as the cleanest in the country's history.

Defense budgets since the early 1980s have shown little change except for measurable increases between 1993 and 1996. Weapons replacement and modernization have been almost abandoned as spending constraints preclude outlays much beyond pay and benefits. As a consequence, the readiness of the armed forces to deal with any threat from abroad is severely limited. They are capable of carrying out most internal security functions, but lack the resources to adequately patrol the country's borders against the flow of illicit drugs.

The armed forces in 1999 consisted of about 24,300 active-duty personnel. The army has seven brigades, most organized along constabulary or tactical infantry lines. The air force operates three flying squadrons, only one of which is armed, and the navy maintains twelve armed patrol vessels. The Dominican military is second in size to Cuba's military in the Caribbean.

The National Police, the National Department of Investigations, and the National Drug Control Directorate also share responsibility for security matters. The latter two groups, which draw personnel from both the military and the police, report directly to the president.

The criminal justice system comes under the jurisdiction of the national government. The system, according to its critics, has many shortcomings, including interference by political authorities, judicial corruption, maladministration of the courts, and scandalously poor prison conditions. Much police misconduct goes unpunished. In addition, the Dominican Republic has become a primary way station in the transport of narcotics between Colombia and the United States. Dominican nationals are leading figures in drug distribution and delivery in New York and throughout the northeastern United States. Rarely do narcotics-related crimes result in prison sentences in the Dominican Republic.

The presidential administration that took office in 1996 had drug corruption and judicial and prison reform on its agenda. Measures have been introduced to make the criminal justice system more humane and effective and independent of politics. As the head of a minority party, the president nevertheless faces an uphill battle in cleansing the bureaucracy, the military, and justice and law enforcement agencies of the influence of the well-entrenched drug interests.

History and Development of the Armed Forces

Spanish colonial militias were the first organized military forces in what is now the Dominican Republic. These forces maintained law and order over the entire island of Hispaniola, which from 1496 was ruled from Santo Domingo, the center of Spanish colonial administration in the New World (see The First Colony, ch. 1). By the mid-1500s, when Spain's interests shifted to the richer colonies of Mexico and Peru, the Dominican colony had a well-established hierarchical social system that was based on authoritarian rule by a small white elite. The colony also included a large black slave population (see Ethnic Heritage, ch. 2).

The shift in Spain's colonial interests and the consequent withdrawal of most of Spain's military from the Dominican colony was followed by a long period of economic and political decay, during which domestic order deteriorated. The colony was threatened by pirates along the coast as well as by periodic encroachment by the forces of France and England, which were competing with each other and with Spain for territory and power in the New World.

As a result of this competition, Spain was forced in 1697 to cede the western third of Hispaniola to France. Nevertheless, border disputes continued, and by 1797 France had prevailed on Spain to cede the rest of the island.

Before French rule became established in the Dominican colony, however, a slave revolt broke out in the western portion of the island, which came to be known as Haiti. In what proved to be the first in a series of Haitian incursions into Dominican territory, the rebellious Haitians invaded the poor and less populous eastern side of the island in 1801. Haitian forces were repelled, but the rebellion within Haiti continued, and the French were forced to withdraw from the island by 1804. In 1809, helped by Britain, Spain regained control of the Dominican portion of the island. Spain ruled only until 1821, however, when the Dominican colonists revolted. Independence lasted just a few weeks before Haiti invaded in 1822. The Dominicans were not able to expel the Haitian forces until 1844 (see The Struggle for Formal Sovereignty, ch. 1).

The long-delayed achievement of independence did not bring peace to the new Dominican Republic, nor did it improve public order. Political power was extremely decentralized, and competition among factions of the landowning white elite produced a level of national disunity that had disastrous effects on public safety. Although the central government had established a national army, this force essentially consisted of a small group of officers who were interested chiefly in personal enrichment and whose duties were largely ceremonial. The national army was far outnumbered by armed militias that were organized and maintained by local caudillos, who had set themselves up as provincial governors. Using these militias, the caudillos waged bloody civil wars as they contended for regional and national power. National political life was characterized by repeated coups and military uprisings against whichever caudillo—usually self-promoted to general-officer status—had gathered enough power to seize the presidency.

The continuous civil war, political upheaval, and misrule that characterized the republic's early years were punctuated by repeated Haitian attempts to invade. During such periods of danger, forces larger than the small national army were needed to defend the country. These forces, hastily raised and poorly equipped, were essentially conglomerations of regional militias that had been filled out by poor farmers or landless plantation workers who had been pressed into service. Once the threat had subsided and Haitian forces had been repelled, the militias would return to advancing the cause of particular regional leaders. The impressed troops would return home, where some would contribute to the general state of disorder by taking up banditry.

During its first thirty years of independence, the Dominican Republic was run directly, or indirectly, by General Pedro Santana Familias and General Buenaventura Báez Méndez, whose bitter rivalry was played out in civil wars that resulted in alternating Santana and Báez regimes (see Ambivalent Sovereignty,

Dominican troops participating in a parade
Courtesy Embassy of the Dominican Republic, Washington

Caudillo Rule, and Political Instability, ch. 1). Each of the two generals used his position to enrich himself, his relatives, and his followers at public expense. To deal with the national bankruptcy caused by civil war, corruption, and mismanagement, Santana called on Spain in 1861 to restore colonial rule. The Dominicans soon had enough of Spanish control, and in 1865 Spain was again forced out. As a result of army restructuring after the restoration, existing military tendencies in Dominican society became more pronounced.

General Ulises Heureaux became president in 1882. During his brutal, dictatorial rule, factionalism was repressed, and the nation enjoyed relative internal peace. The army emerged as a standing organization for the first time, based on a system of conscription that affected mainly peasants. The number of officers increased sharply, and military expenditures dominated the state budget. By 1897 Heureaux was able to boast of a disciplined army with 14,000 Remington rifles and six artillery batteries. With the country's newly built rail lines and a modest navy, the force had considerable mobility.

After Heureaux was assassinated in 1899, political factions again contested for power and for access to the national treasury. By 1904 the economy was in shambles, and foreign governments were threatening to use force to collect defaulted loans. Citing the need to avert European intervention, the United States assumed control of Dominican customs receipts in 1905. Amid continuing disorder, a force of 750 United States Marines landed in 1912, and in 1916 they were authorized by President Woodrow Wilson to take full control of the Dominican government (see From the United States Occupation (1916–24) to the Emergence of Trujillo (1930), ch. 1).

The marines disbanded the regional militias and ruled the nation directly for eight years, acting as police in cities and in rural areas. As part of its effort to build effective institutions of government in the Dominican Republic, the United States formed a new Dominican Constabulary Guard of about 2,000 officers and men to replace the old national army. Up to this time, both the civilian and the military elites had been drawn from the same wealthy landowning class. Intense resentment among the elites against the United States presence, however, made it impossible to find recruits for the new constabulary among the landowning class. The ranks became filled by the lower strata of Dominican society and, as a result, the new force had neither ties nor debts to the traditional elite. The most notable representative of the new military leadership was Rafael Leónidas Trujillo Molina, who entered the Dominican Constabulary Guard in 1919 as a second lieutenant. By curtailing the power of regional caudillos, the constabulary gave the country a sense of political unity and provided the structure for the emergence of a new elite that would eventually control political life.

In 1924, after the Dominican Republic had adopted a new constitution and had elected a civilian president, the United States forces withdrew. The same year, the constabulary was renamed the Dominican National Police, a somewhat misleading title for what had become more a military entity than a law enforcement organization. By that time, Trujillo had risen to the rank of major and had assumed one of the nation's two field commands. He had also emerged as one of the most influential voices within the force, increasingly able to mold its development to suit his personal ambitions. In 1928 when the National Police was renamed the National Army (Ejército Nacional), Trujillo became a lieutenant colonel and army chief of staff. In this role, Trujillo was the most powerful individual in the nation even before his election to the presidency in 1930 (see The Trujillo Era, 1930–61, ch. 1)

By the 1930s, the new Dominican military establishment had developed into a centrally controlled and well-disciplined force that was both larger and far better equipped than any previous Dominican army. New rifles and machine guns were purchased, and an artillery element was fashioned by combining Krupp 77mm guns from the old Dominican army with newer 37mm and 77mm guns. The unified, apolitical, and professional force that had been envisioned by the United States military government had not been realized, however. Instead, traditional Dominican patterns of military service persisted, including factionalism, politicization, and the perception that position entitled one to personal enrichment. Trujillo encouraged and strengthened these patterns, and used them both to retain the support of the armed forces and to control them. Military officers became an elite class, gaining wealth, favors, prestige and power, and developing an esprit de corps that Trujillo carefully nurtured. Under these conditions, a career in the military came to be esteemed as an avenue of upward mobility. The services themselves were built up, large quantities of arms were imported, and a defense industry was established. The country was divided into three military zones, each garrisoned by a two-battalion brigade.

Trujillo rationalized maintenance of a large military by citing the purported need for vigilance against Haiti and, particularly after the Cuban Revolution of 1959, against communism. For the most part, however, Trujillo used the large and powerful military establishment to maintain internal control over the nation. The army and the navy intelligence services were among the numerous agencies Trujillo employed to maintain close surveillance and rigid control over the population. In 1957 the intelligence and secret police organizations were unified into the State Security Secretariat. With a personnel strength of 5,000, this new organization was larger than either the regular National Police, the air force, or the navy.

The military establishment claimed an increasingly greater share of the national budget. Part of the military costs were offset by basing privileges granted to the United States during World War II. The basing agreement enabled the Dominican Republic to qualify for Lend-Lease aid. However, only limited equipment transfers took place, mostly light weapons and lightly armored vehicles. After the war ended, the country acquired larger quantities of surplus stocks, including 105mm howitzers, light tanks, and half-track armored personnel carriers. Sweden and Brazil became important suppliers of matériel; combat, training, and transport aircraft were acquired from Britain and the United States.

Trujillo did not rely solely on rewards to keep control over the military. He maintained personal command of all aspects of military organization, including promotions, logistics, assignments, and discipline. He constantly shuffled personnel from assignment to assignment to prevent any potential rival from gaining an independent power base. Trujillo also used the tactic of frequent inspections, sometimes in person and sometimes by undercover operatives, to keep tabs on both men and operations. In addition, he brought many of his relatives and supporters into the armed forces, promoting them rapidly as a reward for loyalty.

As part of his effort to maintain control over the armed forces, Trujillo built up the air force as a political counterbalance to the army, and he encouraged factionalism in all the services. A full armored battalion was formed at San Isidro Air Base outside Santo Domingo. This battalion, which was directly subordinate to the Ministry of Defense, essentially constituted a fourth armed force, further splintering power within the military. The total complement of 10,000 men was supplemented by a call-up of reservists after Fidel Castro Ruz established his communist dictatorship in Cuba in 1959. The government acquired many additional weapons from a variety of sources, notably 106mm recoilless rifles from the United States and AMX–13 tanks from France. The Dominican army easily crushed an invasion from Cuba of anti-Trujillo Dominicans in July 1959.

After Trujillo was assassinated in 1961, the military, as the nation's most powerful and best-organized interest group, claimed a major role in the political competition that followed. It soon became clear, however, that the factionalism encouraged by Trujillo prevented the military from acting as a unified institution. Instead, elements of the armed services allied with various civilian politicians. After Juan Bosch Gaviño of the center-left won the presidential election in 1962, portions of the military became alarmed over his reforms and his tolerance of leftists and legal communist parties. In 1963 armed forces officers, led by Elías Wessin y Wessin (a colonel at the time), overthrew Bosch and replaced him with a civilian junta. Another faction of officers calling themselves Constitutionalists favored the return of Bosch. In 1965 this faction overthrew the civilian junta. In the following days, civil war erupted as the armed forces split into warring camps. The majority within the armed forces united behind Wessin y Wessin (by this time a general) and attacked the new government with armored and air support. The Constitutionalists armed their civilian supporters in order to defend the capital (see Democratic Struggles and Failures, ch. 1).

United States intervention in the conflict halted the fighting, but subsequent efforts to reunify the armed forces were only partly successful. The agreement to reintegrate those officers who had supported Bosch was never fully implemented, and only a few gained readmission. Politically, the outlook of the officer corps remained right of center after the civil war.

Although the armed forces continued to be a significant factor, their influence on national political life steadily declined. This decline began during the administration of Joaquín Balaguer Ricardo (1966–78; 1986–96), who made effective use of some of the same tactics employed by Trujillo to maintain control over the military, including the encouragement and manipulation of factionalism within the officer corps and the frequent shuffling of top assignments. He also increased the number of general officers from six in 1966 to forty-eight by 1978. At the same time, Balaguer gave senior officers a stake in his regime by appointing many to positions in government and in state-run enterprises. He also extended valuable sugar-growing concessions for government mills.

The process of reining in the military advanced significantly during the terms of Balaguer's successors, Silvestre Antonio Guzmán Fernández (1978–82) and Salvador Jorge Blanco (1982–86), each of whom made an effort to institutionalize the armed forces and to remove the powerful group of officers who had supported Trujillo and Balaguer. The partial success of their efforts was demonstrated in the period from 1984 to 1985, when the armed forces leadership repeatedly and publicly supported Jorge Blanco's government in the face of social unrest provoked by adverse economic conditions. Although Jorge Blanco had not been the military's preferred candidate in the 1982 elections, the leadership chose to support him as constitutional head of state rather than to take power itself.

Military capability in the years after the 1965 civil war declined to an even greater extent than did the armed forces' national political role. After that time, each administration faced increasing national economic constraints that forced stringent limits on defense spending. Although force levels and personnel budgets were generally left untouched, aging equipment was not replaced. As a result, as of 1999 equipment in all three services was outmoded, in short supply, and of doubtful operational utility.

Role of the Military in Public Life

The 1966 constitution describes the armed forces as "essentially obedient and apolitical and without the right to deliberate. The purpose of their creation is to defend the independence and integrity of the republic, to maintain public order, and to uphold the Constitution and the laws." By law, members of the armed forces are denied the right to vote and the right to participate in the activities of political parties and organized labor.

Since the early 1960s, the political influence of the military has declined. And military officers have largely accepted their status as defenders of national sovereignty and their subservience to the civilian government hierarchy. During Balaguer's first two terms (1966–78), the president reinforced his control by accommodating high officers, helping them to become landowners, merchants, and industrialists, positions they could not have attained had they remained in the purely military sphere. When Balaguer left office in 1978, the officers were reluctant to see power handed over to Antonio Guzmán, fearing a threat to their profitable positions. Their fears were justified. Guzmán retired some forty pro-Balaguer generals and introduced a period of military professionalization. When Balaguer resumed power in 1986, however, the retired generals were reintegrated into the military and offered a financial stake in the regime. Although friendly to the military establishment, Balaguer's authoritarian style enabled him to keep it on a tight leash (see Interest Groups and Social Actors, ch. 4).

After disputed elections marred by fraud in 1994 between José Francisco Peña Gómez of the Dominican Revolutionary Party (Partido Revolucionario Dominicano—PRD) and Balaguer of the Reformist Social Christian Party (Partido Reformista Social Cristiano—PRSC), the Dominican military openly supported the election board's declaration of Balaguer's victory. (Balaguer had won elections in 1966, 1970, and 1974; was voted out of office in 1978; and was reelected in 1986 and 1990.) An official communique warned against attempts to

*President Fernández attending the
graduation of various infantry classes, 1997
Courtesy Embassy of the Dominican Republic,
Washington*

undo the decision, saying that the armed forces "would not
omit efforts to guarantee public peace and the tranquillity and
serenity that the Dominican family enjoys."

A post-election agreement in 1994 limited Balaguer's term to
two years, and lawyer Leonel Fernández Reyna, new head of
the PRD, won in a run-off election. Soon after taking office in
1996, President Fernández undertook efforts to reprofessional-
ize the military leadership, which had become preoccupied
with its own enrichment under Balaguer's policy of granting
economic and commercial privileges. He retired twenty-four of
the country's seventy generals, most of whom were considered
allies of Balaguer. The president also replaced the head of the
navy, the head of the air force, the head of the state intelligence service, and the commander of the second brigade.
Admiral Rubén Paulino Álvarez continued as secretary of state
for the armed forces. Although Fernández faces opposition
from pro-Balaguer factions in the officer corps, he may be able
to count on a more liberal group of officers to support him in
the transition to a more democratic style of government.

Missions

No valid purpose exists for armed forces structured to defend the Dominican Republic's security because the country faces no foreseeable external military threat. The principal justification for the military establishment is the containment of possible civil unrest. The military is thus largely organized as an internal security force. The armed forces also constitute a principal line of defense against international drug trafficking. However, in spite of help from the United States, the flow of narcotics has not been stemmed because of equipment and budget limitations as well as insufficiently motivated personnel.

The Dominican Republic has a tradition of enmity toward Haiti although the military officers of the two countries have maintained friendly relations. On a personal level, President Balaguer had little incentive to enforce the United Nations (UN) embargo against the Haitian military regime in 1994 because it was intended to help restore the government of President Jean-Bertrand Aristide, whom Balaguer personally disliked. The unhindered movement of goods, particularly gasoline, across the lightly patrolled border with Haiti undercut the effectiveness of the embargo. Only after coming under heavy international pressure did Balaguer agree to seal the border by replacing corrupt border guards with 10,000 or more troops. The United States provided radios and night vision equipment, and a UN observer force was dispatched to help stiffen the Dominican effort. The Dominican army cut down embargo violations by day but was unable to prevent activity at night. It was also alleged that many of the border troops were less interested in interdicting gasoline than in ensuring their share of the bribe money changing hands.

After the return of the Aristide government in 1994, several of the more notorious of the Haitian military coup leaders took refuge in the Dominican Republic, where their presence became a source of tension between the two governments. In 1996, however, they were deported by the Dominican authorities and left for Central America.

Dominican army troops and observation posts are thinly located along the length of the 388-kilometer frontier. Border forces are principally concerned with illegal border crossings and contraband, especially narcotics. Haitian military capability has been clearly unequal to that of Dominican forces, and incursions in whatever form could be handled. Any latent Haitian threat became even more improbable after the Haitian armed forces were abolished in 1995. The renewal of upheaval in Haiti would present a danger of large-scale refugee movements, however. The several hundred thousand legal and illegal Haitian immigrants who work in the nation as agricultural laborers are already a recurring source of tension, and the Dominicans would face increasing difficulty in controlling border movement if the economic situation in Haiti caused more Haitians to flee conditions in their own country (see Foreign Relations, ch. 4).

After Castro's assumption of power in 1959, the Dominican Republic saw Cuba as a potential external threat. This view, which was rooted in the anticommunist sentiments espoused by Trujillo, is still held by most military officers. It also has a basis in the 1959 Cuban-based invasion attempt by anti-Trujillo Dominicans. Cuba itself, however, has never taken overt military action against the nation. Critics have charged the armed forces with justifying attacks on leftist political groups and on political and labor activists by falsely accusing them of having ties with Cuba.

Until the mid-1970s, the military occasionally conducted operations against limited insurgencies, but by the late 1970s the country was relatively free of insurgent groups. In 1990 eight terrorist attacks, mainly bomb explosions, were directed against United States targets in the Dominican Republic. None of the attacks resulted in the death of a United States citizen. Some were linked to the United States military action against Panama. A group calling itself the Revolutionary Army of the People claimed responsibility for several of the attacks. The government blamed the National Union of Revolutionary Students and other communist organizations for attempting to organize a campaign of terror and subversion.

As part of its mission to assist the police in maintaining public order, the military keeps watch on political groups deemed to be possible sources of instability, including opposition parties of the far left that have little following but operate freely.

Interdiction of illegal immigration is another mission of the armed forces. The country has become an important way station for would-be immigrants to the United States who attempt to cross the 175-kilometer-wide Mona Passage to Puerto Rico. Refugees from many corners of the world congregate on the country's northern coast to make contact with boat captains. Local officials are often bribed to overlook the activity. Although the armed forces cooperate with the United States in intercepting the refugees, the navy's tight budget hampers its interdiction efforts.

Article 93 of the constitution states that an objective of the armed forces is the pursuit of civic-action programs and, at the direction of the executive branch, participation in projects that promote national, social, and economic development. The armed forces hence conduct civic-action activities in the form of well-digging; road, home, and school construction; and the provision of sports and educational equipment to rural schools. The military also runs the most important vocational school system in the nation. Navy schools train diesel mechanics, for example, and the army is largely responsible for forest conservation. In addition, military medical and dental teams pay visits to remote areas, and the air force has transported medicine, doctors, and supplies to areas damaged by hurricanes and other natural disasters. The navy also plays a role in transporting fuel oil.

Armed Forces Organization, Training, and Equipment

Under the constitution, the president of the republic is the commander in chief of the armed forces. The chain of command extends from the president to the secretary of state for the armed forces and then to deputy secretaries of state for the army, navy, and air force (see fig. 6). The secretary and the three deputies are all military personnel. In the past, the secretary has usually been an army lieutenant general although an admiral held the post in 1998 and the incumbent in 1999 was a major general, Manuel de Jesús Florentino. The secretary is appointed by the president and also serves as chief of the armed forces general staff. The deputies, normally holding the rank of major general or rear admiral, are appointed by the secretary with the approval of the president.

Each deputy controls his service through a chief of staff and a general staff that consists of five principal sections: personnel, intelligence, operations, logistics, and public affairs. In addition, an administrative judge advocate section for each service handles military legal matters. Except in emergencies, the chiefs of staff exercise operational control over the three services of the armed forces.

The army is responsible for the nation's land territory and for the border with Haiti. The navy is responsible for coastal waters, port areas, dams, rivers, and lakes. The air force is responsible for the operation and security of international airports, local airports, and landing strips.

The Secretariat of State for the Armed Forces operates several schools, including the three military academies. It also runs the General Juan Pablo Duarte Military Institute of Advanced Studies located in Santo Domingo, which operates a one-year command and staff program for senior officers and a six-month course of advanced strategic studies. The institute also offers fourteen specialized courses, including military intelligence, foreign languages, and military law. Another school at the same location, the General Directorate for Military Training, gives a specialized course for captains and first lieutenants, with a branch for noncommissioned officers. It has introduced courses on human rights, environmental protection, and forestry.

The secretariat also administers the Vocational School of the Armed Forces and Police, which is headquartered in Santo Domingo and has twenty-three branches throughout the country. With a student body primarily composed of civilians, its offerings include courses in carpentry, electricity, auto mechanics, industrial mechanics, plumbing, and leather and metal working. Some courses are also taught in prisons. The school operates a job placement program for its graduates.

The armed forces maintain an integrated judicial system for courts-martial for officers, and each branch conducts courts for minor offenses. All persons subject to military jurisdiction who commit a crime or misdemeanor while on military duty are accountable to military authorities. Those not on military duty are liable to prosecution by civilian authorities.

Army

As of 1999, the Dominican army had a strength of approximately 15,000, about twice the size of the navy and air force combined. The army is organized into seven brigades composed of battalions that fall into one of two categories—administrative, which perform constabulary functions, and tactical, which are organized as combat units. Purely tactical brigades are generally composed of three battalions, while administrative brigades have no fixed number of battalions and may have as many as five or six.

The first brigade, headquartered in the capital, is a combat brigade with two battalions in the capital and one at San

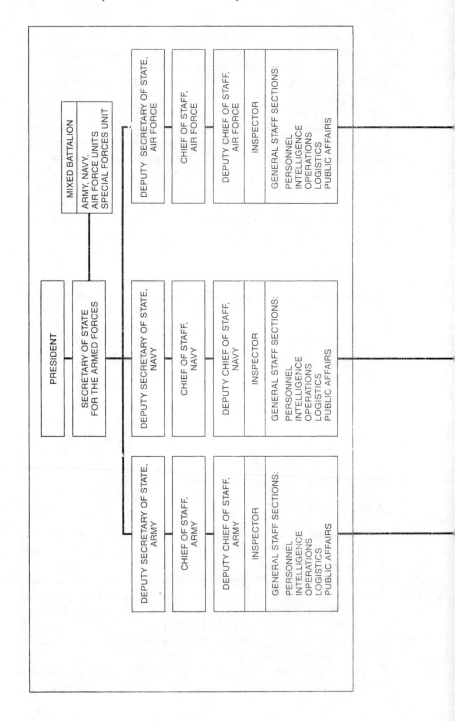

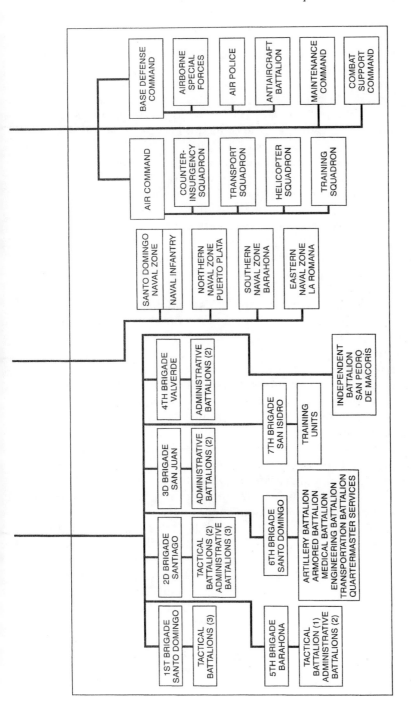

Figure 6. Dominican Republic: Organization of the Armed Forces, 1999

Cristóbal nearby (see fig. 7). The second brigade, with headquarters in Santiago, has three administrative and two tactical battalions, the first in Santiago and the second, a Special Force, in the central mountains at Constanza. The third brigade is an administrative brigade at San Juan in the west. One of its battalions patrols the frontier with Haiti. The fourth brigade has its headquarters in Valverde. One of its two battalions patrols the northern part of the border with Haiti. The fifth brigade has headquarters at Barahona, with one tactical and two administrative battalions scattered in the southwest. The sixth brigade is designated as combat support. It has five battalions—artillery, armor, medical, engineering, and transportation—and quartermaster services. The seventh brigade is designated as a training brigade.

One independent battalion, headquartered at San Pedro de Macorís, has four companies stationed at provincial capitals at the eastern end of the island. A mixed tactical battalion of army, navy, and air force infantry units headquartered in Santo Domingo reports directly to the secretary of state for the armed forces. It includes a mixed Special Forces unit trained in antiterrorism.

The army's principal small arm is the German G3 7.62mm rifle. Its armored assets include twelve French AMX–13 tanks and twelve American M–41A1 light tanks, all mounting 76mm guns. Eight Cadillac Gage V–150 Commando armored vehicles and twenty half-tracks serve as armored personnel carriers. The artillery units maintain twenty-two 105mm towed howitzers and are also equipped with 81mm and 120mm mortars (see table 12, Appendix). Most of the foregoing weapons date from the post-World War II period, and their present operational utility is considered doubtful.

Army enlisted personnel receive basic training at the Armed Forces Training Center near San Isidro, ten kilometers east of the capital. Advanced and specialized training is also provided to relevant units. Officer candidates are required to be high-school graduates and to meet strict physical requirements. Officer cadets attend the four-year Military Academy at San Isidro. A six-month course for infantry captains and lieutenants is conducted to prepare young officers to function as company commanders. Senior officers attend the Armed Forces Staff College in Santo Domingo to prepare for battalion-level and higher commands.

Navy

A Dominican navy was first established in 1873, when the country acquired a gunboat built in Scotland. By the time the navy was disbanded in 1916 during the United States Marine occupation, the fleet had acquired only two more gunboats and four armed launches. Several elements of the navy were incorporated into the Dominican Constabulary Guard in 1917 to function as a small coast guard. The navy remained an element of the National Army until 1943, when the Dominican National Navy was formally established as a separate service. During the next year, the navy began activities at the naval base at Las Calderas; in 1948 a separate naval school opened there.

The navy received a number of coast guard cutters from the United States just before the outbreak of World War II. Three additional cutters were transferred after the transport *Presidente Trujillo* was sunk by a German submarine in 1942. The Dominican Republic was not actively involved in the war although it made base facilities available to the United States. As a consequence of the purchase of numerous war-surplus vessels as part of a postwar expansion program, the Dominican navy became the most powerful in the Caribbean, with personnel numbering 3,000, including one marine battalion. Naval strength had leveled off by the time of the 1965 civil war when naval units participated in the shelling of Constitutionalist positions in Santo Domingo. After 1965, aging vessels were not replaced, and the naval inventory steadily declined.

As of 1999, the active naval complement was 3,800 officers and men, a reduction of 25 percent from ten years earlier. Navy headquarters are located at the 27 de Febrero Naval Base in Santo Domingo. The other principal base is at Las Calderas. The navy also has facilities at the ports of Barahona, Haina, La Romana, Monte Cristi, Pedernales, Puerto Plata, Samaná, and San Pedro de Macorís.

The navy chief of staff supervises the operations of the regional commands. The Santo Domingo Naval Zone includes the naval headquarters and the various naval organizations located in the capital. The headquarters of the Northern Naval Zone, at Puerto Plata, are responsible for the Atlantic coast from the northern border with Haiti to the Mona Passage. The Southern Naval Zone, headquartered at Barahona, covers the southwest coastal area to the Haitian border. The Eastern Naval Zone, with headquarters at La Romana, covers the eastern end of the island.

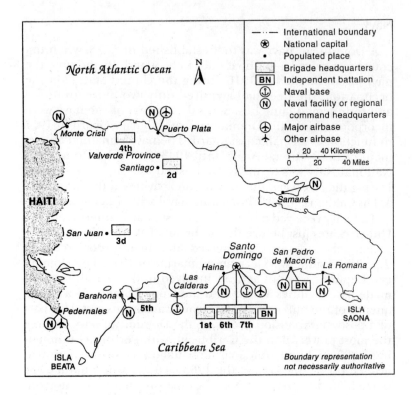

Figure 7. Dominican Republic: Military Bases and Headquarters, 1999

By 1999 national economic constraints had reduced the Dominican fleet to twelve armed patrol vessels and thirteen support ships, tugboats, and sail training ships. Most of the armed vessels are World War-II vintage craft of United States origin. The largest is a 1,000-ton (fully loaded) patrol vessel of the Balsam class, formerly a United States Coast Guard cutter transferred to the Dominican Republic in 1995 for antinarcotics patrols. Only limited use has been made of the new vessel because of insufficient fuel supplies. The most heavily armed are two 855-ton corvettes sold to the Dominican Republic in 1976. Each mounts two 76mm guns. An Admiral-class gunship of 905 tons, a former United States minesweeper, and a Satoyomo-class vessel of 860 tons are each mounted with a single 76mm gun. Smaller patrol craft are fitted with Bofors 40mm machine guns and Oerlikon 20mm machine guns (see table 13, Appendix). The navy has at its disposal two Alouette III helicopters and five Cessna T–41D aircraft for inshore coastal reconnaissance. Naval aircraft are operated by air force liaison personnel. A battalion-sized naval infantry unit is headquartered at Santo Domingo.

The Dominican Navy undertook a concerted effort in 1999, in cooperation with the United States Coast Guard, to intercept illegal shipments to Puerto Rico of persons, weapons, and drugs. In addition, the navy created a motorized company to interdict illegal crossings. The company consists primarily of fifty-five naval officers who patrol the coasts on all-terrain motorbikes, equipped with night vision and communications gear.

Naval enlisted personnel receive instruction at the training center at Las Calderas. The Naval Academy at Las Calderas offers a four-year course to officer cadets.

Air Force

The air force traces its origins to 1928, when the government, inspired by the use of air power in World War I, authorized the creation of an aviation school. The first military aviation element was formed in 1932 as an arm of the National Army. The air force became an independent service in 1948. After several name changes, it has been officially designated as the Dominican Air Force since 1962.

Beginning in 1942, with the grant of base facilities to the United States, the Dominican Republic received shipments of aircraft under the Lend-Lease program, mostly light trainers. Later, after the signing of the Rio Treaty in 1947, the United States provided twenty-five F–47 fighter-bombers, plus C–46 and C–47 transports and additional trainers. Trujillo later purchased two B–17 and two B–25 bombers from commercial sources. In 1952 he made a large purchase of jet fighter-bombers from Sweden and F–51Ds from the United States. By the mid-1950s, the air force had some 240 aircraft and some 3,500 uniformed personnel. After Trujillo's assassination, however, funds were not forthcoming for the replacement of aging aircraft, and the air force's capabilities dwindled rapidly.

Air force headquarters are located at San Isidro Air Base near Santo Domingo. Most aircraft are based at San Isidro as well. The second large base is La Unión at Puerto Plata on the north coast. Smaller bases are at Barahona, La Romana, and

Pedernales, with airstrips at Constanza in the central mountainous area and Dajabón, on the Haitian border. The air force administers the general military medical center located in San Isidro. The air force also runs the nation's Civil Aeronautics Directorate, and air force officers oversee the operation of the nation's airports.

The air force, numbering some 5,500 personnel in 1998, is organized into three flying squadrons. The counterinsurgency squadron is equipped with eight Cessna A–37B Dragonflies. The A–37B, developed from the T–37 jet trainer, can land on short, unimproved airstrips. It is armed with a machine gun and can carry a light load of bombs or other munitions. The transport squadron uses three C–47 Douglas Dakotas and one Commander 680, and the helicopter squadron has as its principal units eight Bell 205s for search-and-air rescue and transport. Various small aircraft are used for liaison and training purposes (see table 14, Appendix). The air force carries out routine antidrug reconnaissance patrols, but is often grounded because of lack of fuel and spare parts.

The Base Defense Command provides security for all bases and aircraft. It includes an airborne Special Forces unit and an air police unit, both of approximately battalion size, and an antiaircraft battalion equipped with four 20mm guns. The Maintenance Command is responsible for maintenance and repair. The Combat Support Command supplies all base services. Air force cadets attend the Army Military Academy at San Isidro for three years, then spend their fourth year at the Frank Feliz Miranda Aviation School, also at San Isidro.

Manpower

The combined strength of the three armed services in 1998 was 24,300. This figure represents a ratio of 2.8 military personnel for every 1,000 citizens, which conforms to the average for all Latin American states. The armed forces had expanded about 10 percent over the previous decade.

The armed forces no longer have the strength and the military potential they enjoyed under Trujillo, but the military continues to be a popular career. The constitution provides for compulsory military service for all males between the ages of eighteen and fifty-four. However, the ranks are easily filled by volunteers, and the military does not impose a strain on national manpower. Officers, noncommissioned officers (NCOs), and many enlisted personnel, as well, look on the military as a long-term career. As a result, all three services consist largely of experienced and well-trained professionals.

Entry into the officer corps is competitive, and most entrants are drawn from the middle and the lower-middle classes. Most enlisted personnel come from rural areas. The military has a very small number of females; most serve in positions traditionally reserved for women, such as nursing. Women first gained admittance to positions traditionally held only by men in 1981, when a few female personnel were commissioned as medical officers.

Pay and conditions of service compare well with opportunities available in civilian occupations. Larger installations maintain a number of commissaries and exchanges, and each of the three services operates officer and enlisted clubs. Military personnel also benefit from free medical service. Under the armed forces' generous retirement program, all members who have served thirty years are entitled to receive a pension based on 75 percent of their active-duty pay at the time of retirement. Certain officers, such as pilots and naval engineers, may apply for a full pension after twenty years of service.

Defense Spending

Estimated defense expenditures for 1998 were US$180 million, representing 1.1 percent of gross national product (GNP—see Glossary), according to the United States Central Intelligence Agency. The levels of spending reported by the International Institute for Strategic Studies in London, presumably calculated on a different basis, were significantly lower, averaging US$109 million annually for the years 1994–96 and US$120 million in 1997. Military expenditures averaged about 7 percent of central government expenditures during the decade 1986–95 and were slightly in excess of 1 percent of GNP in most years of that decade.

The level of military spending measured in Dominican currency rose steadily during the late 1970s, remained at relatively constant amounts during the early 1980s, then tended to be somewhat higher from 1992 onward. When adjusted for inflation, however, there was no real increase in military outlays until 1993. The sharp decline in the value of the peso in the mid-1980s weakened the nation's ability to finance the arms imports necessary for modernization, not to mention replacements and spare parts for existing equipment.

The problem was made even more acute by the fact that the military budget is preponderantly allocated to current operations. Capital expenditures are believed to account for well under 10 percent of total military spending. The low proportion of the budget devoted to funding capital improvements is illustrated by the fact that reported arms and related imports during the 1986–95 period totaled only about US$40 million, constituting 0.35 percent of the nation's total imports. The United States has been the most important source of military equipment although, during the 1982–87 period, the nation's principal arms supplier was France.

Trujillo established the nation's defense industry just after World War II. By the late 1950s, the Dominican Republic had the capacity to be nearly self-sufficient in small weapons. Although that capability has deteriorated, the nation still has a modest arms-manufacturing capacity. The arsenal at San Cristóbal, twenty-four kilometers west of Santo Domingo, produces small arms ammunition and can repair heavier weapons and vehicles. Smaller wooden-hulled craft have in the past been produced by domestic shipbuilders for the navy.

Between fiscal year (FY—see Glossary) 1950 and FY 1996, United States grant military assistance to the Dominican Republic totaled US$36.5 million. No grant assistance has been provided in recent years except for the transfer to the Dominican Republic in 1995 of a United States Coast Guard cutter to assist the antinarcotics effort. Training for the Dominican military in the United States or elsewhere in Latin America under the International Military Education and Training (IMET) program is provided at a cost of about US$35,000 annually. Financing of Dominican purchases under the Foreign Military Sales Program totaled US$34.5 million between FY 1950 and FY 1996. The Dominican Republic used this credit program for only US$441,000 worth of matériel in FY 1996.

Ranks, Uniforms, and Insignia

The rank structure of the armed forces follows traditional lines and largely conforms to the pattern of the United States services, with minor variations reflecting the disparity in force levels. The army has eight enlisted grades, six company and field-grade ranks, and three ranks for general officers (see figs. 8 and 9). The air force has seven enlisted grades; its officer ranks are identical to those of the army. Naval personnel are separated into six enlisted grades, six ranks for officers, and three ranks for flag-rank officers (admirals). The highest rank attainable is lieutenant general (army and air force) or admiral in the navy (comparable to vice admiral in the United States Navy).

Uniforms resemble those of United States counterparts in cut, design, and material. The ground forces wear olive green uniforms; the air force, blue; and the navy either navy blue or white. Enlisted personnel in all three services also have khaki uniforms. The three categories of uniform include full dress, dress, and daily. The dress uniform is worn off-duty as well as on semiformal occasions. The basic uniform for officers consists of a short-sleeve or long-sleeve shirt, tie, trousers, belt, and black shoes. The basic uniform for army and air force enlisted personnel is an olive green fatigue uniform with combat boots. Navy enlisted personnel wear denim shirts and dungarees for work and middy blouse and trousers when off duty.

Army and air force company-grade officers wear one, two, or three silver laurel leaves as their insignia of rank. For field-grade officers, rank insignia consist of one to three gold stars. Brigadier, major, and lieutenant generals wear one, two, and three silver stars, respectively. Naval officer ranks are indicated by gold stripes worn on the lower sleeve of the uniform jacket. Army and air force enlisted personnel wear green chevrons on the upper sleeve; navy enlisted personnel wear red chevrons.

Internal Security and Public Order

The Dominican Republic historically has depended on the export of its sugar and other agricultural products. By the late 1970s, however, markets for these crops had plummeted, and the consequent agricultural crisis forced thousands of farmers to migrate to the cities. Although some employment was created by setting up industrial trade zones and promoting tourist trade, sufficient jobs did not materialize, and workers, peasants, and even middle-income families expanded the ranks of the unemployed. Many of the unemployed emigrated to the United States, mainly during the late 1970s and the 1980s.

The Dominican population has traditionally turned to the state to relieve social distress. In the past, political parties distributed contracts and found jobs for their followers, but in the late 1990s the government had only a limited capacity to deal with the wider needs of material relief. About half the people live below the poverty line. Access to potable water and sewerage is limited, and electric power outages are common. The

DOMINICAN REPUBLIC RANK	SEGUNDO TENIENTE	PRIMER TENIENTE	CAPITÁN	MAYOR	TENIENTE CORONEL	CORONEL	GENERAL DE BRIGADA	MAYOR GENERAL	TENIENTE GENERAL
ARMY	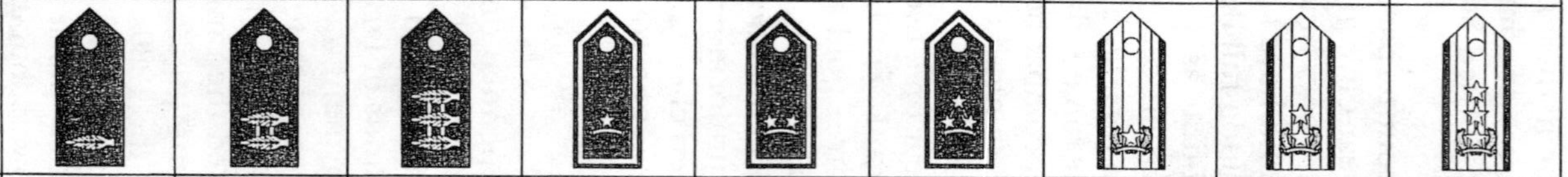								
U.S. RANK TITLES	2D LIEUTENANT	1ST LIEUTENANT	CAPTAIN	MAJOR	LIEUTENANT COLONEL	COLONEL	BRIGADIER GENERAL	MAJOR GENERAL	LIEUTENANT GENERAL
DOMINICAN REPUBLIC RANK	SEGUNDO TENIENTE	PRIMER TENIENTE	CAPITÁN	MAYOR	TENIENTE CORONEL	CORONEL	GENERAL DE BRIGADA	MAYOR GENERAL	TENIENTE GENERAL
AIR FORCE	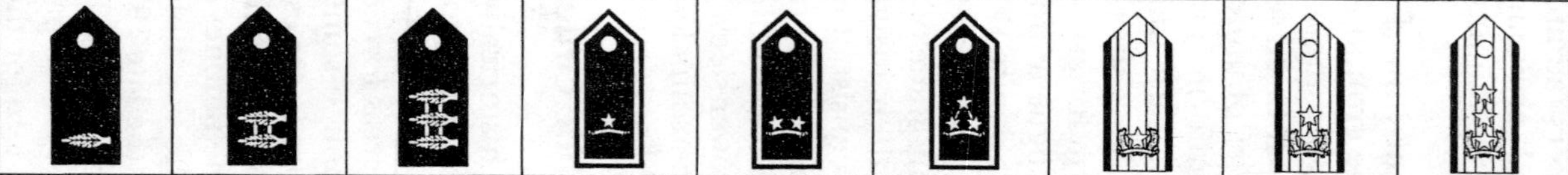								
U.S. RANK TITLES	2D LIEUTENANT	1ST LIEUTENANT	CAPTAIN	MAJOR	LIEUTENANT COLONEL	COLONEL	BRIGADIER GENERAL	MAJOR GENERAL	LIEUTENANT GENERAL
DOMINICAN REPUBLIC RANK	ALFÉREZ DE FRAGATA	ALFÉREZ DE NAVÍO	TENIENTE DE NAVÍO	CAPITÁN DE CORBETA	CAPITÁN DE FRAGATA	CAPITÁN DE NAVÍO	CONTR-ALMIRANTE	VICE-ALMIRANTE	ALMIRANTE
NAVY	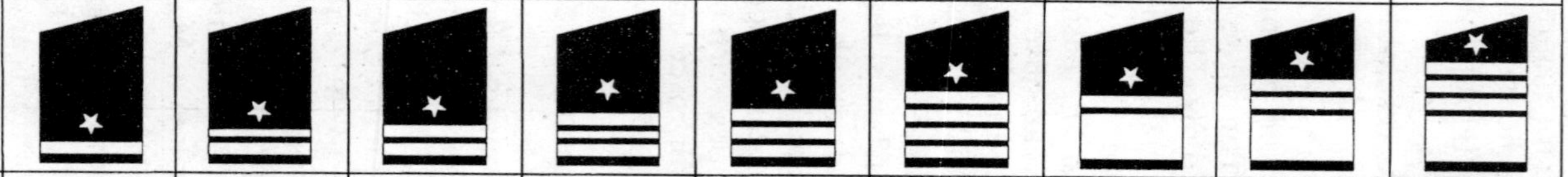								
U.S. RANK TITLES	ENSIGN	LIEUTENANT JUNIOR GRADE	LIEUTENANT	LIEUTENANT COMMANDER	COMMANDER	CAPTAIN	COMMODORE ADMIRAL	REAR ADMIRAL	VICE ADMIRAL

Figure 8. Dominican Republic: Officer Ranks and Insignia, 1999

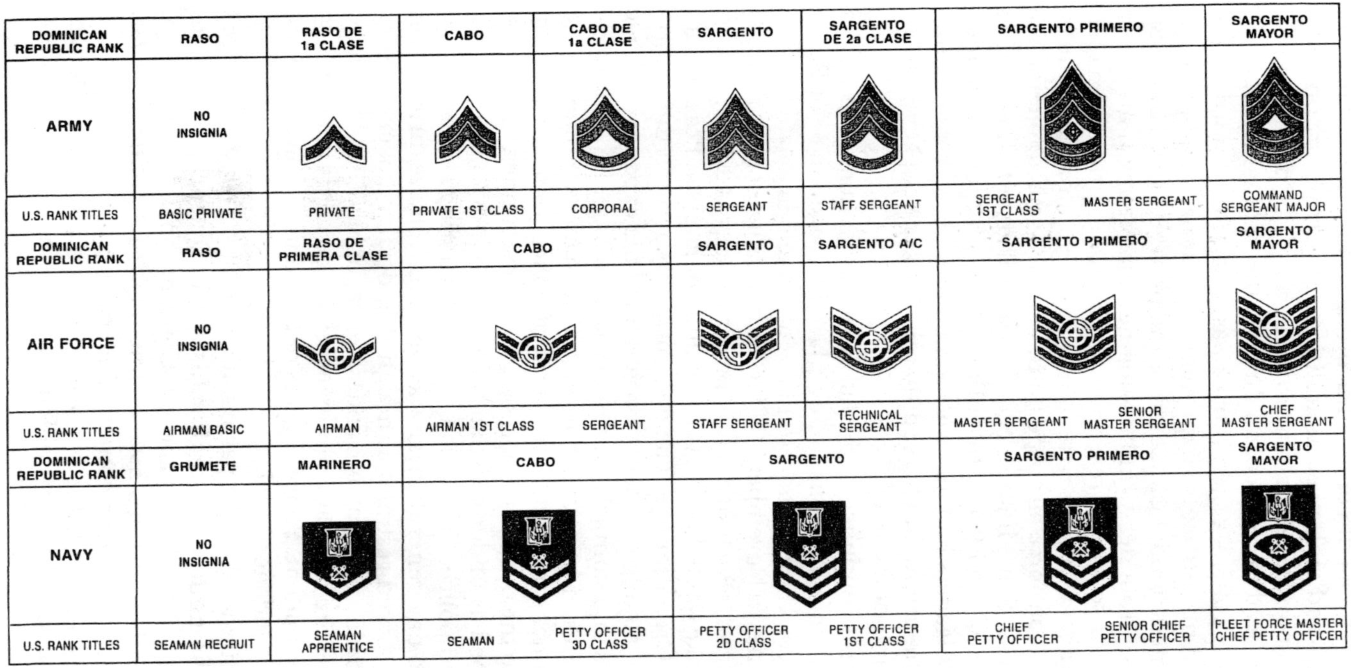

DOMINICAN REPUBLIC RANK	RASO	RASO DE 1a CLASE	CABO	CABO DE 1a CLASE	SARGENTO	SARGENTO DE 2a CLASE	SARGENTO PRIMERO	SARGENTO MAYOR
ARMY	NO INSIGNIA							
U.S. RANK TITLES	BASIC PRIVATE	PRIVATE	PRIVATE 1ST CLASS	CORPORAL	SERGEANT	STAFF SERGEANT	SERGEANT 1ST CLASS / MASTER SERGEANT	COMMAND SERGEANT MAJOR
DOMINICAN REPUBLIC RANK (AIR FORCE)	RASO / NO INSIGNIA	RASO DE PRIMERA CLASE	CABO		SARGENTO	SARGENTO A/C	SARGENTO PRIMERO	SARGENTO MAYOR
U.S. RANK TITLES	AIRMAN BASIC	AIRMAN	AIRMAN 1ST CLASS	SERGEANT	STAFF SERGEANT	TECHNICAL SERGEANT	MASTER SERGEANT / SENIOR MASTER SERGEANT	CHIEF MASTER SERGEANT
DOMINICAN REPUBLIC RANK (NAVY)	GRUMETE / NO INSIGNIA	MARINERO	CABO		SARGENTO		SARGENTO PRIMERO	SARGENTO MAYOR
U.S. RANK TITLES	SEAMAN RECRUIT	SEAMAN APPRENTICE	SEAMAN	PETTY OFFICER 3D CLASS	PETTY OFFICER 2D CLASS	PETTY OFFICER 1ST CLASS	CHIEF PETTY OFFICER / SENIOR CHIEF PETTY OFFICER	FLEET FORCE MASTER CHIEF PETTY OFFICER

Figure 9. Dominican Republic: Enlisted Ranks and Insignia, 1999

resulting social discontent has brought periodic outbreaks of turmoil and violence. In addition, grassroots groups have shown an increasing ability to organize major protest actions that can lead to conflict and threaten the internal order.

In July 1997, a general strike was called in the northeast to demand infrastructure improvements that had been promised in the presidential campaign of the previous year. Power cuts resulting from delays in building new generating units were a particular source of resentment. The rising prices of staples like rice and chicken were also at issue. Hundreds of soldiers, as well as air force airborne units, were dispatched to reinforce the police. Some injuries occurred as strikers set off explosives and exchanged fire with police. Although the strike ended after its leaders had met with a team of high government officials, the president charged that the strikes were being led by "remnants of the left."

Protests continued in the fall of 1997, with numerous violent street demonstrations taking place in the suburbs of Santo Domingo. These demonstrations culminated in a national general strike in November 1997 to protest failure of the national power grid, which had led to power outages and rising prices. The strike was led by the Coordination of Popular, Peasant, and Union Organizations. The demonstrators accused the government of aiming for high growth rates at the expense of public services and controls on the prices of fuel and food staples. The series of local and national disturbances prompted the government to deploy thousands of police, reinforced by soldiers, to the poor neighborhoods of the main cities, which were described as under a virtual state of siege. Although ten civilians and police officers had been killed during earlier clashes, the two-day general strike was peaceful. The security forces demonstrated restraint although they detained many persons on suspicion of vandalism and violence. In July 1998, the police used live fire in an attempt to disperse a demonstration, killing one law student. Police officers detained in the incident were arrested and faced trial.

Dominican Marxist parties, illegal under Trujillo, emerged from the underground after his death. During the civil war, they supported Bosch and the Constitutionalists. Since then, most of these groups have operated as legal political parties. Although they have contested elections, they are small and weak and have failed to win seats in the legislature. The Dominican Communist Party, which has had a legal existence since

1977, was one of fifty-three political organizations and trade unions that formed the Dominican Leftist Front in 1983 but which still retain their individual structures. The government has often detained members of organizations and populist groups thought to be preparing public disturbances, especially during election campaigns. For example, the authorities detained hundreds of opposition party figures, members of other antigovernment groups, and journalists, ostensibly to foil possible violence, following the disputed 1994 elections.

The presence of Haitians living illegally in the Dominican Republic has been a source of recurrent disturbances. Large numbers of Haitians come to the country, some legally but most undocumented, searching for economic opportunity. Security forces, particularly the army, round up and repatriate thousands of these Haitians each year. Persons with legal residence and those of Haitian ancestry with possible claims to Dominican citizenship have complained of being included in the expulsions without being given a chance to prove their status. Ill-treatment of Haitian sugarcane cutters working under contract has also been a source of resentment and violence. Forced recruitment of Haitians to work on the sugar plantations has been reported. After as many as 25,000 Haitians were deported in early 1997, the presidents of the two countries met to set up a mechanism for the repatriations to be carried out under humane conditions.

National Police

The nation's security forces consist of the National Police, the National Department of Investigations (Departamento Nacional de Investigaciones—DNI), the National Drug Control Directorate (Dirección Nacional de Control de Drogas—DNCD), and the armed forces. The National Police is under the secretary of state for interior and police, the military is under the secretary of state for the armed forces, and the DNI and DNCD report directly to the president.

The country's first police organization was a municipal force set up in 1844 in Santo Domingo. Beginning in 1847, other towns formed similar organizations. Eventually, every province had independent police forces. The national executive branch had only nominal influence over these forces, which were largely controlled by local caudillos. The local forces were disbanded in 1916 during the United States occupation; at that time, the United States Marines, and later members of the

Dominican Constabulary Guard, assumed police duties. The National Police was created in 1936. Since then, police activities in the nation have been completely centralized, and no independent provincial or municipal forces have existed.

In 1998 the National Police numbered some 15,000. The force's current strength reflects an enlargement by 50 percent in less than a decade. A further 2,000 personnel from the military were reportedly transferred to the police in September 1997 to help deal with civil disturbances. The director general of the National Police is a police major general, who is directly subordinate to the secretary of state for interior and police (see fig. 10). The police maintain a close relationship with the armed forces, and, until the 1980s, the chief of the National Police was often a senior officer from one of the armed services. The director general is assisted by a deputy director general and directly supervises two sections: Internal Affairs and Planning, and Special Operations. Three other sections, Administration and Support, Police Operations, and Territorial Zones, are headed by the deputy director general.

The deputy director general of police has overall responsibility for territorial police operations. He supervises five regional directors, usually police brigadier generals, who are responsible for five zones: the Northeastern Zone (headquartered at San Francisco de Macorís), the Northern Zone (Santiago), the Southern Zone (Barahona), the Central Zone (San Cristóbal), and the Eastern Zone (San Pedro de Macorís). The police zones each cover several provinces; forces within the zones are broken down into provincial sections, companies, detachments, and local police posts.

An assistant director general under the director heads the Special Operations Section, which is responsible for the administration of the secret service, generally headed by a police brigadier general. The secret service performs undercover surveillance of domestic political groups and foreigners suspected of espionage or of inciting political or economic disorder. In October 1997, Special Operations took more than 500 persons into custody because it was believed they might incite violence during the planned general strike. The secret service coordinates its efforts with the DNI, which reports to the president. Created in 1962, the DNI is authorized to "investigate any act committed by persons, groups, or associations that conflict with the constitution, laws, or state institutions, or that attempt to establish any totalitarian form of government." The DNI is an investigative body and, unlike the police, generally does not have arrest authority. The functions of the DNI are closely coordinated with those of the armed forces intelligence units, as well as with the functions of the police. The DNI is often commanded by a retired military general.

Approximately half of all police personnel are stationed in the capital area, both because Santo Domingo is by far the nation's largest city and because police headquarters, as well as several special police units, are located there. Among the special units garrisoned in the capital is a paramilitary Special Operations battalion with some 1,000 personnel armed with teargas and shotguns. The unit is used for riot control in Santo Domingo, although elements also can be deployed rapidly to any section of the country. Other specialized police units include a special Bank Guard Corps and a Sappers Corps that performs firefighting and civil defense duties.

The public image of the police has improved since the 1970s, but excesses on the part of police personnel, including beatings of suspects, continue to spark controversy. The government has adopted several measures to monitor police behavior and has taken corrective steps, but complaints about such abuses continue to surface (see Respect for Human Rights, this ch.).

Criminal Justice System

The Dominican criminal justice system is basically an inquisitorial arrangement in which a court and its staff take general charge of a criminal case, and the judge gathers evidence to supplement that produced by the prosecution and the defense. Evidence is largely committed to writing, and the final stage of the proceedings consists of the judge's examining all the combined written material and then deciding whether he or she is convinced, beyond doubt, of the guilt of the accused. The criminal courts do not, therefore, operate under a system of trial by jury.

The 1966 constitution guarantees several basic legal rights to all citizens. These include the rights of due process, public trial, and habeas corpus protection. An accused person is also guaranteed protection against double jeopardy and self-incrimination. A written order from a competent judicial authority is required if any person is to be detained more than forty-eight hours or if an individual's home or property is to be searched. Security forces have frequently violated these provisions by

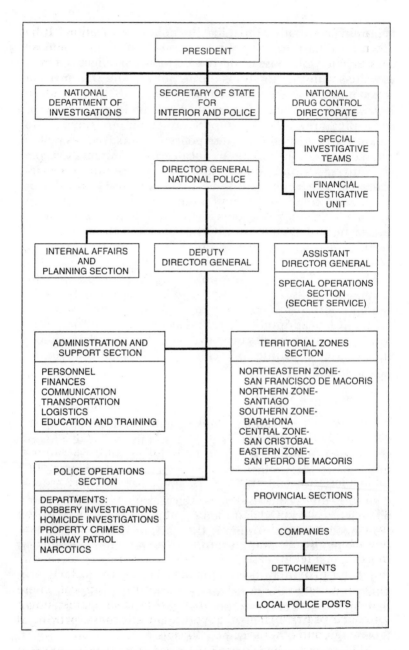

Figure 10. Dominican Republic: Organization of Internal Security Agencies, 1999

detaining suspects for "investigation" or "interrogation." It has been customary for the police to detain both suspects and witnesses in a crime, deciding only after investigation which merit release and which should be held further. Since the new government took office in 1996, an effort has been made to reduce abuses of the forty-eight-hour rule by placing lawyers from the prosecutor's office in police stations.

During the closed pretrial investigative phase of the criminal justice process, the state does not provide counsel to indigent prisoners. A small public defender organization was introduced in 1998 to assist indigent defendants in the Santo Domingo area. Other indigent cases are assigned to part-time, private attorneys. The courts rarely appoint defense lawyers in misdemeanor cases.

Defendants awarded bail rarely face an actual trial. Those denied bail may serve their entire sentences while awaiting trial. Accordingly, the decision to grant bail often determines whether an accused person will ever serve a prison sentence.

The justice system suffers seriously from chronic delays. Many suspects undergo a long period of pretrial detention that sometimes exceeds the maximum possible criminal sentence. In 1998 the proportion of the prison population awaiting trial was more than 75 percent. In the Santo Domingo National District, which accounts for approximately 45 percent of all criminal cases, the average pretrial detention declined from 13.8 months in 1996 to 6.5 months in 1998. However, the rest of the country did not experience corresponding improvement.

In addition to the Supreme Court of Justice, the constitution established three basic types of courts: courts of appeal, courts of first instance, and justice of the peace courts. There are special courts for labor, traffic, administrative, and land matters. Most misdemeanor offenses are tried by the justice of the peace courts, of which there is one in each municipality or township. The courts of first instance have original jurisdiction for criminal felony cases. There are twenty-nine of these, one for each province. Decisions may be, and regularly are, appealed to one of the nation's seven courts of appeal. These courts also have original jurisdiction over cases against judges of courts of first instance, government attorneys, provincial governors, and other specified officials.

Military and police courts have jurisdiction over members of the security forces, but a military or police board frequently remands cases involving capital crimes to civil courts. In 1996 police referred two cases of extrajudicial killings to civilian criminal courts.

The constitution stipulates an independent judiciary, but in the past interference from other entities, including the executive branch, has undermined judicial independence. The Senate previously appointed all justices by majority vote for four-year terms, except members of the Supreme Court. This procedure subjected judges to undue political influence and often resulted in a wholesale turnover of judicial personnel when control of the Senate changed hands. The result was a highly politicized process, sometimes bringing incompetent jurists to the bench who could not be supervised effectively by the executive authorities.

Under a constitutional reform enacted in 1994, the judiciary was granted a fixed percentage of the national budget, thus weakening legislative control. A Council of the Magistrature was created to appoint justices of the Supreme Court (see The Judiciary, ch. 4).

The constitution requires all judges to have law degrees, and judges at each level of the judiciary are required to have practiced law for a specified number of years. Supreme Court justices, for instance, must have a minimum of twelve years of experience, and judges of the courts of first instance must have two years of experience. Justices of the peace are also required to have a law degree; exceptions are permitted, however, in rural areas where it might be impossible to appoint a trained lawyer.

Respect for Human Rights

The government observes the protections guaranteed to citizens under the constitution. It grants individuals and groups of all political points of view the freedom to speak, respects the constitutional right of peaceful assembly and association, normally grants permits for public marches and meetings, and imposes no restrictions on domestic or international travel. The government also adheres to the constitutional protections against invasion of the home, and conducts wire tapping and other forms of surveillance under provisions provided by law.

Dominican internal security forces are generally responsive to the authority of the civilian executive branch, but frequent instances of human rights abuse have occurred. Misuse of the police for political motives is relatively rare, however. There are no political prisoners, and deliberate political murders have not occurred in recent years. However, the 1994 disappearance of university professor Narciso González, a prominent critic of the government of President Balaguer, has been a source of discord in the country, with suspicion falling on senior military officers. After President Fernández took office in 1996, he reopened the investigation of the case.

In 1997 President Fernández dismissed the heads of the National Police and the DNCD after both officers had been criticized by the attorney general for use of torture in criminal investigations and excessive force in attempting to control crime. Extrajudicial executions, described as "exchanges of fire," were said to have occurred. In addition, valuable assets seized in drug cases—cars, planes, and boats—were said to have disappeared.

Numerous deaths have resulted from police use of excessive force on persons in custody, during civil disturbances, or in pursuing suspects. In 1995 eighty-five such cases were reported; in 1998 seventy-five extrajudicial killings were ascribed to the police or the DNCD, a sharp increase over the previous year. Police personnel involved in such incidents may be tried by police courts or remanded to civilian courts. During 1998 police courts convicted and sentenced fifty members of the police for serious crimes. Numerous other officers were dismissed and their cases remanded to the civilian court system. As a rule, sentences in serious cases of abuse have ranged from a one-month suspension to six months' incarceration. In 1997 the narcotics police of the DNCD were accused of numerous cases of torture. The DNCD initially failed to cooperate with efforts to impose civilian supervision over the investigative process; the monitoring program resumed when the DNCD director was removed. When soldiers were transferred to the National Police in 1997, the human rights issue was high profile enough that the government mandated that those transferred receive several weeks of human rights training.

The National Police and narcotics police are reported to engage in the practice of rounding people up indiscriminately in poorer neighborhoods; most detainees are released after several hours. The security authorities continue to detain relatives and friends of suspected criminals to coerce a suspect into surrendering. Detentions of hundreds of persons occurred in 1994 and in earlier years at election time, ostensibly to prevent violent demonstrations. The individuals involved were released within the legal forty-eight-hour period.

Penal System

With a countrywide prison population of about 14,814 in 1997, the largest penal facility is the national penitentiary, La Victoria, in Santo Domingo. All individuals sentenced to more than two years of imprisonment serve their sentences there. A warden is supposed to run each prison and report to the attorney general through the Directorate of Prisons. In practice, however, the police or military colonel assigned to each prison to provide security is in charge of the prison and neither the wardens nor the Directorate of Prisons has much power.

The corrections system has received inadequate financing and suffers from unsanitary conditions and gross overcrowding. Medical supplies and services of physicians are deficient. Most prisoners find it necessary to supplement the prison diet with food supplied by relatives or purchased. Rioting to protest overcrowding and food shortages is an almost annual occurrence, often accompanied by loss of life. Gangs operating inside the prisons supply drugs and run prostitution rings. Prison officers reportedly engage in extortion and other forms of corruption.

Under the Fernández government, which took office in 1996, some reforms have been instituted. The government instituted a census of all prisons, and the attorney general's office began a case-by-case review of prisoners. Minors, the mentally ill, and the infirm were also segregated from other prisoners. In addition, a renovation program has begun at La Victoria and several other prisons to supply improved sanitation and more comfortable quarters, medical teams have been sent to each prison, and telephone access and recreation programs have been instituted.

As of the end of 1997, the number of inmates at La Victoria penitentiary had been reduced to 2,100 from a peak of 3,500. However, as a result of a crackdown against crime, the prison's population had risen to 3,300 by the end of 1998. Najayo, the second largest prison, built in 1994 to house 700 inmates, had a population of 2,290. Some 300 juveniles found by investigators to be incarcerated in La Victoria were removed in 1997. An inspection by a government reform commission continued to find many incidents of violations in other prisons, including 156 juveniles jailed with adults at Najayo. Females are held in separate prison wings under conditions that are, in general, superior to those found in the male wings; few abuses by guards have been reported.

Narcotics Trafficking

The Dominican Republic is a major transshipment country for cocaine from Colombia destined for the United States and Puerto Rico. The country's long, underpatrolled border with Haiti and its poorly paid and ill-equipped police and armed services make it an ideal linkage point for drug deliveries. Although the Dominican Republic is not a drug-producing country, the profits of drug trafficking support a significant part of the construction and business sectors, and are responsible for much of the personal spending on luxuries.

Dominican citizens are heavily involved in the street narcotics networks in New York and other cities of the Northeast and Miami. They are believed to be responsible for one-third of the 300 tons of cocaine reaching United States markets each year —a share that has doubled since the early 1990s. Loads of drugs from Colombia are delivered by ships and planes, often offshore air drops for pickup by small Dominican vessels. The drugs are then transferred directly to Puerto Rico by specially designed speedy small craft and yachts, or to the mainland United States hidden in legitimate cargoes. Aircraft are used for flights to the Bahamian islands. Profits from drug transactions are sent back to the Dominican Republic by bulk transfers of cash concealed in commercial shipments and camouflaged as remittances from Dominican workers in the United States.

The Dominican Republic has demonstrated considerable determination in the conduct of its counternarcotics effort. Senior officials engage in neither drug trafficking nor money laundering. The counternarcotics effort is normally in the hands of the DNCD and the military. Composed of more than 800 officials from the police, the three armed services, and the civilian sector, the rapidly growing DNCD has done an excellent job of battling drug trafficking along the southwest and east coasts and in the Santo Domingo area. However, lack of experience among operational-level personnel and low salaries hamper its overall effectiveness. The DNCD is aided by Special Investigative Teams of the DNCD, trained and equipped by the United States; these teams supply valuable intelligence on major international narcotics operations. A Financial Investigative Unit was formed in 1997 to uncover money laundering. The two other mechanisms for controlling drug trafficking are not as effective. Neither the police nor the military are sufficiently motivated or equipped to impose consistently effective controls. The army has had little success in interdicting shipments along the porous border with Haiti, across which thousands of kilograms of cocaine are smuggled annually. In 1998, however, a new border check station was established on the easiest route for smuggling drugs for transshipment to the United States, and two more stations were planned to be opened in 1999. The navy and air force, however, lack sufficient resources to give full support to the DNCD, and patrol planes obtained from the United States can perform only limited coastal reconnaissance because of fuel and parts shortages.

The United States is engaged in a program to furnish equipment and training in support of the Dominican counternarcotics effort. Under the terms of a bilateral agreement concluded in 1988, the United States has supplied US$4,200,000 in counternarcotics assistance. In 1998 US$300,000 was provided, including support for a canine detection program and the Haitian border initiative. A United States policy of linking denial of visas with drug-related corruption has also proven effective in thwarting corruption.

Although the DNCD is said to be relatively untainted, the United States Department of State reported in 1998 that corruption continued to be widespread among lower-level law enforcement officials; bribery of immigration officers and airline personnel by drug dealers is also common. Of 10,000 drug cases over a seven-year period, only 100 ended in jail sentences. Rumor had it that family ties between Dominican officials and narcotic traffickers have led to delayed arrests, early release, and loss of evidence to prevent conviction.

Charges of corruption have arisen in the DNCD over the disposition of confiscated assets of drug traffickers. Numerous incidents of torture of prisoners by the DNCD have also been alleged, in some cases with leaders of the DNCD present. After the rear admiral heading the DNCD was dismissed in 1997, a new agency was formed to take charge of seized assets and placed under the direct control of the governmental coordinating body, the National Drug Council (Consejo Nacional de Drogas) rather than the DNCD.

As regards criminal cases, 1,942 Dominicans were deported from the United States as criminals in 1997. More than 100 Dominican nationals wanted in the United States are believed to have taken refuge in their homeland. In 1998 the Dominican Republic enacted legislation repealing the prohibition on the extradition of Dominican nationals and subsequently extradited three Dominicans, in one case for narcotics-related racketeering. In 1999 the Dominican government had yet to act on a number of other extradition requests from the United States. Dominican gang members in the United States have been considered notoriously violent, confident they could escape punishment by fleeing to their homeland.

Since taking office in 1996, President Fernández has made strenuous efforts to reduce narcotics-related corruption among the judiciary and the police, military, and customs services. Nevertheless, his party is weak in Congress, and the political opposition has become increasingly dependent on funds from major drug dealers. Drug money infiltrates into legitimate business enterprises, casinos, banking, and the media, thereby turning illicit profits into legitimate assets. The influence of the traffickers grows as more and more of the economy becomes dependent on them.

Fernández has made a promising beginning by introducing partial reforms to the criminal justice system and attempting to motivate the military and the police to join more wholeheartedly in the struggle against narcotics. While improving cooperation with the United States on this issue, his political priorities oblige him to turn first to the reduction of social tensions induced by poverty and breakdowns in public services, matters of primary importance to the Dominican electorate.

*   *   *

No recent studies that deal comprehensively with national security in the Dominican Republic are available. Two works published in 1983–84 survey the history and development of the armed forces until that period. One is Adrian English's *Armed Forces of Latin America,* and the other is the section on the Dominican Republic in John Keegan's *World Armies* (second edition). A recent study of the institutional evolution of the armed forces is *Las fuerzas militares en la República Dominicana desde la Primera República hasta los comienzos de la Cuarta República* by Jose Miguel Soto Jimenez.

Current order of battle data are available in *The Military Balance* published by the International Institute of Strategic Studies in London and in Jane's *Fighting Ships.* The conduct of the internal security forces, the reform of the judicial system, and problems of human rights and public order are reviewed in *Country Reports on Human Rights Practices,* a report submitted annually by the United States Department of State to the

United States Congress. The Department of State's *International Narcotics Control Strategy Report* provides an annual appraisal of the Dominican effort to curtail drug trafficking. Mention of other matters pertaining to the military and internal security can often be found in *Caribbean Insight* and *Latin American Regional Reports: Caribbean and Central America Report*. Both of these periodicals are published in London. (For further information and complete citations, see Bibliography.)

Haiti: Country Profile

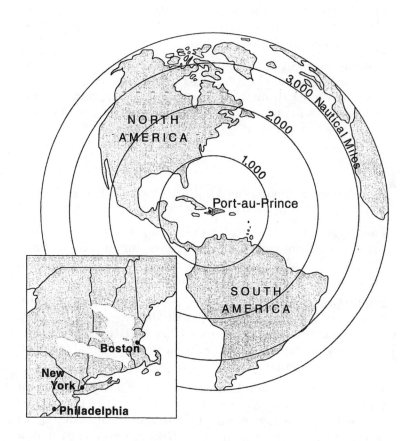

Country

Formal Name: Haiti.

Short Form: Haiti.

Term for Citizens: Haitians.

Capital: Port-au-Prince.

Geography

Size: Approximately 27,750 square kilometers.

Topography: Five mountain ranges divide country into three regions: northern, central, and southern. Highest peak, Morne de la Selle, located in south, reaches an altitude of 2,715 meters. No navigable rivers. Largest lake is Étang Saumâtre, brackish body in southern region.

Climate: Tropical climate influenced by northeast trade winds. Wet season generally lasts from March through May, dry season from December through February. Rainfall irregular because of mountainous topography. Temperature in lowland area 15°C to 25°C in winter, 25°C to 35°C in summer.

Society

Population: Estimated at 8 million in year 2000. Estimated growth rate 2.08 percent annually 1995–2000.

Language: 1987 constitution recognizes both French and Creole as official languages. Languages linguistically distinct, not mutually comprehensible. Creole spoken by vast majority, but facility with French connotes higher social status.

Ethnic Groups: Population almost entirely black and mulatto as result of historical origin as slaveholding agricultural colony. Economic and political elite mainly mulatto. Only ethnic minority "Arabs"—Syrian, Lebanese, and Palestinian immigrants—most of whom work in export-import sector.

Education and Literacy: In academic year 1996–97, enrollment rate 64 percent for six- to twelve-year-olds and 15 percent for twelve- to eighteen-year-olds. Private schools attended by 75 percent of school enrollment. Ninety percent of urban children but only 23 percent of rural children attend school. University of Haiti major institution of higher learning. National literacy estimates range from 20 to 53 percent.

Health: Children twelve to twenty-four months old at high risk for malnutrition. Infant mortality high at seventy-two per 1,000 live births in 1996, a decline since mid-1980s. Principal causes of death for children one to five years old diarrheal illnesses (37 percent), malnutrition (32 percent), and respiratory illness (25 percent). Common causes of adult deaths malaria, tuberculosis, parasitic diseases, and typhoid fever. National incidence of human immunodeficiency virus (HIV) projected at 5.4 to 7.7 percent for 2000; rate of males to females with acquired immune deficiency syndrome (AIDS) one to one.

Religion: Roman Catholicism official religion according to 1860 concordat with Vatican. Voodoo more widely practiced than Catholicism, could be considered national religion. Much overlap of believers, with most voodooists considering themselves Roman Catholics. Although church joined in several antivoodoo campaigns in course of Haiti's history, its opposition to folk religion more sporadic and ambivalent than that of Protestant missionaries, who condemn voodoo as diabolical. Rapid growth of Protestantism since 1950; some estimates 25 percent of population Protestant in late 1990s.

Economy

Gross Domestic Product (GDP): From 1991 coup to 1994, real GDP plunged 30 percent and per capita GDP dropped from US$320 to US$260. In late 1990s, US$225 per capita GDP made Haiti poorest country in Western Hemisphere.

Agriculture: Employed 66 percent of total workforce of almost 3 million in 1990s and accounted for some 25 to 30 percent of GDP and less than 10 percent of exports. In late 1990s, agriculture sector produced only 20 percent of Haiti's domestic food requirements. Constantly deteriorating rural infrastructure, primitive farming techniques, migration out of rural areas, deforestation, and natural disasters, including Hurricane Georges in September 1998, have taken a toll.

Industry: Manufacturing 14 percent of GDP in 1991, suffered following Jean-Bertrand Aristide's overthrow and ensuing embargo imposed by United Nations (UN) and Organization of American States (OAS). Of 180 companies operating in four free zones (more than 150 of these, mostly United States-controlled, engaged in assembly production), 130 closed factories after 1991 coup. Some thirty plants reopened after reestablishment of constitutional government in October 1994. Plants generated about 60,000 jobs producing processed foods, electrical and electronic equipment, textiles, clothing, toys, sporting goods, and handicrafts. Assembly industry prospects hampered by underdeveloped infrastructure, illiterate workforce, scarce managerial personnel, and highest utility costs in Caribbean. Chronic political instability prompted many firms to relocate to more stable Caribbean areas, mostly to free zone in neighboring Dominican Republic. By late

1990s, Haiti's assembly sector operating at fraction of capacity. In mid-1999 Prime Minister Alexis decided to resume privatization process of various enterprises after a two-year hiatus.

Currency: Gourde (G). Official exchange rate originally set at G5 to US$1 in 1919. Black market trading began in early 1980s in response to high inflation and fiscal shortfalls. Political crises of early 1990s, international embargo, and sharp drop in government revenues reduced value of gourde by about 80 percent by 1994. Although the Central Bank pumped more than US$37 million into foreign exchange market in 1996, gourde continued to fall to G16.9 = US$1 in August 1997. In 1999 gourde fluctuated between 17.5 and 18.3 to US$1.

Imports: Primarily food, tobacco, chemicals, machinery, and transportation equipment; fell from US$449 million in 1991 to US$141 million in 1994.

Exports: Mainly coffee and manufactured goods from assembly plants; declined from US$202 million in 1991 to US$57 million in 1994.

Balance of Payments: Since mid-1960s and continuing into late 1990s, Haiti has incurred substantial trade deficits. Deficits partially offset by remittances from Haitians working abroad and official aid. During 1992–94 international trade embargo, public deficit financed mainly by Central Bank credit and accumulation of arrears. External current account deficit, estimated at 19 percent of GDP in FY 1994–95, projected to drop gradually to 10 percent of GDP by FY 1999–2000.

Fiscal Year (FY): October 1 through September 30.

Fiscal Policy: Effects of gourde depreciation, together with rising food prices, raised inflation rate from 15.6 percent in December 1996 to 17.2 percent in July 1997. To protect gourde stability, government adopted stringent fiscal policy and aggressive tax collection program. New legislation broadened base of sales tax and unified its rates, reduced tax evasion among larger companies, and minimized number of tax and customs exemptions.

Transportation and Communications

Roads: Of 1999 total of 4,050 kilometers of roads, 950 kilometers are paved, another 950 kilometers are gravel or otherwise improved, and 2,150 kilometers are unimproved and almost impassable during rainy season. Two paved highways link northern and southern regions.

Ports: Port-au-Prince is major port, with container facilities and berths for large liners. Remaining thirteen ports, largely provincial and small, centers of imported contraband in 1990s.

Airports: Haiti's main international airport is located ten kilometers north of Port-au-Prince. Some ten other airfields are operational but are only grass strips.

Railroads: One rail line, used for transporting sugarcane. No passenger rail service.

Telecommunications: With a ratio of six telephones per 1,000 inhabitants in 1998, Haiti ranks below some poorer African nations (eight telephones per 1,000 people). The 39,000 telephone lines of the 1980s increased to 64,000 in late 1990s, with 80 percent concentrated in capital area, where only 25 percent of population live. Subscribers with international service can dial directly to United States and Europe via satellite station at Sabourin. Telephone service in rural areas so poor that many resort to two-way radios.

Government and Politics

Government: Internationally monitored national election in November 1990 ended four years of military-dominated rule that followed end of Duvalier family dictatorship. Jean-Bertrand Aristide, elected president in a landslide, inaugurated to five-year term February 7, 1991. 1990 election overturned in September 1991 by military coup. De facto military government of General Raoul Cédras failed to achieve international recognition; ousted by UN-sanctioned multinational force in September 1994 with Aristide restored to power after three years in exile. Internationally monitored parliamentary and municipal elections of 1995 brought to office candidates affiliated with Aristide's Lavalas political movement. Majority had run under Lavalas Political Organization (Organisation Politique Lavalas—OPL) banner. René Garcia Préval, OPL's candidate, won December 1995 presidential election, succeeding Aristide February 7, 1996. Prime Minister Rosny Smarth formed OPL-dominated cabinet. In January 1997, Aristide formed new political party, Lavalas Family (La Famille Lavalas—FL), creating schism within ruling

OPL. In June 1997, Smarth resigned. In December 1998, deeply divided parliament confirmed Jacques Édouard Alexis as prime minister. In January 1999, Préval initiated rule by decree, dismissing parliament and appointing municipal officials "interim executive agents" of Ministry of Interior. In March, following successful negotiations between Préval and a coalition of political organizations that did not include FL or OPL, Prime Minister Alexis formed interim government and Préval named a Provisional Electoral Council with mandate to organize overdue parliamentary and municipal elections by late 1999. Elections held in May 2000, with Aristide's Lavalas Family party gaining victory. OAS Election Observation Mission questioned validity of Senate elections, and United States, Canada, and European Union threatened to withhold aid if results not revised. As of August 2000, Haitian government has refused to accept OAS recommendations.

Politics: Tentative progress toward pluralistic democratic government after long history of rule by military leaders and dictators. Tradition of political movements or upheavals and strong presidency inhibit development of political parties and of power sharing among executive, legislature, and judiciary. Late 1980s Lavalas movement of Aristide promoted a participatory and decentralized democracy as opposed to more urban-centered, representative forms of democratic governance. Movement splintered several times since gaining power in 1990 elections. National political institutions and organizations decimated during three years of de facto military rule (1991–94). Political void following 1995 dismantling of Haitian army filled by OPL. Emergence in 1997 of Aristide's FL shattered OPL, creating bitter rivalry between country's two dominant political groups. Other political parties small and weak. Adherents of authoritarian rule abound, but lack stable institutions and popular support. Church, business, and civil society lack formal political institutions, but often have been influential political actors. Charismatic leadership, currently in person of Aristide, remains dominant political trait in Haiti.

International Relations: Focused mainly on United States, country's leading trade partner and major source of foreign aid, and on neighboring Dominican Republic. Haiti's longstanding regional and international isolation diminished following greater involvement by Caribbean Community and Common Market (Caricom), OAS, and UN beginning with 1990 elections and increasing following international condemnation of 1991 military coup and subsequent multi-national intervention of September 1994. Argentina, Canada, France, and United States especially active since the coup, maintaining active presence through UN peacekeeping and police training missions between 1994 and 1999. Haiti recognized Cuba in 1996 and initiated exchange missions. Presidents Aristide and Préval decreased Haiti's isolation through participation in international summits. Haiti hosted its first OAS General Assembly in 1995. Haiti's growing overseas population gave country vocal presence in many North American and European cities.

International Agreements and Memberships: Member of UN, OAS, Caribbean Community, Association of Caribbean States, Inter-American Development Bank, World Bank, International Monetary Fund, World Trade Organization, and Lomé Convention.

National Security

Armed Forces: Armed Forces of Haiti (Forces Armées d'Haïti—FAd'H) disbanded January 1995, after return of President Aristide from exile. Strength of armed forces including police elements 8,000 before Aristide's return.

Police: Haitian National Police (Police Nationale d'Haïti—PNH) with approximately 6,000 members only functioning security force in late 1999.

Police Organization: Main components Administrative Police, Judicial Police, and Office of Inspector General. Specialized units include presidential and ministerial guards, crowd control unit, Coast Guard, and Counternarcotics Unit. Nine departmental directorates supervise city and rural divisions. UN-sponsored police trainers helped form PNH in 1995; about 280 trainers from eleven countries as of late 1999.

Police Equipment: Ordinary police carry sidearms. Special units have shotguns, semiautomatic rifles, and submachine guns. Some riot equipment, vans, and radio equipment.

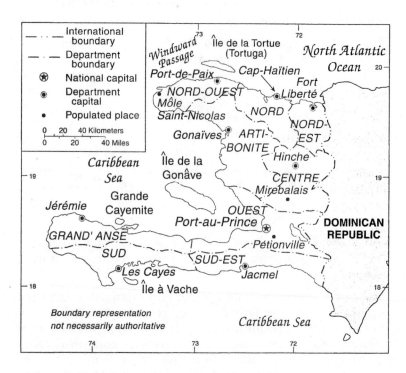

Figure 11. Haiti: Administrative Divisions, 1999

258

Table B. Haiti: Chronology of Important Events

Period		Description
1492		Columbus lands at present-day Môle Saint-Nicolas, Haiti; establishes first permanent Spanish New World settlement at site of Santo Domingo.
1492–1697		Spain colonizes Hispaniola.
1503		Nicolás de Ovando named governor and supreme justice; institutes *encomienda* system. Importation of African slaves begins.
1697		Treaty of Ryswick: Spain cedes western part of Hispaniola, known as Saint-Domingue, to France following War of the Grand Alliance.
1791–1803		Slave rebellion in Saint-Domingue leads to revolution under Toussaint Louverture against French expeditionary force.
1804	January 1	Haiti becomes independent, with Jean-Jacques Dessalines as president and, subsequently, emperor.
1806		Dessalines assassinated.
1807		Haiti partitioned.
1807–18		Alexandre Pétion president in the south.
1807–20		Henry Christophe president and during 1811–20 king in the north.
1818–43		Jean-Pierre Boyer presidency; Boyer reunites Haiti 1820, invades and occupies Santo Domingo 1822; abolishes slavery.
1843–1915		Period of political instability in Haiti.
1860		Concordat restores relations between the Vatican and Haiti.
1862		United States recognizes Haiti.
1915–34		United States marines occupy Haiti.
1937		Dominican military kills 5,000–12,000 Haitians along Haitian-Dominican border.
1941–42		Roman Catholic Church organizes anti-superstition campaign.
1946–50		Dumarsais Estimé presidency; new 1946 constitution and reforms launched.
1950	May 10	Military coup overthrows regime of Dumarsais Estimé and leads to period of instability.
1950–56		Paul Magloire presidency.
1957–71		François Duvalier presidency/dictatorship.
1966		Revision of concordat between the Vatican and Haiti allows François Duvalier to nationalize the Roman Catholic Church.
1971–86		Jean-Claude Duvalier presidency.
1983		Pope John Paul II visits Haiti; advocates justice, more egalitarian society.
1985–86		Haitians demonstrate against Jean-Claude Duvalier.
1986	January	United States withholds recertification of Haiti for foreign assistance.
	February 7	Jean-Claude Duvalier leaves Haiti.
1986–88		Lieutenant General Henri Namphy heads National Council of Government.[1]
1990	December	Free parliamentary and presidential elections.
1991	February 7	Jean-Bertrand Aristide assumes presidency.

Table B. *(Continued) Haiti: Chronology of Important Events*

Period		Description
	September 25	Aristide addresses United Nations General Assembly.
	September 31	Haitian military overthrows Aristide; he leaves for Venezuela, later goes to United States.
1991–94		Raoul Cédras military regime.
1993	July 3	Aristide and Haitian armed forces commander General Raoul Cédras sign Governors Island Accord, providing for Aristide's return to power in Haiti on October 30, 1993.
	July 16	United Nations Security Council imposes worldwide oil and arms embargo on Haiti.
	October 11	Armed gangs prevent the *USS Harlan County* from docking in Port-au-Prince.
1994	April 12	Randall Robinson, Executive Director of TransAfrica, begins hunger strike to protest United States policies toward Haiti.
	April 29	Ambassador Lawrence Pezzullo is dismissed as United States envoy to Haiti; former United States Congressman William Gray III replaces him.
	May 21	United Nations levies comprehensive embargo on Haiti.
	July 31	United Nations Security Council passes resolution (S/Res/ 940) approving United States plan to raise a multilateral force to remove the military junta from power in Haiti.
	September 16–18	Team consisting of former President Jimmy Carter, former chair of the United States Joint Chiefs of Staff General Colin Powell, and United States Senator Sam Nunn of Georgia negotiates the peaceful departure from Haiti of junta leaders.
	September 19	United States forces land unopposed in Port-au-Prince.
	October 4	Haitian police chief Michel François leaves Haiti for the Dominican Republic.
	October 13	General Cédras and General Biamby leave Haiti for Panama.
	October 15	President Aristide returns to Haiti.
	October 16	United Nations lifts all sanctions on Haiti.
1995	June 25	Contentious municipal and parliamentary elections held.
	August 13	Rerun of contended municipal and parliamentary elections.
1996	February 7	René Préval assumes presidency.

Chapter 6. Haiti: Historical Setting

Figure from a painting by Prosper Pierrelouis

AFRICAN SLAVES IN THE French colony of Saint-Domingue rebelled against their French masters, defeated a powerful Napoleonic military force, and founded the independent nation of Haiti in January 1804. This overthrow of a government by slaves is the only such revolution in history. It also made Haiti the second oldest independent nation in the Western Hemisphere, after the United States. However, since this auspicious beginning, Haitian history has seen perennial political, economic, and racial problems.

Haitian rulers have emulated the French colonial system. They have exploited racial, religious, and class differences, and retained armies and personal security forces to control the population and remain in power. At various times they have favored either blacks or light-skinned Haitians (mulattoes), Roman Catholics or voodooists, the elite or the masses, each at the expense of the other.

As a consequence of the French colonial legacy, Haiti has had a history of dictatorial leaders who have defied constitutions, ruled through reliance on their military and security forces, and often come into power or left it through violent means. Of the few presidents who were popularly elected, such as Dumarsais Estimé (1946–50), François Duvalier (1957–71), and Jean-Bertrand Aristide (1991–95), only the last named left office voluntarily after completing his term of office. The popular revolt that deposed President-for-Life Jean-Claude Duvalier (1971–86), the military coup that deposed President Aristide in 1991, and the United States/United Nations actions that reinstated Aristide in 1994 suggest that violence continues to be the usual route to change.

Spanish Discovery and Colonization, 1492–1697

The island of Hispaniola (La Isla Española), which today is occupied by the nations of Haiti and the Dominican Republic, is located about eighty kilometers from Cuba, 200 kilometers from Jamaica, and 1,120 kilometers from the United States. Haiti has an area of about 27,750 square kilometers, comparable in size to the state of Maryland. Evidence exists of human habitation in Haiti as early as the fourth millennium B.C. by people of Central American origin. The Taino emerged as an ethnic group in Hispaniola around A.D. 1200, and the Caribs arrived just before the Spanish landed at Môle Saint-Nicolas in 1492.

Christopher Columbus received a friendly reception from the Indians when he disembarked on Hispaniola in what is today Haiti, near Cap-Haïtien. However, when Columbus returned on his second voyage in 1493, he found that his first settlement, Navidad, had been destroyed and its inhabitants slain. Undeterred, Columbus established a second settlement, Isabela, farther to the east, and continued his mission to spread Roman Catholicism, claim new lands for Spain, and discover gold.

Hispaniola, or Santo Domingo, as it became known under Spanish dominion, became the first outpost of the Spanish Empire. When the quest for gold failed, the island became important as a seat of colonial administration and a starting point for other conquests. It was in Santo Domingo that the system of allotments of land (*repartimiento*) was introduced, whereby Spanish-born persons residing in the New World (*peninsulares*) received large grants of land and the right to compel labor from the Indians who lived there.

Christopher Columbus was the first administrator of Santo Domingo. He and his brother, Bartolomé Columbus, fell out of favor with the settlers and the Indians as a result of their harsh demands and discipline. They also lost favor with the crown for failure to maintain control of the colony, bring gold back to Spain, or discover a new route to Asia. Both brothers were briefly held in a Spanish prison. The colony's new governor, Nicolás de Ovando, laid the groundwork for the island's development. During his tenure, the *repartimiento* system gave way to a system in which all the land was considered to be the property of the crown (*encomienda*). This new system granted stewardship of land to the crown's agents (*encomenderos*), who were entitled to employ (or, in practice, to enslave) Indian labor.

The Indians were the first and greatest victims of colonial rule. Although the exact size of the indigenous population of the time is not known, contemporary observers have estimated it to be between several thousand and several million. By most accounts, however, there were between 60,000 and 600,000 Indians on the island. Within fifty years, almost all had been killed outright, died as a result of overwork in the mines, or succumbed to diseases to which they were not immune.

Several years before the Indians were decimated, Santo Domingo had lost its position as the preeminent Spanish colony in the New World. Its lack of mineral riches caused it to be neglected by the mother country, especially after the conquest of New Spain (Mexico). In 1535 Santo Domingo was incorporated into the Viceroyalty of New Spain, which included Mexico and the Central American isthmus; its status dwindled further after the conquest of the rich kingdom of the Incas in Peru. Agriculture became the mainstay of the island's economy, although the colony did not reach the high level of productivity that was subsequently to characterize it under French rule.

Although Hispaniola never realized its economic potential under Spanish rule, it remained strategically important as a gateway to the Caribbean. The Caribbean provided the opportunity for pirates from England, France, and the Netherlands to impede Spanish shipping, waylay galleons filled with gold, and establish a foothold in the hemisphere, which had been divided by papal decree between Spain and Portugal. This competition for spoils occurred throughout the Caribbean, but nowhere as intensively as on Hispaniola.

England's Sir Francis Drake led one of the most famous forays against the port of Santo Domingo in 1586, just two years before he played a key role in the English navy's defeat of the Spanish Armada. Drake failed to secure the island, but his raid, followed by the arrival of corsairs and freebooters who established scattered settlements, was part of a pattern of encroachment that gradually diluted Spanish dominance.

Beginning in the 1620s, Frenchmen, reportedly expelled by the Spanish from Saint Christopher (Saint Kitts), began to use Tortuga Island (Île de la Tortue), located off the northwest coast of Hispaniola, as a base to attack English and Spanish shipping. They came to be called buccaneers, a term derived from the Indian word, *boucan*, meaning spit, on which they cooked their meat. Skirmishes with Spanish and English forces were common. As the maintenance of the empire drained the energies of a declining Spain, the buccaneers' intervention became more effective on behalf of France. The first permanent settlement on Tortuga was established in 1659 under the commission of King Louis XIV of France. The subsequent establishment of the French West India Company to direct the expected commerce between the colony on Tortuga and France underscored the seriousness of the enterprise.

In time, the buccaneers began to cross to the western side of Hispaniola to hunt for cattle and wild boar, and some settled there, assuming they would be safe because of the area's relative remoteness from the Spanish capital city of Santo Domingo. By 1670 the buccaneers had established a permanent settlement at Cap-François, now Cap-Haïtien (see fig. 11). At that time, the western third of the island was commonly referred to as Saint-Domingue, the name it bore officially after Spain relinquished sovereignty over the area to France following the War of the Grand Alliance, which officially ended with the Treaty of Ryswick in 1697.

French Colony of Saint-Domingue, 1697–1803

More French citizens arrived in Saint-Domingue in the 1720s. They hoped to get rich by farming indigo, coffee, or sugar and then to return to France. Many succeeded in their goal. By the mid-eighteenth century, this territory, largely neglected under Spanish rule, had become the richest and most coveted colony in the Western Hemisphere. Between 1783 and 1789, agricultural production on the island almost doubled, creating more wealth than the rest of the West Indies combined, and more than the United States. Sugar was the principal source of its wealth. Saint-Domingue produced 40 percent of the sugar imported by France. The colony played a pivotal role in the French economy, accounting for almost two-thirds of French commercial interests abroad and 40 percent of foreign trade.

This flourishing economy was based on slavery. The first African slaves were brought from Portugal and Spain, but by 1513, shipping lines had been established exclusively for slaving, and its victims were imported directly from Africa. Although most of the slaves came from West Africa, their origins were diverse, representing at least thirty-eight regions in Africa and 100 tribes. With time, Saint-Domingue became the principal slave-importing island in the West Indies. According to historian Moreau de St. Méry, who wrote in 1797, based on census figures there were 452,000 slaves in Saint-Domingue in 1789 out of a total population of 520,00—the remainder consisted of 40,000 whites and 28,000 *affranchis* (free men and women of color) or descendants of *affranchis*. Between 1764 and 1771, 10,000 to 15,000 new slaves arrived in Saint-Domingue annually, while countless others died at sea en route. Most who survived the crossing subsequently perished in

Saint-Domingue, some because of the island's tropical heat, humidity, and diseases, and others as the result of brutal treatment by plantation owners. Statistics show that there was a complete turnover of slaves every twenty years. In 1789 two-thirds of all the slaves in the colony had been born in Africa.

The colony was hierarchically structured, based on color, class, and wealth. At the bottom of the social ladder were the slaves who had just arrived in Saint-Domingue and spoke only African languages. As field laborers, they had the hardest work and were despised by everyone else. On the next rung were the Creole slaves, Africans whose source of pride was that they had been born in the New World. Above them came the mulatto slaves, who often worked in the plantation house and viewed themselves as superior to the freed black slaves because of their indoor work and lighter skin color. At the top were the *affranchis*, usually mulattoes, or people of color (*gens de couleur*), neither whites nor slaves. Whites were on a separate social ladder; at the bottom were the shopkeepers, referred to as the small whites (*petits blancs*). At the top were the plantation owners, wealthy merchants, and high officials, who were known as the big whites (*grands blancs*).

Social and racial dissatisfaction and tensions among planters, free blacks, and slaves became widespread in Saint-Domingue in the last years of the colony. In addition, the planters chafed at regulations imposed by the mother country. France appointed the colonial governors, quartered militia in the colony, and required that all cargo travel on French ships.

The free blacks protested their second-class status. Beginning in the 1770s, the white colonists imposed laws that precluded blacks from being called "mister," from wearing certain clothes, or from sitting wherever they liked in churches and theaters. The free blacks wanted equal rights with whites, and most of all the right to hold citizenship and to own slaves.

The slaves on Saint-Domingue, who were badly mistreated by the planters, became increasingly restive, spurred on by the French Revolution, with its endorsement of freedom and equality and by campaigns by British and French anti-slavery organizations. Violent conflicts between white colonists and black slaves were common in Saint-Domingue. Bands of runaway slaves, known as maroons (*marrons*), entrenched themselves in bastions in the colony's mountains and forests, from which they harried white-owned plantations, both to obtain provisions and weaponry and to avenge themselves against the inhabitants. As their numbers grew, these bands, sometimes consisting of thousands of people, began to carry out hit-and-run attacks throughout the colony. This guerrilla warfare, however, lacked centralized organization and leadership. The most famous maroon leader was François Macandal, whose six-year rebellion (1751–57) left an estimated 6,000 dead. Reportedly a *boko*, or voodoo sorcerer, Macandal drew from African traditions and religions to motivate his followers. Only one instance is known of an organized plan to free slaves during the 100 years prior to 1791. The instigator was Macandal. His attempt failed before it got started, but as the number of slaves, free blacks, and escaped slaves increased, so, too, did the potential for insurrection.

In 1790 the National Assembly in Paris required that the white Colonial Assembly grant suffrage to landed and tax paying free blacks; the planters' refusal to comply led to the first rebellion in Saint-Domingue. A white militia, reinforced by a corps of black volunteers, contributed to the racial tensions by brutally putting down the revolt, which was led by Vincent Ogé.

Fight for Independence, 1791–1803

The slave rebellion that finally toppled the French colony began with a voodoo ceremony. It was organized by Boukman, a maroon voodoo priest (*houngan*), on August 14, 1791, at the Turpin plantation near Bois Cayman. Among those who participated in that ceremony and later became leaders of the revolution and new nation were Toussaint Louverture (also seen as L'Ouverture), Georges Biassou, and Jean-François.

The slave rebellion began little more than a week after the voodoo ceremony. The slaves slaughtered whites and torched property, fields, and factories in northern settlements, including Acul, Limbé, and Flaville. When news of the uprising reached Cap-Français (formerly Cap-François), whites retaliated at random against non-whites. In response, they were attacked by thousands of blacks. The rebellion ended with an estimated 10,000 slaves and 1,000 whites dead, and 1,200 coffee estates and 200 sugar plantations ruined.

The attack on Cap-Français failed, but elsewhere the planters were unable to regain control. Mulatto forces under André Rigaud, Alexandre Pétion, and others, reinforced by black slaves, continued to clash with white militia in the west and south. The rebellion set in motion events that culminated in the Haitian Revolution.

After the French National Assembly declared in favor of enfranchisement of free blacks and enforcement of equal rights, commissioners were dispatched to Saint-Domingue to implement the policy. Whites in Saint-Domingue, who had had little respect for royal governance in the past, now rallied behind the Bourbons and rejected the radical egalitarian notions of the French revolutionaries. A convoluted situation developed in different regions of the colony, which resulted in divisions within the white, mulatto, and black communities as well as among the various groups. Black slaves battled white colonists while blacks who supported the French king, known as black royalists, fought white and mulatto French republicans, and still other mulattoes struggled against white troops. The Spanish and British took advantage of the instability, and their intervention became another chapter in the revolution.

The leader of the slave rebellion in Saint-Domingue was Toussaint Louverture. Toussaint was born between 1743 and 1746 on the Bréda plantation in northern Saint-Domingue, one of a small number of slaves who were well treated and allowed to become literate. Toussaint served on the Bréda plantation as a steward; when the rebellion began, he arranged safe conduct for his master's family out of the colony and joined the army. He soon emerged as the preeminent military strategist, reportedly in part because of his reading of works by Julius Caesar and others, and in part because of his innate leadership ability.

In April 1793, Cap-Français fell to the French republican forces, who were reinforced by thousands of blacks who had joined them against the French royalists on the promise of freedom. In August Commissioner Léger-Félicité Sonthonax abolished slavery in the colony.

Two black generals refused to commit their forces to France. Instead, Jean-François and Georges Biassou accepted commissions from Spain and, in coordination with Spanish forces, sought to take the north of Saint-Domingue. Toussaint joined the Spanish in February 1793. Commanding his own forces, he cut a swath through the north, swung south to Gonaïves, and by the end of the year had taken control of north-central Saint-Domingue. At this point, Toussaint changed his surname to Louverture meaning "opening," perhaps a commentary on his ability to find openings on the battlefield, or an allusion to his role in creating an opening for slaves.

Some historians believe that Spain and Britain may have reached an informal arrangement to divide the French colony between them—with Britain taking the south and Spain the north. British forces landed in Jérémie and Môle Saint-Nicolas, besieged what is now Port-au-Prince, and took it in June 1794. Meanwhile, the Spanish launched an offensive from the east. The French forces checked Spanish progress toward Port-au-Prince in the south, but the Spanish pushed rapidly through the northern part of the country, occupying most of it by 1794. Spain and Britain appeared poised to seize Saint-Domingue but were foiled by epidemics of tropical diseases.

Toussaint's centrally located forces became the key to victory. After three years of service with Biassou and Jean-François, Toussaint joined forces with France on June 25, 1794, presumably because the French National Assembly had decided on February 4, 1794, to abolish slavery whereas Spain showed no sign of keeping its promise to end slavery in territories it controlled, and Britain had reinstated slavery in places it had occupied. Toussaint took the Artibonite region following a number of raids against his former allies. André Rigaud's mulatto forces had some successes in the south, and the tide turned toward the French republicans. On July 22, 1794, a peace agreement was signed between the principal contenders, France and Spain; Britain was not involved, having no legitimate claim to Hispaniola. Although not implemented until the next year, the Treaty of Basel directed Spain to cede its holdings on Hispaniola to France. The Spanish forces were left without supplies, funding, or avenues of retreat. The armies of Jean-François and Biassou disbanded, and many of their forces joined Toussaint.

In March 1796, Toussaint rescued the French commander, General Étienne-Maynard Laveaux, from a mulatto-led effort to depose him as the primary colonial authority, and the grateful Laveaux appointed Toussaint lieutenant governor of Saint-Dominque. Subsequent French governors made Toussaint commander in chief of all French forces on the island. From this position, Toussaint attempted to create an autonomous state under black rule by getting rid of the French and the mulattoes. He expelled Sonthonax, the French commissioner, and defeated Rigaud's forces in the so-called War of the Castes (1799–1800).

After capturing the port of Santo Domingo in May 1800, Toussaint controlled all of Hispaniola. Then, he turned his attention to domestic issues. In 1800 the plantations were operating at only two-thirds of their former productivity. Toussaint sought to maintain an export economy by putting his generals in charge of the plantations. He reinstated forced labor, *fermage*, in order to grow sugar, coffee, and other crops; made Roman Catholicism the official religion; and outlawed voodoo, the religion of most of the population. Toussaint also declared divorce illegal and demanded monogamy and marital fidelity of his subjects, although he himself kept mistresses.

According to a constitution approved by the Colonial Assembly in 1801, Toussaint was made governor general for life and given the authority to choose his successor. This did not please slave-holding countries, such as the United States and Britain, and threatened French ambitions for a western empire. With the French victorious in Europe, on October 23, 1801, Napoleon ordered his brother-in-law, General Charles Victor Emmanuel Leclerc, to retake the colony and restore slavery.

A 20,000-man French-led expeditionary force, which included Polish, German, Dutch, and Swiss mercenaries and was joined by white colonists and mulatto forces under Pétion and others, landed on the north coast of Saint-Domingue in January 1802. Their numbers were later doubled. Toussaint held out for several months, but two of his chief lieutenants, Jean-Jacques Dessalines and Henry Christophe, held separate talks with the French and went over to their side. On May 6, 1802, Toussaint surrendered, perhaps believing that blacks would be allowed to retain their freedom or that tropical diseases would work their earlier magic and allow him to regain control. However, despite French assurances of his safety, Toussaint was arrested in June 1802 and sent to the Fort de Joux prison in the Jura mountains of France, where he died on April 7, 1803.

Following Toussaint's betrayal, Dessalines, Christophe, and Pétion regrouped to oppose Leclerc and his diseased army. Leclerc requested reinforcement but died of yellow fever two months later, in November 1802. Once his replacement, General Donatien Rochambeau, arrived, fierce fighting continued for another year, during which 55,000 more people were killed, including most of the remaining whites. Many plantations and villages were also destroyed. By September 1803, Rochambeau wrote to Napoleon Bonaparte advising him that the only way for France to win would be to kill everyone over twelve in Saint-Domingue. Meanwhile, more than 20,000 of his own forces were dead. War had resumed in Europe, and consequently Rochambeau was never adequately supported. Following the French defeat at Vertières, Rochambeau fled to Jamaica in November 1803, where he surrendered to the British, ending French colonial rule in Saint-Domingue. After a decade of violence, 300 years of foreign domination had come to an end.

Early Years of Independence, 1804–43

On January 1, 1804, Jean-Jacques Dessalines proclaimed the birth of a new nation. Its name would be Haiti, taken from an Arawak word for "mountainous," and its flag would be red and blue like the French tricolor, but minus the white stripe.

The new nation faced major challenges. Its black and mulatto population of 480,000 in 1789 had been reduced to 250,000 by 1804. Its plantation-based economy was in shreds, and few of the 170,000 who could still do agricultural work wanted to return to the plantations, the symbol of slavery. Even if a supply of labor were found, credit would be required, and it would not be obtainable from the hostile, slave-owning surrounding states. The population was uneducated and largely unskilled, and commerce was almost nonexistent.

Dessalines, the first leader of Haiti, was born in the north, on the Corers plantation, where he served as a field hand prior to being sold to a freeman. Both his masters were brutal, and Dessalines developed a hatred for whites, mulattoes, and authority. When the revolt began, he joined forces with Toussaint Louverture, and proved to be a successful and ruthless leader in battle. As the leader of Haiti, Dessalines governed with a firm hand just as Toussaint had done and, like Toussaint, reimposed the plantation system and used the military to ensure that laborers stayed on the plantations and worked. The quality of life for blacks did not improve much during Dessalines's rule. His extensive use of the military set a pattern that lasted until the army was disbanded in 1995.

In 1803 Dessalines became governor general for life, and, in 1804, he crowned himself Emperor Jacques I. Dissatisfaction with his rule increased and became widespread. Cultured Haitians objected to his ignorance and illiteracy, the mulattoes felt threatened by his racism, and most Haitians objected to his corruption and poor economic judgment.

Dessalines was assassinated on October 17, 1806. En route to Port-au-Prince with a column of troops to crush a mulatto-led rebellion, Dessalines was ambushed, shot, and hacked to pieces

Artist's rendering of Henry Christophe's palace
Sans Souci at Cap-Haïtien
Courtesy Library of Congress Prints and Photographs Division

by people probably hired by mulatto opponents. The perpetrators were never apprehended. His assassination contributed to a legacy of racial friction, and led to a popular connection between Dessalines and black power. It was the first in a long series of violent deaths of Haitian heads of state.

Although Dessalines had not designated a successor prior to his murder, a number of candidates presented themselves after his death. The leading contender from the north was Henry Christophe, but he was not popular enough in the south to offset the desire there for a mulatto leader. Consequently, the Constituent Assembly worked out an arrangement that created a weak presidency and a strong legislature. Christophe would be president, and Alexandre Pétion would head the legislature, thus beginning a tradition of "politics by understudies" (*politique de doublure*), where, typically, a black president would be manipulated from behind the scenes by a mulatto. However, this arrangement failed because Christophe was not content to be a figurehead president.

Partition of Haiti, 1811–20

After military attacks to displace Pétion failed, the country split into two parts. Christophe ruled the north from Cap-Haï-tien, while Pétion governed the south and west. In 1811 Christophe crowned himself King Henry I of Haiti, and the northern dominion became a kingdom. He installed a nobility of mainly black supporters, who assumed titles of earl, count, and baron.

Christophe, who was born a slave in Grenada and served masters at sea, in Georgia, and in Saint-Domingue, remained a life-long anglophile. He spelled his first name, Henry, with the English orthography. As president, he hired English teachers to establish national schools, and encouraged British investment in Haiti.

Christophe's career was also influenced by his association with Toussaint Louverture. During the Haitian Revolution, Christophe had become a protégé of Toussaint and helped develop the *fermage* program that returned Haitians to the plantations as paid laborers. When Christophe became president, he also attempted to restore the sugar plantations, using workers who were bound to the land.

Christophe sought to open up international trade, but he was afraid such trade would encourage foreign invasions. He brought 4,000 warriors from Dahomey in West Africa, the Royal Dahomets, as a security force to protect himself and Haiti and to encourage honesty and morality among his subjects. Christophe remains conspicuous among Haitian leaders for his emphasis on public and personal morality.

Meanwhile, in the south and west, Alexandre Pétion was head of a military oligarchy. He ruled under two constitutions. Under the first, he was president of the republic from 1807 to 1816, and under the second, he became president for life.

An important difference between the northern kingdom and the southern republic was the treatment of land ownership. Christophe gave the bulk of the land to the state and leased large tracts to estate managers. Pétion distributed state-owned land to individuals in small parcels. He began distributing land to his soldiers in 1809, and later extended the land grant plan to other beneficiaries, lowering the selling price to a level that almost anyone could afford. Pétion's motivation was to reward people for the travails of slavery. A legacy of this well-intentioned program has been to create a region of family-owned farms, which have become increasingly unproductive through subdivision according to inheritance laws.

To Christophe's chagrin, his subjects continued to defect from the harsh conditions in the north to the more benevolent situation in the south. In 1818, when Pétion, known to his citizens as Father Good Heart (Papa Bon Coeur), died without naming a successor, the Senate selected General Jean-Pierre Boyer to fill his post. Boyer was a mulatto, who had been born in Port-au-Prince and joined the revolutionary forces with Toussaint. After independence, he served Pétion as secretary and commander of the Presidential Guard.

After Pétion's death in 1818, Christophe sought to reunite Haiti, but the south rejected the prospect of domination by a black leader. In October 1820, following a stroke that had caused him to lose control of the army, his principal power base, Christophe committed suicide. Boyer immediately took advantage of the situation, and on October 26, he entered Cap-Haïtien with 20,000 troops and reunited the country.

Jean-Pierre Boyer Reunites Haiti, 1820–43

Boyer inherited a country with diminishing agricultural production caused by Pétion's policy of land distribution. He tried to revive the plantation system through the enactment of the Rural Code (Code Rural). Its regulations included forced labor to produce export crops and the use of rural police to restrict the movement of peasants and make them work. However, government laxity and lack of cooperation from plantation owners caused the system to fail and led to the ultimate demise of the plantation economy. Sugar production continued to decline as a result of the move toward small subsistence farms. Throughout the nineteenth century, coffee remained the principal export, while food crops were raised for local consumption.

Like previous Haitian rulers, Boyer feared another invasion of Haiti. To eliminate foreign presence on the island, he seized the Spanish colony of Santo Domingo in 1822. This ended slavery in Hispaniola but created a legacy of poor relations between the French and Spanish-speaking sides of the island.

Three years later, Boyer undertook another measure intended to remove the threat of foreign invasion and open Haiti to international commerce. He agreed to compensate France for its losses during the revolution. In return for a 150-million-franc indemnity and halving customs charges for French trade, Haiti received diplomatic recognition from France. Britain recognized Haiti the following year. This act ended Haiti's diplomatic isolation, but did not preclude intervention. Although the indemnity was reduced in 1838 to 60 million francs, the payments had a disastrous effect on the Haitian economy and led to years of French domination of Haiti's finances.

Social and class divisions based on color and property ownership hardened during Boyer's rule. Despite his efforts to appoint blacks to responsible positions, his government increasingly fell into the hands of the mulatto elite. Uneducated rural blacks found few opportunities in the bureaucracy and turned to the army.

Nevertheless, the immediate threat to Boyer came from mulattoes opposed to the political and social status quo. In the late 1830s, Hérard Dumesle, a mulatto member of Congress, founded the Organization for the Social Rights of Man and Citizen, which was critical of the economy, corruption, and nepotism and called for an end to Boyer's rule. Although Dumesle and his congressional sympathizers were expelled from the legislature, dissatisfaction with the government continued. On January 27, 1843, Charles Rivière-Hérard, a cousin of Dumesle, overthrew Boyer in what is referred to as the Revolution of 1843. Boyer sailed to Jamaica, the destination of other displaced Haitian rulers in the nineteenth century. The Dominicans took this opportunity to declare their independence.

Boyer's presidency was remarkable for its length, the longest in Haitian history, and for its relative placidity. During his rule, the nation was reunited internally and internationally. However, Boyer's presidency also saw a hardening of class and social divisions based on skin color and property ownership. Blacks, who had been excluded from power under Boyer, reasserted themselves after his overthrow. The subsequent struggle for power led to a succession of short-lived governments.

Increasing Instability, 1843–1915

The period between 1843 and 1915 was marked by a pattern of political instability and struggle in which a succession of incompetent or brutal leaders came and went rapidly and violently. Of the twenty-two heads of state between 1843 and 1915, only one served out his prescribed term of office. Three died while serving. One was blown up in the palace, one was poisoned, one was hacked to pieces by a mob, one resigned, and fourteen others were deposed by coups.

This was also a period of economic stagnation. Revenues from agriculture declined as the ill-tended and subdivided land yielded less and less. Payments to France emptied the federal reserves, and the national treasury was chronically in default. Presidents appealed to foreign countries for loans and help to stay in power. A new and lucrative business emerged: coup-making. German merchants funded rebellions on speculation, and Haitian mercenaries, known as *cacos*, carried out the coups.

Interspersed among these short-lived presidencies were a few longer-lasting dictatorships in which black leaders were manipulated by elite mulatto politicians or merchants. Another phenomenon was a growing rivalry between Liberal (mulatto) and National (black) parties.

The life of most Haitians was dismal. As late as 1915, more than 90 percent of the population was illiterate. The average annual income was only US$20. Not only were people poor, but tropical diseases such as malaria, hookworm, yaws, and intestinal infections were endemic, leading to high mortality rates.

The presidency of Charles Rivière-Hérard (1843–44) was cut short because of international and domestic difficulties. In March 1844, Hérard returned from a failed effort to take Santo Domingo to diminished support. Two months later, bands of peasants called *piquets* (a term derived from the stakes they carried as weapons) overthrew Hérard at the behest of an army officer, Louis Jean-Jacques Acaau, who demanded an end to mulatto rule.

As property values declined, politics became more lucrative. Between 1844 and 1849, mulattoes in the Senate, including Beaubrun Ardouin and his brothers, ruled behind the scenes, installing a series of black leaders and taking the profit. The first was the eighty-seven-year-old Philippe Guerrier (1844–45), who had been a member of the peerage under Christophe. In short order, he was succeeded by Jean-Louis Pierrot (1845–46) and Jean-Baptiste Riché (1846–47).

The fourth mulatto presidential choice, Faustin Soulouque (1847–59), was a little-known black from the Presidential Guard, whom the Ardouin brothers had selected. Soulouque was ambitious and ruthless. After arresting, exiling, and killing his sponsors, he established a secret police force, the *zinglins*, to terrorize adversaries; he used *piquets* to frighten the merchants of Port-au-Prince and then executed the *piquet* leader, who had become too powerful.

A year after taking office, Soulouque crowned himself Emperor Faustin I. Perhaps fear of foreigners prompted his renewed attacks on the Dominican Republic. Both of his incursions were defeated, however, and they contributed to his overthrow by General Nicholas Geffrard. Soulouque was the last Haitian leader to have been a slave.

Geffrard, a dark-skinned mulatto, restored the old order of elite rule. His relatively long rule (1859–67) was peaceful and progressive, in contrast to that of his predecessor. He is credited with a number of accomplishments: he produced a new constitution based on Pétion's 1816 document, promoted education and organized a medical school, cut the army by half, and tried to improve the quality of cotton production. He also signed a concordat with the Vatican in 1860 that ended a sixty-year schism with Rome, led to abler clergy, and gave Roman Catholicism a privileged position among religions in Haiti. Geffrard also won recognition for Haiti from the United States in 1862.

The 1860s were a difficult decade for Haiti politically and economically. Geffrard was harassed by the elites and the *piquets* throughout his rule. Under siege in Cap-Haïtien, Geffrard called in the British for support. He was the first Haitian president to stay in power with foreign support, but not the last. In 1867 General Sylvain Salnave, a light-skinned mulatto populist with support from northern blacks and the poor in Port-au-Prince, forced Geffrard to leave the country for Jamaica.

Salnave, however, lacked the support of the *cacos*. After waging several unsuccessful battles against them, he was pursued to the Dominican border, captured, tried, and executed on January 15, 1870.

After setting up an interim provisional government, the National Assembly selected Nissage Saget as president. Saget completed his term of office (1870–74) and stepped down voluntarily. His successor, President Boisrond Canal, resigned in 1879 in the absence of legislative cooperation. All of the subsequent presidencies until 1915 began and ended with force or the threat of it.

Rebellion, intrigue, and conspiracy continued to be commonplace even under the rule of Louis Lysius Félicité Salomon (1879–88), the most notable and effective president in the late nineteenth century. From a political southern black family, he was well educated, well traveled, and politically experienced. After living in France following his expulsion by Hérard, he had returned to Haiti and served as minister of finance under Soulouque.

President Salomon was a populist. He established a national bank, brought some order to public administration, revived agriculture to an extent, linked Haiti to the outside world through the telegraph, opened rural schools, and imported French teachers. Salomon also paid off the indemnity to France. Although known as a nationalist, Salomon encouraged investment by permitting foreign companies to own Haitian land.

Salomon's support of the rural masses and efforts to contain elite-instigated plots kept him in power longer than the strongmen who preceded and followed him; however, when he tried to stay in office beyond his term, Salomon was evicted by Liberal Party forces and other opponents.

The final exception to the short-lived presidencies of the late 1800s was that of Florvil Hyppolite (1889–96). Hyppolite is remembered for his Ministry of Public Works, which built bridges, docks, iron markets, and public buildings throughout Haiti and installed telephone and telegraph lines. After Hyppolite, Haitian politics became even more unstable and the governments particularly short-lived. This was the case until the United States occupation in 1915.

United States Involvement in Haiti, 1915–34

The turn of the century was a period of expansion for the United States. It was becoming an extraterritorial economic and military power, accumulating possessions in the Caribbean and Central America that included Cuba, Puerto Rico, and parts of Panama. The Monroe Doctrine in 1823 and the Roosevelt Corollary in 1904, the opening of the Panama Canal in 1914, the beginning of World War I, and Admiral Alfred Mahan's doctrines concerning the strategic importance of sea-lanes of communications all contributed to a growing view that the Caribbean was an American lake in the United States' own backyard.

One of the Caribbean countries where the United States had interests was Haiti. By 1915 the United States controlled Haiti's banking and railroads and accounted for most of the country's imports. Only Germany, which had considerable business and strategic interests in the area, provided real competition. Germany was rumored to be interested in acquiring Môle Saint-Nicolas as a refueling station, a prospect that concerned the

United States because it would place a potential European enemy in relative proximity.

Between 1849 and 1915, the United States Navy sent warships to Haiti on twenty-six occasions to extract debt payments from reluctant Haitian governments and to prevent the British, French, and Germans from gaining a greater foothold. After the fall of President Antoine Simon in 1910, six Haitian leaders seized power during the next four years, four of whom were killed in office. In December 1914, following news of additional *caco* revolts, a United States ship entered Port-au-Prince, removed US$500,000 from the Haitian Bank, a sum that the United States claimed it was due, and deposited it in the National City Bank of New York. This action was regarded as a significant affront by Haitians.

The event that caused the United States Marines to invade Haiti occurred on July 27, 1915. Seeing that his downfall was imminent, President Vilbrun Guillaume Sam ordered the killing of 167 political prisoners in the national penitentiary and then sought refuge in the French embassy. However, an irate crowd stormed the embassy, dragged Guillaume Sam out, pulled him apart, and then paraded parts of him through the streets. The next day, the United States deployed 330 marines aboard the *USS Washington* to protect its citizens, stabilize the Haitian government, and secure United States financial interests. The United States Marines remained in Haiti for the next nineteen years.

The marines took rapid control of Haiti. They imposed martial law, disbanded the Haitian army, installed Philippe Sudre Dartiguenave, a mulatto from an elite family, in the presidency, and then appointed lesser officials.

On September 15, 1915, the marines announced complete political and administrative control of Haiti. A treaty, the Haitian-American Convention, decreed that United States citizens would collect customs and oversee all government outlays, approve all debt requests, advise the treasury, direct public works and health programs, and launch an agricultural training campaign. Article 10 decreed that the United States would create and head a new constabulary. Not surprisingly, Haitians resented this treaty, which was originally to be in force for ten years but which, in March 1917, was extended for another ten years.

The marines also changed the Haitian constitution. After the Haitian congress refused the first draft proposed, the

President Philippe Sudre Dartiguenave (seated at center)
with ministers and bodyguards
Courtesy National Archives

marines dissolved congress and resubmitted the draft to a closely monitored national plebiscite, which accepted it almost unanimously. The authorship of this constitution is still debated. Some argue that the author was the young assistant secretary of the navy, Franklin Delano Roosevelt.

The 1918 constitution included a novel provision for Haiti—white foreigners would be permitted to own land. Many North American companies took advantage of this opportunity to lease large tracts of Haitian land.

During the nineteen-year occupation, the marines undertook numerous initiatives under the presidencies of Philippe Sudre Dartiguenave (1915–22) and Louis Borno (1922–30). They attempted to improve the country's infrastructure by building roads, bridges, wharves, lighthouses, and irrigation systems. They tried to improve health conditions by upgrading the sanitation system and providing clean water. They brought in United States physicians to create a public health program that included the establishment of hospitals, clinics, and training schools for doctors and nurses and mounted campaigns against syphilis, yaws, malaria, and hookworm. They tried to modernize agriculture by creating an agricultural-technical system, the Service Technique, with the help of United States agricultural experts. They sought to professionalize the security forces by replacing the constabulary, or gendarmerie, with a National Guard. They attempted to stabilize the Haitian currency, the gourde, by linking it to the dollar.

Whatever initial Haitian enthusiasm existed for the United States invasion dimmed quickly. Haitians increasingly disliked the marine presence and governance. They resented the legalization of land ownership by foreigners and the forced drafts of peasants for road building, known as corvée.

A particular problem was the racial prejudice of the United States Marines. The marines favored the predominantly light-skinned mulatto elite and installed a series of mulatto presidents that lasted through Sténio Vincent (1930–41).

The marines were charged with promoting stability. As part of this mission, they created and trained a gendarmerie, which came to be called the Garde d'Haïti, and was a precursor to the Haitian army. The Garde was increasingly employed to hunt down and kill Haitians who opposed the occupation and may ultimately have killed as many as 6,000 and put another 5,500 into labor camps. The intolerance of North American whites of the occupying force caused indignation, resentment, and eventually a racial pride that was reflected in the work of a new generation of Haitian historians, ethnologists, writers, artists, and others, many of whom later became active in politics and government.

In 1918 Charlemagne Péralte, a former military officer from a rural, middle-class family, proclaimed himself leader of the *cacos* (mercenary bands) and announced that he was determined "to drive the invaders into the sea and free Haiti." Péralte attacked outlying military establishments and then, on October 7, 1919, Port-au-Prince itself. Péralte became a national hero, but, shortly afterward, he was betrayed, ambushed at gunpoint, killed, and then publicly displayed as a warning to other rebels. Benoît Batraville took his place, but after his murder in 1920, armed resistance to the occupation ended.

The marine occupation continued after World War I, although it was an embarrassment to President Woodrow Wilson at the Versailles Peace Conference in 1919, where national self-determination was a major topic. It was not until 1929, after many Haitians were killed and wounded in student uprisings and a strike at Les Cayes, that the United States Congress demanded an inquiry into the occupation.

President Herbert Hoover appointed W. Cameron Forbes, a former governor general of the Philippines, to head an investigatory commission. The commission found that although the marines had made material improvements, they had excluded Haitians from a real role in government and from the Garde d'Haïti. The commission concluded that "the social forces that created [instability] remained—poverty, ignorance, and a lack of a tradition or desire for orderly free government." The commission recommended withdrawal of the occupation forces, and United States withdrawal was underway by 1932, when Franklin D. Roosevelt became president. The last contingent of marines departed in August 1934, after a formal transfer of authority to the Garde; a financial mission remained until 1941 to safeguard United States holdings. The departure was welcomed by Haitians of all colors, classes, and sectors of society.

Although the United States occupation was intended to bring political and financial stability to Haiti, dictatorships soon returned, and the improvements to the country's infrastructure made by the marines were allowed to deteriorate.

Racial prejudice in Haiti dates from the colonial experience, but the Revolution of 1946, which brought black leaders to power, was a direct reaction to the United States occupation. Historically, educated Haitians had taken pride in their familiarity with France, ability to speak French, and their Roman Catholicism. After the occupation, increasingly, Haitians came to reject anything to do with whites and the West. They began to explore and take pride in their African roots and in Haitian history, and openly to practice voodoo, the religion of most Haitians. In 1957 François Duvalier played on these anti-white, anti-Western, pro-black and pro-voodoo sentiments to gain the presidency and hold power.

The occupation led to another unforeseen and tragic result. In October 1937, some 5,000 to 12,000 Haitians were killed by the Dominican military on orders from dictator Rafael Leónidas Trujillo. These Haitians were living in an area on the Haitian-Dominican border that the United States Marines had incorporated into Haiti during the occupation. Historically difficult relations between Haiti and the Dominican Republic worsened because of the killings and because of Dominican resentment of previous Haitian control.

From the End of the United States Occupation to Duvalier, 1934–57

The 1930 presidential election was the first since the occupation began in which the marines did not interfere. The winner was Sténio Vincent, a former senator with populist tendencies. A charismatic speaker, Vincent was the first Haitian head of state to make official speeches in Creole rather than French.

Beyond efforts to remove the marines from Haiti and improve infrastructure and services, President Vincent increasingly used his office and the Garde to increase his own power and wealth. In 1935 he forced a new constitution through Congress that allowed him sweeping powers to dissolve the legislature, reorganize the judiciary, appoint ten out of twenty-one senators, and rule when the legislature was not in session. Then, he held a plebiscite that transferred economic matters from the legislature to the executive. Vincent repressed opposition and censored the press, but when he sought to remain in office for a third term, the United States objected. He relinquished the presidency to Élie Lescot in 1941.

Élie Lescot was a light-skinned mulatto like his three predecessors. His previous experience as ambassador to the Dominican Republic and in other government jobs seemed promising. However, Lescot exacerbated racial sensitivities by placing light-skinned people at all levels of the government irrespective of their competence. He exacerbated religious sensitivities by facilitating an anti-superstition campaign (1941–42) that the Roman Catholic Church organized against voodoo. Lescot also became increasingly authoritarian. He declared himself commander in chief of the military, repressed the people, censored the press, and compelled Congress to grant him extensive powers to handle the budget and fill legislative vacancies without elections.

Lescot's declining popularity sank further when correspondence was made public that revealed that he had been under the influence and pay of Dominican President Trujillo when he was ambassador to the Dominican Republic, and that Trujillo's money might have helped get him elected. After Lescot jailed the Marxist editors of a journal called *La Ruche* (The Beehive) in early January, students took to the streets to protest and demand more civil liberties. Then, on January 11, 1945, army officers, led by Major Paul E. Magloire, forced Lescot to resign, and the Garde took power. The Garde acted in a singular fashion, on behalf of the nation rather than an individual. Further, it pledged to hold free elections and did.

The Revolution of 1946, as the elections were called, was the result of incompetent, dishonest, and repressive governance and exasperation at mulatto domination. The spectacle of mulattoes everywhere in the administration turned many blacks into pro-black activists, or *noiristes*. A contemporary writer, Roger Dorsainville, described the popular mood, saying, "I was a *noiriste*. And I will add that anyone in my social class in Haiti, after Lescot, under Lescot, whoever was not a *noiriste* would have been scum . . . ."

In May 1946, Haitians elected a National Assembly whose purpose was to select a president on August 16, 1946. The three major candidates were black. The leading candidate, Dumarsais Estimé, was from a modest black family in Verrettes. He had been a school teacher, assembly member, and minister of education under Vincent. Félix d'Orléans Juste Constant was leader of the Communist Party of Haiti (Parti Communiste d'Haïti—PCH). Démosthènes Calixte was a former Garde commander and a stand-in for Daniel Fignolé, head of the progressive coalition that included the Worker Peasant Movement (Mouvement Ouvrier Paysan—MOP); Fignolé was too young to run himself.

Dumarsais Estimé was anti-elitist and therefore regarded as anti-mulatto. His base of support came from blacks, particularly from the emerging middle class and the north. Although Estimé was a civilian, he had the blessings of the Garde d'Haïti and won easily on the second round of polling.

Dumarsais Estimé enjoyed broad support in the early years of his presidency. Under a new constitution in November 1946, he launched a series of reforms intended to improve the condition of life in the cities and countryside. He brought more middle-class and lower-class blacks into the public sector, increased the daily minimum wage, raised salaries of civil servants, and proposed the nation's first social security laws. He expanded the school system, encouraged rural cooperatives, sent agronomists to Puerto Rico to study farming techniques, and encouraged the United States and the Export-Import Bank to invest in a Haitian Tennessee Valley Authority for the Artibonite River.

However, President Estimé made enemies, who finally contributed to his overthrow. He alienated the elites by purging mulatto officials from his administration and pursuing an agenda that encouraged labor unions and forced people to pay income tax for the first time. Although Estimé was a practicing Roman Catholic, he disturbed Catholics and the church with his endorsement of voodoo. Finally, even some blacks deserted him, characterizing the regime as ineffectual.

President Estimé had sought the support of the Garde by turning it into the Haitian army, but when he attempted to amend the constitution in 1950 to prolong his presidency, the new army, under Colonel Paul Magloire, sent him to exile in Jamaica, with the tacit support of the elite and little public opposition. The people who had ensured the transfer of power from Lescot to Estimé called for new elections.

Colonel Magloire resigned from the junta to run for president. With the blessings of the military and the elite and the absence of electoral opposition, he won a term in the first elections in Haiti in which all men over twenty-one could vote.

President Magloire was an appealing figure who managed to captivate blacks while restoring the elites to prominence. Under his presidency, the business community and government benefited briefly from favorable economic conditions, as did the country's infrastructure, agricultural sector, and school and health systems, all with the help of foreign loans.

By Haitian presidential standards, Magloire was firm but not harsh. He jailed political opponents, prohibited labor strikes, and periodically shut down printing presses. On the other hand, he allowed unions and sometimes the presses to function.

However, Magloire's increasing corruption disillusioned many Haitians. He controlled the sisal, cement, and soap monopolies and built mansions for himself. Then, after Hurricane Hazel devastated Haiti in 1954, Magloire appropriated relief funds that had been earmarked for recovery. In May 1956, after an attempt to prolong his stay in office, protesters demanded that he step down. In December 1956, after strikes shut down Port-au-Prince, Paul Magloire fled to Jamaica.

The period between the ouster of Magloire in December 1956 and the election of François Duvalier in September 1957 was marked by political instability. During that interval, there were three provisional presidents, one of whom resigned, and two others who were ousted by the army.

François Duvalier, 1957–71

François Duvalier came from a modest but upwardly mobile black family in Port-au-Prince. He attended the Lycée Pétion, a good state school, with other children of academically ambitious parents of limited means. After graduation, Duvalier studied medicine in Haiti. Then, he took an internship at Saint François de Sales Hospital near the capital. Afterward, he took a post that attempted to eradicate yaws and became director of a clinic. In August 1944, Duvalier briefly attended Michigan State University to study public health, but before completing the program returned to Haiti to continue his work against yaws.

François Duvalier's interest in literature, ethnography, and politics led him to start the Haitian negritude movement in 1929 with Lorimer Denis, a black lawyer, nationalist, and mystic. He founded a pro-voodoo, African-focused organization, Les Griots (a Guinean term meaning The Bards) in the late 1930s. Then he helped Dr. Price Mars form the Bureau of Ethnology, an organization dedicated to the study and propagation of indigenous Haitian customs and values.

François Duvalier's first overtly political act was to become general secretary of Daniel Fignolé's party of young professionals, the MOP. In 1946 he became a protégé of Dumarsais Estimé, then the MOP candidate. When Estimé was elected president, Duvalier entered the cabinet as minister of labor. When Estimé was ousted from office in 1950, Duvalier also lost his job. In September 1956, François Duvalier entered the race for president as the heir to Dumarsais Estimé.

Although François Duvalier was not everyone's favorite candidate, he had broad support. His proponents saw him as educated, mild mannered, lacking in undue political ambition, and having good international connections. He had worked with poor and sick Haitians, he was a pro-black nationalist, and he cared about voodoo and ethnicity. This father-figure demeanor and manner caused him to be refered to as "Papa Doc." Finally, he had the support of the Haitian army.

The election was historic. All Haitians over the age of twenty-one were eligible to vote for a president. However, whether the peoples' will was done is debatable. There were no official election observers, the army disqualified the most popular candidate, Fignolé, and there were claims of fraud. In any case, François Duvalier claimed a decisive victory, and his followers captured two-thirds of the legislature's lower house and all the seats in the Senate. In September 1957, François Duvalier was installed as president.

In his first speech on October 22, 1957, President Duvalier promised government unity, reconciliation, and financial redistribution. However, within weeks, he began to destroy all past or potential opposition in order to centralize power in himself and remain in power.

Duvalier's apparent lack of political ambition was a sham. In October 1961, he extended his presidency another six years and replaced the bicameral legislature with a unicameral body. In June 1964, unwary voters in a plebiscite discovered that they had approved a constitutional change making François Duvalier president for life.

President Duvalier reigned supreme for fourteen years. Even in Haiti, where dictators had been the norm, François Duvalier gave new meaning to the term. Duvalier and his henchmen killed between 30,000 and 60,000 Haitians. The victims were not only political opponents, but women, whole families, whole towns. Duvalier also used other techniques to eliminate opposition, including imprisonment, intimidation, and exile. Many left in what became the first wave of Haitian emigration.

To protect himself against the military, Duvalier repeatedly reshuffled the high command and promoted junior black officers. In July 1958, when a coup attempt occurred, Duvalier created a separate Presidential Guard within the army for one purpose only, to enable him to remain in power. In 1959 Duvalier created the Volunteers for National Security (Volontaires de la Sécurité Nationale—VSN), or *makout*, as they were dubbed, in reference to mythical Haitian bogeymen who carry off sleeping children in sacks. The VSN was a secret, private, armed paramilitary group reporting directly to the palace, whose members used terror and blackmail to get patronage for the regime and themselves (see The Duvalier Era, 1957–86, ch. 10). Duvalier used religion as a form of control. He co-opted voodoo priests as spies in the countryside, and for added protection, he himself dressed as a well-known voodoo figure. Finally, the president created a new elite, who owed its wealth and status to him.

President Duvalier weathered a series of foreign political crises early in his tenure, which enhanced his power and contributed to his view of himself as the "personification of the Haitian fatherland." By 1961 Duvalier had received US$40.4 million in foreign assistance, mainly as gifts from the United States. However, in mid-1962, President John F. Kennedy cut aid to Haiti after Duvalier arrogantly refused to account for its disbursement. Even so, Duvalier continued to receive funds secretly. After Kennedy's death, Duvalier again received aid openly. In return, he remained outside the communist camp and voted with the United States to expel Cuba from the Organization of American States (OAS).

In April 1963, when an army officer suspected of trying to kidnap two of Duvalier's children took refuge in the Dominican chancery, Duvalier ordered the Presidential Guard to occupy the building. The Dominicans were incensed; President Juan Bosch Gaviño ordered troops to the border and threatened to invade. However, the Dominican commanders were reluctant to enter Haiti, and Bosch was obliged to turn to the OAS to settle the matter.

After the government, the military and the Roman Catholic Church were the two most powerful institutions in Haiti, and President Duvalier sought to weaken both. Although he was less violent with the church, he employed similar techniques with both institutions. Duvalier co-opted clergy, arrested those who opposed him, exiled several bishops, a papal nuncio, and numerous clergy, and confiscated church property. Despite such actions, on October 25, 1966, he succeeded in having the Vatican sign an accord that allowed him to nationalize the church, effectively putting himself at the head of the church in Haiti. The most significant change in the concordat was that the president was given the power to name archbishops and bishops, with the approval of the Holy See. Duvalier nominated five bishops, four of whom, including the archbishop, were black. According to the president, the new church would promote Haitian unity. The church would no longer be a white, largely French, institution with foreign loyalties. For the remainder of his presidency, Duvalier continued to control the church and expel those, such as the Holy Ghost Fathers, whom he accused of being antigovernment. With regard to the army, Duvalier exiled or eliminated officers who opposed him, closed the Military Academy because he considered it a potential source of opposition, and expelled the United States mission in 1963, fearing its influence (see The Duvalier Era, 1957–86, ch. 10).

The social and economic liabilities of the François Duvalier government far outweighed its marginal benefits. The attrition of the population through exile and murder was a terrible blow to the country's economic and political development and to its image in the world. Religious and racial tensions increased as a result of Duvalier's endorsement of voodoo and his support for the black urban middle class at the expense of the mulatto elite. Despite substantial multilateral and bilateral economic support, the economy stagnated as a result of neglect and the diversion of as much as 10 million dollars a year from the treasury. Among the few positive things that can be said about his presidency is that François Duvalier provided some new opportunities for the black urban middle class. Before his presidency, the army command had been a bastion of the mulatto elite. Duvalier turned it into a medium for black upward mobility. Another progressive aspect of his presidency was the Haitianizing of the Catholic hierarchy, which acted as a stimulus to Haitianize the rest of the church.

Jean-Claude Duvalier, 1971–86

Only nineteen years old in 1971, when his father died peacefully in his sleep, Jean-Claude Duvalier (referred to as "Baby Doc") protested that he was too young and inexperienced to be president. Although it is unclear whether he was in fact mentally prepared to be president, there is near unanimity that he was ill-suited for it. For the first few years, Jean-Claude's politically ambitious mother, Simone Ovide, ran the government, while he lived the life of a playboy.

For many Haitians and foreign observers, Jean-Claude's youth, approachability, and his political promises were encouraging. The United States was heartened when the new president announced that "his father had accomplished the political revolution, and his administration would realize the economic revolution."

There were initial signs of political openings that included more freedom of the press and respect for human rights. By neglecting his role in government, however, Jean-Claude squandered a considerable amount of domestic and foreign goodwill and facilitated the dominance of Haitian affairs by a clique of hard-line Duvalierist cronies, who later became known as dinosaurs.

On May 27, 1980, Jean-Claude Duvalier married Michèle Bennett. The wedding made the *Guinness World Book of Records* for lavishness and highlighted for most Haitians the disparities between their lives and that of the Duvaliers. Everything about the wedding was contentious. Although the bride was a divorcée, the couple was married in the Port-au-Prince cathedral by an archbishop. In addition, she was a light-skinned

*Jean-Claude Duvalier (third from right) with wife Michèle
and others at a military ceremony*

mulatto, whose former husband was the son of a man who had
attempted a coup against François Duvalier. Michèle's father,
Ernest Bennett, had a reputation for shady business deals,
including narcotics trafficking.

The marriage alienated many Haitians, particularly blacks
and Duvalierists, the very people François Duvalier had cultivated. Increased political repression added to the volatility of
the situation, which continued until 1986.

Jean-Claude's personal interest in government was extractive. His principal source of revenue was the Tobacco and
Matches Administration (Régie du Tabac et des Allumettes),
established by President Estimé as a tobacco monopoly. Jean-
Claude expanded the monopoly to include profits from other
state-owned industries. Over the years, he drew hundreds of
millions of dollars from this "nonfiscal account." An additional
source of income for the first family was the business community, which Jean-Claude's wife, Michèle Bennett, canvassed and
from which donations were extorted.

Corruption and intimidation extended well beyond the first
family. The *makout* and section chiefs, or *chefs de section* (the
paramilitary rural constabulary), also used a method of extortion called "squeeze and suck" (*peze souse*) referring to the way

291

Haitian popsicles are eaten by squeezing the bottom and sucking from the top).

At the beginning of the 1980s, a period of economic decline and stagnation set in. Based on all the economic indicators, Haiti fell to the bottom of the group of least-developed nations. Bad governance, combined with a series of natural disasters, increased discontent and misery. By 1986 nearly half of all Haitians were unemployed, and many more were underemployed. Many people were not getting enough to eat and were dying of treatable illnesses.

In the first half of the 1980s, Haiti's problems intensified. In 1982 Hurricane Allen destroyed plantations growing coffee, one of Haiti's principal agricultural products. In 1982 and 1983, droughts further devastated agricultural production. In 1983 Reynolds Aluminum, which mined bauxite in Haiti, left. The same year, the worldwide economic crisis hit Haiti. Then, acquired immune deficiency syndrome (AIDS) became associated with Haiti, causing tourism to plummet and some foreign-owned assembly plants to leave. To avoid the spread of African swine fever, Haitian black pigs were all eradicated by 1984. These pigs had been the major protein source for Haitians and, in effect, their savings account (see Livestock and Fishing, ch. 8). In addition, high population growth caused the subdivision of land into plots too small to support a family. Overcultivated and deforested terrain was causing soil erosion and depletion of charcoal, the major energy source.

Dissatisfaction with Jean-Claude increased following a one-day visit by Pope John Paul II on March 9, 1983. The government encouraged the visit, hoping it would revive the president's declining reputation. The president, his ministers, and a crowd estimated at 200,000 met the pontiff at the airport. Jean-Claude spoke first, conceding his concordatory right to name the church hierarchy. Then the pope spoke. He recalled that Haiti was the first Latin American country to proclaim liberty and added how important it was to have liberty. The Eucharistic and Marial Congress he had come to attend reminded him that the meaning of the Eucharist was service and love, and the Haitian church needed to serve everyone, especially the poorest. The slogan of the Congress was "something has to change here," and the pope agreed. He continued, saying that there was a "deep need for justice, a better distribution of goods, more equitable organization of society and more participation. There was a legitimate desire for freedom of expression, access to food, care, schools, literacy, honest and dignified work, social security, and the fundamental rights of man." All of this had to be done "without violence . . . out of respect and love of liberty." Many Haitians were deeply moved by the papal visit. The government was not. The papal message seemed to provide permission to the clergy and laity to pressure the government for reform, and ultimately, if it could not change, for Jean-Claude Duvalier to leave office.

Subsequently, the popular church, or small church (*ti-legliz*), and the Catholic radio station, Radio Soleil, sought to make Haitians aware of the role that government should have and to urge people to protest when anyone's rights were usurped. The response of the government to increased public discontent and demands for openness was more repression. Demonstrators were shot. Meetings and church services were invaded. Newspaper publishers and owners of radio stations, including Radio Soleil, which became the symbol of anti-Duvalierist resistance, were killed or deported, and their newspapers were closed.

In early 1985, the government passed legislation that would allow political parties, and it released some political prisoners. That July the government held a referendum on the presidency, but the patently sham ballot did not fool Haitians, and these staged events, including the October firing of Roger Lafontant, the brutal minister of interior, served only to reconfirm opinion that the government was beyond repair.

On November 26, 1985, the commemoration of a 1980 government crackdown turned the next day into a demonstration for "an end to misery, the Constitution, and the Duvalier government." On November 28, troops intervened in Gonaïves and randomly opened fire, killing three previously uninvolved students. The government announced the formation of a commission to investigate the events at Gonaïves but closed Radio Soleil to prevent its broadcasts. These events convinced Haitians that Duvalier had to go. Antigovernment protests, marches, and school and university strikes spread to other cities.

In last-ditch efforts to save his presidency, Duvalier revamped his cabinet, lowered the cost of cooking oil and several other basic consumer items, invited the church for talks, announced a military reform and the dissolution of the political police, and promised to bring to trial those presumed responsible for the killings in Gonaïves. The public was neither appeased nor intimidated. Demonstrations spread, paralyzing the whole country.

In January 1986, the Reagan administration began to pressure Duvalier to leave Haiti, as did Congressman Walter Fauntroy, chair of the Congressional Black Caucus, who had been interested in Haiti since 1979. The United States refused a request to provide asylum for Duvalier, but offered to assist with the dictator's departure. Duvalier had initially accepted the offer on January 30, but then changed his mind.

On January 31, the United States prematurely announced Duvalier's departure, and Haitians were overjoyed. Jean-Claude responded to the demonstration by declaring a state of siege, dispatching the *makout* and the army. Despite these threats, Haitians continued to demonstrate all over the country. On that same day, the United States Department of State reduced its US$56 million aid package to Haiti. This action distanced Washington from the Duvalier regime and denied the regime a significant source of income. At this point, two leading officers who had devised a plot to remove the Duvaliers, army chief of staff Lieutenant General Henri Namphy and Military Academy head Colonel Williams Regala, confronted the Duvaliers and demanded their departure. Left with no bases of support, Jean-Claude agreed.

After hastily naming a National Council of Government (Conseil National de Gouvernement—CNG), made up of Namphy, Regala, and three civilians, Jean-Claude and his family, his entourage, and a caravan of trucks loaded with possessions departed Haiti on the night of February 7, 1986, aboard a C–141 transport provided by the United States. Spontaneous street demonstrations and church masses were held all over Haiti to celebrate. People felt free. A popular slogan was "the muzzle is off." Graffiti on walls thanked Radio Soleil, and many Haitians wore a teeshirt emblazoned on the front with the newly restored Haitian red and blue flag and the words "Liberation of Haiti, February 7, 1986", and on the back, "operation to uproot evil accomplished."

Post-Duvalier Era, 1986–90

The widespread joy and expectations for a new Haiti soon dimmed. Haitians had hoped to rid the country of Duvalierists and *makout* and bring to trial those who had committed crimes. Instead, a number of high-ranking officers, including the head of the *makout* and the former army intelligence chief, managed to slip out of the country. Others known to have committed crimes were freed after army courts found insufficient evidence to convict them. Some Duvalierists remained in high positions. Haitians described the situation they were experiencing as "Duvalierism without Duvalier." As a result, some took the law into their own hands. In the weeks after Duvalier fled, mobs killed a number of known *makout*. Crowds looted the home of former secret police chief Luc Désir and prevented him from leaving the country. A Creole term for this vigilante justice was *dechoukaj*, "uprooting evil." *Dechoukaj* was particularly focused on *makout* and voodoo priests and priestesses, *houngans* and *mambos*, who were presumed to have been associated with the *makout* or Duvaliers. The spokesperson for the national voodoo organization, however, blamed the Roman Catholic Church, accusing it of inciting a new anti-superstition campaign.

Haitians were also concerned about the composition and agenda of the CNG, which was charged with preparing the way for elections. The interim government was led by Lieutenant General Henri Namphy, army chief of staff. The group consisted of four other Duvalierists: three military officers (colonels Prosper Avril, Williams Regala, and Max Valles), and one civilian (Alex Cinéas, former minister of public works under Duvalier). In addition, the CNG had two civilians known for their opposition to Duvalier: Gérard Gourgue, an educator, lawyer, and president of the Haitian League for Human Rights; and Rosney Desroches, a well-known and respected educator. These last two members had short-lived tenures in office, however. Gourgue resigned after two months to protest army repression, and Desroches was removed a year later, when the CNG abandoned its reformist facade and moved sharply to the right. Before long, the CNG became a military junta composed of Duvalierists.

Initially, the CNG dismantled some of the unpopular vestiges of the Duvalier era. It rescinded the 1983 constitution providing for a presidency for life, disbanded the VSN, restored the original red and blue flag of 1804 that François Duvalier had replaced by a red and black banner, replaced the Duvalierist National Assembly with a new thirteen-member ministerial cabinet, nationalized properties belonging to the Duvaliers, freed political prisoners, permitted political organizations to exist and political exiles to return to Haiti, and pledged to respect human rights and freedom of the press. However, the CNG did not attempt to uproot Duvalierism, as the public demanded, because the army was still full of Duvalierists; and by dismantling the VSN, the CNG restored the army to its dominant position in Haiti.

Within months, the CNG embarked on a policy of repression. On April 26, 1986, police shot into a peaceful crowd led by Jean-Bertrand Aristide, gathered to commemorate prisoners killed and incarcerated at Fort Dimanche, Haiti's most infamous Duvalier prison. In November, police disrupted a demonstration protesting the abduction and murder of two literacy workers. By the end of its first year in office, the CNG was responsible for the deaths of more civilians than in fifteen years of Jean-Claude Duvalier's government.

Hopes for greater freedom revived briefly in March, when a CNG working committee produced a new constitution that Haitians readily approved by referendum on March 29, 1987. It put planning and execution of presidential elections in the hands of a Provisional Electoral Council (Conseil Électoral Provisoire—CEP), to be composed of civilians. It reduced the powers of the presidency, and Article 291 prohibited the participation in government for ten years of anyone who had been "an architect of dictatorship and its maintenance during the past twenty-nine years."

However, the CNG, the military, and Duvalierists were not happy with the new constitution and prospective presidential elections, seeing them as a challenge to their continued political dominance. Soon afterward the CNG announced that it would dissolve the CEP and take over its functions. Although Haitians were outraged, military strength triumphed.

The political environment was gloomy. However, on election day, November 29, 1987, prospects of a new constitution and president combined with a sense of security offered by the presence of international observer teams and reporters, brought people to the polls. When they opened that morning, Duvalierist thugs and soldiers shot openly at the lines of waiting voters, killing between 22 and 200 and seriously wounding many others. The CNG immediately canceled the elections and disbanded the CEP. According to Namphy, this action was to prevent the CEP from handing the presidency to a leftist, insinuating that Gourgue of the National Cooperative Front (Front National de Concertation—FNC) was a leftist and would have won, although an August opinion poll indicated that World Bank (see Glossary) economist Marc Bazin was the leading candidate.

As a consequence of what came to be called the "election-day massacre," the four principal candidates condemned the CNG, called for the restoration of an independent CEP, and agreed to abstain from any new elections organized by the CNG. Responding to domestic and international pressure, the CNG agreed to hold new elections in January, under an electoral council of its choosing.

The candidate preferred by the military and the United States in the rescheduled presidential elections was Leslie François Manigat. The military anticipated that he would be malleable, and the United States viewed the Haitian academic and anti-communist, who had left the country a generation earlier and had ties to the United States and the Caribbean, as more qualified than the other candidates. When the CNG-orchestrated elections took place on January 17, 1988, the major candidates and most Haitians boycotted them; less than 10 percent of those eligible voted. Manigat was declared the winner of elections marked by fraud and abstention.

Leslie Manigat held office for five months, during which he made some powerful enemies, including the Roman Catholic Church, drug traffickers, and the military. After the church had boycotted the presidential elections, Manigat did not invite the bishops to his inauguration. Wearing a Masonic sash, he had a voodoo priest give the blessings. Several months later, Manigat informed the church that he was going to change the concordat, implying a reduction in its power.

President Manigat's initially cordial relations with the military soon soured. Unable to obtain foreign military and economic assistance, as he had promised, Manigat attempted to find other sources of income. He initiated legal mechanisms to recover hundreds of millions of dollars allegedly stolen by Jean-Claude Duvalier. Haiti had become a major transshipment point for drugs en route to the United States from Latin America. Manigat tried to stop the corrupting flow. Both of these actions threatened vested interests within the armed forces. On June 20, 1988, when President Manigat attempted to gain civilian control over the military and remove top army officers, he was removed from office by noncommissioned officers, and General Namphy took control. On the same day, General Namphy dissolved the National Assembly, suspended the 1987 constitution, placed the country under strict military control, and, because he felt the country was not ready for elections or democracy, declared himself president.

Namphy was supported by the army as president of the new military government, but divisions existed in the army command, and each faction vied for control of the presidency. As a consequence of his lack of support within the military hierarchy, Namphy sought additional support outside, from henchmen of the Duvalier regime and former *makout*. To intimidate civilian resistance, Namphy unleashed a campaign of terror. Victims included Lafontant Joseph, a distinguished lawyer and human rights advocate, and members of the activist sector of the church. In one week, three churches were stormed. The first assault was particularly vicious. Armed men burst into St. Jean Bosco on September 11, killing eleven worshipers and wounding seventy others in an unsuccessful attempt to reach Jean-Bertrand Aristide, the officiating priest.

On September 17, 1988, noncommissioned officers ousted General Namphy in a coup, dispatched him to the Dominican Republic, and took charge—arresting and demoting officers with Duvalierist connections. Hope grew, and talk about housecleaning to complete efforts begun in February 1986 unleashed new efforts to uproot *makout* all over Haiti.

This coup was different from previous ones. The noncommissioned officers had more in common with most Haitians than their officers. Excluded from perquisites and poorly paid, they issued a list of demands that called for restoration of the 1987 constitution, legislative and presidential elections, respect for human rights, removal of *makout* from the army, the disarming of paramilitary gangs, separation of the army from the police, and an end to political brutality.

Inexplicably, the noncommissioned officers turned over control of the government to Brigadier General Prosper Avril. Within a short time, he accused them of planning a coup against him and arrested fifteen of the leaders. By December 1988, President Avril, who had been installed by the army in September 1988, was in full control of the government.

President Avril was an astute politician and tactician, skills he had learned from service to the Duvaliers. Prior to becoming a member of the CNG, the general had commanded Duvalier's Presidential Guard, been financial manager for the Duvalier family, and served as a personal aide to Jean-Claude Duvalier.

Avril cultivated loyalty by giving a share of the goods that Haiti imported to his friends for resale, a practice that contributed to a US$60 million increase in the budget deficit. He also co-opted potential enemies by including various sectors of society in his cabinet. However, Avril, who used spies to create an atmosphere of fear in the country, increasingly used force to remain in power, initiating a wave of assassinations, arrests, torture, and deportations that led to growing opposition to his rule. Twenty-five political organizations formed a common Front Against Repression (Front Contre la Répression) and six political parties called for Avril's departure and a transfer of power to the Supreme Court. Haitians were outraged when three political activists were arrested, tortured, and publicly displayed on Halloween 1989. When the army attacked an anti-Avril demonstration in Petit Goâve, resulting in the death of an eleven-year-old girl on March 5, 1990, Haitians demonstrated throughout the country. To avoid further bloodshed, United States ambassador Alvin Adams encouraged Avril to leave office. On March 12, Avril resigned and was flown to Florida by the United States.

Following Avril's departure, the 1987 constitution was restored and used as a basis for a transition government. The constitution called for the appointment of an interim president from the Supreme Court, and Ertha Pascal Trouillot, whose political leanings were relatively unknown, was selected. It also called for a ministerial cabinet and a Council of State (Conseil d'État) consisting of representatives of the political parties to oversee the government.

Although Trouillot was obliged to cooperate with the Council of State, she began to act unilaterally in selecting members of the cabinet, including choosing a Duvalierist to be minister of finance, and allowing some notorious Duvalierists to return to Haiti. These included General Williams Regala, who was accused of complicity in the November 1987 election massacre, and Roger Lafontant, head of the *makout* accused of torturing prisoners while he was minister of interior. When Lafontant formed a political party, the Union for National Reconciliation, and announced his candidacy for president, outraged Haitians went on strike and called for his arrest. After the government had issued an arrest warrant for him and the military police had refused to execute it, Trouillot dropped the matter. Her action, showing lack of democratic resolve, led the council to say it could no longer work with her and to demand her resignation.

The Council of State turned to the 1987 constitution for guidance in preparing for elections. Using Article 191, it created an independent Permanent Electoral Council (Conseil

Électoral Permanent) to develop electoral laws and organize and support elections. Under Article 291, which prohibited close collaborators of the former government from holding public office for a decade, it barred Roger Lafontant's candidacy. Then, the Permanent Electoral Council announced the parliamentary and presidential elections for December 16, 1990. Prospects for successful elections looked poor, given a new wave of violence that included the murder of a council member and associate, and a record since 1986 of delayed, canceled, or rigged elections.

Aristide Presidency, February 7, 1991–September 30, 1991

The two leading presidential candidates were Marc Bazin and Jean-Bertrand Aristide. Bazin, a former World Bank economist and right of center candidate of his party, the Movement for the Installation of Democracy in Haiti (Mouvement pour l'Instauration de la Démocratie en Haïti—MIDH), was referred to as the "American candidate" because he was seen as being the choice of the United States, where he had lived for many years. By contrast, Aristide was an outspoken anti-Duvalierist and a priest who entered the race at the last minute with tangential links to the National Front for Change and Democracy (Front National pour le Changement et la Démocratie—FNCD).

The campaign was punctuated by violence and derogatory rhetoric directed at Aristide—one rally was interrupted by a grenade explosion that killed seven and wounded fifty others. However, the December 16, 1990, elections went smoothly and were judged to be honest. For both reasons, they were unprecedented in Haitian election history. The elections were monitored by international observer teams from the United States led by Jimmy Carter, the OAS, and the UN. Aristide, or "Titid," as he was affectionately called by his supporters, won a landslide victory. Seventy-five percent of the eligible voters had gone to the polls, and 66.48 percent had voted for him while 14.22 percent voted for Bazin. Having condemned *makoutism*, Duvalierism, the excesses of the elite, and conservatism of the church, Aristide had won a clear mandate to create a more just, equal, and democratic Haiti.

Although most Haitians were jubilant, there were efforts to sabotage Aristide even before he took office. On January 1,

1991, Archbishop François Wolff Ligondé gave a homily in the Port-au-Prince Cathedral in which he called the president-elect a "socio Bolshevik," and wondered whether this was the beginning of a dictatorship. But he urged his parishioners not to be afraid, saying "this, too, shall pass." On January 6, Roger Lafontant attempted a coup. He arrested President Trouillot, forcing her to resign, then went on television saying he had the support of the army. Infuriated Haitians took to the streets in two days of clashes with the police and army, and violence against church property before the military arrested Lafontant and restored President Trouillot to office. On January 27, Haitians stifled the threat of a coup involving the imprisoned Lafontant. On February 3, someone fire-bombed Aristide's orphanage, Family Is Life (Lafanmi Selavi), killing four children. In the seven weeks prior to the inauguration on February 7, 125 people died of street violence and clashes with the army and police.

The transfer of power on February 7, 1991, from President Trouillot to an elected president, was unexpected and unprecedented. Few people expected that Aristide would be allowed to take office or that his presidency would last. They were half-right.

Jean-Bertrand Aristide was born in 1953 to a property-owning peasant family from Port-Salut in southern Haiti. He was sent to Port-au-Prince to be educated by the Salesian Order; then, in 1966, to a seminary in Cap-Haïtien. Thereafter he became a novice in the Dominican Republic. Before ordination in 1982, Aristide studied in Canada, Israel, Greece, and Italy. Returning to Haiti in 1985, Father Aristide helped oust Jean-Claude Duvalier and, subsequently, worked to eliminate residual traces of Duvalierism.

Aristide's efforts created enemies. In 1986 his march to commemorate victims of the notorious prison, Fort Dimanche, was interrupted by bullets intended for him. In 1987 his jeep ride to Jean Rabel to commemorate the peasants murdered by the military almost cost him his life. In 1988 his mass at St. Jean Bosco was halted by the military and by thugs who killed thirteen, wounded seventeen others, and burned the church. In 1988 the Salesians removed him from their order for "incitement of hatred and violence, glorifying class struggle, and profanation of the liturgy." Aristide emerged stronger from each of these confrontations. His popularity was reflected at the polls, and witnessed to by the huge crowd outside the palace on inauguration day.

Aristide's skilled use of language and symbolism was evident at his inauguration. A peasant woman helped put on the presidential sash, and most of the speech was in Creole, the only language of most Haitians. In his speech, Aristide noted that there were people under the table and on top of it but that everyone should be at the table together (the next morning, he served breakfast to hundreds of homeless people and street children at the palace). He called for a marriage between the army and people to oppose the *makout* and anti-democrats, and said that since marriages require sacrifices, he would retire the high command, reassign several top-ranking officers, and promote and commission others. Among the promoted was Colonel Raoul Cédras, who would lead the coup against him seven months later. Because no party had won a majority in the National Assembly, President Aristide selected a friend, René Garcia Préval, as prime minister and minister of interior and national defense. For the cabinet, he chose friends and allies—mostly university educated and progressive technocrats.

In lieu of a political party, President Aristide formed an organization called Lavalas, a Creole phrase meaning "cleansing flood" (Organisation Politique Lavalas—OPL), which drew support from the masses, including the rural and urban poor. OPL produced the Lavalas Development Model, which contained Aristide's goals. The goals included "transition from misery to poverty with dignity" and promotion of social democracy in Haiti based on the European model. After the inauguration, Aristide announced his priorities. They included addressing poverty and corruption, improving the infrastructure, decentralizing the role of Port-au-Prince, achieving food self-sufficiency, bringing criminals to justice, collecting taxes, and instituting essential public spending programs.

During his first seven months, President Aristide made progress against military-related corruption, drug trafficking, and human rights abuses. He dismantled the section chief system found in rural areas (see Role of the Army in Law Enforcement Prior to 1995, ch. 10) and closed Fort Dimanche. He created a human rights commission and commissions to investigate and bring to justice those accused of crimes between 1986 and 1990. He curbed waste and corruption by closing offices and agencies and reducing budgets and salaries, including his own.

President Aristide achieved a positive balance in the treasury for the first time in years through the collection of taxes and arrears; invitations to the "10th Department," as he called the Haitian diaspora, to invest in Haiti; and foreign assistance. By July 1991, he had accumulated US$511 million in grants and concessionary loans and by September, a US$48 million appropriation in standby loans from the International Monetary Fund (IMF—see Glossary).

Aristide and his achievements did not meet with everyone's approval. The military feared reduction of its budget, demobilization of its infamous Leopard Corps, establishment of a separate presidential security force, interruption of its lucrative drug trade, and investigations into its involvement in the election day and Jean Rabel massacres and the destruction of St. Jean Bosco. The rich were afraid of the empowerment of the social classes they had historically dominated and the prospect of paying taxes and obeying laws. The Roman Catholic Church hierarchy was apprehensive about the *ti-legliz* movement and its loss of influence in a more egalitarian institution. The United States had misgivings about Aristide because he had been critical of "the frigid north."

Opposition to Aristide and his government became increasingly evident. Several plots were devised by former or current *makout* and former military officers. Civilians and soldiers attempted to assassinate or overthrow him. On April 16, *makout* burned the Hyppolite Public Market in Port-au-Prince while former supporters complained that the effort to curb the *makout* and lower the cost of living was too slow.

On September 26, 1991, Aristide learned that a coup was planned for his return from the UN, where he had just proclaimed that "democracy (in Haiti) has won out for good." In Haiti the next day, Aristide addressed the nation, denouncing the *makout* and elites. He urged the people to give the elites what they deserved, a burning tire around their necks, or "necklace" (*père lebrun*), and extolied the device, "What a beautiful tool! It has a good smell." Such statements alarmed civil libertarians as examples of presidential intimidation of the legislature and courts and abuse of presidential power.

Military Coup Overthrows Aristide, September 30, 1991–October 1994

The coup began on September 29, 1991, when soldiers

attacked Aristide's residence. Although Aristide escaped, on September 30 he was captured at the palace, delivered to Brigadier General Cédras, flown to Venezuela, and soon thereafter was in Washington. Violence and terror spread across the country as soldiers hunted down Aristide supporters. One victim was Silvio Claude, the ardent anti-Duvalierist and perennial Protestant presidential candidate, who was "necklaced." Approximately 1,500 people were killed in the first few days after the coup.

On October 3, 1991, the military held a news conference. According to Cédras, head of the junta, the coup was justified because Aristide had abused power by undermining the constitution, preaching class warfare, and encouraging violence and mob rule. Yet, opposition to the coup continued, and the army responded with more violence. Amnesty International reported murders, arrests, torture, disappearances, and attacks against community and church organizations.

The junta reversed Aristide's reforms. It restored the section chiefs, fired Aristide-appointed prosecutors and judicial officers, and released prisoners convicted of human rights violations. It created a civilian government, appointing an eighty-year-old Supreme Court justice, Joseph Nérette, president and former Duvalier minister of tourism Jean-Jacques Honorat as prime minister.

Foreign reaction was swift and negative. United States Secretary of State James Baker condemned the coup leaders and informed them that "this coup will not stand." Then the United States imposed a series of penalties on the regime. The OAS also condemned the coup. It called for Aristide's reinstatement, attempted to have a dialogue and hold meetings with the junta, and imposed hemispheric trade sanctions on Haiti. Additionally, the UN Security Council condemned the coup, refused to recognize its leaders, and issued a statement of moral support for President Aristide's return.

The junta thwarted efforts to negotiate and countered with an attack on Aristide, quoting statements by him that endorsed "necklacing." The Haitian bishops then weighed in. They favored a state of law and a democratic society in Haiti but denied that restoring Aristide would result in a return to democracy. This propaganda had an effect. Initial enthusiasm for returning the president diminished as these critical reports about him began to circulate.

Haitians, meanwhile, were suffering from the brutality of the junta and the effects of sanctions and embargoes. There were food shortages, 65,000 Haitians lost jobs, fuel shortages paralyzed public services, and unprecedented numbers of Haitians tried to leave Haiti—crossing the border to the Dominican Republic or attempting to go by boat to the United States, which turned back most of them.

On June 23, 1993, frustrated by failed diplomatic initiatives, the UN Security Council imposed a worldwide fuel and arms embargo on Haiti; this action succeeded in bringing the junta to the negotiating table. On July 3, Aristide and Cédras signed an accord at Governors Island, New York, that provided for Aristide's return, suspension of the embargo, installation of a new prime minister and government, separation of the army and police, the presence of a UN force in Haiti, and amnesty for the military high command on its resignation.

Once the embargo was lifted, violence recurred against partisans of democracy. Five men were gunned down outside city hall as they waited to welcome the new prime minister. Antoine Izméry, an associate of Aristide, was pulled out of church and shot in the street in front of an international team. A new organization, the Revolutionary Front for the Advancement and Progress of Haiti (Front Révolutionnaire pour l'Avancement et le Progrès d'Haïti—FRAPH), composed of armed civilian supporters of the junta, took credit for some of the violence.

On October 11, 1993, the *USS Harlan County* was prevented by armed thugs from docking in Port-au-Prince. It had been transporting a lightly armed contingent of United States and Canadian troops, the vanguard of the UN force, to oversee the return of democracy to Haiti. The incident ended the Governors Island Accord and led to resumption of economic sanctions. The junta displayed its contempt for the forces attempting to restore democracy by gunning down François Guy Malary, Aristide's minister of justice, along with his driver and bodyguard, and allowing some of the worst Duvalierist torturers to return to Haiti.

In the United States, President Aristide, President William J. Clinton, and Congress differed on what to do. The situation was compounded after Aristide called for a total embargo on Haiti. Some called Aristide callous. The *New York Times* implied that he had brought the coup on himself by forcing out newly elected officials who had opposed Duvalierism. Moreover, a leaked Central Intelligence Agency report described Aristide as mentally unstable, which contributed to the clamor against him in Washington and beyond.

Initiatives by a few individuals forced the United States and the UN into action. On April 22, 1994, six congressmen, five of them members of the Congressional Black Caucus, demonstrated in front of the White House to protest United States policy toward Haiti and were arrested. On April 12, Randall Robinson, executive director of TransAfrica, a lobbying organization on Africa and the Caribbean, began a hunger strike that he announced would last until the administration fired special envoy to Haiti Larry Pezzullo and changed its policies toward the Haitian military and the refugees. Twenty-seven days later, Pezzullo was fired, and the hospitalized Robinson received assurances that his other demands would be met. Robinson then ended his strike.

The Department of State named a new special envoy to Haiti and promised asylum hearings for Haitian refugees aboard United States ships. President Clinton took new steps to cut off the junta from oil supplies and their foreign bank accounts. On April 28, President Clinton gave the junta an ultimatum: a global trade embargo or resignation within fifteen days. On May 6, the UN Security Council approved a near total trade embargo on Haiti along with restrictions on the junta, with a deadline of May 12.

The junta demonstrated that it had no intention of relinquishing power. On May 11, it installed Émile Jonaissant, an eighty-one-year-old Duvalierist Supreme Court justice, as provisional president; he selected his own prime minister and cabinet. When President Clinton applied additional pressure, ending United States-Haitian commercial flights and urging United States citizens to leave the country, the junta attempted to provoke nationalist and anti-United States sentiments by airing television films of the 1915 invasion. The situation led President Jonaissant to declare a state of emergency and impose a curfew. Infantrymen paraded through the streets.

In response, the United States asked the UN to endorse a United States-led military intervention in Haiti, and on July 31, 1994, the UN Security Council passed a resolution (S/Res/ 940) approving a plan to raise a Multinational Force, Operation Uphold Democracy, which would "use all necessary means to facilitate the departure from Haiti of the military dictatorship."

Preparations for both forcible and permissive entries proceeded. The United States, Canada, France, and Venezuela (referred to as the Friends of Haiti) played a key role. Ten countries ultimately agreed to participate, and the United States deployed a battleship, the *USS Eisenhower* to the Caribbean, increasing pressure on General Cédras.

On September 15, President Clinton addressed the United States public, justifying the need for an invasion by citing the terrorism of the military regime. The next day, Clinton made a final effort to avoid a military invasion of Haiti by sending former president Jimmy Carter, former chair of the United States Joint Chiefs of Staff General Colin Powell, and Senator Sam Nunn of Georgia to Haiti to arrange a peaceful departure of the junta. On September 18, with airplanes headed toward Haiti, Carter phoned Clinton to say that the junta would step down in return for an amnesty for themselves and the Haitian military. President Aristide gave his approval.

On September 19, 1994, United States troops entered Haiti peacefully and unopposed. Haitians greeted the United States forces warmly but cautiously, fearing reprisals from the Haitian military. However, as the people became more festive, Haitian police killed two people while United States forces watched, unsure of their mandate. Other incidents occurred in Cap-Haïtien and Gonaïves.

The junta left Haiti within a month. On October 4, former police chief Joseph Michel François fled to the Dominican Republic. On October 10, General Cédras resigned in a brief ceremony in which he had to be protected from jeering crowds, and on October 13, generals Cédras and Biamby left for exile in Panama.

Democracy Restored, 1994–96

President Aristide made a triumphal return to Haiti on October 15, 1994. For the first time, an exiled Haitian president was restored to office. A jubilant crowd, estimated at 10,000, gathered in front of the presidential palace to see and hear him. President Aristide spoke to them about reconciliation and justice, repeating the phrase, "No to violence, no to vengeance, yes to reconciliation." The next day, October 16, the UN Security Council lifted all economic sanctions against Haiti.

A sense of disillusionment soon set in among many of Aristide's followers, however. Their champion of social justice entertained the wealthy, contemplated privatization of state industries, and selected a businessman as prime minister. His obvious wealth, his move to a mansion, marriage and subsequent fatherhood were disturbing changes in the former priest.

Haitians had also changed. Most were much worse off than before 1991. The economy had been destroyed by sanctions; the departure of the pivotal assembly industry left 70 to 80 percent of Port-au-Prince unemployed; and the infrastructure and agricultural sectors had collapsed. Many educated, technically skilled, and formerly politically involved Haitians had left, and 3,000 to 4,000 others had been killed.

President Aristide faced multiple challenges on his return to Haiti, not the least of which were the high expectations of his supporters and a mere fifteen months left of his term. He announced a detailed economic recovery program designed to streamline the bloated and corrupt public sector and renew private-sector job creation. In response, the international community pledged a major emergency economic aid package of US$1.2 billion. Aristide used this assistance to support the government, and create temporary public works jobs for the immediate alleviation of poverty, avoiding unpopular and controversial measures. In view of the magnitude of Haiti's economic problems, the reforms needed time to succeed.

President Aristide took bold action in dealing with the issue of domestic security. In early 1995, he disbanded the military and paramilitary organizations that had tyrannized Haitians and prevented a society based on laws. A new Haitian National Police under the Ministry of Justice and Public Security superseded the armed forces as the agency dealing with the nation's serious problem of maintaining law and order. Meanwhile, the international force, which consisted in large measure of United States troops, remained to guarantee basic security and assist in training the Haitian National Police. A beginning was made on the reform of the judicial system by weeding out corrupt and incompetent judges, and measures were taken to improve prison conditions (see Justice System, ch. 10). As one of his first actions, Aristide created a National Commission of Truth and Justice to investigate and write a report on some of the worst crimes committed between 1991 and 1994. The commission finished its investigation and presented its findings to the Ministry of Justice in January 1997; no further action has been reported. In the area of social reform, President Aristide created a National Secretariat for Literacy and began land reform.

The June 25, 1995, municipal and parliamentary elections were contentious. The elections were delayed twice, and the Provisional Electoral Council reviewed candidates and printed ballots up to the last minute, leading to a boycott by three political parties, and a low turnout. Despite UN monitoring, some fraud occurred, necessitating a rerun on August 13. Except for Lavalas, which did well, nearly all of the other political parties called for an annulment.

Presidential elections followed in November. Aristide campaigned for René Préval, his prime minister and friend, until the last moment, when Aristide himself appeared to consider staying in office. Thereafter, neither Aristide nor his disappointed supporters, who had hoped that Aristide would run again, showed much enthusiasm for Préval. Only 30 percent of the eligible voters went to the polls, and 80 percent of those who did voted for Préval on the OPL ticket. Regardless of the turnout, the election was unprecedented. When Préval took office on February 7, 1996, for the first time in Haitian history power was transferred from one democratically elected president to another.

President Préval (1996–) is an agronomist, who was a baker in Port-au-Prince before Jean-Bertrand Aristide selected him to be prime minister. Viewed as a hard worker, his main appeal came from his association with Aristide. Over time, however, the relationship became strained, and Préval's popularity decreased.

President Préval inherited a daunting array of problems. As of early 1996, the depressed economy continued to decline while the astronomical unemployment rate continued to climb. Inflation had already reached 30 percent and was expected to increase. In response to these indicators and because of the new openness and availability of weapons, common crime was increasing, straining the capabilities of the new National Police. Foreign assistance had declined drastically— from US$230 million in fiscal year (FY—see Glossary) 1995 to US$90 million in FY 1996, depriving President Préval of an external cushion.

Although Haitians carried out an historic transition from one democratically elected president to another, the future of democracy in Haiti remained uncertain. Upcoming congressional elections would give Haitians the opportunity to correct the marred 1995 congressional elections and create a permanent electoral council. Although President Préval seemed committed to the privatization of state-owned industries, as of early 1996 it remained to be seen whether he would be able to overcome congressional and public opposition. To date, Haiti had not begun the process of economic recovery nor reached a consensus on how it might be achieved.

*   *   *

Historical works on Haiti traditionally have focused on the leaders of the war of independence, the early heads of state, François Duvalier, and voodoo. Recently, however, a number of comprehensive studies on Haiti have appeared. Among these are David Nicholls' *From Dessalines to Duvalier,* Robert and Nancy Heinl's *Written in Blood: The Story of the Haitian People, 1492–1995,* James Leyburn's *The Haitian People,* Selden Rodman's *Haiti: The Black Republic,* and Robert Rotberg and Christopher Clague's *Haiti: The Politics of Squalor.* For precolonial and colonial history, see M.L.E. Moreau de Saint-Méry, *A Civilization that Perished.* For the revolution, consult C.L.R. James, *The Black Jacobins, Toussaint L'Ouverture and the San Domingo Revolution.* The United States occupation of Haiti is chronicled in Hans Schmidt's *The United States Occupation of Haiti, 1915–1934.* For more about François Duvalier, see Bernard Diederich and Al Burt's *Papa Doc et les Tontons Macoutes.* For the Duvalier dynasty, consult Elizabeth Abbott's *Haiti: The Duvaliers and Their Legacy.* For a chronology of efforts to restore Jean-Bertrand Aristide to power, see *Haitian Democracy Restored: 1991–1995* by Roland I. Perusse. For the role of religions in Haiti, look at Anne Greene's *The Catholic Church in Haiti: Political and Social Change* and for voodoo, consult *Voodoo and Politics in Haiti, Voodoo Heritage,* and *Études sur le vodou haïtien* by Michel S. Laguerre. (For further information and complete citations, see Bibliography.)

Chapter 7. Haiti: The Society and Its Environment

Figure from a painting by Prosper Pierrelouis

IN 1804 HAITI EMERGED FROM thirteen years of revolution as the New World's second republic, having attained independence from France. Sharply defined social distinctions in the colonial system set the stage for Haiti's evolution as an independent but deeply divided society—a majority of peasant freeholders, formerly slaves, dominated by a small ruling class, formerly free men of color. These social distinctions fostered the creation of contrasting cultural and linguistic forms.

Peasant society emerged as largely self-regulating and defensive in response to military rule in rural areas and the absence of a voice in government. The exclusion of peasants from national institutions created the opportunity for a flowering of local cultural forms, including the Creole language and the voodoo religion. A rich Haitian tradition of cultural innovation has long coexisted with the French language and the Roman Catholic Church favored by the urban elite.

As a post-colonial state in 1804, Haiti was ahead of its time and was treated by the outside world as a pariah state. Consequently, Haiti went its own distinctive way far more than other countries in the region. Culturally, it continues to be marked far more than other New World societies by African cultural influences as well as its Franco-Haitian heritage, and by linguistic and cultural isolation from its neighbors. Haiti's remarkable cultural heritage includes a sophisticated repertoire of traditional dance, music, religion, oral literature, and artistic expression.

In the early nineteenth century, small yeoman farmers supplanted the plantation system as the dominant mode of production. Haitian agriculture shifted rapidly from large-scale monocropping for export to a diverse mix of food and cash crops produced on thousands of dispersed plots. Haiti's emergent elite moved from plantation production into mercantile pursuits based on agricultural exports and industrial imports. The economically powerful also gained control of the apparatus of state. Newly independent Haiti maintained a sizable standing army inherited from the revolutionary period, and up to the 1990s the Haitian army consistently exercised a powerful political role.

With a total population of around 7.6 million, Haiti in 1998 was the most rural, the poorest, and the most densely populated country in the hemisphere. Most Haitians continue to be small peasant farmers. Intense class stratification persists despite the growth of intermediary classes since the 1950s, significant out-migration, and a phenomenal rate of urban growth centered on Port-au-Prince, a metropolitan area of around 2 million people. Despite a high rate of rural out-migration, the rural population continues to expand. Demographic pressures exert acute stress on the country's natural resource base.

By international standards, the majority of Haitians are very poor. This alarming level of poverty reflects the poor distribution of national wealth, the precipitous decline of agriculture in the past few decades, acute land scarcity, a highly degraded environment, weak institutions of government, and prolonged political and economic crisis since the mid-1980s. Efforts in the 1990s to decentralize and democratize the state have yet to make a palpable difference in the daily lives of most people.

In the late 1990s, even the most remote rural areas of the country have significant contact with the outside world. This contact is the result of the growth of influence of foreign missionaries and nongovernmental agencies since the 1950s, significant out-migration since the 1970s, rapid growth of Creole-language radio programs and stations since the early 1980s, turbulent political struggles since the mid-1980s, and international political and military intervention in Haiti in the mid-1990s (see Multinational Security Assistance, ch. 10).

Geography

Haiti occupies the mountainous western third of Hispaniola (La Isla Española), the second largest island of the Greater Antilles. The island is divided between Haiti and the Dominican Republic (see fig. 1). The two countries share a 388-kilometer border established in a series of treaties, the most recent being the 1936 Protocol of Revision of the Frontier Treaty of 1929. Haiti's eastern border runs along mountain ranges and the Pedernales River in the south and the Massacre River in the north. The Atlantic Ocean borders Haiti to the north, and the Caribbean Sea borders it on the west and south. The Windward Passage separates Haiti from Cuba. Haiti's close neighbors also include Jamaica and Puerto Rico.

Haiti occupies an area of about 27,750 square kilometers, about the size of Maryland. Two large peninsulas in the north and south dominate Haiti's mainland. The country has around

1,300 kilometers of coastline. The land area includes numerous small islands and four large islands: Île de la Gonâve (680 square kilometers) adjoining the Baie de Port-au-Prince, Île de la Tortue (180 square kilometers) off the north coast, and Île à Vache (fifty-two square kilometers) and Grande Cayemite (forty-five square kilometers) off the southern peninsula.

Haiti has very few plains; they make up only 22 percent of the national territory. Slopes in excess of 20 percent cover 63 percent of this rugged, mountainous land, and only 29 percent of the country has less than a 10 percent slope. The northern tier of the country includes the Plaine du Nord—the country's largest coastal plain—an area of 2,000 square kilometers, and the smaller Plaine des Moustiques and Plaine de l'Arbre in the arid northwestern peninsula. The northern mountain range, the Massif du Nord, is an extension of the Cordillera Central of the Dominican Republic. It varies in elevation from 600 to 1,100 meters and extends from Haiti's eastern border into the northwestern peninsula.

Haiti's geographic center includes the Central Plateau, around eighty-five kilometers long and thirty kilometers wide. To the southwest of the plateau lies the range of Montagnes Noires with a maximum elevation of 1,400 meters, and the lower Artibonite River Valley measuring around 800 square kilometers. The Artibonite delta is the country's major rice-producing area. Other important lowland areas include the Plaine de l'Estère and Plaine des Gonaïves. South of the Artibonite Valley are the mountains of the Chaîne des Matheux and Chaîne du Trou d'Eau—an extension of the Sierra de Neiba range of the Dominican Republic.

The southern tier of Haiti includes the Plaine du Cul-de-Sac and the Plaine de Léogane near Port-au-Prince, the Plaine des Cayes, other small coastal plains, and the high mountain ranges of the southern peninsula. The Plaine du Cul-de-Sac is a natural depression twelve kilometers wide that extends thirty-two kilometers from the Dominican border to the coast of the Baie de Port-au-Prince. The mountains of the Massif de la Selle are an extension of the Sierra de Baoruco range in the neighboring republic and run in an east-west direction in the upland interior of the southern peninsula. The Morne de la Selle (Montagne Terrible) is the highest point in Haiti with an elevation of 2,684 meters. In the southwestern portion of the peninsula, the steep and rugged Massif de la Hotte rises to 2,347 meters on Pic de Macaya.

315

Haiti has a large number of streams that carry torrential flows during the wet season and slow to a trickle in the dry season. Streams tend to be short and swift flowing because of the narrow peninsulas and numerous mountain ridges. Five rivers generate most of the country's water catchment: the Artibonite, Grande-Anse, L'Estère, Trois Rivières, and Cavaillon. The Artibonite is the largest drainage system in the country. Its headwaters are the Libon River in the foothills of the Massif du Nord. The Libon crosses the border into the Dominican Republic and then forms part of the border before reentering Haiti as the Artibonite River. At the border, the river expands into the Lac de Péligre formed by a dam in the southern part of the Central Plateau. Péligre Dam, constructed in 1956, is the country's major hydroelectric facility. The Artibonite drains some 10,000 square kilometers, including 6,570 square kilometers in Haiti. The 400-kilometer river is only one meter deep during the dry season and may dry up completely in certain spots. During the wet season, it is more than three meters deep and subject to flooding.

The 150-kilometer Trois Rivières is the most important river in the northern region. It has an average width of sixty meters, and is three to four meters deep. The ninety-five-kilometer Guayamouco River flowing through the Central Plateau is one of the principal tributaries of the Artibonite River. It has an average width of sixty meters and a depth of three to four meters. The most prominent body of water in the southern tier of the country is the Étang Saumâtre in the Plaine du Cul-de-Sac. A brackish lake that is gradually becoming less salty, it has an elevation sixteen meters above sea level and is twenty kilometers long and six to fourteen kilometers wide.

Haiti lies within the Low Subtropical Region at 18 to 20 degrees North latitude. The Holdridge Life Zone Classification System identifies nine subtropical life zones in Haiti: Thorn Woodlands, Dry Forest, Moist Forest, Wet Forest, Rain Forest, Lower Montane Moist Forest, Lower Montane Wet Forest, Lower Montane Rain Forest, and Montane Wet Forest. The Moist Forest, filled by growths of mahogany and tropical oaks, is the most commonly represented natural life zone. Temperatures are almost always high in lowland areas, ranging from 15°C to 25°C in the winter months and 25°C to 35°C during the summer.

The period from December through February is generally a dry season with little or no rainfall. Most of the country has a major rainy season in the spring and minor rains in the fall. Northeast trade winds and mountainous terrain create extreme weather conditions and highly variable temperatures. Tropical storms, drought, floods, and hurricanes are common. Rainfall patterns range from 300 millimeters in the northwest to more than 3,000 millimeters on Pic de Macaya in the high mountains of the southwest. One-fourth of the country has annual precipitation less than 1,200 millimeters. Most areas have at least 1,000 millimeters of annual precipitation, and a substantial percentage of the country receives 1,500 millimeters or more.

Geologists hold that Hispaniola was formed by three distinct land masses that collided over geologic time and were formed by the uplifting of oceanic crust. Exposed rock formations are sedimentary, metamorphic, or igneous; in Hispaniola sedimentary limestone deposits are by far the most abundant (80 percent). These limestone-based soils are more fertile than igneous-derived soils; the most fertile soils are alluvial deposits in river valleys and coastal plains. The permanent rise in sea level over geologic time has given rise to a notable degree of local endemism, resulting in a number of plant species peculiar to the region.

Natural Resources

Land Use and Water

The amount of arable land is small in relation to the size of the population. The rich soil tends to be found in small, noncontiguous areas and is concentrated along the coast or valley bottoms. Four large parcels of contiguous good land dwarf all others: the Plaine du Nord, the river basins of the lower Artibonite and of L'Estère, and the Plaine des Cayes and the Plaine du Cul-de-Sac.

By agronomic standards, 63 percent of all land in Haiti is too steep for sustainable agricultural production; however, land-use data indicate that two-thirds of all cultivated land is on mountain slopes and that the bulk of production on mountain slopes takes the form of erosion-intensive, annual food crops. Therefore, the scale of mountain cultivation is double that considered suitable even for perennial crops.

Land-use studies show roughly 80 percent of the country occupied by an agricultural landscape, including land actively farmed, fallow lands, farmhouses and compounds, pastures,

317

and wood lots. Experts classify at most 11 percent of the land, and perhaps only 7 percent, suitable for crop production under present techniques of cultivation. This analysis further suggests that no more than 28 percent of the land should be cultivated if using optimum techniques for soil and water conservation. These numbers are remarkable since survey national data from 1995 show 48 percent of total land area under active cultivation. Assuming a total population of 7,630,997 in 1998, the overall population density is 581 individuals per square kilometer of cultivated land, or 989 per square kilometer of land deemed cultivable.

This situation is clearly untenable and has catastrophic consequences for the environment and for rural livelihood. Data from the 1980s show a pattern of negative growth in agricultural production combined with ongoing population increase in the rural sector. Agriculture's share of total exports fell from around 90 percent in the 1950s to less than 10 percent in the late 1990s (see Agriculture, ch. 8). In terms of food consumption, the data also show a decline of 33 percent in the number of calories consumed per person per day since 1980.

Haiti's most acute environmental problem is undoubtedly soil erosion. A high proportion of cultivated land is farmed far beyond its carrying capacity, and forest cover has been largely decimated for agricultural use. By deforesting the landscape and degrading the land, agricultural forces have imposed acute pressure on the resource base. By some estimates, the equivalent of 6,000 hectares or more of arable land is lost annually because of erosion. Perhaps 88 percent of erosion stems from the cultivation of slopes that exceed 50 percent incline. Furthermore, the application of landscape-wide conservation techniques is complicated by the fragmentation of holdings. Recent data suggest that average farm size is 1.8 hectares divided into 3.7 noncontiguous plots.

The productive potential of irrigated land is significantly underused in Haiti; irrigated land is estimated to be less than 40,000 hectares. Technically, an additional 22,000 hectares could be rehabilitated and brought back into production. By some estimates, new investment in this sector could develop an additional 80,000 hectares. A limiting factor is a decrease in the quantity of surface water available for irrigation as a result of the effects of reduced vegetative cover on river discharge. There is evidence that base flows in Haiti's rivers and streams are diminishing. Aside from its use in irrigation, surface water is also the primary source of water used by most Haitians for domestic household needs. In general, groundwater is significantly underused for both household use and irrigation. The use of groundwater for irrigation is mostly limited to the Plaine du Cul-de-Sac.

Forestry and Fuelwood

There is a paucity of current data on forest cover. The most reliable national data are based on aerial photographs dating back to 1978. However, the United Nations Food and Agriculture Organization (FAO) has made some estimates based on the rate of deforestation prevalent in the late 1980s (see Forestry, ch. 8). In general, Haiti's forest cover is fast disappearing because of the press of people on the land, the clearing of land for food production, growth in the demand for construction material, and the harvest of fuelwood. In the case of many tree species, only a few relic stands of natural forest remain.

Several important stands of mangrove forest can be found in Haiti's coastal areas and estuaries. The most notable pine tract is the pine forest of the Massif de la Selle, a 28,000-hectare tract of state land that has been severely disturbed by illicit wood harvest and agricultural incursions. Much of Haiti was originally covered by broadleafed forest. Important stands remain in the northern region of Le Borgne-Anse-à-Foleur and around Pic de Macaya. Semi-arid forest, indicated by natural stands of mesquite, is found near the Étang Saumâtre and around Grand Gosier and Côtes de Fer. Natural stands of arid-land scrub, characterized by cactus, succulents, and thorny shrubs, are found between in the Savane Désolée between Gonaïves and Anse Rouge.

In the sixteenth century, forests of various types covered much of the island of Hispaniola although some observers estimate that less than half of Haiti was then covered by merchantable forest. Haiti exported precious woods throughout the nineteenth and early twentieth centuries and was for a time the largest exporter of logwood in the hemisphere. In addition, Haiti exported considerable quantities of mahogany, Spanish cedar, and lignum vitae. Since at least the 1940s, significant wood product shortages and growing wood imports have been . reported. Perhaps 8 percent of the territory was covered by natural forest in 1954.

Reliable national data from 1978 indicated that only 6.4 percent of the country was covered by forest—roughly one-third dense forest canopy and two-thirds open forest. Between 1978 and 1984, monitoring of three representative sites character- ized as degraded, open, and closed forest showed rates of deforestation ranging from 1.0 to 3.4 percent. It is clear that the process of deforestation has continued unabated since 1978; it was thought in 1993 that forests represented as little as 2.2 percent of the land. In general, the remaining parcels of forest today are highly fragmented and concentrated along watershed divides and on steep slopes vulnerable to erosion.

The primary cause of deforestation is the sheer scale of agri- cultural occupation of the landscape; however, demand for woodfuels is another significant contributor to deforestation. Per capita consumption of fossil fuels is the lowest in the hemi- sphere. Haiti is currently 80 percent self-sufficient in energy— based on wood as the primary cooking fuel in rural areas and wood charcoal in urban areas.

Fuelwood alone constitutes 70 percent of the national supply of energy. Residential consumption makes up more than 50 percent of total energy demand. Fuelwood, bagasse, and wood charcoal also supply 63 percent of industrial demand. Two- thirds of national charcoal consumption is attributed solely to Port-au-Prince. Ninety percent of Port-au-Prince households use wood charcoal for cooking. To a certain extent, growing national demand for charcoal parallels the growth of Port-au- Prince as an urban center.

Charcoal production is an important source of off-season employment for an estimated 67,000 small farmers. Its produc- tion is decentralized and produced by traditional methods. Since the 1970s, production has shifted from traditional supply zones of the arid northwest and Île de la Gonâve to a much broader range of production sites in all nine administrative departments of the country. Charcoal is generally acquired at prices far below its actual replacement cost. This fact signifi- cantly limits market incentive to manage wood as a renewable resource base for charcoal production. The mining of wood resources therefore contributes to degradation of the environ- ment.

Mining

There is little mining activity in Haiti except for construction materials. Deposits of bauxite on the Rochelois Plateau near Miragoâne and copper near Terre Neuve were mined in the past; the bauxite mine closed in 1982 and the copper mine in

1971. Some copper can be found in Vallières, some gold in Faille-Perches, and some lignite with a high sulfur content on the Central Plateau and Azile. Salt flats exist in Gonaïves and Caracol. High-grade calcium carbonate has been identified at Miragoâne and Dufort, and marble has been found in the Artibonite, Camp Perrin, Jacmel, and Margot. Deposits of clay in Hinche and the Plaine du Nord have good characteristics for pottery and tile manufacture. There are also numerous sites where gravel, limestone, and river sands are extracted for use as construction material for roads and buildings. Such mining, which is virtually unregulated, disfigures the landscape and creates a high risk of erosion and landslides.

Coastal and Marine Resource

Haiti's impressive coastal and marine habitats include mangrove wetlands, seagrass meadows, coral reefs, and numerous protected bays and estuaries. The diverse coastal system has white coral sand beaches, limestone cliffs, and rocky shorelines. Haiti's near-shore underwater landscapes are considered to be spectacular. These habitats are well developed and could potentially be managed as renewable resources for fishing and tourism.

The country's insular shelf (0–200 meters in depth) is quite narrow and covers an area of 5,000 square kilometers. This sedimentary platform generally extends no more than 300 meters offshore, then drops abruptly to the ocean floor to depths of 300 to 4,000 meters. The waters surrounding Haiti are not naturally productive because of the narrowness of the insular shelf, the unusual depth of the adjoining Caribbean, the warmth of surface waters, and the limited supply of nutrients. There is relatively higher production of fish stocks off the western tip of the southern peninsula.

An estimated 180 square kilometers of coastal areas are covered by mangrove forests. The mangroves are valued for their wood products and serve an extremely important role as reservoirs of plant and animal species. Significant stands of mangroves are found along the north coast between the Baie de l'Acul and Fort Liberté, the Artibonite estuary, and the offshore islands of Île de la Gonâve, Grande Cayemite, and Île à Vache. The mangroves are largely unaffected by coastal development but are subject to growing pressures as a result of unregulated harvest for polewood and charcoal.

In general, the mangroves are a critical habitat for threatened or endangered animal species, including the American crocodile, green sea turtle, hawksbill turtle, loggerhead turtle, American flamingo, roseate spoonbill, reddish egret, West Indian tree duck, masked duck, white-crowned pigeon, Hispaniolan trogon, peregrine falcon, and West Indian manatee. Critical marine and coastal habitats deserving of special protection include the following: Les Arcadins, a group of small islands and reefs in the Baie de Port-au-Prince; the Baie de Baradères and the Cayemites archipelago, including 1,200 hectares of mangroves; Île à Vache, an island south of Les Cayes with mangroves, reefs, crocodiles, and numerous shorebirds; and the small bays of Labadie and Cadrasses on Haiti's Atlantic coast in the north.

An estimated 8,000 to 10,000 fishermen practice small-scale traditional fishing using small boats. A fleet of some 3,000 sailboats and rowboats operates within a radius of about five kilometers from shore; there is widespread over-fishing in nearshore areas and underuse of other resources at a greater distance (see Agriculture, ch. 8). Most fishermen are oriented primarily to consumption needs. The major species found in local markets are snapper, spiny lobster, conch, shrimp, and parrot fish. Haiti exports significant quantities of coral, sea turtles, aquarium fish, and shells.

Biodiversity

Haiti's ecological diversity has created a rich and varied flora. Some 5,000 species of plants have been identified, including more than 3,000 woody plants, trees, and shrubs; 600 species of fern, and 160 orchids. Thirty-six percent of all plants are endemic. Plant species have adapted to a broad diversity of life zones, including dry desert and high mountain rainforest. Selecting for species utility, adaptability, and tradition, peasant farmers have retained a diverse range of tree and shrub species within the densely occupied agricultural landscape.

Haiti also has a rich fauna, especially the more than 220 bird species including seventy-five resident species and endemics such as the La Selle thrush, Hispaniolan trogon, Hispaniolan parrot and parakeet, chat tanager, palmchat, black-crowned palm tanager, and the gray-crowned palm tanager—a species unique to Haiti. The country is also home to significant numbers of water birds, including American flamingos, frigate birds, white-tailed tropicbirds, and the nearly extinct black-capped petrel, a seabird that nests in the high cliffs of La Selle and the Massif de la Hotte.

The island has few remaining endemic mammals. There are relic populations of two unusual rodents, the hutia and the long-nosed solenodonte. A small population of manatees survives in coastal waters. Reptiles include significant numbers of the American crocodile, iguanas, and a variety of unusual boas and other snakes.

The major threats to wildlife are population pressure; habitat destruction; hunting; non-native species such as rats and mice, feral dogs and cats, and the mongoose; lack of government regulation; and weak national institutions for biodiversity protection and management. Inadequate regulation of biological exports also poses a risk to wildlife. Haiti exports live reptiles, amphibians, arachnids, and tortoise shell and has been the largest Caribbean supplier of raw coral and ornamental fish to the United States.

Government decrees of 1980 and 1983 created three major protected areas—the Pine Forest Reserve, La Visite National Park, and Pic de Macaya National Park—but the government does not effectively manage these resources. All three sites are located in the southern highlands of Massif de la Selle and Massif de la Hotte and include the nation's two highest points, Pic de Macaya and Morne de la Selle. All three have a high rate of species endemism. Collectively, these sites are by far the most significant remnants of high mountain forest habitats, including the rainforest of Pic de Macaya. In the mid-1990s, the government initiated new programs to protect the environment and launched a national system for direct management of protected areas. The Pine Forest is managed as a mixed-use facility, and the two parks are operated for protection of biological diversity and upper watersheds.

Environmental Crisis

Haiti's resource base is under acute stress. The Haitian peasantry is faced with overwhelming challenges to its way of life. Agricultural production per capita has dropped at least 33 percent since 1980 and produces a declining share of the gross national product (GNP—see Glossary). Recent broad-based surveys classify the vast majority of peasant farmers as indigent according to standards of the FAO. The anarchic growth of urban areas also reflects the crisis in rural livelihood and contributes to deterioration of the resource base.

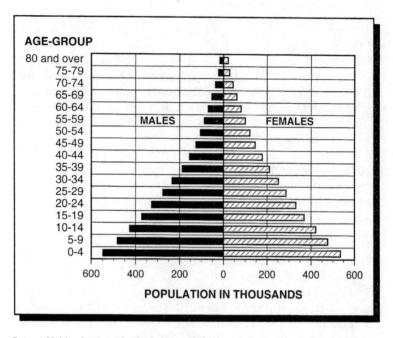

Source: Haitian Institute for Statistics and Information Technology in Pan American
   Health Organization, *Health Situation Analysis: Haiti, 1996*, Port-au-Prince,
   1996, 153.

Figure 12. Haiti: Population Distribution by Age and Sex, 1995

Sustainable agriculture in lowland areas requires vastly
increased forest cover in Haiti's upper watersheds. From an
environmental perspective, a significant portion of the highlands should be returned to forest and perennial crops, and
existing forest cover should be protected and better managed.
The decline in quality of water resources reflects the destruction of forest cover. According to one report, the volume of
spring water in the Port-au-Prince area has declined by more
than 50 percent within a five-year period. The decline of natural forest cover also has a serious impact on the remaining
endemic species of flora and fauna.

Haiti is faced with a number of pollution problems. The two
most pressing pollution-related problems are assuring safe
water and the sanitary disposal of human waste. Contamination
of surface and groundwater from human waste and other solid
and liquid wastes is increasing. Water-related diseases are preva-

lent. An estimated 53 percent of the population of Port-au-Prince has access to safe water. Growing levels of air pollution in the Port-au-Prince metropolitan area also pose a threat; the problem has been exacerbated by a dramatic increase in automobile imports since the mid-1990s.

Population

Demographic Profile

According to census-based projections, the estimated population of Haiti in 1998 was about 7.6 million with an average density of 282 people per square kilometer. Since 1985 Haiti's annual rate of population growth has been estimated to be around 2.2 percent. Life expectancy in the late 1990s was sixty-one years compared to an average of sixty-nine years in the Latin America region. The crude birthrate in the mid-1990s was estimated to be 44.5 per 1,000 and the crude death rate 12.2 per 1,000. Haiti's population pyramid shows 40 percent of the total population to be less than fifteen years of age (see fig. 12). Sex distribution data indicate a predominance of females because of higher male mortality and emigration rates.

Haiti has conducted only a few censuses throughout its history. At the time of independence in 1804, Haiti had a total population estimated to be well under 500,000, increasing to 780,000 in 1850 and to 1.6 million by 1900. A survey in 1918–19 reported 1.9 million people. In 1950 Haiti's first formal census indicated a total population of 3.1 million. In 1971 the second census estimated a population of 4.2 million, a figure that rose to 5.1 million in the country's third and most recent national census (1982). Critics have argued that Haiti's censuses are inadequate and tend to undercount the population. The country's census information is clearly out of date. Old geographic definitions of urban areas, for example, do not reflect the territorial expansion of urbanization in the 1980s and 1990s (see table 15, Appendix).

Port-au-Prince and other cities, including Cap-Haïtien, Saint-Marc, Gonaïves, and Les Cayes, report significant expansion in the 1990s (see table 16, Appendix). Assuming a redefined metropolitan area, an unprecedented 41 percent of the population may now be living in urban areas—primarily Port-au-Prince and its urbanized environs—and only 59 percent in rural areas. Despite rapid urbanization, Haiti still has one of the lowest urban-to-rural population ratios in the region. The country's rural population has been estimated at 2.7 million in 1950, 3.4 million in 1971, 3.8 million in 1982, and 4.5 million in 1998.

Between 1980 and the late 1990s, annual growth rates of metropolitan Port-au-Prince averaged 4.4 percent—more than double the estimates of national growth and three times the average rate of rural growth (1.2 percent). Census-based projections indicate that some 66 percent of the country's urban population is concentrated in the metropolitan area of Port-au-Prince. In 1998 the city and its environs were estimated to have 2 million inhabitants. In 1995 the city of Cap-Haïtien had an estimated population of 108,294, Saint-Marc 75,507, Gonaïves 72,109, and Les Cayes 54,252. These projections are likely underestimated because they rely on 1982 data and exclude new urban agglomerations around the old city centers.

Migration

The rate of population growth in Haiti's rural areas is less than one-third that of urban areas despite a much higher rural fertility rate. The main reason for this disparity is out-migration. Some 29 percent of rural households reported out-migration of one or more household members in a recent comprehensive survey of rural Haitians. The most common destinations are urban areas or other countries.

In the 1990s, the Haitian diaspora is estimated to number around 1.5 million people residing primarily in the United States, the Dominican Republic, and Canada. Census surveys of the 1980s identified the United States as the primary destination between 1950 and 1985, with the United States receiving 68 percent of Haitian emigrants during this period. There were also significant levels of emigration to the Dominican Republic, Canada, the Bahamas, Guadeloupe, Martinique, French Guiana, and France.

Haitian emigrants in the 1950s and 1960s were commonly urban middle- and upper-class opponents of the François Duvalier government (see François Duvalier, 1957–71, ch.6). In the 1970s, the profile of emigrants to the United States shifted to include growing numbers of lower-class Haitians from both rural and urban areas. By the mid-1980s, there were sizable numbers of Haitians in New York, Miami, Boston, Chicago, and Philadelphia, including an estimated 20 percent with illegal immigration status. Census data from 1990 indicate that although small numbers of Haitians live in widely dispersed areas of the United States, most live in only four states. According to the 1990 census, nearly three-fourths of immigrant Haitians and Haitian-Americans lived in New York and Florida and most of the rest in Massachusetts and New Jersey. The vast majority immigrated to the United States after 1970, and the largest number entered between 1980 and 1986. In the 1980s, the primary United States destination shifted away from New York to Florida; during this period immigrants were more commonly single, female, and less well-educated compared to earlier immigrants.

Since the early 1970s, thousands of Haitians have sought to emigrate to the United States in small boats and without documentation. Between 1972 and 1981, the United States Immigration and Naturalization Service (INS) reported more than 55,000 Haitian "boat people" arriving in Florida. The INS estimated that up to 50 percent of the arrivals escaped detection. About 85 percent of "boat people" from this period settled in Miami.

Small-craft departures from Haiti continued throughout the 1980s and early 1990s but declined after 1992. In September 1981, the United States entered into an agreement with Haiti to interdict Haitian boats and return prospective immigrants to Haiti. Between 1981 and 1992, some 54,000 Haitians were picked up at sea under the interdiction program. During the first eight months of the Raoul Cédras military regime (1991–94), some 34,000 Haitians were interdicted at sea. Thousands made application for refugee status and were held at the United States military base at Guantanamo Bay, Cuba, pending resolution of their status. This period also saw an immense rate of internal displacement within Haiti as a result of army repression and the extended political crisis.

Haiti has a longstanding history of temporary and seasonal migration of workers to neighboring countries. Between 1915 and 1929, an estimated 220,000 Haitians migrated to Cuba and thousands more to the Dominican Republic for seasonal employment in sugarcane fields. In the late 1950s and 1960s, the government of François Duvalier recruited 30,000 Haitian canecutters annually for the Dominican sugar harvest. The Dominican Republic continues to be an important destination for temporary and permanent Haitian migrants. Much of this migration is undocumented. In the late 1990s, an estimated 800,000 Haitians and Dominico-Haitians resided in the Dominican Republic. Americas Watch and other observers report that

Haitian workers in the Dominican Republic are subject to abusive working conditions and forced labor practices.

Out-migration tends to moderate Haiti's population growth. Internal rural-urban migration, for example, softens the impact of the high fertility rate in rural areas but also imposes acute stress on Haiti's urban communities and public services. An estimated 70 percent of Haiti's internal migrants are between ten and twenty-nine years of age. Migration is clearly an escape valve and has an overall moderating effect on Haitian poverty. At the same time, emigration causes heavy loss of professional and skilled personnel from both urban and rural areas. Remittances from abroad, however, do support thousands of poor families and inject a massive infusion of capital into the Haitian economy. Overseas remittances are estimated to be between US$350 million and US$500 million annually— some 12 to 15 percent of Haiti's GNP. Urban households are more likely to benefit from overseas remittances than rural households. Migration studies suggest that women are more likely to migrate to cities and men to go abroad.

The large number of Haitians living abroad is playing a growing role in domestic cultural, social, and political trends. Emigration creates greater latitude for upward social mobility. Hence emigration has an impact on social relations within Haiti, a society traditionally marked by rigid social distinctions. The use of English as a second language has also expanded considerably because of the preponderance of United States influence and its role as the primary destination for emigrants. Emigration also tends to increase the number of female-headed households in Haiti. In the 1990s, the Haitian diaspora has been a notable factor in domestic Haitian politics. As early as 1990, presidential candidate Jean-Bertrand Aristide referred to the Haitian diaspora as Haiti's "Tenth Department." After the return of constitutional government in late 1994, the Aristide government created a new ministry devoted to the Haitian diaspora.

Social Structure

The indigenous population of Haiti first came into contact with Europeans when Christopher Columbus landed in the country in 1492. The encounters with Europeans, first the Spanish and then the French, proved disastrous for the inhabitants; by the first decade of the seventeenth century, the Amerindian population was extinct (see Spanish Discovery and

Colonization, 1492–1697, ch. 6). As a result, the social structure implanted in colonial Saint-Domingue was determined primarily by French colonial policy, slave labor, and the highly stratified plantation system. Major planters and government officials dominated the colonial ruling class and carefully controlled all segments of the population, especially African slaves and their descendants. Society was structured around the rapid production of wealth for the planters and French investors.

The French imposed a three-tiered social structure in Saint-Domingue. A small European elite (*grands blancs*) controlled the top of the social pyramid, and African slaves (*noirs*) and their descendants occupied the lowest rung of society. An intermediary class of free men and women of color (*affranchis*) emerged as a result of sexual unions between slaves and slave owners and also from ex-slaves who purchased their freedom or were given their freedom by former slave owners. Some mulatto freedmen inherited land, became relatively wealthy, and owned slaves. Perhaps one-fourth of all slaves in Saint-Domingue belonged to freedmen. Nevertheless, racial codes kept the *affranchis* socially and politically inferior to Europeans. Another intermediary class was made up of poor whites (*petits blancs*), who considered themselves socially superior to mulattoes although they were generally inferior in economic terms. In 1791 the total population of Saint-Domingue was 519,000— 87 percent slaves, 8 percent white, and 5 percent free men and women of color. Because of the brutality of the slave regime and harsh working conditions, many slaves died, and new slaves were constantly imported. At the time of the slave rebellion in 1791, most slaves had been born in Africa rather than Saint-Domingue.

The Haitian Revolution changed the country's social structure. The colonial ruling class and white population were eliminated, and the plantation system was largely destroyed. The earliest black and mulatto leaders attempted to restore a plantation system based on free labor under strict military control, but the system collapsed under the presidency of Alexandre Pétion (1807–18) (see Early Years of Independence, 1804–43, ch. 6). The newly independent state confiscated old colonial estates and distributed land to former slaves, revolutionary soldiers, and army officers. In this process, the new Haitian upper class lost control over agricultural land and labor, the economic base during colonial times. To maintain its economic and social position, the new Haitian upper class turned away from agricultural pursuits in favor of urban-based activities, particularly government, the professions, and the export trade.

The nineteenth-century Haitian ruling class consisted of two groups, the urban elite and the military leadership. The urban elite was primarily a closed group of educated, comparatively wealthy, French-speaking mulattoes. Birth was an important determinant of elite social position; intermarriage and shared values reinforced class solidarity. The military was an avenue of social mobility for disadvantaged black Haitians. In a shifting, uneasy alliance with the military, the urban elite ruled the country and isolated the peasantry from national affairs. The urban elite promoted French norms and models as a means of separating itself from the peasantry. French language and manners, orthodox Roman Catholicism, and light skin were important criteria of high social position. The elite disdained manual labor, industry, and local commerce in favor of genteel professions such as law and medicine.

A small, politically important middle class emerged during the twentieth century. Opportunity for social mobility increased slightly, but the traditional elite retained its social and economic preeminence. François Duvalier presided over an expanding black middle class based in part on increased access to government patronage and corruption. Since the 1980s and 1990s, peasants have been somewhat less isolated from national politics. Economic hardship in rural areas has heightened rural-urban migration and expanded the lower and middle classes of urban areas. Despite these changes, the peasantry as a social sector continues to be dominated by urban political and economic interests.

The Upper Class

By some estimates, Haiti's upper class constitutes 4 percent of the total population and controls 67 percent of national income in contrast to the poor majority—70 percent of the population with control over 20 percent of the nation's resources. The upper class includes the traditional elite and others who have gained wealth and power through the political system. Others have moved into upper ranks through wealth accrued in industry or export-import businesses.

Members of the traditional elite hold key positions in trade, industry, real estate, and the professions. They are identified by membership in "good families" with recognized status over a period of generations. Elite membership generally entails a knowledge of European cultural refinements and French language and customs. Light skin and straight hair are important characteristics of this group although there are important phenotypical exceptions, particularly among old elite families originating in the northern region. French surnames are common among the mulatto elite, but increased immigration from Europe and the Middle East in the late nineteenth and the early twentieth centuries introduced names of other national origins to the roster, including German, English, Danish, and Arabic.

To a certain extent, people of Arab origins in Haiti are identified as an ethnic minority; these people include descendants of Syrian, Lebanese, and Palestinian traders who first arrived in the late nineteenth century. From their beginnings as itinerant peddlers of fabrics and other dry goods, Arab merchants moved into the export-import sector, engendering the hostility of Haitians and foreign rivals. Many have Haitian citizenship and use French and Creole as their preferred languages. Formerly spurned by elite mulatto families, families of Arab origins in the 1990s commonly intermarry with Haitians and take part in all aspects of upper-class life, including the professions and industry.

The Middle Class

The middle class was essentially nonexistent during the nineteenth century. It became somewhat more sharply defined around the time of the United States occupation (1915–34). Occupation policies fostered the growth of intermediary classes, including the creation of a professional military and expansion of government, urban growth, and increased centralization of economic and political power in Port-au-Prince. Educational reform in the 1920s, an upsurge in nationalism and black consciousness, and the wave of economic prosperity after World War II also fostered the emergence of an expanded middle class. The mulatto elite dominated government in the 1930s and the early 1940s, however, and thwarted the political aspirations of the black middle class. Under Dumarsais Estimé (1946–50) and François Duvalier (1957–71), an active member of the negritude movement, and his son Jean-Claude Duvalier (1971–86), the black middle class grew in size and political influence. Since the 1970s, broad-based emigration has tended to expand the Haitian middle class as a result of upward mobility, overseas remittances, and a stream of return migration in the 1980s and 1990s. Nevertheless, the middle class remains a small minority in the late 1990s, perhaps 15 percent of the population.

Despite greater access to political power, the middle class tends to be insecure in its social position and culturally ambivalent, subject to conflict between Franco-Haitian and Afro-Haitian cultural traditions. Social characteristics of members of the middle class include a moderate income, literacy, knowledge of French, a preference for occupations that do not require manual labor, and upward mobility through education and urban residence. Despite their emulation of the upper class, middle-class Haitians resent the social preeminence and class and color prejudice of the elite.

Peasants

Since 1950 the population of rural Haiti has increased by an estimated 167 percent to a total of 4.5 million people, mostly small peasant farmers. During this period, rural areas dropped proportionally from 88 percent to only 59 percent of the population. Current evidence indicates that rural poverty is more severe than urban poverty. The majority of rural households are highly vulnerable to food shortages, and more than 80 percent fall below the poverty line according to FAO standards.

Peasant occupation of the agricultural landscape is based on widely dispersed homesteads and several noncontiguous plots within each farm unit (see Natural Resources, this ch.). Most farms include productive activity on sites the farmer does not own. Farmers are simultaneously owner-operators, landlords, and tenants, depending on the plot. Many are land poor, but the number of landless farmers who rely solely on wage labor is relatively small. Landless peasants are likely to migrate to urban areas.

Unlike peasants in much of Latin America, most of Haiti's peasants have owned land since the early nineteenth century. Land is the most valuable rural commodity, and peasant families go to great lengths to retain it and to increase their holdings.

Peasants in general have control over their landholdings, but many lack clear title to their plots. Haiti has never conducted a cadastral survey, but it is likely that many families have passed on land over generations without updating land titles. Division of land equally among male and female heirs has resulted in farm plots that are too small to warrant the high

A house-raising
Courtesy Inter-American Foundation
Haitian peasants
Courtesy Pan-American Development Foundation

costs of a surveyor. Heirs occasionally survey land before taking possession of it, but more frequently heirs divide plots among themselves in the presence of community witnesses and often a notary. Undivided plots are often used for grazing or farmed on a rotating basis. Families commonly sell land to raise cash for such contingencies as funerals or to pay the expenses of emigration. Purchasers often hold land with a notarized receipt rather than formal registration and transfer of title.

Peasants have a strong sense of identity as Haitians and cultivators of the land. However, they have little or no sense of class solidarity, and rivalries among peasant families and local factions are common. Since the 1940s, small rotating labor groups have tended to replace large labor societies more common earlier in the century. Peasants organize work parties and exchange labor to supplement family labor and meet the intensive labor requirements of peasant agriculture. Peasants also buy and sell daily wage labor.

Rural social arrangements are firmly rooted in kin ties, fictive kinship, patron-client relations, other special ties and obligations, and competing factions. Community solidarity is weakly developed. In the late 1950s, outside development agencies began to organize peasant councils as a self-help strategy to promote community development. By the 1980s, such councils had been organized in most of rural Haiti. In the early 1980s, the government of Jean-Claude Duvalier sought to politicize and control this widespread network of rural councils. Despite rhetoric of local autonomy and democratic representation, peasant councils came to be dominated by traditional power holders and outside interests.

In the 1960s and 1970s, church leaders and other reformers promoted small pre-cooperative groups called *gwoupman* in lieu of the old community councils. The most successful of these groups were built on indigenous sociocultural forms oriented to kinship, labor exchange, or traditional rotating credit groups. In the period since 1986, the *gwoupman* movement and other peasant organizations have been severely persecuted under various military regimes, especially under the de facto government of Raoul Cédras (1991–94). With the return of constitutional rule in late 1994, this persecution ceased. In the latter 1990s, few of the older community councils remained active, and the small group movement has expanded into many areas of rural Haiti. In a distinct break with the past, numerous members of local peasant organizations have been elected to public office as parliamentarians, mayors, and members of new rural governing councils in keeping with the constitution of 1987.

For most of Haiti's history, the Haitian peasantry has been notably isolated from national institutions, excluded from a voice in government, and subject to unfair taxation and urban domination. In the late twentieth century, especially in the period since 1986, peasants have become highly politicized. Rural areas have civilian local government bodies for the first time in history. Peasants have unprecedented contact with the outside world for a variety of reasons, including radio, the Creole media, severe economic crisis in rural Haiti leading to high rates of out-migration to Port-au-Prince and abroad, political turbulence for more than a decade, and the presence of international civilian and military personnel.

Urban Lower Class

The urban lower class is concentrated in Port-au-Prince and the sprawling slums of major coastal towns, especially Cap-Haïtien, Gonaïves, and Les Cayes. An estimated two-thirds of Port-au-Prince is concentrated in slum districts, some dating back to colonial times and others dispersed more recently into ravines and lowland flood plains. High rates of rural-urban migration feed the growth of high-density neighborhoods. As early as 1976, field research found the average density of Port-au-Prince slums to be 890 inhabitants per hectare, with a quarter of this population exceeding 1,200 persons per hectare. In contrast, high-income neighborhoods of the city averaged 100 persons per hectare.

Urban slums are composed largely of displaced peasants, primarily young people. Many residents maintain contact with home communities in rural Haiti. Rural points of reference influence urban social organization in low-income districts. Studies of Cité Soleil—the capital's well-known coastal slum district—found only 9 percent of residents native to the district, 67 percent rural born, 50 percent single young people, and 33 percent made up of households headed by single-parent females. There is evidence of high demand for education in slum districts, and a much higher than average rate of literacy—75 percent—compared to the nation as a whole (at most 50 percent). In the politically turbulent period since 1986, pressure groups have emerged in urban slum neighborhoods. Despite problems of internal disunity and fragmentation, these groups have successfully organized mass demonstrations and exercised a degree of political influence.

The urban lower class operates primarily within the informal sector. Access to water and electricity is controlled privately rather than by official utilities. Fewer than 40 percent of Port-au-Prince residents have access to potable water. In the 1990s, many unoccupied lands of the city were taken over for housing; however, studies of Cité Soleil suggest that most residents are renters not squatters. Sixty-seven percent of the housing is rented or built on rented sites; however, rents are paid to a class of speculative landlords who acquire land by taking over unoccupied state land or other lands left vacant because of exile, political looting, or theft.

A large percentage of the active labor force is self-employed, working part-time, or working in the services sector—traditionally the largest employment sector in the city. Perhaps 25 percent of workers in Port-au-Prince are employed in domestic service. Reports in the latter half of the 1990s indicate that 35 to 45 percent of actively employed slum residents are engaged in commerce. An estimated 67 percent of the population lives on less than US$25 a month. In the 1980s, a high percentage of residents in the St. Martin slum district borrowed money at interest rates ranging from 15 to 95 percent per month.

Gender Roles and Marriage

Haiti's population is disproportionately young and female. Demographic data suggest a shortage of men in most age-groups older than age ten—a tendency more pronounced in urban than in rural areas. Females are economically active at a young age, including an estimated 10 percent of all girls between the ages of five and nine years old and 33 percent of ten- to fourteen-year-old girls. Rural-urban migrants are far more likely to be women than men. Female heads of household are much more common in urban areas. Official 1996 data indicate that 26 percent of rural households and 46 percent of urban households are headed by women. By some estimates, 50 to 70 percent of households in Port-au-Prince are headed by women responsible for their own livelihood. In any case, Haitian women are the central figures in sustaining families under the prevailing conditions of economic decline and poverty.

In general, Haitian women participate in the labor force to a far greater extent than is the case in other countries in the

Boats arriving for market day in Restel, southern Haiti

region. Women dominate Haiti's internal market system. Some women specialize as market intermediaries, buying and selling produce and serving as links between local markets and regional or urban markets. Women with enough capital to be full-time market traders are often economically independent of men. An estimated 70 percent of women in the services sector are employed as servants, especially in Port-au-Prince. In the assembly industry, more than 50 percent and perhaps as much as 75 percent of factory workers are women, according to various estimates.

In rural areas, men and women play complementary roles. Men assume primary responsibility for farming, especially the heavy field labor. Women commonly assist in weeding and harvesting. Women assume primary responsibility for selling household agricultural produce in local markets. In peasant farming, the income generated through agricultural production belongs to both husband and wife. Women may own or inherit land, but men usually control land transactions and the primary land base for peasant farming. Women are responsible for most household tasks, including cooking, laundry, gathering wood, and carrying water. Haitian families are patriarchal, but women play a key economic role—ultimately the pivotal role in day-to-day operations of the household economy.

The most common marital relationship is based in *plasaj*, a form of customary marriage. Such relationships are considered normal and proper in peasant families and the urban lower class. Spouses generally have an explicit economic agreement at the beginning of either legal or customary marriage. In rural Haiti, this understanding is negotiated, oftentimes between the families of the two parties to a marital union, and usually requires the husband to provide a house and cultivate at least one plot of land for his new wife.

For the most part, lower-class men and women undertake legal marriage primarily for social prestige. Given the significant expense of weddings, many couples in *plasaj* unions delay legal marriage for many years. In the 1960s, this pattern began to change among Protestant families who belonged to churches that strongly promote legal marriage and provided affordable weddings. It is not unusual for men to have extramarital relationships. Some enter into polygamous marriages by custom, although most men cannot afford the expense. Men and women both value children and contribute to childcare, but women bear most of the burden.

Women's rights are not the equal of men's in a court of law. Women do not inherit from their partners' *plasaj*. In addition, legal sanctions for adultery are far greater for women than for men. Women are also subject to physical abuse. According to one study, 29 percent of women reported that their first sexual experience was non-consensual. A legal reform in 1983 accorded adult rights to married women for the first time, and the constitution of 1987 expanded legal protection for all families whether or not based on legal marriage.

Among the traditional elite, civil and religious marriages are the norm. Divorce was once rare, but has become more acceptable. Upper-class wives have entered the labor force in growing numbers since the 1970s. In general, social trends, rapid urbanization, and out-migration have extracted a severe toll on marital unions and family life across class boundaries.

There have been associations of urban women since the 1930s. A number of women's organizations were established in the 1960s and 1970s. Since 1986 there has been dynamic growth in women's groups, greater media interest in women's issues, and somewhat greater participation of women in politics and government. After the return of constitutional government in 1994, the Aristide administration created a new government ministry devoted to women's issues. The ministry acts

Woman going to market,
Port-au-Prince
Courtesy Anne Greene

primarily as an advocacy and policy-making institution. Women's groups are playing a growing role within grassroots peasant organizations and rural savings and loan associations.

The Language Question

French and Creole

Two languages are spoken in Haiti: Creole and French. The social relationship between these languages is complex. Perhaps nine out of ten Haitians speak only Creole—the everyday language for the entire population. Only about one in twenty is fluent in both French and Creole. Thus, Haiti is neither francophone nor bilingual. Rather, two separate speech communities exist: the monolingual majority and the bilingual middle and upper classes.

All classes value verbal facility. Public speaking plays an important role in political life; the style of a speech is often more important than its content. Repartee enlivens the daily parlance of monolingual peasant and bilingual urbanite alike.

Small groups gather regularly to listen to storytellers. The social status of French and Creole helps define the Haitian social and cultural dilemma.

Language serves as a complicating factor in interactions between members of the elite and the masses. Haitians of all classes take pride in Creole as the national language. Nevertheless, some Haitians regard Creole as a non-language, claiming that "it has no rules" in contrast to the high-status mystique of French. At the same time, most bilingual Haitians harbor ambivalent feelings about French. In Creole the phrase "to speak French" means "to be a hypocrite."

Fluency in French is more important than skin color as an indicator of elite social status. Public use of French tends to exclude the Creole-speaking majority from political discourse, government, legal documents, the judicial system, and intellectual life. Bilingual families use French primarily on formal and public occasions. Creole is a language of open self-expression, informal gatherings, storytelling, slang, and jokes. Haitian French generally lacks these relaxed, informal qualities. Monolingual Creole speakers avoid formal situations requiring the use of French. In certain social contexts, some monolingual Creole speakers use French-sounding phrases to impress their audience. Middle-class bilinguals in Port-au-Prince frequently encounter social situations where French would be appropriate, but imperfect mastery of the language may betray lower-class origins. Because of the defining social role of language, middle-class use of French is often stiff and self-conscious in comparison to its use by upper-class speakers.

The origins of Creole are still debated. Some scholars believe it arose from a pidgin used for communications between French colonists and African slaves. Others believe that Creole came to the colony of Saint-Domingue as a fully developed language that originated as a maritime trade language. Whatever its origins, Creole is linguistically a distinct language, not a French dialect. The Creole lexicon is derived primarily from French, but Creole grammar is not like French, and the two languages are not mutually comprehensible.

There are regional and class variations in Creole. Regional variations include lexical items and sound shifts, but the grammatical structure is consistent throughout the country. Bilingual speakers tend to use French phonemes in their Creole speech. The Port-au-Prince variant has attained special status and influence as the emerging standard form of the language.

The use of French and Creole during the colonial era set speech patterns for the postindependence period. During the colonial period, French was spoken mainly by whites and mulatto freedmen. With the collapse of slavery and the plantation system, French became a status marker distinguishing those who had attained personal freedom before the revolution (*anciens libres*) and those who achieved freedom during the revolution. After independence French became the language of government, commerce, culture, and refinement. Even the most ardent nationalists of the nineteenth century placed little value on Creole.

In the twentieth century, attitudes toward Creole began to change, especially after the United States occupation in 1915. The occupation forced Haitian intellectuals to confront their non-European heritage. A growing black consciousness and nationalism led many Haitians to consider Creole as the nation's "authentic" language. Written Creole first appeared in 1925, and the first Creole newspaper was published in 1943.

In the 1950s, a movement to give Creole official status began to evolve. The constitution of 1957 reaffirmed French as the official language but permitted Creole in certain public functions. In 1969 Creole attained limited legal status; the language could be used in the legislature, the courts, and clubs, but it was not allowed in accredited educational institutions. In 1979 a decree permitted Creole to be used as the language of instruction in classrooms. The constitution of 1983 declared both Creole and French to be national languages but specified that French would be the official language. Creole attained full status as a national language in the constitution of 1987.

Changes in Language Use

Since the 1970s, use of Creole in public has greatly increased even on formal occasions. Conversations at elite dinner tables, once held strictly in French, now switch fluidly between French and Creole mid-sentence. Use of Creole by radio and television media increased rapidly as advertisers learned the value of marketing products in the native tongue of growing numbers of consumers in the Port-au-Prince region. In 1986 Creole newscasts played an important political role in the fall of Jean-Claude Duvalier. Creole was the primary vehicle for political campaigns in the Haitian elections of the 1980s and 1990s. Since the mid-1990s, a rapidly growing network of local and regional radio stations has broadcast entirely in Creole.

English has become far more important than ever before and competes in some respects with French as the high-status language. It is the key language for international trade in an island economy dependent on exports, imports, light industry based on United States contracts, and overseas remittances from the United States. The sheer scale of Haitian emigration to the United States promotes the use of English, as does a smaller stream of return migration. Members of the elite now commonly send their children to study in United States institutions of higher education.

Use of English cuts across class lines. Hundreds of French-speaking elite families spent years of exile in the United States during the Duvalier period and returned to Haiti fluent in English. Most migrants to the United States have settled there permanently; however, there has been significant travel back and forth and a small stream of permanent migration back to Haiti since 1986. Monolingual Creole speakers emigrated to the United States and returned to Haiti as literate speakers of English with little or no knowledge of French. The presence of so many Haitians in the United States has deeply marked the Creole lexicon with new words and expressions. For Creole monolinguals, learning English may seem more practical than learning French, and English poses fewer social and psychological obstacles. English-language television programs are now readily available on Haiti's private cable service and have helped familiarize Haitians with the language. In addition to English, Spanish is a common second or third language in Haiti, largely because of seasonal Haitian migration to the Dominican Republic and some return migration to Haiti of long-term residents.

Creole, Literacy, and Education

Haiti's national language policy has been inconsistent as a result of conflicting political interests. Former governments that claimed to represent the masses hesitated to give Creole and French equal legal status. In the late 1970s and early 1980s, however, the government approved the use of Creole in education, the National Pedagogic Institute announced an official orthography for Creole, and the Ministry of National Education, Youth, and Sports announced national reforms in education (see Education, this ch.).

The most controversial aspect of these reforms was the introduction of Creole as a medium of instruction in primary schools. In many rural and urban schools, textbooks were in French, but classroom discussion took place in Creole. The education reform was intended to boost performance through instruction in the native language, but many opposed the use of Creole. Bilingual families believed the use of Creole would erode their linguistic advantage in society by de-emphasizing French. Elements of the upper class opposed Creole instruction since they did not support mass popular education. Many poor people also opposed the reform because they preferred the social status of French rather than Creole. The government eventually declared that students would initially study in Creole and shift to French when they entered the fifth grade. Most private schools simply ignored the curriculum reforms. As of the late 1990s, the education reforms of the late 1970s and early 1980s had never really been implemented as national policy.

In 1996 the Ministry of National Education, Youth, and Sports completed a draft National Education Plan and held a national conference to plan for the future of education in Haiti. The draft plan proposed to expand access to education, especially in rural areas, and to implement curriculum reform in keeping with the education reform of 1982.

Adult literacy programs in Haiti have generally emphasized Creole rather than French. Catholic and Protestant missionaries first promoted adult Creole literacy in the 1930s and 1940s. In the 1960s, the government established adult literacy programs in Creole, and in the mid-1980s the Roman Catholic Church sponsored nationwide literacy programs. In the late 1990s, grassroots peasant organizations continued to sponsor adult literacy training in Creole. Community leaders and development workers use the language in recording the minutes of meetings and project reports. Growing numbers of monolingual speakers regularly use Creole to write letters and personal notes.

There is a small but growing written literature in Creole. Earlier, most Creole texts were produced by church groups or community development organizations. Many of these texts were training materials or church newsletters. Both the Old Testament and the New Testament are available in Creole. Publications in Creole now include a broader range of topics, including news, history, sociopolitical analysis, and sophisticated literary works, poetry, and novels by well known authors such as Frank Étienne and Félix Morisseau-Leroy.

343

Religious Life

Roman Catholicism is the official religion of Haiti, but voodoo may be considered the country's national religion. Most Haitians believe in and practice at least some aspects of voodoo. Most voodooists believe that their religion can coexist with Catholicism. Most Protestants, however, strongly oppose voodoo.

Voodoo

Misconceptions about voodoo have given Haiti a reputation for sorcery and zombies. Popular images of voodoo ignore the religion's basic character as a domestic cult of family spirits intimately linked to sickness, health, and well-being. Adherents of voodoo do not perceive themselves as members of a separate religion; most consider themselves Roman Catholics. In fact, there is no word for the voodoo religion in the Creole language of rural Haiti. The Creole word *vodoun* refers to a kind of dance and in some areas to a category of spirits. Roman Catholics who are active voodooists say that they "serve the spirits," and they do not consider that practice to be inconsistent with Roman Catholicism. Haitians also distinguish between the service of family spirits and the practice of magic and sorcery. The belief system of voodoo revolves around family spirits (often called *loua* or *mistè*) who are inherited through maternal and paternal lines. The *loua* protect their "children" from misfortune. In return, families must "feed" the *loua* through periodic rituals in which food, drink, and other gifts are offered to the spirits. There are two basic kinds of services for the *loua*. The first is held once a year; the second is conducted much less frequently, usually only once a generation. To save money, many poor families wait until they feel a need to restore their relationship with their spirits before they conduct a service. Services are usually held at a sanctuary on family land.

In voodoo, there are many *loua*. Although there is considerable variation among families and regions, there are generally two groups of *loua*: the *rada* and the *petro*. The *rada* spirits are mostly seen as "sweet" *loua*, while the *petro* are seen as "bitter" because they are more demanding of their "children." *Rada* spirits appear to be of African origin while *petro* spirits appear to be Haitian.

Loua are usually anthropomorphic and have distinct identities. They can be good, evil, capricious, or demanding. Because *loua* most commonly show their displeasure by making people sick, voodoo is used to diagnose and treat illnesses. *Loua* are not nature spirits, and they do not make crops grow or bring rain. The *loua* of one family have no claim over members of other families, and they cannot protect or harm them. Voodooists are therefore not interested in the *loua* of other families.

Loua appear to family members in dreams, and more dramatically through trances. Many Haitians believe that *loua* are capable of temporarily taking over the bodies of their "children." In voodoo men and women enter trances during which they assume the traits of particular *loua*. People in such a trance feel giddy and usually remember nothing after they return to a normal state of consciousness. Voodooists say that the spirit temporarily replaces the human personality. Possession trances usually occur during rituals such as services for *loua* or a *vodoun* dance in honor of the *loua*. When *loua* appear to entranced people, they may bring warnings or explanations for the causes of illnesses or misfortune. *Loua* often engage the crowd around them through flirtation, jokes, or accusations.

Ancestors (*lèmò*) rank with the family *loua* as the most important spiritual entities in voodoo. Elaborate funeral and mourning rites reflect the important role of the dead. Ornate tombs throughout the countryside also reveal how much attention Haiti gives to its dead. Voodooists believe the dead are capable of forcing their survivors to construct tombs and sell land. In these cases, the dead act like family *loua* that "hold" family members to make them ill or bring other misfortune. The dead also appear in dreams to provide their survivors with advice or warnings.

Voodooists make a strong distinction between inherited family spirits and purchased spirits. They believe that *loua* can be paid to bring good fortune or protection from evil and that dead souls can be paid to attack enemies by making them ill. The "purchase" of spirits in this manner has an instrumental or manipulative character. People view this type of transaction as dangerous and antisocial.

Folk belief includes zombies and witchcraft. Zombies are either spirits or people whose souls have been partially withdrawn from their bodies. Some Haitians resort to *bòkò* specialists in sorcery and magic. Secret societies whose members practice sorcery can also be found in Haiti. Witchcraft and charges of witchcraft are rooted in social relationships, and reflect the real-life conflicts between people. In this sense, witchcraft is a kind of social leveler and is used to protect personal or property rights.

Witchcraft is also important in diagnosing illness and performing healing rites. Voodoo specialists, male *houngan* and female *mambo*, mediate between humans and spirits through divination and trance. They diagnose illness and reveal the origins of other misfortunes. They can also perform rituals to appease spirits or ancestors or to repel magic. In addition, many voodoo specialists are accomplished herbalists who treat a variety of illnesses.

Unlike Roman Catholicism and Protestantism, voodoo lacks a fixed theology and organized hierarchy. Each specialist develops his or her own reputation for helping people. Former president François Duvalier recruited voodoo specialists to help him control all aspects of Haitian life. Although Duvalier indicated that he retained power through sorcery, voodoo is essentially a decentralized, family-based cult, and Duvalier failed to politicize the religion to any great extent.

Roman Catholicism

Before the Haitian Revolution, the church played a minor role in colonial life. Plantation owners feared that religious education for slaves could undermine their basis for control, and they expelled the education-oriented Jesuits in 1764. Roman Catholicism gained official status in several postindependence Haitian constitutions, but there was no official Roman Catholic presence in the country until the signing of a concordat with the Vatican in 1860. The Vatican had previously refused to recognize the Haitian government. The concordat provided for the appointment of an archbishop in Port-au-Prince, designated dioceses, and established an annual government subsidy for the church. An amendment to the concordat in 1862 assigned the Roman Catholic Church an important role in secular education.

Initially, a small number of priests and members of religious orders ministered primarily to the urban elite. Until the mid-twentieth century, the majority of priests were francophone Europeans, particularly Bretons, who were culturally distant from their rural parishioners. Roman Catholic clergy were generally hostile toward voodoo, and they led two major campaigns against the religion in 1896 and 1941. During these campaigns, the government outlawed voodoo services, and Catholics destroyed voodoo religious objects and persecuted practitioners. Catholic clergy have not been consistently militant in opposing voodoo, and they have not been successful in eradicating or diminishing the popular religious practices of the rural and urban poor. The clergy have generally directed their energies more toward educating the urban population than eradicating voodoo. Since the 1970s, the use of drum music has become common in Roman Catholic services. Incorporating folk elements into the liturgy, however, did not mean the Roman Catholic Church's attitude toward voodoo had changed.

Nationalists and others came to resent the Roman Catholic Church in the 1940s and 1950s because of its European orientation and alliance with the mulatto elite. François Duvalier opposed the church more than any other Haitian president. Between 1959 and 1961, he expelled the archbishop of Port-au-Prince, the Jesuit order, and numerous priests. In response to these moves, the Vatican excommunicated Duvalier. When relations with the church were restored in 1966, Duvalier prevailed. He succeeded for the first time in having a Haitian named an archbishop and also gained the right to nominate bishops.

The mid-1980s marked a profound change in the church's stance on issues related to peasants and the urban poor. Reflecting this change was the statement by Pope John Paul II during a visit to Haiti in 1983 that "things must change here." Galvanized by the Vatican's concern, Roman Catholic clergy and lay workers called for improved human rights. Lay workers fostered an emerging peasant rights movement. The Roman Catholic radio station, Radio Soleil, played a key role in disseminating news in Creole about government actions during the 1985–86 crisis and encouraged opponents of the Duvalier government. The bishops, particularly in Jérémie and Cap-Haïtien, actively denounced Duvalierist repression and human-rights violations.

In the aftermath of Jean-Claude Duvalier's departure in 1986, the church took a less active role in Haitian politics. The church hierarchy, however, strongly supported the 1987 constitution that granted official status to Creole and guaranteed basic human rights, including the right to practice voodoo. The alliance with the lower classes in the 1980s left the Roman Catholic Church internally divided in the late 1990s. These divisions reflect in part the church hierarchy's ambivalent relationship to the political movement it supported in the 1980s, including the dramatic role of a former priest, ex-president Jean-Bertrand Aristide, who continues to play an active role in Haitian politics (see Aristide Presidency, February 7, 1991–September 30, 1991, and Democracy Restored, 1994–96, ch. 6).

Protestantism

Protestantism has existed in Haiti since the earliest days of the republic. By the mid-nineteenth century, there were small numbers of Protestant missions in the country, principally Baptist, Methodist, and Episcopalian. Protestant churches, mostly from North America, have sent many foreign missions to Haiti. Almost half of Haiti's Protestants are Baptists; pentecostals are the second largest group. A range of Protestant denominations includes Nazarenes, Seventh Day Adventists, Jehovah's Witnesses, the Salvation Army, Mennonites, and Presbyterians. Protestantism in Haiti has grown rapidly since the 1950s. By some estimates, around 25 percent of the population are Protestant. The number of Protestant adherents, especially pentecostals, continues to grow.

Protestantism appealed initially to the middle and the upper classes, and has long played an important role in education. Protestant churches subsequently focused their attention on the poor and did so far earlier than the Roman Catholic Church. Protestant churches and clergy are found even in remote areas. Having long used Creole rather than French, Protestant clergy promote adult literacy in Creole. They have also established numerous schools and clinics in communities otherwise without access to these much-needed services. Protestant congregations encourage baptisms and marriages and generally perform them free.

Protestantism actively opposes voodoo and for many Haitians provides an alternative to serving voodoo spirits. Most Protestant denominations consider all *loua*, including family spirits, as demons. When people convert to Protestantism, they often come to view the folk religion as diabolical. Some Haitians convert to Protestantism when they reject family spirits that have failed to protect them. Others become Protestants as a way to gain new forms of protection from misfortune.

In his struggle with the Roman Catholic Church, François Duvalier welcomed Protestant missionaries, especially from the United States. Although Protestants tend to compete with the Roman Catholic Church and other Protestant churches for adherents, in 1986 in an unusual show of interreligious solidarity Protestant leaders and radio media joined Roman Catholics in public opposition to the government during the political troubles leading to the fall of Jean-Claude Duvalier.

Education

Haiti's postcolonial leaders announced progressive education policies, and the constitution of 1805 called for free and compulsory primary education. Although policy goals were never fully implemented, early rulers Henry Christophe (1807–20) and Alexandre Pétion (1807–18) constructed schools. By 1820 there were nineteen primary schools and three secondary lycées. The Education Act of 1848 created rural primary schools with a more limited curriculum and established colleges of medicine and law. A comprehensive education system was never developed, however, and the emergent elite who could afford the cost sent their children to school in France. The signing of the concordat with the Vatican in 1860 resulted in the arrival of clerical teachers, further emphasizing the influence of the Roman Catholic Church within Haiti's best-educated social class. The Roman Catholic Church became a state church, and Catholic schools turned into public schools jointly funded by the Haitian government and the Vatican.

The new teachers, mainly French clergy, concentrated on developing the urban elite, especially in the excellent new secondary schools. In the classroom, they promoted an attachment to France and expounded on Haiti's backwardness. In the nineteenth century, few priests ventured to rural areas to educate peasants. In both urban and rural settings, the schools run by clergy followed a classical curriculum emphasizing literature and rote learning. The curriculum changed little over time except during the United States occupation, when authorities established vocational schools. The elite resisted these efforts, and the government restored the old system in 1934.

In the 1970s, the Haitian government, with support from the World Bank (see Glossary) and the United Nations Educational, Scientific, and Cultural Organization (UNESCO), began to reform its educational system, mostly at the primary level. In 1978 the government unified educational administration for the first time by putting rural schools under the same authority, the Department of National Education, as urban schools.

At the end of the nineteenth century, there were 350 public schools in Haiti. This number increased to 730 schools in 1917; the schools, however, served a mere 11 percent of the country's school-age children. The 1940s saw some expansion of public education. Public schools grew very slowly between 1960 and 1971, a trend that has continued to the present. To compensate, religious communities and private individuals have opened a growing number of schools. Private education represented 20 percent of enrollment in 1959–60 and 57 percent of primary school enrollment in 1979–80. By 1996–97, private schools accounted for more than 75 percent of primary and secondary school enrollment. Therefore, private education is the norm in Haiti today, and public schools cater to less than 10 percent of the school-age population.

More than 67 percent of Haiti's private schools are religious, including 10 percent Roman Catholic and some 59 percent Protestant and nondenominational. There are a number of secular community schools, and a rapidly growing number of schools that operate as commercial enterprises, mostly unlicensed and unmonitored. According to the 1996–97 school census, 42 percent of all primary schools and 64 percent of secondary schools are less than ten years old. An estimated 67 percent of private schools are affiliated with the Haitian Private School Foundation (Fondation Haïtienne d'Enseignement Privé—Fonhep), founded in the late 1980s with support from the United States Agency for International Development.

Access to quality education in Haiti runs parallel to the class-based structure of Haitian society. The best schools serve about 5 percent of total enrollment. These are mostly religious schools in urban areas, such as the venerable Collège St. Louis de Gonzague in Port-au-Prince. The public school system, an increasingly small proportion of all schools, constitutes a middle range in quality. The remaining vast majority of private schools fall into the bottom category, offering poor instruction and limited materials. As a result, the overall quality of education is low.

Parents and families—and most families are poor—bear the primary financial burden of getting an education in Haiti. According to figures from 1996–97, families cover a phenomenal 61 percent of all educational expenditures, compared to 7 percent from the national budget and 32 percent from nongovernmental organizations and large donor agencies.

Classroom, University of Haiti, Faculty of Medicine and Pharmacy,
Port-au-Prince
Partially completed addition to an elementary school
Courtesy Inter-American Development Bank

More than 33 percent of this youthful country is of school age (five to eighteen years); the number is estimated at 2,460,160 for the year 1995. Statistics on enrollment show relatively little evidence of gender discrimination in enrollment; girls make up 48 percent of the enrollment in both primary and secondary schools. Some evidence exists of changing patterns in which families enroll all or nearly all of their children in school rather than sending just one or two as has been reported in the past.

There is a strong urban bias in both the quality of education and in access to schools. Only 23 percent of rural children have access to formal education compared to more than 90 percent of urban children of school age. Furthermore, only 20 percent of educational expenditures goes to rural areas where the vast majority of the population lives. At the secondary school level, 82 percent of schools are located in urban areas and 55 percent of all secondary school enrollment is in the Port-au-Prince area.

For more than a decade, Haiti's protracted political crisis caused sporadic disruption of school operations, especially during the years 1986–88 and 1991–94. Despite this turbulence, school enrollment has grown tremendously overall. Since 1988, primary school enrollment has increased by 39 percent in public schools and 103 percent in private schools. During this same period, secondary school enrollment increased by 198 percent in public schools and 93 percent in private schools; however, only 15 percent of those between the ages of twelve and eighteen were enrolled in school in 1996–97.

This growth in enrollment takes place in a context of high illiteracy and immense demand, especially by the poor majority, who invest heavily in education despite meager resources. Estimates of illiteracy range from 47 to 80 percent. Illiteracy in Haiti is far higher than in other countries in the region, which average 15 percent.

The Ministry of National Education, Youth, and Sports sponsors a program in supplementary education, including literacy training. Most non-formal training in Haiti is offered by nongovernmental organizations and focuses primarily on adult literacy, community organization skills, civic education, public health, and various types of community development.

Primary Schools

The school year begins in October and ends in July, with two-week vacations at Christmas and Easter. Regular primary education consists of six grades, preceded by two years of kindergarten (*enfantin*). Primary education consists of preparatory, elementary, and intermediate cycles, each of which lasts two years. Promotion between grades depends on final examinations and c'ass marks recorded in trimesters. At the end of the sixth year, students who pass final examinations receive a graduation certificate (*certificat d'études primaires*). After receiving the certificate, students can take examinations for entry into either secondary school (seven-year cycle) or higher-primary school (three-year cycle).

The Ministry of National Education, Youth, and Sports estimates that 64 percent of primary school-age children (six to twelve years old) were enrolled in school in 1996–97, compared to 25 percent in 1971 (ages six to eleven) and 40 percent in 1982. These figures show rapid expansion; however, Haiti still has the lowest rate of primary-school enrollment in the hemisphere. The Ministry of Education estimates a total enrollment of 1,429,280 primary-school students in 1996–97.

According to the National Education Plan, 43 percent of students entering first grade reach fifth grade, and only 38 out of 1,000 children who enter first grade finish secondary school. The overall dropout rate is 17 percent in primary schools and 10 percent in secondary schools. There is a high proportion of overage students, including 75 percent of primary school students, 80 percent of public secondary school, and 90 percent of private secondary school students.

Statistics from 1996–97 report 9,528 primary schools in Haiti and 41,170 primary school teachers (see table 17, Appendix). Private school teachers are generally less qualified than public school teachers. About 33 percent of public school teachers have diplomas from teacher training colleges, but only 5 percent of private school teachers hold such credentials. The tremendous growth of private schools has broadened general access to schooling, but the quality of this expanded education is generally poor. In addition to primary schools, in 1996–97 Haiti had 409 public preschools and 4,949 private preschools (see table 18, Appendix).

Secondary Schools

General secondary education consists of a three-year basic cycle and a four-year upper cycle that leads to a baccalaureate (*baccalauréat*) certificate and possible university matriculation.

The curriculum emphasizes the classics and the arts to the detriment of the sciences. Despite these limitations, general secondary education is often of high quality. Secondary-school graduates usually qualify for admission to the University of Haiti or institutions of higher learning abroad.

In 1996–97, approximately 15 percent of twelve- to eighteen-year-olds, some 327,980 students, attended 1,170 secondary schools. In addition to general secondary schools, several vocational and business schools exist, most of them in metropolitan Port-au-Prince.

Higher Education

Unlike primary and secondary school, enrollment at the university level is primarily in public schools. Haiti's most important institution of higher education is the University of Haiti. Its origin dates to the 1820s, when colleges of medicine and law were established. In 1942 the various faculties merged into the University of Haiti. Enrollment at the state university has more than doubled since the early 1980s. In 1994–95 there were close to 10,000 students at the University of Haiti. About 25 percent of university students were enrolled in the Faculty of Law and Economics; 33 percent at the National Institute of Administration, Management, and International Studies; and the remainder in agriculture, education, ethnology, applied linguistics, medicine, pharmacy, science, and human sciences. Most professors work part-time, teach several courses at different institutions, and are paid on an hourly basis, leaving little time available for broader contact with students. The University of Haiti is an urban system dispersed into a number of small facilities. It has chronic shortages of books, equipment, and materials.

Since the 1980s, a new trend has developed in higher education, the establishment of small, private, multidisciplinary institutions. Such institutions include the Université Quisqueya in Port-au-Prince with 1,100 students (1995) and the Haitian Adventist University (Université Adventiste d'Haïti) with 500 students (1995). Several other smaller institutions have a combined enrollment under 1,300 (1995), including the Caribbean University (Université Caraïbe), American University of the Caribbean, Haitian Southern Baptist Evangelical Mission University (Université Mission Evangélique Baptiste du Sud d'Haïti), the University of King Christophe (Université du Roi Christophe) (Cap-Haïtien), and the Jean Price Mars University

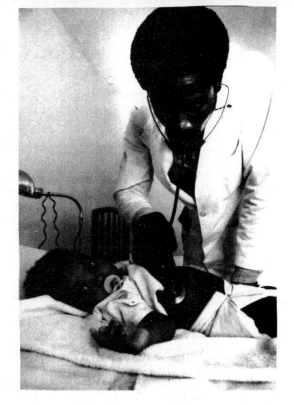

Doctor examining infant,
Miragoâne
Courtesy Inter-American
Development Bank

(Université Jean Price Mars). In addition, Haiti has seven private law schools located in provincial towns, including Gonaïves, Les Cayes, Jacmel, Hinche, Fort Liberté, Saint-Marc, and Cap-Haïtien. Total enrollment in law schools in secondary cities is estimated to be around 800 students, including the Law School of Gonaïves with an enrollment of 524 in 1995. Ten small private schools offer training in engineering, and more than two dozen offer specialized training in religion (Catholic and Protestant seminaries), business and commerce, journalism and communications, medical programs, and education.

Health

Fertility and Family Planning

In view of intense population pressure, fertility and family planning are critical issues in Haiti. In the 1990s, studies show an overall decline in Haiti's fertility rate since the 1960s despite rising rates reported for the 1980s. The total fertility rate in 1996 was 4.8 percent—far higher than the regional average of 2.8 percent. In rural Haiti, the rate of fertility is 5.9 children per woman compared to 3.0 in Port-au-Prince. Studies show a strong correlation among urban residence, literacy, and declining fertility. The reduced fertility rate in urban areas is closely tied to a lower rate of marital unions for urban women, and double the rate of unstable unions for urban women compared to rural women.

Rates of contraceptive use are up since the late 1980s. In the mid-1990s, reported rates of contraceptive use were 13 percent for women and 17 percent for men. Rates of contraceptive use are higher in urban than rural areas. Studies suggest that the demand for family planning services exceeds available programs and that many women lack access to modern contraceptives and birth-control information.

Nutrition and Disease

According to mid-1980s surveys, average daily nutritional consumption was estimated to be 1,788 calories per person, 80 percent of the FAO daily minimum requirements. An estimated 50 percent of Haitians consume less than 75 percent of recommended caloric intake. Cereals and vegetables supply more than 50 percent of food energy, and meat and dairy products supply about 5 percent. One study found that 25 percent of households had consumed no animal products in the preceding week. Millet and starchy roots are key sources of nutrition in low-income households, and bread is tending to replace other cereal foods in urban areas. Peasant households confronting chronic malnutrition are inclined to adopt agricultural strategies that limit risk and ensure short-term survival rather than long-term well-being. Witness the shift away from cereals into higher production of starchy root crops since 1950. Inadequate nutrition is an important factor in Haitian disease. Anemia, for example, is common among children and women.

Infant and child health is poor. Infant mortality in 1996 was seventy-two per 1,000 live births, about double the regional average. Although comparative data show evidence of a decline in infant mortality in recent decades, almost half of all deaths occur within the first five years. Children ages twelve to twenty-four months are at high risk for malnutrition because of increased vulnerability during weaning. The proportion of one-year-old children who die before reaching age five has increased somewhat since the late 1980s, a period that coincides with severe economic and political crisis.

For children ages one to five, the principal causes of death are diarrheal illnesses (37 percent), malnutrition (32 percent), and acute respiratory illness (25 percent). In this age-group, the mortality rate of children born to women with no education is three times that of children born to women who have completed secondary school. Smaller family size and wider spacing between children correlate with lower child mortality rates.

Acute respiratory infections and diarrheal diseases are the most common illnesses treated at primary health care clinics. Other serious diseases are bronchopneumonia, malaria, syphilis, tetanus, typhoid, tuberculosis, parasitic diseases, meningococcemia, measles, and xerophthalmia. In addition to malnutrition, poor sanitation is a key contributor to poor health indicators. Investment in this area has not kept pace with urban growth. Access to safe water declined in the mid-1990s, going from 60 percent in 1985 to less than 30 percent of urban residents and 25 percent of rural residents. In 1984 less than 20 percent of the population had toilets or latrines. In the 1980s and 1990s, violence has been a major public health problem, especially political violence.

The earliest cases of Kaposi's sarcoma in Haiti, later identified as AIDS (acquired immune deficiency syndrome), were diagnosed in Port-au-Prince in 1979 and the early 1980s. In response, Haitian physicians and scientists formed the Haitian Study Group on Kaposi's Sarcoma and Opportunistic Infections in 1982. Review of the evidence suggests that the virus was then new to Haiti, and that the emergent Haitian epidemic was closely related to an earlier North American epidemic of AIDS. In its early stages, the Haitian epidemic affected men more than women, and tended to be correlated with prostitution and contact with non-Haitians or returned Haitians.

The total number of confirmed cases of AIDS in Haiti is unknown at present because there has been no systematic reporting of AIDS diagnosis since 1992. Human immunodeficiency virus (HIV) studies were carried out in rural and urban zones in 1986 and 1992. Some monitoring of Red Cross blood transfusion centers has occurred. The Centers for Disease Control (CDC) studied the incidence of HIV among Haitian refugees at Guantanamo in 1992. In the absence of systematic study of the broader population of Haiti, the best data on the incidence of HIV and AIDS stem from studies of pregnant women. Such data have been used as the basis for broader population projections.

According to projections for the year 2000, the national incidence of HIV is estimated at 5.4 percent to 7.7 percent (260,000 to 365,000 people), or 8.4 to 12 percent HIV positive in urban areas and 4.1 to 5.8 percent HIV positive in rural areas. The ratio of males to females with AIDS has shifted over time from five to one in 1982 to one to one in the late 1990s. Some 30 percent of children born to infected women contract the virus. AIDS is having a significant impact on the life expectancy of Haitians, estimated at 47.4 to fifty-one years as opposed to sixty-one years without the AIDS effect. Deaths resulting from AIDS are estimated at 125 persons per day. Cumulative deaths from AIDS may rise to 1 million by the year 2010. According to current estimates, Haiti has between 163,000 and 235,000 AIDS orphans. Tuberculosis is the primary cause of death for people who test positive for HIV; 40 to 50 percent of people who are HIV positive also have tuberculosis.

Health Services

Modern health services in Haiti are inadequate, mostly private, and largely urban. Some 660 facilities provide the nation's health services, including public facilities (30 percent), private nonprofit (30 percent), mixed public/private (30 percent), and for-profit facilities (10 percent) (see table 19, Appendix). Nongovernmental organizations provide about 70 percent of the health services in rural areas. There are some 400 dispensaries, 140 health centers providing outpatient services, sixty health centers with beds, and fifty departmental and national hospitals. Since the late 1980s, per capita spending on public health has dropped 50 percent.

In 1994 the country had 773 physicians, 785 nurses, and 1,844 auxiliary nurses; Haiti had a ratio of 1.6 physicians, 1.3 nurses, and 0.4 dentists for every 10,000 inhabitants. Health services are strongly concentrated in the area of the capital. About 52 percent of hospital beds, 73 percent of physicians, and 67 percent of the nation's nurses are concentrated in the region of the capital city. An estimated 50 percent of the population is served by modern health-care facilities. Some 80 percent of women give birth at home. Vaccination coverage affects about 25 percent of the population.

The majority of people use traditional religious practices and healers to diagnose and treat illness. Herbal medicine is widely used, especially in rural areas, although environmental deterioration has made some herbs more difficult to obtain. In addition to home remedies, herbal specialists (*doktè fey*) provide massage and remedies. Many voodoo specialists and diviners (*houngan*) are also experts in herbal remedies. An estimated 11,000 traditional midwives attend most rural births. Some midwives receive training in modern methods from public and private community health programs. Home remedies and traditional healers provide important services in the absence of modern medical facilities for the majority of rural people.

Welfare

Social security and welfare services are very limited. The government provides pensions to some retired public officials, but there are no guaranteed pensions for civil servants. A social-insurance system for employees of industrial, commercial, and agricultural firms provides pensions at age fifty-five after twenty years of service and compensation for total incapacity after fifteen years of service. A system of work-injury benefits also covers private and public employees for partial or total disability. The Ministry of Social Affairs administers these programs.

The dearth of government social programs forces most Haitians to rely on their families. Individuals without kin or land in rural areas are truly destitute. A large number of international donors and nongovernmental organizations provide public goods and services in the absence of state services. In general, Haitians cultivate personalized networks of kinship and other traditional ties and obligations in order to cope with hardship, scarcity, and the limited availability of public services.

*   *   *

Classic works on Haiti in English include James G. Leyburn's *The Haitian People*, an excellent social history, especially the 1966 edition with a forward by anthropologist Sidney Mintz; *Life in a Haitian Valley* by Melville J. Herskovits, detailing the life of peasants and townspeople in the 1930s; Harold Courlander's interesting study of Haitian folklore in *The Drum and the Hoe: Life and Lore of the Haitian People*; Alfred Métraux's landmark study, *Voodoo in Haiti*; and the pioneering work of Haitian ethnologist Jean Price-Mars, *Thus Spoke the Uncle (Ainsi parla l'oncle)*, which appeared in 1928 and was published in English in 1983.

The work of David Nicholls, *From Dessalines to Duvalier: Race, Colour, and National Independence in Haiti*, is an insightful history of Haitian political and social ideologies since the early nineteenth century. The volume of essays edited by Charles R. Foster and Albert Valdman, *Haiti—Today and Tomorrow: An Interdisciplinary Study*, continues to be a useful source for various aspects of Haitian society especially the sections devoted to cultural perspectives, language and education, and rural development. Mats Lundahls's *Peasants and Poverty: A Study of Haiti* is an important general work that views Haitian economic decline in terms of overpopulation, environmental degradation, and government passivity. Simon Fass's *Political Economy in Haiti: The Drama of Survival* is the first detailed examination of the urban lower class and remains current.

In the 1990s, several authors have treated contemporary themes. Some examples are physician-anthropologist Paul Farmer, who wrote a social analysis of acquired immune deficiency syndrome, *AIDS and Accusation: Haiti and the Geography of Blame*; Alex Dupuy's *Haiti in the World Economy: Class, Race, and Underdevelopment since 1700*; former United States Ambassador Ernest H. Preeg's *The Haitian Dilemma: A Case Study in Demographics, Development, and U.S. Foreign Policy*; and the treatment of Haitian migration and poverty by Anthony Catanese in *Haitians: Migration and Diaspora*.

Recent works also include medical anthropologist Paul Brodwin's *Medicine and Morality in Haiti: The Contest for Healing Power*, examining the role of Haitian religion in defining strategies for dealing with sickness and healing; a theological treatment of Haiti's popular religion by Leslie Desmangles, *The Faces of the Gods: Vodoun and Roman Catholicism in Haiti*; a collection of articles on Haitian religion and artistic expression, *The Sacred Arts of Haitian Vodou*, edited by Donald Consentino; and a literary treatment of Haitian history and religion, *Haiti, History, and the Gods*, by Joan Dayan.

The best synthesis of information on the Haitian natural environment is still the *Haiti Country Environmental Profile: A Field Study* prepared by Marko Ehrlich and other authors for the United States Agency for International Development. Joel Timyan's recent *Bwa Yo: Important Trees of Haiti* amasses a considerable amount of information on useful tree species of Haiti. The World Bank has published a series of technical papers with current information on Haitian poverty, health, education, and governance, *Haiti: The Challenges of Poverty*

Reduction. (For further information and complete citations, see Bibliography.)

Chapter 8. Haiti: The Economy

Figure from a painting by Prospèr Pierrelouis

ONLY ONE YEAR AFTER Christopher Columbus landed on Hispaniola in 1492, the Spanish established themselves as the dominant European colonial presence on the Caribbean island. With the decline of Spain as a colonial power in the late seventeenth century, however, the French moved in and started their colonization of the western part of Hispaniola, sustaining themselves by curing the meat and tanning the hides of wild game. What is now known as Haiti was used by French buccaneers to harass British and Spanish ships until Spain ceded the western third of the mountainous island to France and agreed to the borders delineated by the Treaty of Ryswick in 1697.

As piracy was gradually suppressed, more and more Frenchmen became planters and made Saint-Domingue—as the French portion of the island was called then—one of the richest colonies of the eighteenth-century French empire. Another factor contributing to this success was the large number of African slaves being imported to work the sugarcane and coffee plantations. But it was this same slave population, led by Toussaint Louverture (also seen as L'Ouverture), Jean-Jacques Dessalines, and Henry Christophe, that revolted in 1791 and gained control of the northern part of Saint-Domingue.

After a bloody, twelve-year rebellion by descendants of African slaves, Haiti became the world's first independent black republic on January 1, 1804. It is also the second oldest republic in the Western Hemisphere, after the United States. It occupies an area about the size of Maryland—27,750 square kilometers—with a population variously estimated at between 7 and 8 million. The World Bank (see Glossary) estimated in mid-1997 that approximately 80 percent of the rural population lives below the poverty level. The majority of these people do not have ready access to safe drinking water, adequate medical care, or sufficient food. With a gross domestic product (GDP—see Glossary) per capita of US$225, in the late 1990s Haiti had the dubious distinction of being the poorest country in the Western Hemisphere and the fourteenth poorest nation in the world.

Stages of Development

The Haitian Revolution (1791–1803) devastated agricultural

output. The leadership of the new nation faced the daunting task of reviving economic activity without relying on slavery. After the 1806 assassination of Haiti's first national leader, Jean-Jacques Dessalines, Haiti operated under a dual economy, with forced labor on large plantations in the north and small-scale farming in partitioned land in the south. The 1820 unification of the nation entailed the abandonment of plantation agriculture and the establishment of a peasant-based agricultural economy. Although policies of land redistribution and limited social and economic reform improved the lives of the former slaves, the policies also produced a severe and ultimately irreversible decline in agricultural production.

Haiti's slave-based plantation economy, which had made the island France's most lucrative overseas possession, with thousands of profitable large plantations producing massive amounts of sugar, coffee, and cotton, was badly shattered by the dismantling of the large estates. The products produced on these estates accounted for almost 65 percent of French commercial interests abroad and about 40 percent of foreign trade. They also accounted for 60 percent of the world's coffee and 40 percent of the sugar imported by Britain and France. The sharp decline in economic productivity was largely caused by the fact that small landholders lacked the motivation to produce export crops instead of subsistence crops. Although coffee dominated agriculture in the south because of its relative ease of cultivation, the level of production was too low to generate worthwhile quantities of exports. Sugar production, which was primarily in the north, also dropped off, and when sugar was no longer exported in substantial quantities, the cultivation of cane ceased and sugar mills were closed.

Despite the lowered productivity, this system lasted until plantation agriculture was replaced by a peasant-based agriculture economy. The shift took place after the rival regimes of Henry Christophe's kingdom north of the Artibonite River and Alexandre Pétion's republic in the south were unified in 1820 (see Early Years of Independence, 1804–43, ch. 6). Land redistribution policies and limited social and economic reform improved the lot of the peasantry, but these same policies also resulted in a severe and irreversible decline in agricultural production.

In 1825 Haiti's economy was crippled when its leaders agreed to pay France a staggering indemnity of 150 million francs in exchange for recognition. United States recognition occurred in 1862 during the American Civil War. Meanwhile, social conditions deteriorated seriously, and heightened conflicts between the black majority and the ruling mulattoes produced severe economic disorders and alarming political instability. The ensuing government chaos and the steady decline of the economy led to gradual involvement in Haiti's affairs by European and United States interests. In 1915, concerned about European—especially German—economic competition and political rivalry in the Caribbean, the United States used the opportunity of an internal crisis and numerous government changes during a particularly unstable period of Haiti's history to intervene militarily and occupy the Caribbean island nation. The immediate pretext for the intervention was the execution on July 27 of more than 150 political prisoners, provoking an angry mob to parade the dismembered corpse of the president through the streets of Port-au-Prince. This shocking spectacle prompted the United States to land military forces in Haiti's capital exactly one day later, on July 28, 1915 (see United States Involvement in Haiti, 1915–34, ch. 6).

The nineteen-year occupation ended in 1934, when United States forces were withdrawn at the request of the elected government of Haiti. That the occupation's impact was of a lasting—and significant—nature, was evidenced by the fact that within only six weeks of the landing, Marine Corps commanders were serving as administrators in the provinces. Civilian United States representatives also were in control of Haitian customs and other administrative institutions. However, United States occupation forces aroused sharp resistance and strong nationalist sentiments among black intellectuals, who resented the entrenchment of the mulatto minority in power by what they perceived to be United States connivance.

On the government-to-government front, nevertheless, a treaty passed by the Haitian legislature in November 1915 gave the United States authority to appoint financial advisers and receivers and to run the country's public works and public health programs. Among the positive economic aspects of the occupation were major infrastructure projects carried out by United States forces, occasionally employing forced labor. The forces concentrated on constructing hospitals, schools, roads, bridges, wharves, and lighthouses, and creating clean water facilities and telephone systems. United States financial advisers and receivers also managed to keep Haiti current on its foreign debt payments at a time when default by other borrowers was common. The administration of the country's fiscal and monetary policies was considered such a success that United States economic advisers continued to manage the national treasury for seven years after the withdrawal of United States troops.

Haiti's mulatto ruling class made a special effort during the following decade to strengthen its position: a new professional military establishment was created and dominated by mulatto officers, and successive governments were run almost totally by mulatto ministers. The mulattoes' entrenchment in power, however, ended in 1946, when president Elie Lescot (1941–45) was overthrown by Dumarsais Estimé (1946–50), a black leader who resented the stranglehold of the mulatto minority on the economy and who aroused nationalist and leftist sentiments among disaffected black intellectuals. The brief hold on power of Estimé and his liberal trade unions was terminated by a military coup on May 10, 1950, amid deteriorating domestic conditions.

The same junta that had taken over from Lescot reinstated itself, and one of its members, Paul E. Magloire, won the country's first direct elections and assumed office in December. He managed to make some infrastructure improvements and to establish a good working relationship with the business community, while allowing labor unions to function. But when he tried to dispute the termination date of his presidential term in 1956, labor leaders and thousands of other Haitians took to the streets and forced him to flee to Jamaica, leaving the task of restoring order to the army.

In 1957, a year of turmoil in Haiti's history during which six different governments held power, another black nationalist and a former labor minister in Estimé's cabinet, François Duvalier, was elected president. One of his declared objectives was to undermine the mulattoes' political influence and limit their economic dominance. A small black middle class emerged, but the country suffered from economic stagnation, domestic political tension, and severe repression under Duvalier. After a seven-year period of dynastic rule, Duvalier extended his tenure in office by amending the constitution in 1964 and declaring himself president for life. All economic and military assistance from the United States was suspended in 1963 after Duvalier expelled the United States ambassador. Aid was not resumed until 1973.

Shortly before his death in April 1971, Duvalier bequeathed power to his nineteen-year-old son, Jean-Claude, also making him president for life. "Baby Doc" continued many of his father's economic development policies. Although these projects were intended in most instances to contribute to his personal enrichment, the country experienced a brief period of economic recovery. But Jean-Claude ultimately failed to provide the leadership necessary for Haiti's sustained development. The country was precipitously plunged into economic stagnation, with famine spreading in rural areas and thousands of "boat people" fleeing to the United States. As popular demands for reform aimed at alleviating the suffering of the vast majority of the population living in poverty were ignored by the government, public discontent kept mounting until the first antigovernment riots in twenty years broke out, and food warehouses were looted. The ensuing and heightened civil disorder, which lasted for months without letup, finally forced Jean-Claude Duvalier into exile in France (arranged by the United States) on February 7, 1986.

Political turmoil following the demise of the twenty-nine-year dictatorship of the Duvaliers caused the economy to decline sharply, with devastating effects on the poorest segments of the population. A constitution providing for an elected two-chamber parliament, as well as an elected president and prime minister, was adopted in 1987. But when Duvalierist gangs attacked polling stations on election day, November 29, the election was canceled. Most major aid donors, including France, Canada, and the United States, suspended their assistance and investment programs in protest. The United States and the Organization of American States (OAS) brought pressure for another election, which occurred in 1988, and resulted in the election of Leslie Manigat, a professor. Manigat, who had been elected in a low turnout, was overthrown four months later, and during the next two years, a series of military leaders played musical chairs.

In elections held in December 1990, a Roman Catholic priest and long-time opponent of the Duvalier regimes, Jean-Bertrand Aristide, won 67 percent of the vote (see Aristide Presidency, February 7, 1991–September 30, 1991, ch. 6). The installation of Haiti's first freely elected president on February 7, 1991, prompted a group of Western countries to promise more than US$400 million in aid. Aristide responded by initiating a reform program aimed at collecting more taxes and reducing inflation, corruption, and smuggling. When he was overthrown by dissatisfied elements of the military only seven months later, on September 30, 1991, he left his homeland first for Venezuela, then for the United States. Almost immediately upon his departure, Haiti's foreign assets were frozen and an international trade embargo was imposed on all items, with the exception of basic food and medical supplies.

The impact of the trade embargo on the country's economy was very severe. More than 100,000 jobs were lost. Starvation spread through most rural areas and into provincial towns. The flight of approximately 300,000 people from Port-au-Prince to the countryside worsened poverty and health conditions. Thousands of boat people managed to flee the country. Smuggling and evasion of sanctions continued to increase to an alarming degree.

From October 1991 to October 1994, Haiti was ruled by a succession of military-backed regimes of which Raoul Cédras was the principal figure (see Military Coup Overthrows Aristide, October 1991–October 1994, ch. 6). They perpetuated repression and terror, tolerated human rights violations, and sanctioned widespread assassinations in open defiance of the international community's condemnation. The international embargo and suspension of most external aid caused inflation to rise from 15 percent to 50 percent. A dramatic drop in exports and investment also took a toll on the country's industrial productivity and further damaged its already weak infrastructure.

Economic Policies

At the time of the military coup in 1991, Haiti's per capita GDP had fallen steadily by 2 percent a year since 1980. The country's economic stagnation was caused by permissive policies that tolerated massive corruption and inefficiency in the public sector, and by social polarization, mismanagement, and total neglect of human resources. From 1991 to 1994, real GDP fell 30 percent and per capita GDP dropped from US$320 to US$260.

Aristide's return to power on October 15, 1994, after a complex process that included threats of military intervention by the United States and a coalition of multinational forces, raised the hope of economic revival. With the situation gradually stabilizing, a conference of international donors held in Paris in August 1994 produced approximately US$2 billion—including

US$425 million from the United States—in pledges of assistance by 1999 in exchange for a commitment from the Haitian government to adhere to a program of economic reform, trade/tariff liberalization, privatization, macroeconomic stabilization, and decentralization. But implementation of these programs was slowed down by parliamentary bickering, opposition to structural reform, and public dissatisfaction with the lack of progress in the stagnating economy. Negotiating an International Monetary Fund (IMF—see Glossary) offer of US$1 billion in aid, with stringent conditions relating to structural adjustment and privatization of nine major state enterprises, proved to be tortuous. Other attempts at economic and social reform, such as implementing an increase in the minimum wage, also proved to be futile.

Faced with popular demonstrations against the controversial concept of privatization while he was trying to tackle the daunting challenge of rebuilding his country's crumbling physical infrastructure, Aristide decided in October 1995 not to proceed with the privatization of a state-owned cement plant and a flour mill. As a result, no further progress on privatization was possible during his term. Moreover, lack of commitment to civil service reform and other structural reforms tied to loans from the World Bank and IMF derailed the signing of two credit agreements with those international organizations and prompted Aristide's prime minister to resign in October 1995.

Structural Policy

When President René Garcia Préval took office in February 1996, he vowed to implement the structural adjustment program that had been suggested to Aristide. His government initiated a program to reduce expenditures and eliminate thousands of civil service jobs occupied by "ghost employees." Another acute problem was the huge budget deficit caused by central government support for inefficient state-owned enterprises and a bloated public sector in general. Parliament eventually enacted economic reform legislation authorizing the executive branch to proceed with privatization. The new legislation allowed the granting of management contracts for forming joint ventures with private investors through partial divestiture of state-owned enterprises.

The government also put in motion an Emergency Economic Recovery Plan (EERP) whose main objective was to achieve rapid macroeconomic stabilization and to attend to the

most pressing needs in health, nutrition, sanitation, and infrastructure. A medium-term strategy to address the country's
urgent needs for rehabilitation and economic development
also was supported by an IMF stand-by agreement. Economic
performance improved significantly under the EERP: real GDP
grew by 4.5 percent in fiscal year (FY—see Glossary) 1994–95
and the twelve-month rate of consumer price increases
declined to 30 percent from 40 percent in FY 1993–94. In spite
of a stronger than projected revenue performance, however,
the government deficit for FY 1994–95 was higher than contemplated. The deficit may have resulted, however, from
higher expenditures on a job-training program and larger than
anticipated wage adjustments in the priority Ministry of Public
Health and Population and Ministry of National Education,
Youth, and Sports. As the government started to improve its
historically poor record of tax collection and exercise better
control over expenditures, it also managed to meet IMF
requirements to sign an Enhanced Structural Adjustment Facility (ESAF) agreement in October 1996.

The government's role in the country's market-oriented
economy has been sharply reduced since 1987, when government attempts to control prices or supplies were undercut by
contraband or overwhelmed by the great number of retailers.
Even when the government sets prices for such basic items as
flour and cement, consumer prices are governed by supply and
demand. Gasoline prices and utility rates, which are more
effectively regulated, are the exception to the rule—perhaps
because gasoline prices are required by law to be adjusted to
reflect changes in world petroleum prices and exchange rate
movements.

Because Haiti's tax system is inefficient, direct taxes amount
to only about 13 percent of government receipts. Tax evasion is
so rampant and so few taxpayers are registered with the tax
bureau (Direction Générale des Impôts—DGI) that the government has made improved revenue collection a top priority.
The DGI has a large taxpayers' unit that focuses on identifying
and collecting the tax liabilities of the 200 largest taxpayers in
the Port-au-Prince area, which are estimated to account for
more than 80 percent of potential income tax revenue. Efforts
are also being made to identify and register other taxpayers. In
addition, the value-added tax has been extended to include
sectors previously exempt, such as banking services, agribusiness, and the supply of water and electricity. Collection remains

weak and inefficient, and the DGI is frequently forced to physically collect payments.

Otherwise, the role of the government in the economy continues to be minimal. There are few government subsidies, and goods are traded at market prices. Indeed, the government has made a special effort to reduce tariff and nontariff barriers and has reiterated its commitment to further trade liberalization. During the three years of the international embargo following the military coup of 1991, the country's imports dropped from US$449 million to US$141 million, declining more than 65 percent in 1994 alone. By the late 1990s, the government had eliminated many of the steps formerly involved in importing goods and simplified the import process to such an extent that more than 70 percent of all goods on the Haitian market were imported. Pent-up demand also may have contributed to the steady rise in imports.

Inducing private-sector participation in state-owned enterprises was another policy issue the government had to tackle. A presidential commission of seven government officials and fifteen private-sector representatives was established in 1994 to recommend measures for "modernization of the economic and financial infrastructure" of the country. The law on the modernization of public enterprises, as proposed by the Council for the Modernization of Public Enterprises (Conseil de Modernisation des Entreprises Publiques—CMEP), prompted the government in 1997 to target nine of Haiti's inefficient parastatals for privatization, including the telephone company (Télécommunications d'Haïti—Teleco), electric company (Électricité d'Haïti—EdH), airport authority, and two commercial banks.

The original aim was to complete the privatization process by March 1998. However, by mid-1998, even such a small company as Cimenterie d'Haïti, which was to be one of the first to be privatized, had not been sold. Claims by about 42,000 state employees and some members of the governing Lavalas coalition that the government's plan was tantamount to "putting the country up for sale" seemed to send another signal to slow down implementation of the privatization process.

In mid-1999, hundreds of striking longshoremen shut down the Haitian capital's port for three days running in protest against the government's plan to put the port authority up for sale by the end of 1999. They also accused the port director of mismanagement and demanded an audit of his accounts. The airport union membership, who feared they would lose their jobs, accused the airport authority director of incompetence and demanded his resignation. Most of the street demonstrations that followed, which involved setting fire to tire barricades—and cost millions of dollars in lost business and customs duties—were led by supporters of former President Aristide, who reportedly remains opposed to the government's privatization program.

Despite these protests, Prime Minister Jacques Édouard Alexis decided in mid-1999 to resume the privatization process after a two-year hiatus. He transferred majority ownership of the Cimenterie d'Haïti to private hands for US$15 million. The cement company was the second enterprise to be privatized. The first was La Minoterie flour mill, which was turned over to private ownership in September 1997. It had been closed, and hundreds of its workers, who were not hired back when it reopened, blocked the entrance to the mill with flaming tires and demanded compensation for their toil and lost income.

Lack of progress on the privatization front was only one of the many concerns of the international community trying to help Haiti. The international community, including the United States, repeatedly voiced impatience with the slow pace of both economic and political reforms. United States displeasure at Haiti's sluggish pace of reform was bluntly expressed by then-Deputy Secretary of the Treasury Larry Summers at the annual meeting of the Inter-American Development Bank in March 1998. Former chairman of the United States National Security Council, Anthony Lake, also visited the island nation several times in 1998, trying to energize Haitian reform efforts. On the congressional side, many Republican members showed no enthusiasm for approving administration requests for more assistance to Haiti. On the contrary, most members strongly criticized the lack of progress on judicial reform, the continuing corruption of the police force, and the increasing amounts of drugs entering the United States through Haiti.

Fiscal Policy

The banks mentioned on the privatization list did not include the Bank of the Republic of Haiti (Banque de la République d'Haïti—BRH), which was founded in 1880 as a public-sector institution and which started functioning as a central bank in 1934, when it became known as the National Republic Bank of Haiti (hereafter Central Bank). The other two state-owned commercial banks are the National Credit

Bank (Banque Nationale de Crédit) and the Haitian People's Bank (Banque Populaire Haïtienne). Other commercial banks operating in Port-au-Prince include two from the United States (Citibank and First National Bank of Boston), one Canadian (Bank of Nova Scotia), and France's National Bank of Paris (Banque Nationale de Paris). After a new banking law issued in 1979 empowered the Central Bank with monetary-management responsibilities, it became involved in controlling credit, setting interest rates, assessing reserve ratios, restraining inflation, and issuing Haiti's national currency, the gourde (G; for value of the gourde—see Glossary).

The gourde has been pegged to the United States dollar since 1919 at the rate of five gourdes to the dollar. The value of this fixed exchange remained strong for decades, fluctuating only with the movement of the dollar. No black market existed for gourdes until the early 1980s, when unusually high inflation and large budget deficits eroded the value of the gourde and brought premiums of up to 25 percent for black-market transactions. The political crises of the early 1990s and the ensuing uncertainty, however, exerted heavy downward pressure on the gourde, despite the Central Bank's efforts to halt the decline. The effects of the international embargo and the sharp drop in government revenues reduced the value of the currency by about 80 percent by 1994. In the year after Aristide's return in October 1994, the gourde fluctuated between G14 and G15.5 to US$1. Although the Central Bank pumped more than US$37 million into the foreign exchange market in 1996, the gourde fell from 15 gourdes to the United States dollar in September of that year to 16.9 gourdes to the United States dollar in August 1997. The effects of the depreciation, together with rising food prices, raised the inflation rate from 15.6 percent in December 1996 to 17.2 percent in July 1997.

In an effort to reduce the rate of inflation and to protect the stability of the gourde without trying to fix the nominal exchange rate, the government decided to embark on a stringent fiscal policy and an aggressive tax collection program. The government took a number of measures relating to the fiscal program for FY 1996–97. To cite one example: an important piece of legislation provided for broadening the base of the sales tax and unifying its rates, reducing tax evasion among larger companies, minimizing the number of tax and customs exemptions, and introducing new mechanisms to help control public expenditures. Although statistical data in Haiti are, in general, of poor quality, there are reliable Central Bank statistics showing that tax revenues rose by 58 percent from G2.25 billion in October 1996 to G3.54 billion in June 1997. (The ESAF agreement signed in October 1996 calls for enacting a new law to strengthen the role and effectiveness of the Haitian Statistical Institute and the Central Bank.)

The constantly diminishing external budgetary support—especially with US$150 million being frozen pending resolution of political squabbles—made the Central Bank resort to a tight monetary policy to counteract the destabilizing effect of fiscal imbalances caused by high-interest bonds issued earlier. The salutary outcome was a 3.8 percent drop in the inflation rate to 11.8 percent by mid-1998 (from 15.6 percent the previous year). The IMF anticipated a further drop to 9 percent in 1999.

Restructuring the country's tax system to increase government revenues and reduce reliance on external aid is only one ingredient in the government's fiscal reform agenda. A second key element is that the growth in current expenditures be consistent with available domestic and external resources and be allocated mainly to priority sector programs. Realizing that the unusually high level of external support for the budget in the immediate post-crisis period of the early 1990s could not be expected to be sustained indefinitely, the government feels that its budgetary savings would need to be increased considerably from their level of -3.4 percent of GDP in FY 1995–96. Third, the country's civil service system needs to be restructured, not only to improve the efficiency of the public administration but also to reduce its burden on the budget. Civil service reform legislation proposing a 16 percent reduction of 7,000 jobs from a total of 42,000 jobs was approved at the end of 1996, but political resistance has stalled implementation. (The IMF estimate of the needed reduction in civil service jobs goes as high as 22 percent: "In FY 1996/97 government employment will be reduced by at least 7,500 persons, plus 3,500 'ghost workers,' from a total of some 50,000 by means of attrition, voluntary separation, and early retirement.") Fourth, public investment, which dropped to negligible levels during the army's three-year rule in the early 1990s, needs to be raised to a level high enough to rebuild the infrastructure and encourage private investment. International financial institution estimates suggest that public investment would need to total about 6 to 7 percent of GDP.

Another problem facing the government in FY 1996–97 was the proliferation over the years of tax and customs duty exemptions given nongovernmental organizations (NGOs) and other humanitarian and religious organizations. Although recognizing the valuable contributions of these organizations in addressing the country's dire social needs, tax authorities have expressed concern about the effect of the many exemptions on their revenue. To ascertain that requests for tax exemption from these organizations are legitimate and that exempt items are not traded commercially, tax authorities have instituted a recertification procedure to ensure that only bona fide organizations are granted exemptions. To ensure the transparency of the process, the Ministry of Economy and Finance has been publishing monthly information on exemptions and the resultant loss of revenue.

Finance

All these revenue-generating programs notwithstanding, as of 1999 Haiti's budget had failed to reverse a historical trend of very large deficits—even after adding external assistance as a source of revenue. As far back as the Duvalier era, public finances were openly used for the benefit of the president and his family and friends, without regard to their negative impact on the economy. In the early 1980s, when Jean-Claude Duvalier expanded public-sector investments in poorly managed flour mills, sugar factories, and oil processing plants, these investment decisions were based mainly on how much they would benefit him and his entourage. Such gross misallocations of public finances had a negative impact on the flow of external assistance, which dropped further after the November 1987 election massacre (see Post-Duvalier Era, 1986–90, ch. 6). As a result, the government was forced to try to curtail deficit spending and to reduce further its meager allocations for economic and social development. But the continuing need to finance large public-sector deficits and to allocate more resources to military spending forced the government to increase its domestic borrowing, thereby adding to the deficit.

The revenue-deficit picture in the 1990s may have been caused by a different set of circumstances, but it did not differ significantly. The budget process remained cumbersome and continued to suffer from poor management and lack of effective controls. Expenditure control procedures were constantly being circumvented through the use of at least 250 discretionary ministerial spending accounts. In addition, the lack of oversight controls in the form of audits and accountability was bound to result in the misappropriation and misallocation of public funds. Although the government had agreed to the IMF structural adjustment program in 1996, Haiti lacked the cash to implement the program. In view of Haiti's bad financial situation, the United States advanced it US$10 million in budget support in 1997. Lack of funding from other foreign sources, as well as rapidly growing public expenditures, added considerably to the budget deficit and compelled Haitian authorities to resort to Central Bank funding. By the end of FY 1995–96, internal debt was G9.2 billion, about 21 percent of GDP.

In early 1996 at the behest of international financial institutions, the Haitian government instituted tight controls over the budget, trying to turn it into a policy instrument. The budget was under the jurisdiction of two different ministries and was not treated as a consolidated central government budget. The Ministry of Economy and Finance was charged with preparing the operational budget, relying on domestic resources. However, investment outlays financed from external sources were not included in the operational budget but rather were the responsibility of the Ministry of Planning and External Cooperation. Hence, in order to verify all expenditures, especially those from the various ministries' discretionary accounts (*comptes courants*), the government introduced strict expenditure control procedures. The verification procedure led to the closing of two-thirds of such accounts. Another policy decision—to freeze for three years the government wage bill calling for pay-scale raises—was designed to divert more funds to higher priority social programs. The government also started to seriously implement a fiscal reform agenda that would further restructure the tax administration system and simplify it in such a way as not only to raise tax revenues substantially but also to reduce reliance on external donors.

In an effort to raise the revenue-to-GDP ratio, the government decided to reduce exemptions from taxes and customs duties. By the end of 1996, the rates of the sales tax (*taxe sur le chiffre d'affaires*—TCA) were unified at 10 percent, and the base of this tax was extended to cover most goods. (According to IMF estimates, TCA-related measures would amount to almost 1 percent of GDP annually.) Other taxes and fees were raised, including airport taxes, car registration fees, and passport fees. The government failed in 1998 to introduce scheduled legislation to tighten the eligibility criteria for fiscal incentives under the investment code. Nor did action occur with regard to initiating a plan to energize provincial revenue collections. The intent was not only to broaden the tax base but also to strengthen public-service delivery in the interior of the country outside Port-au-Prince, which had been long neglected. Strengthening local administrations and expanding public services beyond the capital and a few other major urban areas remained an objective of the government's decentralization efforts. Problems related to relocating personnel to rural areas and scarcity of resources generated locally, however, continued to present almost insurmountable obstacles as late as 1999.

Balance of Payments

Foreign trade as such has not constituted a major factor in the Haitian economy in recent decades. However, foreign trade deficits represent a significant element in Haiti's balance of payments and will be considered in that context here. Haiti has traditionally registered substantial trade deficits, a trend that dates back to the mid-1960s, lasted through the 1980s, and has continued into the late 1990s. The deficits were partially offset by generous remittances from the many Haitians working abroad and by official aid. But such inflows tend to dry up sporadically, as was the case after the 1987 election violence and in the wake of the 1991 military coup and the ensuing international trade embargo. During the three-year embargo, the public deficit was financed mainly by Central Bank credit and the accumulation of arrears. Net Central Bank credit to the public sector rose by an average of 65 percent annually from 1992 to 1994. According to data from the IMF, Haitian exports in 1997 were valued at 1,995 million gourdes, whereas imports cost 10,792 million gourdes, indicating a very unfavorable trade balance (see table 20, Appendix).

Haiti's balance of payments is particularly sensitive to changes in the rate of trade development, import prices, and the rate of export growth—more so than many other countries with similar economic problems. For example, if the country's export growth slows as a result of a decline in a major sector such as the assembly industry, the overall balance of payments would register a significant deficit. Similarly, if the terms of trade deteriorate one year because of lower prices for an export such as coffee and higher petroleum product prices, the overall balance of payments would be weaker. This scenario

played itself out in FY 1995–96 when the terms of trade deteriorated as a result of higher food and oil prices, adversely affecting the balance of payments.

The external current account deficit, which was estimated to
be 19 percent of GDP in FY 1994–95, is projected to drop gradually until it reaches 10 percent of GDP by FY 1999–2000, a rate
below its 1990 level. An anticipated sharp rise in exports from
the light manufacturing assembly sector is expected to push
total export receipts from their level of 4.2 percent of GDP in
FY 1995–96 to 7.6 percent of GDP by FY 1998–99. Following a
reversal of the initial surge related to restocking and rehabilitation needs in the wake of lifting the embargo, imports
increased considerably in FY 1996–97, returning to 1990 levels.

External Debt

Haiti's foreign debt has fluctuated little over the years and
has been relatively manageable, especially when compared to
that of neighboring countries. The country's total external
debt was about US$726 million in 1991, almost US$770 million
in 1993, and US$778 million in 1995 (see table 21, Appendix).
Haiti's sluggish economy may be the reason why most of Haiti's
debt has been in the form of concessional loans—favorable
interest rates and long grace periods. Private loans have
accounted for a negligible percentage of the debt. However,
debt-service payments, as a percentage of exports, have been
rather high and continued to be so in the late 1990s, depending on the performance of the economy.

When Aristide was elected in 1990, most bilateral official
creditors decided to cancel Haiti's debts. But three years after
the military coup, the debt-service payments were so far behind
that arrears to multilateral commercial lenders alone
amounted to more than US$82 million. At the end of 1994,
after the restoration of the legitimate government, the United
States and nine other countries paid off the arrears. In May
1995, Haiti reached a debt rescheduling agreement with its
Paris Club (see Glossary) creditors on concessional terms,
whereby the Paris Club canceled two-thirds of Haiti's debt,
about US$75 million, and rescheduled the other third over
twenty-three years.

Haiti's external debt stood at 34 percent of GDP in FY 1995–
96 and was projected to rise to about 40 percent of GDP in FY
1998–99. However, since most of the debt is to multinational
institutions mainly on concessional terms and future external

Unloading flour, Port-au-Prince harbor
Courtesy Inter-American Development Bank
Section of National Highway Two near Miragoâne
Courtesy Inter-American Development Bank

assistance is expected to be provided as grants or concessional loans, the country's debt-service payments were projected to drop from 26 percent of exports of goods and services in FY 1995–96 to 18 percent in FY 1998–99 and to about 13 percent in FY 1999–2000 (see table 22, Appendix).

Foreign Aid

Haiti's history of chronic political instability, ill-advised economic policy, and constant environmental deterioration, as well as its lack of good arable land, has made it heavily dependent on external assistance. Because the cour.try's economic problems have been caused by a succession of unstable regimes, international assistance has—not surprisingly—paralleled the political situation. Although Haiti had received a considerable amount of development aid until 1991, external contributions dropped dramatically after the September coup of that year, when almost all economic aid ceased, except for limited shipments of humanitarian items (see table 23, Appendix).

The amount of humanitarian assistance rose from a total of US$65 million in 1992 to almost US$110 million for two years running. The United States contribution accounted for 66 percent of the total; the United Nations (UN) and the European Union (EU) provided 13 percent each. Canada contributed about 4 percent, and France provided approximately 2 percent.

After the Aristide administration returned to power in 1994, most donors resumed aid to Haiti; 45 percent of the country's operating budget for 1994–95 came from foreign sources. The World Bank provided an emergency loan of US$400 million. At a meeting held in Paris in January 1995, fourteen countries and nineteen multinational institutions pledged a US$1.2 billion aid package over an eighteen-month period. The international community also promised US$500 million of assistance annually through the year 2000.

Because of its keen interest in shoring up Haiti's fragile stability, the United States has been the largest single bilateral donor, providing US$100 million in aid in FY 1995 and US$135 million in FY 1996. The World Bank, the Inter-American Development Bank (IDB), and the EU are the major multilateral donors. In addition to financial support, United States efforts to strengthen the Haitian economy have included restarting the Peace Corps program in 1996 (the Corps had first entered

Haiti in 1983), and establishing the United States-Haitian Business Development Council and an Overseas Private Investment Corporation commercial loan program.

Haiti's share of the FY 1998 appropriations for the United States Agency for International Development (USAID) totaled US$140 million, consisting of US$72 million in Economic Support Funds, US$26 million in development assistance, and US$42 million in Public Law–480 (see Glossary) food aid. Channeled through NGOs to circumvent public-sector inefficiencies and vagaries, these funds are used to provide humanitarian aid, increase agricultural productivity, promote health projects, strengthen private-sector economic growth, redirect relief efforts toward developmental activities, and help Haiti pay its arrears to international institutions. Humanitarian assistance from NGOs has included food for approximately 1 million Haitians and help in upgrading the planning and management capabilities of the Ministry of Public Health and Population. Over and above sponsoring vaccination programs, the United States has financed basic health services for more than 2 million people.

As the poorest nation in the Western Hemisphere, Haiti has been the recipient of generous economic assistance from numerous multilateral and bilateral development agencies and financial institutions. However, historically, the United States has been the major aid source. United States aid, which began in 1944, three years after the last United States economic advisers of the occupation left Haiti, has, however, been punctuated by interruptions dictated by political developments. Because President John F. Kennedy terminated all but humanitarian aid to the François Duvalier government in 1963, Haiti did not participate in the Alliance for Progress development program for Latin America. United States assistance resumed ten years later during Jean-Claude Duvalier's regime, and it continued until January 1986, a month before the end of the Duvalier era. United States aid was restored in unprecedented amounts three weeks after Duvalier's exile, only to be suspended again when President Ronald Reagan stopped nonhumanitarian aid flows after the electoral violence of November 1987. Development assistance resumed in the late 1980s but was terminated after the 1991 military coup. The United States joined other major donors in resuming aid in 1994, when a constitutional government returned to Haiti.

As the only country that has maintained a resident aid mission in Haiti since the 1970s, the United States has made significant contributions to the country's economy through USAID. USAID's efforts have concentrated on such programs as nutrition, family planning, watershed management, agro-forestry, and improving rural conditions through soil conversion. USAID also has pursued narcotics interdiction, migration control, and political reform. United States assistance between 1982 and 1987 accounted for 35 percent of Haiti's total external aid and 60 percent of its bilateral aid.

USAID was credited in 1982 with setting a new trend of distributing larger amounts of its assistance through NGOs rather than through Haitian ministries. By the late 1980s, other donors followed suit, and more and more humanitarian aid was distributed through a network of NGOs. When Haitian officials complained about lack of coordination among these organizations, USAID financed the creation of the Haitian Association of Voluntary Agencies (HAVA), an umbrella NGO whose function is to coordinate all aspects of humanitarian aid and whose membership exceeds 100. As a result, in the late 1990s most aid continued to be distributed through NGOs.

Labor

Haiti's labor force was estimated to be 2.94 million in 1992, according to the Food and Agriculture Organization (FAO) of the United Nations. About two-thirds of the workers are engaged in agriculture, despite the shift to services and manufacturing over the past several decades. More than two-thirds of Haitians are still not part of the formal economy, however, and continue to live by subsistence farming. Assembly plants, most of which are concentrated in the Port-au-Prince area, provide the bulk of manufacturing employment. Approximately 150,000 manufacturing jobs were lost after the military coup of 1991. Although some thirty plants were reopened after Aristide's return to power in 1994, unemployment in the late 1990s was estimated at between 60 percent and 70 percent, compared with 49 percent in the late 1980s. As with other statistics, unemployment figures vary, depending on the methodologies used in gathering such data.

Figures vary widely as to the numbers of Haitians living and working in the Dominican Republic (see Haitians, ch. 2). Two United States analysts believe there were some 500,000 Haitians and Dominico-Haitians (Dominicans of Haitian ancestry)

Planting beans at Gallette Chambon in the Cul-de-Sac Plain Courtesy Inter-American Development Bank

in the Dominican Republic in 1995. Historically, more than 20,000 Haitians have worked annually in the Dominican sugar-cane fields during the harvesting season, although the number of such workers has decreased in recent years. But in bad times, greater numbers of indigent Haitians travel to the Dominican Republic, imposing a heavy burden on their neighbor's social services. For this reason, periods of political tension between the two countries are occasionally punctuated by calls for more stringent immigration regulations; these occasions usually result in the forced expulsion of many undocumented Haitians from the Dominican Republic. Most of those expelled manage to return fairly quickly, however, mainly because of the lack of adequate controls on both sides of the border.

In fairness it should be noted that the Haitian community resident in the Dominican Republic makes significant contri-butions to the Dominican economy by performing many menial jobs that the average Dominican worker tends to shun. Indeed, the ambivalence of Dominicans toward their Haitian neighbors is seen in the stance of some senators representing Dominican frontier provinces who have expressed concern over a possible avalanche of illegal Haitian immigration (trig-gered by dire socioeconomic conditions); they have called on the international community to promote social and economic development in Haiti instead of concentrating only on institu-tionalizing democratic rule. Other Dominicans have gone so far as to suggest that their country might be wise to encourage more Dominican investment in Haiti. After all, the Dominican Republic's exports to Haiti exceed US$30 million a year, while its imports from Haiti fall short of US$1 million; moreover, Haiti buys 77 percent of all Dominican exports to the Carib-bean.

Haiti established a labor code in 1961, but revised it in 1984 to bring legislation more in line with standards set by the Inter-national Labour Organisation (ILO). Conformity with ILO guidelines was a prerequisite for certification under the Carib-bean Basin Initiative (CBI—see Glossary) enacted by the United States Congress in 1983. The country's most fundamen-tal labor law, the minimum wage, is the most controversial. Low wage rates have attracted foreign assembly operations. In 1989 the average minimum wage stood at the equivalent of US$3 a day, with small variations for different types of assembly work. The minimum wage in the late 1980s was below the 1970 level in real terms, but assembly manufacturers and government officials refused to increase wages because they needed to remain competitive with other Caribbean countries. Although labor laws include an array of provisions protecting workers, the government does not enforce many of these provisions.

Haiti's constitution and its labor code guarantee the right of association and provide workers the right to form unions without prior government authorization. However, the law requires unions to register with the Ministry of Social Affairs within sixty days of their formation. Six labor federations represent about 5 percent of the total work force. The labor code protects trade union organizing activities and stipulates fines for those who interfere with this right. Organized labor activity is concentrated in the Port-au-Prince area, in state-owned public enterprises, the civil service, and the assembly sector. The high unemployment rate and anti-union sentiment among some factory workers have limited the success of union organizing efforts, however. Collective bargaining is nearly nonexistent, especially in the private sector, where employers can generally set wages unilaterally.

The minimum employment age in all sectors is fifteen years; fierce adult competition for jobs ensures that child labor is not a factor in the industrial sector. However, as in other developing countries, rural families in Haiti often rely on their children's contribution of labor to subsistence agriculture, and in urban environments children under the age of fifteen usually work at informal-sector jobs to supplement family income. Despite the labor code's prohibition of forced or compulsory labor, some children continue to be subjected to unremunerated labor as domestic servants. This situation appears to be true primarily for rural families. Because such families are often too large for adult members to support all family members, children are sometimes sent to work at informal-sector jobs to supplement family income. The ILO has criticized as inadequate the Ministry of Social Affairs' enforcement of child labor laws.

Agriculture

Much of Haiti's countryside is mountainous, and its soil fertility is low, mostly because of erosion and drought but partly because of population density. Perhaps 28 percent of the land is considered arable, but population pressure puts 48 percent of it under cultivation, mostly in small plots. Of a total arable area estimated at 771,500 hectares, about 142,000 hectares are deemed suitable for irrigation, but only some 40,000 hectares are served by irrigation systems. Indeed, irrigation is rare, except in the main valley, the Artibonite, and the Port-au-Prince and Les Cayes plains in the southwest.

Nevertheless, agriculture remains the mainstay of the economy and continues to account for two-thirds of the total work force, followed by commerce and manufacturing. The significance of the agricultural sector in the 1980s and 1990s differed, however, from that in the 1950s, when it employed 80 percent of the labor force, represented 50 percent of GDP, and contributed 90 percent of exports. Agriculture in the mid-1980s accounted for 35 percent of GDP and for 24 percent of exports, compared with about 30 percent of GDP and less than 10 percent of exports in the late 1990s. In the late 1990s, the sector barely produced 20 percent of the country's domestic food requirements. The constantly deteriorating rural infrastructure, continuing fragmentation of land holdings, primitive farming techniques, migration out of rural areas, insecure land tenure, and deforestation as well as other ecological and natural disasters are among the problems that have taken a toll on the sector. Population pressure also has caused a shift from the production of cash crops such as coffee and sugar to the production of food crops such as rice and beans. Nevertheless, food production has not kept pace with the increase in population, and the situation has resulted in higher food-importing bills. Malnutrition is another problem facing the country. Malnutrition was so widespread in 1994 that relief organizations were feeding about 700,000 people daily.

The agriculture sector suffered a more devastating blow than originally thought when Hurricane Georges hit the island on September 22–23, 1998. The government estimated the number of deaths at no fewer than 400 and the cost of damage at more than US$300 million. Most of the losses were incurred through the destruction of crops and the indirect damage to supporting infrastructure, with the main problem being flooding in flat and low-lying areas. Irrigation and drainage systems of the important Artibonite area also were damaged, adversely affecting future production. Almost 70 percent of the second rice crop in this largest rice-growing valley was destroyed.

The United States committed US$12 million for the emergency reconstruction effort, and the IMF agreed to offer a US$20 million loan. The IDB could have offered additional badly needed disaster relief, but the lack of a prime minister

*Cleaning drinkers at a
chicken farm
Courtesy Inter-American
Development Bank*

and the refusal of parliament to ratify foreign loans prevented the IDB from disbursing any loans. The only silver lining in Hurricane Georges was that the reconstruction drive in its wake was expected to stimulate the island's construction sector.

Land Tenure

During the colonial period, runaway slaves, or maroons (*marrons*), had already established themselves as independent agriculturists in remote areas. After 1804 ex-slaves expanded this pattern and laid informal claim to unoccupied land as small peasant farmers. The newly independent Haitian state formally confiscated French colonial holdings and asserted state ownership of all unclaimed lands. Early rulers of Haiti distributed land to thousands of newly independent citizens, ex-soldiers, and former officers in the revolutionary army. Because of these early patterns of land reform and dispersion, landholdings in Haiti today are significantly more egalitarian than elsewhere in the Latin American region.

National census data on land distribution in 1950 and 1971 are unreliable and out of date. USAID has played a key role in generating more current information, including the Agricultural Development Support survey of 1,307,000 parcels (1988), a national survey of 5,000 households under the Interim Food Security Information System (1995), and a national baseline survey of 4,026 households in 1994–96, including data on land tenure. The latter survey noted that 90 percent of farmers surveyed have access to land, they own two-thirds of the land they farm, average farm size is 1.7 hectares, and farms average 3.7 dispersed plots. The largest 1 percent of farms in the survey occupy 10 percent of the land.

In addition to private land, Haiti has large state holdings farmed by tenant farmers and squatters. By some estimates, there are around 35,000 leaseholders on state lands, including large and small holdings. Small farmers undertake most agricultural activity on state lands. Such activity amounts to perhaps 5 percent of rural households and 10 percent of all agricultural land. Estimates of state land vary from 100,000 to 300,000 hectares; there are, however, no reliable inventories of state land.

Community studies and surveys find that landholding in rural Haiti has the following characteristics. Private property is the rule. Peasant smallholdings predominate over large holdings and are made up of several distinct parcels. The vast majority of peasant farmers are owner-operators of their own land. Most peasant farmers are both landlords and tenants, and inherited land is divided equally among all children of the deceased. Land is readily bought and sold without updating title. Formal entitlement to land is commonly avoided or postponed, and land is most often held on the basis of customary arrangements.

There is immense pressure on the land as an agricultural resource. Agriculture is in decline while population pressures show marked increase. Overall population density has increased from about 207 people per square kilometer of arable land in 1900, to 401 people in 1950, and 989 people per square kilometer in 1998. Clearly, the cultivable land base has far surpassed its carrying capacity (see Land Use and Water, and Demographic Profile, ch. 7).

Since 1986 a series of highly politicized land disputes and land invasions have occurred in the aftermath of the Duvalier regime and subsequent military governments. In the 1990s, the rapid growth of Port-au-Prince and other urban areas has been marked by a notable increase in urban squatting. Land disputes in Haiti are generally not well served by the national system of justice. The traditional or customary system of land tenure continues to function fairly well, especially at the local level in most rural areas. Some grassroots peasant organizations have organized around land rights and dispute resolution. In 1995 the Aristide government created the National Institute of Agrarian Reform (Institut National de la Réforme Agraire—Inara), whose mission is policy reform and restructuring of the national land tenure system.

Cash Crops

Grown by some 380,000 peasants, coffee has had a prominent role in Haiti's agriculture since it was introduced by the French from Martinique in 1726. Production of the colony's main cash crop, which peaked in 1790, declined steadily after independence. It fell precipitously during the 1960s. After a boom in prices and in production in the late 1970s, output declined again from 42,900 tons in 1980 to 30,088 tons by 1987. Coffee trees covered an estimated 133,000 hectares in the 1980s, with an average annual yield of 35,900 tons. Haiti's coffee is sold through a system of intermediaries, speculators, and large-scale merchants. The high taxes involved in the system make production erratic and compel farmers to alternate between coffee and food crops, depending on price fluctuations and profit expectations. Although Haiti is a member of the International Coffee Organization (ICO), it was unable to fulfill its ICO export quota, which stood at 300,000 bags of 60 kilograms each (18,000 tons) in 1988. Total coffee production fell from 697,000 bags of 60 kilograms (41,820 tons) in 1982 to 359,000 bags (21,540 tons) in 1994, but it registered a rise to 496,000 bags (29,760 tons) in 1995. Coffee export earnings, however, amounted to only US$9.1 million in 1991–92 (latest figures available), which represented barely 10 percent of export revenue, compared with 35 percent five years earlier.

Soon after Columbus brought sugarcane to Haiti on his second voyage to Hispaniola, sugar became one of the island's most important cash crops. But after 1804, production never returned to pre-independence levels, perhaps because it was in the hands of small peasants rather than large plantations. The sugar harvest fell to under 4 million tons by the early 1970s, but a sharp increase in the world price of the commodity helped it rebound to nearly 6 million tons by the middle of the decade. Lower prices and structural problems combined to cause a drop in sugar output in the 1980s. By the end of the decade, sugarcane covered fewer than 114,000 hectares of the coastal plains, and sugarcane planting yielded fewer than 4.5 million tons annually. Only about 45,000 hectares were planted in the late 1990s. The production cost of Haitian sugar was three times more than the world price in the 1980s.

Shifts in the world sugar market, caused mainly by international substitution of corn-based fructose for sugarcane, exerted further pressure on Haitian producers, and production stagnated. Total sugar exports dropped from 19,200 tons in 1980 to 6,500 tons in 1987. In 1988 Haiti exported no sugar. The country's three major industrial sugar mills, including the oldest one, the Haitian American Sugar Company (HASCO) near Port-au-Prince, have ceased operations, citing losses caused by competition from cheap legal and illegal imports. Another industrial mill, the Centrale Dessalines, produced 20,000 tons of sugar in 1994. In addition, Haiti has almost 1,000 peasant-run mills. Total production of raw sugar in 1994 was estimated at 30,000 tons. Sugar export earnings fell from G22.7 million in 1986–87 to G2 million in 1990–91. Haiti is now a net importer of sugar.

Other cash crops include cocoa, cotton, sisal, and essential oils. Cacao plants covered an estimated 10,400 hectares in 1987 and yielded about 4,000 tons of cocoa a year. But cocoa has been declining in importance, as shown by the drop in its export earnings from US$4 million in 1987–88 to US$660,000 in 1995–96.

Cotton cultivation peaked in the 1930s, before Mexican boll weevil beetles ravaged the crop. In the 1960s, growers introduced a higher quality of cotton, which was processed in local cotton gins and then exported to Europe. But when cotton prices fell in the 1980s, cotton plantings shrank from 12,400 hectares in 1979 to under 8,000 hectares by 1986, and exports ceased.

Sisal, exported as a twine since the 1920s, peaked in the 1950s, when industries spawned by the Korean War used up much of the nation's 40,000-ton output. As the substitution of synthetic fibers for sisal reduced most large-scale growing of the plant in the 1980s, however, Haiti exported an average of only 6,500 tons a year, mainly to the Dominican Republic and Puerto Rico.

The export of essential oils, derived from vetiver, lime, amyris, and bitter orange for the cosmetics and pharmaceutical industries, peaked in 1976 at 395 tons. Exports gradually leveled off at a little more than 200 tons, generating an average of US$5 million in foreign exchange.

Cleaning mud from an old irrigation canal in the Artibonite Valley
Making mountainside terraces at Dofourmi, above Port-au-Prince,
for reforestation planting
Courtesy Inter-American Development Bank

Food Crops

The fall in prices for cash crops in the 1980s was accompanied by a rise in the output of food crops, such as corn, sorghum, rice, bananas, beans, and potatoes. Real per capita food production, however, declined, and Haiti continued to import millions of tons of grains. The trend toward increased production of food crops also has had negative ecological consequences because the planting of more tuber staples has accelerated soil erosion. But underfed farmers realistically could not be expected to grow tree crops in place of these badly needed staples.

Corn, the leading food crop, is sown on more hectares—about 220,000—than any other crop. It is grown separately in the south and interspersed with legumes in other areas. Sorghum often replaces corn during the second growing season as the leading crop, but total hectares planted average only 156,000. Rice became an increasingly common cereal beginning in the 1960s, and its production increased considerably in the 1980s as a result of improved irrigation schemes in the Artibonite Valley. Rice production, however, has fluctuated considerably and remains dependent on government subsidies. An estimated 60,000 hectares yielded an average of 123,000 tons, from 1980 to 1987 (latest data available). But the sharp reduction of protective tariffs in the mid-1990s led to increased imports of rice, mostly from the United States, and a corresponding decrease in production. The reopening of ports also led to large-scale smuggling of cheap rice and reductions in the planted area to less than 36,000 hectares.

Other food crops cultivated in Haiti include a variety of red and black beans, which provide the main source of protein in the diet of millions. As many as 129,000 hectares provided 67,000 tons of beans in 1987 (latest data available). Potatoes, one of the country's largest food crops, grow on an estimated 100,000 hectares and yielded 260,000 tons of produce a year in the 1980s. Banana palms are also common and provide, on the average, more than 500,000 tons of produce annually, almost entirely for domestic consumption. Although the flimsy trees are vulnerable to hurricanes and droughts, rapid replanting has helped sustain the crop. The significant lowering of import tariffs, decreed by IMF reforms in 1994, has increased smuggling of cheaper food products from the Dominican Republic, particularly bananas.

Forestry

Haiti has had a long and sad history of deforestation, which has had a devastating effect on the country's economy. The most direct effect of deforestation is soil erosion. In turn, soil erosion has lowered the productivity of the land, worsened droughts, and eventually led to desertification, all of which have increased the pressure on the remaining land and trees. As far back as the 1950s, it was becoming obvious that environmentally unsound agricultural practices, rapid population growth, and increased competition over scarce land were accelerating deforestation problems uncontrollably. Intensified demand for charcoal has worsened the situation by accelerating logging operations. The FAO estimated that deforestation was destroying 6,000 hectares of arable land a year in the 1980s. As a result, an impetus to act came from abroad. USAID's Agroforestry Outreach Program, Projè Pyebwa, was the country's major reforestation program in the 1980s. Between 1982 and 1991, the project distributed some 63 million trees to more than 250,000 small peasant farmers. Later efforts to save Haiti's trees—and thus its ecosystem—focused on intensifying reforestation programs, reducing waste in charcoal production, introducing more wood-efficient stoves, and importing wood under USAID's Food for Peace program. Much of the tree cover continued to be cut down indiscriminately for use as charcoal until the cutting reached alarming proportions in the 1990s. Only an estimated 60,000 hectares, 2.2 percent of the total land area, were forested in 1993.

Livestock and Fishing

Most peasants possess a few farm animals, usually goats, pigs, chickens, and cattle. Few holdings, however, are large, and few peasants raise only livestock. Many farm animals, serving as a kind of savings account, are sold or are slaughtered to pay for marriages, medical emergencies, schooling, seeds for crops, or a voodoo ceremony. Haiti had an estimated 200,000 pigs in 1994, compared with a record high of 1.2 million in the early 1980s. In the late 1970s, the island's pig stock became infected with the highly contagious African swine fever, which had spread from Spain to the Dominican Republic and then to Haiti via the Artibonite River. Panicked farmers first slaughtered their own infected animals, about one-third of the total pig population. Fear of further infection eliminated another third. Then a government eradication program almost wiped out what remained of the 1.2 million pigs by 1982. Angry farmers complained about the government's inadequate compensation for their slaughtered livestock and about its restocking program using pigs imported from the United States. The large imported pink sentinel strain of pig offered as a replacement for the hardy creole breed was considered unsuitable for Haiti's environment. Farmers also complained that the United States variety required a level of upkeep they could not afford. To supplement the sentinel pigs, Jamaican creole pigs were added to Haiti's livestock population. After the swine-fever epidemic, chicken replaced pork as the most widely consumed meat in the Haitian diet.

Goats are one of the most plentiful farm animals in Haiti and, like the creole pigs, adapt well to the terrain and sparse vegetation. Their numbers increased from 400,000 in 1981 to more than 1 million by the end of the 1980s (latest figures available). Approximately 54 percent of all farmers own goats. Sheep are raised in some areas, but they are not particularly well adapted to the island's climate.

Some 8,000 to 10,000 Haitians fish the 1,500-kilometer coastline on a full-time or part-time basis, netting an average annual catch of 5,000 tons of fish. Although Haiti's immediate coastal waters are over-fished, deep-sea fishing is underdeveloped because most Haitian fishers lack the modern equipment required for profitable fishing on the high seas. Thus, fishing in general has remained undeveloped into the late 1990s, even though it potentially could have been a major source of badly needed protein in the population's diet. The country imports more than 12,000 tons of fish products a year to satisfy domestic demand.

Industry

Manufacturing

Like almost everything else in Haiti, manufacturing, which was the most dynamic sector of the economy in the 1980s and which accounted for more than 18 percent of GDP in 1980 (and almost 14 percent of GDP in 1991), suffered several crippling blows in the wake of Aristide's overthrow and the ensuing embargo imposed by both the UN and the OAS. Of 180 companies operating in four free zones, 130 closed their factories in the aftermath of the 1991 coup. However, almost thirty

Women making rugs at Fort Jacques, near Port-au-Prince
Courtesy Inter-American Development Bank

Plaiting banana tree bark for baskets at Port-au-Prince Industrial Park
Courtesy Inter-American Development Bank

plants reopened within a year after the reestablishment of constitutional government in October 1994. The sector managed to revive slowly; by mid-1997 (latest data available), it employed approximately 23,000 people—considerably fewer than the 100,000 employed prior to the miliary coup—and its contribution to GDP had reached 11 percent.

Manufacturing recorded strong growth that averaged about 10 percent per year in the 1970s and almost 12 percent per year by 1980. Manufactured goods replaced agricultural commodities as the country's leading exports during this decade. In 1991 manufacturing accounted for 14 percent of GDP. By the end of the 1980s, the manufacturing sector comprised 500 enterprises, most of which were family owned and small or medium-sized (latest available data). Major products include processed foods, electrical equipment, textiles, toys, sporting goods, clothing, and handicrafts. Most of these items are not destined for local consumption, however. Principal production for the local market is in the area of food and beverages.

Assembly Sector

In the late 1980s, attracted to Haiti by the prevalence of extremely low wages, more than 150 firms, mostly United States-controlled, set up operations on the edge of Port-au-Prince to assemble light industrial products for re-export. The factories generated about 60,000 jobs (two-thirds held by women) for workers assembling electronic components, toys, sporting goods, and clothing. Their contribution to government revenue was insignificant, however, since they were exempted from taxation for up to fifteen years and were free to repatriate profits. In its attempt to attract the assembly industry, Haiti had benefited from both its proximity to the United States and its access to such organizations as the Generalized System of Preferences (GSP—see Glossary) and the CBI. Its special position in assembly production was eventually eroded, however, as other countries in the region, such as the Dominican Republic, Jamaica, and Costa Rica, began to capitalize more aggressively on the advantages of the CBI. Haiti's prospects in the assembly industry were hampered by a combination of factors, including an underdeveloped infrastructure, an illiterate work force, scarce managerial personnel, and—perhaps most important—the highest utility costs in the Caribbean. The country's chronic political instability was another major factor that prompted many companies to relocate their

Twine factory
Courtesy Inter-American
Development Bank

assembly operations to more stable countries in the Caribbean, mostly to the free zone in the neighboring Dominican Republic. By the late 1990s, Haiti's once-thriving assembly sector was operating at a fraction of its capacity.

Construction

It was not surprising that the demise of the assembly manufacturing subsector would deal Haiti's construction industry as devastating a blow as it did in the 1990s. Construction had depended heavily on industrial structures related to assembly manufacturing since the 1970s. It had also concentrated heavily on extravagant houses being built in the residential areas of Port-au-Prince and its exclusive suburb of Pétionville; these construction projects almost halted during the political instability and economic turmoil of the 1990s. Meanwhile, the country's disadvantaged majority continued to labor and build their own dwellings with a mixture of raw materials, mostly wood and palm thatch in rural areas and corrugated metal, cardboard, or wood in urban shantytowns.

Mining

Haiti has few natural resources; they include small amounts

of gold, silver, copper, iron, nickel, and marble. The country's insignificant mining sector, which accounted for less than 1 percent of GDP and employed less than 1 percent of the labor force in the early 1980s, all but vanished in 1983, when a United States firm, Reynolds Company, decided to close its bauxite mine at Miragoâne after forty years of operation. The plant produced an average of 500,000 tons of bauxite a year, but the declining metal content of the ore, coupled with high production costs and the oversupplied international bauxite market, made it a losing business venture.

A Canadian mining company, Sainte Genevieve, which started prospecting for gold in the northern part of the island in 1995, decided to relocate its operations to the Dominican Republic in late 1997. Although it had created more than 300 jobs, the local community expressed strong concerns about the adverse effects the mining operation could have on their agricultural output. Their demands that the company finance rehabilitation of irrigation systems, bridges, and dams in their region prompted the firm's decision to depart.

Energy

Haiti had limited energy resources in the late 1990s. The country has no petroleum resources, little hydroelectricity potential, and rapidly diminishing supplies of wood fuels. Local timber and charcoal account for 75 percent of the total energy used in the country, imported petroleum for 15 percent, bagasse (sugarcane residue) for 5 percent, and hydroelectric power for 5 percent. In addition, only a meager 10 percent of the country had access to electricity in 1995. Even in Port-au-Prince, where almost half the population has electricity, the supply is so limited that many industries must resort to private generators. Although most provincial towns have intermittent electricity, only 3 percent of the rural population has any.

The Haitian Electricity Company (Électricité d'Haïti— EdH), established in 1971, operates the Péligre hydroelectric plant above the Artibonite Valley, which provides approximately one-third of the island's public electricity. Four thermal plants in the Port-au-Prince area provide the other two-thirds. Tapping illegally into power lines has long been a fairly common practice, and almost half of the current produced by the EdH was stolen.

Haiti imports all of its petroleum. When a petroleum embargo was imposed in 1993, thousands of people made a living smuggling gas across the border from the Dominican Republic. The fuel embargo also increased the population's need for timber and charcoal, the major household fuel, resulting in greater deforestation as well.

By the mid-1990s, the country's installed electric power capacity was approximately 210 megawatts. The power industry's performance is far below par, however, because of the dilapidated condition of production and transmission equipment, lack of maintenance, silting at the Péligre Dam, and low stream discharge during the dry season. Power interruptions resulting from generation and transmission equipment failures occur frequently. Blackouts are even more common in the provinces. The hydroelectric potential is estimated at 120 megawatts, of which fifty-four megawatts have been installed. Peak demand in Port-au-Prince is capped at 100 megawatts because that is all the supply that is available. But the potential demand from Port-au-Prince could be higher than 200 megawatts, if there were reliable supplies and adequate distribution systems. Generation capacity was largely rebuilt after 1995, which has enabled the EdH to supply eighteen to twenty-four hours a day of electric power to almost all of Port-au-Prince during the rainy season. Power supplies are usually unreliable between December and March, when production at the Péligre dam declines.

Transportation and Communications

Haiti's transportation system remains inadequate in the 1990s, in spite of the major infrastructural improvements that accompanied the growth period of the 1970s (see fig. 13). Poor transportation hinders economic growth, particularly in the agricultural sector. Like other services in the economy, transportation—when it is available—is prohibitively expensive for most citizens.

Roads are considered the most important part of the country's transportation system. Of a total of 4,050 kilometers of roads, 950 kilometers are paved, another 950 kilometers are gravel or otherwise improved, and 2,150 kilometers are unimproved and almost impassable during the torrential rainy season. Besides the paved streets in Port-au-Prince, Haiti has only two main highways. These highways, which were paved in 1973, link the northern and southern regions of the country. National Highway One extends north from the capital to Cap-Haïtien via the coastal towns of Montrouis and Gonaïves.

Figure 13. Haiti: Transportation System, 1999

National Highway Two proceeds south from Port-au-Prince to Les Cayes by way of Miragoâne with a spur to Jacmel. Road travel outside these two arteries, which themselves had badly deteriorated by the mid-1990s because of poor road maintenance and lack of repair, is quite difficult and requires four-wheel-drive vehicles that are equipped to travel on the washed-out roads that are especially common during the rainy season.

In view of the condition of Haiti's roads, the World Bank approved a US$50 million loan program for road construction. However, the loan program was suspended in late 1998 when auditors uncovered major irregularities in contract awards— but only after the Bank had disbursed almost US$23 million. Subsequently, in January 1999 the Bank decided to halt the program altogether because of mismanagement and suspected corruption. A spokeswoman for the Bank confirmed that at least a US$6 million portion of the loan was declared a "mis-procurement," adding that the Bank was demanding repayment.

The government provides extremely limited and unreliable public transportation, leaving road transport in the hands of small operators who run trucks, vans, and taxis without much regard to safety concerns. In the late 1990s, most Haitians were continuing to use "tap-taps," brightly colored and overcrowded jitneys that service almost every corner of the island. Nearly all vehicles in Haiti are imported; an estimated 50,000 vehicles were in use in 1991, compared with 36,600 vehicles ten years earlier.

Ports are another major component of the country's transportation sector. Haiti has fourteen ports. Although most of these ports are provincial and small, they have turned into major centers of imported contraband, especially after the upheavals of the 1990s. Port-au-Prince remains the major port, and is equipped with container facilities and berths for large liners. It also remains the island's central shipping site for most registered imports and exports. Beside its container capability, it offers a roll-on/roll-off facility, a thirty-ton gantry crane, and a fifty-ton mobile crane in addition to its older mechanical handling equipment and two transit warehouses. Port fees are so expensive, however, that the port is underused. Wharfage costs are four times higher than those of the neighboring Dominican Republic. Also, most of the port's equipment is in very poor condition. Perhaps for this reason, legislation relating to the modernization of public enterprises had recommended that management of the port be turned over to a private operator. The legislation was still pending in parliament in late 1999.

Cap-Haïtien was the second major port until the end of the 1980s, handling most cruise-ship traffic as well as domestic and international merchant ships. In the 1990s, it was replaced by Miragoâne, which in 1999 remained a major export port. Lesser used ports include Les Cayes, Fort Liberté, Gonaïves, Jacmel, Montrouis, and Jérémie. They play a role in internal commerce, mainly as an alternative to the island's poor road system and as a conduit for contraband trade out of the Dominican Republic and Miami. Although smuggling may have stimulated economic activity at these small provincial ports, it has resulted in the loss of millions of dollars in import duties. The porous border with the Dominican Republic also continues to be a favorite route for imported contraband.

Haiti's main, and only international, airport is located about ten kilometers north of Port-au-Prince. Opened in 1965, it is equipped for international flights and handles most domestic flights as well, with the exception of Cap-Haïtien. The country's other airfields (about ten) are operational, but they are no more than grass strips. The government-owned Air Haiti is the only airline that services these provincial airports. Air Haiti operates under the control of the National Civil Aviation Office (Office National de l'Aviation Civile—ONAC). The National Airport Authority (Autorité Aéroportuaire Nationale—AAN) regulates the country's airports. Air links abroad were suspended in July 1994, as part of internationally imposed sanctions, but were restored before year's end. Some ten airlines from Europe, the Caribbean, and the Americas regularly schedule services to Port-au-Prince airport.

Haiti, with a 1998 ratio of six telephones per 1,000 people, the same as in the mid-1980s, ranks below some of Africa's poorer nations—eight telephones per 1,000 inhabitants. The 39,000 telephone lines of the 1980s increased to 64,000 in the late 1990s, but 80 percent of them remained concentrated in the Port-au-Prince area, where only about 25 percent of the total population live. Telephone service to provincial towns remains so unreliable that many rural areas must depend on two-way radios. By contrast, subscribers with international service (again, almost all in the capital area) can dial directly to the United States and Europe via a satellite station at Sabourin; rates are high, however. The country's telephone system is operated by Teleco, under the Ministry of Public Works, Transportation, and Communications. Teleco, 96 percent of which is owned by the government, is on the list of public enterprises to be privatized.

Approximately sixty amplitude modulation (AM) and frequency modulation (FM) stations and twenty television stations operated in Haiti in the late 1990s. In 1997 Haiti had some 38,000 television sets and some 415,000 radios. The only radio station whose signal covers the entire country is Radio Nationale d'Haïti, which is government-operated and located in the capital. Another radio station that also has a large audience is Radio Soleil, which is run by the Archdiocese of Port-au-Prince and broadcasts in both Creole and French. Cable television service, carrying several United States channels, is a pay-cable station broadcasting on thirteen channels in French, Spanish, and English; it is owned by a private operator, Télé-Haïti. Télévision

Riders on a "tap-tap" (jitney)
near Gonaïves
Courtesy Inter-American
Development Bank

Colorful "tap-taps" on Avenue
Dessalines, Port-au-Prince
Courtesy Inter-American
Development Bank

Nationale d'Haïti is the state television station, broadcasting on four channels in Creole, French, and Spanish.

Tourism

A new international airport in 1965 and improved relations with the United States helped Haiti's tourism industry to flourish in the 1970s. Tourist arrivals (139,000 by air and 163,000 by sea) peaked in 1980, and net expenditures on tourism (US$44 million) reached their highest level in 1981 before a series of events made Haiti unpopular among tourists. One of these events was publicity surrounding Haiti as a possible origin of acquired immune deficiency syndrome (AIDS) and the high number of AIDS cases among Haitians. The former allegation proved false, but the portrait lingered along with television images of political violence, dire poverty, "boat people," and general instability. As political instability spread to many parts of the island, tour operators began to express concerns about their customers' security, and the number of cruise ships visiting Haiti declined considerably. The number of tourist arrivals fell sharply after the September 1991 coup. According to the Central Bank, the number of visitors in 1991–92 was down to 82,493 (latest figures available). The declining number of tourists forced many hotels to close. The number of hotel rooms available to tourists also dropped consistently, from 3,000 in 1981 to 1,500 in 1987 to 800 by mid-1996.

Trouble with the island's tourism continued into the late 1990s. Radio Galaxie announced in April 1999 that Haiti Club Med would close almost immediately. Although the closure was supposed to be "temporary," the government's quick response was to announce that it was taking steps to encourage more tourists to visit Haiti. The measures included the abolition of visa requirements, which raised concerns as to the degree this would facilitate illegal traffic from Haiti to the United States via the Bahamas.

Outlook

The critical situation in which Haiti finds itself stems mainly from its chronic political instability, which occasionally borders on chaos. This instability has scared away international donors and dried up the external aid on which the country has depended for decades. In turn, lack of aid has adversely affected an economy stagnant for some years and taken a

Market scene, Port-au-Prince
Courtesy Inter-American
Development Bank

severe toll on a population already living in abject poverty. Haiti also has other deep-rooted endemic problems: an unskilled population, lack of resources, maldistribution of wealth, marked disregard for social justice among traditional power holders, a dysfunctional judiciary, growing scarcity of productive land, lack of off-farm labor opportunities, paucity of investment in human and social capital, deficits in capital and credit markets, an ingrained tradition of corruption, unemployment and underemployment of unskilled labor, an entrenched and inefficient bureaucracy, and—perhaps most important—a lack of will on the part of the country's leaders to stop the political infighting and start implementing whatever reforms have been legislated.

Both the United Nations secretary general and the United States secretary of state have voiced on separate occasions their concern over the Haitian government's inaction, which caused the suspension of badly needed international aid. In urging Haiti's political leaders to "resolve their differences," the secretary of state said in April 1998 that the Haitian people "deserve the ability to have the fruits that the international community is trying to give them." Similarly, in early 1998 members of the Foreign Relations Committee of the United States House of Representatives warned that United States funding for Haiti would be suspended if Haitian leaders did not make more serious efforts to reach a political solution. Meanwhile, substantial amounts of aid from other foreign donors were withheld for the same reason.

Important as it may be for any Haitian leader to renew the flow of external aid, it is far more important for Haiti to be committed to the concept that economic development must be based on trade and investment and institutional reforms. Such measures involve factors that include job creation and the improvement of social services for the disadvantaged, rather than a growing dependence on international assistance. R. Quentin Grafton of the University of Ottawa and Dane Rowlands of Carlton University make the point that Haiti's political instability is "symptomatic of its institutional arrangements where the powers of the state are viewed as a means to personal enrichment." Haiti's institutional structure is such that it has encouraged economic exploitation and intimidation, as well as political repression and stark inequities between the privileged and disadvantaged segments of the population. To reverse these tendencies, a leadership is needed that acknowledges that appropriate institutional reform is essential for Haiti's development. The country's social, economic, and political structure needs to be modified so as to assure the poor their fair share of resources and social services and to ensure the participation of the less advantaged communities in shaping their institutional environment.

The role of leadership need not be the government's exclusive domain. A good example of private initiative was a three-day economic conference held in April 1998 in Jacmel. A group of Haitian mayors and some forty Haitian-Americans, including ten businessmen from New York, met to discuss ways of energizing Haiti's development process. They chose to hold their encounter at some distance from the capital to show that private efforts can be mounted without state sponsorship. Bringing together elected officials of small provincial towns, who had been accustomed to obeying directives of the central government, with a group of potential investors and business leaders also made the point that thousands of Haitian emigrants living abroad could be tapped for financial assistance to development projects in rural communities. Haitians living in the United States alone reportedly send home an estimated US$3 million a day.

Two World Bank projects provide another example of a different approach to socioeconomic development in Haiti. When the country's gross domestic product fell by about 40 percent during the 1991–94 embargo years, and large numbers of jobs were lost, the World Bank initiated a two-year Employment Generation Project, which provided short-term jobs for 325,000 of Haiti's poorest. Another social safety-net program geared toward directly assisting the underprivileged and improving social services is known as the Basic Infrastructure Project, which involves the poor in its design and implementation. The project's goal is the rebuilding of critical infrastructure in serious disrepair (roads, sanitation facilities, and flood controls) in provincial towns. The objective is achieved through consultation with local communities and use of local labor in construction, thereby providing opportunities for more sustained employment.

Whatever approach the Haitians choose to reform their country's basic institutional structure and to embark on a coherent economic development program, their task is bound to be daunting. Dealing with an economy in ruins, a population in despair, an administrative system in shambles, and a government at a standstill will not be easy and may take years, even with substantial aid from the international donor community.

* * *

Reliable statistical data on Haitian economics are hard to obtain. Most publications acknowledge that their figures are based largely on estimates. For example, despite the obvious breadth and depth of their research, the International Monetary Fund and the World Bank note that they have little confidence in the statistical data provided on Haiti.

Perhaps the best source on Haiti's economy is the Economist Intelligence Unit, which publishes an annual country profile as well as four quarterly country reports on the island nation. The profile typically includes a comprehensive analysis of the country's economic developments, while providing an insightful political backdrop to put them in perspective. The quarterly updates furnish what is tantamount to a running chronicle of economic and political events as they unfold on the Haitian scene. It is also useful to consult publications by major donors such as the World Bank, the Inter-American Development

Bank, and the United States Agency for International Development. These and other donors issue reports of surveys, policy
research, and other current information on Haiti. A good
recent collection of such reports is available from the World
Bank, *Haiti: The Challenges of Poverty Reduction.*

Mats Lundahl, a Swedish economist, has written an economic history, *Peasants and Poverty: A Study of Haiti,* and other
useful books and articles on Haiti; and Simon Fass has published an interesting study on the economics of survival and
informal credit among the urban poor, *Political Economy in
Haiti: The Drama of Survival.* Development initiatives are treated
in a collection of articles edited by Derrick Brinkerhoff and
Jean-Claude Garcia-Zamor, *Politics, Projects, and People: Institutional Development in Haiti.*

More recent works include *The Haitian Dilemma: A Case Study
in Demographics, Development, and U.S. Foreign Policy* by Ernest H.
Preeg, an economist and former United States ambassador to
Haiti. A conference on Haiti after the return of Aristide generated a collection of papers edited by Robert I. Rotberg, *Haiti
Renewed: Political and Economic Prospects.* There is also a recent
volume on political economy by Alex Dupuy, *Haiti in the New
World Order: The Limits of the Democratic Revolution,* and an earlier
volume entitled *Haiti in the World Economy: Class, Race, and
Underdevelopment since 1700.* (For further information and complete citations, see Bibliography.)

Chapter 9. Haiti: Government and Politics

Figure from a painting by Dieuseul Paul

AS HAITI APPROACHES ITS 200th anniversary of independence from France, it is struggling to discard deeply rooted legacies of centralized government based on authoritarian rule and of politics predicated upon elitism, cronyism, and exclusion. Historically, the Haitian state has ignored the need to develop institutions and to enact programs required to advance the nation's well-being, and to be accountable to citizens. Haiti's leaders have neglected to build political institutions with a numerically significant or sustained citizen involvement. Rather, since independence in 1804, the country's governments, led by military strongmen, charismatic leaders and/or elites whose interests were shared by the army, generally have done little more than seek to maintain power and prey upon those over whom they exercised such power. Particularly vulnerable to state-sponsored predation and political exclusion have been the urban poor and the country's demographic majority: its peasants.

From the February 1986 demise of the twenty-nine-year Duvalier family dictatorship up to the September 1994 international intervention that dislodged a brutal de facto military regime, Haiti's deeply dichotomized political system experienced a period of profound transition (see table 24 and table 25, Appendix). Characterized by constant turmoil and protracted violence, these eight years witnessed a struggle between two largely juxtaposed groups with fundamentally different visions of their country's future. Supporters of Haiti's traditional political power structure—often simply referred to as *makout* and composed of the army and other henchmen, and their allies among the political and economic elites—sought to maintain the status quo or, under international and domestic pressure, to accept at least cosmetic change. Traditionalists were challenged by a cacophony of voices calling for social, economic, and political reform. Those voices were led by individuals who emanated principally from community and religious groups, and the middle-class nongovernmental organizations and professional associations of Haiti's increasingly organized civil society. These new political actors saw the Ayiti Libere (Liberated Haiti) of 1986 as an opportunity to end authoritarianism, to democratize and decentralize the state, and, as such, to provide political access to the largely disenfranchised *moun andeyo* (outsiders)—the rural and urban poor and working classes. Two popular political slogans that sprang up in 1986 illustrate the differences between these two groups and their aspirations. The slogan *Chaque quatre ans* (Every four years), calling for regular elections and implying participatory democratic governance, was embraced by those seeking reform. *Vive l'armée* (Long live the army) was adopted by those opposing change.

The 1986–94 post-Duvalier transitional period witnessed an incessant tug-of-war between these two tendencies. Political recidivists, significantly outnumbered by their opponents, resorted to the raw power of weapons and violence when necessary, to maintain their position. An early example of this tactic was the massacre of voters that led to the abandonment of the 1987 presidential election. This incident and the instances of intimidation and murder that followed were eclipsed by the slaughter of some 3,000 Haitians that accompanied the late September 1991 military coup d'état and the subsequent three-year reign of terror led by the Armed Forces of Haiti (Forces Armées d'Haïti—FAd'H).

Confronting the grim reality of brute force, Haiti's incipient reformers relied upon determination, resilience, and sheer strength of numbers throughout the transitional period. They early achieved such key victories as the 1986 election of a constituent assembly and the 1987 ratification of a new, democratic constitution. Ultimately, they resisted the "Duvalierism without Duvalier" of the late 1980s to build a national reformist political movement—Lavalas (a Creole phrase meaning "cleansing flood")—that coalesced around an outspoken Roman Catholic priest, Jean-Bertrand Aristide. With complementary support from international players, Haiti's reformers achieved a transcendent milestone in Haiti's political history: the free, fair, and internationally recognized parliamentary and presidential elections of December 1990.

Although that accomplishment was reversed with the 1991 military coup, it was not erased. The coup leader, General Raoul Cédras, and his co-conspirators succeeded in grasping power during three years of despotic rule, but they were unable to consolidate their hold on power and to gain the national and international legitimacy they desperately sought. The strength and depth of Haitian support for the government of President Jean-Bertrand Aristide, and the legitimacy granted to it as a result of the 1990 elections, ultimately enabled Haiti's nascent democratic political process to triumph over the attempt by the putschists to return Haiti to its past.

By late 1994, following eight difficult years of post-Duvalier transition, Haiti's formula of governance by military strongmen symbiotically linked with the country's elites had entered into an advanced state of disintegration. The influence of political charisma, however, especially in the presence of Jean-Bertrand Aristide, had not decreased. As the junta's leaders were escorted from power following the United Nations (UN)-sanctioned and United States-led multinational military intervention of September 1994, and Haiti's legitimately elected officials were restored to office, the country exploded with relief and joy. Once those emotions subsided, Haiti and its leaders turned their attention to an uncertain political future. Was the country witnessing an end to the difficult transition from predatory rule and political exclusion to an era when accountability and the politics of inclusion would characterize patterns of governance, and the Haitian state would serve the nation? Or, would Haiti witness the re-emergence of patterns of politics and governance that would do little more than replicate those of the past?

From an International Intervention to the Presidency of René Préval, September 1994–December 1999

Restoration of Constitutional Government, September 1994–September 1995

On September 19, 1994, the first contingents of what would become a 21,000-strong Multinational Force (MNF) landed in Haiti to oust the de facto regime and restore Haiti's legitimate government to power. Because a last-minute permissive intervention had been negotiated, bloodshed was averted, and damage to Haiti's urban and rural infrastructure—already crumbling from years of neglect—did not occur. As Haiti's putschists were escorted from power, or fled on their own, however, they left behind a country in total shambles. Public coffers were empty. The economy, under international sanctions for most of the previous three years, had shriveled. Damage to Haiti's already fragile natural environment had worsened. Political parties and civil society organizations were in varying states of disarray, and most citizens carried either physical or psychological scars of violence and terror.

415

The infrastructure and institutions of government were equally in ruin. Key government posts, including that of prime minister, were vacant. During the three years of de facto rule, most public officials elected in 1990 or appointed by the elected government either had fled the country or had gone into hiding. As they returned en masse—many via a chartered aircraft that flew back home dozens of parliamentarians who had sought asylum in the United States and Canada—they found dysfunctional conditions for governance. Not only were state coffers empty, but reforms initiated prior to the coup to streamline and upgrade the civil service had been reversed as the FAd'H placed cronies in public office and padded the civil service payrolls with thousands of supporters. Government offices had been stripped clean, as the army and its allies took vehicles, equipment, furniture, supplies, and even light bulbs from offices as they vacated them. When President Aristide was restored to his office and quarters in the National Palace in mid-October, there was one functioning telephone, and, because the furniture had been stolen or destroyed, he had to sleep on a cot.

Regardless of these conditions, the Aristide government, with massive assistance from the international community, had to move with haste to confront a broad array of challenges. The first order of business was to address the quandary of what to do about the discredited FAd'H. The army, although removed from power and stripped of its heavy weapons by the MNF, remained as an institution whose legitimacy was established in the 1987 constitution. President Aristide wasted little time completing the dismantling process begun by the MNF and, as such, removed the institution from its role as political arbiter. He nevertheless found a way to respect the constitution. Following a violent demonstration in December 1994 by members of the FAd'H over salary and pensions, the Haitian executive initiated a series of steps that emasculated the force. By May 1995, all that was left of the Armed Forces of Haiti was a small military band. Without an army to block the way, Haiti now stood before an unprecedented clear path for political reform.

The disappearance of the FAd'H meant that Haiti no longer had a police force. That fact, which called for urgent attention, opened up space for genuine reform of the country's public safety apparatus. Once again with significant international assistance, steps were taken quickly not only to reform the police, but also to fulfill the as-yet unmet constitutional mandate to place the police under the civilian control of the Ministry of Justice and Public Security. Following the creation by the MNF of an Interim Public Security Force (IPSF) composed principally of former FAd'H personnel vetted for blatant human rights abuse, and under the supervision of UN-affiliated International Police Monitors (IPMs), international experts began training new recruits for the Haitian National Police (Police Nationale d'Haïti—PNH). As the PNH began to deploy in mid-1995, it gradually replaced the IPSF. Decommissioned IPSF members were invited to join other former FAd'H personnel in an internationally supervised program of reintegration through skills training. Ultimately, 5,482 of the FAd'H's 6,250 demobilized soldiers enrolled in that program. By February 1996, the 5,200-member PNH was fully trained and deployed under the watch of UN-affiliated civilian police mentors (Civpols).

Haitian officials also had to confront the complicated status of elected officials. While exiled officials who were elected in 1990 were reclaiming their offices in the aftermath of the intervention, others who had sympathized with the coup leaders or had been installed by them were vacating their posts. Among the latter were the nine senators, who had been "elected" to six-year terms in 1993, but whose legitimacy was unrecognized. By late 1994, the terms of all officials elected in 1990 either had expired or were about to end, with the exception of nine senators elected to six-year terms and the president of the republic, whose term would expire in February 1996. Hence, after incumbent office holders were restored to office, there was a pressing need to conduct nationwide general elections for almost all elected posts.

Before elections could be conducted, key preparatory actions were required. A prime minister had to be nominated and confirmed, his cabinet installed, and a new Provisional Electoral Council (Conseil Électoral Provisoire—CEP) selected. The Lavalas movement and smaller political parties, in varying states of disarray following the three years of de facto rule, had to reorganize themselves and identify qualified candidates. The electoral infrastructure, destroyed by the FAd'H, had to be recreated, beginning with voter registration.

In October 1994, Smarck Michel, a businessman and former minister of commerce, was nominated by Aristide as the new prime minister, received parliamentary ratification, and formed a new government that began to restore order and function to the executive branch. Subsequently, a CEP was formed and, working with massive international assistance, gradually oversaw the creation of a framework for parliamentary, municipal, and communal section elections. Between June and September 1995, the elections were held. International observers deemed the elections "free, fair, and flawed," the latter characterization resulting principally from the commission's mixed performance (see Democracy Restored, 1994–96, ch. 6). Thousands of candidates from dozens of political parties stood for election to communal section councils, municipal councils, and the parliament—a total of 2,192 positions. Few incumbents won re-election. Swept into office was a new generation of political leaders, practically all of whom ran either as candidates of Lavalas Political Organization (Organisation Politique Lavalas—OPL) or one of the three other political parties that had joined the OPL to form the Lavalas Political Platform (Plate-forme Politique Lavalas—PPL), or simply as Lavalas independents. In a break with Haiti's political past, the victorious candidates were residents of the constituencies they were elected to represent or to govern, and few counted themselves as members of the traditional political class (*classe politique*).

Presidential Transition, October 1995–March 1997

As Haiti's newly elected officials took office, Smarck Michel resigned in October 1995, largely over issues linked to economic policy. Michel had endorsed macroeconomic policies promoted by the multilateral and bilateral donors who in January 1995 had pledged approximately US$2.8 billion in aid for Haiti's recovery. That policy, based largely on such reform measures as the divestiture of state enterprises ("privatization") and reduced tariffs ("free trade"), became a contentious issue among Lavalas partisans who did not want to undermine the state, but rather to make it finally render services to citizens. Michel was quickly replaced by Claudette Werleigh, the sitting minister of foreign affairs, nominated by Aristide, whose position on macroeconomic policies was enigmatic, and confirmed by the new, pro-Lavalas parliament. Werleigh's government, however, did not move on economic reform policies, thus precipitating a slow-down in aid flows, as internationally identified conditionalities to disbursements went unmet.

Attention to this crisis was diverted, however, by a growing focus on the status of the presidential election scheduled for late 1995. As the election date drew near, speculation centered around two questions: would President Aristide seek to extend his term by three years to make up for the time spent in exile, and, if not, to whom would he give the Lavalas nod as candidate. Both questions remained unanswered until several weeks prior to the election date. Ultimately, Aristide did not respond to pressure from among his partisans for his additional three years and endorsed his close friend and first prime minister, René Garcia Préval, as the Lavalas candidate. Running under the *Bò Tab la* (Everyone Around the Table) symbol of Lavalas, Préval easily defeated the handful of barely known opposition candidates from small political groups. Although his margin of victory was huge, voter turnout, at just 28 percent, was significantly lower than the 51 percent for the parliamentary and municipal elections held just months earlier. Haiti experienced the first peaceful transition in its history of democratically elected presidents at Préval's inauguration on February 7, 1996. As Jean-Bertrand Aristide handed over the presidential sash, his successor assumed the difficult roles of leading a country still reeling from decades of bad governance and of succeeding an enormously popular, and young, national hero.

Préval chose agronomist and OPL partisan Rosny Smarth as his prime minister nominee. Smarth easily won parliamentary confirmation as the post-intervention international military presence continued to diminish. The MNF had already withdrawn on March 31, 1995, handing over its authority to a much smaller UN peacekeeping mission, the United Nations Mission in Haiti (UNMIH), whose mandate was set to end a year later. Through a series of UN Security Council resolutions responding to requests from the government of Haiti, however, UNMIH's mandate was extended to July 1996. The UN peacekeepers ultimately remained in Haiti until November 1997, however, through a vastly scaled down United Nations Support Mission in Haiti (UNSMIH) between July 1996 and July 1997, and an even smaller United Nations Transition Mission in Haiti (UNTMIH) from August to November 1997.

While the international military presence was diminishing and the PNH was assuming complete responsibility for Haiti's public safety, the Préval/Smarth government enacted programs and policies aimed at addressing Haiti's most pressing social and economic problems. To emphasize its advocacy of decentralization, the government spotlighted programs that would move resources out of Port-au-Prince to the countryside.

President Préval placed a strong emphasis on agrarian reform, winning parliamentary support for an increased budget for the National Institute of Agrarian Reform (Institut National de la Réforme Agraire—Inara) and mandating it to focus primarily on the Artibonite Valley, Haiti's breadbasket. Préval himself traveled frequently to the countryside to promote his agricultural reform programs.

Concurrently, international economic assistance resumed principally as a result of the Smarck government's advocacy of economic reform measures that included policies for the modernization of state enterprises. This approach called for the reform of state enterprises through public-private sector partnerships rather than outright privatization. Still, key parliamentary leaders resisted modernization and managed to garner enough support for their position to block or delay passage of required economic reform legislation.

In January 1997, the ruling Lavalas political movement was shaken to its roots, when a new political party personally identified with former President Aristide, the Lavalas Family (La Famille Lavalas—FL), was formally registered. This development further complicated the political picture. As the new organization coalesced around the still-popular, charismatic leader, the Lavalas movement began to splinter into two principal groups. Elected officials and political activists either gravitated to the FL or stayed loyal to the OPL, which soon changed its name to the Organization of Struggling People (Organisation de Peuple en Lutte), a name that enabled the organization to distance itself from Lavalas while maintaining its highly recognized acronym. Rumors and speculation swirled around the political allegiance of President Préval and the ability of the OPL-led government of Prime Minister Smarth to win support for its programs and policies in a now starkly divided parliament.

Balance of Power and Political Gridlock, April 1997–January 1999

The first opportunity for the FL to demonstrate its political power would be the elections set for April 6, 1997, that would renew one-third of the Senate and that would create two key institutions in the decentralization of government: the communal section assemblies and town delegations. As voting day neared, controversy surrounding several FL senatorial candidates, particularly one with prior FAd'H affiliation, overshadowed the fact that the FL was fielding slates of candidates (*cartels*) for most of the communal section assemblies and town delegation races. The dismally low 5 percent turnout on April 6 reflected a growing trend of voter fatigue, frustration, apathy, and confusion. The election was plagued not only by a negligible turnout, but also by controversy surrounding the extremely poor management of the process by the allegedly pro-FL CEP and resultant fraudulent vote counts in many races, including several close senatorial races where CEP determinations related to spoiled ballots pushed the FL candidate to outright victory. Pointing to widespread allegations of fraud, few international observers recognized the elections as free and fair. The government, yielding to this pressure, as well as that applied vehemently by the OPL, refused to recognize the results, but did little to resolve the matter quickly.

While the election controversy festered, the country tumbled into an unprecedented political crisis. Government became gridlocked, as relations between the executive and parliamentary branches worsened and the Chamber of Deputies and the Senate, fraught with internal divisions, failed to reach consensus on most pressing legislative matters, including the passage of the government's budget and legislation related to economic reform. In June Prime Minister Smarth, unable to work effectively with the parliament and personally disgusted by the way political in-fighting had paralyzed the country— "power is a disease in this country," he stated—resigned, throwing the executive branch into a turmoil. Although many members of his cabinet followed him, leaving their posts, others remained in caretaker roles to manage ongoing programs. However, they were unable to initiate programs until a new government was formed. As remaining ministers combined portfolios, spreading a thin executive branch even thinner, external assistance once again began to dry up, a significant development in a country whose budget is approximately two-thirds derived from foreign aid. Alarmingly, by October 1997, only US$1 billion of the US$2.1 billion pledged almost three years earlier had been disbursed.

In the meantime, President Préval, standing somewhere between the FL and the OPL, appeared to be unable to find a way out of the electoral crisis. Indeed, many viewed him as remaining surprisingly aloof from it. After a delay of several months, he nominated Ericq Pierre, an agronomist and Haiti's representative to the Inter-American Development Bank

(IDB), as his next prime minister. Pierre failed to win confirmation, however, because many parliamentarians were uncomfortable with his links to an organization viewed as promoting Haiti's controversial economic policies. In late 1997, Préval sent his second nomination, Hervé Denis, to the legislative body for confirmation. Denis, an economist and playwright with close ties to Aristide, was denied the post as the OPL rallied against him.

In July 1998, Préval sent his third nomination, Jacques Édouard Alexis, an educator and minister of national education, youth, and sports in the Smarth cabinet, to parliament. Initially, with strong national and international pressure building for the confirmation of Alexis as a pivotal first step toward resolution of the increasingly debilitating political crisis, it appeared that Haiti would finally have a new prime minister. Once in office, Alexis and his government would face not only the task of forging the government's role in rebuilding the nation, but also the challenge of organizing the municipal and parliamentary elections mandated by the end of 1998. Alexis was eventually confirmed by the severely divided parliament, but not until December 17, much too late to organize the elections. Before the new prime minister completed the required next steps of the parliamentary ratification process—presenting his general policy statement and his cabinet—Haiti's political crisis deepened even further.

On January 12, 1999, President Préval, citing the 1995 electoral law that identified January 11 as the expiration date of the term of public officials elected in 1995, issued a presidential decree dismissing the entire Chamber of Deputies and Senate, with the exception of the nine senators who had been elected to six-year terms. On January 22, Préval issued another decree, converting the positions of elected mayors and communal section council members, whose terms also expired, into "interim executive agents" assigned to the Ministry of Interior. The Haitian chief executive's actions ushered the country into yet another period of governance by decree, albeit this time by a legitimately elected president and prime minister who had been confirmed personally, but whose government had not completed the confirmation process. Haiti's defunct lawmakers vehemently protested Préval's decision, citing constitutional irregularities and calling for the populace to rally to their cause. Ultimately, however, Haiti's Supreme Court failed to rule against the president's actions, and ordinary Haitians, "disillusioned with their dysfunctional democracy," failed to respond to the parliamentarians' call.

Unbalanced Power: January–December 1999

Following what Préval's critics labeled a "political coup d'état," Haiti entered into a period characterized by protracted, tedious, and often byzantine political negotiations, and by spasms of demonstrations and politically related unrest. The next twelve months were also characterized by widespread speculation of veiled political intrigue, particularly as it related to the involvement of former President Aristide and his partisans, and uncertain progress toward the resolution of the political deadlock that had all but derailed the country's meandering march toward democratic governance.

Shortly after the president's dismissal of parliament, six political parties, including the OPL, formed the Coalition to Defend Democracy (L'Espace de Concertation pour la Sauvegarde de la Démocratie) and opened negotiations with the executive branch to resolve the crisis. In late February, the OPL withdrew from the coalition, just prior to the murder of still-sitting Senator Yvon Toussaint, a member of the party. On March 6, the remaining five members of the coalition signed an accord with the executive to resolve the crisis. The agreement mandated the quick creation of a CEP to begin organizing the overdue municipal and parliamentary elections. On March 16, Préval named by decree a nine-member CEP that included three members chosen by the coalition. Reaction to Préval's actions varied. The coalition members and the FL welcomed the formation of the CEP. The OPL and several conservative political organizations reacted coolly, noting that while the members appointed to the body were individuals of integrity, the body itself had not been formed in consultation with parliament, as required by law. Next, on March 24 Préval named a government. Led by Prime Minister Alexis, the cabinet of ministers, sworn in on March 26, was viewed by the government's critics as composed principally of supporters of President Préval and former President Aristide.

Before the CEP could move toward elections, it was obligated to resolve the still-festering controversy surrounding the outcome of two Senate seats contested in April 1997 and claimed by the FL. On June 11, the CEP effectively annulled the results of those elections by announcing that the upcoming Senate race would include the two contested seats. It then set the date for the first round of municipal and parliamentary elections as November 28. Although a number of political organizations, notably the OPL, refused to commit to the elections, the FL quickly announced that it would participate. The task facing the nascent electoral body was enormous. In addition to the need to obtain the support and participation of the Haitian people, it had to obtain funding and then oversee such complex tasks as voter and candidate registration and the creation of the election's administrative infrastructure, including the appointment of officials to administer the decentralized process.

In view of the enormity of these tasks, few were surprised when the election date was changed to December 19 and then to March 19, 2000. As the dates for municipal and parliamentary elections edged into the new century, however, another issue emerged: whether these elections would ultimately be held separate from the end-of-2000 election for the person who would succeed President Préval on February 7, 2001. Delays in progress toward bifurcated municipal/legislative and presidential elections were widely viewed as playing into the hands of the FL, whose leader had already announced his candidacy for the presidency. In spite of widespread speculation that the popularity of President Aristide, who had left the priesthood, married, and had a family, had slipped somewhat from its 1990 levels, political observers in Port-au-Prince still viewed his electoral coattails as long enough to assure an FL municipal and parliamentary sweep in a combined, general election. At issue, also, was that of the level of voter turnout. Having declined to 5 percent in April 1997, election officials, civil society leaders, and politicians faced the need to identify effective strategies to return voter participation to the levels experienced a decade earlier.

As the country crept toward either one or two elections in 2000, other issues continued to weigh upon those of politics and governance. The ability of Haiti's National Police force to remain independent from partisan politics was tested repeatedly as various political factions called upon the force to support their position and cause. Although informed observers remained cautiously optimistic that the police, under the leadership of Director General Pierre Denizé, were maintaining their autonomy, they also acknowledged the fragility of this status, particularly in view of increased corruption within the force, mostly linked to Haiti's increased role as a conduit for international cocaine trafficking, and the late 1999 resignation, following months of pressure from FL partisans, of Robert Manuel, secretary of state for public security and close ally of President Préval. The severe and continuing lack of progress in judicial reform also continued to plague the PNH's ability to conduct its mission. An additional challenge facing the PNH was that of providing security for upcoming elections. Undermanned, thinly spread, and confronting an increasingly armed society, the spectre of isolated or general election-related violence—and the PNH's ability to face it—loomed as a large question mark on the horizon.

Concurrently, as Haiti continued to strain under the enormity of the tasks before it, international presence continued to taper off. In August 1999, Washington announced the early 2000 withdrawal of the United States Support Group, a 500-soldier training mission remnant of the 20,000 strong MNF force sent to Haiti in 1994. In December the United Nations announced a final extension of its 280-member Civilian Police Mission in Haiti and the eighty-member International Civilian Mission to March 2000. A new, smaller, and entirely civilian UN umbrella mission with a year-long mandate to cover civilian police, human rights, and judicial reform, functioning in tandem with the UN development mission and under the auspices of the UN General Assembly, however, would follow. In all, Haiti's political landscape at the dawn of the new century could best be described as "fluid and fragile."

Toward Municipal, Parliamentary, and Presidential Elections

As debilitating as the political crisis that prevailed in Haiti following the April 1997 elections was, it can be viewed as an indicator of considerable progress toward the reform of Haiti's system of government and politics, particularly in the use—or lack thereof—of power or force to resolve a political crisis. Indeed, the absence of the army as the traditional means to resolve political problems has given birth in Haiti to the phenomenon of political gridlock. Unfortunately, however, the ability of Haiti's political leaders to dialogue and use political compromise as a non-violent, democratic means to resolve disputes remains underdeveloped. Nevertheless, the fact that disputes were confronted, if not resolved, by debate and political maneuvering, not by violence or weapons, is a positive change in Haiti's political culture.

Less clear during the crisis has been irreversible progress in the evolution of Haiti's political culture from one based on an all-powerful president to one based on principles of democracy, the balance of power, and stable political institutions. The dismissal of parliament in early 1999, the assignment of local elected officials to the Ministry of Interior, and the renewal of presidential rule by decree are all troublesome indicators in the country's struggle to divest itself of the dominant role played by the person who occupies the Presidential Palace.

Given these mixed signals, the future of Haiti's nascent and fragile democracy as it moves toward the next round of elections is far from guaranteed. Thirteen years after the resounding approval by the populace of a new constitution, many of its envisaged institutions of decentralized and responsive government are not in place. The elections instrumental to achieving them are still uncertain exercises, involving increasing controversy and decreasing voter participation. In addition, those elections are still subject to apparent manipulation and postponement, hindering the implementation of important election calendars that correspond with the duration of terms in office.

Perhaps the most problematic aspect of Haiti's quest for political reform and democratization is what former Prime Minister Smarth referred to as the "disease of power" that is deeply rooted in the country's political culture. Haiti's struggle to systematize free and fair elections is an example of the debilitating effects of that disease. Before this disease can be cured, the country must achieve the emplacement of a permanent electoral council (Conseil Électoral Permanent) that can conduct elections according to schedule and objectively. Also, as Haiti's political leaders maneuver to ensure their advantage, they must find effective and efficient means of reaching workable solutions of compromise with their political opponents. The disease of power appears to manifest itself in the continuing tendency among many Haitians to seek solutions in the form of a charismatic leader rather than from a political process that builds strong institutions and seeks progress through negotiation, compromise, and consensus.

As Haiti struggles toward the full implementation of the reformed government and politics sought by most citizens after 1986, many obstacles remain in its path. An examination of the country's constitutional framework provides some understanding of the reforms sought by many Haitians, but that have proven extremely elusive.

Constitutional Framework

Haitian heads of state, often drafting and abolishing the nation's constitutions at will, have treated the documents as their own personal charters. The 1987 constitution, although drafted by an independent commission and ratified by referendum, initially suffered the same treatment. Repeatedly, governments that held power in Haiti between 1986 and 1994 either ignored constitutional provisions, applied them selectively, or suspended them altogether. Only following the restoration of legitimate government in late 1994 was the constitution fully reinstated.

The 1987 constitution is a modern, progressive document. It guarantees a series of basic rights to the citizenry. It declares the intent to establish and maintain democracy in Haiti and includes ideological pluralism, electoral competition, and the separation of powers. Mindful of the perfidious manipulation of constitutions by previous governments, the Haitian jurists who crafted the 1987 constitution carefully prescribed a complex process that requires a two-thirds majority approval of amendments by two consecutive sessions of the National Assembly (Assemblée Nationale) prior to their enactment (Articles 282–1 to 284–1). The articles also ban a sitting president from initiating and enacting amendments during his term of office (Article 284–2) and eliminate the practice of amendment by popular referendum (Article 284–3).

Key provisions of the exacting document, which contains 298 articles, have begun to reshape the governmental system and political tradition bequeathed to Haiti by previous generations of leaders. In particular, the reduction of the president's constitutional powers, the decentralization of governmental authority, and the creation of elected councils for local government have initiated processes of profound change. The constitution establishes the segregation of police and army functions, a point that has become somewhat moot given the 1994–95 dismantling of the Armed Forces of Haiti, but a key provision at the time of ratification. The constitution also establishes an independent judiciary. An extremely popular provision of the 1987 document barred from public office for ten years individuals who had served as "architects" of the Duvalierist dictatorship, enriched themselves from public funds, inflicted torture on political prisoners, or committed political assassinations (Article 291). The constitution abolishes the death penalty and focuses on the protection of civil rights through detailed restrictions on the arrest and detainment of citizens. It calls for the establishment of a career civil service based on merit and for job security, and it recognizes both Creole and French as official languages.

The constitution established a complex system of government based upon three major independent branches of government: legislative, executive, and judicial. Legislative powers are vested in two houses, the Chamber of Deputies and the Senate. Deputies and senators are elected by direct suffrage. Eighty-three deputies are elected to represent electoral districts, and twenty-seven senators represent Haiti's nine geographic departments. In the executive branch, the president of the republic serves as head of state. A prime minister, chosen by the president from the majority party in the legislature, heads the government. Other components of the executive branch include cabinet ministers and secretaries of state. The judiciary consists of a Supreme Court (the Court of Cassation), courts of appeal, and other lower courts. The president appoints judges on the basis of nominations made by various elected bodies, including departmental and communal assemblies.

The constitution also provides for several special institutions and autonomous governmental offices that include the Permanent Electoral Council (Conseil Électoral Permanent), the Superior Court of Auditors and Administrative Disputes, the Conciliation Commission (a body responsible for settling disputes between the executive and legislative branches and between the two houses of the legislature), the Office of Citizen Protection (an ombudsman organization established to protect citizens against abuse by the government), the University of Haiti, the Haitian Academy (responsible for standardizing the Creole language), and the National Institute of Agrarian Reform. The constitution contains a number of provisions intended to guide the country during transitions between elected governments. These provisions include granting the Permanent Electoral Council sufficient autonomy to hold local and national elections, free of outside interference.

The application of constitutional provisions has occasionally been the focus of vigorous political debate, both within the National Assembly and between the legislative and executive

*Presidential Palace with statue of the Unknown Maroon in foreground,
Port-au-Prince
Courtesy United States Agency for International Development*

branches. Particularly protracted and animated has been the
debate surrounding the creation and functioning of the Provisional Electoral Council (Article 289) and its transition to a
Permanent Electoral Council (Articles 191–199), mandated to
take place following the inauguration of the first democratically elected president. Although that event occurred in February 1991, as of late 1999, the Permanent Electoral Council was
still not in place.

Governmental System

At the turn of the century, the complex system of government created by the 1987 constitution was still not completely
in place, although progress had been made since the 1994
ouster of de facto military rule by way of parliamentary and
municipal elections in 1995, the presidential election of 1995,
and programs for judicial reform. The disputed election of
April 1997, the subsequent resignation of the prime minister,
the protracted failure of the executive and legislative branches
to agree on his replacement, and the resultant dismissal of parliament and postponement of parliamentary and municipal
elections have significantly stalled the completion of the gov-

ernmental system and the initiation of a regular electoral calendar based upon the duration of the terms of office of elected officials. Progress toward the emplacement of a reformed judiciary capable of functioning as an independent branch of government has likewise been stalled, in part because of delays in creating the government bodies responsible for nominating judges.

Governmental Institutions

Haiti's complicated system of government is premised on the need to decentralize governmental functions through the composition of a series of executive and legislative bodies that correspond to the country's geopolitical units. Those units are *départements*, of which there are nine; *communes* (municipalities), of which there are 133, approximating United States counties; and *sections communales* (communal sections), of which there are 565, corresponding roughly to United States towns or districts.

Voters in each of the 565 communal sections elect to four-year terms a three-member Communal Section Administrative Council and a seven- to twenty-five-member Communal Section Assembly. Communal section assemblies serve a parliamentary function; they are charged with advising and assisting the communal section administrative councils, which are responsible for administering the affairs of the communal section and, hence, serve as the executive branch of local government. Communal section assemblies also nominate justices of the peace and appoint a representative to the Municipal Assembly, which is the next legislative level of government (see table 26, Appendix).

Each of Haiti's 133 municipalities has both a Municipal Assembly and a Municipal Council. The assemblies are composed of one member per communal section, plus a town delegation whose members are elected to four-year terms. Municipal assemblies serve an essentially parliamentary function, overseeing the three-member Municipal Council, which is elected to a four-year term and functions in an executive role. The president of the Municipal Council serves as mayor.

The legislative and executive bodies in each of Haiti's nine departments are the Departmental Assembly and the Departmental Council, respectively. The assembly is constituted first, comprising one member from each Municipal Assembly within the department. The Departmental Assembly in turn elects three people to serve four-year terms on a Departmental Council. Members of the council do not have to be chosen from among assembly members. In addition to its role in electing members to the council, the Departmental Assembly nominates candidates for the CEP and judges for the courts of appeal and the courts of first instance. It also selects a representative to serve on the Interdepartmental Council. The nine members of the Interdepartmental Council become members of the Council of Ministers, which also includes the prime minister and his cabinet of ministers. Representatives of the departmental assemblies who become members of the Council of Ministers carry ministerial rank and voting rights on issues of decentralization and development.

The executive branch is headed by a president elected by popular vote to a five-year, non-renewable term. The president names a prime minister, who, once confirmed by the National Assembly, or parliament, heads the government, selecting a council of ministers or cabinet and appointing their secretaries of state. The cabinet of Prime Minister Jacques Édouard Alexis in December 1999 was composed of fifteen ministers (see table 27, Appendix). The president presides over the Council of Ministers, which must be composed of no fewer than ten members. He or she also appoints representatives to coordinate and control public service functions, excluding public safety, in each department.

The legislative branch is headed by the National Assembly composed of a Senate (Sénat) and a Chamber of Deputies (Chambre de Députés). The three senators of each department are elected to staggered six-year terms, with one-third of the Senate coming up for election every two years. The eighty-three deputies are elected from smaller electoral districts determined by population distribution. Large urban areas can be represented by no more than three deputies.

Haiti derived the formal aspects of its legal system from Roman law, the Napoleonic Code, and the French system of civil law. Like the executive and legislative branches of government, the judiciary is also decentralized, based on an ascending order of courts, beginning at the municipal level with the Court of the Justice of the Peace and rising to the Court of Cassation (Supreme Court). Justice of the peace courts are located in each of Haiti's municipalities. Each court has at least one judge and other officials. To be nominated as a justice of the peace, an individual must have a law degree, be at least twenty-five years old, be in good legal standing, and have completed a probationary period of at least one year. Justices of the peace hear civil law cases, including those that involve limited sums of money, and landlord and tenant disputes. Their jurisdiction in criminal matters extends only to cases where the penalty does not exceed six months in jail.

Courts of first instance are either civil or criminal tribunals located in major cities. Each court has one judge and various other officers. The courts hear civil cases and all criminal cases, including those sent by the inspector general of the Haitian National Police. For nomination to this court, an individual is required to have practiced law for at least two years. Sitting above the courts of first instance are courts of appeals, of which there are four, located in Port-au-Prince, Les Cayes, Gonaïves, and Cap-Haïtien. The appeals court in the capital has a president and five judges; those in the other cities have a president and four judges. These courts hear both civil and criminal cases, including all appeals from courts of first instance and criminal appeals from justice of the peace courts. For appointment to a Court of Appeals, judges must have been on the bench of courts of first instance for at least three years.

Haiti's highest court, the Court of Cassation, consists of a president, a vice president, and ten judges. It generally functions in two chambers with five judges each, but functions as a whole when hearing appeals and pleas concerning the unconstitutionality of laws and decrees. Judges of the Court of Cassation must be at least thirty years old and must have held the position of judge or public attorney for at least seven years.

In addition to these courts, there are also a Superior Court of Auditors and Administrative Disputes and special courts that oversee matters concerning property rights, juveniles, and labor conflicts. The Senate may constitute itself into a High Court of Justice to preside over crimes of state treason, embezzlement, or abuse of power involving high state officials in the discharge of their duties. In 1996 a School of the Magistrature opened in Port-au-Prince to provide judicial training for current and new judges.

Functions of Government

Historically, most Haitians have viewed government functionaries as beneficiaries of patronage and the spoils system rather than as public servants. Governments traditionally supported and maintained the established political order and extracted wealth from the population. Citizens therefore expected little or nothing from the state. Rather, reflected by the fact that the Creole word for state—*leta*—also means "bully," they saw government as an entity that confiscated, taxed, prohibited, or imprisoned. The notion of government working in partnership with its people, respecting a social contract to help improve all citizens' standing within the society, has been an abstraction.

The Haitian government also traditionally served as a source of jobs. Payrolls of state ministries and state enterprises were inflated by leaders with cronies and family members, some of whom, the infamous *zonbi* (zombie) employees, appeared only to collect their salaries. Political favoritism and bribery plagued the system. Social scientists have used terms such as *kleptocracy, predatory state, government-by-franchise,* and *autocolonization* to describe the Haitian system of taxation, patronage, corruption, public monopolies, and private monopolies protected by the state.

The Haitian state developed a relatively elaborate apparatus for taxing average citizens, but it provided them few public services. As a result, Haitians have relied heavily on foreign-assistance agencies, nongovernmental organizations (NGOs), and remittances from abroad to receive or purchase services provided by most other governments. Education, for example, has been the Haitian government's most elaborate public-service sector, but the majority of children attend costly private schools. The state's abdication of its role as service provider created a situation in which foreign-assistance agencies and the NGOs they support served as a kind of shadow government.

Government institutions in Port-au-Prince have provided the facade of public services through the Ministry of Public Health and Population; the Ministry of Agriculture, Natural Resources, and Rural Development; the Ministry of National Education, Youth, and Sports; and others. These ministries have had no representatives in most rural areas, however, and they have provided relatively few services even in Port-au-Prince. Government budgets for public services generally accounted for salaries, but they provided little or no support for program implementation.

In addition to the armed forces, the main Haitian institution bringing in revenue has been the customs house. The state also extracted wealth through its control over certain essential services and through public and private monopoly ownership of key commodity-based enterprises. Since the restoration of elected government, the dismantling of the army, and subsequent progress in the democratic political process, the state's image as predator and bully is changing. State monopolies and franchises have disappeared or are in the process of being restructured. The oppressive section chief system that epitomized the state as bully no longer exists (see Aristide Presidency, February 7, 1991–September 30, 1991, ch. 6, and Role of the Army in Law Enforcement Prior to 1995, ch. 10).

The government's income tax agency (Département Général des Impôts—DGI) has become the object of reform efforts and has been restructured as part of an overall effort to collect taxes equitably from all citizens (wealthy Haitians have generally paid little, if any, government taxes). The government's relationship with other institutions in the society, particularly NGOs, is in flux as public policies now advocate a lead role for government in the provision of citizen services. In this regard, some elected and public officials, recollecting the cozy relationship that existed between certain NGOs and the Haitian army, have also vocalized their desire to dismantle the "Republic of NGOs."

Haitians held high expectations that government would quickly demonstrate an improved capacity to serve its citizens following the end of de facto military rule. The renewed flow of bilateral and multilateral funding following the 1994 intervention heightened those expectations. Thus far, however, stated policies and initial efforts to decentralize governmental structure and function have not been widely matched by a flow of government resources from Port-au-Prince, an improved capacity of public officials to collect and manage public revenues, or an improved standard of life for ordinary citizens. While mayors, other local officials, and citizens struggle to find resources to sponsor or support local development activities, they see an inept and struggling national government that continues both to be the country's principal employer and to spend most of its resources on itself. Although government is no longer necessarily perceived as a repressive and extractive entity, many have taken to viewing it as a *grand mangeur* (big eater) that uses public resources to feed only itself.

Urban Dominance, Rural Exclusion: Confronting Entrenched Patterns

First-time visitors to the country are often told that Haiti is actually two distinct countries—the Republic of Haiti and the Republic of Port-au-Prince—that have little contact with each other. The sharp division between them and between the outsiders of rural Haiti and the city dwellers is reflected in the dominance of the capital city. National political institutions and decisions, steadfastly focused on Port-au-Prince, have been far removed from the lives of most Haitians. The political system affects all Haitians, but changes in government have had little direct impact on the lives of rural dwellers. Governments have concentrated themselves in the capital, allocating two-thirds or more of their revenues to be spent in a city that traditionally has held fewer than 20 percent of Haiti's people. Foreign assistance has tended to exacerbate rural-urban differences because about 40 percent of all foreign aid has directly benefited Port-au-Prince.

In contrast to the relative, albeit selective and uneven, development of Port-au-Prince, provincial cities and towns and rural hamlets have remained undeveloped, lacking such basic twentieth-century amenities as electricity, piped water, sanitation services, and adequate roads. They offer their inhabitants little more than primitive conditions, few opportunities, and a place from which to try to escape, an option taken by ever-increasing numbers seeking perceived greater opportunities in Port-au-Prince and farther afield. As a result of shifting populations, Haiti's rural and urban demographics have begun to change, Port-au-Prince and its environs have expanded significantly, in all possible directions, and in 1998 held approximately 2 million inhabitants (see Population, ch. 7).

Following the demise of the Duvalier dictatorship in 1986, decentralization became a catch phrase of those seeking greater public-sector attention to secondary cities, small towns, and villages, and a reversal of historical trends of government investment. In the succeeding years of military rule, decentralization came principally in the form of opening regional ports that had been closed by the dictatorship and fallen into disrepair. The port openings, which could have increased customs revenue and fueled local development, resulted instead in the generation of wealth for those linked to the contraband trade that flowed in and out of the reopened ports. Key public institutions responsible for controlling trade and overseeing revenue collection, notably the customs bureau, port authority, and coast guard, were either corrupt, inept, or nonexistent.

With the restoration of elected government and the subsequent renewed process toward a decentralized governmental system prescribed by the constitution, renewed attention has been placed on entrenched patterns of urban dominance and rural exclusion, and on developing or strengthening government institutions. Debates over the allocation of scarce public resources and the priority use of foreign assistance amid desperate and growing needs in both of Haiti's "republics" now are joined by parliamentarians who originate from long-neglected areas, and are fueled by pressure from local elected officials and the voters who elected them. Although this dynamic of governance is still at an early and uncertain phase of development, it represents a fundamental change from the traditional and unchallenged domination of the capital and its political class.

As debates continue, progress toward developing or strengthening government capacity, in both Port-au-Prince and elsewhere, has been minimal. Revenue generation for enhanced public investment remains ineffective as contraband continues to flourish. State institutions charged with the responsibility for overseeing measures of effective decentralization remain weak and/or disproportionately focused on Port-au-Prince. The Ministry of Agriculture, Natural Resources, and Rural Development, for example, has more employees in the capital than elsewhere in the country. Port-au-Prince, with its increased growth and myriad of highly visible and urgent problems brought on by a deteriorated infrastructure and ever-increasing overcrowding, continues to receive a disproportionate amount of public attention and investment.

Still, the preeminence of the capital in setting Haiti's political agenda is being challenged by the emergence of a decentralized governmental system. Heightened attention among the country's elected leaders to issues of urban dominance and rural exclusion, brought on in large part by shifting patterns of political participation, suggests that a change in the uneven relationships between Haiti's two "republics" is beginning to take place.

Political Dynamics

The Haitian political system historically has displayed certain enduring features. In recent years, especially since late 1994, many of these features have begun to change.

*Poster bidding farewell to Jean-Bertrand Aristide, following his
1994 overthrow
Courtesy Anne Greene*

Political Players and Patterns of Participation

Involvement in Haitian politics traditionally has been the
domain of the army and urban elites. Other members of the
society, the demographically dominant urban poor and the
rural masses, largely excluded from meaningful participation
in the country's political life, have been the target of Haiti's
political players, particularly when they could be mobilized to
serve ulterior motives of political leaders. The Duvaliers were
masterful at mobilizing the masses to serve their ends: trucking
peasants to the capital so they could demonstrate their "support" of the regime; creating festive events and holidays during
which the poor could receive hand-outs from their munificent
leader such as food, currency in the form of five-gourde notes
thrown at them from passing cars, and T-shirts emblazoned
with a likeness of the president.

With the demise of the Duvaliers, Haiti's political outsiders
struggled to gain meaningful participation in their country's
political process. The clear parameters for the equal participation in political life for all citizens established by the 1987 constitution facilitated a tidal wave of outside voter registration in
1990 immediately after their man, Jean-Bertrand Aristide,
declared his candidacy for the presidency. Haiti's political elites

were forced to confront an unexpected and sobering reality when the populist priest came from nowhere to defeat resoundingly their candidate and expected victor, Marc Bazin, on the strength of the independent participation of voters whose views and participation previously had not counted. Indeed, many observers have attributed the subsequent support of the military by Haiti's established political class at least in part to the fact that they could not accept a political scenario where their votes were equal to those of their maids and illiterate peasants.

Since 1990 the inclusion in Haiti's political life of its former political outsiders has expanded to include their participation as candidates in local and national elections, and their ascension to various elected posts. These trends have resulted in the emergence of a heretofore largely unknown dynamic in Haitian politics, that of increased accountability of elected officials to their constituents. Port-au-Prince continues to be the center of Haiti's political life, and political players based there loom large in determining the country's political dynamics. Nevertheless, the ascension of outsiders to meaningful inclusion in the country's politics, combined with the disappearance of the army as a political player and the partial eclipse of the dominant power of urban political elites, has created an important and fundamental alteration of Haiti's political dynamics.

Maintenance and Transfer of Power

During the twenty-nine-year rule of the Duvaliers, Haiti resembled not a republic, but a dynastic monarchy, where a leader extended his term of office at will, ultimately to become "president-for-life," and power was transferred from father to son. The Duvalier achievement of hereditary succession was new to Haiti, but arbitrary term extensions and for-life presidencies were not. Duvalier's immediate predecessors all tried to extend their prescribed terms in office, and nine of his predecessors had designated themselves chiefs of state for life. In short, the primary goal of most Haitian leaders has been to maintain themselves in power for as long as possible.

The governmental system prescribed by Haiti's 1987 constitution, although still incomplete in its implementation, was created in large part to constrain such presidential perfidy. The five-year, nonconsecutive term of the top executives is only one of a number of constraints aimed at ensuring regular and orderly transitions of power. When President Aristide opted not to attempt to extend his term in office by three years to make up for the time lost in exile, but rather stood down and transferred power peacefully to René Préval, he established a positive precedent for his successors. In a country, however, where a well-known proverb reminds all that "Laws are made of paper, bayonets are made of steel," it was the dismantling of the army, not the constitution by itself, that enabled such a pre-scribed transition to occur. Unless this now-obsolete proverb can find its way back into Haiti's political lexicon, the mainte-nance and extension of the personal power of a president, if now achieved, must take place by a combination of nonconsec-utive terms and a political proxy, and under the watchful eyes of a parliament that may not be prone to making such a maneuver easy.

The Presidency and Political Culture

Although hundreds of positions were open in the 1990 elec-tions, it was only one—the presidency—that seemed to matter. In 1994 the restoration to power of one person, President Aris-tide, overshadowed all other issues linked to Haiti's three-year, post-coup crisis. Underscored by this attention to one office or to one person was a deeply ingrained Haitian political reality: the focus has always been on the presidency, the crown jewel—some might say the only jewel—in Haitian politics. For genera-tions, the aspiration of Haitian political leaders has been to achieve the all-powerful position of the presidency. Haitian writers have often described in pathological terms the obses-sion of Haiti and its political leaders with the presidency. Prior to becoming president, François Duvalier wrote about the his-torical "mania for the presidency" as the disease of "presidenti-tis." State and nation merged in the person of the president, an often godlike figure with life-and-death power over the citi-zenry. Presidents rarely represented a coalition of interest groups; instead they usually headed a faction or political move-ment that seized control of the state by any means possible, with the support, or at least the tolerance, of the army.

These perceptions, and the reality of weakly developed polit-ical institutions and separation of powers, have reflected the disproportionate power of the country's chief executive and the existence in Haiti of a political culture based on who would be the president. Political parties or movements organized around a charismatic or powerful leader who could ascend directly to the position. Legislative bodies and elections, which have existed for centuries in form if not in substance, have generally done little except assist the chief of state in obtaining whatever he wished.

More than a decade after 1986's pivotal event, which unleashed the country's pent-up desire to modernize its government and politics, there remains the fundamental challenge to move from a political culture based on the presidency to one based on democracy. As Haiti's political institutions have strengthened themselves, governmental structure and function have begun to decentralize and devolve certain responsibilities from Port-au-Prince. As a result, separation of powers has gained real meaning, and the supremacy of the presidency has begun to decline. President Préval has endured much criticism—from both within and beyond Haiti—as a weak president. Although few would argue that he lacks the charisma of his predecessor, it is also true that his is the first administration to confront fully the realities of the constitutionally weakened presidency. As Haiti moves toward the election of Préval's successor, the weakened presidency may be challenged by the return of Jean-Bertrand Aristide.

Perceptions of Democracy

After the fall of Jean-Claude Duvalier in 1986, talk of democracy was everywhere in Haiti. Average Haitians expected that life would improve dramatically with the muzzle of dictatorship gone and democracy at their doorstep. For most Haitians, however, democracy was an abstract concept. They had not experienced anything close to real democracy, having been excluded from a voice in the political process. The political role models for most Haitians emerged during the Duvalier era. For many, notions of democracy meant only a change in the factions and the personalities of the people in power. For others, democracy meant their finally being able to take their turn at the spoils system. Some people believed that democracy meant an opportunity to do what one pleased—liberty without responsibility. Many felt that a democracy should provide everyone with jobs, food, and material goods.

Between 1986 and 1991, Haitians had an opportunity to become better acquainted with the concept of democracy through their participation in a constitutional referendum and in election processes, and through their involvement in a spectrum of political organizations, whose activities ranged from neighborhood committees to political parties. They also had an opportunity to experience democracy as a slow and difficult process, especially in a context such as Haiti's, and not as a sudden elixir to eliminate problems. Between 1991 and 1994, when Haitians suffered painful setbacks to the fitful process of political change they had been able to put in motion, their commitment to what remained largely an abstraction was profoundly tested. Regardless of varying perceptions of what democracy was or would be, Haiti's people stood firm behind their commitment to it.

Since the 1994 restoration of democratic governance, Haiti's experience with the democratic process has deepened, but the results have disappointed many. Although voters have shown thus far a penchant for denying new candidates or those standing for re-election who appear susceptible to the deeply ingrained political role models of the past, fewer and fewer are voting; participation in elections has declined precipitously with each election. Voter disenchantment with the results of those exercises is a key factor contributing to the growing apathy. In spite of their participation in the process, few Haitians have seen improvement in their economic conditions. Indeed, most have seen their quality of life worsen as they witness, instead, titanic political struggles among factions in parliament and between the executive and legislative branches. As long as Haiti's democratic process fails to produce political results that can bring tangible improvements in overall and individual well-being to Haiti's citizens, it will remain fragile, nascent, and susceptible to setbacks.

The Mass Media and the Spread of Information

The mass media in Haiti expanded rapidly between the 1950s and the 1990s, with radio leading the way. The transistor radio brought news and information to previously isolated rural areas. Joining state-owned radio during the Duvalier years were stations established by private entrepreneurs and by Protestant missionaries and the Roman Catholic Church. The latter's station, Radio Soleil, which emphasized educational broadcasts, played an important role in the fall of Jean-Claude Duvalier in 1986. Following that event, the approximately two dozen radio stations broadcasting in Haiti, at least half of which operated from Port-au-Prince, became the principal source of information on breaking political developments through their use of mobile units equipped for direct broadcast. Stations also became the venue used by political leaders and activists to issue declarations and demands. In 1996 Haiti had more than sixty radio stations, including twenty-nine in the Port-au-Prince area.

Under 1991–94 de facto military rule, several radio stations were ransacked, and outspoken announcers were kidnapped and/or killed. Fearing the consequences of political reporting, stations undertook a mode of self-censorship. Objective reports on the political crisis reached Haiti via shortwave Voice of America (VOA) broadcasts, from stations broadcasting in Creole from the Dominican Republic, and, at one point, from United States military aircraft equipped with radio transmitters. Since late 1994, Haiti's radio stations have resumed their pre-coup role as outlets for news, political commentary, declarations, and discussions. Their number has expanded considerably with the advent of low-power, community-based radio stations.

In 1996 Haiti's print media were dominated by two daily newspapers published in Port-au-Prince with an estimated combined circulation of 29,000, four weekly newspapers including three edited in New York and Miami and sold in Haiti, and a variety of monthly publications. The number of publications varies over time, with some produced irregularly. Circulation outside Port-au-Prince is limited. Unlike radio, which broadcasts principally in Creole, Haiti's print media are primarily in French. In 1996 Haiti had six publishing houses and several dozen bookstores.

In 1996 some twenty television stations, including a cable network, were broadcasting in Haiti. With the advent of small, independent stations in Haiti's secondary cities, broadcasts are much more available than before outside of Port-au-Prince. Those with means own satellite dishes that pick up television signals from abroad. During de facto military rule, international broadcasts picked up by these dishes played a major role in disseminating information. Telephones, faxes, and E-mail also played a key role in diffusing information, both during de facto military rule and after it. Their utility, however, is circumscribed by the irregularity and low quality of Haiti's telephone service, and the limited number of available telephone lines. In 1996 President Préval disbanded the government's Ministry of Propaganda and Information. Taking its place have been public relations offices and information officer positions in key government ministries and departments.

Technology and modern communications notwithstanding, *zen,* that is, information and rumors passed from one person to the next, continues to play a key role in the reporting and dissemination of news in Haiti. News of incidents occurring in far reaches of the country is often spread through *zen* more rapidly than by electronic or print media, which, given their own resource limitations, depend to a certain extent on *zen* networks as their sources. If not carefully checked for accuracy, however, reporting based on *zen* can result in the spread of incomplete or distorted information.

Creole has become Haiti's principal language of communication in radio and television, and among officials in public positions and civil society organizations. Many candidates elected to office since 1995 speak only Creole. In recent years, ever since its orthography became standardized, written Creole has been used much more frequently. It has become the language of preference in adult literacy classes and has been more thoroughly incorporated into the formal education system. The production of materials written in Creole also has expanded tremendously since the 1980s. French, however, remains widely represented in the press, commercials, advertisements, street names, and the cultural scene.

Interest Groups

Since the 1986 demise of the Duvalier dictatorship, a variety of such interest groups as political parties, political activist organizations, private-sector and professional associations, and civil society organizations, including NGOs, regional peasant movements, and community groups, have become a greater part of the Haitian political landscape. The groups function with varying degrees of freedom, visibility, and effectiveness. Since late 1994, their ability to function freely, in accordance with the law, has been guaranteed.

Political Parties

Political parties in Haiti have existed in name since the nineteenth century, but have not exerted independent influence on the political system. As a rule, they have been dominated by an elite, self-described political class based in the Republic of Port-au-Prince. Parties have been most active during presidential election campaigns, when they have organized under the banner of specific individuals serving as their campaign vehicles. Parties have tended to be institutionalized around their founder/leader, to thrive or perish according to that individual's political status. This historical tendency has changed slightly in recent years, particularly as parties have begun to try to build national constituencies and to compete for lesser offices.

In the 1870s and 1880s, the emergence of the Liberal Party (Parti Libéral—PL) and the National Party (Parti National—PN) reflected the polarization between black and mulatto elites. In the wake of the United States occupation (1915–34), nationalist parties organized around the issue of resistance to foreign occupation. During the presidential campaign of 1946, there were many candidates and parties, including the Popular Socialist Party (Parti Socialiste Populaire—PSP), Worker Peasant Movement (Mouvement Ouvrier Paysan—MOP), Communist Party of Haiti (Parti Communiste d'Haïti—PCH), and a federation of groups known as the Haitian Revolutionary Front (Front Révolutionnaire Haïtien—FRH).

The presidential campaign of 1956–57 included candidates who ran under the banners of the National Agricultural Industrial Party (Parti Agricole et Industriel National—PAIN), the MOP, the PN, and the National Unity Party (Parti Unité National—PUN), which was led by François Duvalier. Both Duvalier governments banned, or severely restricted, opposition political parties. As a result, about a dozen opposition parties operated in exile, including the established PAIN and MOP, and such newcomers as the National Political Assembly of Democrats (Rassemblement Démocratique National Politique—RDNP) formed by Leslie Manigat in Venezuela, the Unified Haitian Communist Party (Parti Unifié des Communistes Haïtiens—PUCH) based in France, and the National Progressive Revolutionary Haitian Party (Parti National Progressiste Révolutionnaire Haïtien—Panpra) headed by France-based Serge Gilles.

With the ouster of the Duvalier dictatorship, exiled parties shifted their activities to Haiti, often coinciding with the "triumphal" return home of their leaders. During the presidential campaign of 1987, more than 100 individuals announced their candidacy. As of August 1987, twenty-one political parties had registered. None of these parties, however, developed a nationwide organization, although four of them stood out from the rest prior to the violence that sabotaged the election: the Christian Democrat Party of Haiti (Parti Démocrate Chrétien d'Haïti—PDCH), led by Sylvio Claude; the Movement for the Installation of Democracy in Haiti (Mouvement pour l'Instauration de la Démocratie en Haïti—MIDH), led by Marc Bazin; PAIN, led by its founder's son, Louis Dejoie II; and the National Cooperative Front (Front National de Concertation—FNC), represented by Gérard Gourgue. The FNC, a loose federation of parties, community groups, and trade unions that had previously joined forces as the Group of 57, had the broadest and most diverse following. It included two well-structured parties with some national membership—the National Committee of the Congress of Democratic Movements (Comité National du Congrès des Mouvements Démocratiques—Conacom) and Panpra.

By the 1990 elections, the FNC had expanded its coalition to include the Unified Democratic Committee (KID, based on the Creole name) and its charismatic leader Evans Paul, altered its name to the National Front for Change and Democracy (Front National pour le Changement et la Démocratie—FNCD), and become affiliated with Jean-Bertrand Aristide's amorphous Lavalas movement when it persuaded him to be its standard-bearer. Although twelve other parties fielded presidential aspirants and slates of candidates for other posts, Marc Bazin of the MIDH was considered the chief rival to Aristide. Bazin, however, drowned in Lavalas's cleansing flood as Aristide swept to office. His political ally and KID leader, Paul, captured what was perhaps the elections' second largest prize: Port-au-Prince City Hall. The victors of other parliamentary, municipal, and local offices were divided among the FNCD, MIDH, and other parties.

Most political party activities shifted out of Haiti following the 1991 coup d'état. However, three developments in Haiti affected the country's political party dynamics. First, in 1991 Sylvio Claude was assassinated, effectively ending the PDCH. Second, in 1992 MIDH leader Bazin accepted an appointment as the military government's prime minister, inflicting the same fundamental damage to his future and that of his party as Leslie Manigat inflicted on himself and his RDNP when he accepted the presidency offered by the military in rigged elections in 1988. Third, in 1993 supporters of Aristide in Haiti announced the formation of the Lavalas Political Organization (OPL), headed by political scientist Gérard Pierre-Charles, peasant movement leader Chavannes Jean-Baptiste, and agronomist Yrvelt Chéry.

Following the return of Aristide, the OPL became the leading institution of the Lavalas movement, as Aristide broke with the FNCD and his ally, Evans Paul. In the 1995 parliamentary and municipal elections, the FNCD presented itself as the main opposition to the Lavalas Political Platform, a coalition that pulled together the OPL, MOP, and two newer parties, the Open Gate Party (Pati Louvri Baryè—PLB), which had its strongest following in the North Department, and the Resistance Committee of Grand' Anse (KOREGA, based on the Creole name), a Lavalas group based principally in the Grand' Anse and South departments. Most other marginal political parties boycotted the elections, although some individuals affiliated with them presented their candidacies. Their absence was not felt; voters endorsed the PPL or independent candidates linked with Lavalas by large margins of victory in most races. Without the Lavalas endorsement, Evans Paul failed to gain re-election as mayor of Port-au-Prince, and the FNCD was almost shut out.

Of the fourteen candidates who ran in the December 1995 presidential election, four were independents; nine were affiliated with political parties. The landslide winner, René Préval, ran simply as Lavalas. As noted elsewhere, since those elections the Lavalas movement has splintered in two directions: toward Jean-Bertrand Aristide's Lavalas Family, created in 1997, and toward the OPL, which altered its name to the Organization of Struggling People to symbolize its break from Aristide's Lavalas. The OPL is headed by Gérard Pierre-Charles. The other parties that formed the 1995 PPL coalition—MOP, PLB, KOREGA—remain active, although they are currently overshadowed by the FL-OPL division. The marginal parties, now including the FNCD and sometimes lumped together as "the opposition," still exist, but they are characterized by small followings. They are plagued by their inability to distinguish themselves from political pasts that do not appeal to most voters, or to form effective coalitions. Since the contested elections of April 1997, the OPL has occasionally taken a common position with these parties.

Duvalierists and *Makout*

Support for the de facto military regime was strong among a network of individuals and organizations that had participated in the well-developed patronage system of the Duvalier dictatorships and the military regimes that followed. Among them were the former members of the infamous nationwide paramilitary organization, the *tonton makout*, and Duvalierist or military sympathizers who lost their jobs when ministries were down-sized in 1990. Still others included the sons of past military and *makout* leaders, who, in 1993, organized the Revolutionary Front for the Advancement and Progress of Haiti (Front Révolutionnaire pour l'Avancement et le Progrès d'Haïti—FRAPH), a paramilitary group that backed the military regime. Following the MNF intervention, decommissioned members of the FAd'H and some of their political allies joined this loose, anti-democracy network. With the abolition of the FAd'H, how-ever, the disparate groups and individuals that make up this network, although representing a destabilizing factor, have no established institutional base for coordination or support.

The Elite

The system of public and private monopolies, including par-astatals and import-substitution industries, developed under the Duvaliers and sustained by subsequent military regimes generated great wealth for a handful of powerful families in Port-au-Prince. Viewing itself threatened by changes in the political status quo, this elite sector backed the military govern-ments likely to protect their lucrative business privileges estab-lished under the old regime. Characterized as MREs (Morally Repugnant Elites) by international actors during the de facto military period, Haiti's upper crust has had to adapt to the country's altered political framework following an interna-tional intervention that came not to their assistance, but to the assistance of those they opposed.

Not all of Haiti's elite can be assigned MRE status. Some, feeling the pinch of international sanctions and perhaps dis-gust with the FAd'H's mounting human rights atrocities, exhib-ited a willingness to work toward the restoration of the Aristide government prior to the intervention, as evidenced by their participation in a widely publicized meeting in Miami with Aris-tide and his supporters in early 1994. Since the restoration of democratic governance, they and others have opened relations with the Aristide and Préval administrations, seeking mutually beneficial relations and upholding the deeply established prac-tice of *politique de doublure* (political understudies) (see Early Years of Independence, 1804–43, ch. 6). Since 1994 some gov-ernment officials have privately expressed displeasure with the MRE characterization, feeling that it maintains polarization at a time when reconciliation is required. "This country will not develop without their participation," one high-ranking official stated. Some in government and among the elites emphasize the importance of recognizing generational differences and supporting the efforts of younger generations to "play by the rules." The creation of revamped chambers of commerce in the country's secondary cities and the work of the Center for Free Enterprise and Democracy (Centre pour la Libre Entreprise et la Démocratie—CLED), a private-sector association founded in 1993, are cited as examples of these efforts.

Some of these younger members have emerged from the intermediate classes (those between the wealthy elite and the impoverished masses) that grew significantly during the Duvalier era, principally as a result of Papa Doc's political strategy of providing avenues of patronage to the black middle class as a means for creating a new political constituency. Others are the educated sons and daughters of middle-class professionals who emigrated from Haiti in droves to Europe, Africa, Latin America, and the Caribbean, and, most commonly, to North America during the Duvalier years, or who have been educated abroad. Returning home, they bring resources, experience, expertise, attitudes, and values that reinforce Haiti's efforts to change.

Civil Society

In a report issued in 1992, the Inter-American Development Bank estimated that between 800 and 1,000 development NGOs were active in Haiti prior to the coup d'état. Not included in the bank's figures were the thousands of community-based religious, social, and economic groups that had emerged by 1991 to become involved in improving the lives of their members and communities. The groups, and the national and international NGOs that work with them, tended to coalesce around such interests as literacy, agricultural production and marketing, credit, the status of women and children, civil and legal rights, and access to improved social and economic services. They should be distinguished from the so-called popular organizations that arise in response to timely issues; these organizations are more informally structured, and sometimes do little more than serve as mouthpieces for various politicians.

During the 1990s, particularly since 1994, civil society organizations also have been deeply involved in reforming Haiti's political process and making the government responsive to citizens. Haitians in organized civil society associations formed the core of the Lavalas political movement's strength. By 1995, having seen their associations disintegrate, their leaders forced into exile or hiding, and their programs damaged or destroyed during the three years of de facto military rule, civil society activists seemed determined to engage the political system more profoundly—as candidates for political office or as appointees in public posts. As a result, many mayors, members of communal section administrative councils and of the parliament, and government technicians throughout Haiti have their roots in grassroots groups or the NGOs that work with them. Their experience as grassroots activists has infused Haitian government, especially at the communal and municipal levels, with new and, at least initially, idealistic leadership that is well informed of the challenges that government needs to confront. Given access to supporting resources, they are well positioned to work in partnership with organized civil society and the modernizing business sector to begin to confront them. It is yet to be seen, however, if this new generation of leaders will change the entrenched political system or if the system will, indeed, change them.

Foreign Relations

A Haitian religious leader recently stated that his country's relative importance on the world stage is like an accordion: sometimes it is small; sometimes it is large. Although Haiti's relative isolation through most of its history has constrained its foreign relations, keeping the imagined accordion small, at times Haiti has occupied a prominent place on the world stage. This was particularly the case between 1991 and 1996, when a violent military coup d'état against the internationally recognized Aristide government, followed by three years of brutal de facto rule, led to international sanctions, intense multilateral diplomacy, a refugee crisis, and, ultimately, an international military intervention and peacekeeping operation sanctioned by the United Nations (UN) and led by the United States. The intense attention given to Haiti during this period not just by the UN and the United States, but also by the Organization of American States (OAS), member states of the Caribbean Community and Common Market (Caricom), a grouping within the UN referred to as The Friends of Haiti (Argentina, Canada, France, the United States, and Venezuela), and the governments of the thirty-four countries that contributed personnel to the UN peacekeeping operation, has placed the relatively small Caribbean country on the world stage as never before,

449

perhaps to such an extent that its isolation from the world community has ended.

Haiti achieved some prominence as a result of its successful revolution, but the governments of slaveholding countries either ignored or decried the country during the first half of the nineteenth century. In the United States, the question of recognizing Haiti provoked sharp debate between abolitionists, who favored recognition, and slaveholders, who vehemently opposed such action. The advent of the Civil War, however, allowed President Abraham Lincoln to recognize Haiti without controversy. Haiti became a focus of interest for the great powers in the early twentieth century mainly because of the country's strategic location. Competition among the United States, Germany, France, and Britain resulted in the breaching of Haiti's sovereignty and the nineteen-year occupation (1915–34) by United States forces (see United States Involvement in Haiti, 1915–34, ch. 6). Subsequent isolation stemmed from Haiti's cultural and linguistic uniqueness, its economic underdevelopment, and international condemnation of the Duvalier dictatorship and subsequent military regimes.

Relations with the United States

Haiti has maintained a long-standing relationship with the United States. Economic ties to the United States are vital, as the latter country is Haiti's primary trading partner for both exports and imports. The United States is also Haiti's most important source of bilateral foreign assistance and the primary target for Haitian emigration. A large number of United States private voluntary agencies and religious groups are active in Haiti, for example. The Haitian private sector is closely tied to the United States economy. In short, the economic and political influence of the United States in Haiti has been more extensive than the influence of any other country.

United States diplomatic interest in Haiti has been uneven. Washington's interest in its neighbor arose chiefly because of the country's proximity to the Panama Canal and Central America. Haiti borders the Windward Passage, a narrow body of water on which maritime traffic could be easily disrupted. During World War I, the United States undertook a military occupation of Haiti, along with a number of other countries in the Caribbean and Central America. During the Cold War, Washington viewed Haiti as an anti-communist bulwark, partly because of the country's proximity to Cuba. François Duvalier

United Nations mission personnel in Moulin sur Mer, 1996
Courtesy Anne Greene

exploited United States hostility toward the Cuban regime of Fidel Castro and United States fears of communist expansion in the Caribbean basin in order to deter the United States government from exerting excessive pressure on his own dictatorship.

Since the 1980s, the United States has been particularly interested in curbing illegal Haitian immigration. Washington also has focused on Haiti as a transshipment point for narcotics destined for United States markets and has undertaken various efforts to curtail shipments. Between 1986 and 1994, Haitian army involvement in drug trafficking reduced the effectiveness of United States efforts. Following the 1996 departure of UN peacekeeping troops, United States attention to narcotics trafficking in Haiti has intensified because Haitian coasts have become particularly vulnerable to international traffickers seeking to land their product on Hispaniola for transfer to proximate United States ports of entry, notably Puerto Rico.

From the 1970s until 1987, United States assistance to Haiti grew. Between 1987 and 1994, however, the flow of assistance to Haiti was disrupted on several occasions, notably following the 1987 election massacre and during the 1991–94 period of de facto military rule. Following the restoration of Haiti's legitimate government in late 1994, the United States added a pledge of US$458 million to the US$2.342 billion pledged by other bilateral and multilateral donors for the rehabilitation and development of the country over five years. Four years later, the majority of those funds (approximately US$1.5 billion) remained undisbursed, largely as a result of factors in Haiti (see Economic Policies, ch. 8).

Relations with the Dominican Republic

The second most important country to Haiti is the Dominican Republic, with which it shares the island of Hispaniola. An enormous amount of trade, much of it informal, crosses the border. The Haitian economy has proved to be a desirable market for Dominican products. During the 1991–94 period of international economic sanctions on Haiti, the flow of goods from the Dominican Republic provided a lifeline for the de facto military regime and facilitated the market penetration of Dominican products as never before. By the mid-1990s, an estimated US$50 million in products flowed annually from the Dominican Republic into Haiti.

Until recently, political relations between Haiti and the Dominican Republic have been strained. For generations, Haitians had informally crossed into the Dominican Republic in search of work. The perceived "blackening" of the Dominican population resulting from this population flow motivated dictator Rafael Trujillo (1930–61) to carry out a notorious massacre of Haitians in 1937. Nevertheless, more than 250,000 people of Haitian parentage now live in the Dominican Republic.

In recent decades, Haiti has supplied cheap labor to the Dominican Republic, mostly to harvest sugarcane and coffee, and, until 1986, through a formal intergovernmental exchange. The question of the status and treatment of those laborers, a prickly issue between the two countries, occasionally has spilled onto the international stage. In July 1991, for example, when United States congressional hearings on the treatment of Haitian laborers in the Dominican Republic exposed abusive treatment of Haitian children in the canefields, Dominican President Joaquín Balaguer responded by pushing thousands of poor, dark-skinned people, mostly Haitians, but also some Dominican-Haitians born in his country, across the border, creating a refugee crisis in the hemisphere's already poorest country. Although the issue of Haitians in the Dominican Republic remains a difficult one, since the mid-1990s and the election of Presidents René Préval in Haiti and Leonel Fernández in the Dominican Republic, relations between the two countries have improved considerably. The two governments now explore cooperation on such issues as the environment, drug trafficking, and economic development.

Relations with Other Countries

Ties with other Caribbean nations have been limited. Historically, Britain and France strove to limit contacts between their dependencies and Haiti, in order to discourage independence movements. Haiti's cultural and linguistic distinctiveness also prevented close relations in the Caribbean. Haitian labor migration to the Bahamas since the 1970s has resulted in strained relations with that country in the late 1990s because in recent years Bahamian authorities have returned undocumented migrants to Haiti. Following the election of Aristide and the 1991 coup, a new awareness of Haiti arose in the Commonwealth Caribbean, however. In 1994 Caricom troops were the first international contingent to land in Haiti following the entry of United States soldiers. By 1998 Haiti had achieved membership status in Caricom. In general, Haiti's relations with Latin America, historically limited, have expanded since Haiti became part of a broader movement toward democracy in the region in 1990, and then intensified as Latin American nations, especially Venezuela, Argentina, and Chile, assumed leadership roles in the resolution of the Haitian crisis of 1991–94.

Other countries important to Haiti include the primary donor countries for foreign assistance, especially Canada, France, Germany, and the Republic of China (Taiwan). Increasingly, European assistance to Haiti has been coordinated under the auspices of the European Union, which, by 1998, was the largest single donor of aid to Haiti. Haiti has maintained special cultural ties to France, even though the two countries are not major trading partners. Haiti also has enjoyed a supportive relationship with the Canadian province of Quebec, one of the few linguistically compatible entities in the Western Hemisphere and the home of a significant number of Haitian émigrés. The importance of Haiti to Quebec and to Canada is reflected in Canada's leadership in the resolution of Haiti's political crisis and its deep involvement in UN peacekeeping and public safety programs since. Haiti's membership in international and multilateral organizations includes the UN and its associated organizations, the OAS, the Inter-American Development Bank, the World Bank (see Glossary), the Lomé Convention (see Glossary), the International Monetary Fund (see Glossary), and the World Trade Organization.

The Haitian diaspora, or Haitians living outside of Haiti, several million strong and concentrated principally in South Florida, New York, and other North American cities, has become an important focus of Haitian foreign relations. Although Haitians overseas are prohibited from voting in Haitian elections, members of what is now referred to as Haiti's "Tenth Department" play influential roles in the transfer of resources, knowledge, and skills from their metropolitan base to the homeland. Additionally, they play key roles in advocating policies toward Haiti in Washington and Ottawa.

Haitians have been proud of their history, particularly the accomplishments of such revolutionary figures as Jean-Jacques Dessalines and Toussaint and, in more recent years, such figures as Charlemagne Péralte, Jean-Marie Vincent, François Guy Malary, and others who fought for freedom from foreign or authoritarian rule. Haiti has suffered not only from its uniqueness and from its similarity to other less developed nations, but also from the abuse of its own leaders. Since the demise of the Duvalier dictatorship, most Haitians have demonstrated a strong desire for the reform of the systems of governance and politics that have abused the country and its people. They steadfastly clung to their commitment to democracy through the shock of the 1991 coup and the repression and violence that followed. Although Haiti can now count itself among the democratic nations of the hemisphere, as it approaches the twenty-first century the country and its leaders face the enormous challenges of eschewing the past and completing reform processes of government and politics that run contrary to the country's history.

*   *   *

Among studies of Haiti's government and politics, two stand out in providing the comprehensive historical framework required for understanding contemporary issues: *Haiti in the World Economy: Class, Race, and Underdevelopment since 1700*, by Alex Dupuy, and *Haiti, State Against Nation: The Origins and Legacy of Duvalierism*, by Michel-Rolph Trouillot. The analysis of politics and government in both of these works covers the period up to, and including, the demise of the Duvalier dictatorship. Dupuy's more recent book, *Haiti in the New World Order*, provides a detailed description and analysis of political developments between 1986 and the late 1994 intervention and restoration of the Aristide government, with a parallel analysis of economic policies promoted and applied in Haiti during the post-Duvalier era. *Libète: A Haitian Anthology*, edited by Charles Arthur and Michael Dash, provides an insightful array of short essays on Haiti and its political culture. Finally, the writings of Jean-Bertrand Aristide offer many useful insights into Haiti's political culture and its best-known contemporary political leader. *In the Parish of the Poor* offers essays from the pre-presidential era, whereas *Dignity* includes assessments from the period of de facto rule and the author's restoration to the post of president.

Several works focus more exclusively on the period of 1990–94, covering Jean-Bertrand Aristide's government prior to the military coup and the subsequent three years of de facto military rule. *The Haiti Files: Decoding the Crisis*, edited by James Ridgeway, compiles essays on the principal political players both in Haiti and internationally, including the Haitian diaspora. A number of its essays relate politics and government to drugs, migration, and international assistance. *Haitian Frustrations: Dilemmas for US Policy*, edited by Georges Fauriol, also focuses on key political sectors, placing its emphasis on international actors and their involvement in Haiti's political crisis, and includes the texts of key political documents. *Haitian Democracy Restored: 1991–1995*, by Roland I. Perusse, provides a succinct description of developments during these crisis years. *Haiti Held Hostage: International Responses to the Quest for Nationhood, 1986–1996*, by a team of researchers led by Robert Maguire, places the 1991 military coup d'état and period of de facto rule in a broader perspective, examining both developments leading up to it, and the role of international actors in the period following the military intervention. It offers a concluding chapter on lessons learned for future crises and interventions.

Although material on the evolution of Haiti's politics and governance since 1994 exists principally in the form of individual reports and articles, one published volume, *Haiti Renewed: Political and Economic Prospects*, edited by Robert Rotberg, provides analyses by leading scholars and several political activists on an array of political and economic challenges confronting Haiti and offers policy recommendations. The World Bank's

March 1998 report, *Haiti: The Challenges of Poverty Reduction*, includes technical papers that offer information on Haiti's political economy and analyses of overcoming obstacles to economic and political development. Finally, the *Haiti Info Circular*, compiled three times annually since 1995 under the auspices of the Georgetown University Caribbean Project's Haiti Program and available on the project's website, reproduces reports and analysis on Haiti and United States Haiti policy written and published by a wide array of Washington-based government agencies, scholars, and private policy analysis organizations. (For further information and complete citations, see Bibliography.)

Chapter 10. Haiti: National Security

BORN OF REVOLUTIONARY violence and plagued by socio-economic deterioration, Haiti has not succeeded in building permanent civilian institutions capable of exercising control over the military establishment. Until 1994 the armed forces had been a pillar of Haitian society based on an institutional cohesion that other organizations lacked. The military leadership acted with relative autonomy as a kind of government in reserve, ready to intervene in crises when civilian authority broke down.

Upon his return to power in 1994 after three years of military rule, the elected president, Jean-Bertrand Aristide, took the bold step of abolishing the armed forces. Although Haiti never before had a police force independent of the army, the country's security was entrusted to the newly created Haitian National Police (Police Nationale d'Haïti—PNH) under the supervision of civilians having no previous experience in matters of public safety. The evolution of the PNH into a professional, competent force for public order may be pivotal to the future of democratic government in Haiti.

Until the United States occupation in 1915, much of Haiti's history had been the story of competing mercenary bands (*cacos*) and peasant groups (*piquets*), who fought a ramshackle military. The most visible product of the occupation turned out to be the Garde d'Haïti, which evolved into the Armed Forces of Haiti (Forces Armées d'Haïti—FAd'H).

Under his autocratic rule, François Duvalier (1957–71) shrewdly brought the FAd'H under his control while ruthlessly suppressing all opposition groups. As a counterweight to the army's power, a sinister paramilitary organization was created—the Volunteers for National Security (Volontaires de la Sécurité Nationale—VSN)—to protect the regime and enforce its directives. During the tenure of François Duvalier's son, Jean-Claude Duvalier (1971–86), a reconstituted officer corps emerged, restoring the balance with the VSN.

After popular discontent forced Duvalier into exile, a succession of military coups and periods of internal military feuding were followed by the election of Aristide in 1990 (inaugurated 1991). Although police functions traditionally had been the responsibility of the army, Aristide's intention to introduce a separate police force was unacceptable to the FAd'H leadership and contributed to his ouster in a military-led coup nine months after he took office. During the subsequent three years of military rule (1991–94), the armed forces deteriorated sharply as a result of the poor economic state of the country, an international arms and fuel embargo, and growing corruption and competition for spoils among members of the officer corps. When Aristide returned, supported by a United Nations (UN) force, he ordered a rapid demobilization. Some soldiers were transferred to an interim police force, but most found themselves suddenly deprived of their careers and incomes. Embittered and in many cases still armed, they formed a potentially dangerous dissident element.

With international assistance, the government swiftly introduced a training program for the new national police, the first units of which took up their posts in mid-1995. As of late 1999, the police were close to their targeted strength of 6,732, a modest number for a country with Haiti's population and severe security and crime problems. All PNH recruits are obliged to go through a nine-month course at the police academy after meeting mandated educational standards and rigorous testing. Some officers and enlisted members of the FAd'H were accepted into the PNH after screening but have been required to undergo the same testing and training as civilian candidates. Former army officers remain a minority in the ranks of supervisory police.

The remaining small UN military contingents were withdrawn between August and November 1997, leaving a mission of some 290 civilian police officers to train and provide mentoring to the young PNH recruits. A separate United States contingent of mainly engineering troops provides assistance in the construction of roads, schools, bridges, and other public works.

The PNH is organized into two main elements: the Administrative Police, which, operating through nine departmental directors, staffs city police stations, subprecincts, and rural posts; and the Judicial Police, which investigates cases on behalf of examining magistrates. Separate specialized units deal with crowd control and narcotics violations, and act as protective forces to guard the president and high officials. The small Haitian Coast Guard is being trained in intercepting narcotics shipments and already cooperates with the United States Coast Guard in this regard. The staff of the inspector general investigates allegations of human rights abuses and crimes by the police, and regularly surveys the operation of police stations.

Four years after it was first deployed, the PNH had achieved measurable success in a country that had no civilian police tradition. It has for the most part been politically impartial, refraining from involvement in the political dispute that paralyzed the government in 1998 and 1999. Nevertheless, individual police commanders have been accused in incidents of harassment and intimidation of critics of the government.

This positive assessment of the PNH is clouded by a significant number of abuses, including the unnecessary use of force that has often resulted in deaths, mistreatment of detainees, failure to observe legal procedures in making arrests, and arrogance in dealing with the public. At supervisory levels, officers of both civilian and military backgrounds demonstrate numerous weaknesses.

The police are ill-equipped to deal with the country's rapidly growing role as a transshipment point for narcotics between Colombia and the United States. Although a number of police have been dismissed for drug corruption, the integrity of the force is seriously endangered by the influence of the traffickers.

In spite of programs of international assistance, the justice system in Haiti remains barely functional and is afflicted with rampant corruption. Many judges are poorly educated, untrained, unqualified, and open to bribery. In addition, the legal process is extremely slow; only a small proportion of crimes reaches the trial stage. In 1998 some 80 percent of prison inmates were being subjected to illegal or prolonged detention. Because of the public's lack of confidence in the judicial process, vigilante activity against suspected criminals is commonplace.

Aristide's daring move to do away with the armed forces has proved to be a major achievement. The civilian national police, in spite of its many shortcomings, is improving, and, although serious problems remain, they are being addressed by the authorities and are not on the massive or systemic scale that existed under the de facto military regime of 1991–94. Ex-soldiers and other disaffected elements, as well as mounting criminal and narcotics activity, present continuing dangers to the regime. If the new police force can weather its current challenges and remain apolitical, future civilian governments should be able to conduct the country's affairs without the risk of another military takeover.

The Military in Haitian History

The origins of Haiti's military lie in the country's revolution, which began with a slave rebellion in 1791 and culminated in French withdrawal in 1803 (see Fight for Independence, 1791–1803, ch. 6). A decade of warfare produced a military cadre from which Haiti's early leaders emerged. Defeat of the French demonstrated Haiti's considerable strategic stamina and tactical capabilities, but Haiti's victory did not translate into a successful national government or a strong economy. Lacking an effective constitution, Haiti was usually ruled by force. The armed forces, which had been united against the French, fragmented into warring regional factions. The military soon took control of almost every aspect of Haitian life, and officers assumed responsibility for the administration of justice and for municipal management. According to a Haitian diplomat, the country in its earlier days was "an immense military camp." Without viable civilian institutions, Haiti was vulnerable to military strongmen, who permanently shaped the nation's authoritarian, personalist, and coercive style of governance.

During the latter half of the nineteenth century, the army either failed to protect the central government or directly caused the government's collapse by means of a coup. In addition, rural insurgent movements led by *piquets* and *cacos* limited the central government's authority in outlying areas. These groups carried on guerrilla warfare into the twentieth century; they remained active until put down by the United States Marines in 1919.

Prolonged instability weakened the army. By the end of the nineteenth century, Haiti's military had become little more than an undisciplined, ill-fed, and poorly paid militia that shifted its allegiances as battles were won or lost and as new leaders came to power. Between 1806 and 1879, an estimated sixty-nine revolts against existing governments took place; another twenty uprisings or attempted insurrections broke out between 1880 and 1915. At the beginning of the twentieth century, Haiti's political problems attracted increasing foreign involvement. France, Germany, and the United States were the major actors. In 1915, as mob violence raged, the United States occupied the country (see United States Involvement in Haiti, 1915–34, ch. 6).

During the occupation, the United States Marines disbanded Haiti's army, which consisted of an estimated 9,000 men, including 308 generals. In February 1916, the Haitian Constabulary (Gendarmerie d'Haïti) was formed. United States Marine Corps and United States Navy officers and noncommissioned officers (NCOs) commanded the group. The gendarmerie attempted to assure public safety, initially by subduing the *cacos*; to promote development, particularly road construction; and to modernize the military through the introduction of a training structure, a health service, and other improvements. The gendarmerie became the Garde d'Haïti in 1928; the Garde formed the core of Haiti's armed forces after the United States administration ended in 1934.

The United States had sought to introduce a modern, apolitical military establishment in Haiti. On the surface, it succeeded; the organization, training, and equipment of the Garde all represented improvements over the military conditions existing before the occupation. What the United States did not (and probably could not) reform was the basic authoritarian inclination of Haitian society, an inclination antithetical to the goal of military depoliticization.

Some professionalization of the army continued for a few years after the United States occupation; however, Haiti's political structure deteriorated rapidly after 1934, weakening civil-military relations and ultimately affecting the character of the armed forces. After the coup that ended the populist government of Dumarsais Estimé and led to Colonel Paul E. Magloire's election to the presidency in 1950, the army resumed a political role. This development divided the army internally and set the stage for François Duvalier's ascent to power in late 1957 (see François Duvalier, 1957–71, ch. 6).

The Duvalier Era, 1957–86

When François Duvalier came to power in 1957, the armed forces were at their lowest point professionally since 1915. Duvalier's establishment of a parallel security apparatus posed the most serious challenge to the crumbling integrity of the armed forces. In 1959 the regime began recruiting a civilian militia (Milice Civile) drawn initially from the capital city's slums and equipped with antiquated small arms found in the basement of the Presidential Palace. The militia became the Volunteers for National Security (Volontaires de la Sécurité Nationale—VSN) after 1962. Its control extended into the countryside through a system of information, intelligence, and command tied directly to the Presidential Palace. Both François Duvalier and his son, Jean-Claude, lacked military experience; still, they managed to neutralize the army's influence through intimidation, bribery, and political maneuvering. The Duvaliers also managed to stave off a number of low-level opposition plots and invasion attempts, mostly during the 1960s.

During the early 1960s, François Duvalier pursued measures to overpower the mainstream military establishment, often by ruthlessly eliminating or exiling any officers who opposed him. The Military Academy, a professional and elitist institution that represented a potential source of opposition to the regime, was closed down in 1961. Officers who attempted to resist Duvalier forfeited their careers. In 1963 Duvalier expelled the United States military mission, which he had invited to Haiti in 1959; Duvalier feared that the military-modernization values imparted by United States instructors could lead to resistance to the government's restructuring of the armed forces.

Although referred to as a militia, the VSN in fact became the Duvaliers' front-line security force. As of early 1986, the organization included more than 9,000 members and an informal circle of thousands more. The VSN acted as a political cadre, secret police, and instrument of terror. It played a crucial political role for the regime, countering the influence of the armed forces, historically the regime's primary source of power. The VSN gained its deadly reputation in part because members received no salary, although they took orders from the Presidential Palace. They made their living, instead, through extortion and petty crime. Rural members of the VSN, who wore blue denim uniforms, had received some training from the army, while the plainclothes members, identified by their trademark dark glasses, served as Haiti's criminal investigation force.

When Jean-Claude Duvalier ("Baby Doc") came to power in 1971, the country's security forces became less abusive, but they still resorted to some brutality. During Jean-Claude's regime, a realignment of power between the VSN and the armed forces was achieved, ensuring him greater control over the nation's security apparatus. Jean-Claude's half-hearted attempt to open Haiti to the outside world and to qualify for renewed foreign assistance from the United States suggested a need to restrain the abuses of the VSN.

With United States support, the government created the Leopard counterinsurgency unit, which provided the regime with a relatively modern tool for responding to internal threats. By placing a capable new force under Baby Doc's command, the Leopards reduced his dependence on the allegiance of the armed forces and the VSN. In 1972 the Military Academy reopened, and the first class since 1961 graduated in 1973. Because the lower classes could not meet the academy's educational requirements, the students were drawn from the middle class and were usually sponsored by active-duty officers or other officials. The reopening of the academy represented a small step toward reprofessionalizing the military. Some modernization of army equipment was also undertaken during this period.

The armed forces largely escaped the immediate wrath of a population clearly bent on putting an end to Duvalier rule. Popular violence had erupted in 1984, and it continued into early 1986 in an expanding sequence of local revolts. In its waning days, the regime relied heavily on the VSN and on limited local police capabilities to curb violence. Many Haitians detected the fissures growing in the nation's security apparatus, and some rumors held that the army would move against Duvalier. These rumors, however, proved incorrect; still, Duvalier's inability to contain the widespread rioting through political measures and the VSN's failure to control the unrest placed the military in a pivotal position. Conscious of his precarious hold on power, Duvalier reshuffled the cabinet and the military leadership in the last days of 1985, but to no avail. Reports of brutal excesses by the increasingly desperate VSN further weakened Duvalier's position.

The army's discontent with the crumbling regime became evident when troops refused to fire on demonstrators, and, in a few instances, army personnel turned against the VSN. With last-minute assistance from the United States, Haiti's leading generals provided the political transition required to ease Duvalier out of power in February 1986. In pushing for Duvalier's abdication, the army was not expressing genuine concern for the best interests of Haiti. Rather, the army sought to shield itself from responsibility for the explosive sociopolitical situation.

The Post-Duvalier Period

Jean-Claude Duvalier left behind a hastily constructed

interim junta, controlled by the armed forces. After Jean-Claude's departure, Lieutenant General Henri Namphy, army chief of staff, became head of the interim National Council of Government. The interim government officially disbanded the VSN a few days after Duvalier's departure but avoided the politically difficult measure of effectively halting the VSN's activities. The failure to do so led angry mobs to set upon members of the VSN and set in motion a cycle of instability. Despite the popular backlash, some VSN agents managed to survive by integrating themselves into military circles. By 1987 the initial positive view of the armed forces had given way to anger because of the army's failure to dismantle the VSN, which continued to thwart proposed government reform. Worse, the senior military command was blamed for the failed elections of 1987 and 1988, isolating the Haitian military from the international community, which had grown skeptical about the role of the armed forces.

In September 1988, another coup brought Lieutenant General Prosper Avril of the Presidential Guard to power. The armed forces continued to face problems. Within a six-month period, 140 officers reportedly were retired or were fired, some because they were suspected of drug smuggling. Political rifts within the senior command split the officer corps into warring factions. After a week of internecine conflict in April 1989, Avril was able to prevail because he held the loyalty of the Presidential Guard and enjoyed support from many NCOs. But the military was left in a state of crisis, without a clearly defined political program.

Under pressure from the United States and facing severe dissension at home, Avril fled to Florida in March 1990. Elected president in fair elections nine months later, Jean-Bertrand Aristide entered office in February of 1991 without opposition from the army. He introduced an ambitious program of reforms, several of which were bound to disturb the military leadership. The top ranks were purged, steps were taken to separate the police from the army as called for by the 1987 constitution, and the position of section chief—key to the FAd'H's power in the provinces—was abolished.

Increasingly perceived as a radical by the military, Aristide found it difficult to exert his authority over the military command. The return to Haiti of Duvalier supporters and the evidence of drug-dealing among a number of officers heightened civil-military friction. A military-led coup, backed by the economic elite and right-wing elements, overthrew Aristide in September 1991, less than eight months into his five-year term.

A puppet civilian government installed by the armed forces effectively dominated the weak and divided civilian politicians and managed the country. The main military figure was Lieutenant General Raoul Cédras, who had been appointed chief of staff of the armed forces by President Aristide, but who was generally believed to have engineered the coup against Aristide. Cédras installed his friend, Brigadier General Philippe Biamby, as chief of staff of the army. Both Cédras and Biamby came from prominent families that had supported the Duvalier regime. Another leading coup figure was Lieutenant Colonel Joseph Michel François, in charge of the Port-au-Prince military zone, with control over the capital's police. François also was thought to have been responsible for building up a force of 1,500 plainclothes auxiliaries, known as "attachés," who committed most of the abuses and intimidation of opponents of the military regime. The attachés were abetted by the provincial section chiefs and a new group that emerged in 1993, the Revolutionary Front for the Advancement and Progress of Haiti (Front Révolutionnaire pour l'Avancement et le Progrès d'Haïti—FRAPH).

As international pressures mounted against the de facto government, the armed forces became less and less a professional military organization and more a violent business enterprise with numerous criminal features. According to an exiled former Haitian officer, Kern Delince, "The hierarchy and most of the principles upon which armies are organized have vanished. What you have left is a force of mercenaries and predators, a military institution that is in its terminal phase. . . ."

The army developed close links with wealthy families and controlled most state-owned businesses, such as the telephone and electricity companies, the port, and imports of basic goods like cement and flour. It was widely believed that the army was permeated with officers profiting from the narcotics trade. Because the officers were making so much money and because of their dislike of Aristide, they had little incentive to end the stalemate. In response to the situation, the international community instituted an international embargo, which had severe effects on the country. The embargo hit the poor the hardest, and, ironically, enabled the military to profit from the sale of scarce fuel supplies smuggled into the country. Eventually, however, the presence of armed civilian gangs, the lack of funds to pay soldiers' salaries and the growing dependence of senior and junior officers on the proceeds of drug trafficking contributed to the breakdown of military discipline.

As a result of these economic pressures and the worsening domestic situation, in July 1993, a Cédras-led delegation accepted a plan, known as the Governors Island Accord for the place where it was negotiated, to restore the Aristide government. As one element of the accord, 1,100 police trainers and military personnel under UN control were to supervise the reform of the Haitian army and to introduce the constitutionally mandated separate police force. The accord did not go smoothly. When the first Canadian and United States military personnel were about to go ashore from the cargo ship, the *U.S.S. Harlan County*, they were discouraged from landing by a FRAPH-led dockside demonstration. With the Governors Island Accord thus repudiated, the UN embargo was reimposed, and a renewed campaign of terror was instigated by the FAd'H and FRAPH.

A year later, with stiffened international sanctions that targeted all trade except food and medicine, and a UN-endorsed United States intervention imminent, the Haitian military leadership capitulated and accepted the "permissive intervention" plan negotiated by a delegation headed by former United States president Jimmy Carter.

Disintegration and Demobilization of the Haitian Army, 1993–95

On September 19, 1994, a day after the Carter agreement was signed, the first units of the United States-led Multinational Force (MNF) landed in Haiti. The military leaders, including General Cédras, resigned, as called for by the agreement, and went into exile, leaving the FAd'H leaderless and demoralized. Aristide, who resumed his presidential term in October 1994, quickly moved to reduce the size of the discredited army, announcing a reduction in personnel from 6,000 to 3,500. Some of the former soldiers were enrolled in a United States-sponsored program to ease their return to civilian life by providing them with job training and referrals, but few found employment. To reduce the danger of violence from weapons among civilians and demobilized soldiers, the MNF instituted a buy-back program that attracted thousands of firearms but failed to uncover all the hidden arms that could be used in a future uprising against the legitimate government. Many ordinary soldiers were permitted to serve in the Interim Public Security Force (IPSF), which acted as a stopgap until the new civilian national police force could be trained and deployed. Some 3,300 soldiers were ultimately accepted into the IPSF.

By January 1995, all officers' commissions had been revoked, and the remaining FAd'H personnel who had not been accepted into the IPSF were demobilized. Aristide announced his intention to ask parliament to take up a constitutional amendment to formally abolish the armed forces. Under the constitution, action to this effect was not possible until the end of the legislative term in 1999. In addition to the weapons collected by the occupying troops under the buy-back program, the military's heavy weapons were impounded and destroyed.

Structure and Capabilities of the Pre-1995 Armed Forces

Haiti's internal upheavals had repeatedly caused the armed forces to assume a decisive role in the conduct of the political institutions of the state. Domestic security concerns greatly outweighed external defense considerations in the operations and organization of the armed forces. The FAd'H constituted the military arm of the Ministry of Interior and National Defense. The commander of the FAd'H served a renewable three-year term. Under him, the general staff had the usual staff offices for operations, intelligence, logistics, and training. Among other important officers were the inspector general, an adjutant general, and commanders of the military regions of the north and south, and of the metropolitan military region (Port-au-Prince).

The nine military departments under the northern and southern military regions operated principally as district police. Only the forces assigned to the metropolitan military region had a significant tactical capability. The strongest of these units was the 1,300-member Presidential Guard, which was relatively well-trained and disciplined. Many members of the guard were stationed on the grounds of the Presidential Palace as a protective force for the president. The Dessalines Battalion, with barracks behind the Presidential Palace, was a light infantry force of some 750 men. The Leopard Corps was an internal security unit of some 700 men equipped with United States help. Both the Dessalines Battalion and the

Leopard Corps were disbanded after the 1989 conflict within the army.

The FAd'H controlled the Port-au-Prince police and the prison system. The capital's police force of about 1,000 ill-trained members was in effect a low-level constabulary under military command. The armed forces administered the capital city's firefighters and the country's customs, immigration, and narcotics-control programs.

Haiti's security services consisted of about 8,000 military and police when military rule was ended in 1994. The FAd'H itself had a strength of about 6,200. Most officers began their careers at the Military Academy at Frères (near Pétionville). After a three-year course in a class of about sixty students, academy graduates became career officers with the opportunity of rising to the most senior FAd'H positions. In the final years of the regime, the academy program degenerated. The training was only nominal, and officers were selected and promoted not on the basis of their records and capabilities but on family ties and political orientation. Graduates of the NCO school and training camp at Lamentin (near Carrefour) outside Port-au-Prince served in mainstream army units or were assigned to rural police duties, but the NCO school, too, was not fully operational in the last years of the military government. Basic training was conducted at the unit level. Although Article 268 of the 1987 constitution required all men to serve in the military when they reached their eighteenth birthday, enlistment was in reality voluntary. Women were limited to participating in the medical corps.

Prior to demobilization of all the armed forces—army, navy, and air force—the principal small arm for most of the army was the Garand M1 rifle of World War II vintage. Some German G3 and American M16 rifles were distributed to elite units, as were Israeli Uzi submachine guns. The Presidential Guard had a few armored vehicles and artillery pieces at its disposal. As reported by *The Military Balance, 1995–96*, these consisted of V–150 Commando and M2 armored personnel carriers and nine 75mm and 105mm towed howitzers. The army also had a small inventory of 60mm and 81mm mortars, 37mm and 57mm anti-tank guns, 20mm and 40mm antiaircraft guns, and some 57mm and 106mm rocket launchers.

The Haitian navy was formed in 1860 and by the turn of the century was theoretically the largest naval force in the Caribbean, with two cruisers and six gunboats, manned largely by foreign mercenaries. The navy ceased to exist after the United States military occupation in 1915 but reappeared as a coast guard unit in the late 1930s. During and after World War II, Haiti received several coast guard cutters and converted submarine chasers from the United States. After the three major units of the Haitian coast guard mutinied in 1970, shelling the Presidential Palace, the ships were disarmed by the United States at Guantanamo, Cuba, where they had fled, and returned to Haiti. François Duvalier subsequently announced plans for a major expansion by the purchase of twenty-four vessels, including motor torpedo boats, but the project was not consummated and was in any event probably beyond the support capabilities of the Haitian navy.

During the 1970s, after Duvalier's death, most of the existing fleet units were disposed of or returned to the United States. Five small patrol craft were purchased privately in the United States, as was an armed tugboat from the United States Navy; the tugboat was converted for offshore patrol use. This vessel plus two coastal patrol craft were all that remained of the navy when the 1991–94 military regime ended. The navy had a single base at Port-au-Prince and a complement of 340 officers and men.

The Haitian air force was formed in 1943 with a number of training aircraft and help from a United States Marine Corps aviation mission. After World War II ended, several transport aircraft, including three Douglas C–47s, were added to form a transport unit. In 1950, after the arrival of a United States Air Force mission, a combat unit was formed with six F–51D Mustangs. The F–51s were instrumental in the defeat of the 1970 naval mutiny when they strafed the rebel vessels bombarding the capital. By the early 1980s, the combat units consisted of six Cessna 337 counterinsurgency aircraft. Haiti also had a variety of transport aircraft and trainers and a unit of eight helicopters. By the end of the military regime in 1994, the operating aircraft were listed as four Cessna 337s, two light transport aircraft, and twelve training aircraft. The helicopters were no longer in service. The air force's only base was at Port-au-Prince, and its personnel strength as of 1993 was estimated at 300.

Military Spending and Foreign Assistance

According to estimates published by the United States Arms Control and Disarmament Agency (ACDA), military expenditures averaged about US$40 million annually under the military regime. In 1994, the final year of the military government, the spending level of US$45 million amounted to 30.2 percent of central government expenditures and 2.3 percent of gross national product (GNP—see Glossary). However, because of the deteriorating economy resulting from government mismanagement and the international embargo, the share assumed by the military was relatively higher than in more normal times. Any analysis of spending data is subject to many uncertainties. Portions of the nation's expenditures for military purposes probably have been unrecorded, or allocated funds may have been siphoned off by corrupt officers.

Between 1975 and 1985, under the Duvaliers, military spending averaging US$30 million a year represented about 8 percent of government expenditures. Between 1987 and 1991, when Aristide was ousted by the military, the share of military expenditures in the national budget rose from 10.6 percent to 15.3 percent. Recorded military outlays did not exceed 2 percent of GNP during the Duvalier era or under any subsequent regime.

Throughout the twentieth century, the United States was the primary source of foreign military support in terms of matériel and financing. United States military missions to Haiti during and after World War II helped to maintain links between the two countries.

Overall, between 1950 and 1977, the United States provided US$3.4 million in military aid, which included the cost of training for 610 Haitian students in the United States. During the 1980s, no direct military aid was provided, although some credits were advanced to permit commercial military purchases. The financing program amounted to about US$300,000 a year, but the Duvaliers spent a much greater amount in direct commercial transactions, primarily for crowd-control equipment. All forms of military assistance ended when the elections of 1987 failed. ACDA has recorded no imports of military equipment since 1987, when US$500,000 worth of military items entered the country, presumably acquired through commercial channels.

Role of the Army in Law Enforcement Prior to 1995

Although the 1987 constitution mandated a separate police corps and a new police academy under the jurisdiction of the Ministry of Justice and Public Security, political realities prevented the implementation of these changes. The army feared that a separate police would compete for funds and influence and would threaten its opportunities for profit. The armed forces continued to act as the nation's ultimate law enforcement agency in spite of their lack of competence in this area. The only identifiable police force in Haiti operated in Port-au-Prince, its members assigned to it by the armed forces. This 1,000-member force had few operational or technical capabilities, even though it was responsible for criminal investigations, as well as narcotics and immigration control. Members of the FAd'H detailed for police duties received no specific training in police methods. They did not have regular beats, investigate crimes, or carry out other normal police functions. The police could be hired to arrest persons on flimsy evidence. Warrantless arrest was common, as was incommunicado detention.

There was no true rural police. Small garrisons, operating under military department command, with some cooperation from the lowest central government administrative heads, the military section chiefs, were responsible for rural security. In effect, the 562 section chiefs functioned not only as police chiefs but also as primary government representatives in rural areas. Thus, with little or no oversight from the capital and without special training, the officers assigned to keep order often acted as prosecutors, judges, and tax assessors in a brutal system whose main purpose was to prevent any grassroots opposition from developing.

In addition to its failure to establish a nationwide police force as called for in the constitution, the military leadership failed to subdue the VSN and other vigilante groups. Direct links between the senior army command and remnants of the VSN enabled many VSN agents to infiltrate FAd'H units and the cadres of the Port-au-Prince police force. Many of the paramilitary groups simply were engaged in a career of banditry with no political motivation. The Avril government made some effort to crack down on abuses in the internal security services, but members of the FAd'H and its various affiliates continued to use their monopoly of power to subjugate and mistreat the Haitian citizenry. It has been estimated that some 3,000 Haitians died in the 1991–94 period as a result of the FAd'H's oppressive governance.

Haiti's External and Domestic Security Concerns

Defense of the nation against external threats was never a

prominent factor in the mission of Haiti's armed forces. Since the efforts of the French to reconquer the island in the early years of the nineteenth century, the country has not been seriously challenged by any foreign power. In 1822 Haiti occupied the eastern part of the island of Hispaniola, which had declared itself independent of Spain as the Republic of Santo Domingo. Controlling the whole island, however, drained the national treasury, and internal struggles so weakened the army that it was unable to pursue missions beyond its borders. Nonetheless, under Faustin Soulouque, Haiti made repeated attempts to reconquer the eastern part of the island between 1847 and 1859, following its ejection in 1844.

The principal sources of the nation's safety until the twentieth century were the jealousies among the great powers and the increasing interest of the United States in a stable order in Haiti. The United States Navy deployed to the country's ports fifteen times between 1876 and 1913 in order to protect United States lives and property. Occupation of Haiti by the United States Marines beginning in 1915 was designed to ensure domestic law and stability. During this period, the United States helped establish the Garde d'Haïti, which was intended to be a modern, apolitical military establishment oriented toward this goal.

As a noncommunist country situated only eighty kilometers from Cuban territory, Haiti's security falls within the wider framework of United States strategic interests in the Caribbean. The Marine occupation and a succession of American training missions have in effect placed Haiti under a United States security umbrella. The Duvaliers' tight control eliminated all Marxist influence, and it was not until 1986 that a small communist party began to operate openly in the country. Cuba has not tried to interfere in Haitian affairs, deterred by the severity of Haiti's political and economic difficulties and the high profile of the United States in the region.

Relations with the Dominican Republic, Haiti's neighbor on the island of Hispaniola, have been marked by recurrent differences, but neither country presents a threat to the other's territorial integrity or security. The Dominican Republic was an important source of smuggled gasoline and other goods during the 1991–94 international embargo against Haiti. Under pressure from the United States, however, the Dominicans strengthened their military border posts, reducing if not shutting off the movement of contraband. By agreement, several thousand Haitian cane cutters migrate annually to assist in the harvest of Dominican sugar plantations. Nevertheless, the issue of legal and illegal Haitian workers in the Dominican Republic is a source of friction. During a visit by Haitian president René Garcia Préval to the Dominican capital of Santo Domingo in 1996, the first such event in decades, the authorities of the two countries agreed to set up a joint commission on trade, immigration, and other problems.

Traditionally, the military has seen its role as an autonomous force available to intervene in crises that threaten lawful authority. It has, however, been subject to chronic instability traceable in part to generational and political differences among members of the officer corps and the complicating role of the VSN and other paramilitary groups. As of 1999, the former military leaders and agents of the paramilitary groups still presented a latent threat to the post-1994 government. Many of these figures live in exile in the Dominican Republic or in one of the Central American countries. Other former soldiers are employed by private security companies and as personal bodyguards of wealthy families. The private security firms are larger and better armed than the Haitian police. Arms are easily available to dissident elements. Only about 30,000 of roughly 175,000 guns in Haiti have been seized or turned in under the United States-sponsored buy-back program.

Armed groups could potentially bring about the collapse of Haiti's civilian government by assassinations of leading politicians, aiding plots by disaffected elements, or taking advantage of mounting turmoil growing out of street violence and economic distress or politically manipulated demonstrations. The continued presence of small United States military contingents and UN-sponsored personnel acts as a limited deterrent on actions intended to overturn domestic institutions.

Government officials have charged that former military figures have encouraged paramilitary gangs to demoralize and destabilize the political situation by demonstrating that the PNH is unable to ensure the nation's internal security. An incident in May 1999 in which eleven detainees were gunned down by the police in Port-au-Prince has been cited as a deliberate plot to tarnish the image of the PNH. Seven officers were arrested, including the Port-au-Prince police commissioner, a former army officer.

Episodes of violence are common in Haiti, particularly in the slum area of Port-au-Prince known as Cité Soleil, which the police are often reluctant to penetrate. Most of this crime is associated with five or six criminal gangs. Although these gangs are formless and undisciplined, they represent a danger to the established order by contributing to a sense of chaos and lawlessness that weakens public confidence in the government's power to maintain control. Most of the lawless behavior lacks a political motivation, although the police have been the target of a number of attacks, some resulting in their deaths. In early 1998, the station chief in Mirebalais was lynched by a gang of young men linked to Aristide's political movement.

Violence has spread from gang-ridden areas to more prosperous parts of the city and to the countryside, driven by increasing economic desperation and a limited police presence. The looting of warehouses, truck hijackings, and holdups of buses are among the most common forms of armed crime. A rash of kidnappings and robberies of wealthy and middle-class Haitians has been a further feature of the crime wave. Vigilante groups, sometimes organized with government approval, act to enforce rough "street justice" where the police are unable or unwilling to act, or where confidence is lacking in the court system. Angry mobs often kill suspected thieves, murderers, and rapists. According to police records, some 100 deaths resulted from such incidents in the first half of 1998. Occasionally, timely police intervention has prevented lynchings.

Some armed, unemployed ex-FAd'H soldiers have turned to crime. Other demobilized troops with legitimate grievances over the loss of their careers and pensions and the lack of jobs and army severance pay present a potentially dangerous antigovernment element. Several hundred ex-soldiers staged a protest in the capital in 1996, threatening to take up arms if their demands were not met. Subsequently, the police arrested twenty members of the extreme right-wing Mobilization for National Development, most of whose members were ex-soldiers, on charges of plotting the assassination of public officials. Two of the group's leaders were later found murdered, apparently by members of the Presidential Guard. René Préval, who became president in February 1996, came under United States pressure to purge his bodyguard unit but, apparently fearful for his own safety, was unwilling to do so until a security detail from the United States and Canada was assigned to guard him. The detail was withdrawn a year later.

Internal Security since 1994

Upon President Aristide's return to Haiti in October 1994, the military was divested of all of its previous internal security functions, and steps were immediately undertaken to replace it with a separate national police force as stipulated in the constitution. As an initial measure, the Interim Public Security Force (IPSF) was formed under the supervision of more than 1,000 international police monitors. Nearly 1,000 of the IPSF members were drawn from Haitian migrants in the United States safe haven in Guantanamo, Cuba. Most of the remainder, about 3,300, were former FAd'H personnel who had been screened to eliminate any suspected of human rights abuses or criminal conduct. After an inadequate six-day training period that emphasized human rights, the interim police were deployed to cities and larger towns with the international monitors serving as mentors to the untried new officers and helping to reduce violations of human rights.

The effort to establish a permanent professional police force got underway with the opening of a police academy in January 1995 at Camp d'Application outside of Port-au-Prince. A series of four-month courses was instituted to enable the newly trained policemen to begin replacing the IPSF in June 1995. In December 1995, the government phased out the IPSF by incorporating its remaining 1,600 members into the permanent police force.

National Police

The Haitian National Police (Police Nationale d'Haïti— PNH) reached its targeted strength of 6,500 by early 1998, but, by late 1999, its strength had fallen to 6,000 as a result of dismissals. Its goal is to have 9,500–10,000 policemen by 2003, a goal that many observers doubt is attainable. For a nation of Haiti's size, the police complement is considered modest in comparison with other countries of the region. New York City, with a similar population, has a police force five times the size of Haiti's.

The PNH represents a signal departure from Haiti's historical reliance on the army to maintain internal security. Under the police law passed by the Haitian congress in November 1994, the PNH falls under the immediate jurisdiction of the Ministry of Justice and Public Security and the secretary of state for justice and public security. Ultimate authority rests

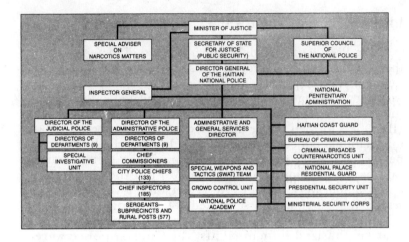

Figure 14. Organization of the Haitian National Police, 1999

with the Superior Council of the National Police, which includes the ministers of justice and interior, and the director general and inspector general of police. Pierre Denizé, a civilian lawyer with a reputation for being tough on crime and corruption, was appointed director general of police in 1996. The director general is chosen by the president from police directors or divisional commanders for a renewable three-year term. His appointment is subject to Senate approval.

Recruitment to other command positions has been opened to both military officers and civilian university graduates. Both groups are required to go through the same examination process and training. No more than one-third of PNH officers are former military, and the highest posts at PNH headquarters and departmental directorates are all held by civilians.

Neither military nor civilian officers have proven to be well qualified, with wide differences in capacities of individual officers. Deployed after the first agents were already in place, the officers have had difficulty gaining the respect of their subordinates. Many officers meeting the academic criteria have shown poor leadership skills. In addition, many have failed to enforce discipline against the agents under their command and have failed to implement regulations and codes of discipline.

The PNH is divided into two main units, the Administrative Police with responsibility for day-to-day public security and crime prevention, and the Judicial Police, a detective force that assists the courts in carrying out criminal investigations (see fig. 14). A separate unit, the Office of the Inspector General, which reports to both the director general and the minister of justice, investigates complaints against the police of human rights abuses. The Office of the Inspector General also conducts periodic inspections of police establishments and the Police Academy to assure compliance with police regulations and to evaluate the PNH's effectiveness. The office had seventy-two people assigned to it in 1997, and more personnel were being added. Its head was said to be seriously committed to purging the PNH of abusive and criminal elements, but the staff was overwhelmed as a result of trying to pursue cases of police misbehavior while at the same time carrying out its on-site inspection schedule.

Each of Haiti's nine departments has a departmental police director. Beneath them are the positions of chief commissioners (*commissaires principaux*) and some 130 posts of city police chiefs or municipal commissioners (*commissaires municipaux*). The next subdivisions are the 185 subcommissariats under chief inspectors (*inspecteurs principaux*) and, finally, 577 supervisory positions of sergeants (*inspecteurs*) in the sub-precincts of smaller towns and the smallest police divisions in rural and urban areas. These smallest offices may be staffed by as few as three policemen.

Specialized forces—the 200-member National Palace Residential Guard, the eighty-seven member Presidential Security Unit, and the Ministerial Security Corps—provide protection to the political leadership. There is also a crowd control unit, the Company for Intervention and Maintaining Order (Compagnie d'Intervention et Maintien d'Ordre—CIMO), and a SWAT team, the Intervention Group of the Haitian National Police (Groupe d'Intervention de la Police Nationale d'Haïti—GIPNH). Each of the nine administrative regions also has its own crowd control force. Two specialized units that had been undergoing training began to be deployed in 1997. One was the Haitian Coast Guard with ninety-four members; the other was the Counternarcotics Unit under the Bureau of Criminal Affairs with only twenty-five members.

The government has established a Special Investigative Unit under the director of the Judicial Police to look into notorious homicides—generally politically motivated—dating back to the mid-1980s. About seventy such cases have been brought under investigation, including deaths that occurred under the military regime after 1991, and high-profile killings following Aristide's return to office. However, the unit is ill-equipped and inexperienced and had made only limited progress on these cases by the close of 1999.

Some mayors have formed quasi-official forces to supplement the work of the PNH in their communities. These forces remain small and lack legal standing or the right to carry weapons. The municipalities have openly resisted the national government's demands that their arms be turned in to the PNH. In some cases, they assume arrest authority without the sanction of the law. The Port-au-Prince extra-legal force is believed to number several dozen persons, and the adjoining suburb of Delmas has about thirty. Other communities have smaller corps.

Recruitment, Training, and Equipment

Initial recruitment for the PNH was carried out by traveling teams that tested thousands of applicants. Only a small percentage was able to pass the examination, in part because literacy in French and the equivalent of a high-school diploma were required. This relatively high education level created some problems for the police in dealing with the mostly illiterate population, especially in rural areas, and the education requirement has since been reduced to a tenth-grade level. Members of the IPSF were allowed to apply on the basis of recommendations from international police monitors but were still required to pass the entrance test.

The academy course has been expanded from four to nine months, although, realistically, adequate training would require twelve to eighteen months. The program includes instruction in police procedures, tactical skills, police management and administration, law, and a course in "human dignity." Under pressure to train large numbers of recruits rapidly, the initial classes were brought to Fort Leonard Wood, Missouri, for the portion of the program dealing with practical police skills. Short-term specialized courses also have been introduced to sharpen the skills of police and officers in the field.

The training program was developed by the United States Department of Justice's International Criminal Investigative Training Assistance Program (ICITAP). Haitian lawyers focus on the constitution and Haitian laws, while personnel of ICITAP, together with Canadian and French police trainers, deal

National Police, Port-au-Prince
Courtesy United States Agency for International Development

with patrol, arrest, and investigative techniques. Haitian instructors are scheduled to fill all positions at the academy.

The highest 10 percent of the members of the initial classes received additional training for supervisory positions. Other members of each class were selected to receive additional investigative training for service in the Judicial Police. Women comprised about 7 percent of the original classes and were assigned to regular patrol duties after graduation.

The monthly salary ranges between US$250 and US$400, with sergeants earning US$500–600. These wages are generous by Haitian standards. Nevertheless, the police have demonstrated for higher rates on the grounds that higher salaries will reduce a force member's temptation to resort to bribery and drug trafficking. However, it seems unlikely that the Haitian government can afford to maintain this pay scale if the economy continues to decline. In 1998 consideration was being given to establishing a separate rural police force that would be less well paid and have lower entrance standards. Many PNH recruits are reluctant to serve outside Port-au-Prince, in some cases because they are concurrently continuing university studies. However, a policy of redeployment has been instituted to bring police who have served in rural areas for several years into towns and making members of the PNH in the Port-au-Prince area subject to reassignment to the provinces.

Each new officer is provided with a gun, shoes, and one uniform. The uniform consists of blue trousers with a vertical yellow stripe and a pale tan shirt, usually short sleeved. Rank insignia are worn on epaulets. Members of CIMO wear distinctive black uniforms.

The police are restricted by law to carrying only sidearms. Special units are equipped with shotguns, M16 semiautomatic rifles, and Uzi submachine guns, but in some cases police on routine assignments are seen with them as well. Some riot shields and bulletproof vests have been distributed. Maintenance of equipment, including firearms, is poor, and control systems are described as embryonic. Vehicles are in seriously short supply. A number of new vans were donated to the police, but most quickly became inoperable because of insufficient maintenance and repair and the high accident rate attributed to the inexperience of the recruits. Radio communication exists between the capital and the departmental directors and major urban areas, but communications remain poor in rural areas. The police stations were at first in wretched condition, some entirely uninhabitable, especially outside the capital. They lacked furniture, office equipment, and holding cells. Typewriters, filing cabinets, and some other equipment have since been made available with the aid of outside agencies.

Among the problems still confronting the new police force are weak leadership and political influence over appointments and promotions. Excessive use of force continues to be at a worrisome level (see Respect for Human Rights, this ch.). Police often also display an arrogant attitude toward the local community. PNH personnel are reluctant to descend from their vehicles, to carry out routine patrolling, or to thoroughly investigate crimes. In addition, supervisors are frequently absent from their posts. However, Rachel M. Neild of the Washington Office on Latin America, who has closely followed the emergence of the PNH, observed in early 1998 that in spite of these problems the PNH had gained confidence in 1997, its second full year, and had become less dependent on foreign police monitors in carrying out its operations."

The United States Department of State observed in 1999 that the PNH was continuing to gain experience and to benefit from training. Nevertheless, the PNH found itself still grappling with problems of attrition, corruption, incompetence, narcotics trafficking, and human rights abuses within its ranks.

Respect for Human Rights

State violence and terror have been features of Haitian life since the nation broke away from colonial rule in 1804, and even before. Between Aristide's overthrow in 1991 and his restoration in 1994, the use of paramilitary groups against individuals thought to be opposed to the regime became common. Control of the populace was enforced by acts of kidnapping, extrajudicial killings, rape, and "disappearances." Mutilated bodies were left in the streets as warnings against disobedience. A pattern of judicial corruption, arbitrary arrest, and prolonged detentions was inherited from the previous Duvalier era as a method of governance. The FAd'H and its various affiliates used their monopoly to subjugate and abuse the Haitian citizenry. Their abuses escalated in the final months of the military regime's existence.

The arrival in 1994 of the international military and police missions and the return of President Aristide brought a dramatic reduction in the level of institutional violence. The shift in responsibility for law enforcement from the FAd'H to a new police organization and the subsequent disbanding of the FAd'H introduced fundamental changes to the human rights landscape. The transformation has by no means been complete, however. Continuing political feuds and bitter hatreds, combined with the inexperience of the new police force, have accounted for many brutal criminal acts, but far beneath the scale of the past. In the first three years following the entry of the international forces in September 1994, about two dozen executions were recorded that may have been politically motivated. The most notorious cases in which a government role was suspected were those of Mireille Bertin, the spokeswoman for an opposition party, in 1995, and two right-wing extremist leaders the following year. In October 1999, Jean Lamy, a former army colonel who was slated to become secretary of state for justice (public security), was assassinated by unknown gunmen.

There were sixty-six cases of extrajudicial killings by the police in 1999, according to the Organization of American States (OAS)/UN International Civilian Mission (ICM). Although a continuing problem, these killings were not political but resulted from excessive use of force and lack of professionalism on the part of the police. Many were believed to be summary executions of suspects and detainees. Others occurred during police actions against gangs and mobs. Cases of police executions and serious police crimes were investigated by the Office of the Inspector General, although police beatings were likely to be overlooked.

In January 1999, the secretary of state for justice and public security announced that 500 police implicated in various infractions had been removed from the force. However, the weakness of the judiciary has precluded successful prosecutions of police for unjustified deaths. This apparent impunity was underscored in 1997, when an investigative judge released without trial six members of the PNH who had been charged with participating in three separate incidents of summary executions. The judge involved was later removed from office, and Haitian authorities were making efforts to reinstitute charges.

Police mistreatment of detainees appears to be on the increase. The ICM recorded 191 such incidents in 1998. This rise, which went up nearly five times in a single year, may have been linked to the beatings of large groups of inmates in connection with escape attempts at two prisons. Many reports involved beatings of armed gang members, excessive force in dealing with demonstrators, application of psychological pressures, and administration of shock treatment to prisoners while they were under questioning. However, these incidents of human rights violations by the PNH failed to substantiate a policy of deliberate or systematic abuse. The inspector general has focused most of his resources on police criminal activities and has not punished many cases of abuse. Complaints against indiscriminate use of firearms by the police have declined in spite of the increase in the number of police deployed. The inexperience and youth of the recruits as well as training shortcomings and fears for their own safety accounted for many of the problems of the new force.

Multinational Security Assistance

The coup of September 1991 against Haiti's first democratically elected president brought condemnation by the UN Security Council and the imposition of sanctions by the OAS. Diplomatic efforts by the OAS to restore the Aristide government lacked force in part because the OAS embargo was so porous. It was not until June 1993, when the Security Council imposed a worldwide fuel and arms embargo, that the leaders of the illegal Haitian military regime agreed to negotiations to restore democracy to the country. However, the ten-point Governors Island Accord of July 3, 1993, failed when an advance team of the UN-sponsored police trainers and military personnel was prevented from coming ashore (see The Post-Duvalier Period, this ch.)

More resolute pressures by the United States and the UN, plus preparations by the United States for an actual invasion, finally persuaded the de facto Haitian leaders to agree to the landing of troops on the basis of "permissive intervention." The United States-led Multinational Force (MNF) quickly grew to 21,000 troops, of which 2,500 were from other countries.

The MNF was welcomed as a liberating force by ordinary Haitians, who celebrated their restored freedom and the hope of a resumption of democratic government. Relations with the Haitian military were less cordial. The MNF was obliged to send patrols into the countryside to replace Haitian troops carrying out rural police functions. In the cities, the FAd'H was confined to barracks and divested of its arms. The coup leaders soon departed the country, leaving the army demoralized and leaderless.

In March 1995, the MNF was formally replaced by the UN Mission in Haiti (UNMIH) under the terms of a UN resolution providing for a force of 6,000 military peacekeepers. The 3,300 United States military personnel then remaining in Haiti formed the core, with most of the other troops coming from Bangladesh, Pakistan, Nepal, and Canada. The UNMIH was organized into five infantry battalions, including a United States quick-reaction force, a military police battalion, and engineering, aviation, logistics, military intelligence, and civil affairs units. The group had its headquarters in Port-au-Prince, with six subheadquarters. United States Special Forces were detailed to twenty-five rural areas to supervise ad hoc arrangements with local army units.

In 1996 Canada assumed a principal role in the operation, agreeing to supply the UNMIH force commander. The mission was gradually drawn down until its last contingents of 650 Canadian and 550 Pakistani troops began their departures in November 1997. A separate United States contingent of 480 active-duty soldiers and reservists remained in Haiti from the original force of 20,000 in 1994. Mainly civil engineers and medical personnel, they helped with construction of schools, roads, and bridges and provided medical assistance. The troops were scheduled to be withdrawn in January 2000, to be replaced by reserve and National Guard forces on short assignments to continue medical programs and engineering projects.

The UN was also responsible for some 900 police trainers from more than twenty countries, who assisted in the formation and professionalization of the PNH. This multinational mentoring and training force had been reduced to 290 civilian police specialists from eleven countries by 1998, of whom twenty-three were detached from the Royal Canadian Mounted Police and from local police forces in Canada, thirty from the United States, many of them of Haitian origin, and thirty-five from France. Argentina supplied 140 federal police to provide security for the police trainers. The training mandate was scheduled to expire March 15, 2000, with a follow-up technical support program planned.

Justice System

Haiti's legal system reflects its colonial origins. It has a French structure superimposed on a traditional African-Caribbean society and thus lacks the parallel or indigenous legal system often found in modern Africa. The civil law system is based on the Napoleonic Code. The Criminal Code dates from 1832 (see Governmental Institutions, ch. 9).

For nearly 200 years, the justice system has been noted for its rampant corruption. Most crimes go unsolved and unpunished. The Duvalier dictatorships and the military regimes that followed left a judicial system that was barely functioning. The best judges and lawyers fled the country, in some cases to serve as judicial officials of newly independent francophone African states.

The OAS/UN International Civilian Mission to Haiti delivered a devastating indictment of the judicial system after the monitors had completed a study of the system's most pressing weaknesses in 1993 while the military was still in power. Their report found that judges, prosecutors, and lawyers had been threatened, beaten, and killed for attempting to follow the rule of law. Judges and prosecutors were afraid even to investigate cases involving the military, the attachés, or their supporters. Corruption and extortion permeated every level of the judicial system. Despite the requirement that justices of the peace have a law degree and complete a minimum one-year probationary period, many justices of the peace did not know how to read and write. People viewed the court system with contempt and avoided it by settling disputes on their own, sometimes by "vigilante justice." The impunity of the most powerful sectors of Haitian society fed the country's cycle of violence. Judicial procedures and protections were systematically breached by detentions and warrantless arrests that amounted simply to abduction.

The restored civilian government has undertaken limited measures to redress the abuses of the 1991–94 period, but as of 1999 the judicial system remained weak and corrupt. Sweeping judicial reforms are planned. Congress passed a judicial reform law in 1998, but it did not contain sufficiently precise measures to produce material changes. Persons are still detained for long periods without trial, and normal protections against arbitrary arrest are routinely violated. A large proportion of crimes, including grave political offenses, are never brought to trial even when strong evidence could be presented against the presumed perpetrators.

With the help of international donors, the Ministry of Justice and Public Security has opened a magistrates' school offering a twenty-four-week course. The first two classes in 1998 and 1999 trained a corps of 100 new magistrates. In addition, 120 justices of the peace attended training seminars. The ministry has improved the functioning of the public prosecutor's office and brought about better case presentation and judicial supervision. In spite of some salary increases, there have been repeated strikes of justices of the peace and prosecutors demanding pay raises and better working conditions. Many lower courts are barely functional, lacking proper quarters, electricity, record-keeping, or stationery. Corrupt judges from the coup period, many regarded as irredeemable, continue on the bench. Failure to reform the code of criminal procedure contributes to a large backlog of cases. The code stipulates that the fifteen courts of first instance hold only two criminal court sessions per year, each lasting for two weeks, to try all major crimes, primarily murder, requiring a jury trial.

At the end of 1999, about 80 percent of prison inmates were unsentenced and awaiting trial. No compensation is granted to those ultimately found innocent. A new Office to Control Preventive Detention was formed by the Ministry of of Justice in 1998 to accelerate the review and processing of cases stagnating in the prison system. By improving judges' access to detainees, this office facilitated the review of 1,198 cases and the release of 477 prisoners and referral of 160 detainees to the courts.

The constitution stipulates that a person may be arrested only if apprehended during commission of a crime or if a warrant has been issued. The detainee must be brought before a judge within forty-eight hours of arrest. The police often take a cavalier attitude toward the legal requirements for the issuance of valid search and arrest warrants, adequate evidence for arrests, and presentation of suspects before a judge within forty-eight hours. The constitution prohibits the interrogation of those charged with a crime unless the suspect has legal counsel present or waives this right. Most accused cannot afford counsel, and, despite efforts of local and international human rights groups to provide legal aid, many interrogations continue to be held without counsel present. During actual trials, most defendants have access to counsel. Notwithstanding the order of the minister of justice that Creole be used in the courts, most legal proceedings continue to be conducted in French, which only about 10 percent of the population speaks.

Under the post-1994 civilian regime, there were no reported cases of the previously common practice of secret detention. The number of arbitrary arrests also declined significantly. The government has detained political opponents and persons associated with the former military regime, often on vague charges of plotting against the state. In some cases the authorities have responded to court orders to release such prisoners, but in others political prisoners have continued to be held contrary to court rulings.

The Ministry of Justice and Public Security is said to have made a sincere effort to overcome the stagnation of the trial system, releasing those who had already served more time than if they had been found guilty. As part of a new project, law students assist detainees to prepare their cases. The constitution provides protection against unnecessary force, psychological pressure, or physical brutality to extract confessions. However, police mistreatment of suspects at the time of arrest remains common.

Prison System

Haiti's prisons have long been notorious for their inhumane conditions and often cruel treatment of inmates. A United States Marine Corps report described them in 1934 as "a disgrace to humanity." Under the military regime of 1991–94, the prisons deteriorated still further. Detainees suffered from a lack of the most basic hygiene as well as from inadequate food and health care. Prisoners had to rely on families for food and medicines. Most of the seventeen prisons were remnants of garrisons built for United States troops in the 1920s and lacked electricity, potable water, and toilets; many prisoners were forced to sleep on the floor in densely overcrowded quarters.

The civil governments of Aristide and Préval have taken some measures to improve the situation, with the help of international humanitarian bodies. The government created Haiti's first civilian prison agency, the National Penitentiary Administration (Administration Pénitentiare Nationale—Apena), and formed a corps of trained prison guards. The agency was placed under the PNH in 1997 but retained most of its autonomy. The prison population was 3,494 in late 1998. One section of Fort National, the main penitentiary in Port-au-Prince, has been refurbished to house women and juveniles. In other prisons, overcrowding often prevents strict separation of juveniles from adults or convicts from those in trial detention. In 1998 prisoners generally received one or two adequate meals a day, often supplemented by food brought by family members. In police station holding cells, where politically sensitive prisoners have often been kept, detainees continued to be dependent on their families for food. Prisoner health is a serious problem. The International Committee of the Red Cross (ICRC) paid for the installation of rudimentary clinics, but the government has failed to keep them adequately staffed with medicines. Human rights groups such as the ICRC and the Haitian Red Cross are freely permitted to visit prisons and police stations to monitor treatment of prisoners and to provide needed medical care, food, and legal aid.

Narcotics Trafficking

Haiti's geographic location between Colombia and the United States, coupled with its long, unpatrolled coastline, mountainous interior, and the presence of numerous airstrips, makes the country an ideal transshipment and storage point for Colombian cocaine suppliers. A lesser amount of marijuana also transits Haiti. Haiti itself is not an important producer of illegal drugs, nor has domestic drug consumption been a significant problem. Narcotics shipments from Colombia reach Haiti's southern coast via high-speed boats and by land and sea drops from light aircraft. A portion of the drugs are exported

489

directly, but most are smuggled across the border to the Dominican Republic for onward transit to the United States, Canada, and Europe.

The de facto military government of 1991–94 maintained a minimal drug enforcement effort, with the primary responsibility for antidrug operations assigned to the army and police units under army control. The air force and navy did not have the resources to make a material contribution to drug interdiction. Rumors abounded of senior officials linked to drug trafficking, although direct evidence was lacking. After the army command announced that any member linked to drug trafficking would be expelled from the military and subjected to civil prosecution, some low-ranking officers and enlisted personnel were reassigned or dismissed. However, the civil judicial system declined to prosecute military personnel on drug charges. United States efforts to help the Haitian counternarcotics effort were suspended while the military regime was in power.

Under the Préval government, primary responsibility for drug suppression was brought under the Ministry of Justice and Public Security's special adviser on narcotics matters. Enforcement is primarily the responsibility of the Counternarcotics Unit of the national police. The Haitian Coast Guard, activated with United States help, cooperated with the United States Coast Guard in several significant seizures in 1997, its first year. As a result of these operations, the Haitian Coast Guard was able to add to its inventory three high-speed vessels that had been confiscated from drug dealers.

Although Haiti's role is secondary to that of the Dominican Republic in the drug transit trade, the feeble resources of the PNH and the corruption of the Haitian justice system have made Haitian territory increasingly inviting for illegal narcotics shipments. Oceangoing speedboats can leave Colombia at dusk and arrive at the Haitian coast before daybreak with little risk of detection. Drug loads can then be carried across the border to the Dominican Republic or smuggled to Florida on freighters. United States authorities have estimated that nearly sixty-seven tons of cocaine passed through Haiti in 1999. This figure represented 14 percent of the total amount of cocaine produced in South America in that year.

In 1998 the PNH made eighty-six drug-related arrests; none of those arrested were considered major drug traffickers. Of those detained, thirty-four were Colombians. None of those brought before the courts in 1997 or 1998 resulted in successful prosecutions. Although 100 PNH officers were dismissed for drug-related offenses and ten arrested as a preliminary to prosecution, internal corruption persists. Seized cocaine is believed to be marketed by the police. Poorly paid customs agents and judges (whose salaries are often lower than those of the police) contribute to the difficulty of preventing official corruption.

Haiti's enforcement effort remains beyond the capacity of the Haitian security forces alone to control. Haiti's laws are strong, but the country's weak judicial system has brought few traffickers to trial. The Office of the Special Adviser has drafted new legislation to improve narcotics control and to introduce the first law to combat money laundering, but the political impasse of 1998–99 prevented enactment of these measures by parliament.

As of 1999, the Haitian government was still struggling in its attempts to establish functioning internal security and justice administrations in place of systems that had never enjoyed any credibility with the Haitian people. The police continued to be prone to unwarranted abuses, and their inexperience in confronting criminal behavior has led to numerous unjustified killings. Nevertheless, hundreds of police have been cited for misconduct, many have been discharged, and some even jailed. Such efforts to impose a standard of behavior on the security forces have been almost unknown in Haiti's history.

The new police force faces serious challenges in controlling major crime, violence directed against the democratic government, and international commerce in narcotics. It must also build and uphold professional standards against the threats of corruption and politicization. Although the Haitian army and its affiliated organizations have all been dissolved, many of their former members are armed and capable of creating chaotic conditions endangering the regime. As the sole agency in Haiti dedicated to the maintenance of law and order, the PNH is essential to the preservation of a secure environment for democratic government.

*   *   *

Among the considerable number of scholars who have examined the collapse of the military regime in Haiti in 1994 and the resumption of civilian government, the reports by Rachel M. Neild published by the Washington Office on Latin

491

America are notable for their detailed record of the development of the Haitian National Police, based on periodic visits for personal observation. In several studies, Donald E. Schulz of the Army War College analyzes the country's internal security problems in a broader framework. The 1998 United Nations report on its civilian police mission appraises the success of its efforts to improve the police and judicial systems three years after the return of civilian rule. A vivid account by Elizabeth Rubin in the *New York Times Magazine* relates the experiences of a Haitian-born New York City policeman helping to deal with the enormous problems of bringing order to a society with no tradition of law and justice.

The political role of the army from the close of the Duvalier era in 1986 until the restoration of democratic rule in 1994 is recounted in *Haitian Frustrations: Dilemmas for U.S. Policy*, edited by Georges A. Fauriol. The deplorable state of the Haitian judicial system is addressed by William G. O'Neill in a contribution to *Haiti Renewed: Political and Economic Prospects*.

A treatment of the structure, internal conflicts, and ultimate breakdown of the armed forces can be found in the Fauriol work. Two earlier publications, *Armed Forces of Latin America* by Adrian J. English and *World Armies*, edited by John Keegan, provide historical background on the evolution of the FAd'H. (For further information and complete citations, see Bibliography.)

Appendix

Table 1. Metric Conversion Coefficients and Factors

When you know	Multiply by	To find
Millimeters..........................	0.04	inches
Centimeters	0.39	inches
Meters..............................	3.3	feet
Kilometers	0.62	miles
Hectares...........................	2.47	acres
Square kilometers	0.39	square miles
Cubic meters	35.3	cubic feet
Liters..............................	0.26	gallons
Kilograms..........................	2.2	pounds
Metric tons.........................	0.98	long tons
....	1.1	short tons
....	2,204	pounds
Degrees Celsius (Centigrade)..........	1.8 and add 32	degrees Fahrenheit

Table 2. Dominican Republic: Population and Percentage Increase, 1981 Census and 1993 Census

Region Subregion Province	Population		Increase (in percentages)
	1981	1993	
Cibao			
Central Cibao			
Espaillat................	163,860	202,376	23.5
La Vega	277,018	344,721	24.4
Puerto Plata	201,893	261,485	29.5
Santiago	533,102	710,803	33.3
Monseñor Nouel[1]	112,932	149,318	32.2
Total Central Cibao......	1,288,805	1,668,703	29.5
Eastern Cibao			
Duarte..................	227,798	281,879	23.7
María Trinidad Sánchez....	99,731	124,957	25.3
Salcedo	94,173	101,810	8.1
Samaná	64,537	75,253	16.6
Sánchez Ramírez	119,866	163,166	36.1
Total Eastern Cibao	606,105	747,065	23.3
Western Cibao			
Dajabon.................	54,675	68,606	25.5
Monte Cristi	83,124	95,705	15.1
Santiago Rodríguez	56,144	62,144	10.7
Valverde................	94,579	152,257	61.0
Total Western Cibao	288,522	378,712	31.3
Total Cibao..........	2,183,432	2,794,480	29.5
Southwest			
Enriquillo			
Bahoruco	78,042	105,206	34.8
Barahona...............	141,313	164,835	16.6
Independencia	35,908	39,541	10.1
Pedernales	15,493	18,054	16.5
Total Enriquillo........	270,756	327,636	21.0
De Valle			
Azua...................	140,914	199,684	41.7
Elías Piña..............	61,895	64,641	4.4
San Juan de la Maguana ...	231,509	252,637	9.1
Total De Valle	434,318	516,962	19.0
Total Southwest	705,074	844,598	19.8
Southeast			
Valdesia			
National District..........	1,540,786	2,193,046	42.3
Peravia.................	169,067	201,851	19.4
San Cristóbal............	289,340	420,820	45.4

Table 2. *(Continued) Dominican Republic: Population and Percentage Increase, 1981 Census and 1993 Census*

Region Subregion Province	Population		Increase (in percentages)
	1981	1993	
Monte Plata[1]	155,608	167,148	7.4
Total Valdesia	2,154,801	2,982,865	38.4
Yuma			
El Seybo	83,230	96,770	16.3
La Altagracia	96,009	115,685	20.5
La Romana	107,021	166,550	55.6
San Pedro de Macorís.	147,777	212,368	43.7
Hato Mayor[1]	68,397	80,074	17.1
Total Yuma	502,434	671,447	33.6
Total Southeast.	2,657,235	3,654,312	37.5
TOTAL.	5,545,741	7,293,390	31.5

[1] These provinces became a part of the category after the 1981 census.

Source: Based on information from Dominican Republic, Oficina Nacional de Estadística, *República Dominicana en Cifras, 1997,* Santo Domingo, 1998, 47.

Table 3. *Dominican Republic: School Attendance, Population Five Years of Age and Older by Level of Instruction,*
1993 Census

Region Subregion Province	Preschool	Primary	Secondary	Technical University	University	Total
Cibao						
Central Cibao						
Espaillat...........	2,242	58,372	13,436	2,598	1,625	78,273
La Vega............	3,576	93,109	20,963	4,493	2,977	125,118
Puerta Plata........	2,880	61,052	12,782	1,995	1,066	79,775
Santiago............	8,184	132,967	33,109	4,114	5,990	184,364
Monseñor Nouel.....	1,518	41,385	10,768	1,934	1,333	56,938
Total Central Cibao...	18,400	386,885	91,058	15,134	12,991	524,468
Eastern Cibao						
Duarte.............	3,321	66,488	13,680	2,640	1,029	87,158
Maria Trinidad Sánchez.	1,221	26,594	4,552	419	215	33,001
Salcedo............	1,243	21,398	5,543	632	363	29,179
Samaná............	661	15,531	1,829	194	62	18,277
Sánchez Ramírez.....	1,252	34,419	5,850	899	410	42,830
Total Eastern Cibo...	7,698	164,430	31,454	4,784	2,079	210,445
Western Cibao						
Dajabon...........	816	17,430	3,241	283	258	22,028
Montecristi.........	1,422	20,111	4,414	425	336	26,708
Santiago Rodríguez....	761	13,771	2,430	203	149	17,314

Table 3. (Continued) Dominican Republic: School Attendance, Population Five Years of Age and Older by Level of Instruction, 1993 Census

Region Subregion Province	Level of Instruction					Total
	Preschool	Primary	Secondary	Technical University	University	
Valverde................	1,817	29,487	7,348	1,431	741	40,824
Total Western Cibao....	4,816	80,799	17,433	2,342	1,484	106,874
Total Cibao	30,914	632,114	139,945	22,260	16,554	841,787
Southwest						
Enriquillo						
Bahoruco............	1,136	24,507	3,636	330	214	29,823
Barahona...........	1,926	39,078	8,082	1,121	705	50,912
Independencia	470	9,189	1,355	62	54	11,080
Pedernales	201	3,949	480	17	13	4,660
Total Enriquillo....	3,733	76,673	13,553	1,530	986	96,475
Del Valle						
Azua	1,886	40,713	6,979	726	462	50,766
Elías Piña.........	673	15,176	1,338	82	68	17,337
San Juan..........	2,688	59,475	8,941	744	689	72,537
Total Del Valle ...	5,247	115,364	17,258	1,552	1,219	140,640
Total Southwest.....	8,980	192,037	30,811	3,082	2,205	237,115
Southeast						
Valdesia						
National District	32,203	443,724	144,334	23,919	24,812	668,992
Peravia	1,900	40,009	5,682	809	280	48,680
San Cristóbal	4,821	92,674	18,773	2,015	1,158	119,441

Table 3. (Continued) Dominican Republic: School Attendance, Population Five Years of Age and Older by Level of Instruction, 1993 Census

Region Subregion Province	Level of Instruction					Total
	Preschool	Primary	Secondary	Technical University	University	
Monte Plata..........	1,499	39,176	4,767	552	278	46,272
Total Valdesia..........	40,423	615,588	173,556	27,295	26,528	883,385
Yuma						
El Seybo..........	755	24,650	3,461	856	401	30,123
La Altagracia..........	1,076	32,971	6,495	1,774	923	43,239
La Romana..........	1,939	47,353	12,763	2,640	1,896	66,591
San Pedro de Macorís..........	2,705	40,615	9,845	1,079	548	54,792
Hato Mayor..........	844	16,896	2,220	177	163	20,300
Total Yuma..........	7,319	162,485	34,784	6,526	3,931	215,045
Total Southeast..........	47,742	778,068	208,340	33,821	30,459	1,098,430
TOTAL..........	87,636	1,602,219	379,096	59,163	49,218	2,177,352

Source: Based on information from Dominican Republic, Oficina Nacional de Estadística, *República Dominicana en Cifras, 1997*, Santo Domingo, 1998, 67.

Table 4. Dominican Republic: Health Facilities and Personnel,
1996–97

Facility	Personnel
Health facilities	1,334
Hospitals...	213
Hospital beds.......................................	15,236
Medical schools	10
Dental schools	8
Nursing schools	5
Physicians..	17,460
Dentists..	1,898

Source: Based on information from Pan American Health Organization, *Health Condi-*
tions in the Americas, 2, Washington, 1994, 183–84; *Health in the Americas,* 1,
Washington, 1998, 269, 284–86, 293, 308, and 2, Washington, 1998, 237–38.

Table 5. Dominican Republic: Leading Causes of Death by Sex, 1994
(in percentages)

Causes of Death	Sex	
	Female	Male
Cardiovascular and circulatory diseases................	38.2	30.7
Malignant neoplasms	13.6	10.8
Communicable diseases	11.9	11.3
Accidental injuries and violence......................	5.8	18.0
Other causes	30.5	29.2
TOTAL..	100.0	100.0

Source: Based on information from Pan American Health Organization, *Health in the*
Americas, 2, Washington, 1998, 229–30, 232.

Table 6. Dominican Republic: Employment by Sector, 1996

Sector	Employees
Agriculture	310,500
Commerce.	545,700
Construction	126,600
Energy	13,700
Manufacturing	428,400
Mining	8,800
Transportation and Communications.	185,700

Source: Based on information from Banco Central de la República Dominicana.

Table 7. Dominican Republic: Agricultural and Livestock Production,
1997
(in tons)

Product	Production
Beef	79,000
Cocoa.	56,000
Coffee	96,000
Poultry.	156,000
Rice	521,000
Sugarcane	6,296,000
Tobacco	38,000

Source: Based on information from Banco Central de la República Dominicana.

Table 8. Dominican Republic: Mineral Production, 1993–97

Mineral	1993	1994	1995	1996	1997
Gold (troy ounces)	8,000	49,000	106,000	118,000	76,000
Silver (troy ounces).	39,000	296,000	677,000	547,000	399,000
Nickel (tons)	13,000	.31,000	31,000	30,000	33,000

Source: Based on information from Banco Central de la República Dominicana.

Table 9. Dominican Republic: Tourism, 1993–97

	1993	1994	1995	1996	1997
Number of stopover visitors	1,719,000	1,766,800	1,490,200[1]	1,930,000	2,211,000
Number of hotel rooms	26,800	28,965	32,475	35,750	38,250

[1] Non-Dominican only.

Source: Based on information from Dominican Republic, Secretariat of State for Tourism.

Table 10. Dominican Republic: Imports and Exports, 1988–97
(in millions of United States dollars)

Year	Imports	Exports
1988	1,608	889
1989	1,963	924
1990	1,792	734
1991	1,728	658
1992	2,174	562
1993	2,118	110
1994	2,883	644
1995	2,588	766
1996	3,205	816
1997	3,582	881

Source: Based on information from International Monetary Fund, *International Financial Statistics, 1998*, Washington, 1998, 377.

Table 11. Dominican Republic: United States Assistance, FY 1962–97[1]
(in millions of United States dollars)

FY[1]	Development Assistance	PL–480 Programs[2]	ESF[3]	Total
1962	24.7	23.9	22.8	71.4
1963	2.1	9.6	0.0	11.7
1964	0.0	0.0	4.9	4.9
1965	1.4	3.3	84.3	89.0
1966	21.8	5.4	72.5	99.7
1967	21.5	4.3	32.2	58.0
1968	27.1	14.2	16.4	57.7
1969	12.3	13.2	0.0	25.5
1970	5.2	14.0	0.0	19.2
1971	13.5	12.8	0.0	26.3
1972	7.4	19.0	0.0	26.4
1973	1.0	14.2	0.0	15.2
1974	12.6	4.2	0.0	16.8
1975	5.6	5.5	0.0	11.1
1976	16.1	11.4	0.0	27.5
1977	0.9	11.9	0.0	12.8
1978	1.3	3.9	0.0	5.2
1979	26.4	20.7	0.0	47.1
1980	34.6	19.7	0.0	54.3
1981	17.4	18.6	0.0	36.0
1982	19.0	20.6	41.0	80.6
1983	26.5	25.3	8.0	59.8
1984	27.8	21.6	34.0	93.4
1985	30.1	45.1	95.0	170.2
1986	26.5	34.6	40.0	101.1
1987	19.5	85.3	0.0	104.8
1988	18.6	33.3	13.0	64.9
1989	20.1	25.0	0.0	45.1
1990	18.0	4.4	0.0	22.4
1991	13.9	3.3	0.0	17.2
1992	11.0	4.5	5.0	20.5
1993	17.8	2.4	1.7	21.9
1994	10.7	4.8	0.0	15.5
1995	9.0	4.3	0.0	13.3
1996	9.7	3.3	0.0	13.0
1997	11.0	0.0	0.3	11.3
TOTAL	542.1	557.6	471.1	1,570.8

[1] FY—fiscal year, e.g., October 1, 1962–September 30, 1963.
[2] PL—Public Law (see Glossary).
[3] ESF—Economic Support Funds.

Source: Based on information from US Agency for International Development.

Table 12. Dominican Republic: Major Army Equipment, 1998

Description	Country of Origin	Inventory
AMX–13 light tanks, 76mm gun....................	France	12
M–41A1 light tanks, 76mm gun	United States	12
V–150 Commando armored personnel carriers	United States	8
M–2/M–3 half-track armored personnel carriers	United States	20
M–101 105mm howitzers, towed	United States	22
Mortars, 120mm	United States	24
Mortars, 80mm	United States	n.a.[1]

[1] n.a.—not available.

Source: Based on information from *The Military Balance, 1998–99*, London, 1998, 222.

Table 13. Dominican Republic: Major Navy Equipment, 1999

Description	Country of Origin	Inventory
Corvettes		
Cohoe class, 855 tons, two 76mm guns	United States	2
Patrol forces		
Balsam class cutter, 1,034 tons, two 12.7mm machine guns.........................	United States	1
Admiral class gunships, 905 tons, one 76mm gun	United States	1
Satoyomo class patrol boat, 960 tons, one 76mm gun	United States	1
Canopus class large patrol craft, 95 tons, one 40mm gun...........................	United States	2
PGM–11 class large patrol craft, 145 tons, one 20mm machine gun....................	United States	1
Bellatrix class coastal patrol craft, 60 tons, three 12.7mm machine guns..................	United States	4

Source: Based on information from *Jane's Fighting Ships, 1999–2000*, Alexandria, Virginia, 1999, 169–71.

Table 14. Dominican Republic: Major Air Force Equipment, 1998

Description	Country of Origin	Inventory
Counterinsurgency aircraft		
Cessna A–37B Dragonfly.....................	United States	8
Transport		
C–47 Douglas Dakota	United States	3
Aero Commander 680	United States	1
Liaison		
Cessna 210................................	United States	1
PA–31 Navajo..............................	United States	2
Beechcraft Queen Air 80	United States	3
Beechcraft King Air..........................	United States	1
Helicopter		
Bell 205	United States	8
Aérospatiale SA–318C........................	France	2
Aérospatiale SA–365	France	1
Trainer		
North American AT–6........................	United States	2
Beech T–34B Mentor	United States	6
Beech T–41D Mescalero......................	United States	3

Source: Based on information from *The Military Balance, 1998–99*, London, 1998, 222.

Table 15. Haiti: Estimated Population by Geographic Department and Rural-Urban Residence, 1995[1]

Department	Population	Percent	Percent Urban	Percent Rural
Artibonite..............	1,013,779	14	23	77
Centre.................	490,790	7	14	86
Grand' Anse............	641,399	9	13	87
Nord..................	759,318	11	27	73
Nord-Est..............	248,764	3	25	75
Nord-Ouest	420,971	6	14	86
Ouest	2,494,862	35	60	40
Sud	653,398	9	14	86
Sud-Est	457,013	6	8	92
TOTAL................	7,180,294	100	33	67

[1] Population projections are based on national census data from 1950 and 1982. The population of urban areas may be underestimated, especially for the Port-au-Prince metropolitan area (Ouest). The most recent national census of Haiti occurred in 1982.

Source: Based on information from Institut Haïtien de Statistique et d'Informatique, *Tendances et perspectives de la population d'Haïti au niveau régional (département, arrondissement, et commune), 1980–2005,* Port-au-Prince, 1992, 12, 15, 35.

Table 16.   *Haiti: Estimated Population by Department and Arrondissement, 1995*[1]

Department	Arrondissement	Population
Artibonite		
	Gonaïves	188,930
	Gros Morne	142,675
	Saint-Marc	235,808
	Dessalines	311,545
	Marmelade	134,821
Total Artibonite		1,013,779
Centre		
	Hinche	148,186
	Mirebalais	150,217
	Lascahobas	124,817
	Cerca la Source	67,570
Total Centre		490,790
Grand' Anse		
	Jérémie	189,237
	Anse-d'Hainault	82,742
	Corail	114,800
	Miragoâne	97,506
	Anse-à-Veau	157,114
Total Grand' Anse		641,399
Nord		
	Cap-Haïtien	173,779
	Acul du Nord	125,126
	Grande Rivière du Nord	62,534
	Saint-Raphaël	129,674
	Borgne	91,619
	Limbé	57,227
	Plaisance	119,359
Total Nord		759,318
Nord-Est		
	Fort Liberté	41,849
	Puanaminthe	82,763
	Trou du Nord	69,168
	Vallières	54,984
Total Nord-Est		248,764
Nord-Ouest		
	Port-de-Paix	174,550
	Saint-Louis du Nord	77,022
	Môle Saint-Nicolas	169,399
Total Nord-Ouest		420,971

Table 16. (Continued) Haiti: Estimated Population by Department and Arrondissement, 1995[1]

Department	Arrondissement	Population
Ouest		
....	Port-au-Prince	1,639,774
....	Léogane	295,675
....	Croix des Bouquets	315,175
....	Arcahaie	155,471
....	Île de la Gonâve	88,767
Total Ouest		2,494,862
Sud		
....	Cayes	264,426
....	Port-Salut	73,971
....	Aquin	166,955
....	Coteaux	56,910
....	Chardonnières	91,136
Total Sud		653,398
Sud-Est		
....	Jacmel	248,462
....	Bainet	128,650
....	Belle-Anse	79,901
Total Sud-Est		457,013

[1] Population projections are based on national census data from 1950 and 1982. The population of urban areas may be underestimated.

Source: Based on information from Institut Haïtien de Statistique et d'Informatique, *Tendances et perspectives de la population d'Haïti au niveau régional (département, arrondissement et commune), 1980–2005*, Port-au-Prince, 1992, 38–62.

Table 17. Haiti: Education Facilities and Personnel by Department, 1996–97[1]

Department	Primary Schools			Secondary Schools	
	Schools	Students	Teachers	Schools	Students
Artibonite	1,667	222,754	6,901	129	28,127
Centre	653	83,258	2,215	60	12,607
Grand' Anse.........	1,099	149,799	3,552	60	15,439
Nord...............	1,027	162,962	4,613	119	23,796
Nord-Est............	320	62,173	1,459	34	8,339
Nord-Ouest	744	103,912	2,941	71	13,727
Ouest	2,332	419,166	12,814	557	191,558
Sud................	987	128,870	3,935	97	23,381
Sud-Est.............	699	96,386	2,740	43	11,007
TOTAL.............	9,528	1,429,280	41,170	1,170	327,981

[1] These figures are based on statistics drawn from the education census of 1996–1997.

Source: Based on information from Haiti, Ministry of National Education, Youth, and Sports, *Annuaire statistique des écoles fondamentales et secondaires d'Haïti*, Port-au-Prince, 1998, 12, Annex A, tables 1 and 12, Annex B, tables 1 and 11.

Table 18. Haiti: Education Facilities by Level of Instruction and Sector, 1996–97[1]

Level	Public	Private	Total
·Preschool........................	409	4,949	5,358
Primary	1,071	8,457	9,528
Secondary	144	1,026	1,170
Higher..........................	7	52	59

[1] Data on preschool, primary, and secondary education are based on the education census of 1996–97 undertaken by the Ministry of Education. Data on higher education are from 1994–95.

Source: Data on preschool, primary, and secondary education based on information from Haiti, Ministry of National Education, Youth, and Sports, *Annuaire statistique des écoles fondamentales et secondaires d'Haïti*, Port-au-Prince, 1998. Data on higher education based on information from Research Triangle Institute, Academy for Educational Development, and Educat, S.A., *Technical Diagnosis of the Haitian Education System*, Port-au-Prince, Projet d'élaboration du plan national d'éducation 2004, 1997.

Table 19. Haiti: Health Facilities and Personnel by Department, 1994[1]

Department	Health Facilities	Hospitals and In-patient Facilities	Beds	Beds/ 100,000 Population	Physicians	Nurses
Artibonite	84	15	572	56	69	33
Centre	44	3	205	42	14	9
Grand' Anse	60	11	421	66	13	22
Nord	52	11	776	102	31	52
Nord-Est	22	5	113	45	15	11
Nord-Ouest	59	8	261	62	19	29
Ouest	235	42	3,372	135	561	527
Sud	71	12	581	89	30	61
Sud-Est	36	3	172	38	21	41
TOTAL	663	110	6,473		773	785

[1] Figures are based on 1994 data for physicians and nurses and population projections for 1995.

Source: Based on information from Pan American Health Organization, *Health Situation Analysis*, Haiti, Port-au-Prince, 1996, 93, 102.

Table 20. Haiti: Imports and Exports, 1988–97
(in millions of Haitian gourdes)[1]

Year	Imports	Exports
1988	1,721	896
1989	1,455	720
1990	1,661	801
1991	2,414	1,005
1992	2,727	719
1993	4,555	1,029
1994	3,783	1,236
1995	9,866	1,666
1996	10,448	1,413
1997	10,792	1,995

[1] For value of gourde, see Glossary.

Source: Based on information from International Monetary Fund, *International Financial Statistics, 1998*, Washington, 1998, 469.

Table 21. Haiti: External Debt, Fiscal Years 1991–95
(in millions of United States dollars)

Year	Long-term	Short-term
1991	621	105
1992	638	112
1993	648	121
1994	635	47
1995	752	26

Source: Based on information from World Bank, *Global Development Finance*, Washington, 1997.

Table 22. Haiti: Grants Received, FY 1991–92–FY 1996–97
(in millions of Haitian gourdes)[1]

Year	Grants Received
FY 1991–92	14.0
FY 1992–93	1.1
FY 1993–94	2.2
FY 1994–95	696.7
FY 1995–96	354.3
FY 1996–97	694.6

[1] For value of gourde, see Glossary.

Source: Based on information from International Monetary Fund, *International Financial Statistics*, Washington, 1997.

Table 23. Haiti: Sources and Amounts of Development Assistance, 1990–99
(in millions of United States dollars)

Year	United States	France	Canada	European Union
1990	54			
1991	78.5			
1992	63.6	16.6	9.4	12.6
1993	49.8	16.5	14.6	10.0
1994	90.6	14.9	14.9	13.6
1995	193.7	31.1	18.4	85.8
1996	135.6	29.6	24.4	67.4
1997	99.1			
1998	97.3[1]			
1999	97.0[1]			

[1] Planned.

Source: Based on information from United States Agency for International Development, Washington, and Organization for Economic Cooperation and Development, Paris, 1998.

Table 24. Haiti: Heads of State, 1971–99

Name	Period	Title
Jean-Claude Duvalier	1/1/71 – 2/7/86	President-for-Life
General Henri Namphy	2/7/86 – 2/7/88	Chairman, National Council
Leslie F. Manigat	2/7/88 – 6/20/88	President
General Henri Namphy	6/20/88 – 9/17/88	President, Military Government
General Prosper Avril	9/17/88 – 3/12/90	President, Military Government
General Hérard Abraham	3/10/90 – 3/13/90	President, Provisional Military Government
Ertha Pascal-Trouillot	3/13/90 – 2/7/91	President, Provisional Government
Jean-Bertrand Aristide	2/7/91 – 10/1/91	President
Jean-Bertrand Aristide	10/1/91 – 10/11/94	President-in-exile
General Raoul Cédras	10/1/91 – 10/10/91	President, Military Junta
Joseph C. Nerette	10/10/91 – 6/19/92	Provisional President under Military Rule
Marc-Louis Bazin	6/19/92 – 6/15/93	Provisional President and Prime Minister under Military Rule
Jean-Bertrand Aristide	6/15/93 – 5/12/94	President recognized by Military Junta following the Governors Island Agreement
Émile Jonassaint	6/11/94 – 10/12/94	Provisional President under Military Rule
Jean-Bertrand Aristide	10/12/94 – 2/7/96	President
René Garcia Préval	2/7/96 –	President

Table 25. Haiti: Prime Ministers, 1988–99

Name	Period
Martial Celestine	1988
René Garcia Préval	1991
Jean-Jacques Honorat	1991 – 1992 (interim)
Marc Bazin	1992 – 1993
Robert Malval	1993 – 1994
Smark Michel	1994 – 1995
Claudette Werleigh	1995 – 1996
Rosny Smarth	1996 – 1997
— vacant —	1997 – 1999
Jacques-Édouard Alexis	1999 –

Table 26. Haiti: Civil Jurisdictions and Government Institutions, 2000

ADMINISTRATIVE JURISDICTION	LEGISLATIVE BRANCH	EXECUTIVE BRANCH	THE JUDICIARY
National	National Assembly	President	Court of Cassation (Supreme Court)
	– Senate	Council of Ministers	
	– Chamber of Deputies	*Permanent Electoral Council*[1]	
	Interdepartmental Council[1]	Delagates and Vice Delegates	
Departments (9 *départements*)	*Departmental Assembly*[1]	*Departmental Council*[1]	Courts of Appeal
			Courts of First Instance
Municipalities (133 communes)	*Municipal Assembly*[1]	Municipal Council	Justice of the Peace Courts
Communal Sections (565 *sections communales*)	*Communal Section Assembly*[1]	Communal Section Administrative Council	

[1] Not yet formally in place.

Table 27. Haiti: Cabinet Ministers, December 1999

Office	Incumbent
Prime Minister, Minister of Interior and Territorial Collectivities	Jacques Édouard Alexis
Minister of Agriculture, Natural Resources, and Rural Development	François Séverin
Minister of Commerce and Industry	Gérald Germain
Minister of Culture	Jean-Robert Vaval
Minister of Economy and Finance	Fred Joseph
Minister of Environment	Yves Cadet
Minister of Foreign Affairs	Fritz Longchamp
Minister of Haitians Living Overseas	Jean Généus
Minister of Justice and Public Safety	Camille Leblanc
Minister of National Education, Youth, and Sports	Paul Antoine Bien-Aimé
Minister of Planning and External Cooperation	Anthony Dessources
Minister of Public Health and Population	Michaëlle Amédée Gédéon
Minister of Public Works, Transportation, and Communication	Max Alcé
Minister of Social Affairs	Mathilde Flambert
Minister of Women's Affairs	Nonie Mathieu

Bibliography

Chapter 1

Atkins, G. Pope, and Larman C. Wilson. *The United States and the Trujillo Regime*. New Brunswick, New Jersey: Rutgers University Press, 1972.

Betances, Emelio. *State and Society in the Dominican Republic*. Boulder, Colorado: Westview Press, 1995.

Black, Jan Knippers. *The Dominican Republic: Politics and Development in an Unsovereign State*. Boston: Allen and Unwin, 1986.

Calder, Bruce. *The Impact of Intervention: The Dominican Republic During the U.S. Occupation of 1916–1924*. Austin: University of Texas Press, 1984.

Campillo Pérez, Julio A. *Elecciones dominicanas: Contribución a su estudio*, 49. Santo Domingo: Academia Dominicana de la Historia, 1982.

Crassweller, Robert. *Trujillo: The Life and Times of a Caribbean Dictator*. New York: Macmillan, 1966.

Cross Beras, Julio A. *Sociedad y desarrollo en la República Dominicana, 1844–1899*. Santo Domingo: Instituto Tecnólogico de Santo Domingo, 1984.

Espinal, Rosario. *Autoritarismo y democracia en la política dominicana*. San Jose, Costa Rica: CAPEL, 1987.

Espinal, Rosario. "An Interpretation of the Democratic Transition in the Dominican Republic." In Giuseppe Di Palma and Laurence Whitehead, eds., *The Central American Impasse*. New York: St. Martin's Press, 1986.

Espinal, Rosario, and Jonathan Hartlyn. "Dominican Republic: The Long and Difficult Struggle for Democracy." Pages 469–518 in Larry Diamond, Jonathan Hartlyn, Juan J. Linz, and Seymour Martin Lipset, eds., *Democracy in Developing Countries: Latin America*, 2d ed. Boulder, Colorado: Lynne Rienner, 1999.

Ferguson, James. *Dominican Republic: Beyond the Lighthouse*. London: Latin American Bureau, 1992.

Galíndez, Jesús de. *The Era of Trujillo: Dominican Dictator*. Ed., R.H. Fitzgibbon. Tucson: University of Arizona Press, 1973.

Gleijeses, Piero. *The Dominican Crisis: The 1965 Constitutionalist Revolt and American Intervention.* Trans., L. Lipson. Baltimore: Johns Hopkins University Press, 1978.

Guerrero, Miguel. *El golpe de estado: Historia del derrocamiento de Juan Bosch.* Santo Domingo: Editora Corripio, 1993.

Hartlyn, Jonathan. "The Dominican Republic: Contemporary Problems and Challenges." Pages 150–72 in Jorge I. Domínguez, Robert A. Pastor, and R. Delisle Worrell, eds., *Democracy in the Caribbean: Pol tical, Economic, and Social Perspectives.* Baltimore: Johns Hopkins University Press, 1993.

Hartlyn, Jonathan. *The Struggle for Democratic Politics in the Dominican Republic.* Chapel Hill: University of North Carolina Press, 1998.

Hoetink, H. *The Dominican People, 1859–1900: Notes for a Historical Sociology.* Trans., S.K. Ault. Baltimore: Johns Hopkins University Press, 1982.

Hoetink, H. "The Dominican Republic, c. 1870–1930." Pages 287–306 in *The Cambridge History of Latin America,* 5. Ed., Leslie Bethell. Cambridge: Cambridge University Press, 1986.

Lowenthal, Abraham. "The Dominican Republic: The Politics of Chaos." In Robert Kaufman and Arpad von Lazar, eds., *Reform and Revolution: Readings in Latin American Politics.* Needham Heights, Massachusetts: Allyn and Bacon, 1969.

Martin, John Bartlow. *Overtaken by Events: The Dominican Crisis from the Fall of Trujillo to the Civil War.* Garden City, New York: Doubleday, 1966.

Martínez Fernández, Luis. "The Sword and the Crucifix: Church-State Relations and Nationality in the Nineteenth-Century Dominican Republic," *Latin American Research Review,* 30, No. 1, 1995, 69–93.

Mateo, Andrés L. *Mito y cultura en la era de Trujillo.* Santo Domingo: Libreria La Trinitaria e Instituto del Libro, 1993.

Moya Pons, Frank. *The Dominican Republic: A National History.* New Rochelle, New York: Hispaniola Books, 1995.

Moya Pons, Frank. "The Dominican Republic since 1930." Pages 509–44 in Leslie Bethell, ed., *The Cambridge History of Latin America,* 7. Cambridge: Cambridge University Press, 1990.

Moya Pons, Frank. "Haiti and Santo Domingo, 1790–c. 1870." Pages 237–76 in Leslie Bethell, ed., *The Cambridge History of Latin America*, 3. Cambridge: Cambridge University Press, 1985.

Moya Pons, Frank. *Manual de historia dominicana*. 7th ed. Santo Domingo: Pontificia Universidad Católica Madre y Maestra, 1983.

Moya Pons, Frank. *El pasado dominicano*. Santo Domingo: Fundación J.A. Caro Alvarez, 1986.

Sáez, José Luis. "Catolicismo e hispanidad en la oratoria de Trujillo," *Estudios Sociales*, 21, No. 3, July–September 1988, 89–104.

Sang, Mu-Kien A. *Buenaventura Báez: El caudillo del sur (1844–1878)*. Santo Domingo: INTEC, 1991.

Sang, Mu-Kien A. "Entre el autoritarismo y la aspiración de libertad," *Estudios Sociales*, 27, No. 95, January–March 1994, 27–47.

Sang, Mu-Kien A. *Ulises Heureaux: Biografía de un dictador*. Santo Domingo: INTEC, 1966.

Vega, Bernardo. *Control y represión en la dictadura trujillista*. Santo Domingo: Fundación Cultural Dominicana, 1986.

Vega, Bernardo. *En la década perdida*. Santo Domingo: Fundación Cultural Dominicana, 1990.

Vega, Bernardo. *Trujillo y el control financiero norteamericano*. Santo Domingo: Fundación Cultural Dominicana, 1990.

Vega, Bernardo. *Trujillo y las fuerzas armadas norteamericanas*. Santo Domingo: Fundación Cultural Dominicana, 1992.

Welles, Sumner. *Naboth's Vineyard: The Dominican Republic, 1844–1924*, 1 and 2. Mamaroneck, New York: Paul P. Appel, 1966.

Wiarda, Howard J. *Dictatorship, Development, and Disintegration*, 1, 2, and 3. Ann Arbor: Xerox University Microfilms, 1975.

Wiarda, Howard J. *The Dominican Republic: Nation in Transition*. New York: Praeger, 1969.

Wiarda, Howard J., and Michael J. Krzanek. *The Dominican Republic: A Caribbean Crucible*. Boulder, Colorado: Westview Press, 1982.

Chapter 2

Americas Watch, National Coalition for Haitian Refugees, Caribbean Rights. *Haitian Sugar Cane Cutters in the Dominican Republic.* New York: 1989.

Americas Watch, National Coalition for Haitian Refugees, Caribbean Rights. *Half Measures: Reform, Forced Labor, and the Dominican Sugar Industry.* New York: 1991.

Americas Watch, National Coalition for Haitian Refugees, Caribbean Rights. *Harvesting Opposition: Forced Haitian Labor in the Dominican Republic.* New York: 1990.

Atkins, G. Pope, and Larman C. Wilson. *The Dominican Republic and the United States: From Imperialism to Transnationalism.* Athens: University of Georgia Press, 1998.

Balmori, Diana, Stuart F. Voss, and Miles Wortman. *Notable Family Networks in Latin America.* Chicago: University of Chicago Press, 1984.

Baud, Michiel. "The Origins of Capitalist Agriculture in the Dominican Republic," *Latin American Research Review,* 22, No. 2, 1987, 135–53.

Bell, Ian. *The Dominican Republic.* Boulder, Colorado: Westview Press, 1981.

Betances, Emelio, and Hobart Spalding, Jr., eds. *The Dominican Republic Today: Realities and Perspectives.* New York: Bildner Center for Western Hemisphere Studies, City University of New York, 1996.

Black, Jan Knippers. *The Dominican Republic: Politics and Development in an Unsovereign State.* Boston: Allen and Unwin, 1986.

Bray, David. "Economic Development: The Middle Class and International Migration in the Dominican Republic," *International Migration Review,* 18, No. 2, Summer 1984, 217–36.

Cambeira, Alan. *Quisqueya la Bella: The Dominican Republic in Historical and Cultural Perspective.* Armonk, New York: M.E. Sharpe, 1997.

Carvajal, M.J., and David T. Geithman. "Migration Flows and Economic Conditions in the Dominican Republic," *Land Economics,* 52, No. 2, May 1976, 207–20.

Castillo, José del, and Martin F. Murphy. "Migration, National Identity, and Cultural Policy in the Dominican Republic," *Journal of Ethnic Studies,* 15, No. 3, Fall 1987, 49–69.

Corten, André, and Isis Duarte. "Five Hundred Thousand Haitians in the Dominican Republic," *Latin American Perspectives*, 22, No. 3, Summer 1995, 94–110.

Dominican Republic. Oficina Nacional de Estadística. *República Dominicana en Cifras, 1997.* Santo Domingo: 1998.

Ferguson, James. *The Dominican Republic: Beyond the Lighthouse.* London: Latin America Bureau, 1992.

Garza, Rodolfo de la. "Binational Impact of Latino Remittances," Policy Brief. Claremont, California: Tomas Rivera Policy Institute, Scripps College, March 1997.

Georges, Eugenia. *The Making of a Transnational Community: Migration, Development, and Cultural Change in the Dominican Republic.* New York: Columbia University Press, 1990.

Grasmuck, Sherri. "Migration Within the Periphery: Haitian Labor in the Dominican Sugar and Coffee Industries," *International Migration Review*, 16, No. 2, Summer 1982, 365–77.

Grasmuck, Sherri, and Patricia R. Pessar. *Between Two Islands: Dominican International Migration.* Berkeley: University of California Press, 1991.

Hartlyn, Jonathan. *The Struggle for Democratic Politics in the Dominican Republic.* Chapel Hill: University of North Carolina Press, 1998.

Hitt, Deborah S., and Larman C. Wilson. *A Selected Bibliography of the Dominican Republic: A Century after the Restoration of Independence.* Washington: Center for Research in Social Systems, American University, 1968.

Hoetink, H. *The Dominican People, 1859–1900: Notes for a Historical Sociology.* Trans., S.K. Ault. Baltimore: Johns Hopkins University Press, 1982.

Kryzanek, Michael J., and Howard J. Wiarda. *The Politics of External Influence in the Dominican Republic.* New York: Praeger/Hoover Institution Press, 1988.

Lemoine, Maurice. *Bitter Sugar: Slaves Today in the Caribbean.* Trans., Andrea Johnston. Chicago: Banner Press, 1985.

Lernoux, Penny. *Cry of the People.* Garden City, New York: Doubleday, 1980.

Logan, Rayford W. *Haiti and the Dominican Republic.* New York: Oxford University Press, 1968.

"Mirrors of the Heart: Race and Identity," *Americas* series, program No. 4. WBGH Boston and Central TV Enterprises in association with Columbia University, Florida International University, and Tufts University, 1992.

Mones, Belkis, and Lydia Grant. "Agricultural Development, the Economic Crisis, and Rural Women in the Dominican Republic." Pages 35–50 in Carmen Diana Deere and Magdalena León, eds., *Rural Women and State Policy: Feminist Perspectives on Latin American Agricultural Development.* Boulder, Colorado: Westview Press, 1987.

Morrison, Thomas K., and Richard Sinkin. "International Migration in the Dominican Republic: Implications for Development Planning," *International Migration Review,* 16, No. 4, Winter 1982, 819–36.

Moya Pons, Frank. *The Dominican Republic: A National History.* New Rochelle, New York: Hispaniola Books, 1995.

Moya Pons, Frank. *El pasado dominicano.* Santo Domingo: Fundación J.A. Caro Alvarez, 1986.

Murphy, Martin F. *Dominican Sugar Plantations: Production and Foreign Labor Integration.* New York: Praeger, 1991.

Pan American Health Organization. *Health Conditions in the Americas,* 2. Washington: 1994.

Pan American Health Organization. *Health in the Americas,* 1 and 2, 1998. Washington: 1998.

Perusek, Glenn. "Haitian Emigration in the Early Twentieth Century," *International Migration Review,* 18, No. 1, Spring 1984, 4–18.

Pessar, Patricia R. "Dominican Transnational Migration: Uneven Benefits Back Home and the Contingency of Return." Pages 151–76 in Emelio Betances and Hobart Spalding, Jr., eds., *The Dominican Republic Today: Realities and Perspectives.* New York: Bildner Center for Western Hemisphere Studies, City University of New York, 1996.

Pessar, Patricia R. "The Linkage Between the Household and Workplace of Dominican Women in the U.S.," *International Migration Review,* 18 No. 4, Winter 1984, 1188–211.

Ramírez, Nelson, Isis Duarte, and Carmen Gómez. *Población y salud en la República Dominicana.* Estudio No. 5. Santo Domingo: Instituto de Estudios de Población y Desarrollo de Profamilia, 1986.

Rodríguez Sepúlveda, Bienvenida. *Evaluación de la encuesta nacional de fecundidad de la República Dominicana de 1980.*

World Fertility Survey, Scientific Reports, No. 63. London: World Fertility Survey, October 1984.

Schoenhals, Kai, comp. *Dominican Republic.* World Bibliographical Series No. 3. Santa Barbara, California: CLIO Press, 1990.

Sharpe, Kenneth Evan. *Peasant Politics: Struggle in a Dominican Village.* Baltimore: Johns Hopkins University Press, 1977.

Statistical Abstract of Latin America, 32 and 33. Eds., James W. Wilkie, Catherine Komisaruk, and José Guadalupe Ortega. Los Angeles: University of California Press, 1996 and 1997.

Torres-Saillant, Silvio, and Ramona Hernández. *The Dominican Americans: The New Americans.* Westport, Connecticut: Greenwood Press, 1998.

Ugalde, Antonio. "Where There Is a Doctor: Strategies to Increase Productivity at Lower Costs," *Social Science and Medicine*, 19, No. 4, 1984, 441–50.

UNAIDS/WHO. *Dominican Republic. Epidemiological Fact Sheet on HIV/AIDS and Sexually Transmitted Infections: 2000 Update.* Geneva: 1999.

United States. Department of Health and Human Services. Social Security Administration. Office of Policy, Office of Research, Statistics, and International Policy. *Social Security Programs Throughout the World, 1985.* Research Report No. 60. Washington: GPO, 1986.

Walker, Malcolm T. *Politics and the Power Structure: A Rural Community in the Dominican Republic.* New York: Teachers College Press, 1972.

Wiarda, Howard J. *The Dominican Republic: Nation in Transition.* New York: Praeger, 1969.

Wiarda, Howard J., and Michael J. Kryzanek. *The Dominican Republic: A Caribbean Crucible.* 2d ed. Boulder, Colorado: Westview Press, 1992.

Chapter 3

Economist Intelligence Unit. *Country Profile, 1996–97: Dominican Republic, Haiti, Puerto Rico.* London: 1996.

Economist Intelligence Unit. *Country Profile, 1997–98: Dominican Republic, Haiti, Puerto Rico.* London: 1997.

Economist Intelligence Unit. *Country Profile, 1998–99: Dominican Republic, Haiti, Puerto Rico.* London: 1998.

Economist Intelligence Unit. *Country Report, 3rd Quarter 1997: Cuba, Dominican Republic, Haiti, Puerto Rico.* London: 1997.

Economist Intelligence Unit. *Country Report, 4th Quarter 1997: Cuba, Dominican Republic, Haiti, Puerto Rico.* London: 1997.

Economist Intelligence Unit. *Country Report, 1st Quarter 1998: Cuba, Dominican Republic, Haiti, Puerto Rico.* London: 1998.

Economist Intelligence Unit. *Country Report, 2nd Quarter 1998: Cuba, Dominican Republic, Haiti, Puerto Rico.* London: 1998.

Espinal, Rosario. "Economic Res ructuring, Social Protest, and Democratization in the Dominican Republic." *Latin American Perspectives*, 22, No. 3, 1995.

The Europa World Year Book, 1997. London: Europa, 1997.

International Monetary Fund. *Consultation with the Dominican Republic.* Washington: 1997.

International Monetary Fund. *International Financial Statistics, 1998.* Washington: 1998.

Moya Pons, Frank. "The Dominican Republic since 1930." Pages 509–44 in Leslie Bethell, ed., *The Cambridge History of Latin America*, 7. Cambridge: Cambridge University Press, 1990.

Political Handbook of the World, 1997. Binghamton: State University of New York, 1997.

South America, Central America, and the Caribbean, 1997. London: Europa, 1997.

United States. Agency for International Development. *Dominican Republic: Program Priorities.* Santo Domingo: 1997.

United States. Agency for International Development. *Dominican Republic: Results Report and Resource Request, FY 1995–1998.* Santo Domingo: 1996.

United States. Agency for International Development. *USAID Strategic Plan, 1997–2002.* Santo Domingo: 1997.

United States. Department of Commerce. *Dominican Republic: 1998 Country Commercial Guide.* Washington: 1997.

United States. Department of State. Bureau of Public Affairs. *Background Notes: Dominican Republic.* Washington: GPO, 1994.

United States. Department of State. Bureau of Public Affairs. *Background Notes: Dominican Republic.* Washington: GPO, 1997.

United States. Department of State. *Dominican Republic: Overview.* Washington: GPO, 1996.

United States. Embassy in Santo Domingo. *Dominican Republic: Economic Management.* Santo Domingo: 1997.

United States. Embassy in Santo Domingo. *Dominican Republic: General Policy Framework.* Santo Domingo: 1997.

World Bank. *Annual Report, 1996.* Washington: 1996.

World Bank. *The Dominican Republic - Growth with Equity: An Agenda for Reform.* Washington: 1995.

World Bank. *Global Development Finance.* Washington: 1997.

World Economic Factbook, 1997–98. London: Euromonitor, 1997.

(Various issues of the following publication were also used in the preparation of this chapter: International Monetary Fund, *International Financial Statistics.*)

Chapter 4

Atkins, G. Pope. *Arms and Politics in the Dominican Republic.* Boulder, Colorado: Westview Press, 1981.

Bell, Ian. *The Dominican Republic.* Boulder, Colorado: Westview Press, 1981.

Betances, Emelio, and Hobart Spalding, et al. "The Dominican Republic—after the Caudillos," *North American Congress on Latin America Report on the Americas,* 30, No. 5, March–April 1997.

Black, Jan Knippers. *The Dominican Republic: Politics and Development in an Unsovereign State.* Boston: Allen and Unwin, 1986.

Brea Franco, Julio. *El sistema constitucional dominicano,* 1 and 2. Santo Domingo: Editorial CENAPEC, 1983.

Brea, Ramonina, Isis Duarte, Ramón Tejada, and Clara Báez. *Estado de situación de la democracia dominicana (1978–1992).* Santo Domingo: Pontificia Universidad Católica Madre y Maestra, 1995.

Campillo Pérez, Julio A. *Elecciones dominicanas: Contribución a su estudio,* 49. Santo Domingo: Academia Dominicana de la Historia, 1982.

Castillo, José del. *Ensayos de sociología dominicano.* Santo Domingo: Ediciones Siboney, 1981.

Conaghan, Catherine M., and Rosario Espinal. "Unlikely Transitions to Uncertain Regimes? Democracy Without Compromise in the Dominican Republic and Ecuador," *Journal of Latin American Studies*, 22, October 3, 1990, 553–74.

Crassweller, Robert. *Trujillo: The Life and Times of a Caribbean Dictator.* New York: Macmillan, 1966.

Duarte, Isis, Ramonina Brea, Ramón Tejada, and Clara Báez. *Cultura política y democracia en la República Dominicana: Informe final de la encuesta cultura política y democracia (DEMOS 94).* Santo Domingo: Pontificia Universidad Católica Madre y Maestra, 1996.

Espinal, Rosario. *Autoritarismo y democracia en la política dominicana.* San Jose, Costa Rica: CAPEL, 1987.

Espinal, Rosario. "Electoral Observation and Democratization in the Dominican Republic." In Kevin J. Middlebrook, ed., *Electoral Observation and Democratic Transitions in Latin America.* La Jolla: Center for U.S.-Mexican Studies, University of California, San Diego, 1998.

Espinal, Rosario. "An Interpretation of the Democratic Transition in the Dominican Republic." In Giuseppe Di Palma and Laurence Whitehead, eds., *The Central American Impasse.* New York: St. Martin's Press, 1986.

Espinal, Rosario, and Jonathan Hartlyn. "Dominican Republic: The Long and Difficult Struggle for Democracy." Pages 469–518 in Larry Diamond, Jonathan Hartlyn, Juan J. Linz, and Seymour Martin Lipset, eds., *Democracy in Developing Countries: Latin America*, 2d ed. Boulder, Colorado: Lynne Rienner, 1999.

Galíndez, Jesús de. *The Era of Trujillo: Dominican Dictator.* Ed., R.H. Fitzgibbon. Tucson: University of Arizona Press, 1973.

Gleijeses, Piero. *The Dominican Crisis: The 1965 Constitutionalist Revolt and American Intervention.* Trans., L. Lipson. Baltimore: Johns Hopkins University Press, 1978.

Guerrero, Miguel. *El golpe de estado: Historia del derrocamiento de Juan Bosch.* Santo Domingo: Editora Corripio, 1983.

Hartlyn, Jonathan. "The Dominican Republic: Contemporary Problems and Challenges." Pages 150–72 in Jorge I. Domínguez, Robert A. Pastor, and R. Delisle Worrell, eds., *Democracy in the Caribbean: Political, Economic, and Social Perspectives.* Baltimore: Johns Hopkins University Press, 1993.

Hartlyn, Jonathan. *The Struggle for Democratic Politics in the Dominican Republic.* Chapel Hill: University of North Carolina Press, 1998.

Jiménez Polanco, Jacqueline. *Los partidos políticos en la República Dominicana: Actividad electoral y desarrollo organizativo.* Santo Domingo: Editora Centenario, 1999.

Kryzanek, Michael J., and Howard J. Wiarda. *The Politics of External Influence in the Dominican Republic.* New York: Praeger/Hoover Institution Press, 1988.

Kurzman, Dan. *Santo Domingo: Revolt of the Damned.* New York: Putnam, 1965.

Latorre, Eduardo. *Política dominicana contemporánea.* Santo Domingo: Ediciones Intec, 1975.

Lowenthal, Abraham. *The Dominican Intervention.* Cambridge: Harvard University Press, 1972.

Lowenthal, Abraham. "The Dominican Intervention in Retrospective," *Public Policy,* 18, Fall 1969, 133–48.

Lowenthal, Abraham. "The Dominican Republic: The Politics of Chaos." In Robert Kaufman and Arpad von Lazar, eds., *Reform and Revolution: Readings in Latin American Politics.* Needham Heights, Massachusetts: Allyn and Bacon, 1969.

Martin, John Bartlow. *Overtaken by Events: The Dominican Crisis from the Fall of Trujillo to the Civil War.* Garden City, New York: Doubleday, 1966.

Mitchell, Christopher. "Urban Elections in the Dominican Republic, 1962–1994." In Henry Dietz and Gil Shidlo, eds., *Urban Elections in Democratic Latin America.* Wilmington: SR Books, 1998.

Mitchell, Christopher. "U.S. Foreign Policy and Dominican Migration to the United States." Pages 89–123 in Christopher Mitchell, ed., *Western Hemisphere Immigration and United States Foreign Policy.* University Park: Pennsylvania State University Press, 1992.

Moya Pons, Frank. *The Dominican Republic: A National History.* New Rochelle, New York: Hispaniola Books, 1995.

Moya Pons, Frank. "The Dominican Republic since 1930." Pages 509–44 in Leslie Bethell, ed., *The Cambridge History of Latin America,* 7. Cambridge: Cambridge University Press, 1990.

Moya Pons, Frank. *Manual de historia dominicana.* 7th ed. Santo Domingo: Pontificia Universidad Católica Madre y Maestra, 1983.

Moya Pons, Frank. *El pasado dominicano.* Santo Domingo: Fundación J.A. Caro Alvarez, 1986.

Rivera-Cire, Tirza. *El sector justicia en República Dominicana: Diagnóstico y recomendaciones para la acción.* Santo Domingo: Fundación Institucionalidad y Justicia, 1996.

Sang, Mu-Kien A. "Entre el autoritarismo y la aspiración de libertad," *Estudios Sociales,* 27, No. 95, January–March 1994, 27–47.

Slater, Jerome. *Intervention and Negotiation: The United States and the Dominican Republic.* New York: Harper and Row, 1970.

Vega, Bernardo. *En la década perdida.* Santo Domingo: Fundación Cultural Dominicana, 1990.

Vega, Bernardo. "República Dominicana, economía y política al término del siglo XX," *Ciencia y Sociedad,* 18, No. 3, 353–63.

Wiarda, Howard J. *Dictatorship and Development: The Methods of Control in Trujillo's Dominican Republic.* Gainesville: University of Florida Press, 1968.

Wiarda, Howard J. *Politics and Social Change in the Dominican Republic. Dictatorship, Development, and Disintegration,* 1, 2, and 3. Ann Arbor: Xerox University Microfilms, 1975.

Wiarda, Howard J., and Michael J. Krzanek. *The Dominican Republic: A Caribbean Crucible.* Boulder, Colorado: Westview Press, 1982.

Chapter 5

Amnesty International. *Amnesty International Report, 1996.* London: 1996.

Anderson, George M. "Darkness in the Dominican Republic," *America,* 173, No. 16, November 18, 1995, 10–11.

Atkins, G. Pope. *Arms and Politics in the Dominican Republic.* Boulder, Colorado: Westview Press, 1981.

Betances, Emelio. *State and Society in the Dominican Republic.* Boulder, Colorado: Westview Press, 1995.

Betances, Emelio, and Hobart Spalding Jr. "The Dominican Republic—after the Caudillos," *North American Congress on*

Latin America Report on the Americas, 30, No. 5, March–April 1997, 16–19.

Black, Jan Knippers. "The Dominican Military's Conditional Retreat." Pages 176–94 in Constantine P. Danopoulos, ed., *From Military to Civilian Rule*. New York: Routledge, 1992.

Buckman, Robert T. *Latin America 1997*. The World Today Series. Harpers Ferry: Stryker, 1997.

Dominican Republic. *Constitution*. Constitutions of the World Series. Dobbs Ferry, New York: Oceana, 1973.

"Dominican Republic," *Military Technology*, No. 1, 1997, 51–52. World Defence Almanac, 1996–97.

Echevarria, Vito. "Dominicans Respond to Police Ban," *Hispanic*, 10, No. 3, March 1997, 12–13.

English, Adrian J. *Armed Forces of Latin America*. London: Jane's, 1984.

Farley, Christopher John. "Dangerous Tides," *Time*, 145, No. 15, April 10, 1995, 56–57.

Human Rights Watch. *Human Rights Watch World Report, 1997*. New York: 1998.

Jane's Fighting Ships, 1999–2000. Ed., Richard Sharpe. Alexandria, Virginia: Jane's Information Group, 1999.

Keegan, John, ed. *World Armies*. Detroit: Gale Research, 1983.

Kraus, Clifford, and Larry Rohter. "Dominican Drug Traffickers Tighten Grip on the Northeast," *New York Times*, May 11, 1998, A1, A16.

Marquis, Christopher. "U.S. to Send Troops, Equipment to Help Dominican Republic Seal Border with Haiti," *Knight-Ridder Tribune News Service*, June 21, 1994.

The Military Balance, 1998–99. London: International Institute for Strategic Studies, 1998.

Rohter, Larry. "Dominicans Face Strike as Hardship Fans Unrest," *New York Times*, November 9, 1997, A9.

Rohter, Larry. "Hispaniola's 'Sugar-Cane Curtain' Is Starting to Come Down," *New York Times*, November 26, 1996, A5.

Rohter, Larry, and Clifford Kraus. "Dominicans Allow Drugs Easy Sailing," *New York Times*, May 10, 1998, A1, A6.

Soto Jimenez, José Miguel. *Las fuerzas militares en la República Dominicana desde la Primera República hasta los comienzos de la Cuarta República*. Santo Domingo: Ediciones Grupo 5, 1996.

Tamayo, Juan O. "Dominican Now Ranks as Third-Leading Nation in Drug Smuggling," *Knight-Ridder Tribune News Service*, May 23, 1997.

United States. Arms Control and Disarmament Agency. *World Military Expenditures and Arms Transfers, 1996*. Washington: GPO, 1997.

United States. Department of Defense. *Foreign Military Sales, Foreign Military Construction Sales, and Military Assistance Facts as of September 30, 1996*. Washington: 1996.

United States. Department of State. *Country Reports on Human Rights Practices for 1996*. Report submitted to United States Congress, 105th, 1st Session, Senate, Committee on Foreign Relations, and House of Representatives, Committee on Foreign Affairs. Washington: GPO, 1997.

United States. Department of State. *Country Reports on Human Rights Practices for 1997*. Report submitted to United States Congress, 105th, 2d Session, House of Representatives, Committee on Foreign Affairs, and Senate, Committee on Foreign Relations. Washington: GPO, 1998.

United States. Department of State. *Country Reports on Human Rights Practices for 1998*. Report submitted to United States Congress, 106th, 1st Session, Senate, Committee on Foreign Relations, and House of Representatives, Committee on Foreign Affairs. Washington: GPO, 1999.

United States. Department of State. Bureau of International Narcotics Matters. *International Narcotics Control Strategy Report*. Washington: GPO, 1997.

United States. Department of State. Bureau of International Narcotics Matters. *International Narcotics Control Strategy Report*. Washington: GPO, 1998.

United States. Department of State. Bureau of International Narcotics Matters. *International Narcotics Control Strategy Report*. Washington: GPO, 1999.

United States. Department of State. Bureau of Public Affairs. *Background Notes: Dominican Republic*. Washington: GPO, 1997.

(Various issues of the following publications also were used in the preparation of this chapter: *Caribbean Insight* [London]; *Latin American Regional Reports: Caribbean and Central America Report* [London]; *New York Times*; and *Washington Post*.)

Chapter 6

Abbott, Elizabeth. *Haiti: The Duvaliers and Their Legacy.* New York: McGraw-Hill, 1988.

Aristide, Jean-Bertrand. *Aristide: An Autobiography.* Maryknoll, New York: Orbis Books, 1993.

Aristide, Jean-Bertrand. *In the Parish of the Poor: Writings from Haiti.* Maryknoll, New York: Orbis Books, 1990.

Auguste, Yves. *Haïti et les États Unis.* Port-au-Prince: Henri Deschamps, 1987.

Averill, Gage. *A Day for the Hunter, a Day for the Prey: Popular Music and Power in Haiti.* Chicago: University of Chicago Press, 1997.

Balch, Emily G. *Occupied Haiti.* Rev. ed. New York: Garland, 1972.

Baskett, J. *History of the Island of St. Domingo from Its First Discovery by Columbus to the Present Period.* Westport, Connecticut: Negro University Press, 1971.

Bazin, Marc. *Construire ensemble: Discours et messages,* 2. Port-au-Prince: Henri Deschamps: 1990.

Bohning, Don. "Aristide's Next Job: Set Course for Haiti," *Miami Herald,* February 10, 1991, 20A.

Bonhomme, Colbert. *Révolution et contre-révolution en Haïti de 1946 à 1957.* Port-au-Prince: Fardin, 1984.

Boswell, Thomas D. "The New Haitian Diaspora," *Caribbean Review,* 11, No. 1, 1982, 18–21.

Buell, R.L. *The American Occupation of Haiti.* New York: Foreign Policy Association, 1929.

Casimir, Jean. *Le Caraïbe: Une et divisible.* Port-au-Prince: Henri Deschamps, 1991.

Castor, Suzy. "L'expérience démocratique haïtienne." In Suzy Castor, Micha Gaillard, Paul Laraquée, and Gérard Pierre-Charles, eds., *Haïti: A l'aube du changement.* Port-au-Prince: Centre de Recherche et de Formation Économique et Sociale pour le Développement, 1991.

Castor, Suzy. *L'occupation américaine d'Haïti.* Port-au-Prince: Société Haïtienne d'Histoire, 1988.

Castor, Suzy. *La ocupación norteamericana de Haiti y sus consecuencias (1915–1934).* Mexico: Siglo Veintiuno, 1971.

Cobb, Charles E., Jr. "Haiti Against All Odds," *National Geographic*, November 1987, 645–47.

Cole, Hubert. *Christophe: King of Haiti*. New York: Viking, 1967.

Colon, Yves, Lizette Alvarez, and Christopher Marquis. "U.S. to Open Guantanamo for Haitians," *Miami Herald*, June 29, 1994, 1A, 12A.

Corvington, Georges. *Port-au-Prince au cours des ans: La capitale d'Haïti sous l'occupation, 1915–1922*. Port-au-Prince: Henri Deschamps, 1984.

Corvington, Georges. *Port-au-Prince au cours des ans: La capitale d'Haïti sous l'occupation, 1922–1934*. Port-au-Prince: Henri Deschamps, 1984.

Danner, Mark. "A Reporter at Large: Beyond the Mountains-I," *New Yorker*, November 27, 1989, 55–100.

Danner, Mark. "A Reporter at Large: Beyond the Mountains-II," *New Yorker*, December 4, 1989, 68–78, 111–41.

Danner, Mark. "A Reporter at Large: Beyond the Mountains-III," *New Yorker*, December 11, 1989, 100–31.

Daudet, Yves, ed. *La crise à Haïti*. Paris: Editions Montchestien, 1996.

Davis, H.P. *Black Democracy: The Story of Haiti*. Rev. ed. New York: Biblo and Tannen, 1967.

Désinor, Carlo. *De coup d'état en coup d'état*. Port-au-Prince: L'Imprimeur II, 1988.

Diederich, Bernard, and Al Burt. *Papa Doc et les Tontons Macoutes*. Port-au-Prince: Henri Deschamps, 1986.

Dupuy, Alex. *Haiti in the New World Order: The Limits of the Democratic Revolution*. Boulder, Colorado: Westview Press, 1997.

Duvalier, François. *Mémoires d'un leader du Tiers Monde: Mes négotiations avec le Saint Siège ou, une tranche d'histoire*. Paris: Hachette, 1969.

Farmer, Paul. *The Uses of Haiti*. Monroe, Maine: Common Courage Press, 1994.

Fauriol, Georges. "The Duvaliers and Haiti," *Orbis: A Journal of World Affairs*, 32, No. 4, Fall 1988, 587–607.

Fauriol, Georges, ed. *Haitian Frustrations: Dilemmas for U.S. Policy*. Washington: Center for Strategic and International Studies, 1995.

Ferguson, James. *Papa Doc, Baby Doc: Haiti and the Duvaliers*. Oxford and New York: Basil Blackwell, 1987.

Fowler, Carolyn. "The Emergence of the Independent Press in Haiti: 1971–1980," *Black Collegian*, 11, No. 5, April–May 1981, 149–51.

Greene, Anne. *The Catholic Church in Haiti: Political and Social Change.* East Lansing: Michigan State University Press, 1993.

Greene, Graham. *The Comedians.* New York: Viking, 1966.

"Haiti: Manigat Ousted in Clash with Namphy," *Latin American Newsletter* [London], RC–88–06, July 21, 1988.

Heinl, Jr., Robert Debs. "Haiti: A Case Study in Freedom," *New Republic*, 150, No. 20, May 16, 1964, 15–21.

Heinl, Jr., Robert Debs, and Nancy Gordon Heinl. *Written in Blood: The Story of the Haitian People, 1492–1995.* 2d ed. Rev. by Michael Heinl. Lanham, Maryland: University Press of America, 1996.

Hockstader, Lee. "Even with Nowhere to Go, Haitians Are Taking to the Sea," *International Herald Tribune*, November 22, 1991.

Hurbon, Laënnec. *Dieu dans le vaudou haïtien.* Port-au-Prince: Henri Deschamps, 1987.

Institut Haïtien des Statistiques et d'Information, *Health Situation Analysis, Haiti 1996.* Pan American Health Organization/World Health Organization: June 1996.

James, C.L.R. *The Black Jacobins, Toussaint L'Ouverture and the San Domingo Revolution.* 2d ed. New York: Random House, 1963.

Joseph, Raymond. "Haitian Religious and Business Leaders Stop Pampering Baby Doc," *Wall Street Journal*, February 7, 1986, 21.

Keegan, John E. "The Catholic Church in the Struggle Against Duvalierism," *America*, 158, No. 16, April 23, 1988, 429–32.

Laguerre, Michel S. *Études sur le vaudou haïtien: Bibliographie analytique.* Montreal: Centre de recherches caraïbes, 1979.

Laguerre, Michel S. "The Haitian Political Crisis," *America*, 155, December 27, 1986, 416–20.

Laguerre, Michel S. *The Military and Society in Haiti.* Knoxville: University of Tennessee Press, 1993.

Laguerre, Michel S. "The Place of Voodoo in the Social Structure of Haiti," *Caribbean Quarterly*, 19, No. 3, September 1973, 36–50.

Laguerre, Michel S. *Voodoo and Politics in Haiti.* New York: St. Martin's Press, 1989.

Laguerre, Michel S. *Voodoo Heritage.* Beverly Hills, California: Sage, 1980.

Lawless, Robert. *Haiti's Bad Press.* Rochester, Vermont: Schenkman Books, 1992.

Leyburn, James. *The Haitian People.* Rev. ed. Westport, Connecticut: Greenwood Press, 1980.

Lionet, Christian. *Haïti: L'année Aristide.* Paris: L'Harmattan, 1992.

Logan, Rayford W. *The Diplomatic Relations of the United States with Haiti: 1776–1891.* Chapel Hill: University of North Carolina Press, 1941.

Logan, Rayford W. *Haiti and the Dominican Republic.* New York: Oxford University Press, 1968.

Maguire, Robert, Edwige Baluntansky, Jacques Fomerand, Larry Minear, William G. O'Neill, Thomas G. Weiss, and Sarah Zaidi. *Haiti Held Hostage: International Responses to the Quest for Nationhood, 1986–1996.* Occasional Paper No. 23. Providence, Rhode Island: Thomas J. Watson Jr. Institute for International Studies and the United Nations University, 1996.

Manigat, Leslie F. *Haiti of the Sixties, Object of International Concern.* Washington: Washington Center of Policy Research, 1964.

Manigat, Leslie F. *La crise haïtienne contemporaine ou les années 1990s: Une grille d'intelligibilité pour la crise présente.* Port-au-Prince: Centre Humanisme Démocratique en Action, 1995.

Manigot, Anthony P. "Haiti: Problems of a Transition to Democracy in an Authoritarian Soft State," *Journal of Interamerican Studies and World Affairs,* 28, No. 4, Winter 1986–87.

Métraux, Alfred. *Voodoo in Haiti.* New York: Schocken Books, 1972.

Millspaugh, A.C. *Haiti Under American Control, 1915–1930.* Boston: World Peace Foundation, 1931.

Montague, Ludwell L. *Haiti and the United States, 1714 to 1938.* Durham, North Carolina: Duke University Press, 1940.

Moreau de Saint-Méry, Méderic-Louis Elle. *A Civilization That Perished: The Last Years of White Colonial Rule in Haiti.* Trans.

and ed., Ivor D. Spencer. Lanham, Maryland: University Press of America, 1985.

Morse, R.M., ed. *Haiti's Future: Views of Twelve Haitian Leaders.* Washington: Wilson Center Press, 1988.

Nicholls, David. *From Dessalines to Duvalier: Race, Colour, and National Independence in Haiti.* London: Cambridge University Press, 1979.

Nicholls, David. *Haiti in the Caribbean Context: Ethnicity, Economy, and Revolt.* New York: St. Martin's Press, 1985.

Nicholls, David. "Haiti: The Rise and Fall of Duvalierism," *Third World Quarterly,* 8, No. 4, October 1986, 1239–52.

Nicholls, David. "Past and Present in Haitian Politics." In Charles R. Foster and Albert Valdman, eds., *Haiti—Today and Tomorrow: An Interdisciplinary Study.* Lanham, Maryland: University Press of America, 1984.

Organization of American States. *Report on the Situation of Human Rights in Haiti.* Washington: November 1990.

Ott, Thomas O. *The Haitian Revolution, 1789–1804.* Knoxville: University of Tennessee Press, 1973.

Paley, William. "Haiti's Dynastic Despotism: From Father to Son to ...," *Caribbean Review,* Fall 1985.

Parkinson, Wenda. *'This Gilded African,' Toussaint L'Ouverture,* London: Quarter Books, 1978.

Perusse, Roland I. *Haitian Democracy Restored: 1991–1995.* Lanham, Maryland: University Press of America, 1995.

Plummer, Brenda Gayle. *Haiti and the United States: The Psychological Moment.* Athens: University of Georgia Press, 1992.

Preeg, Ernest H. *The Haitian Dilemma: A Case Study in Democratic Development and U.S. Foreign Policy.* Washington: Center for Strategic and International Studies, 1996.

Preeg, Ernest H. "Haiti's Aid-Fueled Economy," *Journal of Commerce,* January 16, 1996, 6A.

Preeg, Ernest H. "Introduction." In Charles R. Foster and Albert Valdman, eds., *Haiti—Today and Tomorrow: An Interdisciplinary Study.* Lanham, Maryland: University Press of America, 1984.

Price-Mars, Jean. *So Spoke the Uncle (Ainsi parla l'oncle).* Translation and introduction by Magdaline W. Shannon. Washington: Three Continents Press, 1983.

Rodman, Selden. *Haiti: The Black Republic: The Complete Story and Guide.* 6th ed. New York: Devin-Adair, 1984.

Rotberg, Robert I. "Haiti's Past Mortgages Its Future," *Foreign Affairs,* 67, No. 1, Fall 1988, 93–109.

Rotberg, Robert I., and Christopher Clague. *Haiti: The Politics of Squalor.* Athens, Georgia: Houghton Mifflin, 1971.

Samway, Patrick H. "Rebuilding Haiti: An Interview with Jean-Bertrand Aristide," *America,* 176, No. 5, February 15, 1997, 12–16.

Schmidt, Hans. *The United States Occupation of Haiti, 1915–34.* New Brunswick, New Jersey: Rutgers University Press, 1971.

Seabrook, W.B. *The Magic Island.* New York: Paragon House, 1989.

Steiff, William. "Haitian Hell: A Government Gone Awry," *Multinational Monitor,* 6, December 18, 1985, 3–10.

Trouillot, Michel-Rolph. *Haiti, State Against Nation: The Origins and Legacy of Duvalierism.* New York: Monthly Review Press, 1990.

United States. Agency for International Development. "Position Paper for the U.N. General Assembly, 40th Session," *Economic Assistance to Haiti,* October 31, 1985.

Weinstein, Brian, and Aaron Segal. *Haiti: Political Failures, Cultural Successes.* New York: Praeger, 1984.

White, Robert E. "Haiti: Policy Lost, Policy Regained," *Cosmos,* 1996, 83.

"Who's a Genuine Refugee?," *Washington Post,* December 30, 1991, A12.

Wilentz, Amy. *The Rainy Season: Haiti since Duvalier.* New York: Simon and Schuster, 1989.

Chapter 7

Americas Watch, National Coalition for Haitian Refugees. *Half the Story: The Skewed U.S. Monitoring of Repatriated Haitian Refugees,* 4, No. 4. New York: June 1992.

Americas Watch, National Coalition for Haitian Refugees. *A Troubled Year: Haitians in the Dominican Republic.* New York: 1992.

Americas Watch, National Coalition for Haitian Refugees, Caribbean Rights. *Harvesting Oppression: Forced Haitian Labor in the Dominican Sugar Industry.* New York: 1990.

Americas Watch, National Coalition for Haitian Refugees, Jesuit Refugee Services/USA. *No Port in a Storm: Misguided Use of In-Country Refugee Processing in Haiti,* 5, No. 8. New York: September 1993.

Barthélémy, Gérard. *Dans la splendeur d'un après-midi d'histoire.* Port-au-Prince: Henri Deschamps, 1996.

Barthélémy, Gérard. *Le pays en dehors: Essai sur l'univers rural haïtien.* Port-au-Prince: Henri Deschamps, 1989.

Barthélémy, Gérard. *Paysans, villes, et bidonvilles en Haïti: Aperçus et réflexions.* Port-au-Prince: GRET, 1996.

Barthélémy, Gérard, and Christian Girault, eds. *La république haïtienne: État des lieux et perspectives.* Paris: ADEC - Karthala, 1993.

Bastien, Rémy. *Le paysan haïtien et sa famille.* Paris: Karthala, 1985.

BDPA-SCETAGRI. *Gestion des ressources naturelles en vue d'un développement durable en Haïti.* Paris: Haiti, Ministry of Economy and Finance and the International Development Association, 1990.

Brinkerhoff, Derrick W., and Jean-Claude Garcia-Zamor, eds. *Politics, Projects, and People: Institutional Development in Haiti.* New York: Praeger, 1986.

Brodwin, Paul. *Medicine and Morality in Haiti: The Contest for Healing Power.* Cambridge: Cambridge University Press, 1996.

Bureau of Applied Research in Anthropology. *A Baseline Study of Livelihood Security in the Departments of the Artibonite, Center, North, Northeast, and West, Republic of Haiti.* Conducted in collaboration with the Haiti Adventist Development and Relief Agency and the Interim Food Security Information System. Tucson: University of Arizona, 1997.

Bureau of Applied Research in Anthropology. *A Baseline Study of Livelihood Security in the Southern Peninsula of Haiti.* Conducted in collaboration with Haiti Catholic Relief Services and the Interim Food Security Information System. Tucson: University of Arizona, 1996.

Bureau of Applied Research in Anthropology. *A Study of Livelihood Security in Northwest Haiti.* Conducted in collaboration with CARE/Haiti and the Interim Food Security Information System. Tucson: University of Arizona, 1996.

Burns, L. Vinton. *Report to the Government of Haiti on Forest Policy and Its Implementation.* Rome: Food and Agriculture Organization of the United Nations, 1954.

Castor, Suzy. *Les femmes haïtiennes aux élections de 1990.* Port-au-Prince: CRESFED, 1994.

Catanese, Anthony V. "Changing Demographics of Haitian-American Immigrants." Paper presented at Annual Meeting, Haitian Studies Association, October 1997.

Catanese, Anthony V. *Haitians: Migration and Diaspora.* Boulder, Colorado: Westview Press, 1999.

Cayemittes, Michel, Antonio Rival, Bernard Barrère, Gérald Lerebours, and Michaele Amédée Gédéon. *Enquête mortalité, morbidité et utilisation des services (EMMUS II), Haïti 1994/95.* Pétionville, Haiti: Institut Haïtien de l'Enfance, Macro International, 1995.

Consentino, Donald, ed. *The Sacred Arts of Haitian Vodou.* Los Angeles: UCLA Fowler Museum of Cultural History, 1995.

Conway, Frederick J. "Pentecostalism in the Context of Haitian Religious and Health Practice." Ph.D. dissertation. Washington: American University, 1978.

Correia, Maria. "Gender and Poverty in Haiti." Annex 2, pages 1–21 in *Haiti: The Challenges of Poverty Reduction, 2: Technical Papers.* Report No. 17242–HA. Washington: World Bank, 1998.

Courlander, Harold. *The Drum and the Hoe: Life and Lore of the Haitian People.* Berkeley: University of California Press, 1960.

D'Ans, André. *Haïti, paysage et société.* Paris: Karthala, 1987.

Dayan, Joan. *Haiti, History, and the Gods.* Berkeley: University of California Press, 1998.

Delince, Kern. *Les forces politiques en Haïti: Manuel d'histoire contemporaine.* Paris: Karthala, 1993.

Desmangles, Leslie. *The Faces of the Gods: Vodoun and Roman Catholicism in Haiti.* Chapel Hill: University of North Carolina Press, 1992.

Dupuy, Alex. *Haiti in the New World Order: The Limits of the Democratic Revolution.* Boulder, Colorado: Westview Press, 1997.

Dupuy, Alex. *Haiti in the World Economy: Class, Race, and Underdevelopment since 1700.* Boulder, Colorado: Westview Press, 1989.

Efron, Edith. "French and Creole Patois in Haiti." Pages 215–39 in Lambros Comitas and David Lowenthal, eds., *Consequences of Class and Color.* West Indian Perspectives Series. Garden City: Anchor Books, 1973.

Ehrlich, Marko, Nicolas Adrien, Fred Conway, Herman Lauwerysen, Francis LeBeau, Lawrence Lewis, Ira Lowenthal, Yaro Mayda, Paul Paryski, Glenn Smucker, James Talbot, and Evelyn Wilcox. *Haiti Country Environmental Profile: A Field Study.* Port-au-Prince: United States Agency for International Development, 1985.

Energy Sector Management Assistance Program. *Haiti Household Energy Strategy.* Washington: United Nations Development Programme and the World Bank, 1991.

Farmer, Paul. *AIDS and Accusation: Haiti and the Geography of Blame.* Berkeley: University of California Press, 1992.

Farmer, Paul. *The Uses of Haiti.* Monroe, Maine: Common Courage Press, 1994.

Fass, Simon. *Political Economy in Haiti: The Drama of Survival.* New Brunswick, New Jersey: Transaction Books, 1988.

Fass, Simon. "Port-au-Prince: Awakening to the Urban Crisis." Pages 155–80 in W. Cornelius and R. Kemper, eds., *Metropolitan Latin America: The Challenge and the Response.* Beverly Hills: Sage, 1978.

Foster, Charles, and Albert Valdman, eds. *Haiti—Today and Tomorrow: An Interdisciplinary Study.* Lanham, Maryland: University Press of America, 1984.

Gagnon, Gerard. "Food Security Issues in Haiti." Annex 3, pages 1–36 in *Haiti: The Challenges of Poverty Reduction, 2: Technical Papers.* Report No. 17242–HA. Washington: World Bank, 1998.

Gaillard, Eric. *Estimation de la séroprévalence chez les adultes en Haïti. VIH-SIDA, méthodologie pour projeter le cours et l'impact de l'épidémie du VIH.* Port-au-Prince: Policy Project and the GHESKIO Centers, August 1998.

Gaillard, Eric, Eddy Génécé, Bernard Liautaud, Laurent Eustache, and Jean W. Pape. *Impact du SIDA: Mise à jour des projections épidémiologiques du VIH et du SIDA en Haïti.* Port-au-

Prince: Policy Project and the GHESKIO Centers, September 1998.

Haiti. Ministry of Environment. *Haïti dans le dernier carré, actes du colloque sur la gestion des aires protégées et le financement de la conservation de la biodiversité en Haïti.* Port-au-Prince: L'Imprimeur II, 1997.

Haiti. Ministry of National Education, Youth, and Sports. *Annuaire statistique des écoles fondamentales et secondaires d'Haïti.* Port-au-Prince: 1998.

Haiti. Ministry of National Education, Youth, and Sports. *Plan national—Éducation 2004.* Port-au-Prince: Projet d'Élaboration du Plan National—Éducation 2004, 1995.

Herskovits, Melville. *Life in a Haitian Valley.* Garden City: Anchor Books, 1971.

Human Rights Watch/Americas Watch, National Coalition for Haitian Refugees, Caribbean Rights. *Half Measures: Reform, Forced Labor, and the Dominican Sugar Industry.* New York: 1991.

Human Rights Watch/Americas Watch, National Coalition for Haitian Refugees, Jesuit Refugee Service/USA. *Fugitives from Injustice: The Crisis of Internal Displacement in Haiti,* 6, No. 10. New York: 1994.

Institut Haïtien de Statistique et d'Informatique. *Health Situation Analysis, Haiti 1996.* Pan American Health Organization/World Health Organization, June 1996.

Institut Haïtien de Statistique et d'Informatique. *Tendances et perspectives de la population d'Haïti au niveau régional (département, arrondissement, et commune), 1980–2005.* Port-au-Prince: Ministry of Economy and Finance, 1992.

James, C.L.R. *The Black Jacobins: Toussaint L'Ouverture and the San Domingo Revolution.* 2d ed. New York: Random House, 1963.

Jean-Pierre, Jean. "The Tenth Department," *North American Congress on Latin America Report on the Americas,* 27, No. 4, January–February 1994, 41–45.

Labelle, Micheline. *Idéologie de couleur et classes sociales en Haïti.* Montreal: Presses Universitaires de Montréal, 1978.

Laguerre, Michel S. "The Role of the Diaspora in Haitian Politics." Pages 170–82 in Robert I. Rotberg, ed., *Haiti Renewed:*

Political and Economic Prospects. Cambridge: World Peace Foundation, 1997.

Lawless, Robert. *Haiti's Bad Press.* Rochester, Vermont: Schenkman Books, 1992.

Leyburn, James G. *The Haitian People.* Rev. ed. New Haven: Yale University Press, 1966.

Logan, Rayford W. *Haiti and the Dominican Republic.* New York: Oxford University Press, 1968.

Lowenthal, Ira P. "Labor, Sexuality, and the Conjugal Contract in Rural Haiti." Pages 15–33 in Charles Foster and Albert Valdman, eds., *Haiti—Today and Tomorrow: An Interdisciplinary Study.* Lanham, Maryland: University Press of America, 1984.

Lowenthal, Ira P. "'Marriage Is 20, Children Are 21': The Cultural Construction of Conjugality and the Family in Rural Haiti." Ph.D. dissertation. Baltimore: Johns Hopkins University, 1987.

Lundahl, Mats. *Peasants and Poverty: A Study of Haiti.* London: Croom Helm, 1979.

Lundahl, Mats. *Politics or Markets: Essays on Haitian Underdevelopment.* London: Routledge. 1992.

Métraux, Alfred. *L'homme et la terre dans la vallée de Marbial, Haïti.* Paris: UNESCO, 1951.

Métraux, Alfred. *Voodoo in Haiti.* New York: Schocken Books, 1972.

Mintz, Sidney W. "Pratik: Haitian Personal Economic Relationships." In *Proceedings of the 1961 Annual Spring Meetings of the American Ethnological Society.* Seattle: 1961.

Mintz, Sidney W. "The Rural Proletariat and the Problem of Rural Proletarian Consciousness," *Journal of Peasant Studies,* 1, 1974, 291–325.

Moral, Paul. *Le paysan haïtien: Étude sur la vie rurale en Haïti.* Port-au-Prince: Fardin, 1978.

Nicholls, David. *From Dessalines to Duvalier: Race, Colour, and National Independence in Haiti.* London: Cambridge University Press, 1979.

Nicolas, Schiller. "Forestry and Forest Resources in Haiti," *Caribbean Forester,* 1, No. 3, 1940, 20–22.

Pan American Health Organization. *Health Situation Analysis, Haiti 1996.* Port-au-Prince: Ministry of Public Health and Population and World Health Organization, 1996.

Pillot, Didier, ed. *Stratégies et logiques sociales, 2: Paysans, systèmes, et crise: Travaux sur l'agraire haïtien.* Port-au-Prince and Pointe-à-Pitre: SACAD/FAMV, 1993.

Preeg, Ernest H. *The Haitian Dilemma: A Case Study in Demographics, Development, and U.S. Foreign Policy.* Washington: Center for Strategic and International Studies, 1996.

Price-Mars, Jean. *Lettre ouverte au docteur René Piquion: Le préjugé de couleur est-il la question sociale?* Port-au-Prince: Éditions des Antilles, 1967.

Price-Mars, Jean. *So Spoke the Uncle (Ainsi parla l'oncle).* Translation and introduction by Magdaline W. Shannon. Washington: Three Continents Press, 1983.

Record, S.J., and D.M. Clayton. *Timbers of Tropical America.* New Haven: Yale University Press, 1924.

Research Triangle Institute. Academy for Educational Development, and Educat S.A. *Technical Diagnosis of the Haitian Education System.* Port-au-Prince: Projet d'Élaboration du Plan National d'Éducation 2004, 1997.

Rotberg, Robert I., ed. *Haiti Renewed: Political and Economic Prospects.* Cambridge: World Peace Foundation, 1997.

Saint-Louis, René. *La présociologie haïtienne: Haïti et sa vocation nationale (éléments d'ethno-histoire haïtienne).* Ottawa: LEMEAC, 1970.

Salmi, Jamil. "Equity and Quality in Private Education." Annex 6, pages 1–17 in *Haiti: The Challenges of Poverty Reduction, 2: Technical Papers.* Report No: 17242–HA. Washington: World Bank, 1998.

Schmidt, Hans. *The United States Occupation in Haiti, 1915–1934.* New Brunswick, New Jersey: Rutgers University Press, 1971.

Schneidman, Miriam, and Ruth Levine. "Health and Nutrition Sectors." Annex 5, pages 1–11 in *Haiti: The Challenges of Poverty Reduction, 2: Technical Papers.* Report No: 17242–HA. Washington: World Bank, 1998.

Sergile, Florence, Charles Woods, and Paul Paryski. *Final Report of the Macaya Biosphere Reserve Project.* Gainesville: Florida Museum of Natural History, 1992.

Smucker, Glenn R. "Peasant Councils and the Politics of Community." Pages 93–113 in Derrick Brinkerhoff and Jean-Claude Garcia-Zamor, eds., *Politics, Projects, and People: Institutional Development in Haiti.* New York: Praeger, 1986.

Smucker, Glenn R. "Peasants and Development Politics: A Study in Haitian Class and Culture." Ph.D. dissertation. New York: New School for Social Research, 1983.

Smucker, Glenn R. "The Social Character of Religion in Rural Haiti." Pages 35–56 in Charles R. Foster and Albert Valdman, eds., *Haiti—Today and Tomorrow: An Interdisciplinary Study.* Lanham, Maryland: University Press of America, 1984.

Smucker, Glenn R. *Trees and Charcoal in Haitian Peasant Economy.* Port-au-Prince: United States Agency for International Development, 1979.

Smucker, Glenn R., and Dathis Noriac. *Peasant Organizations in Haiti: Trends and Implications.* Arlington, Virginia: Inter-American Foundation, 1996.

Smucker, Glenn R., T. Anderson White, and Mike Bannister. *Land Tenure and the Adoption of Agricultural Technology in Rural Haiti.* Washington: International Food Policy Research Institute, 1999.

Tardif, Francine. *La situation des femmes haïtiennes.* Port-au-Prince: United Nations, Inter-Agency Committee on Women and Development, 1992.

Timyan, Joel. *Bwa Yo: Important Trees of Haiti.* Washington: SECID, 1996.

Trouillot, Michel-Rolph. *Haiti, State Against Nation: The Origins and Legacy of Duvalierism.* New York: Monthly Review Press, 1990.

United Nations Children's Fund. *L'école haïtienne: Évolutions et tendances récentes (L'universalisation au prix de la qualité).* Port-au-Prince: UNICEF Haiti, 1996.

United Nations. Department of International Economic and Social Affairs. *Monographies sur les politiques de population: Haïti.* Document No. 25. New York: 1990.

United States. Agency for International Development. *USAID Monitoring Report, August–October 1995.* Port-au-Prince: 1995.

Valme, Gilbert, and J-A Victor, eds. *Les actes du premier colloque national sur les parcs et les aires protégées d'Haïti.* Port-au-Prince:

Institut National de Sauvegarde du Patrimoine National (ISPAN) and Fédération des Amis de la Nature (FAN), 1995.

White, T. Anderson, and Glenn R. Smucker. "Social Capital and Governance in Haiti: Traditions and Trends." Annex 9, pages 1–18 in *Haiti: The Challenges of Poverty Reduction, 2: Technical Papers*. Washington: World Bank, 1998.

Wiens, Thomas, and Carlos Sobrado. "Rural Poverty in Haiti." Annex 1, pages 1–15 in *Haiti: The Challenges of Poverty Reduction, 2: Technical Papers*. Washington: World Bank, 1998.

Woods, Charles A., Florence Sergile, and Jose Ottenwalder. *Stewardship Plan for National Parks and Natural Areas of Haiti*. Gainesville: Museum of Natural History, University of Florida, 1992.

Woodson, Drexel G. "Introduction: Livelihood Systems and Food Security in Haiti." Pages 1–25 in Bureau of Applied Research in Anthropology, *A Baseline Study of Livelihood Security in the Departments of the Artibonite, Center, North, Northeast, and West, Republic of Haiti*. Tucson: University of Arizona Press, 1977.

World Bank. *Haiti: The Challenges of Poverty Reduction*. Report No. 17242–HA. Washington: Latin America and the Caribbean Region, 1998.

World Bank. *Haiti: The Challenges of Poverty Reduction, 2: Technical Papers*. Report No. 17242–HA. Washington: Latin America and the Caribbean Region, 1998.

Zuvekas, Clarence. *Land Tenure, Income, and Employment in Rural Haiti: A Survey*. Working Document Series. Washington: United States, Department of Agriculture, 1978.

Chapter 8

Brinkerhoff, Derrick W., and Jean-Claude Garcia-Zamor, eds. *Politics, Projects, and People: Institutional Development in Haiti*. New York: Praeger, 1986.

Cox, Ronald. *Private Interests and United States Foreign Policy in Haiti and the Caribbean Basin: Contested Social Orders and International Politics*. Ed., David Skidmore. Nashville: Vanderbilt University Press, 1997.

Dupuy, Alex. *Haiti in the New World Order: The Limits of the Democratic Revolution*. Boulder, Colorado: Westview Press, 1997.

Dupuy, Alex. *Haiti in the World Economy: Class, Race, and Underdevelopment since 1700.* Boulder, Colorado: Westview Press, 1989.

Economist Intelligence Unit. *Country Profile, 1996–97: Dominican Republic, Haiti, Puerto Rico.* London: 1996.

Economist Intelligence Unit. *Country Profile, 1997–98: Dominican Republic, Haiti, Puerto Rico.* London: 1997.

Economist Intelligence Unit. *Country Profile, 1998–99: Dominican Republic, Haiti, Puerto Rico.* London: 1998.

Economist Intelligence Unit. *Country Report, 3rd Quarter 1997: Cuba, Dominican Republic, Haiti, Puerto Rico.* London: 1997.

Economist Intelligence Unit. *Country Report, 4th Quarter 1997: Cuba, Dominican Republic, Haiti, Puerto Rico.* London: 1997.

Economist Intelligence Unit. *Country Report, 1st Quarter 1998: Cuba, Dominican Republic, Haiti, Puerto Rico.* London: 1998.

The Europa World Year Book, 1997. London: Europa, 1997.

Fass, Simon. *Political Economy in Haiti: The Drama of Survival.* New Brunswick, New Jersey: Transaction Books, 1988.

"For Haitians, Hope Is Still a Rare Commodity," *Washington Post,* December 9, 1997, A16.

"Get House in Order to Open Door to More Aid, Albright Tells Haiti," *Washington Post,* April 5, 1998, A27.

Grafton, R. Quentin, and Dane Rowlands. "Development Impeding Institutions: The Political Economy of Haiti," *Canadian Journal of Development Studies,* 17, No. 2, 1996.

"Haitian Economic Conference," *New York Times,* May 11, 1998, A3.

International Monetary Fund. *International Financial Statistics, 1998.* Washington: 1998.

International Monetary Fund. *International Financial Statistics.* Washington: 1997.

Lundahl, Mats. *Peasants and Poverty: A Study of Haiti.* London: Croom Helm, 1979.

Political Handbook of the World, 1997. Binghamton: State University of New York, 1997.

Preeg, Ernest H. *The Haitian Dilemma: A Case Study in Demographics, Development, and U.S. Foreign Policy.* Washington: Center for Strategic and International Studies, 1996.

Rotberg, Robert I., ed. *Haiti Renewed: Political and Economic Prospects.* Cambridge: World Peace Foundation, 1997.

Schulz, Donald E. "Haiti: Will Things Fall Apart?," *Parameters,* Winter 1997–98, 73–91.

Smucker, Glenn R., T. Anderson White, and Mike Bannister. *Land Tenure and the Adoption of Agricultural Technology in Rural Haiti.* Washington: International Food Policy Research Institute, 1999.

United States. Agency for International Development. *Economic Assistance to Haiti.* Washington: GPO, 1998.

United States. Agency for International Development. *Haiti: Development Assistance Program, Fiscal Year 1997.* Washington: GPO, June 1997.

United States. Department of Commerce. *Haiti: 1997 Country Commercial Guide.* Washington: GPO, 1997.

United States. Department of State. *Country Reports on Economic Policy and Trade Practices for 1996.* Report submitted to the Senate Committee on Foreign Relations and Committee on Finance. Washington: GPO, January 1997.

United States. Department of State. *Haiti: Background Notes.* Washington: GPO, March 1995.

United States. Department of State. *Haiti: Background Notes.* Washington: GPO, October 1997.

United States. Department of State. *Haiti: Economic Background.* Washington: GPO, 1997.

United States. Department of State. *Haiti: Political Overview.* Washington: GPO, 1997.

"With U.N. Troops Departing, Haiti Faces Same Old Woes," *Washington Post,* December 1, 1997, A1, A22.

World Bank. *Global Development Finance.* Washington: 1997.

World Bank. *Haiti Project: Basic Education.* Washington: 1997.

World Bank. *Haiti Project: Emergency Economic Recovery Credit.* Washington: 1995.

World Bank. *Haiti Project: Second Economic and Social Fund.* Washington: 1998.

World Bank. *Haiti: The Challenges of Poverty Reduction.* Report No. 17242–HA. Washington: Latin America and the Caribbean Region, 1998.

The World Economic Factbook, 1997–98. London: Euromonitor, 1997.

The World Factbook, 1997. Washington: Central Intelligence Agency, 1997.

Chapter 9

Americas Watch, National Coalition for Haitian Refugees. *Silencing a People: The Destruction of Civil Society in Haiti.* New York: February 1993.

Aristide, Jean-Bertrand. *Aristide: An Autobiography.* Maryknoll, New York: Orbis Books, 1993.

Aristide, Jean-Bertrand. *Dignity.* Charlottesville: University of Virginia Press, 1996.

Aristide, Jean-Bertrand. *In the Parish of the Poor: Writings from Haiti.* Maryknoll, New York: Orbis Books, 1990.

Arthur, Charles, and Michael Dash, eds. *Libète: A Haiti Anthology.* Princeton, New Jersey: Marcus Wiener, 1999.

Averill, Gage. *A Day for the Hunter, A Day for the Prey: Popular Music and Power in Haiti.* Chicago: University of Chicago Press, 1997.

Bailey, Michael, Robert Maguire, J. O'Neil, and G. Pouliot. "Haiti: Military-Police Partnership for Public Security." Pages 215–52 in Robert B. Oakley, et al., eds., *Policing the New World Disorder: Peace Operations and Public Security.* Washington: National Defense University Press, 1998.

Ballard, John R., and John J. Sheehan. *Upholding Democracy.* Westport, Connecticut: Praeger, 1998.

Bellegarde-Smith, Patrick. *Haiti: The Breached Citadel.* Boulder, Colorado: Westview Press, 1990.

Benesch, Susan. "Haitian Army Trades Truncheons for Trumpets," *Miami Herald,* June 12, 1995, A1.

Bohning, Don. "Haiti Risks Loss of Support as Crisis Festers," *Miami Herald,* October 7, 1998.

Brice, Kim. *Bouche Pe: The Crackdown on Haiti's Media since the Overthrow of Aristide.* New York: Committee to Protect Journalists, September 1992.

Center for International Policy. "Haiti: Democrats vs. Democracy," *International Policy Report,* November 1997.

Dash, Michael. "Paved with Good Intentions: Relations Between Haiti and CARICOM." Pages 304–14 in Brian L. Moore and Swithin R. Wilmot, eds., *Before and After 1865: Education, Politics and Regionalism in the Caribbean.* Kingston, Jamaica: Ian Randle, 1999.

Dupuy, Alex. *Haiti in the New World Order: The Limits of the Democratic Revolution.* Boulder, Colorado: Westview Press, 1997.

Dupuy, Alex. *Haiti in the World Economy: Race, Class, and Underdevelopment since 1700.* Boulder, Colorado: Westview Press, 1989.

Dworken, Jonathan, Jonathan Moore, and Adam Siegel. *Haiti Demobilization and Reintegration Program.* Alexandria, Virginia: CNA, 1992.

Farah, Douglas. "Haiti's Nascent Prospects Turn Suddenly Bleak," *Washington Post,* November 25, 1995, A1.

Farmer, Paul. *AIDS and Accusation: Haiti and the Geography of Blame.* Berkeley: University of California Press, 1992.

Farmer, Paul. *The Uses of Haiti.* Monroe, Maine: Common Courage Press, 1994.

Fauriol, Georges A., ed. *Haitian Frustrations: Dilemmas for U.S. Policy.* Washington: Center for Strategic and International Studies, 1995.

Foster, Charles R., and Albert Valdman, eds. *Haiti—Today and Tomorrow: An Interdisciplinary Study.* Lanham, Maryland: University Press of America, 1984.

Gibbons, Elizabeth D. *Sanctions in Haiti: Human Rights and Democracy Under Assault.* Westport, Connecticut: Praeger, 1999.

Girault, Christian. "Society and Politics in Haiti: The Divorce Between the State and the Nation." Pages 185–206 in Colin Clarke, ed., *Society and Politics in the Caribbean.* London: Macmillan, 1990.

Haiti. *Konstitsyon Repiblik d'Ayiti.* Port-au-Prince: 1987.

Haitian-Americans for Economic Development. *Estimate of Haitians and Americans of Haitian Origin in the United States.* Silver Spring, Maryland: 1996.

Inter-American Development Bank. *Haiti Country Programming Paper.* Washington: June 1992.

International Republican Institute. *Elections in Haiti: Attitudes and Opinions.* Washington: February 10, 1999.

International Republican Institute. *Haiti Election Update.* Washington: June 1997.

International Republican Institute. *Haiti Pre-Election Assessment Mission Report No. 1.* Washington: February 27, 1997.

Kovaleski, Serge F. "Cai tels 'Buying' Haiti," *Washington Post*, February 16, 1998, A22.

Kovaleski, Serge F. "A Nation in Need: After 5-Year U.S. Intervention, Democracy in Haiti Looks Bleak," *Washington Post*, September 21, 1999, A13.

Lane, Charles. "Island of Disenchantment: Haiti's Deteriorating Democracy," *New Republic*, 217, No. 13, September 29, 1997, 17–24.

Lawyer's Committee for Human Rights. *Learning the Hard Way: The UN/OAS Monitoring Operation in Haiti, 1993–1994.* New York: 1995.

Maguire, Robert. "Bootstrap Politics: Elections and Haiti's New Public Officials." Hopkins-Georgetown Haiti Project, Haiti Papers, No. 2. Baltimore: Johns Hopkins University, 1996.

Maguire, Robert. "Standing Tall: Balanced Development in Haiti," *Grassroots Development*, October 2, 1986, 8–11.

Maguire, Robert, Edwige Baluntansky, Jacques Fomerand, Larry Minear, William G. O'Neill, Thomas G. Weiss, and Sarah Zaidi. *Haiti Held Hostage: International Responses to the Quest for Nationhood, 1986–1996.* Occasional Paper No. 23. Providence, Rhode Island: Thomas J. Watson Jr. Institute for International Studies and the United Nations University, 1996.

Malone, David. *Security Council Decision-Making: The Case of Haiti, 1990–1997.* Oxford: Oxford University Press, 1999.

Marshall, Toni. "Haitian Political Chaos Holds Up Aid," *Washington Times*, May 5, 1998, A16.

McDonald, Kim A. "Unearthing Sins of the Past," *Chronicle of Higher Education*, 42, No. 6, October 6, 1995, A12, A20.

Morrell, James R., Rachel Neild, and Hugh Byrne. "Haiti and the Limits to Nation-Building," *Current History*, 98, No. 626, March 1999, 127–32.

Neild, Rachel. *Can Haiti's Police Reforms Be Sustained?* New York: National Coalition for Haitian Rights; and Washington: Washington Office on Latin America, 1998.

Nelson, Sue. "Postconflict Elections in Haiti." In *From Bullets to Ballots: Electoral Assistance to Postconflict Societies.* Washington: Center for Development Information and Evaluation, United States Agency for International Development, 1998.

Nicholls, David. *From Dessalines to Duvalier: Race, Colour, and National Independence in Haiti*. Rev. ed. New Brunswick, New Jersey: Rutgers University Press, 1996.

Norton, Michael. "Another Power Struggle Hits Haiti," *Washington Times*, November 8, 1997, A1, A8.

Norton, Michael. "Haiti's New Leader Slow to Take Control: Foreign Aid Investment Could be Lost," *Washington Times*, February 14, 1996, A11.

Perusse, Roland I. *Haitian Democracy Restored, 1991–1995*. Lanham, Maryland: University Press of America, 1995.

Pierre, Ericq. "Haiti: Thoughts on the Present Situation," *Haiti Study Group Information Circular*. Washington: Georgetown University Haiti Program, August 1999.

Ribadeneira, Diego. "A Frail Haiti Awaits Aristide," *Boston Globe*, October 15, 1994, 1, 6.

Ridgeway, James, ed. *The Haiti Files: Decoding the Crisis*. Washington: Essential Books, 1994.

Robberson, Tod. "Haitian Capital Positively Chaotic," *Washington Post*, October 30, 1994, A31.

Robberson, Tod, and Douglas Farah. "Aristide Rebuilding His Government; Haitians Rebuilding Their Lives," *Washington Post*, October 17, 1994, A10.

Rohter, Larry. "Haiti Paralysis Brings a Boom in Drug Trade," *New York Times*, October 27, 1998, A1, A4.

Rohter, Larry. "Split Between Aristide and His Successor Imperils Haiti's Governing Party," *New York Times*, May 12, 1996, 6A.

Rotberg, Robert I., ed. *Haiti Renewed: Political and Economic Prospects*. Cambridge: World Peace Foundation, 1997.

Schulz, Donald E. "Haiti: Will Things Fall Apart?," *Parameters*, Winter 1997–98, 73–91.

Simpson, Glenn R., and Steve Stecklow. "World Bank Halts $50 Million Loan to Haiti Over Suspected Corruption," *Wall Street Journal*, January 26, 1999, A13, A15.

Theriot, Lawrence H. "Combating 'Franchise' Food Smuggling .n Haiti," *Haiti Study Group Information Circular*. Washington: Georgetown University Haiti Program, April 1996.

Trouillot, Michel-Rolph. *Haiti, State Against Nation: The Origins and Legacy of Duvalierism*. New York: Monthly Review Press, 1990.

Trouillot, Michel-Rolph. "Haiti's Nightmare and the Lessons of History." In *Dangerous Crossroads: NACLA Report on the Americas*, 27, January–February 1994.

United States. Congress. 102d, 1st Session. House of Representatives. Committee on Foreign Affairs. Subcommittee on Human Rights and International Organizations. *The Plight of Haitian Sugarcane Cutters in the Dominican Republic.* Washington: GPO, June 11, 1991.

White, Robert E. *Haiti: Democrats vs. Democracy.* Washington: Center for International Policy, 1997.

World Bank. *Haiti: The Challenges of Poverty Reduction.* Report No. 17242–HA. Washington: Latin America and the Caribbean Region, 1998.

Wucker, Michele. *Why the Cock Fights: Dominicans, Haitians, and the Struggle for Hispaniola.* New York: Hill and Wang, 1999.

Chapter 10

Albright, Madeleine K. "Keeping Faith with the People of Haiti," *United States Department of State Dispatch*, 6, No. 7, February 13, 1995, 93.

Amnesty International. *Amnesty International Report, 1996.* London: 1996.

Bain, James. "Haiti's Huge Challenge Now Is to Go It Alone," *Jane's Defence Weekly* [London], 29, No. 2, January 14, 1998, 21–22.

Bohning, Don. "Security Remains Shaky in Haiti," Knight-Ridder/Tribune News Service, June 29, 1996.

Bohning, Don, and Tim Johnson. "Aristide Legacy: Should International Troops Remain in Haiti?," Knight-Ridder/Tribune News Service, December 27, 1995.

Constable, Pamela. "A Fresh Start for Haiti?," *Current History*, 95, No. 598, February 1996, 65–69.

Delince, Kern. *L'armée, à quoi sert-elle?* Paper presented at a conference at the University of Puerto Rico on Economic and Social Development in Haiti, Mayaguez, Puerto Rico, April 12, 1995.

Delince, Kern. *Quelle armée pour Haïti?* Paris: Karthala, 1994.

Drummond, Tammerlin. "A Constabulary of Thugs," *Time*, 149, No. 7, February 17, 1997, 62–63.

English, Adrian J. *Armed Forces of Latin America*. London: Jane's, 1984.

Fauriol, Georges A., ed. *Haitian Frustrations: Dilemmas for U.S. Policy*. Washington: Center for Strategic and International Studies, 1995.

French, Howard W. "Haitian Police Chief Emerges from the Shadows," *New York Times*, September 9, 1993, A5.

French, Howard W. "In Haiti's Army, Business Is the Order of the Day," *New York Times*, November 12, 1993, A12.

Hackworth, David H. "A Soldier's View," *Newsweek*, 124, No. 8, August 22, 1994, 33.

Holmes, Steven A. "U.S. General Recommends Pullout from Haiti," *New York Times*, March 14, 1999, A17.

Ives, Kim. "The Second U.S. Occupation," *NACLA Report on the Americas*, 28, No. 4, January/February 1995.

Keegan, John, ed. *World Armies*. Detroit: Gale Research, 1983.

Kidder, T. "The Siege of Mirebalais," *New Yorker*, 71, No. 8, 72–80+.

Klepak, Hal. "Badly Armed but Dangerous, Haiti Defies the Sanctions," *Jane's Defence Weekly* [London], 21, No. 24, June 18, 1994, 20.

Klepak, Hal. "Haiti Takes Its Next Step," *Jane's Defence Weekly* [London], 23, No. 19, May 13, 1995, 94–95.

Klepak, Hal. "Keeping Democracy on Schedule in Haiti," *Jane's Defence Weekly* [London], 25, No. 24, June 12, 1996, 33–36.

Kovaleski, Serge F. "Haiti's Police Accused of Lawlessness," *Washington Post*, April 28, 1999, A1.

Kovaleski, Serge F. "Haitian Politics Tinged by Thin Blue Line," *Washington Post*, October 23, 1999, A17.

Kovaleski, Serge F. "With UN Troops Departing, Haiti Faces Same Old Woes," *Washington Post*, December 1, 1997, 22.

Laguerre, Michel S. *The Military and Society in Haiti*. Knoxville: University of Tennessee Press, 1993.

Lane, Charles. "Island of Disenchantment: Haiti's Deteriorating Democracy," *New Republic*, 217, No. 13, September 29, 1997, 17–24.

McFadyen, Deidre, and Pierre la Ramée, eds. *Haiti: Dangerous Crossroads*. Boston: South End Press, 1996.

Maguire, Robert, Edwige Baluntansky, Jacques Fomerand, Larry Minear, William G. O'Neill, Thomas G. Weiss, and

Sarah Zaidi. *Haiti Held Hostage: International Responses to the Quest for Nationhood, 1986 to 1996.* Providence: Institute for International Studies, Brown University, 1996.

Malone, David. "Haiti and the International Community: A Case Study," *Survival*, 39, No. 2, Summer 1997, 126–46.

Mendel, William W. "The Haiti Contingency," *Military Review*, 74, No. 1, January 1994, 48–57.

The Military Balance, 1995–96. London: International Institute for Strategic Studies, 1995.

Morrell, James R., Rachel Neild, and Hugh Byrne. "Haiti and the Limits to Nation-Building," *Current History*, 98, No. 626, March 1999, 127–32.

Myers, Steven Lee. "Full-Time U.S. Force in Haiti to Leave an Unstable Nation," *New York Times*, August 26, 1999, A1.

Nairn, Allan. "Haiti under the Gun," *Nation*, 71, January 8, 1996, 11–15.

Navarro, Mireya. "At Last on Hispaniola, Hands Across the Border," *New York Times*, July 11, 1999, A3.

Neild, Rachel M. *Can Haiti's Police Reforms Be Sustained?* New York: National Coalition for Haitian Rights; and Washington: Washington Office on Latin America, 1998.

Neild, Rachel M. *Overcoming History: Police Reform in Haiti.* Washington: Washington Office on Latin America, 1998.

Neild, Rachel M. *Policing Haiti: Preliminary Assessment of the New Civilian Security Force.* Washington: Washington Office on Latin America, 1995.

Nelan, Bruce W. "Cops for Democracy," *Time*, 144, No. 16, October 17, 1994, 30–31.

O'Neill, William G. "No Longer a Pipe Dream? Justice in Haiti." Pages 199–214 in Robert I. Rotberg, ed., *Haiti Renewed: Political and Economic Prospects.* Washington: Brookings Institution Press, 1997.

Richardson, Laurie. "Disarmament Derailed," *NACLA Report on the Americas*, 29, No. 6, May–June 1996, 62–63.

Robinson, Linda. "Will Haiti Have Law or Disorder?," *U.S. News and World Report*, 121, July 1, 1996, 46–47.

Rohter, Larry. "Pressed by U.S., Haitian President Begins Purge of Guards," *New York Times*, September 16, 1996, A9.

Rohter, Larry. "Questions Grow Over Haiti Peacekeepers' Role," *New York Times*, July 23, 1997, A8.

Rotberg, Robert I., ed. *Haiti Renewed: Political and Economic Prospects.* Cambridge: World Peace Foundation, 1997.

Rubin, Elizabeth. "Haiti Takes Policing 101," *New York Times Magazine,* May 25, 1997, 42–45.

Schulz, Donald E. *Haiti Update.* Carlisle Barracks, Pennsylvania: Strategic Studies Institute, U.S. Army War College, 1997.

Schulz, Donald E. "Haiti: Will Things Fall Apart?," *Parameters,* Winter 1997–98, 73–91.

Schulz, Donald E. "Political Culture, Political Change, and the Etiology of Violence." Pages 93–117 in Robert I. Rotberg, ed., *Haiti Renewed: Political and Economic Prospects.* Washington: Brookings Institution, 1997.

Shacochis, Bob. *The Immaculate Invasion.* New York: Viking, 1999.

Sweeney, John. "Stuck in Haiti," *Foreign Policy,* No. 102, Spring 1996, 142–51.

Talbott, Strobe. "From Restoring to Upholding Democracy: A Progress Report on U.S. Policy Toward Haiti," *United States Department of State Dispatch,* 7, No. 27, June 1, 1996, 348–51.

United Nations. *Report of the Secretary-General on the United Nations Civilian Police Mission in Haiti.* New York: February 20, 1998.

United States. Arms Control and Disarmament Agency. *World Military Expenditures and Arms Transfers, 1996.* Washington: GPO, 1997.

United States. Department of State. *Country Reports on Human Rights Practices for 1994.* Report submitted to United States Congress, 104th, 1st Session, Senate, Committee on Foreign Relations, and House of Representatives, Committee on Foreign Affairs. Washington: GPO, 1995.

United States. Department of State. *Country Reports on Human Rights Practices for 1995.* Report submitted to United States Congress, 104th, 2d Session, Senate, Committee on Foreign Relations, and House of Representatives, Committee on Foreign Affairs. Washington: GPO, 1996.

United States. Department of State. *Country Reports on Human Rights Practices for 1996.* Report submitted to United States Congress, 105th, 1st Session, Senate, Committee on Foreign Relations, and House of Representatives, Committee on Foreign Affairs. Washington: GPO, 1997.

United States. Department of State. *Country Reports on Human Rights Practices for 1997.* Report submitted to United States Congress, 105th, 2d Session, Senate, Committee on Foreign Relations, and House of Representatives, Committee on Foreign Affairs. Washington: GPO, 1998.

United States. Department of State. *Country Reports on Human Rights Practices for 1998.* Report submitted to United States Congress, 106th, 1st Session, Senate, Committee on Foreign Relations, and House of Representatives, Committee on Foreign Affairs. Washington: GPO, 1999.

United States. Department of State. Bureau of International Narcotics Matters. *International Narcotics Control Strategy Report.* Washington: GPO, 1998.

United States. Department of State. Bureau of International Narcotics Matters. *International Narcotics Control Strategy Report.* Washington: GPO, 1999.

Glossary

Caribbean Basin Initiative (CBI)—A major United States foreign economic policy toward Latin America and the Caribbean enacted by the United States Congress as the
Caribbean Basin Economic Recovery Act in 1984. The act
was revised on August 20, 1990, and given an indefinite
life. Primarily a trade promotion program, the CBI provides duty-free access to the United States market for some
3,000 products, provides expanded bilateral economic
assistance, and allows some limited tax breaks for new
United States investments in the region. The CBI has
helped serve as a catalyst toward economic diversification
in a number of Caribbean Basin countries.

Caribbean Community and Common Market (Caricom)—Caricom was formed in 1973 by the Treaty of Chaguaramas,
signed in Trinidad, as a movement toward unity in the Caribbean. The Dominican Republic is an observer; Haiti was
accepted as a full member in July 1997. The organization
is headed by a Community Council of Ministers, which is
responsible for developing strategic planning and coordination in the areas of economic integration, functional
cooperation, and external relations.

colono(s)—As used in the Dominican Republic, refers to a small
independent sugarcane grower. In other Latin American
countries, the word usually designates a settler or a tenant
farmer.

Dominican Republic peso (RD$)—Dominican monetary unit,
divided into 100 centavos. The Dominican government
officially maintained a one-to-one exchange rate between
the peso and the United States dollar until 1985, when the
peso was allowed to float freely against the dollar for most
transactions. After experiments with multiple exchange
rates, all rates were unified in 1997 on a free-market basis
and at an initial rate of US$1 = RD$14. After Hurricane
Georges, official rate dropped to US$1 = RD$15.46. Commercial rate was US$1 = RD$16 in October 1998.

fiscal year (FY)—The Dominican Republic's fiscal year is the
calendar year, except in the case of the State Sugar Council (Consejo Estatal del Azúcar—CEA), which runs in the
cycle of October 1 to September 30. Haiti's fiscal year is

the same as that of the United States government, running
from October 1 to September 30. Fiscal year dates of reference for these two countries therefore correspond to the
year in which the period ends. For example, FY 2000
began on October 1, 1999, and ends on September 30,
2000.

Generalized System of Preferences (GSP)—The United States
Generalized System of Preferences provides preferential
duty-free entry for more than 4,650 products from some
140 beneficiary countries and territories. The program's
intent is to foster economic growth by expanding trade
between the United States and the developing GSP beneficiaries. Instituted January 1, 1976, the GSP authorization
has been renewed by Congress a number of times since.
The latest renewal occurred in December 1999.

gourde (G)—The Haitian monetary unit, divided into 100 cen-
times. The official exchange rate was originally set in 1919
at G5 = US$1. Political crises of the early 1990s, the inter-
national embargo, and the sharp drop in government revenues had reduced the value of the gourde by about 80
percent as of 1994. In 1999 the value of the gourde fluctuated between G17.5 and G18.3 to US$1.

gross domestic product (GDP)—A value measure of the flow of
domestic goods and services produced by an economy
over a period of time, such as a year. Only output values of
goods for final consumption and investment are included
because the values of primary and intermediate production are assumed to be included in final prices. GDP is
sometimes aggregated and shown at market prices, meaning that indirect taxes and subsidies are included; when
these have been eliminated, the result is GDP at factor
cost. The word *gross* indicates that deductions for depreciation of physical assets have not been made. *See also* gross
national product.

gross national product (GNP)—The gross domestic product
(*q.v.*) plus the net income or loss stemming from transactions with foreign countries. GNP is the broadest measurement of the output of goods and services by an economy.
It can be calculated at market prices, which include indirect taxes and subsidies. Because indirect taxes and subsidies are only transfer payments, GNP is often calculated at
factor cost by removing indirect taxes and subsidies.

industrial free zone(s)—Also known as free trade zones, or free zones, these industrial parks play host to manufacturing firms that benefit from favorable business conditions extended by a given government in an effort to attract foreign investment and to create jobs. In the Dominican Republic, free-zone enterprises pay no duties on goods directly imported into, or exported from, the free zone. These enterprises also enjoy exemptions from Dominican taxes for up to twenty years, and they are allowed to pay workers less than the established minimum wage.

International Development Association (IDA)—*See* World Bank.

International Finance Corporation (IFC)—*See* World Bank.

International Monetary Fund (IMF)—Established along with the World Bank (*q.v.*) in 1945, the IMF is a specialized agency affiliated with the United Nations; it is responsible for stabilizing international exchange rates and payments. The main business of the IMF is the provision of loans to its members (including industrialized and developing countries) when they experience balance-of-payments difficulties. These loans frequently carry conditions that require substantial internal economic adjustments by the recipients, most of which are developing countries.

latifundio—A piece of landed property, usually a great landed estate with primitive agriculture and labor, often in a state of partial servitude.

Lomé Convention—A series of agreements between the European Economic Community (EEC, subsequently the European Union—EU) and a group of African, Caribbean, and Pacific (ACP) states, mainly former European colonies, that provide duty-free or preferential access to the EEC market for almost all ACP exports. The Stabilization of Export Earnings (Stabex) scheme, a mechanism set up by the Lomé Convention, provides for compensation for ACP export earnings lost through fluctuations in the world prices of agricultural commodities. The Lomé Convention also provides for limited EEC development aid and investment funds to be disbursed to ACP recipients through the European Development Fund and the European Investment Bank. The Lomé Convention has been updated every five years since Lomé I took effect on April 1, 1976. Lomé IV, which included the Dominican Republic and Haiti for the first time, entered into force in 1990 and was to cover the ten-year period 1990–99.

minifundio—A small landed estate (*see* latifundio).

Organization of American States (OAS)—Established by the Ninth International Conference of American States held in Bogotá on April 30, 1948, and effective since December 13, 1951. Has served as a major inter-American organization to promote regional peace and security as well as economic and social development in Latin America. Composed of thirty-five members, including most Latin American states and the United States and Canada. Determines common political, defense, economic, and social policies and provides for coordination of various inter-American agencies. Responsible for implementing the Inter-American Treaty of Reciprocal Assistance (Rio Treaty) when any threat to the security of the region arises.

Paris Club—The informal name for a consortium of Western creditor countries (Belgium, Britain, Canada, France, Germany, Italy, Japan, the Netherlands, Sweden, Switzerland, and the United States) that have made loans or guaranteed export credits to developing nations and that meet in Paris to discuss borrowers' ability to repay debts. Paris Club deliberations often result in the tendering of emergency loans to countries in economic difficulty or in the rescheduling of debts. Formed in October 1962, the organization has no formal or institutional existence. Its secretariat is run by the French treasury. It has a close relationship with the International Monetary Fund (*q.v.*), to which all of its members except Switzerland belong, as well as with the World Bank (*q.v.*) and the United Nations Conference on Trade and Development (UNCTAD). The Paris Club is also known as the Group of Ten (G–10).

Public Law–480 (PL–480)—Law passed by the United States Congress in 1954 authorizing the shipment of surplus United States agricultural produce to nations in need in return for local currencies at advantageous rates. The local currencies have been used primarily to cover expenses of United States diplomatic installations overseas.

special drawing rights (SDRs)—Monetary units of the International Monetary Fund (*q.v.*) based on a basket of international currencies including the United States dollar, the German deutsche mark, the Japanese yen, the British pound sterling, and the French franc.

World Bank—Name used to designate a group of four affiliated international institutions that provide advice on long-term finance and policy issues to developing countries: the International Bank for Reconstruction and Development (IBRD), the International Development Association (IDA), the International Finance Corporation (IFC), and the Multilateral Investment Guarantee Agency (MIGA). The IBRD, established in 1945, has the primary purpose of providing loans to developing countries for productive projects. The IDA, a legally separate loan fund administered by the staff of the IBRD, was set up in 1960 to furnish credits to the poorest developing countries on much easier terms than those of conventional IBRD loans. The IFC, founded in 1956, supplements the activities of the IBRD through loans and assistance designed specifically to encourage the growth of productive private enterprises in the less-developed countries. The president and certain senior officers of the IBRD hold the same positions in the IFC. The MIGA, which began operating in June 1988, insures private foreign investment in developing countries against such noncommercial risks as expropriation, civil strife, and inconvertibility. The four institutions are owned by the governments of the countries that subscribe their capital. To participate in the World Bank group, member states must first belong to the International Monetary Fund (IMF—*q.v.*).

Index

290, 295, 302, 304, 347, 417, 427, 447, 460–61, 477, 482, 483–84, 488
Human Rights Watch, 205
Hungarians: in Dominican Republic, 74
Hurricane Allen, 292
Hurricane Georges, 4, 118, 119, 121, 130, 133, 151, 152, 153, 388–89
Hurricane Hazel, 286
Hyppolite, Florvil, 279
Hyppolite Public Market, 303

IAD. *See* Dominican Agrarian Institute
IAEA. *See* International Atomic Energy Agency
ICA. *See* International Coffee Agreement
ICAO. *See* International Civil Aviation Organization
ICITAP. *See* International Criminal Investigative Training Assistance Program
ICO. *See* International Coffee Organization
ICRC. See International Committee of the Red Cross
IDA. *See* International Development Association
IDB. *See* Inter-American Development Bank
IDSS. *See* Dominican Social Security Institute
IFC. *See* International Finance Corporation
Île à Vache, 315, 321, 322
Île de la Gonâve, 315, 320, 321
Île de la Tortue, 315
ILO. *See* International Labour Organisation
Imbert, José María, 23
Imbert, Segundo, 31
IMET. *See* International Military Education and Training
IMF. *See* International Monetary Fund
IMF stand-by agreement: with Haiti, 372
immigration: to Dominican Republic, 72–76; to Haiti, 331
imports: to Dominican Republic, 4, 146, 152, 154; to Haiti, 254, 313, 373, 379–80
import-substitution industries: in Haiti, 447
Inara. *See* National Institute of Agrarian Reform

income distribution: in Dominican Republic, 122; in Haiti, 314
independence: Dominican Republic, 6, 19–23, 214; Haiti, 263, 268–72, 313, 365, 391, 413
Independence Day: in Dominican Republic, 23
Independencia, 64
Independent Revolutionary Party (Partido Revolucionario Independiente—PRI), 192
indigenismo, 95
industrial free zones: in Dominican Republic, 63, 64, 69, 111, 122–24, 132, 139, 140–41
Industrial Incentive Law (Law 299), 139, 140
industry: in Dominican Republic, 3, 139–46; in Haiti, 253, 396–400
Inespre. *See* National Price Stabilization Institute
infant mortality rate: in Dominican Republic, 103; in Haiti, 252
inflation: in Dominican Republic, 114, 115, 116, 120; in Haiti, 309, 370, 372, 375
informal sector: in Haiti, 336, 387
INS. See United States Immigration and Naturalization Service
insurgencies: in Dominican Republic, 223
Intelsat. *See* International Telecommunications Satellite Organization
Inter-American Development Bank (IDB), 7, 118, 146, 147, 154, 204, 206, 257, 374, 382, 388–89, 421–22, 448, 453–54
Inter-American Treaty of Reciprocal Assistance (Rio Treaty), 6, 206
Interdepartmental Council: in Haiti, 431
interest groups: in Dominican Republic, 194–204; in Haiti, 443–49
Interim Public Security Force (IPSF), 417, 469, 477, 480
internal security: in Dominican Republic, 235–38; in Haiti, 477–83
International Atomic Energy Agency (IAEA), 206
International Civil Aviation Organization (ICAO), 206
International Coffee Agreement (ICA), 133

Contributors

Anne Greene has written on Haiti in various scholarly publications and taught at a number of academic institut.ions.

Jonathan Hartlyn, professor of political science at the University of North Carolina, is the author of a book on the politics of the Dominican Republic and numerous articles on the country.

Robert E. Maguire, currently director of programs in international affairs at Trinity College, Washington, DC, has been involved with Haiti for some twenty years through work at the Inter-American Foundation, the Department of State, and Georgetown University.

Boulos A. Malik, a retired Foreign Service Officer, has covered the United Nations in New York and taught at the National War College.

Helen Chapin Metz is a senior analyst in the Middle East/Africa/Latin America Unit, Federal Research Division, Library of Congress.

Glenn R. Smucker is a consultant in the field of applied anthropology who has done considerable work on Haiti for the United States Agency for International Development and for foundations.

Jean R. Tartter is a retired Foreign Service Officer who has written widely on various areas of the world for the Country Studies series.

Larman C. Wilson, professor emeritus of international relations at American Universtiy, has specialized in the Caribbean area and published widely on the Dominican Republic and Haiti.

Published Country Studies

(Area Handbook Series)

550–65	Afghanistan	550–36	Dominican Republic
550–98	Albania		and Haiti
550–44	Algeria	550–52	Ecuador
550–59	Angola	550–43	Egypt
550–73	Argentina	550–150	El Salvador
550–111	Armenia, Azerbaijan, and Georgia	550-113	Estonia, Latvia, and Lithuania
550–169	Australia	550–28	Ethiopia
550–176	Austria	550–167	Finland
550–175	Bangladesh	550–173	Germany
550–112	Belarus and Moldova	550–153	Ghana
550–170	Belgium	550–87	Greece
550–66	Bolivia	550–78	Guatemala
550–20	Brazil	550–174	Guinea
550–168	Bulgaria	550–82	Guyana and Belize
550–61	Burma	550–151	Honduras
550–50	Cambodia	550–165	Hungary
550–166	Cameroon	550–21	India
550–159	Chad	550–154	Indian Ocean
550–77	Chile	550–39	Indonesia
550–60	China	550–68	Iran
550–26	Colombia	550–31	Iraq
550–33	Commonwealth Caribbean, Islands of the	550–25	Israel
		550–182	Italy
550–91	Congo	550–30	Japan
550–90	Costa Rica	550–34	Jordan
550–69	Côte d'Ivoire (Ivory Coast)	550–114	Kazakstan, Kyrgyzstan, Tajikistan, Turkmenistan, and Uzbekistan
550–152	Cuba		
550–22	Cyprus		
550–158	Czechoslovakia	550–56	Kenya

550–81	Korea, North	550–115	Russia
550–41	Korea, South	550–37	Rwanda and Burundi
550–58	Laos	550–51	Saudi Arabia
550–24	Lebanon	550–70	Senegal
550–38	Liberia	550–180	Sierra Leone
550–85	Libya	550–184	Singapore
550–172	Malawi	550–86	Somalia
550–45	Malaysia	550–93	South Africa
550–161	Mauritania	550–95	Soviet Union
550–79	Mexico	550–179	Spain
550–76	Mongolia	550–96	Sri Lanka
550–49	Morocco	550–27	Sudan
550–64	Mozambique	550–47	Syria
550–35	Nepal and Bhutan	550–62	Tanzania
550–88	Nicaragua	550–53	Thailand
550–157	Nigeria	550–89	Tunisia
550–94	Oceania	550–80	Turkey
550–48	Pakistan	550–74	Uganda
550–46	Panama	550–97	Uruguay
550–156	Paraguay	550–71	Venezuela
550–185	Persian Gulf States	550–32	Vietnam
550–42	Peru	550–183	Yemens, The
550–72	Philippines	550–99	Yugoslavia
550–162	Poland	550–67	Zaire
550–181	Portugal	550–75	Zambia
550–160	Romania	550–171	Zimbabwe